Judicial Compulsions

JUDICIAL COMPULSIONS

How Public Law Distorts Public Policy

JEREMY RABKIN

Basic Books, Inc., Publishers

NEW YORK

Library of Congress Cataloging-in-Publication Data

Rabkin, Jeremy A.
    Judicial compulsions: how public law distorts public policy/
    Jeremy Rabkin.

        p. cm.
    Includes index.
    ISBN 0–465–03687–2
    1. Judicial review of administrative acts—United States.
2. Admistrative law—United States.   3. Public interest law—United
States.   I. Title.
KF5425.R33   1989
342.73'06—dc19
[347.3026]

                                                      88–47902
                                                      CIP

Copyright © 1989 by Basic Books, Inc.
Printed in the United States of America
Designed by Vincent Torre
89 90 91 92 HC 9 8 7 6 5 4 3 2 1

To the memory of Herbert Storing,

who taught patience for the intractable,

and to the honor of Antonin Scalia,

who still urges intransigence

against the indefensible.

CONTENTS

vii

Contents

PART IV

CONCLUSION

PREFACE

THE ARGUMENT of this book is rather abstract. I have tried to illustrate the force of the argument with detailed case studies in Part III, but many readers may still regard the overall argument as excessively formal or ideological. Faced with an argument of this sort, many readers may quickly begin to wonder about the author's "real" agenda or about the "real" point of the argument. Others, of course, may simply find themselves losing interest.

For suspicious readers, it may be useful to start with a few words about how I came to write this book and what I take to be its real point. For other readers, it may provide encouragement to keep reading if I start with this brief account of what kept me writing. As is often true with formal arguments, this one does have a personal story of sorts behind it. And the story goes back a good number of years.

In the summer of 1976, as a graduate student at Harvard, I received a grant to study the Office for Civil Rights (then in the Department of Health, Education and Welfare). I had originally intended to study a very different agency. The Atomic Energy Commission had recently been divided into separate regulatory and promotional agencies and I had thought it might be interesting to study the way the new arrangements had affected the regulation of the nuclear power industry. But my academic advisor persuaded me that the regulation of nuclear power would be a rather technical and unrewarding subject for a political scientist. It was a remarkably short-sighted judgment, but revealing of how much even the shrewdest observers underestimated the emerging pattern of public interest politics in the mid-1970s.

So I was persuaded to study the Office for Civil Rights instead. OCR was then the subject of much controversy on college campuses because of its efforts to enforce affirmative action hiring requirements on college faculties. But that aspect of its operation was soon transferred to the Labor Department and was not the main thing that absorbed my attention. Instead, as fate would have it, what most engaged my interest was an elaborate suit by various civil rights organizations to redirect the agency's enforcement operations, a suit which already had asserted jurisdiction over some 80 percent of the agency's efforts. In the summer of 1976, OCR officials were boasting of having achieved a final settlement in this litigation. It turned out to be the first of many "final settlements"—as the reader will discover in chapter 5. By chance, I had stumbled on one of the handful of agencies most likely to turn one's attention from the politics of regulation to the new mode of politics by litigation. A summer at the Nuclear Regulatory Commission could not have turned my attention in this direction any more surely.

What bothered me at the time was not that judicial intervention had a terrible effect on the agency; OCR had taken on a whole range of ambitious new regulatory responsibilities in the mid-1970s and would have been a rather disordered and confused agency under any circumstances. What most troubled me was the legal or constitutional question of how a court could claim the authority to embark on such a broad-ranging reform effort in the first place. When I returned to study OCR some years later, it seemed to me that judicial intervention had, in fact, done more harm than good. But at the outset I wondered how a court could try its skill in such matters at all.

To pursue this question, I enrolled in the standard administrative law course at the Harvard Law School in the fall of 1976. By the end of the term, I was no less confused about how a court could claim such authority. But I had learned that leading legal scholars did not regard such an enterprise of judicially directed reform as at all peculiar or problematic. I discovered that law students in Cambridge and practicing attorneys in Washington held to the same view. And I came to realize that the litigation that engulfed the Office for Civil Rights was not, in fact, an aberrant case, but simply the logical culmination of the broad trend in American public law. It took me some years of further study and reflection to conclude that my initial, incredulous reaction was, after all, well grounded and that the trend in public law during the 1970s was fundamentally misguided.

By the early 1980s, however, judicial activism seemed to be in retreat and I began to think that a presentation of the traditional arguments against an inflated judicial role in administrative affairs would amount to beating a dying horse. What persuaded me to return to this project was the realization that the trend of the 1970s had actually gained a second wind during the 1980s, and not even the advent of numerous Reagan appointees to the federal bench had done much to undermine the strange premises of the earlier, general trend. The *Adams* litigation, itself—the litigation against the Office for Civil Rights that had initially engaged my interest in the new trend in administrative law—droned on through the end of the second Reagan administration. So did similar kinds of litigation involving other regulatory agencies, as the case studies in Part III of this book confirm. Patterns of judicial control that might once have been attributed to partisan enthusiasm thus continued through the 1980s under judges of very different leanings. The judiciary seemed in the grip of a strange compulsion.

Preface

This compulsion can be readily described. The policy decisions of regulatory agencies are frequently criticized and disputed, particularly by the most immediately concerned political constituencies or interest groups. And these criticisms are routinely couched in legal terms as claims that the relevant agency is not adhering to its policy obligations "under the law." The compulsion of judges is to believe that if an advocacy group can show that it would obtain better results from a different construction of an agency's legal duties, the group deserves a day in court to urge its own view of what the law requires. And if the judge then thinks there is merit in the legal argument, he feels compelled to push the agency in this direction. The inevitable result is that interest groups are encouraged to regard their policy preferences as claims of legal "right," and policy decisions become mired in legalism. Judicial compulsions become policy compulsions. The way to break the compulsion is to return to the traditional constitutional view that only individual persons have rights and that legally protected rights must involve individualized claims, like liberty or property.

I have tried to set out the argument for this traditional perspective in the course of this book. It is fundamentally an argument about perspective, and for this reason does not descend to detailed doctrinal criticism or doctrinal prescription in the style of the law reviews. I have tried to remain on that middle ground where political theory merges with the broad lines of constitutional doctrine. The book offers an extended argument about how we ought to think about law and courts in general, not an argument about how courts should describe what they are doing or how they ought to manage occasional, necessary exceptions.

The larger target of this book is not the activity of judges but the climate of legalism in which contemporary judicial compulsions have thrived. Even when not dragged into court, the Reagan administration was continually berated—and frequently intimidated—by charges that it was defying or disregarding legal obligations. The Bush administration is likely to encounter similar charges and may well be similarly damaged or similarly intimidated by them. Extended judicial oversight ratifies and stimulates this larger pattern by suggesting that even where no individual rights are involved, "the law" does and should have a commanding force apart from considerations of policy or consequence. The larger point of this book is that such legalism is a distraction from the genuine policy issues that ought to dominate public debate about regulatory performance. It may seem strange to offer a formal or legal argument to counter excessive reliance on legal arguments. In the current climate, however, I believe that this sort of formal argument is necessary to clear the way for debate on more substantive questions of policy.

Much of the response to this book, however, will surely be "realistic" and partisan rather than formal or legal. It will be said that to depreciate legalism in this setting is to imply that administrative officials need not be overly concerned with the legislative intentions behind the laws they implement. And this implication, it will be said, is calculated to inflate the policy preferences of Republican officials as against the legal enactments of a Democratic Congress. There is certainly some truth in this objection. My point is that it is foolish to make long-term constitutional assumptions on the basis of the particular partisan configurations of any particular era. Part of the value of formal or constitutional argument is that, by its abstraction, it helps to check the tendency toward short-sighted partisan calculation.

In the interest of full disclosure, however, I will confess here that my own policy views often do not run parallel with the substantive policy priorities of the Washington advocacy groups described in this book. But I can also say, in all honesty, that I have been continually impressed by the alertness, energy, and dedication of public interest advocates in Washington. At the same time, I have frequently noticed—and lamented—short-sightedness, fecklessness, and confusion among the political appointees of Republican administrations over the past fifteen years. I do not have any great confidence in the supposed expertise of career bureaucrats, either.

But I believe that the argument of this book does not rest on partisan or personal sympathies. Whether one has more sympathy for private advocacy groups than I do or less respect for executive officials than I do, the fact remains that executive officials are responsible for policy and private advocacy groups are not. This fact may seem a mere formal characterization, but it is true and important nonetheless. Advocacy groups cannot be held responsible for their preferences. Officials are supposed to be responsible for their decisions. That is the heart of the matter. Debate over administrative decisions is both inevitable and essential: officials ought to be criticized for poor performance. But they ought to be criticized *for their performance.* It does not advance public policy to channel criticism and debate into legalistic criteria of proper performance. That is what happens, however, when we pretend that "the law" means that responsible officials owe some particular policy to the advocacy groups best situated to claim it.

My argument is not an appeal for unconditional trust in executive policy decisions. If wider acceptance of the constitutional argument advanced in this book were at all likely to have that result, I would have serious misgivings about the argument. But I do not accept the notion that policy debate must be forever vain and vacuous if it cannot grasp hold of fixed legal criteria, for this is a notion that would make one despair altogether of republican government. It seems to me, however, that this is far from what goes on in public policy. The problem is not that contending advocates are forced, in desperation, to cling to the restraining cords of law. The problem is more often a logjam of contending interests and constituencies, fearful of almost any creative or independent initiative on the part of federal agencies. It seems plain to me that we will continue to suffer confused and frustrating policy outcomes if we cannot accept some scope for independent action by executive officials, and that is not likely to happen while contending interests are encouraged to view even the details of policy as legally entailed and precommitted.

I have some hope that this is an argument that can receive more of a hearing in the 1990s than it did in the 1980s. Certainly, the dream of the 1960s and 70s that activist courts can be the agents of social progress has worn very thin. In the past decade, courts have acted as brakes on policy reconsideration, and even most of those who have sought to reach for these brakes seem to understand that there is a long-term cost to administrative paralysis. Critics of the Reagan administration may have hoped to delay change or reconsideration until the onset of a new administration. With the onset of a new Republican administration, even such critics may begin to wonder whether it is worthwhile to allow constituency groups to veto new policies into the indefinite future. Most people may not care very much whether regulatory agencies are performing well. Some of those who most often resort to the courts to control or direct regulatory policy care very much, however, and they may for just this reason be willing to reconsider their earlier views. The argument will not be settled soon or all at once. But it is worthwhile to return to the fundamentals if we want to break out of the legalistic compulsions of the recent past.

Whatever its merits, this book owes much to those who have helped, encouraged, and prodded me over the years. My interest in administrative law was initially stimulated by the late Herbert Storing, long-time professor of political science at the University of Chicago. My initial interest was then further encouraged by another Chicagoan, Antonin Scalia, who was editor-in-chief of the journal *Regulation* during the late 1970s, when I served there as an assistant editor. I have also incurred considerable intellectual debt to members of the Harvard faculty, most particularly to Professor James Q. Wilson for many years of patience and good sense and to Professor Harvey C. Mansfield, Jr., for periodically luring me into the dizzying realm of political thought beyond conventional good sense. At Cornell, I owe most to Professor Werner Dannhauser, for his encouragement and example, in keeping his eyes upward and his feet on the ground. I must also express appreciation to many other colleagues at Cornell for contributing to a tolerant and stimulating scholarly environment, despite the many differences among us.

For helpful comments on the final draft of this book, I would like to thank

Preface

Louis Fisher of the Congressional Research Service, Robert Katzmann of the Brookings Institution, Thomas Christina of the Department of Justice, Terence Pell of the Department of Education, and Michael S. Greve of the Washington Legal Foundation. I have also benefited much over the years from talks about the general subject of this book with William Kristol and Fred Baumann, who understand that sustained argument is a high form of friendship.

Finally, I must express my appreciation to my parents, my wife, and my children. They have all been immensely patient (or just sufficiently impatient) in waiting for this book to be completed, and they have all been constant reminders to me that legal formulas never reach the fundamental things.

Ithaca, New York
January 1989

PART I

INTRODUCTION

1

The Politics of Interest Group Legalism

SCARCELY a decade elapsed between the assassination of President Kennedy and the forced resignation of President Nixon, but that decade—now regarded in cultural chronology as "the sixties"—transformed the landscape of American public life. It was an era of extreme moral passion and defiant political gestures, an era of great expansion in governmental undertakings and sharp decline in public respect for government. Many of the new concerns that first rose to prominence in that era, such as civil rights and the environment and consumer protection, have retained a permanent place in the framework of public policy. Many of the institutional transformations of that era have also endured through the 1980s. This book is about one of them: the extension of judicial controls over federal regulatory operations.

Prior to the mid-1960s, federal regulation was largely preoccupied with stabilizing particular industries or particular economic transactions, and judicial review of regulatory decisions was almost entirely limited to suits by regulated firms. But the dominant political atmosphere of the sixties—spurred by the civil rights movement, then by the antiwar movement, then by the environmental and consumer movements—was contemptuous of interest group politics and suspicious of "bureaucracy." New programs were celebrated for serving the disenfranchised, the "quality of life," or some higher communal concern.[1] The "new politics" of that era encouraged a new approach to judicial controls on regulation, allowing the beneficiaries of regulation to sue agencies to demand more extensive or more rigorous con-

3

trols. And dozens of so-called "public interest" groups sprang up to exploit these new opportunities.

As the passions of the sixties subsided, the new politics began to settle into more traditional patterns. Successive elections brought moderate or conservative presidents, and in Congress, too, after the early 1970s, the prevailing mood turned more cautious about major regulatory initiatives. Advocates for the environment or consumers or civil rights no longer seemed to speak for vast national movements, transcending ordinary politics, but seemed instead to operate as one more set of Washington interest groups. But the pattern of judicial controls developed in the heady days of the sixties remained in place. And it has remained a continuing source of leverage to advocates of greater regulation, allowing them to resist—often with much success—the new policy directions sought by the Reagan administration during the 1980s.

The new system in administrative law has become entrenched because it serves not merely self-styled "public interest" organizations, but trade unions, business trade associations, and other interests with a stake in extending regulatory controls over others in particular policy contexts. Not even the advent of Reagan appointees to the federal bench has made much of a change in the new administrative law. So in 1985, for example, more than one-third of the suits against government regulatory decisions heard by the U.S. Court of Appeals for the District of Columbia Circuit (D.C. Court of Appeals)—the leading court in the country for major regulatory challenges—were brought by litigants seeking to extend or intensify regulatory controls on third parties. In 1987 this proportion was even higher.[2] In the eighties, this system is less often defended with the sixties rhetoric of safeguarding the "public interest" or assuring legal protection for "underrepresented interests." Rather, it is more commonly defended—at least by judges and law professors—as the price we must pay to maintain the rule of law or to retain a constitutional scheme of checks and balances.[3]

This book is an argument for finally abandoning this legal legacy of the fevered 1960s. It argues that the current pattern in administrative law is *not* the price we pay for constitutional government and the rule of law. It is the price we pay for distorting constitutional government and the rule of law to accommodate the claims of interest groups. By the same token, this book argues that the current pattern in administrative law is *not* a check on interest group politics. It is an extension of interest group politics, under legalistic guises. In a number of regulatory fields the system has, in fact, yielded the usual negative consequences associated with interest group politics: deflecting policy toward narrow aims and interests, paralyzing policy initiative, fostering contradictory or confused overall policy patterns.

Pious talk about "law" does nothing to change the underlying reality. Those

4

who challenge regulatory decisions always have an interest in the outcome. They do not bring lawsuits because of abstract reverence for law. If they are not asserting their own rights, in the manner of regulated firms in conventional lawsuits, legal challengers must be understood as asserting the particular interests of the particular group to which they belong—or, in other words, simply practicing interest group politics in a new forum. It is quite irrelevant whether environmental or consumer advocates or other "public interest" organizations conceive their advocacy as benefiting the entire public. There is no a priori reason to assume that the public shares their view of what constitutes a "benefit" or that the public wants as much of such benefits—with all of their associated costs—as do these advocacy groups. Labor, business, and other advocacy groups may also be convinced that in gaining what they seek they will benefit the general public, and these other interests also obtain considerable leverage under the "new administrative law." But it is surely safer to view all litigating groups as advancing their own interests and their own policy aims than to assume that they are truly disinterested or truly qualified advocates for the actual benefit of the entire public.

The current system in administrative law can hardly be defended, moreover, with the claim that judges will prevent advocacy groups from obtaining any more than their due under the law. To conceive the role of the courts in this light is, after all, to concede the most disputable premise of the undertaking— that public law can in fact be conceived as making particular commitments to particular groups. Neither is it any more persuasive to emphasize the public stake in legality rather than the particular interests of the groups who invoke it. This formula implies that the public has more of a stake in legality than in sound policy—which is, to say the least, a rather curious notion of the public interest, one much more likely to appeal to a public interest lawyer than to the ordinary citizen, left to cope with the consequences of such aimless "legality." Even most defenders of contemporary administrative law do not seem entirely serious in appealing to legality, for this appeal is usually coupled—at least in legal literature—with the disclaimer that the law should not be interpreted in overly rigid ways.[4] Thus the most sophisticated arguments suppose that the modern judge can skillfully find his way to just the right policy balance, rejecting excessive interest claims on the one side and avoiding overly rigid legal constructions on the other.

But with all of the interests and advocates who lobby the agencies now enabled to petition the courts, why suppose that the judges will make better decisions about which ones to heed? Some commentators have argued that judges will make better policy decisions because they are politically independent and removed from bureaucratic routine.[5] But such arguments—celebrating the unaccountable, dilettante judge over the full-time, responsible official—are scarcely very credible. In practice, because the involvement of judges is so fragmentary and episodic, contemporary administrative law looks less like a system in which judges balance and manage contending interests than one in which interest advocates manipulate judges and "law" to attain their own ends. Of course, this system does not always allow interest advocates to get their way. But it offers them the opportunity to tie up public policy in distracting legalism, as consolation for not getting their way. In practice, that is, administrative law has a pronounced tendency to collapse into its awkwardly fused components—interest group politics and aimless legalism—unless judges can summon heroic qualities to keep the system in balance.

This book is an argument against reposing such trust in the heroic virtues of judges. It calls instead for a return to the grounding assumptions of the traditional constitutional scheme. The traditional constitutional outlook did not assume any extraordinary virtue or capacity in executive officials. On the contrary, it assumed that executive decisions were always likely to be disputable. The traditional order was prepared to disclaim exaggerated hopes for administration rather than endorse exaggerated pieties about law. It was more concerned with forestalling abuse than with assuring perfection. But that is, after all, the purpose of a constitution.

The Relevance of Constitutional Perspective

It may be worth emphasizing at the outset, then, that this book's argument proceeds somewhat differently from the criticisms raised by social science case studies of the policy making "capacity" of the courts. Such studies, focusing for the most part on institutional reform cases at the state and local level, have certainly provided abundant documentation of the practical limitations on the judicial capacity to manage large public enterprises.[6] In truth, however, it was always quite obvious that litigation would not provide a very appropriate vehicle for the management of ongoing enterprises. At the same time, studies of the "extraordinary" institutional reform litigation of recent decades have also demonstrated that courts sometimes can succeed in prodding state and local authorities into reforming outrageous and barbaric conditions in state prisons or in state hospitals and psychiatric institutions. With all of their managerial limitations, courts may well seem essential and proper last resorts when claims for redress seem morally undeniable.

The question is what claims should be regarded as morally undeniable. And this is not a question that can be answered without reference to underlying

6

constitutional assumptions—without reference, that is, to the morality of constitutionalism. If prison reform cases seem more constitutionally compelling, it is not simply because judges must recoil from the specter of maimed bodies. Regulatory mistakes may also result in maimed bodies. But prison or hospital reform cases concern the plight of known individuals, whose immediate claim is not very far removed from the historic responsibility of courts to protect individuals from unreasonable confinement by government.[7] Regulatory disputes are generally much more complex and confusing, because it is typically very difficult to identify the victims of regulatory mistake or neglect— or the supposed beneficiaries of judicial relief—and very hard to determine what would actually serve their claims. A more rigorous safety standard, for example, may seem likely to prevent future injuries, but we usually cannot identify the potential victims with precision and a more rigorous standard in one area may well impose substantial costs or risks of other kinds on those whom it seeks to protect. This difficulty is what makes regulatory policy disputes much more inherently political, and hence, from the traditional constitutional perspective, so much less appropriate for judicial management.

At this point, however, it may also be worth emphasizing that the argument of this book is not intended to be another contribution to the debate on "original intent" jurisprudence. To grasp the argument, it is not necessary to descend to arcane researches into the debates at the Constitutional Convention of 1787 or to engage in yet a new round of recently fashionable sparring about the metaphysics of textual interpretation. One need only concede that the common sense of constitutional government—the elementary assumptions of more than two centuries of liberal constitutional thought—did not suddenly cease to be applicable in the late 1960s. Where this book invokes the words or actions of the statesmen who framed the federal Constitution, it does so to illustrate the logic of the system they created. The argument does not finally rest on the moral authority of the framers but on the logic of a few elemental premises—premises that even contemporary courts cannot openly disavow because the whole constitutional scheme plainly rests on them. Different premises can certainly be imagined, but they cannot readily be grafted onto the system we have inherited. Piecemeal litigation is not a very effective substitute for revolution. And for that reason the current system turns out to be as dysfunctional in practice as it is confused in theory.

The traditional constitutional perspective starts with a premise so elementary that contemporary public law finds it impossible to take seriously. It is that judges cannot be responsible for public policy because they are, quite literally, not responsible. The traditional constitutional view was that public policy must be left to officials who are responsible because they are accountable to the public. This commonsense view is derided as unrealistic because, it is said, faceless bureaucracies are not really accountable to the public either. In fact, officials who can be dismissed at will by the president—in a system in which presidents face the voters every four years—clearly are more accountable than life-tenured judges in any meaningful sense of the word "accountable." If one wants to engage in "realism," it might be more plausible to question whether congressional enactments can still claim democratic legitimacy in a system in which the privileges and advantages of incumbency have been so extended that there is now less turnover in the U.S. House of Representatives than in the British House of Lords. Because turnover in offices is far more routine in top administrative posts than in Congress, one might even argue that administrators are more in tune with popular feeling than Congressmen and so more entitled to claim the mandate of democracy.

But appeals to democracy are, after all, mostly the stuff of demagoguery. The original defense of the constitutional scheme was filled with cautions against impulsive democratic majorities. The underlying rationale of the traditional constitutional perspective was not that accountability was necessary to satisfy some simple notion of democracy, but that only an accountable government could retain sufficient moral authority in the modern world to make disputable decisions. This requirement is obvious enough in relation to elected legislatures, whose policy choices immediately attain the status of law. But the framers of the Constitution were equally insistent on the need for "energy" in the executive—meaning precisely the capacity to make decisions, even amid uncertainty and dissension. *The Federalist* went so far in its praise of "energy in the executive" as to warn that any government with "a feeble executive . . . must be, in practice, a bad government."[8]

From this perspective, the problem with judicial control of public policy is that judges cannot be "energetic" because they are supposed to be closely bound by law. And they are supposed to be bound by law—rather than accountable to the public for the consequences of their disputable decisions— because the constitutional purpose of courts is to protect private rights. Even in disputes involving government agencies, judicial fidelity to the law is supposed to allow courts to find an impartial basis for decision between executive officials and private citizens. For surely, whatever else it means, constitutional government means that when a judge is called upon to decide the case of *John Doe v. United States,* he is not automatically assumed to take the side of the government. Fairness to John Doe seems to require that the judge assure him his rights under the law, regardless of what government officials may deem most expedient for the public. But just because judicial intervention is bound to restrict executive "energy" and discretion, the traditional constitutional assumption was that, as Chief Justice John Marshall put it, "the province of the court is solely to decide on the rights of individuals."[9]

In deference to this tradition, suits demanding more vigorous regulatory action are sometimes described as efforts to enforce a "right to clean air" or a right to some other regulatory benefit. But inspirational rhetoric cannot make claims to regulatory benefits function in the same way as conventional legal rights. In contrast to conventional legal rights—such as the property rights of regulated firms—claims to regulatory benefits are generally claims on behalf of beneficiaries who are not readily identified. When a business firm asserts its rights in court, for example, it can be assumed to be speaking for the owners of the firm. And even if the firm is a vast corporate conglomerate, lawyers could, if they had the need, rather quickly determine the name and address of every shareholder. When an advocacy group comes to court to assert the "right to clean air" or to enforce some equally general policy goal, it asserts a claim to something over which it does not have exclusive control. In effect, the advocacy group claims to speak for unknown or indeterminate others to whom it has no meaningful accountability at all. To talk of rights in this context is simply to conceal a difficult question of political structure or representation under an empty legal formula.

A second difference follows from the first. When a conventional owner or holder of a right asserts a claim, the court can assume that the owner knows his own interests. This is the purpose of a conventional right, after all: to allow the holder of the right to pursue his own interest as he sees it. So in conventional kinds of litigation, courts need not inquire whether a particular owner will really serve his own ends through the claims he asserts. In principle, rights exclude such paternalism: either the claimant has a right to what he seeks or he does not, and the judge has no independent responsibility for the claimant's well-being, apart from determining his entitlements under the law. By contrast, when regulatory entitlements are at stake, it seems absurd to separate the legal merits of the claim from the actual consequences of the policy, as if a judge were to say, for example, "I will give these environmental activists what I think the law requires—and too bad if that action yields a dysfunctional policy that ultimately frustrates even their own concern to obtain cleaner air." While legal formality has an evident functional logic in relation to property claims, in claims to regulatory benefits it simply conceals difficult managerial or policy questions under distracting legalisms.

Of course, the fact that policy consequences are disputed does not mean that the dispute is merely technical. Similarly, the fact that the putative beneficiaries of a program are dispersed and unidentified does not mean that nothing can be known about their preferences. Most regulatory disputes reflect genuine clashes of interest, in which the technical arguments are mere counters in an evident political struggle between competing preferences and priorities. From this point of view, it may not seem at all formalistic for a court

9

to consider whether environmentalists have the better argument in law, for the dispute is about whether regulatory policy should favor the concerns of environmentalists as opposed, say, to the concerns of the steel industry. And it is just because both sides do think they understand the likely consequences of a disputed policy that they come forward with technical arguments about which policy is required by law.

These considerations do not really remove the underlying difficulty, however. When a steel producer challenges a constraint imposed by the Environmental Protection Agency (EPA), the firm plainly does speak for its own interest, and the court can presume that the firm does know its own interest. An environmentalist advocacy group does not simply speak for itself, and it cannot simply be presumed to represent all of the relevant interests affected by its claim. The group may well speak for many people who share the outlook and priorities of environmentalists. But the fact is that not everyone does share these views and certainly not in every particular application. A steelworker, for example, may like clean air as much as the next person but may still prefer to put up with a bit more air pollution rather than see the closing of the plant in which he works and the elimination of his current livelihood. We cannot say that the public policy at issue "belongs" to the environmentalist advocacy group without thereby excluding or disenfranchising all sectors of the broader public—like the steelworkers.

But that is what we do say when we speak of the "property rights" of a regulated firm. If the law does not authorize constraints on the firm, it is the firm's own business—and not a question of public policy—what the firm does with its own property. The regulated firm thus presents a genuine legal dispute when it opposes its own distinct rights to the government's public policy. The environmentalist suit remains strangely formalistic (or else outrageously biased) by making the public policy decision turn on whether the advocacy group has the better "legal" argument instead of turning on what would actually serve the general interest of the general public, considering all of the general public's diverse and clashing interests.

None of these difficulties is a recent discovery. If regulatory goals could really be achieved by treating them as court-enforced "rights," it would make no sense to have regulatory agencies at all. We would simply pass laws conferring the desired rights on individuals, as civil right laws, for example, allow the victims of discrimination to sue the immediate perpetrators for redress. The creation of a public agency reflects the recognition that some goals or concerns cannot be treated as individual rights but must instead be pursued as public enterprises. At one time, this distinction was evident even to the courts. So, for example, even in dealing with such an openly constituency oriented agency as the National Labor Relations Board, the Supreme Court insisted in the

1940s that union representatives could not bring suit to force the NLRB to pursue a particular complaint against management.[10] The Court was unwilling to allow any individual litigant to be treated as the proper representative for all of "labor" in NLRB policy, and it was unwilling to assume that courts knew better than the Labor Board what would serve the cause of labor–management relations.

The contrary judicial philosophy that took hold in the late 1960s no doubt owes much to the fevered intellectual climate of that turbulent era—wary of authority, suspicious of expertise, eager for participation and citizen activism. All of these themes were certainly prominent in the rhetoric of the public interest lawyers who helped to spearhead the new pattern in administrative law.[11] But the question remains why judges should have given in so readily and so fully to such entreaties. Or perhaps, more to the point, the question remains why judges did not revert to their more modest traditional role in later years.

Dubious Rationales

Many commentators have insisted that the new judicial role is an inevitable response to the changed circumstances of governmental regulation.[12] If true, this claim would suggest that there is no sense in seeking a return to the older constitutional tradition. But neither of the two most prominent versions of this argument really makes much sense.

The more abstract and scholarly version of the argument views the new judicial role as a necessary check on the dangerously enlarged powers of administrative agencies in modern government. In formal terms, this role is described as an appropriate response to the demise of the nondelegation doctrine—the traditional doctrine that the legislature may not delegate its power to others. Administrative agencies, according to this argument, could once be regarded as mere "transmission belts" for the will of the legislature, expressed in precise regulatory enactments. But as regulatory statutes have become more vague, administrators have acquired vastly more discretion. Courts have therefore had to extend their own sphere of control to assure that administrative discretion is properly exercised.[13]

This is by now a well-worn argument, but it happens to be both historically false and logically circular. The nondelegation doctrine was historically conceived as a protection for the *targets* of regulation, for administrative coercion could not be held within statutory bounds unless statutes were reasonably specific. In fact, however, the doctrine was almost always honored in the breach—which allowed more scope for administrative action than if Congress had been forced to endorse specific policies in legislation. The regulatory statutes of the early twentieth century—like the Interstate Commerce Act of 1887, prohibiting "unreasonable rates," or the Federal Trade Commission Act of 1914, prohibiting "unfair methods of competition"—were if anything far more vague than most of the regulatory statutes enacted in more recent decades.[14] This makes it unlikely that the new judicial role of recent years is merely a response to the demise of the non-delegation doctrine.

The more fundamental problem with this claim, however, is that apart from a few isolated circumstances, courts were never willing before the 1960s to accept suits that called for more vigorous or more extensive enforcement by administrative officials. In this sense, administrative officials have always exercised vast discretion in declining to exercise coercive force, regardless of whether statutes were very detailed or not. In other words, the non-delegation doctrine never had much relevance to the beneficiaries of regulation. It may be true that as the goals of regulation have become more extensive and ambitious, the traditional discretion of enforcement officials has extended the power of regulatory agencies to disappoint more would-be beneficiaries of regulation. But an enlarged risk of disappointed expectations only justifies judicial intervention if one assumes in advance the very point in dispute: that large, ill-defined constituencies can have rights to particular regulatory benefits that can be safeguarded by litigation.

The more "realistic" or "political" version of the argument focuses not on the legislative derelictions of Congress (in handing so much policy discretion to administrators) but on Congressional disappointment with administrators of the wrong party. The argument is that New Deal Democrats in Congress were all in favor of administrative discretion when the discretion would be exercised by appointees of Franklin Roosevelt or a like-minded successor, but took a very different view of administrative discretion exercised by appointees of Richard Nixon or Ronald Reagan.[15] There is no doubt a grain of truth to this argument. It is true, for one thing, that the most explicit authorizations for the new administrative law—provisions in environmental statutes authorizing "any citizen" to sue the EPA to force it to comply with its regulatory "duties"—were enacted in the early 1970s, when tensions between a Republican White House and a liberal Democratic Congress were running particularly high.[16]

Still, it remains the historical fact that courts had begun to open their doors to "public interest" advocacy groups and to other unconventional litigants even before President Nixon assumed office. And the courts extended the new patterns of litigation through the Democratic Carter administration with no direct rebuffs from Congress, even when—as in most cases—judges could not claim any clear statutory warrant for their new role. By contrast, when Republicans gained the majority in the Senate after 1980, Senate committees debated a great many proposals to curb judicial involvement in controversial policy issues like abortion, school busing, and school prayer. But Senate Republicans gave no attention to cutting back the new judicial oversight role in federal regulation even though it would have been most logical to do so if the new judicial role were simply a reflection of partisan maneuver.[17] The truth is that, even if "public interest" firms do identify overwhelmingly with liberal Democrats,[18] many of the other specialized beneficiaries of the new administrative law are Republican business constituencies—like trucking firms invoking judicial assistance to force the imposition of regulatory constraints on would-be competitors.

Whatever Congress might prefer, moreover, the question remains why the judges thought it within their constitutional authority to assure that amorphous regulatory constituencies received no less than Congress intended. To argue that the "rights" of regulatory beneficiaries might have been threatened by the neglectful or partisan policies of Republican administrators is again to assume the very point in dispute. Does Congress have the constitutional authority to create "rights" to private control over executive policy decisions? Is the separation of powers merely one of several options in the constitutional scheme, which Congress is free to disregard at will? In earlier times, courts would surely have answered "no" to these questions, even if Congress were frustrated with the performance of particular executive programs. And in earlier times, courts were not at all unwilling to reject statutory conferrals of jurisdiction when they judged them to be constitutionally improper. That is, after all, just what the Supreme Court did when it first asserted its power to review the constitutional validity of legislative enactments in *Marbury v. Madison.* If judicial attitudes have changed, it is surely not because the Nixon or Reagan administrations performed so much more unacceptably than their predecessors or occasioned so much more congressional criticism.

Thus the explanation for the shift in judicial attitudes seems in the end to have less to do with the force of circumstances than with the power of ideas. The new system of administrative law looks most strange when viewed from the traditional constitutional perspective, where the executive is conceived as the agent of the public rather than as the mere instrument of Congress and where private rights are conceived to be quite distinct from public policy. But this perspective had already considerably decayed by the 1960s, perhaps partly in consequence of the concessions courts had long been making to the modern welfare state and its concomitant, the modern administrative state.

Before the late 1930s, constitutional doctrine sought to fix definite limits

13

on the reach of legislative power. Whether the Supreme Court's formal rationale was federalism or "substantive due process," its general aim was to protect private property and to ensure that public authority was not manipulated to enrich some at the expense of others. Almost all of these limiting doctrines were abandoned by the Supreme Court in the aftermath of its bitter confrontation with President Roosevelt in 1937.[19] Since then, federal spending and regulatory programs have proliferated in all directions—with special programs for lime growers and tobacco farmers, for college students and real estate developers, for importers and exporters, for failing cities and failing auto companies, and so on and so on and so on. And the Supreme Court has resolutely stayed its hand, finding no tax or regulatory statute too onerous, no purpose or constituency too narrow to pass constitutional muster. In this setting, it is easy to lose sight of the difference between private property and public policy and begin to regard the entire economy as one vast pool of resources to be distributed or redistributed as government thinks best—and for government to shape its thinking to the clamor of the loudest or best organized constituencies. At the least, constitutional doctrine has given up on the notion that courts should be drawing any lines against sheer redistribution.

Perhaps it has indeed become impossible or undesirable to draw such lines in an era in which so much is expected of government. But it hardly follows that, because substantive limits on government are abandoned by courts, the basic structure of government must also be subverted. One might just as well argue that because public expectations of government are now so high, we ought to dispense with elections or with due process for criminal defendants. These inferences are more extreme but hardly more illogical than the argument that if Congress may respond to any policy preference by any constituency, it should also be able to delegate to particular constituencies the power to force favored approaches on the responsible executive agencies. It would be more logical to suppose that structural safeguards are more important than ever when substantive limits are no longer enforced. But courts have readily lost sight of structural safeguards in their eagerness to ensure that contemporary constituencies get what they are entitled to under new regulatory measures.

This is only one way, however, in which legal history has encouraged a perspective that blinds courts to the very strange character of contemporary administrative law. The past history of administrative law itself has also helped to obscure the very strange character of the current system. From the outset, administrative law was an accommodation to the notion that regulated firms need not be assured the protection of traditional conceptions of due process, which in time encouraged the view that regulated firms simply held "interests" that should be considered by administrators, instead of having "rights" pro-

14

tected by law. And this view finally encouraged the conclusion that other interests, too, should have equal access to the courts for their claims. To put the point succinctly, administrative law has eroded the traditional understanding of what it means to have a legally enforceable claim, thus making it much easier to extend such claims.

Administrative Law, Old and New

As late as the 1930s, even the term "administrative law" seemed strange and unsettling to many American lawyers. "Administration" was associated with ongoing management, with getting the job done. "Law" was associated with fixed rules to protect people from unwanted intrusions—including the intrusions of government officials. "Administrative law" thus suggested that administrative officials must be allowed to operate with a more managerial or policy-oriented notion of law. This was precisely its appeal to the champions of expanded government regulation and precisely what made it unsettling to those who still championed traditional notions about "the rule of law."[20]

In the traditional view, the rule of law was understood to guarantee that administrators would be held accountable to the same legal process as private citizens. And, in form, at least, legal challenges to administrative decisions did work this way in the nineteenth century. Legal challenges to administrative decisions were, in principle, conducted like any other sort of litigation. If a merchant claimed that a customs inspector had wrongly seized some of his cargo, he filed a suit against the inspector. The judge in the case was supposed to consider the factual evidence and the relevant law as he would in litigation between two merchants over disputed ownership claims.

The doctrines of administrative law that developed in the twentieth century were intended to give more weight to the policy decisions of administrative agencies, while still assuring some of the protections associated with law. At the federal level, the development of such new doctrines was a direct accommodation to the enlarged powers of new regulatory agencies, most notably the Interstate Commerce Commission. When it was established in 1887, the ICC could only enforce its judgments about unfair railroad rates by filing suit in the ordinary courts for an injunction against the offender—and courts then insisted on rehearing all of the evidence and arguments considered by the ICC in making this judgment, much the way that antitrust suits by the Justice Department still require government lawyers to persuade a court of their case. To make the ICC more effective, Congress amended the Commerce Act in

1906 to provide that judgments of the commission would be binding unless overturned by a court on appeal. Administrative law thus sought to develop an appellate role for courts that would give weight to administrative judgments, without leaving regulated firms entirely at the mercy of administrative fiat. During the 1930s, when the New Deal established a host of new regulatory programs, courts became habituated to a still more deferential posture. To put the point somewhat crudely, administrative law sought to give more scope to "administration" by restraining the claims of "law."

This pattern of judicial deference was not simply a concession to the specialized expertise of administrative agencies. It was also an acknowledgment of the difficulty in conducting most regulatory operations by strict or well-defined rules. Before the 1960s, the most prominent federal regulatory agencies concentrated on controlling economic relations—determining which firms should be allowed to provide which services at which rates. The subject matter demanded flexibility for, amid changing economic conditions, no one could readily formulate neat rules to decide the competing claims of rival firms and their diverse clienteles. In earlier times, judges may well have looked to larger economic consequences as they juggled precedents in ordinary common law disputes. But in the laissez-faire climate of the nineteenth century, courts could affect a greater respect for precedent and a greater indifference to the social or economic consequences of their decisions.[21] Administrative regulation of particular industries or economic operations implied, on the contrary, that government could and should try to shape economic outcomes in more detail, which was understood by almost everyone to imply that administrators could not adhere as closely to fixed rules as judges professed to do in ordinary common law cases.

Regulatory commissions tried to preserve such flexibility by developing policy on a case-by-case basis. In effect, they were making and applying their standards as they went along, combining the adjudication of individual cases with the policy making prerogatives of legislatures. Or perhaps it would be more accurate to say that commissions combined the implementing responsibility of executive agencies with the legal powers of adjudicators. Regulated firms could contest proposed commission orders. And in the first instance, their arguments would be heard by a hearing examiner, who was supposed to retain the impartiality of an ordinary judge by avoiding contact with ordinary commission staff. But if the firm—or the commission staff—disagreed with the hearing examiner's formal report, the dispute would be resolved by the same commissioners who were also responsible for managing and directing the investigative and prosecutorial work of the commission staff in the first place. In effect, commissioners sat in judgment on their own agencies.

This compromise with the traditional ideal of judicial impartiality was not the only way in which administrative hearings differed from courtroom trials. From the outset, ICC hearings often differed also in the access they afforded to various affected interests, such as rival railroads or various contending shippers, to participate in the proceedings. In traditional judicial proceedings, third parties could be called as witnesses but rarely were allowed to contribute arguments or evidence on their own initiative. In ordinary judicial trials, the court is supposed to focus on a precise legal question: whether the defendant did or did not invade the rights of the plaintiff, whether the defendant did or did not break the law as alleged by the prosecutor. With this focus, the preferences of third parties seem largely irrelevant, perhaps even an unfair distraction. By contrast, the procedure at administrative hearings acknowledged that the ultimate administrative decision involved a good deal of discretion, and the outcome might very properly be adjusted to accommodate the concerns of third parties. Beginning in the 1920s, competing railroads were sometimes even allowed to appeal ICC decisions to the courts, on the grounds that a favorable administrative decision for another railroad would slight the separate "legal interest" they had asserted in the commission's proceedings. A legal interest was understood to be something much less definite than a property right—but then the property rights of regulated firms were already a good deal less definite or clearly protected by administrative due process.[22]

Legal interest cases of this sort, however, were limited to a few specialized regulatory commissions before the 1960s. The thrust of administrative law changed more significantly when judges first began to insist that consumer advocates be allowed to participate in administrative hearings to contest awards of licenses or permits to firms they viewed as threatening to the "public interest." In 1966, for example, a liberal church group was allowed to challenge the decision of the Federal Communications Commission to relicense a television station in Mississippi which, according to the group, had neglected the programming interests of black viewers.[23] Another landmark decision of this era allowed environmental activists to challenge the licensing of a new power plant by the Federal Power Commission.[24] From allowing consumer or environmental advocates to demand formal agency hearings and a right to participate in such hearings, courts naturally moved to allowing these advocates to appeal ultimate commission rulings to the courts. And from allowing outside advocates to challenge decisions granting licenses, the courts moved to allowing outside advocates to challenge decisions not to take any action or—what amounted to the same thing—not to make any decision. So by 1970, the D.C. Court of Appeals felt entitled to issue an order to the Agriculture Department demanding that it explain why it had taken no action to suppress the use of a particular dangerous pesticide.[25]

The logic of opening hearings and courts to advocates of generalized or abstract "interests" was then followed through by refocusing administrative procedure and judicial review on general rules, not just on particular decisions. Under the prevailing doctrines of the old administrative law, general rules were assumed to affect a wide array of interests but not the distinct legal interests of anyone in particular. No one, that is, was acknowledged to have an actionable legal interest in the formulation of the general rule applied to others. Rules were therefore usually adopted by rather informal procedures, and their legal validity could be challenged only when finally enforced against a particular party. And the informal procedures for formulating rules meant that, at that stage, challengers had little documentary evidence to draw on. These procedures seemed acceptable, however, when the rule of law was regarded primarily as a protection against invidious treatment rather than as a guarantee of sound policy. The Administrative Procedure Act (APA), enacted in 1946 as a codification of existing practice, essentially endorsed this view by requiring formal hearings before independent examiners only for contested individual "orders." By contrast, the APA authorized agencies to promulgate general rules after simply offering advance notice of new rules in the *Federal Register* and then allowing time for the public to submit comments, criticisms, or suggestions through the mail. The APA then directed that when the validity of a rule did come before a court, it should be upheld unless deemed "arbitrary and capricious," while individualized orders should be judged by the more demanding standard that they be "supported by substantial evidence."[26]

These distinctions were substantially abandoned under the new administrative law of the 1970s, however. Courts began to allow challenges to new rules from the moment they were promulgated—even though, under the circumstances, no challenger could claim more than a rather generalized, abstract, or hypothetical stake in the validity of the rule. Even a regulated firm potentially affected by the rule would have to be conceived as a representative of all other firms potentially affected by the rule. And, of course, advocates of tighter or more extensive rules were also allowed to challenge new rules from the outset, for their claim would always be rather abstract, in any case. To give the challengers more chance of success, courts began demanding that agencies provide more extensive argument and evidence for the policy choices involved in rules. The intensification of judicial review thus forced agencies to develop a more formal process for developing rules, so that affected interests could force the agency to accommodate their concerns or justify its refusal to do so. In effect, rule making too was transformed into a quasi-judicial venture, in which distinct interests could demand accommodation to their own "legal interests." But legal interests scarcely differed at this point from political interests. So administrative law took on the appearance of a carefully managed political process.

In managing this process, courts can scarcely claim to be indifferent to policy. But their policy vision is refracted by the preoccupations of the litigants before them. As litigants are allowed to pursue more and more general claims, *public* policy thus seems to dissolve into the claims of contending private litigants. The tendency is nicely illustrated by the titles under which many administrative law cases now appear in the case reports. For example, when a new rule of the Occupational Safety and Health Administration is challenged on the one side by labor or consumer advocates seeking greater stringency, and on the other side by business advocates demanding a less onerous standard, the two challenges may be merged in one appellate court proceeding and recorded in the case reports as *AFL-CIO v. American Petroleum Institute.* [27] OSHA, the executive agency actually responsible for the public policy at issue, appears to be a mere passive bystander.

Thus the actual rights of particular regulated firms have dissolved into a general business "interest," while the public interest has melted into the "interest" of labor unions. Public authority as such—along with the public interest that it is supposed to safeguard—disappears in a strangely disembodied struggle between the ghost of property rights and the specter of private government.

Why Judicial Control Is Not Public Control

From the outset, administrative law has introduced various compromises into the traditional conception of the rule of law, by weakening legal safeguards for distinct private rights. It can be argued that these compromises were inseparable from the logic of economic regulation, and perhaps in practice the resulting flexibility gave back to regulated firms with one hand what it took with the other. Some of the modifications involved in the contemporary system of legal controls may also invoke plausible rationales. Thus it is argued that when rules can impose enormous compliance costs on affected industries, it is better for all concerned to allow immediate appeals to the courts—instead of forcing the agency and the affected firms to invest vast resources in implementing a rule that may later be judged invalid. Similarly, it is argued that when rules involve enormous costs and bear only a general relation to statutory enactments, it is only fair to allow firms to contest the need for such rules, and it is only feasible for them to do so if the agencies are required to explain their rationales in some detail at the outset.

Whatever may be said for particular practical adjustments of this kind in contemporary administrative law, the compromises and exceptions have overwhelmed the underlying logic of the legal system. When different constituencies can challenge so many different aspects of agency operations, private rights or "legally protected interests" no longer seem to be an exception from the general flow of public policy, but rather the essential elements of public policy themselves. In other words, public policy seems to reduce to the legally protected claims of contending interest groups. But this conclusion is too unsettling to be openly embraced. Judges do remain at least vaguely aware that sound public policy is not likely to emerge from a system that cedes so much control to particular private constituencies. So contemporary administrative law continually strives to put the brightest face on its own logic: if interest group claims are now inseparably entangled in public policy, then litigation can be viewed as a means to resolve public policy rather than merely as a means to protect private claims.

Thus legal commentators began to speak of "public law" litigation in the 1970s as if it were a device by which private advocates could make administrative agencies accountable to the courts, rather than a device by which courts make agencies accountable to private litigants.[28] In this perspective, it finally seems to be the judicial system that determines the public interest. In accord with this public law perspective, contemporary courts rarely speak about "rights" or "legal interests," at least in relation to claims for regulatory benefits. They speak rather about "standing" to litigate a particular "issue," which implies that the litigant is not making a claim on his own behalf, but merely standing before the court to offer arguments and advice about how *the court* might best resolve this issue.

But these formulations are rhetorical evasions of the underlying reality. Courts are entirely unequipped to act as ongoing, freestanding guardians of administrative performance. Our entire judicial system has developed on the assumption that courts will simply be deciding cases about property rights or personal rights, in the traditional sense. Thus courts have no authority to initiate inquiries on their own or even to gather supplementary evidence on their own. They are limited to judging "cases" brought by litigants and are, indeed, required by their own rules of procedure to consider only such arguments and evidence as the litigants have actually brought before them. Even if judges shrug off these procedural limitations and seek to be more aggressive—as the managerial role would imply—they have no staff resources to pursue empirical research or even to monitor compliance with their directives.

Whatever their ambitions, moreover, and however exalted their notions of law, judges do not actually have sufficient power to manage administrative undertakings in detail. They cannot force Congress to appropriate more funds to undertake the sort of administrative efforts they think necessary. They cannot force the president to fire the officials already appointed to head administrative programs and replace them with officials who espouse views closer to the judge's. In many institutional reform cases in which federal judges have ordered state or local governments to undertake elaborate reform efforts in the name of constitutional rights (as in prison reform or school desegregation cases), judges have appointed "special masters" to oversee the implementation of their decisions and have successfully badgered state and local authorities to appropriate sufficient funds to finance their directives. Nothing so ambitious has ever been attempted in federal regulatory cases, however, probably because judges sense that Congress and the president would not long tolerate such open preemption of their powers. Unlike hapless local officials, Congress and the president do have the power to protect themselves against overly demanding judges.

In a few federal regulatory cases judges have, in fact, attempted to impose considerable affirmative duties on regulatory agencies. But even in such cases, judicial intervention remains far short of taking on full managerial responsibility for the agency's implementation efforts. In most cases, the power of courts remains largely the negative power of obstructing. Judges can declare an administrative decision unlawful and unenforceable. They can order an agency to submit new arguments, to gather new evidence, or to develop a new policy. But they cannot readily supervise the operation of any new policy or program they order—or coax—into being. The judges must depend on the litigants to keep them informed, and the litigants themselves are not always capable of monitoring administrative implementation decisions or the consequences of those decisions in full detail. Indeed, the litigants may not always find it in their interest even to try to keep the judges fully informed of subsequent developments. Even a pure "public interest" suit, then, does not initiate a program of independent management by courts. It sets up a proceeding that, like any judicial proceeding, ends up focusing on the complaints brought forward by the plaintiffs.

Administrative law doctrine tries to accommodate these realities by insisting that the role of courts is not really to direct public policy but merely to guide and channel the essential discretion of administrators or merely to ensure that administrative discretion is exercised in a fair and proper manner. This claim is supposed to soothe doubts about the managerial or policy making capacities of the courts. Perhaps it also quiets doubts about the mortgaging of public policy to particular interest group claimants. The prevailing legal doctrines allow judges to insist that they are not requiring the agencies to secure any particular result to the advocacy groups who come before them. They are merely requiring agencies to offer adequate consideration to the arguments, standards, or evidence urged by the litigants. And in accord with the "public law" perspective, this is often depicted as an obligation of the agencies not so much to the particular litigants as to the policy process. "Due process" is depicted as a guarantee of sound policy deliberation rather than as a procedural safeguard for some distinctive claim that is due to the litigant. Thus some commentators now insist that judicial review should be understood as a device for safeguarding the "republican" commitment to honest, disinterested deliberation about the public interest.[29]

But all of these formulas again evade the underlying reality. Judicial techniques for channeling discretion were developed in the first place to protect the rights of regulated business firms, and they would have no meaning if they did not have some bite. The usual form in a successful challenge is for the court to declare that the agency has not provided an acceptable rationale for its decision and for the court then to remand the issue for the agency to reconsider in light of the court's construction of the relevant standards. In the most important cases, courts will insist that a particular policy consideration must be accounted for—or must be disregarded—to provide a nonarbitrary result. This procedure is supposed to permit discretion, but it is also supposed to limit discretion. That is the point of the exercise. Many modern cases indeed suggest that it is not enough for courts to determine whether the agency's decision could be justified by legal considerations. Instead, courts insist on a hard look at all of the policy alternatives, in order to ensure that the agency actually did try to make the best choice instead of merely offering plausible excuses for policies really preferred for improper political reasons.[30]

Even under the "hard look" doctrine, however—for all of its pretensions to assuring a comprehensive assessment of all relevant considerations—the nature of litigation virtually assures that policy will not be considered in a detached and comprehensive way. The agenda for the court's inquiry—and therefore, to a significant extent, the agency's—will be shaped by the agenda of the challenging parties, their objections being the hurdles the court and the agency must clear to endorse a disputed policy. To characterize this state of affairs as merely assuring a fair hearing or due process to the challenger's arguments or objections is to miss the point. Requiring that agencies offer opportunity for affected interests to challenge their arguments or evidence would have little meaning if courts did not scrutinize the adequacy of administrative responses to these challenges. Due process has, and is meant to have, substantive implications. And in practice, the power to demand due process is essentially the power to obstruct. This point is most evident if one thinks about the due process guarantees for criminal defendants. No one supposes that jury trials and elaborate rules of evidence ensure that the criminal justice system always punishes in accord with moral deserts. Extensive procedural guarantees enable accused criminals to resist the imposition of criminal sanctions and thus serve to ensure that sanctions will not be lightly imposed. The significance of these procedural protections is perfectly illustrated in the phenomenon of plea bargaining, by which defendants agree to give up their right to insist on a trial if the prosecutor will disavow a stiffer charge or a heavier sentence.

The legal system has traditionally given a somewhat similar (if less extensive) power to regulated firms to make it hard for government to interfere with private property. And in most regulatory enforcement cases, regulated firms indeed strike informal bargains of this sort with regulatory agencies, gaining lesser penalties or easier compliance obligations by waiving their legal rights to resist the agency through administrative hearings and judicial appeals. Contemporary administrative law gives a similar bargaining power to selected interest groups or advocacy groups in order to make it hard for public officials to interfere with the public policy preferences of these groups. And like other potential litigants, advocacy groups may avoid formal court proceedings altogether if they can achieve what they seek merely by threatening to pursue a suit. Courts have even insisted that once a suit has been filed, out-of-court settlements between advocacy groups and the agency must be honored, even though no trial and no formal judicial decision has determined that the terms of the settlement are required by statute or by the public interest.[31] The logic of the system, again, is to satisfy the challenging party, not to safeguard the public interest in any larger terms.

One can think of this system as public control only if one somehow assumes that "the public" is adequately represented by advocacy groups or that the public interest is somehow equivalent to the sum total of interest group pressures. But there are many good reasons for thinking that public policy is already too skewed toward accommodation to interest group pressures. In many ways, inserting an overlay of judicial controls does not counter the maladies of interest group politics but simply extends them.

The Problem of Excessive Deference to Special Interests

To begin with, even though Congress has authorized any citizen to resort to the courts to complain of administrative neglect of his concerns, the reality must be far different. The bargaining leverage made available by the new administrative law is available to relatively few groups. In other words, only a relatively few groups can claim the proprietary stakes in the public interest that contemporary administrative law offers to protect.

The first reason is that litigation is time-consuming and expensive. Even to secure an initial court decision typically takes several years and large legal fees.[32] In practice, moreover, the chances of winning even a favorable initial decision seem to be very much affected by the prior litigational experience of challengers. In general, those who appear often in the courts on similar issues have a much better track record than first-time or infrequent litigants, possibly because they are more sophisticated about picking winnable issues on which to litigate and perhaps also because their arguments are treated more respectfully by judges.[33] At all events, while government agencies are upheld by the courts in the vast majority of cases overall, organized public interest groups generally win more than half of their challenges to government decisions.[34] In environmental litigation, the comparative results for which have been carefully tabulated, environmental advocacy groups have almost always won a higher proportion of their cases than business challengers[35]—probably because so many of the latter were one-time or infrequent litigants.

Furthermore, would-be challengers must recognize that a favorable initial decision may provide little more than an early opening for influence. The court may simply direct the agency to reconsider, to supply new evidence, to hold new hearings—and many more years of litigation may be necessary to secure an ultimately favorable result. An initial setback may be enough to inhibit an agency from pursuing policy initiatives that would be challenged again in the courts. But when groups are seeking to direct ongoing government regulatory efforts, even the patience and financing for years of litigation may not be enough to make a significant difference in policy.

This is so because the underlying weakness of courts, along with their hesitancy about detailed policy making, means that a great deal of effective discretion is still left to administrators—if they seek to exercise it. So, for example, years of litigation by groups urging protection for classical music did not succeed in forcing the Federal Communications Commission to prevent radio stations from abandoning classical music programming.[36] Litigation seeking to impose more active regulatory policies is most likely to be effective, therefore, when it seeks to impose policies that are already viewed with some sympathy by the agency involved, or at least when it seeks to impose policies that the agency has no strong incentives to resist. This is just what Joel Handler found in his survey of a wide variety of "law reform" initiatives (mostly at the state level) during the 1970s.[37]

Because federal agencies tend to be quite sensitive to political pressures from Congress, they are likely to be most responsive to advocacy group litigation when the policies—or at least the policy orientations—urged upon them are those which already command significant political support. Put simply, litigation is most likely to prove an effective advocacy technique when the advocacy group involved already has a good deal of political leverage. So, to cite the most pertinent counterexample to the failure of the classical music lovers, the NAACP needed only one suit against the FCC in the early 1970s to secure a long-term program under which minority businessmen were given special preference in the award of broadcasting licenses—at a time when racial preference schemes of this sort had already come to have powerful support in Congress and a high official of the NAACP had already been appointed to serve as a commissioner on the FCC. And when Reagan appointees at the FCC finally sought to abandon the program, minority preference was quickly restored by Congress—in a little provision of the notorious 1988 omnibus budget resolution, amid a vast array of such favors for specialized constituencies.[38]

The pattern of litigation brought by established public interest groups shows a clear recognition of the importance of congressional support. The most frequent target of public interest litigation, the EPA, is also one of the agencies most often scheduled for congressional oversight hearings, most of which are conducted by subcommittees sympathetic to the concerns of environmentalists. In general, public interest groups do not roam at large through the federal bureaucracy like Robin Hoods, striking at unpredictable places for the weak and dispossessed. They sue agencies that are already the subject of a great deal of congressional attention from committees with similar orientations.[39]

While the initial rhetoric of the public interest movement—deriding the "capture" of regulatory commissions by regulated firms—might have suggested a focus on single industry economic regulatory commissions like the ICC, these older agencies have received relatively little attention from organized consumer advocacy groups. Similarly, the protective subsidy schemes of the Agriculture Department received no significant attention from public interest groups.[40] Instead, public interest litigation has concentrated on a handful of agencies directly concerned with safety or environmental concerns. The public interest advocacy groups have concentrated, in a word, on securing their influence with "their" agencies. And just like specialized economic interests, they combine litigational efforts with extensive Washington lobbying efforts. Public interest advocacy groups usually have less staffing for lobbying efforts, but this shortfall does not seem to make their own patrons in Congress any less attentive to their concerns. Neither does it reduce the tendency of congressional oversight to try to insulate the policy concerns of particular constituency groups from larger claims on public policy.

Thus the new litigation is not an alternative to the traditional system of congressional oversight. It is a supplement to it. Congressional oversight of administrative agencies has long been recognized as a powerful brake on the capacity of new presidential administrations to force changes in policy. Together with the agency and its major constituency groups, congressional oversight committees form "iron triangles" of mutual support, according to this hoary lore, which make particular policy subsystems or subgovernments impervious to outside influence. The picture may always have been somewhat exaggerated, but the conclusion is sound enough: new administrations face tremendous political obstacles in trying to change established agency policies. Contemporary administrative law does not so much challenge this pattern as formalize and extend it, with the result of increasing certain kinds of policy inertia and bureaucratic wheel spinning.

The Problem of Bureaucratic Inertia

Critics on both ends of the political spectrum—and ordinary citizens in the middle—deride governmental bureaucracies for wheel spinning and red tape, for sluggishness and rigidity. As with special interest influence, the force of the charge in any particular case is, of course, very much a matter of perspective. For better or worse, a certain amount of inertia or rigidity is simply inescapable. Every organized program must rely on a large number of organizing assumptions and operating routines, taken as unquestioned "givens." The ordinary individual in the conduct of his own affairs cannot continually reconsider basic questions of aim and purpose, beginning each day by recalculating anew his entire stance toward the world. Large organizations, which must coordinate the activities of large numbers of people, must rely even more on fixed routines and perspectives.

Governmental bureaucracies, operating in politically charged environments, have additional, special incentives to adhere to established patterns. The reason is that change attracts notice and invites attack, while adherence to "the rules" or to established patterns is often a very useful response to complaints about performance. This may be particularly true of federal regulatory programs, just because they are left so vulnerable to political attack from legislative committees, in a system in which the legislature is perpetually in session but has no constitutional obligation (or institutional incentive) to support the executive authorities of the day.[41]

Contemporary administrative law reinforces these administrative tendencies to inertia and passivity in several ways. In the most obvious way, it extends procedural and judicial constraints to new fields of policy. Now, not only new exercises of coercive power but also new policies seeking to cut back on coercive controls may be challenged in court. To survive such challenges, policies seeking reduced controls must first be explained, justified, and placed open for criticism in accord with the norms of administrative due process designed to protect property owners. To put the point most sharply, deregulatory initiatives may now be challenged as readily as new regulatory efforts—and a number of early Reagan administration deregulation efforts were indeed overturned in the courts in this way. At least a few other proposed deregulation initiatives were explicitly abandoned on the grounds that the agency was unwilling to commit the necessary resources required to fight the predictable court battles that would follow.[42]

Yet court decisions of the 1980s have celebrated the need for judicial checks on policy change—as if rapid change were the central problem with the federal bureaucracy. In 1982, for example, the D.C. Court of Appeals overturned the Transportation Department's effort to repeal the controversial "airbags" safety rule on the ground that the rule had only recently been promulgated and "sudden" changes in policy ought to be viewed with suspicion—as if the presidential election intervening between the 1980 adoption and the 1981 repeal of the rule should have had no bearing on administrative policy.[43] In fact, as debate—along with hearings and litigation—on the risks and benefits of the airbag device had already proceeded for fourteen years, the court's intervention ultimately secured a perfect perpetuation of a long-established pattern: at the end of the 1980s, the Transportation Department continued to affirm (as it had throughout the 1970s) that the mandatory installation of this safety device might be a very good thing—but not just yet.[44] By contrast, in 1985 the Garment Workers Union brought a successful suit against the Labor Department's attempted repeal of a fifty-year-old regulation prohibiting textile work outside of factories. In this case, the D.C. Court of Appeals pointed to the very age of the measure as grounds for disallowing its repeal.[45] As it is wrong to repeal established regulations "suddenly," it is equally wrong, according to current legal doctrine, to repeal them after waiting too long. No court has yet announced the appropriate time an agency should wait—assuming there is one—before it may have the temerity to repeal an existing rule, if an interested constituency is eager to maintain the status quo.

Yet the significance of the judicial concern with "stability" or "regularity" goes beyond individual deregulation ventures. The point of procedure is to channel discretion, to limit the considerations that can be invoked to justify a decision. The fact that Al Capone, for example, was a notorious gangster may have seemed a sufficiently good reason for federal officials to try to put him behind bars. But the rules of criminal procedure forced the Justice

Department to prove particular charges "beyond a reasonable doubt," and the tax charges it finally pursued against Capone had to stand on their own evidence, apart from the notorious but less demonstrable indications of his wider criminality. Forcing administrators to justify in detail their decisions not to act more broadly forces them, in a similar way, to rely on legally acceptable rationales and legally acceptable kinds of evidence in making their decisions. This requirement not only burdens the revocation of established policies but establishes a presumption that new policies will proceed in roughly the same patterns as already established ones. There may be sensible rationales for differing approaches, but procedural and judicial controls limit the rationales that can be invoked to make distinctions.

As judges look for order, symmetry, continuity, and precedent to guard against "arbitrary" decisions, then, they encourage administrators to do the same. "We changed our mind" is not taken as a sufficiently good reason for new administrative policies, though it might seem to be a perfectly good reason in a country in which times change and voters often change *their* minds along with the times. The frustration of reformers—the horrified protest that "that just isn't done here"—tends to become elevated to a principle of law. "The law remains unchanged" is taken to be a perfectly good reason for blocking administrative policy change—though it is obvious that many laws overextend their usefulness and courts themselves are often urged (and often take the urging) to cut back or overturn antiquated laws, such as the Connecticut birth control statute overturned by the Supreme Court in the *Griswold* case.[46] Contemporary administrative law often seems wedded to the proposition that, whatever may be true for politically unaccountable courts in forcing changes on reluctant or deadlocked legislatures, when policy change comes from politically accountable executive officials, it ought to be viewed with special suspicion by courts.

The Problem of Policy Incoherence

Concerns to avoid attracting attention or provoking controversy create powerful incentives for government agencies to avoid the reconsideration of existing policies or existing policy assumptions. The same concerns operate in a more general way not only to shelter existing policies but to discourage strategic thinking about new policies, even in circumstances in which agencies are compelled to develop new policies. To think strategically, an agency must carefully consider various public needs and its own differing capabilities under a variety of circumstances. To think strategically, an agency must make distinctions: in a word, it must set *priorities*. But agencies are disinclined to set clear priorities for much the same reason that politicians are: a clear set of priorities implies that the concerns of some constituents are less important than those of others. Agencies, like politicians, are always tempted to avoid facing awkward tradeoffs by settling for vague or platitudinous formulas that seem to promise something to everyone.

It is true, of course, that no policy can please everyone (or please everyone equally) and that there are no universally accepted formulas for comparing the relative costs and benefits of different approaches, promising different costs or benefits to differently situated constituencies. In spite of the analytical difficulties, however, it is often possible to demonstrate that some policies will be vastly more effective than others (in terms of overall benefits secured) or vastly less expensive than others (in terms of agency resources or overall economic resources consumed) and so to see the outlines of better and worse choices—at least if one abstracts from the particularized consequences for specific constituencies. It is often possible to demonstrate that alternative *A* shows much promise and alternative *B* shows much promise, but that taking only some parts of *A* and some parts of *B* together is likely to yield self-canceling, unproductive outcomes overall.

But government agencies have few incentives to make the best tradeoffs or to set the most appropriate priorities because government is not the ultimate beneficiary and "the public"—or the relevant beneficiary of government action—is too dispersed to offer much guidance or to impose much accountability. A number of scholars have therefore suggested that over time, government agencies will tend to be most responsive to those interest groups which stand to benefit most directly from government policy, because such groups will find it easiest to organize, can more effectively track the benefits they receive, and can demand that they continue to receive them.

Public interest organizations have seemed to many observers to be helpful devices for countering this tendency insofar as they enable diffuse and unorganized interests to be represented in governmental policy deliberations. But advocacy groups can easily display the defect of their virtue in this respect. Just because they do seek to speak for large, diffuse constituencies, they cannot be readily held to account for their actions. Aaron Wildavsky and Mary T. Douglas have argued that public interest groups are inclined to issue shrill, hysterical, or "sectarian" denunciations because they could not otherwise mobilize their large and diffuse potential constituencies to pay attention, and to make donations to fund the lobbying and litigating efforts of these groups.[47] This claim does not appear to be true of all public interest organizations, though it may well explain the rhetorical intensity of some. Still, shrill rhetoric does not always imply extremist action, as the behavior of many legislative politicians illustrates. But whether the conduct of these organizations is better characterized as "sectarian" or "idealistic," it remains true that the supposed beneficiaries of their efforts have no ready means of determining whether these advocacy groups are actually securing them significant benefits overall.

To maintain their efforts—whether in raising funds from dispersed, passive supporters or in inspiring those who participate directly—advocacy groups must continue to advocate. The consequences of their efforts may be good for almost everyone or merely good for some people and bad for others. But even if the consequences of their efforts are, on balance, bad for most people, there is no very effective check on their advocacy, because the consequences of their efforts are always difficult to trace. Such advocacy efforts may thus be properly described as "ideological" in the sense that people who support their efforts—with direct contributions or merely with favorable responses in opinion polls—are generally registering an abstract or ideological affinity for the outlook or concerns of these groups, instead of informed assessments of the actual results achieved by these groups. To the extent that support is grounded on ideological affinity, these groups may have all the more incentive to take ideological stands even when these do not secure useful results, because their advocacy may seem clearest when most intransigent.

In this respect, the incentives of public interest advocates may not be all that different from the incentives of government agencies, which are also prone to symbolic gestures. What public interest advocates demand as political gestures to their outlook, agencies often find it easy enough to grant—even if their concession complicates or confuses overall policy—because coherent policy is not their overriding concern.

Things are no better when more specialized interests are allowed to contest regulatory decisions on the grounds that they do not give them what they deserve, or on the grounds that their own benefit is the chief object of the public interest. The Garment Workers Union, for example (or the knitwear manufacturers who joined in their suit), may well have calculated quite correctly that the prohibition of piecework by home workers would redound to the benefit of unionized factory workers (and their employers)—as most anticompetitive measures provide financial benefits to those who are allowed to remain in business. The Garment Workers may even have been correct in supposing that this Labor Department measure had been adopted in the 1930s for their special benefit—as New Deal administrators often adopted measures to reward specialized political constituencies. What served the interest of a declining union fifty years later might not have served the public interest on a broader view of the issue, however. But then, focusing on the claims of specialized beneficiaries always tends to obscure broader views of the public interest.

All of these points, moreover, view the problem of coordination or policy coherence from the standpoint of individual agencies. But the ultimate public concern is not simply with the performance of individual agencies but with the outcomes generated by government as a whole. Just as public law litigation tends to isolate particular agency policies from their larger contexts, it works to isolate individual agencies from the still more general policy context for government or for the country as a whole. Thus, to cite one of the more obvious examples, environmental groups have essentially forced a halt to the licensing and construction of new nuclear power plants by raising endless procedural challenges to the licensing of each new plant by the Nuclear Regulatory Commission. These challenges have so protracted licensing proceedings that the cost for utilities has become unacceptable. The result has been to encourage greater reliance on coal-burning power plants, which pose very considerable (and possibly much more serious) health hazards of their own. The relative safety of alternate energy sources is not the business of the Nuclear Regulatory Commission, however, so it is never weighed in such proceedings.[48] At the same time, environmentalists have worked to impede offshore oil drilling—in suits that again pay only scant attention to larger energy concerns. And still other interests have sued the Energy Regulatory Commission to impede the deregulation of natural gas pipeline pricing, which has limited the availability of this cleaner, safer fuel.[49]

The problem is only partly that judges lack the knowledge and skill to assess remote policy implications and so miss the larger context. The way litigation operates, it is not really the judge's responsibility to assess tradeoffs in the larger policy context. Under the logic of litigation, the judge is *supposed* to focus simply on the complaints of the particular challenger in relation to the particular agency and the particular statute involved, taking the policy issue raised by the challenger as *the* issue in dispute. For this reason, again, judicial control is not at all equivalent to genuine public control. And for this reason it aggravates the problem of coordinating diverse policy pleadings on behalf of the general public as a whole.

Reviving the Constitutional Argument

In a free country, people certainly have the right to advocate anything they think is good, whether for themselves or for others. People are certainly free to advocate policies or particular policy applications that most other people would think foolish or unproductive. But the traditional constitutional scheme sought to emphasize the distinction between political advocacy and private rights. Political advocacy was understood as an appeal to the public good, for which government officials would be responsible in the end to the general public. When, by contrast, individuals asserted valid claims about their own private rights, it was understood that government could not be blamed for honoring such claims because they were, after all, "private"—not subject to public debate or public responsibility. One simple way of summarizing the consequence of contemporary administrative law is to say that it makes more and more public policy accountable to private litigants rather than to the public—or, in other words, that it privatizes public policy as it legalizes it.

All of the effects sketched above seem to follow logically and predictably from superimposing the traditional judicial perspective on executive operations. As courts normally seek to provide preemptive protection for private rights or property rights, judicial protection for interest group claims provides preemptive weight to interest groups—that is to say, those interest groups already situated to exploit this additional leverage. As courts normally seek to protect property rights by trying to ensure that governmental coercion of property is confined by stable and predictable formulas, a more extensive system of judicial review tends to impose more stability and predictability on government policy in general—in other words, it tends to make established policy and policy frameworks more resistant to change. As courts normally seek to exclude private rights from the pulling and tugging of competing policy concerns, so judicial protection for particular interest group claims excludes various policies from general efforts to integrate or coordinate policy operations: it encourages fragmented or incoherent policy efforts.

How different would regulatory policy be if the courts did not exercise this new supervisory role? In truth it is difficult to say. For one thing, the influence of courts can never be measured simply by the apparent consequences of particular cases. Particular cases are *supposed* to cast a shadow, influencing expectations and calculations even when courts are not (but might subsequently be) involved. So, for example, no one supposes that elaborate rules of evidence imposed by courts in criminal trials only matter in actual trials: plainly, they make a difference in the calculations of police, prosecutors, and defense attorneys even when they strike bargains altogether apart from the supervision of judges.

The larger difficulty is that the effects of contemporary administrative law are, for the reasons sketched above, likely to parallel many of the effects of the constitutional scheme in its normal workings. To put the point most succinctly, executive energy is bound to be constrained in similar ways by the pressure of congressional oversight, operating at the behest of various constituencies. It was precisely to guard against the distorting effects of congressional factions on executive operations that the framers of the Constitution originally established a powerful chief executive not directly accountable to Congress, with power to exert a countervailing influence on administrative activity. It was precisely to guard against congressional domination of administration that *The Federalist* celebrated the need for "energy" in the executive, and presented "energy" as demanding a focused responsibility for administrative operations at the top of the executive hierarchy. The traditional constitutional perspective acknowledged the political or disputable character of administrative decision making but sought to provide institutional security against fragmented, incoherent, manipulated policy at the behest of particular constituency groups. Instead of forestalling this danger, contemporary administrative law helps to realize it.

The next three chapters seek to flesh out the case for the traditional constitutional perspective against the implicit premises of contemporary administrative law. Chapter 2 thus expands on the conceptual difficulties in viewing claims to regulatory benefits as "rights" and the greater problems that arise when the appeal to "rights" becomes entangled with claims for "representation"—when, that is, the individual powers of control associated with rights are conflated with the political balancing of claims entailed in political representation. Chapter 3 addresses the notion that the law has commanding force, even if no private rights are involved. It argues that, historically, rhetoric to this effect has involved little more than efforts to bolster particular claims on power and policy, because this view of law is so difficult to sustain in the American constitutional system. Finally, chapter 4 offers a brief overview of changing conceptions of the judicial role to suggest that the contemporary judicial preoccupation with upholding "values"—including the "value" of "legality"—is a conceit that makes little sense except as an excuse for the manipulation of public policy to the advantage of particular interest groups.

The case studies in Part III then seek to demonstrate that the consequences we would expect to follow from the constitutional perspective of contemporary administrative law are what we frequently do encounter in practice. Chapter 5 assesses the impact of some two decades of litigation against the Office for Civil Rights in the Department of Education, focusing on the ways in which this litigation simply served to enhance the questionable political priorities of the particular advocacy groups involved. Chapter 6 analyzes the impact of public interest litigation on the Food and Drug Administration, focusing on the ways in which this litigation has exacerbated the problems posed by an entrenched bureaucratic policy perspective at the FDA. Chapter 7 assesses the consequences of public interest litigation against the Occupational Safety and Health Administration, focusing on the ways in which this litigation has exacerbated the incoherence of OSHA's approach to the setting of major health standards. All of these cases involve efforts to secure more vigorous enforcement of regulatory controls. And all show rather broadly similar patterns, for the problems posed by public interest litigation tend to be closely related. It is just because it does enhance the power of particular advocacy groups that such litigation tends to entrench established policies and to frustrate the effective pursuit of sensible policy goals.

Are these case studies representative of contemporary administrative law? As with any selection of cases to illustrate larger patterns, there may be dispute about which cases are typical and which marginal or anomalous. The courts have certainly played a more intrusive role in the regulatory operations of these three agencies than they have in many others, but they have done so because major advocacy groups have been particularly interested in the work of these agencies. Case studies of public interest or public law litigation in other regulatory settings could certainly illustrate similar patterns, as we find indeed in much detail in Shep Melnick's thoughtful study of public interest suits against the EPA under the Clean Air Act.[50]

It is partly because Melnick and others have already devoted considerable study to environmental litigation that this volume does not give separate attention to that subject. Some readers, moreover, may think the environment has unique claims for judicial protection—a notion that Congress itself might seem to have endorsed in authorizing citizen suits in this one field. This form of litigation seems to me no less unconstitutional and no less inappropriate in relation to environmental amenities than elsewhere; but the general argument of this book may be illustrated with less complication (and less redundancy) from the case studies presented here. At the same time, the case studies in Part II do not examine litigation for regulatory benefits by what might generally be conceived as special interests—such as regulated trucking firms seeking to maintain favorable protective policies from the ICC. The reason for excluding such cases is that they are in some ways overly obvious targets, for it is transparent in such cases that specialized interests seek to make special, selfish claims on public policy. The virtue of the cases presented in Part II is that they do not involve special cases—either in the narrow sense of economic "special interests" or in the spiritual sense in which environmentalist advocacy has come to be regarded as "special." They involve intermediate cases, perhaps more revealing of the regulatory patterns that will remain the bread-and-butter concerns of regulatory policy making over the next decade.

The Politics of Interest Group Legalism

The concluding chapter seeks to summarize the argument in slightly broader terms and offers speculation about the likely future course of administrative law. The outlook in coming years may well be for a continuation of interest group legalism. If we continue to put up with the burdens of interest group legalism, however, it will not be because constitutional principles require such concessions but because we choose to ignore the Constitution.

PART II

CONFUSIONS OF THOUGHT

2

Rights or Representation—
or Muddle?

CONTEMPORARY administrative law gives judges a new role in regulatory oversight, apart from their traditional role as guardians of the legal rights of regulated firms or individuals. Simply stated, the new role invites judges to serve as amateur, unaccountable, episodic managers of regulatory performance. Stated in this way, the system seems impossible to defend. But this characterization actually leaves out the most disturbing element in contemporary administrative law, an element that goes far in explaining its survival: stated more accurately, the current system is one of episodic management by amateur, unaccountable judges *acting at the behest of organized interest groups.*

Most judges and legal commentators do not like to emphasize that administrative law has become a formalized system for the management of interest group politics. Instead, they appeal to the authority of a "law" that transcends the preferences of particular interests altogether or—in accord with the more recent trend in legal commentary—they appeal to the authority of "public values" that virtually transcend law. These evasions are more edifying but certainly much less plausible as an account of what contemporary administrative law is really about. And when carefully considered, they are not really very plausible or very compelling even as an idealized vision of the way things ought to be. But consideration of these fallback defenses of contemporary administrative law can be deferred to the next two chapters.

This chapter deals with the underlying reality in administrative law: the extension of legal protections to interest group claims. Most of the practical problems posed by contemporary administrative law do spring from its effort to safeguard the claims of interest groups or to formalize the prevailing Washington patterns of interest group politics. We are most unlikely to get sensible public policy from a system preoccupied with appeasing or safeguarding the claims of particular interest groups—and least of all when this task is left to judges performing as part-time, unaccountable amateurs in the policy process. But the illustration of the perverse outcomes yielded by this formalized system of interest group politics must be left to the case studies in the third part of this book.

This chapter seeks to fix the frame of reference for thinking about law and policy in regulatory operations, which is really the central issue. Particular policy outcomes are bound to be disputed by differently situated observers, and no system can guarantee universally approved results. At the same time, appeals to "law" and "values" are probably not taken altogether seriously even by most of their exponents in contemporary law schools. Almost every observer of regulatory affairs senses that the public interest is often very much up for grabs, and regulatory politics is very often, therefore, a scramble to see which contending interests can grab the most. Thus it is plausible to think that courts have a legitimate role in assuring that the claims of the various contending groups are adequately protected. Almost from the outset, the new system of administrative law has been defended by more candid commentators as a device for representing underrepresented interests in administrative policy making or for assuring particular constituencies their regulatory "entitlements" or their policy "rights."[1]

This chapter explains why these comfortable, commonplace formulas are actually quite confused and perverse. Starting from a "realistic" liberal skepticism about the public interest, they end by entrenching an inflexible, dogmatic commitment to particular interests or interest groups in public policy. They are not a mere adaptation of the traditional constitutional scheme but a perversion of constitutional government, which encourages the mortgaging of public policy to the most nimble or most vociferous interest group claimants. To explain why this is so, we must go back to first principles, to the initial grounding assumptions of liberal constitutionalism.

Why Constitutional Rights Are Individual Rights

The argument for judicial interventions to ensure the representation of under-represented interests assumes that government is essentially about balancing or reconciling the demands of conflicting interest groups. The argument, then, is that underrepresented interests will not get what they need or deserve if they do not have some special representative vehicle. This claim certainly sounds plausible, for so much of contemporary governmental policy making seems to reflect the pressures of competing interest groups, and it is a common observation that the resulting policies are often skewed in favor of more successful competitors at the expense of others who may seem more deserving on the merits of their claims.

Nonetheless, this emphasis on interests or interest groups disregards the perspective of constitutional government. According to *The Federalist*, "the great object" in framing a constitution is to "secure the public good and private rights . . . and at the same time to preserve the spirit and the form of popular government."[2] The authors of *The Federalist* were, of course, quite aware that most political activity is not animated by disinterested concern either for the public good or for private rights. That is why *The Federalist* devoted so much anxious attention to the vulnerability of "popular government" to the vice of "faction." *The Federalist* recognized that such self-seeking interest groups—or factions—would inevitably arise in any political system in which citizens were free to form their own interests and opinions and press them upon the government. But it refused to equate either the public good or private rights with the mere satisfaction of such interest group claims. Thus, the famous definition of "faction" in *The Federalist* pointedly notes that even "a majority . . . of the whole" body of citizens may be a faction, if "united and actuated by some common impulse of passion, or of interest, adverse to the rights of other citizens, or to the permanent and aggregate interests of the community."[3]

The constitutional perspective expounded by *The Federalist* rests on the political theory of liberalism in its broad, historical sense. As a great liberal theorist has observed, "the whole history of constitutionalism, at least since John Locke . . . is the same as the history of liberalism."[4] The connection is obvious: modern constitutionalism, as an ordering framework of institutions, is primarily concerned with constraining power, and liberalism, as a political theory, is above all suspicious of unconstrained power. It is suspicion of power that has made liberal constitutionalism insist on rights, and insist that rights be located in individuals, while coercive power is reserved to public authority.

Critics of liberalism—and there have been critics, as long as there have been

41

advocates of liberal doctrine—have always maintained that the isolated individual is an altogether unnatural, theoretical construction. But the historic appeal of liberal constitutionalism has been to safeguard people from being placed under fixed obligations to social claims—such as those of the clan, the race, the church, or the class—which have often been viewed by some people as more "natural" and by many others as intolerably oppressive. By vesting rights in individuals, constitutional government seeks to make the fewest presumptions about what individuals would or should choose for themselves.

Even in America, it is true, the law has always recognized certain exceptions to the principle that rights can only be claimed and exercised by individuals acting for themselves. But even the historic exceptions have rationales consistent with the underlying principle. A corporation, for example, may be treated as an individual "person" for many legal purposes, which allows the corporation to exercise the property rights of large numbers of individual investors. But this is possible only because the actual, individual investors—those who own the assets of the corporation—have voluntarily and expressly agreed to invest their property in a common structure, operating under previously agreed terms for corporate decision making. So, too, parents are often empowered to speak for their children; special guardians may be empowered to speak for senile or mentally infirm individuals; trustees may be empowered to speak for deceased donors. But in all such cases, someone else is authorized to exercise an individual's rights, because the individual is formally determined to be incapable of speaking for himself.

While seeking to protect individual choice—the range of choice guaranteed by rights—liberal constitutionalism has, historically, been most concerned with limiting the exercise of coercive power. For that reason constitutional government has always been associated with government by consent, that is, with electoral checks on government or with "the spirit and form of popular government." In one sense, this demand for governmental accountability expresses the same suspicion of received formulas that justifies the demand for individual rights: as the structure of individual rights checks others from presuming to know what individuals would want or how they would exercise their rights on their own, electoral accountability is a check on such presumption in government.

It misses the larger point, however, to complain that constitutional government does not assure sufficient or sufficiently direct governmental accountability to the electorate. Public authority can never be the direct counterpart of private rights, simply assuring that people can pursue their preferences as they choose. Among the most obvious reasons is that, while individuals can make relatively clear and consistent choices for themselves, "the people" or "the public"—an enormous number of diverse individuals—almost never can. The point of individualizing or privatizing rights is to leave some sphere of choice in which individuals can act without having to obtain the permission or consent of others. Emphasizing the public or accountable character of public authority finally has the opposite point: to ensure that public authority cannot be exercised with the same disregard of others as can private rights.

"The public" may sound like an artificial entity—even more than "the individual"—but the appeal of constitutional government, again, is precisely to frustrate a too ready identification of government with what some people may be eager to claim as more "natural" groupings. The point of holding government accountable to the public is to preempt visions of government as properly in the service of the church, the race, the class, and so on, without denying that the proper course of public policy must finally be determined by human beings, not by binding formulas derived straight from nature or divine revelation. For that reason *The Federalist* was quite prepared to view even the majority as a potentially dangerous faction, and it praised the scale and complexity of the new constitutional system for resisting the impulses of those more "natural" majorities likely to operate in smaller or simpler democracies.

In its eagerness to protect the claims of interests or interest groups, contemporary administrative law violates the basic principles of constitutional government at both ends. On the one hand, it allows legal advocates to exercise the claims (or, in the rhetoric of the advocates, "the rights") of other people, without the consent of those other people and, most of the time, even without their knowledge. Legal advocates therefore obtain something akin to the authority of medieval lords, speaking for their vassals and serfs as their natural representative.[5] On the other hand, to the extent that contemporary administrative law holds public authority accountable to particular interest groups, it limits or burdens accountability to the general public—as medieval parliaments sought to assure separate representation to distinct social "estates," allowing the church or the nobility to frustrate general measures.

The difficulty is not merely a matter of appearances. In evading the traditional strictures of liberal constitutionalism, contemporary administrative law makes easier just what these strictures were designed to make more difficult: the accumulation of unaccountable private power. By allowing advocates to speak for others without their consent, administrative law makes it easy to exaggerate the number of people who share the advocates' particular preferences—thus attributing preferences to people who do not share them. What is more to the point, in forcing government to account to interest groups, contemporary administrative law makes it easier for particular interest groups or their self-appointed advocates to deflect, distort, or frustrate public policy for their own private purposes.

The fact that interest group advocates can only enforce their claims with the approval of judges does little to affect these evident conclusions. If judges had some mystical gift for discerning just how far "the public good" could accommodate the claims of particular interest groups—or just how far it should be entrusted to the appeals of particular private advocates—then it might, after all, be sensible to view judicial decisions as altogether detached from the parties demanding those decisions. But if administrative law is to be defended as a more realistic mode of policy making than our traditional constitutional scheme, it must forego such mystical appeals to the "charismatic" gifts of judges. In fact, most defenses of contemporary administrative law end up invoking a rather mystical vision of law, akin to the vision that made medieval jurists anxious to maintain that even parliaments were not responsible for making public policy, but simply for finding or refining preexisting "law"—so that neither the interests at stake nor the policies resulting from their maneuvers need be openly acknowledged.[6]

The Functional Meaning of Rights

Judicial decisions provide the sanction of law for the exercise of coercive force. If one assumes that public authority must retain a monopoly on the legitimate or sanctioned use of force,[7] then it may seem plausible to view courts as a kind of ultimate public authority. It requires barely another step in this reasoning to conclude that whenever the law sanctions the exercise of coercive force, it does so for some public purpose, so that judges are simply ensuring the proper application of force for the achievement of public purposes.

A disciplined mind might indeed follow out this reasoning, as mathematicians can follow out syllogisms in non-Euclidean geometry in which parallel lines do cross or theoretical physicists can reason about subatomic particles for which the ordinary laws of time and motion no longer apply. Thus, in adhering to this perspective, one could argue that any time a private person brings a dispute before a court—seeking judicial sanction for the exercise of force to settle the dispute—the litigant is simply seeking to vindicate public purposes or simply offering his own contribution to law enforcement. Then it could be said that the law generally adopts the policy of delegating control over resources to those with the information and incentives to deploy those resources most efficiently through direct, contractual exchanges. And to protect this public policy scheme, the law prohibits the breaking of contracts or the unauthorized interference with persons and property. When courts order the perpetrators of contract breaches or tortious conduct to desist from their

44

derelictions (or to pay damages to the victims), such orders might be viewed, from the same perspective, as a means of vindicating the original public policy scheme for the management of resources. Although the legal system limits appeals for such orders to the victims of contract breaches or tortious conduct, even this limitation might be described as a public policy measure to guard against an inefficient displacement of resources into excessive litigation or an unnecessarily high degree of compliance with the law.

Even today, however, when "realist" perspectives on law continue to exert very great influence, all but the most willfully perverse legal scholars would find this perspective strange and disorienting.[8] Judges, lawyers, and ordinary citizens find it vastly more natural to think that when courts grant relief to victims of unlawful conduct, they are, in fact, upholding the *rights* of the victims, not the interests or policy goals of society at large. We may think it is economically advantageous to society to maintain private control of property or private rights in general. We may think it is politically convenient to acknowledge a protected range of personal liberties, which, by "privatizing" choices, can remove many contentious subjects from public debate. We may insist that private rights must, in any case, be defined in ways that accommodate larger social or public concerns. But whenever we speak of "rights," we imply that the claims of the owner or holder of those rights must be honored, if he chooses to press them before a court.

That is, after all, the point of describing rights as "private": as long as the law does recognize a right, a claim of "right" cannot be a matter for public or political dispute, but rather a direct, overriding imperative. And the point of separating judges from the rest of the political system is precisely to preserve this private or detached character of individual rights. So, in the very decision that first asserted the Supreme Court's claim to judge the constitutionality of congressional enactments—seemingly the most openly public or political role of the judiciary—Chief Justice Marshall insisted that "the province of the court is solely to decide on the rights of individuals."[9] Well into the twentieth century, the Supreme Court could still cite with approval the dictum of the Marshall Court that "It is only where rights of persons or of property are involved . . . that courts of justice can interpose relief."[10]

Once we view courts as upholding private rights (rather than as managing social interests), two limitations on the system come to seem inescapable. At least they seem inescapable if rights are to function as legal guarantees of private or personal control or as guarantees against interference from others. And both of these limitations are, indeed, still acknowledged by courts in private litigation.

The first is that rights must have limits. Otherwise, every right holder could interfere with every other, and rights would no longer protect private spheres of control, guaranteed against interference from others. Thus courts still speak of legal claims arising when rights are "invaded"—implying that a person's rights have distinct boundaries, like property in land. Of course, this spatial image is only a metaphor, but the traditional conception of rights as the "property" of the owner encourages such metaphors. So, for example, a libel suit may seek redress against a journalist who has never set foot on the house or land of the victim, perhaps has never even met the victim—but can still be held accountable for damaging the victim's good name, conceived as a valuable property that has been injured or invaded by the libel. Similarly, a modern product liability suit may force a manufacturer to pay damages to someone injured by one of his products, though the manufacturer has never been anywhere near the victim's home.[11]

Mindful that rights to redress always involved interference with the free action of others, American courts in the nineteenth century were reluctant to acknowledge many such rights. In this century, courts have been less concerned about interference with freedom of action, at least in economic matters, and so inclined to recognize rights to redress in many more circumstances. But it is still true that individuals do not have unlimited rights to seek redress for every kind of harm or disadvantage imposed on them by the actions of others. So, for example—and it is a quite important example, historically—a business firm that opens a new branch or expands its operations may take sales away from competing firms and in that sense impose financial harm on its competitors. But because we generally refuse to acknowledge a right to be free from the effects of business competition, this harm is not a legally recognized injury for which the competitors can seek redress through the courts. As Sir William Blackstone put it, pointing to the Latin derivation of the modern English term, "The contemplation of what is *jus* [right] is necessarily prior to what may be termed [in the legal sense] *injuria.*"[12]

In addition to this fixing of formal, legal limits on what can be claimed in the name of private rights, there is a second limitation on the vindication of rights by courts, namely, that courts only act to redress violations of rights at the behest of the actual victims of such violations. In one sense, this restriction ensures that rights remain truly private by limiting judicial action to cases in which rights have actually been violated. Each person may have a right to be free from libelous attacks or from physical injury inflicted by defective products. But no one can approach a court to demand preventive action against all newspapers or all manufacturers who *might* violate his rights in this way at some unspecified time in the future. In most cases, courts can only grant relief retrospectively, once it is clear precisely who has violated the plaintiff's rights in precisely what way. In effect, the legal system recognizes rights to the redress of particular injuries but not rights to be free from the risk that such injuries may occur.[13] Rights of the latter kind could not remain private, but would instead expand until they merged with a right to the exercise of general regulatory controls over everyone else—so that those who feared they might be libeled could demand a general censorship scheme to protect their rights, and those who feared they might be injured by faulty products could demand a program of supervision over manufacturing to protect their rights. The limitation of judicial action to the actual victims of legal injury avoids this result by keeping rights private.

This same limitation also maintains the private character of rights in a different way. If only the actual victim may sue for redress, then the victim is left to decide for himself how to exercise his rights. The victim of a libel, for example, may decide that, on balance, he would be better off not pressing a suit, for litigation might simply generate more embarrassing publicity, even if the suit did secure financial damages in the end. Similarly, the victim of a defective product may decide to forego litigation, if the manufacturer offers him handsome compensation in order to avoid the bad publicity of an official court judgment against his product. Or the victim of a breach of contract may decide not to press the matter in litigation in order to maintain good business relations in the future with the other party to the contract. In all such cases, if the victim does not want to press his rights in court, no one else may insist that his rights be vindicated in litigation.

It does not matter that others may be disadvantaged by such decisions not to litigate. A publishing company might lose book sales, for example, if one of its authors refused to press a libel action; other consumers might be placed at greater risk by the failure to pursue a product liability suit; a supply firm might lose some business from its client if the client refused to pursue a breach of contract suit against one of its clients. But in general courts will not allow even those suffering derivative harm to bring suits invoking the rights of others. For if third parties could insist on pursuing the legal rights of others, rights would no longer remain under the control of individual owners or holders—the libel victim's good name would, after all, remain at the mercy of others, the business firm could no longer view contracts as merely serving its own interests, and so on. Rights, in short, would cease to be private.

Once these limitations are accepted, what finally gives force to rights is the notion that judges are bound to uphold properly presented claims about rights. In most private litigation, this approach is just what litigants demand and just what judges say they are providing. In deciding a lawsuit in favor of one party or the other, the judge denies that he is actually favoring the winner over the loser; he claims simply to be recognizing what the winner was already entitled to receive by virtue of his rights, quite apart from the judge's personal preferences regarding the outcome. The judge can disclaim any responsibility for determining whether the plaintiff has been selfish, obstinate, petty, or perverse in asserting his rights in the lawsuit: what the plaintiff has a right to demand, he has a right to receive, and the legal validity of his rights stands quite apart from his personal character (or his ultimate moral deserts) as a litigant.

This view of the matter may seem rather formalistic. But formal reasoning is essential to the logic of rights. For that reason, even today those legal theorists who are most insistent about the moral priority of rights—from Ronald Dworkin on the left to Richard Epstein on the right—are also the most unabashed defenders of formal reasoning in judicial decision making.[14] If judges were not compelled to uphold rights, litigants would simply be supplicants for judicial favor, desperately endeavoring to persuade the judge that social advantage would be served by giving them what they seek. And, in fact, formal notions continue to exercise a very considerable hold on the judicial imagination, just because most people would be shocked if judges simply announced that "Yes, you may have presented a valid claim about your rights, but we aren't going to honor it, because we think it would be politically or economically awkward to do so."

As long as litigants are viewed not as lobbyists for particular public policies but as bearers of legally obligatory claims, courts cannot readily step back from these claims to review the exigencies of public policy. But it then becomes a matter of extreme importance to determine who may bring what claims before a court. Contemporary administrative law, by contrast, proceeds on the premise that, when government is the defendant, it is not necessary to worry much about the basis of the plaintiff's claim. The limitations that apply in private litigation no longer apply in public law litigation, so the logic that justifies the formal neutrality of courts in private litigation no longer applies. This state of affairs might be described as giving "rights" a new meaning. It would be more accurate to describe it as allowing rights to escape the limitations ensuring their private character and transforming rights into peremptory claims on public policy.

The Distinctiveness of Public Authority

In ordinary litigation, rights have a negative character in the sense that they only entitle the claimants to the relief of particular injuries in order to "make them whole again"—and making the claimant "whole" has no more substantive meaning than relieving particular incursions prohibited by the rules. Judicial relief for legally recognized injuries may still leave the claimant quite poor and miserable, then, if that was his condition at the outset. This negative quality of rights follows from the fact that private rights can only be pressed against particular individuals who have violated the rules protecting the claimant's own rights. It is this rule bound character that distinguishes private rights from claims to govern others for one's own benefit. If rights were not limited in this way, the rights of potential defendants would be jeopardized, for they could then be held liable for actions they could not have known were wrongful or prohibited.

Because of these limitations, people have always expected more from government than the mere provision of courts to settle claims about private rights; and from the outset, of course, government in the United States has always provided more. From the very beginning the federal government collected taxes, delivered the mails, fielded an army to fight hostile Indians on the frontier and a navy to protect American shipping on the high seas. State and local governments built roads and canals, financed schools, enacted and enforced a variety of criminal measures—notably including prohibitions on "victimless crimes" such as gambling and prostitution, which were judged to be socially intolerable even though no one had any private right to suppress them.

In the nineteenth century, advocates of such government services may sometimes have claimed that citizens had the right to expect these public benefits. But this assertion was simply a form of rhetoric, as no one imagined that a citizen could file suit to enforce such expectations. As the scale of government benefits and services increased in the early twentieth century, politicians may have resorted more readily to such rhetoric in order to emphasize the importance of particular government programs. So, for example, at the end of the New Deal, President Franklin Roosevelt urged the need for a "second Bill of Rights," which would "guarantee to every citizen" the "right to remunerative employment," the "right to decent housing," the "right to an adequate education," and so on.[15] But all of these claims were still surely a rhetorical formula. The New Dealers were generally hostile to courts, precisely because they assumed that judicial solicitude for private rights would impede the progress of the New Deal's larger social vision; and New Dealers thus viewed even judicial enforcement of many guarantees in the old Bill of Rights with considerable hostility and suspicion.

By the 1970s, as expanding social welfare measures had come to seem an entrenched element of American government, serious scholars indeed argued that every citizen should be conceived as having an absolute right to government assistance of various kinds. So, for example, Henry Shue, a leading scholar of philosophy and public affairs, argued that all governments in the world ought to recognize a human right to economic subsistence or to the satisfaction of basic material needs, because personal autonomy—which he viewed as the goal of the classical rights of liberty and property—would be meaningless without such guarantees.[16]

Still, it is easy to explain why rights of this kind were never developed by courts acting on their own. Imagine the destitute person coming before a court to enforce this right to provision for his basic material needs: against whom, exactly, would he bring such a suit, and what exactly would he be entitled to demand? Even the most creative court would have difficulty articulating—let alone purporting to discover in past precedents—the rule that would entitle the destitute claimant to present a bill for his "minimal" needs to some total stranger and then force the stranger to pay for these needs. If anyone in need could pursue enforceable rights of this kind against anyone else with the wherewithal to finance them, no one could be sure of retaining control over his own property. The whole system of private rights would collapse, and all property would be no more than a temporary borrowing of resources from a common pool, reborrowable on demand from the next person in need. It is just because courts do seek to maintain a working system of private rights that they do not openly venture to enforce rights that impose open-ended duties in this way on unconnected strangers.

Only a government, with its vast organizing powers, can transfer resources among unconnected strangers to make good on such rights without unacceptable violence to the rights of others. And advocates of such rights thus look to government to satisfy them. In the late 1970s, Harvard University Law Professor Laurence Tribe thus claimed to foresee the emergence in American constitutional law of a "general doctrine . . . [that] recognizes for each individual a constitutional right to a decent level of affirmative governmental protection in . . . health and housing, work and schooling."[17] Federal courts did elaborate certain procedural protections on a range of existing government benefit programs in the course of the 1970s, but the courts certainly never came close to implementing such an ambitious vision of constitutional protections. A decade later they are no closer at all to doing so.[18] In general, social welfare measures still extend only so far as they are authorized by the positive enactments of elective legislators.

The reason again is plain. If courts could demand the creation, the extension, or the perpetuation of government benefit programs whenever they deemed it necessary to assure "a decent level of affirmative governmental protection," they would have to claim an open-ended power to impose new taxes. Such power would nullify the fundamental constitutional principle that taxation can only be imposed by a representative public body. And this principle *is* fundamental—sufficiently so to have justified the American Revolution—just because taxation does allow resources to be transferred from some citizens to otherwise unconnected strangers. Limiting this power to a publicly accountable body provides at least some institutional assurance that such transfers will only be undertaken when deemed to be for the benefit of the public at large; and the individual taxpayer does, after all, have a real connection to the public at large, a connection which is preserved (or at least acknowledged) by his vote. The mere claim of the needy person cannot give him the right to obtain funds from unconnected others. The promise of constitutional government is that individuals are only answerable to those whose particular rights they have injured—or to the public at large: if it were otherwise, we would have not a system of equal rights under the law, but a system in which some citizens—by staking absolute claims for "affirmative government protection"—could effectively stake claims on the private rights of others, as if needy citizens were governments unto themselves.[19]

For all of that, however, no American jurist has ever denied that governments can indeed create new rights to particular government benefits. Some of the most famous decisions of the Marshall Court in the early nineteenth century were precisely aimed at upholding individual claims to vested rights, created by government, in conferring corporate charters or granting parcels of land.[20] And when the legislature directs the conferral of a specific benefit on a specific individual (or a specified kind of claimant), there is nothing at all contrary to constitutional principles in allowing courts to enforce such claims against the executive—as Chief Justice Marshall concluded in *Marbury v. Madison.* From this point of view, there is no constitutional objection to a legislatively created right to welfare payments for anyone meeting the legislatively enacted qualifications. Thus, even in the heyday of laissez-faire jurisprudence, early twentieth century courts found no difficulty enforcing rights to legislatively created pension benefits.

If legislatures are free to create many new rights to government benefits, however, there remain some important constitutional limitations on this power—just as there are constitutional limitations on the legislative power to abridge or curtail existing rights. Constitutional limitations of the latter sort remain well accepted in contemporary American law, because most people see that unlimited legislative power could pose considerable danger to individual rights. But the framers of the Constitution placed more reliance on structural constraints on legislative power than on enumerated guarantees in the Bill of Rights, and they saw these structural constraints as important equally for safeguarding the public good as for protecting private rights.

The underlying difficulty with creating new rights is that when something is granted to a private person as a right, it is necessarily withdrawn from public control. This point follows, again, from the meaning of private rights: when a person has a legal right to claim or do some thing, the implication is that no one else may legally constrain him from obtaining or doing that thing. If there were no limits on the creation of new rights, then, all aspects of public policy might be transferred to private control in this way. For just this reason, limitations have always been recognized.

Even in the nineteenth century, in the heyday of judicial solicitude for contract claims and vested rights, the Supreme Court insisted that legislatures could not grant binding guarantees to private persons against changes in legislative policy. In the classic case, the Court held that in conferring a charter to operate a lottery, a state legislature could not be understood to have granted the lottery company a right to be exempted from a subsequent law prohibiting lotteries, because the "power of governing is a trust committed by the people to the government, no part of which can be granted away."[21] Similarly, legislatures may not grant away their own lawmaking responsibilities by delegating to private parties the right to make legal rules binding on others. This principle, already emphasized by John Locke in the seventeenth century, was repeatedly affirmed by the Supreme Court in the nineteenth century and finally invoked in the 1930s in striking down several regulatory measures of the early New Deal. The objection to these New Deal measures, the Court emphasized, was not so much that they delegated legislative power to executive agencies (which, the Court acknowledged, might properly exercise some subsidiary rule making powers, pursuant to legislative authorization) but precisely that they delegated public authority to unaccountable private businessmen.[22]

Just as constitutional principles limit the authority of Congress to delegate its own powers to private persons, the same principles must limit the extent to which Congress may delegate executive power to private persons. The separation of powers, after all, is a constitutional requirement, not a mere arrangement of convenience. And the central purpose of the separation of powers is to inhibit abuses of public power by limiting legislative restrictions on rights to general measures, which must then be left to the particular enforcement decisions of constitutionally distinct authorities. The federal Constitution emphasizes this aspect of the separation of powers with an express prohibition on bills of attainder—legislative enactments imposing penalties on particular, named persons—and by conferring an unlimited pardon power (unlimited, at least, in regard to "public" offenses) on the chief executive. This aspect of the separation of powers is further emphasized by the mode of selection for the chief executive, which, instead of making him accountable to Congress, makes him accountable to the public at large. Under the constitutional scheme of separated powers, then, the executive always retains a certain sphere of discretion in the enforcement of coercive measures, because the legislature may never peremptorily direct the executive to undertake particular coercive actions.[23]

Legislation may certainly obligate the executive to honor newly created rights to government benefits of many kinds, such as payments of money, deeds, commissions, patents, or other individualized benefits analogous to property. In fact, Congress can (and frequently has) enacted "private" bills directing executive officials to deliver particular benefits to specific, named individuals. Even when Congress merely enacts general eligibility criteria for the receipt of government benefits, those who meet the criteria may be recognized as having a right to the relevant benefits. And what a private person may claim as a right, executive officials can have no discretion to withhold. But such rights to government assistance cannot be readily extended to the would-be beneficiaries of executive enforcement operations.

The first great difficulty with such an enforcement beneficiary "right" is that, in most circumstances, it cannot be a claim to a distinct, well-defined benefit, comparable to the claim for a particular sum in financial payments. In practice, it is almost always uncertain what the executive should do in enforcing coercive measures, which means that it is almost always uncertain what the executive would have to do to avoid violating such a right. Well into this century, courts acknowledged this difficulty by insisting that they could only order executive officials to take action when such action corresponded to a mandatory rather than a discretionary duty.[24] And coercion of third parties was never viewed as mandatory because no one supposed that any legislative enactments could properly eliminate all executive discretion in such matters.

The larger and more fundamental difficulty with rights of this kind is that they can never be plausibly viewed as private. This problem is what most clearly distinguishes them from other kinds of accepted rights to government assistance. So, for example, when Congress establishes rights to the receipt of government payments, those who claim such rights may be seen as advancing claims that function like ordinary private rights—claims that legally affect no one else or are no one's business but the claimants. This view is plausible because the funding for such claims is already in the public treasury, having been previously collected from the taxpayers in an entirely separate exercise of public power. Whatever objections the taxpayers might have had to the program must already have been settled by the legislative decision to enact the relevant taxes and establish the program.[25]

When a private person claims a right to demand executive enforcement against third parties, however, it can hardly be said that the targets of such enforcement are already under public control or that their objections to enforcement have already been settled in an earlier public decision. Because the executive retains discretion in the enforcement of coercive measures, its decisions on how to exercise its public duty are still open. If someone sought to enforce his right to have the executive proceed in a certain way, the litigation would have to focus on the general question of how the executive should proceed against third parties. Instead of being a private matter—no one's business but the plaintiff's own—a suit of this kind would clearly amount to the injection of particular private preferences into an executive decision about public policy. In consequence, the executive, instead of remaining responsible for the public good above particular private preferences, would become a conduit through which particular private claimants could impose their own private preferences on others.

It is true, of course, that every private suit seeks to impose one party's will on the other. And there is no question that legislation can establish new private rights, enforceable against other private persons, in many circumstances. But the formalism of rights—limiting litigation over rights to the redress of specific, legally recognized injuries—is precisely designed to limit the exercise of such coercive power. Put another way, the formalism of rights seeks to distinguish the power conferred by rights from the power available to government.[26] The whole point of suits demanding executive enforcement is to extend the reach of private rights, so that, in the name of "rights," private persons can wield the power of government to control unconnected strangers. If the plaintiff in such a suit against the government could file his own suits against all of the third parties involved (those he wanted the executive to target for enforcement), he would not, after all, have any need to sue the executive.

When the law does not recognize any direct private right in one person to protest the harms done him by others, the usual reason is that the law assumes it is not in the public interest to suppress such harms—as with the harms resulting to particular firms from ordinary business competition. Sometimes the law does favor the suppression of the harm involved but still refuses to recognize individual, private rights to relief. This refusal may occur because the "harm" involved cannot be well defined, as would be necessary for the recognition of private rights to relief. Or it may occur because the connection between individual perpetrators and individual victims is much too incidental or diffuse or much too entangled in the expectations of numerous intervening persons for the recognition of private rights to relief—as where automobile emissions are known to contribute to unacceptable levels of overall air pollution in a particular urban area, but the contribution of any one auto to the breathing problems of any one victim is impossible to trace. In such circumstances, we usually establish public regulatory programs instead of recognizing private rights in particular victims against particular perpetrators of harm. Either way, what has been placed under public control would be placed at the disposal of private advocates if they were permitted to sue the executive to demand more vigorous enforcement.

In several major regulatory enactments aiming at the control of pollution,

Congress in the early 1970s did expressly authorize "any citizen" to challenge the adequacy of regulatory enforcement by the EPA. If one accepts the preceding argument, it should be clear that such authorizations violated elemental constitutional principles: on a sound reading, the Constitution simply does not permit Congress to authorize the entangling of private preferences in this way with executive decision making on behalf of the public. Far from questioning the constitutional propriety of such rights, however, contemporary administrative law recognizes such claims to influence the implementation of public programs even when Congress has not expressly authorized them.

This perversion of constitutional government may have come to seem plausible and acceptable in recent decades because something of this sort had already been practiced, in much more limited ways, under the old administrative law. But in retrospect these precedents are anything but reassuring. They suggest, on the contrary, that a system of this sort is likely to generate just those policy distortions that one would expect from this confusion of formal roles: the distortion of public policy to satisfy the particular preferences of particular private interests.

The Novelties of Administrative Law

There was no separate system of administrative law in the nineteenth century. Anyone who claimed that a government official had done him an injury (that is, an injury to a legally protected right) could sue the particular offending official for relief or redress. But just as in private litigation, if the action (or inaction) of government officials had not done some injury to the legally protected rights of a would-be challenger, he had no grounds for a lawsuit. It did not matter whether the challenger had been incidentally disadvantaged or harmed by a governmental action, as a domestic manufacturer might be harmed by the decision of a customs inspector to undervalue the duties owed on imported goods. It did not even matter if this harmful action might have violated some valid legal obligation of the government to third parties or to the general public, as might be true in the case of a negligent customs inspector. If the government had not violated its obligations to a would-be challenger, he had no case. There was no separate doctrine of "standing"—of legal capacity to be heard by a court—apart from the rules or doctrines defining particular "actionable" claims. Even the term "standing" was scarcely mentioned at all in federal court decisions until well into the twentieth century.[27]

Administrative law developed in the early decades of this century as Congress began to delegate essentially legislative powers to regulatory commissions, beginning with the ICC. The ICC was given the power to set "just and reasonable" railroad rates and to regulate the routes and services offered by interstate railroads. It was expected to perform these tasks not by extrapolation from preexisting rules, in the manner of a court, but by weighing a variety of shifting considerations urged by a variety of competing interests (different shippers, different railroads, and so on), somewhat in the manner of a legislature.

In the early decades of the twentieth century, however, federal courts still presumed to impose substantive limits even on legislatures to ensure that their enactments, when restrictive of private rights, could be justified by legitimate public purposes. Under the doctrine of "substantive due process," the Supreme Court thus ventured to strike down a good deal of early labor legislation, such as minimum wage and maximum hours laws. In such cases, the Court insisted that it was not attempting to sit in judgment over legitimate exercises of legislative discretion, but was simply ensuring that legislatures acted within their proper powers or constitutional jurisdiction—to enact measures for the public good rather than to manipulate the rights of some citizens for the parochial benefit of others. The premise of such endeavors was that the Constitution—or natural law—already implied distinct limits on legislative discretion, limits clear enough for a court to discern, so that it would still be enforcing law rather than merely applying its own political or policy preferences.

In this context, it seemed perfectly natural for the courts to review the determinations of the ICC in order to ensure their fidelity to the very vague standards of the commission's legislative charter, with courts again insisting that they were not substituting their preferences for the discretion of the commission but simply keeping the commission within the legal bounds of its jurisdiction. If it seemed "natural," it also seemed essential, even for less demanding conceptions of the rule of law, because the commission did not usually regulate by general rules, in the manner of a legislature, but by particular determinations involving particular railroads, in the manner of a court proceeding case by case. At any rate, the distinction between recognizing legal limits on the scope of discretion and evaluating the substance of particular exercises of discretion was very hard to maintain. In practice, therefore, when railroads appealed orders or rulings of the ICC, their legal arguments were entangled in policy arguments about what the public interest really required. The pattern spread to other administrative regulatory programs involving other industries as new regulatory commissions were established.

Most of the time, however, it was altogether unclear where "the public interest"—the vague central term in most of the regulatory statutes—really lay. Contemporary economists indeed doubt that market competition in transportation services—whether in trucks, buses, airlines, or even railroads—yields any systematic inadequacies that need to be corrected by government regulation.[28] If there were important nonefficiency or noneconomic rationales for regulation in such fields, they were rarely well articulated or widely agreed upon. In these circumstances, it was all too easy for regulated businesses to identify the public interest in regulation with their own particular interests, and for regulators to endorse this identification.

The first important "standing" cases—cases recognizing a claim to sue, unconnected with the challenger's own distinct rights—did not, however, arise from judicial efforts to curb such tendencies. On the contrary, the first standing cases sought to formalize such privileged claims on the public interest. In the mid-1920s the first of these cases, the *Chicago Junction* case, recognized the claims of competing railroads to challenge a decision of the ICC, which had authorized another railroad to expand its service.[29] The competitors claimed that this enhanced competition would do them financial injury and that the ICC had not demonstrated a sufficient public interest rationale to justify such injury. Justice Brandeis's opinion for the Supreme Court acknowledged that the competing railroads had no right, as such, to be secure against financial loss from competition. The Court felt obliged to acknowledge this point, for a right of this kind would have imposed intolerable rigidity on a regulatory scheme that was supposed to retain at least some of the flexibility and adaptibility of the market. But the Court claimed to find indications in the relevant regulatory statute that the ICC (in contrast to the free market) was to take such harms into account in making its decisions, thus giving the competing railroads an ambiguous legal interest in protesting such harms.

The legal interest test for standing at least acknowledged that the competitors were asserting their own interests in litigation, even if they could not assert any clear-cut right to any particular standard of treatment. Similar cases in the 1940s authorized broadcasters to challenge license awards to would-be competitors by the FCC. These cases were even more emphatic that regulated firms in this industry had no right per se to be safeguarded against competition. The Supreme Court thus shifted the rationale for competitor standing: it was not that competing broadcasters had a legal interest of their own that would be served by granting standing in such cases, but that they would be effective advocates of the public interest in avoiding destructive competition.[30]

The evasive formulas advanced in these early standing cases labored to soften the uncomfortable truth that regulated firms were being given a privileged claim on the public interest.[31] In so doing, they opened the way for other interests or advocates to assert privileged claims on the public interest. But this development did not follow for some decades. Thus, it was only in the mid-1960s that consumer advocates were first allowed to bring legal challenges to individual licensing decisions by regulatory commissions. At the time this opportunity was still viewed as exceptional. The APA, enacted in 1946 as a codification of existing judicial decisions on administrative authority, provided that judicial review should be available to "any person suffering legal wrong or aggrieved within the meaning of a relevant statute." "Legal wrong" was understood to embrace conventional claims regarding distinct private rights, while the phrase "aggrieved within the meaning of a relevant statute" referred to the specialized standing law applicable to the handful of statutory schemes, such as those covering ICC and FCC licensing regulation, which authorized appeals to the courts by persons "aggrieved."[32]

In 1970 the Supreme Court reinterpreted the law of standing to make the evolving approach in these specialized settings into the universal norm in court challenges to administrative decisions. In *Association of Data Processing Service Organizations v. Camp*, the Court ruled that computer firms could challenge a new regulation by the comptroller of the currency (Camp) that would have allowed commercial banks to offer data processing services in direct competition with nonbanking firms in this industry.[33] The relevant statute, directing the comptroller of the currency to enforce various restrictions on the banking industry, made no provision for judicial review by persons "aggrieved." The statute did not even refer to the interests of nonbanking firms in competition with banks, seemingly imposing its restrictions instead for the sake of bank customers. Nonetheless, the Supreme Court argued that the computer firms should be allowed standing to question the legality of the comptroller's decision. The computer firms were likely to suffer financial loss as a result of the enhanced competition from banks, and "he who is 'likely to be financially' injured," the Court concluded, "may be a reliable private attorney general to litigate the issues of the public interest in the present case."

The Court's opinion in *Data Processing* was quite insistent that the question at issue was not whether the competitors had a distinct, statutorily created legal interest in avoiding competition—as some of the original ICC competitor standing cases had suggested. That claim might be relevant to the substantive arguments presented by the computer companies *after* they received standing, but such a claim, the Court noted, "goes to the merits." As the Court now saw it, "The question of standing is different. It concerns . . . the question whether the interest sought to be protected by the complainant is arguably within the zone of interests to be protected or regulated by the statute or constitutional guarantee in question." This strange passive construction—"the interest sought to be protected"—seemed to portray "the interest" as having an independent claim of its own, with the actual plaintiffs serving as mere formal escorts accompanying "the interest" into court. The Court's formulations suggested that the computer companies, once granted standing, would not indeed argue their own particular interests but "the issues of the public interest in the case"—presumably the issues arising from the connection between the public interest and that strangely disembodied interest in constraining banking services.

But once the issues were conceived in this way, there was not much logic to making standing turn on a preliminary showing that this free-standing interest was "arguably within the zone of interests to be protected by the statute." For surely it could also be said of this argument (the one about whether the statute was actually supposed to protect "the interest" in question) that it "goes to the merits." This point was cogently urged even at the time in a concurring opinion by Justice Brennan, and subsequent standing decisions of the Supreme Court (and of most lower courts) often simply disregarded the "zone of interests" test.[34] If "the interest" was not even "arguably" covered by the statute, after all, the plaintiff's problem would not be that he had no standing but that he had no case.

This was, of course, the pattern with traditional forms of litigation, as it continues to be the pattern in private litigation today. The question in a conventional lawsuit is never whether the would-be plaintiff has standing to advocate an "interest" before a court, but whether he actually has a personal right to what he seeks from the court. There is no separate law of standing— separate from "the merits" of the legal argument—because the whole argument is about what the plaintiff, himself, is entitled to receive. It would seem absurd to question whether a would-be plaintiff is the proper "escort" or vehicle to bring his own right before the court, for it is by definition already his to control. As we have noted, the formality of private rights may indeed allow the court to treat a claim about rights as standing apart from the owner's real character or motives, in the sense that the claim can be found valid even if the owner himself is thought to be a rascal or a fool. But this formalism is built into the classical conception of rights as claims that, for better or worse, must remain under the owner's control. The law of standing after the *Data Processing* decision seemed to transfer this legal formalism from rights to "interests," which would now also seem to stand apart from the real character or motives of those asserting them. There remains a separate and confusing law of standing, however, because courts have been unwilling to follow out this new formalism to its logical conclusion.

The Evasions of Standing

The essential purpose of the law of standing is to separate "the issues" or "the interests" in litigation from the particular claims of the party bringing these issues or interests before the court. When standing is treated as merely a "threshold" or jurisdictional question, the precise legal entitlements of the plaintiff fade from view. The focus of the case is no longer on what the actual plaintiff is actually entitled to receive but rather on how "the interest" involved should be disposed by the court. The court thus seems to settle "the issues of the public interest" as the direct agent of the public.

A number of commentators during the 1970s thus hailed the emergence of a distinctive "public law judiciary," which was no longer trammeled by the formalities of private rights litigation and was now able to pronounce directly on public "issues" for the benefit of the public.[35] As late as the mid-1960s, legal commentators urging the federal courts to allow "public actions"—appeals for rulings removed from the rights of particular parties—had conceded that there were no solid precedents for such claims in the history of the federal judiciary.[36] But by the early 1970s, "public actions" seemed to be accepted in all but name.

The concept was given particular plausibility by its apparent adoption in several fields of constitutional litigation in the late 1960s. In 1968, for example, the Supreme Court ruled for the first time that a "taxpayer" should have standing to question whether federal aid to parochial schools violated the First Amendment prohibition on "establishment of religion." It was clear that the outcome of the case would in no way affect the individual taxpayer's tax liability (as the school aid at stake was a minuscule fraction of spending from general revenues), and the Court went to great lengths to explain that taxpayers would still not have standing to challenge the constitutional validity of other kinds of federal spending unless their own property were significantly affected by the taxes.[37]

If the Court was simply resolving issues of public importance for the benefit of the public—as one justice persuasively characterized the Court's decision at the time—it seemed to follow that the plaintiff was really a political advocate for a public policy standard. From this perspective, it seemed most reasonable to think of standing criteria as a device for selecting the "proper" advocate; and a proper advocate would plainly be necessary because, in presenting an issue of public importance to the court, the advocate in a public action was surely not speaking for himself alone. A standard legal text in the early 1970s could thus describe the question of standing as if it were indeed a political judgment, akin to the judgment made by voters in selecting representatives to their legislatures: "the question of standing . . . is the question whether the litigant . . . is a sufficiently appropriate representative of other interested persons . . . to warrant recognizing him as entitled to invoke the court's decision."[38]

This perspective on the judicial role, which seems to have been inspired by administrative law standing decisions of the 1940s, indeed proved particularly congenial to many commentators on administrative law. It certainly seemed to complement the general regulatory perspective that views the economy, not in terms of the property rights of particular owners, but simply in terms of resources to be distributed or managed by the state. But the difficulty with this perspective is that it seems to cast the courts as the ultimate regulatory managers of society, simply decreeing managerial directives on the advice of counselors of their own choosing. Although such characterizations no doubt captured the effectual reality in many cases—and in some cases the literal reality[39]—the Supreme Court quickly began to display its discomfort with such naked assertions of judicial power. The Court was unwilling in the end to let federal courts assume an entirely independent responsibility to settle "issues" or "interests" on their own initiative.

Thus in 1972 the Supreme Court refused to grant standing to the Sierra Club for a suit that the Club sought to file, simply in its own name as a long-established advocacy organization.[40] The Sierra Club sought to challenge an Interior Department ruling that permitted recreational development in a national forest, under a statute making no provision for "citizen standing." The Supreme Court insisted that "longstanding interest in a subject" was not enough, in itself, to bring the interest before a court. Courts would need more justification to resolve legal issues than the bare fact that capable issue advocates were ready and eager to present such issues. The issues would not, after all, be allowed to stand entirely on their own.

But the Court remained unwilling to go back to limiting litigants to claims about distinct personal rights. It remained convinced that many issues or interests ought to receive judicial attention even if they could not be pressed by plaintiffs asserting anything as formal or rigid as a right. The Supreme Court therefore proceeded to develop an elaborate, general law of standing that purported to distinguish the circumstances in which advocates could bring issues or interests before a court. The main theme in these pronouncements was the need for would-be plaintiffs to demonstrate that they had actually suffered some tangible injury from the governmental practice or policy they sought to bring before the courts. And it must be an injury, the Court emphasized in a string of cases in the late 1970s, of a kind that judicial intervention could actually succeed in relieving.

This emphasis on remediable injuries evidently struck the Supreme Court as providing a satisfyingly plausible rationale for judicial interventions. It seemed to dispell the embarrassing image of courts pursuing their own governing agendas and instead to present the image of courts as detached neutrals, rushing to the relief of the injured with no more political forethought than the Red Cross. This rubric could not quite conceal the political favoritism at the bottom of the new law of standing, however, because the concept of injury remained extremely manipulable. It certainly did not mean injury to something distinctly under the plaintiff's own control, and it certainly was not limited to direct financial or physical injuries.

So, for example, the Supreme Court was quick to acknowledge that "aesthetic injury" could qualify environmental advocates to bring suits challenging environmental threats to public parks they enjoyed, even when statutes did not authorize citizen standing.[41] Naturally, in the few environmental regulatory statutes that did authorize suits by "any citizen," the Court expressed no doubts at all about the constitutional validity of such provisions. Sometimes the Court denied standing because it was "purely speculative" whether a favorable ruling for the plaintiff would really alleviate the plaintiff's injury. For example, the Court denied standing to poor people demanding that tax exemptions for hospitals be made conditional on more extensive free treatment for the poor, because the hospitals might well respond by foregoing tax exemptions instead of providing more free treatment.[42] But in an essentially similar case, in which black parents sought to make tax exemptions for private schools conditional on various affirmative action efforts, the D.C. Court of Appeals simply redefined the pertinent "injury" as the insult of Internal Revenue Service insensitivity to racial discrimination—so that, by definition, the policy demanded by the plaintiffs would relieve their injury.[43] In other cases, as in suits demanding more rigorous safety standards from OSHA, the Supreme Court simply takes it for granted that the nominal plaintiff can speak for large numbers of people, so that some of them, at least, are statistically sure to receive relief from a favorable ruling.[44]

The confusing twists and turns in these standing decisions were a source of particular exasperation to commentators who embraced the vision of a "public law judiciary" that could resolve important issues for the public. Law reviews over the past decade have thus been filled with articles denouncing the Court for manipulating standing criteria to duck the issues it does not want to decide at the moment.[45] But these denunciations miss the essential point, by taking the vision of the public law judiciary too much for granted.

Standing criteria do, in fact, serve the purpose the Supreme Court says they serve—determining who is a "proper party to bring the issue before the court"—even if they are routinely manipulated by courts to discriminate between the issues they want to decide and the issues they want to avoid. For it is only in the legal imagination that "the issue" stands altogether apart from the parties bringing the case. If standing criteria are manipulated to exclude some issues from the courts and allow others to be brought forward, then advocates concerned with the favored issues will indeed be able to invoke judicial power to further their concerns, while advocates concerned with disfavored issues will not. In the real world, the result is that the American Civil Liberties Union may enter the courts to fight government spending it regards as violating the First Amendment, while the National Taxpayers Union is barred from using the courts to fight other sorts of spending it regards as violating other constitutional limitations. In the real world, advocates seeking more extensive or intensive environmental or safety or consumer regulation may invoke judicial power to further their concerns, while advocates for tighter enforcement of laws against obscenity or other vices may not.

In one sense, however, the courts are nicely impartial, at least in administrative law cases. If self-styled "consumer advocates" are granted standing to complain about the weakening of product labeling requirements,[46] businesses and unions demanding tighter regulation to serve their own interests—usually at the expense of consumers—are also granted standing. So in recent years, trucking companies have won suits seeking to obstruct deregulation by the ICC;[47] unionized garment workers and their employers have succeeded in obstructing the Labor Department from allowing competing knitwear firms to contract out piecework to home workers;[48] agricultural businesses succeeded in obstructing the Energy Regulatory Commission from deregulating natural gas pipelines;[49] and so on.[50] What all of the cases have in common is the same tendency to treat public policy questions as the protected preserves of favored interest groups or interest advocates. And as is often true in regulatory politics, seemingly rival interest groups often do not directly confront each other's efforts in the same general policy arenas, but instead pursue separate niches, where each can dominate some aspect of policy in relative isolation.[51]

It is clear, at any rate, that once advocates do have access to the courts, they are not primarily concerned with presenting "the issues" for the court to decide. They are primarily concerned, like anyone else contemplating a lawsuit, with getting their own way in the matter under dispute. If the mere threat to file suit can intimidate a government agency into altering its policy in the way the advocates demand, there will be no lawsuit. If the filing of the case or the initial stages of argument are sufficient to intimidate the agency, the advocates will settle out of court. Even when cases are pressed to a formal judicial decision on the merits, the relief sought—if it is an order to the agency about how to proceed in the future—will then almost invariably be negotiated by the parties and simply ratified by the court. And once specific obligations are imposed on a government agency under a settlement agreement or court order, it is left to the advocates to decide whether the agency is complying or whether it should be hailed back to court for further proceedings.

This procedure is perfectly logical and appropriate in litigation over private rights, because private rights are designed to allow owners to assert them in what they judge to be their own self-interest. It seems rather strange, however, to say that there is no further issue when the issue advocate in public law litigation is satisfied with the result, as if the public issue were, after all, his own private affair.[52] But that is the effectual truth of the new law of standing, at least in administrative cases. It is essentially a means by which courts grant particular private advocates privileged claims on the conduct of public policy.

Responsible Government

This characterization of contemporary administrative law may suggest that it offends constitutional principles of equality. This objection is not, indeed, frivolous. The defenders of expanded access to the courts often celebrate it as a device for checking the arrogance of government officials, bringing government officials down to the level of citizen advocates to account for their policies on more equal terms. But it might just as well be described as a system that inflates the status of some private citizens into "public citizens," elevating these privileged few almost to the level of responsible government officials while leaving all other citizens simply to endure the consequences.

It can be said that this pattern is inevitable in politics. Some citizens are always better organized or better connected or more energetic than others and consequently exert more influence on public policy. No doubt the underlying pattern reflects inevitable realities in human life. Some people are simply more aggressive, determined, capable, or charismatic than others, and they consequently get more of what they want. But the formalism of law is supposed to abstract from personal differences, and not merely as a pious gesture to some abstract egalitarian faith. Legal formalism has always sought to accommodate the quite down-to-earth problem of distinguishing the appeal of the honorable man of conscience and sound judgment from the appeal of the contriving manipulator or the ideological zealot. Legal formalism seeks to expel such distinctions from the realm of rights to the realm of politics, where they are as appropriate as they are inevitable.

In fact, the deeper objection to giving some private advocates a privileged claim to challenge public policy is that, in eroding the formal equality of private citizens, it undermines the distinction between private claims and public responsibilities. The formalities of constitutional government (such as the conferral of power by virtue of office rather than by virtue of ultimate moral claims to rule) are designed to emphasize the difference between public responsibility and private advocacy. Precisely the point of emphasizing the distinctiveness of public office is to emphasize that public office makes the officeholder responsible to the public—not to particular private citizens and not even, in the end, to the majority.

This was the central theme of *The Federalist* in defending the formal arrangement of powers in the U.S. Constitution. *The Federalist* emphasized "faction" as the great threat to republican government, and we are still aware that the grasping of special interest groups can indeed pose threats to "the rights of other citizens, or to the permanent and aggregate interests of the community." But it is usually forgotten that *The Federalist*'s diagnosis of "the causes of faction" does not start with mere selfishness or greed. It starts with the natural "connection" between a man's "reason and his self-love," which causes "his opinions and his passions [to] have a reciprocal influence on each other" and makes a man's opinions into "objects to which [his passions] will attach themselves."[53] The initial problem is not so much selfishness, then, as self-conceit, which makes men passionately opinionated or fiercely dogmatic in their views. It is this initial problem that makes the more routine political problem—the grasping by most people for narrow gains—so intractable.

It remains a common observation that some of the fiercest and most passionate advocates, when speaking as private citizens, turn out to act and speak a good deal more circumspectly when coping with the responsibilities of public office. The framers of the Constitution, however, were plainly unwilling to rely on the mystique of office alone to transform partisans into responsible officials. In fact, the famous discussion of the moderating effects of a multitude of factions in *The Federalist* 10 is grounded on the initial premise that *if there were* a single dominant faction in a republic, the sense of public responsibility among legislators would rarely be strong enough to withstand the demands of that faction. And notwithstanding *The Federalist*'s reassuring prediction of a self-canceling proliferation of private factions in a continental republic, its subsequent praise for a bicameral legislature with extended terms for the senators again presupposes that faction will not cease to operate on American legislators. Finally, *The Federalist* continually emphasizes the danger that, just because they are elected, "the representatives of the people, in a popular assembly, seem sometimes to fancy that they are the people themselves"[54]— conceiving that their own notions of the public good are necessarily identical with the public good—and thus "often appear disposed to exert an imperious control over the other departments" of government.

The remedy for this "imperious" willfulness, of course, is the separation of powers. To ensure the separation of legislative from executive powers, the framers of the Constitution gave the chief executive a fixed term of office, a guarantee against reductions in his salary, and a qualified veto power to resist statutory incursions on his authority. Just as importantly, they contrived, in spite of their fear of direct continental elections, a mode of selecting the chief executive that would trace his primary responsibility back to the people, not to the legislature.

And "responsibility" is the central theme in *The Federalist*'s discussion of executive power. While responsible legislative action is said to be promoted by the multitude of factions, forced to seek influence through a large number of legislators, the key to "responsibility" in the executive, according to *The Federalist*, is unity. *The Federalist* praises the Constitution for concentrating executive authority in a single chief executive who must, therefore, take on himself the ultimate responsibility for executive operations. By the logic of the constitutional scheme, whatever administrative agencies or departments Congress may establish, their heads "ought to be considered as the assistants or deputies of the Chief Magistrate" and "on this account . . . ought to be subject to his superintendence"—so the president will bear the ultimate responsibility for mismanagement.[55] Among the chief concerns of the men who framed the Constitution was the weakness and incoherence of executive authority under the Articles of Confederation, when congressional committees appointed, removed, and continually interfered with individual administrative officers, each operating apart from the others.[56]

The American scheme of formally separated legislative and executive powers is thus intended to fulfill the basic promise of constitutional government. On the one hand, as previously noted, the separation is designed to protect individual rights by forcing legislatures to think about constraints on private rights in general terms, because they cannot fully control the application or implementation of such constraints by officials in the executive. But at the same time, the separation is meant to ensure enhanced protection for "the public good." Implementation or execution requires continual adjustment and coordination among competing considerations in changing circumstances; it requires "decisiveness" and "energy," as *The Federalist* puts it. And the same quality that makes legislatures well suited to crafting general legislative compromises—their capacity to represent a diverse range of interests—makes them very unsuited to directing and coordinating the details of policy implementation: "the differences of opinion and the jarring of parties" in the legislature "may often promote deliberation and circumspection and serve to check excesses in the majority" but "dissension in the executive department" would "constantly counteract . . . the most necessary ingredients in its composition—vigor and expedition."[57]

In enacting a fiscal budget, Congress must automatically reduce competing concerns to the common currency of dollars and reconsider its priorities with each new budget. Even in this arena, the chaos of the contemporary budget process and the chronic problem of deficits demonstrates the legislative incapacity for coordination. When it comes to the implementation or enforcement of a vast array of separate regulatory measures, enacted by different Congresses in different circumstances over many decades, there is plainly no hope for thoughtful coordination or readjustment of policy by a fractious Congress. The formal unity of the executive reflects the inescapable truth that, whatever the hopes or concerns of the particular legislative coalitions responsible for enacting these diverse measures in different eras, the country as a whole must live with the results, year by year. And it is the implementation or enforcement activity of the executive that is held responsible, in the first instance, for the results obtained.

The enactment of a general legislative standard, just because it must be done abstractly and prospectively, always has a certain degree of wishfulness about it, as if the mere expression of legislative will or legislative intentions could alter reality in itself. But the executive is left to cope with the hard fact that not every legislative intention can be realized, certainly not at once, and certainly not when diverse legislative intentions are in practice contradictory. That is the logic of focusing responsibility for execution on a separate branch of government.

The Federalist emphasizes the peculiar character of executive responsibility by its continual resort to military analogies or military references, as in its claim that "Energy in the executive . . . is essential to the protection of the community against foreign attacks . . . [and] not less essential to the steady administration of the law."[58] When the community must be defended against foreign attacks, the whole community has a common stake in the outcome, and that outcome can often be judged with the brute clarity of victory or surrender. Few fields of domestic administration ever present such extreme cases, in which success and failure are so readily distinguished in the end and every citizen hopes for "success" in similar terms. But the analogy underscores the character of the executive as the acting agent for the public as a whole, responsible for exercising power *strategically*, that is, with an eye to actual results.

Just as the individual person must carefully consider his interests in deciding how to exercise his rights from one situation to the next, the executive must give continual thought to the public interest in deciding how to exercise the powers bestowed by legislation. This responsibility requires the executive to make disputable political judgments, but that is why the executive is made responsible to the people—unlike the judiciary, which can simply claim to be following previously fixed rules with no regard for consequences. The separation of powers is designed to make one part of government squarely responsible for the actual consequences that flow from the legislative "intentions" of all of the nation's diverse laws.

As the Supreme Court has recently noted, the framers of the Constitution did not expect Congress to play any significant role in overseeing the conduct of executive operations.[59] They made the executive formally accountable to the public and not to Congress. But congressional committees began prying and probing and prompting administrative officials on the details of their performance as early as the 1790s, much to the disgust of Treasury Secretary Alexander Hamilton. Congressional committees have done so ever since. The number and staff resources of committees and subcommittees have mushroomed in recent decades to maintain a continuously high level of active oversight of a vastly enlarged executive establishment.

Perhaps this active congressional involvement in policy implementation is inevitable, even appropriate, considering that executive "responsibility" to the country as a whole is quite problematic in most fields of domestic administration. For in most policy fields, the country is not really a whole but an array of diverse sectors and interests, differently affected by executive decisions and likely to judge them in a variety of ways. But no serious observer of American government can claim that the federal executive is too removed from the promptings and demands of particular interest groups. There is nearly universal agreement that close alliances between interest groups, their congressional patrons, and the agencies of most concern to them make it extremely difficult to impose policy priorities or overall coordination from the White House on behalf of the "permanent and aggregate interests of the community."[60]

Many legal scholars have viewed contemporary administrative law as a device for checking interest group pressures on administration, making executive operations more truly accountable to the public.[61] This pleasing notion sounds more credible if one disregards the routine applications of administrative law in which business and labor groups try to stifle their competitors. It sounds more credible to those who focus on the activities of public interest advocates like Ralph Nader and take for granted that such advocates have enduringly pertinent and correct insights into the actual interests of the general public or the true needs of deserving minorities. Even so, the argument must claim that consumer (or environmental or civil rights) champions have so few patrons in Congress that the executive would be free to disregard their claims entirely if they could not invoke the additional advocacy resources of the judiciary. This argument would not sound at all convincing to James Watt, Ann Gorsuch, or any other Reagan administration appointee forced out of office by congressional opposition.

In the end, it remains the inescapable fact that when administrative agencies are made more accountable to private advocates through the judiciary, they are made less accountable to the president. The notion that accountability to private advocates will secure the public interest more consistently or reliably than accountability to the president is a notion that runs counter to the basic premises of the Constitution. To accept the official premises of contemporary administrative law, one must assume that the framers were naïve. But in a choice between the authors of *The Federalist* and the authors of contemporary legal commentaries, the former are hardly the more obvious suspects on which to hang the charge of naïveté.

The Enduring Constitutional Perspective

The proof that the traditional constitutional perspective is not at all anachronistic is that it continues to be the perspective adopted by courts in regard to core executive responsibilities. Thus, while we may think that many fields of contemporary regulation are particularly important to public welfare, most people still think that the "protection of the community against foreign attacks" is a good deal more important. We may even say that the public has a right to expect government to offer this protection in a reliable and effective way. Yet critics on both left and right continually warn that our national policies in one defense or foreign policy field or another are dangerously obtuse, negligent, or misdirected. Often, there is indeed evidence that crass electoral or political calculations have contributed to these policy distortions. But courts have steered very far from such issues, because few judges have ever imagined that our defense postures would be improved by allowing citizen activists to litigate the issues of the public interest in such matters—even when statutes, treaties, or executive orders do arguably afford some relevant legal standard against which to judge executive performance. Private critics in this field must simply make their case to voters or to members of Congress and trust that the responsible executive officials will in time respond appropriately.

So it is with the criminal law. Public opinion polls over the past two decades have repeatedly shown that more citizens are concerned about crime than about pollution or workplace safety or any of the myriad of other concerns addressed by federal regulation.[62] And this concern is perfectly understandable. Far more victims lose their lives each year to criminal homicides than to workplace accidents or environmental carcinogens.[63] Despite the great stake that citizens have in adequate enforcement of the criminal law, however, the courts have remained adamant that no private citizen may force the government to commence criminal proceedings against another.

Yet it is well known that not every criminal prohibition is enforced to the fullest extent. The vigor of enforcement varies from one law to another and from one time to another, and some laws receive so little enforcement over long periods that doubts are raised about whether they continue to be binding. Still, not everyone agrees on which laws should receive what degree of attention from prosecutors and police. On the contrary, there are continual disputes, with some critics urging more vigorous prosecution of welfare cheats, others urging more vigorous prosecution of white collar criminals, some deploring the prosecution of minor drug offenders, and others deploring the prosecution of young men refusing to register for the draft.[64] There is no judicial check on the discretion of the Justice Department to refuse to prosecute. But then, in view of the unlimited reach of the president's pardoning authority, neither is there any judicial check preventing the president from "ordering a general jail delivery," as Chief Justice Taft once observed.[65] The check in both cases is the president's sense of responsibility to the public, in what he himself does or in what he allows (and perhaps even encourages) his appointees to do.

Despite all of the potential for bias and mischief in such unfettered discretion, few judges imagine that prosecution policy would be improved by allowing private advocates to challenge the exercise of this discretion. Hence the discretion to bring or not to bring criminal prosecutions has been treated by the courts as an unqualified responsibility of the executive, even when statutes speak of a mandatory duty to prosecute. To this day, the federal courts have steadfastly refused to allow private plaintiffs to challenge the Justice Department's failure to initiate prosecutions—even when the would-be challengers had themselves been victimized or injured by those they wanted the Justice Department to prosecute. Thus the U.S. Supreme Court affirmed in the early 1970s that "the Executive Branch has exclusive authority and absolute discretion to decide whether to prosecute a case."[66] And a slightly earlier Court of Appeals decision, noting that "prosecutorial discretion has long been recognized as sacrosanct," defended the principle in the traditional formulas of liberal constitutionalism:

> The government differs from private persons and its decisional options, exercisable in the interests of the nation as a whole, may limit the applications of individual citizens [to have prosecutions initiated]. . . . The federal government's

decisions concerning enforcement of its criminal statutes compri
pursuit of national policy. If government could be held liable for p
failing to prosecute . . . its choices in this area could quite conceivabl)
by such a suit. Thus a policy decision by the federal government
influenced by a plaintiff with no governmental responsibility.[67]

The difference in regulatory policy is not that regulators have less di
If regulatory agencies appear to be more constrained, that is only because
judges have insisted on interpreting the discretion of regulatory officials more
narrowly. But in truth the central feature of administrative law has always been
its reluctance to impose very clear or fixed duties on administrators—either
to the property owners being regulated or to those supposed to receive the
benefits of regulation. Contemporary court decisions in administrative law
only rarely result in direct, detailed orders telling administrators what to do.
Judges are usually careful to couch their decisions in procedural terms, calling
on administrators to reconsider or produce better rationales for what they have
done or not done, and for what they may be allowed to do or not do later on,
after following the proper procedures. Judges are reluctant to impose clear
rules or particular obligations precisely because they do not want to make
regulation overly rigid. But they inevitably do make it more rigid, more closely
answerable to litigating advocates than it otherwise would be.

This reluctance to pin down regulatory obligations in detail seems to account for the fact that judges have declined to secure rights to regulatory
benefits in the most obvious and direct way, by requiring regulatory agencies
to compensate each person who has suffered harm traceable to regulatory
negligence.[68] The Federal Tort Claims Act, authorizing damage awards
against the federal government for wrongs committed by federal officials, does
include a specific exemption for official decisions involving the "exercise of
discretion."[69] But the Administrative Procedure Act, enacted by Congress in
the very same year as the Tort Claims Act, also excludes judicial review of
actions "committed to agency discretion."[70] The Supreme Court had no
difficulty in interpreting away this latter barrier to judicial intervention in the
early 1970s, when it was intent on imposing closer judicial control on administrative decision making. The barrier to tort claims for regulatory negligence
has continued to be honored by the courts, it seems, because tort liability
would require courts to identify the beneficiaries of regulation, or the standards that they could insist upon, with too much specificity. The courts have
preferred to leave a screen of ambiguity over the question of precisely what,
or for precisely whose benefit, regulatory agencies are supposed to act.

Recent decisions in administrative law have stressed a similar perspective.
Thus the Supreme Court's 1983 decision in *Heckler v. Chaney*[71] seemed to

breathe new life into the APA restriction on judicial review for decisions "committed to agency discretion." The Court ruled that this phrase must exclude judicial review of the FDA's failure to take action against a specific drug (which, the plaintiff charged, was not "safe and effective" under the standards of the Food and Drug Act). The *Chaney* decision reasoned that such individualized regulatory enforcement decisions were akin to the discretion exercised by criminal prosecutors. And the Court stressed that challenging such individualized decisions was inappropriate when they involved decisions not to act, because forcing agencies to act in some cases might preempt resources, making it impossible for them to act in other cases; and courts were not equipped to judge agency priorities in this way. In the *Chaney* case itself, however, this reasoning had earlier been rejected by the D.C. Court of Appeals, and a concurring opinion by Justice Marshall correctly noted many past decisions in which equally particularized decisions of regulatory agencies not to take action had been reviewed by courts over the preceding decade.[72]

From a constitutional perspective, even the reasoning endorsed by the Supreme Court majority in *Chaney* rather missed the point. There is in truth no fundamental difference between action and inaction: if the FDA had denied the manufacturer of the drug permission to market it or if it had simply delayed a decision on issuing marketing approval beyond the statutory deadline for decision, its behavior could equally be described as inaction—and it would certainly be a specific or particularized case of inaction—but the manufacturer would unquestionably have a right to judicial review.[73] This right would exist even though the manufacturer's suit would undoubtedly divert the attention and energies of FDA officials from other decisions that might be of higher priority from the public's point of view. But the manufacturer would be entitled to have judicial review because he would be invoking his own right—and the meaning of a right is that it can be enforced even when it might seem inconvenient to the public to do so. The question in *Chaney* should have been why the plaintiff had any claim to speak for the public, because he plainly could not claim that the FDA owed a personal duty to him.

The general, implicit answer in administrative law is that the plaintiff is entitled to speak for the public when he is in some way regarded as representative of a broadly shared interest. Thus courts have been much more receptive to suits seeking to challenge general regulations or broad enforcement patterns than individual decisions, because the challengers seem to invoke broader interests or concerns than their own personal interests. So, for example, the *Chaney* decision proved no obstacle at all to a subsequent suit by "a consumer of over-the-counter drugs" protesting the FDA's failure to take action against several hundred products.[74] And courts continue to accept public interest suits demanding that OSHA set new or more stringent health standards, even though additional or tighter standards will affect thousands of subsequent enforcement actions.[75]

In the strange logic of contemporary administrative law, suits challenging broad policies are regarded as more appropriate than suits challenging individual decisions. But surely it cannot be said that the former raise fewer questions about management and priorities. Suits challenging broad policies are from almost every point of view less suitable for judicial involvement, except that courts regard them as more deserving of attention because they affect broader interests. But if the question is the public interest, there is really no good reason to suppose that courts will do better than the responsible executive officials in determining the public interest. That a policy or decision affects a broader range of interests or citizens is not enough to justify judicial intervention, unless the premise of judicial intervention is precisely that courts should be intervening on behalf of interests that are somehow more partial or factional than the overall public interest. And then the question again is why such partial or factional interests should be allowed to make preemptive claims on public policy.

The answer to the latter question—the answer tacitly assumed in most of contemporary administrative law—is that interests or interest groups *ought* to have a special claim on public policy, at least some of them, some of the time. If this answer seems plausible and unproblematic to many people today, perhaps it is a reflection of the degree to which the notion of group rights has already come to be taken for granted in some fields of public policy. To take the most notable example, it is now over twenty years since courts began to demand statistical integration of public schools: in rejecting the view that the Constitution should simply guarantee individuals the right to be treated in a colorblind fashion, the landmark decision of the Fifth Circuit Court of Appeals quite deliberately dismissed this notion as an expression of the "abandoned view that [constitutional] rights are exclusively individual rights."[76]

But, of course, not everyone views such ventures with the same satisfaction; for, among other things, "group rights" necessarily mean rights deployed by court-appointed group representatives. In Boston, a city in which a decade of court-ordered busing left the public schools more segregated than before, black parents finally urged the court to release their schools from the NAACP busing plan and return it to a system of individual free choice regarding school attendance.[77] People who take a more favorable view of busing may still wonder whether it is a precedent for group rights we should want to expand upon.

Such special cases apart, American law has never been very comfortable with group rights, just because they do run so contrary to our constitutional presumptions. Rights over which the right holders have no control smack of

73

the kind of democracy offered in "people's democracies." We could, to be sure, give the collective holders of group rights some meaningful say in their rights—or, more aptly, make the representation of group interests more truly "representative"—by allowing the favored groups to elect their own advocates. This is the solution adopted in labor law, in which union officials are recognized as the legal bargaining agents for workers; but they are so recognized only when a majority of workers can hold these union officials accountable through union elections. If we really wanted to declare that particular programs or agencies were entirely for the benefit of particular groups, we could arrange to have these groups elect their top officials in a similar way, thus making them more "responsible" to the people they are supposed to serve.

But a moment's reflection suggests why such a program has never been seriously considered for government regulatory programs. Consider the problems in implementing a program for group representation in agencies supposedly given over to the control of particular interest groups: Who, for example, would be allowed to vote for the regulatory commissioners of workplace safety? Only actual workers in regulated firms, but not managers or stockholders of these firms or consumers of their products? Who would vote for civil rights regulatory officials? Only blacks and women and other special constituencies, but not the majority of white males who supported antidiscrimination laws in the first place?

If we assume that regulatory electorates are restricted to those deemed most concerned, what recourse should there be for electoral minorities within these constituencies? Perhaps the elected workplace safety representative favors stringent controls that put people out of work, or the elected civil rights representative favors divisive quota schemes. Perhaps others within these constituencies favor opposite policies. Should the dissidents be allowed to complain to their congressmen or to the president, and should these representatives of the wider public be allowed to prompt or pressure the elected regulators to change their policies? Or should that activity be regarded as improper interference with specially protected interests?

In the real world, of course, it is most unlikely that we will ever have to confront such dilemmas directly. For it is most unlikely that our constitutional sensibilities will ever be so jaded as to tolerate programs constructed in this way. It is doubtful that black Americans or Americans with physical handicaps or American factory workers would want to be segregated from the rest of the electorate into specialized constituencies. It is still more doubtful that they would want to be locked into these specialized constituencies without the opportunity to appeal to the representatives of the general public. And it is most of all unlikely that the general public would submit to a scheme in which the authority exercised in its name was entirely handed over to special interest

74

groups—or, rather, a scheme in which the name of the public was removed from programs exercising the coercive powers of the public.

Contemporary administrative law tries to avoid this awkwardness by purporting to represent interests instead of directly representing the people assumed to hold those interests. To just that extent it is not really representation, because it implicitly attributes interests to people who never get to endorse or reject these attributions. But it is notorious that people are not always interested in their interests; at the least, people do not always see their interests the way others wish them to see their interests. Thus near majorities of union members have ignored the counsel of their union officials in successive presidential elections over the past two decades.[78] And the reason, in all likelihood, was not that they disagreed with union officials about their interest *as* union members but that they did not see this interest as predominant. This fact ought to remind us that, in general, the central challenge of government is not so much to reconcile the conflicting interests of contending groups, as it is to reconcile the conflicting interests of the same people. For that reason, in constitutional theory Congress and the president represent not particular interests but the public as a whole.

Insisting on the representation of interests in isolation is opposed not merely to the logic of representation but to the logic of responsible government. It virtually guarantees that such interests will receive more attention, more resources, more investment of governmental power and prestige than most people think they deserve. It virtually guarantees that such reified interests will be served less flexibly, less coherently, in the end less responsibly than citizens are entitled to expect.

3

Bureaucratic Idealism or Executive Power?

THIS CHAPTER takes up the principal fallback defense of contemporary administrative law—that it is simply a scheme for ensuring that "the law" is upheld. This view of the enterprise continually appears in legal literature and judicial opinions (and in public rhetoric) because it seems so much less problematic than the more "realistic" defenses of the system. For as the previous chapter demonstrated, the current system cannot, in fact, be plausibly defended as a vehicle for representation in a genuinely public or genuinely political process; neither can it be plausibly conceived as a mechanism for securing rights, in the sense of distinct claims, controlled by individuals. Appealing to "the law" in the abstract seems much safer, just because it does deflect attention from the moving parties in particular cases and the precise nature of their claims on public policy. By deflecting attention away from the usual first question in politics—"at whose behest?"—this legalistic perspective makes it easier to ignore what must often be the final question: "to whose benefit?" Appeals to the judicial responsibility for upholding the law are appeals to the view that, after all, "the law is the law" and must be upheld; and who can quarrel with that in a "government of laws"?

This legalistic perspective on public policy only seems plausible, however, if we think of the law as already containing all of the answers that policy makers need, so that following the law is as simple as following orders. In other words, this perspective assumes that the answers that policy makers take away from the law do not significantly depend on the questions they bring to it—the problems they are most concerned with when they ask themselves, "What does the law require?" But this proposition is plainly wrong, at least in many common circumstances.

If the legalistic perspective were not wrong, there would scarcely be any need for courts or for any separation between the judiciary and the executive. Most litigation between private citizens and government agencies—arising, say, from disputes over tax assessments, licensing decisions, or the requirements of a government contract—do not arise because government officials have willfully and maliciously flouted their obligations under the law. It is the rare case, in fact, in which the judge or even the private litigant charges executive officials with evil intentions. In some cases, no doubt, executive officials are guilty of arrogance, negligence, or extreme bias; but the same is true of judges in some cases, too. If we were to speculate on the relative frequency of such cases, it would probably be more reasonable to fear displays of bad character among life-tenured judges than among politically accountable executive officials.[1]

But the usual (and usually correct) assumption in litigation involving government is not that executive officials are particularly prone to abusive conduct. Rather, the assumption is that executive officials may misread what the law requires (at least from the perspective of the private challenger or the judge) in their eagerness to make the law accommodate their own notions of good policy. The assumption, in other words, is that government agencies will view the law from their own point of view, just as the taxpayer, the licensee, or the contractor will each view it from his own point of view, reflecting his own, distinct interests. The judge in such disputes can then claim a special institutional virtue as a neutral referee, able to read the law impartially, just because he has nothing at stake in the matter himself. But it is only in special circumstances that this detachment may qualify as a special virtue: for in general we *want* government officials to view their responsibilities under the law in an "interested" way. We want them to try to make the law accommodate the public interest as much as they can. We would be exasperated if they felt no stake in choosing between one interpretation of the law that entailed very bad consequences for the public and another that entailed much better consequences.

At the same time, we would think it quite exasperating if government officials insisted on pursuing everything they might be entitled to do under the law, regardless of the consequences. We expect private litigants to invoke their rights under the law only to the extent that they judge it to be in their own interest to do so. Most of the time, private citizens disputing with the government do not pursue their claims to court or demand everything they might be entitled to claim under the law. Most of the time they find it advantageous to compromise, as even the vast majority of criminal defendants find it more advantageous to "plea bargain" with prosecutors than to insist on their rights to a full public trial of the charges against them.[2]

It seems strange to insist that the public must get everything it is entitled to receive, even when the public—or those exercising governmental responsibility on behalf of the public—do not think this course will serve the public interest. More generally, it is hard to see the logic of drawing sharp lines between the law and public policy when only public rights are at stake. When private rights are at stake, the artificial rigor of the law allows individuals to invoke their rights in order to pursue their interests; when public rights are involved, the same rigor seems to open an awkward gap between the formal rights of the public and its actual interests. Insisting on the full reach of the law in this setting seems to be legalism for no good purpose.

And for exactly this reason, courts before the 1960s generally refused to intervene in administrative decision making to impose their own "impartial" view of what the law might require, except when litigants invoking their own rights were entitled to demand an impartial application of the law in their own cases. Exceptions were made to this presumption in certain administrative fields in the decades between the world wars; then, in the late 1960s, the exceptions expanded into a new rule—the new administrative law. But even today we do not think that government will be better run if judges intervene at random, like inspector generals of legality, to ensure that administrative officials follow the judicially approved view of the law. The doctrine of standing is supposed to prevent just this sort of random intrusion of "unbiased"— which may often mean inexperienced or indifferent—judicial constructions of the law.

In fact, standing limitations mean that even many constitutional requirements are not enforced or interpreted by the courts. The Constitution, for example, provides that "a regular Statement and Account of the Receipts and Expenditures of all public Money shall be published from time to time," but the scale and distribution of congressional appropriations for the Central Intelligence Agency have never been published. Does this practice violate the Constitution? The Supreme Court refused to give a ruling one way or the other when taxpayers tried to press the question in litigation.[3] It has been left to Congress to determine what its constitutional obligations may be in this respect, and Congress is satisfied to maintain this exception to the general norm of published budgetary accounting. Yet it is hard to argue that the Constitution has become meaningless or that the integrity of our public life is set at risk because politically responsible officials have interpreted this constitutional requirement to accommodate what they seem to view as an exigency of national security.

Bureaucratic Idealism or Executive Power?

The traditional logic of limiting courts to private rights assumed that private rights would indeed be at risk if courts could not insist on their own, more detached view of the law in cases affecting private rights. A private right is, by definition, private, that is to say, exempted from the broad and ambiguous responsibilities of those who make public policy. If someone can claim a right against the government, he is by definition entitled to insist that it be respected. If it makes little sense to separate the rights of the public at large from the actual interests of the public, then it makes little sense to insist that courts should uphold their views of what the law requires, when private rights are not involved. This insistence only makes sense if we think that judges will actually do a better job than politically responsible officials in accommodating the law to the public interest or if we think that particular interest group advocates should have a privileged stake in public policy, entitling them to press their own favored views of the law before the courts, as if no more than their own rights were at stake.

Beneath the legalism, the latter premise seems to capture the effectual logic of contemporary administrative law: the further privatization of public policy. For people who think that the AFL-CIO simply *deserves* more control over the policies of the Labor Department than it already has, there is a certain logic to this approach, which is not, after all, so legalistic. For people who think that Ralph Nader simply *deserves* to have his criticisms of public policy given special weight, there is a certain logic to this approach. There is even a certain logic to this system for people who think that America is so riven with social tension that violence and chaos will ensue if liberal advocacy groups cannot appeal to the courts to check the policy leanings of elected conservative administrations—even more than they are already checked by Congress. But this is not a logic that most federal judges are willing to embrace in public. It may not even be a logic that many judges have been willing to embrace in private.

What else, then, can account for the expansion of judicial controls in recent decades? In fact, the notion that administrators should be held to the law is not simply a clever rationale for self-seeking interest groups (though it surely is that, too). Such an abstract appeal to the law sounds plausible and reassuring to many people because it resonates with three enduring notions in American political thought, which have become particularly powerful in recent decades, just as they have become particularly convenient for particular interest group advocates. The first is that the will of Congress must prevail in public policy decisions. The second is that extraordinary administrative powers can be justified by special obligations to the law. The third—which is actually an extension of the second—is that, as extraordinary administrative powers become the rule, citizens are entitled to expect that governmental administration will in general be expert and impartial in its approach to statutory mandates. Each one of these notions had been energetically propagated long before the emergence of the new administrative law at the end of the 1960s. Perhaps this fact explains why these notions became so beguiling to judges, in an era in which they became so convenient for litigating advocacy groups.

But each one of these notions runs contrary to the structure and spirit of the American Constitution. In fact, each has its roots in more or less conscious efforts to repudiate the political premises of the traditional constitutional system; and each is impossible to implement in practice because of the enduring characteristics of our constitutional system. In practice, appeals to these notions continue to look like excuses for interest group manipulation, or invitations to a quite dysfunctional legalism, which makes "the law" an end in itself.

Constitutionalism and Legislative Supremacy

The notion that the will of Congress must prevail is the bedrock principle of contemporary administrative law. Before 1937, the Supreme Court insisted that the Constitution placed definite limits on the extent to which congressional enactments could control local policy questions, on the extent to which congressional enactments could control private economic decision making,[4] and on the extent to which congressional enactments could delegate legislative power to administrative agencies.[5] The regulatory apparatus of recent decades has been built on the ruins of these earlier constitutional doctrines. It is hardly surprising, then, that contemporary administrative law starts with a great deal of deference to congressional enactments in regard to regulatory policy.

But even the contemporary Supreme Court has sometimes enforced constitutional limitations against congressional enactments; and every time it has done so in the past decade, it has invoked the constitutional principle of the separation of powers.[6] So, for example, in *INS v. Chadha* (1983), the Supreme Court ruled that Congress could not delegate the power to veto executive decisions (that is, overturn otherwise binding executive decisions) to one house of Congress (or even to both houses). Congress, the Court insisted, may not exercise executive power under the Constitution, and when it exercises legislative power it must operate in the prescribed constitutional manner, by securing majority votes in both houses and then presenting each bill for presidential approval or veto. In its subsequent decision in *Bowsher v. Synar,* the Court held that Congress could not delegate budget-cutting powers to the comptroller general, because such power to execute or implement a congressional directive could not be delegated to an officer under ultimate congressional control. In such decisions, the Supreme Court has quite reasonably insisted that the principle of separation of powers is all the more vital to the conduct of government business if the scale of federal activities in general is no longer to be limited by the courts. This point seems to be forgotten in administrative law, however, where the Supreme Court has been eager to make the federal courts into agents of Congress, holding executive operations to congressional intentions.

Enforcing the will of Congress, of course, can often serve as an excuse for judges to enforce their own notions of good policy. For example, it is widely acknowledged that in interpreting executive duties under the Clean Air Act and other environmental statutes, judges on the D.C. Court of Appeals frequently read statutory provisions as embodying their own views of sound policy, even when there was little evidence for their interpretations in the legislative history (or when the evidence suggested that the chosen policy was at best the preference only of some particular congressional factions).[7] The Supreme Court has occasionally rebuked lower courts for this sort of activism.

But even in its 1983 decision in *Chevron, U.S.A. v. Natural Resources Defense Council,* the most celebrated of such rebukes in recent years, the Supreme Court took it for granted that judges must hold executive operations to those standards which they can discern as being intended by the enacting Congress.[8] Similarly, in invalidating the "legislative veto," the Court insisted that its repudiation of this device would not leave executive power unchecked, because courts would still ensure executive fidelity to statutory limits—as if this fidelity were an end in itself, quite apart from whether anyone's personal rights might be at stake.[9] And on occasion the Supreme Court has indeed insisted on enforcing the letter of the law, or the strict intent of Congress, in such cases, even when this threatened absurd results—as in a 1979 ruling that the Endangered Species Act must be read to prohibit the completion of a public works project in which tens of millions had already been invested, because the dam construction involved might threaten the survival of an obscure, quite undistinguished variant of an otherwise common species of freshwater fish (a threat discovered only when local opponents of the dam solicited biological researchers to find some "species" that might be endangered by the project).[10]

Appeals of this sort to the ultimate authority of Congress may sound convincing because they resonate with a long tradition of populist clamor against executive authority. Demands that the executive be held "to strict confines of the law" indeed echo one of the oldest rhetorical traditions in American constitutional history, because "the law" is among the most natural rallying cries for people seeking to reassert just those populist conceptions of public authority which the framers of the federal Constitution sought to restrain. For apart from claims of private right, the most obvious reason for insisting that executive officials adhere to the law is to ensure their subordination to the representative authority of the legislature.

Partisans of legislative supremacy, therefore, have always found it tempting to invoke the venerable rhetorical tradition associating executive power with monarchical arrogance and legislative assemblies with the will of the people. Rhetoric of this sort appeals to a tradition that stretches at least as far back as the English Civil War of the early seventeenth century, a tradition that was quite heatedly invoked by the Antifederalist opponents of the Constitution in 1787, who warned that the new Constitution would be the "foetus of monarchy."[11]

Ratification of the Constitution certainly did not end the eagerness of party politicians to exploit this rhetorical tradition. As far back as the 1790s, the opposition leaders in Congress styled themselves "Republicans" and tried to stigmatize the followers of Treasury Secretary Alexander Hamilton as "monarchists" or "monocrats."[12] Half a century later, the congressional opposition to President Andrew Jackson called themselves "Whigs" to emphasize the principled basis of their resistance to the high-handed policies of "King Andrew."[13] In more recent times, liberal Democrats castigated the Nixon Administration as an "imperial presidency," popularizing the coinage of the liberal historian Arthur Schlesinger, Jr., who deployed the term precisely to exploit its resonance with older party slogans for modern partisan aims.[14]

Historically, then, the doctrine of legislative supremacy has been advanced as if it were an inevitable corollary of the doctrine of popular sovereignty: "the people" are entitled to have their way; therefore the legislature, as the voice of the people, must have its way. Like all doctrines of sovereignty, popular sovereignty implicitly (and in its original Hobbesian version, quite explicitly) relies on a strictly positivist view of law: the law is what the sovereign commands, and the law is binding just because the all-powerful sovereign commands that it be obeyed.[15] This may be an appealing view for populist demagogues, but it has never been widely accepted in America. In calmer moments, most Americans have resisted the notion that law is simply the formal dressing of power. It is obvious, after all, that power—even dressed up as "sovereignty"—can be exercised foolishly and impulsively, not to say arbitrarily and oppressively. The continuing public acceptance of a judicial power to overrule some legislative enactments suggests that most Americans still do not actually accept the notion of popular sovereignty as the last word on good government.

Whatever the leanings of contemporary public opinion on the theory of popular sovereignty, however, it is quite clear that our inherited constitutional arrangements do not at all correspond with this simple theory. If "the people" are simply sovereign, they should—as the notion of sovereignty implies—face no obstruction to their will. But the American constitutional scheme, requiring the assent of two different legislative chambers and a veto wielding president, all elected at different intervals, plainly poses many obstacles to the enactment of new measures or the legislative repeal of old measures. At any one time, therefore, the content of the law—or at least of the statutory code—is quite unlikely to reflect the contemporaneous "will of the people."

This thought was not, of course, particularly troubling for the framers of the Constitution. They were not simple enthusiasts of the will of the people, but instead argued quite explicitly that the will of impulsive or selfish majorities *ought* to be obstructed in order to safeguard private rights and the public good. From this perspective, it is not at all problematic for a private litigant to demand that courts check the executive from encroaching on his own private rights when this encroachment is not authorized by law. The complaint of the private litigant in such a case is not that the executive has failed to honor the contemporaneous will of the people, but that his own rights may be infringed, in a manner that violates the constitutional guarantee that infringements on rights will only occur following a deliberately cumbersome legislative process. There may also be good reasons for wanting the executive to honor the intent of Congress even when private rights are not involved. But serving the will of the people cannot be one of these reasons, for any enacted statute at best reflects the will of people in the past—often several decades in the past—and even at that, it is unlikely to reflect anything as simple as the will of the actual majority of voters at the time of enactment.

In view of the institutional obstacles to repealing or altering already enacted statutes, what the demand for administrative adherence to enacted measures actually serves is inertia. Such inertia may be good for protecting private rights, but it does not obviously serve the public good, particularly as circumstances change. In fact, courts themselves often alter the meaning of statutes to serve what they regard as changing circumstances. So, to cite the most famous contemporary example, barely a dozen years after Congress enacted the Civil Rights Act of 1964, a majority of the Supreme Court ruled that this statutory prohibition of "discrimination on the basis of race" did not after all prohibit affirmative action policies providing explicit racial preferences to minorities— even though the leading sponsors of the measure had emphatically denied this interpretation in 1964.[16] Justice Blackmun, at least, candidly acknowledged that this reinterpretation was required by changing circumstances.[17] In this case, the Court reinterpreted a statute to take away individual private rights that had been expressly conferred by that statute (or so it had been thought) only a dozen years earlier—which may seem particularly troubling if one cares about rights.

But in general, if we think that statutory schemes should be revised or updated, it is hard to see why politically insulated judges, with no particular experience in the administration of public programs, have more claim to make such modifications than politically accountable and continually involved officials in the executive branch. Even when private rights are not involved, however, contemporary administrative law eagerly embraces the premise that the will of Congress must be upheld, for judges and commentators have come to regard this claim as an unanswerable justification for judicial review.[18] For example, in a 1986 case, agricultural interests charged that the partial deregulation of natural gas pipeline rates by the Federal Energy Regulatory Commission violated the 1906 Hepburn Act, and the D.C. Court of Appeals, in upholding this claim, solemnly reviewed the legislative record of the enacting Congress in its opinion, citing the floor speeches of Henry Cabot Lodge and other allies of then President Theodore Roosevelt to establish the proper lines of public policy in the 1980s.[19]

To every appearance, a case of this sort simply seems to treat the nostrums of eighty years ago as the indefeasible prizes of contemporary interest groups. Almost no one objects when legislative nostrums of that era concerning public morals—such as laws prohibiting the practice of sodomy—go entirely unenforced decades later. But in administrative law cases, courts continue to insist that the will of Congress must be upheld even though no private rights are at stake, as if the will of some bygone Congress is in itself identical with the public good or the will of the people.

The ultimate difficulty with this legalistic perspective on the will of Congress is not a matter of theory, however, but of simple political reality. From the very outset, when the champions of legislative supremacy demanded executive adherence to the law, they did not mean adherence to a judicially ascertained reading of the will of the enacting Congress. Instead, they took it for granted that congressional oversight committees should speak for the will of Congress. Indeed, the same populist outlook that made Jeffersonian Republicans suspicious of executive power made them at least as suspicious of unelected judges (and the same was true for their post–Civil War namesakes in the Reconstruction Congress).[20] In general, congressional factions have wanted not so much the law as *their version* of the law—which has tended to mean the version favored by their own political constituencies.

And this state of affairs has been quite as prevalent in recent decades as it ever was. The scale of administrative operations has vastly increased in recent decades, but so has the number of specialized congressional subcommittees, committee staffs, and congressional investigative, research, and support staffs.

The official premise of congressional oversight continues to be that Congress must monitor ongoing administrative operations so that it can be adequately informed in carrying out its own legislative duties.[21] But little congressional oversight (whether in formal subcommittee hearings, in informal consultations, or in mandated investigations by specialized congressional staff) has any direct connection with impending legislation. Most seeks to determine whether administrative operations are being run in the way that dominant factions in Congress think they should be run. In fact, changes in regulatory legislation are particularly rare, because it is quite difficult to reassemble majorities in both houses to support any particular proposal for change. If there is any significant difference in the character of congressional activity now, compared with that of earlier decades, it is that power in Congress has become much more decentralized and diffused, so that assembling legislative majorities is more difficult than in the past.[22] But this situation simply increases the incentives of congressmen to seek to influence policy by administrative oversight—through particular committees which may have a broadly consistent policy perspective, for all the diversity of opinion in Congress as a whole.[23] And administrators, aware that congressional committees can focus embarrassing publicity, cut their budgets, or block their promotions, tend to pay close heed to the promptings and carpings of congressional factions, unless their inclinations to resist are strongly reinforced by the White House or by powerful rival factions.[24]

Why does Congress, with so many sources of leverage on administrative policy, welcome the intervention of broader judicial controls, which may compete with its own policy promptings? The simplest answer is that powerful constituency groups demand judicial protection—as regulated business interests persuaded Congress to enact a broad provision for judicial review of administrative findings in the late 1930s (which was vetoed by President Roosevelt and not then revived)[25] and as environmental groups successfully lobbied Congress to enact citizen standing provisions in the major environmental statutes of the early 1970s.[26] The longer answer is that Congress has not, in fact, always thought it prudent to give way to such entreaties. In the mid-1970s, for example, it simply refused to give serious consideration to Ralph Nader's proposal for a measure authorizing any citizen to challenge any regulatory decision in civil litigation.[27] For the most part, the expansion of access to the courts has been the work not of Congress, but of courts themselves. Asking why Congress has not cut back on this access through legislation is like asking why it has not cut back on subsidy or entitlement programs that have expanded far beyond expectations: it is politically quite difficult to remove interest group benefits already in place.

But the final reason why Congress has patiently accepted the expansion of judicial oversight in administrative affairs in recent years is probably that judicial review may advance the aims of some interest groups without posing too much of a threat to other constituencies, favored by the dominant factions in Congress. And that is perhaps the case because judicial directives have only a limited capacity to influence administrative operations when congressional factions apply strong opposing pressures. Courts, in short, are too weak to seem very threatening rivals to congressional factions, but they can often be useful allies. Appeals to "legality," after all, can often be a very useful method of politics. Whether they do anything to further the public good is another question.

The Progressive Tradition and the Independent Commissions

Champions of congressional power, however, have not been the only advocates drawn to a legalistic conception of administrative responsibilities—not at least in this century. Paradoxical as it may seem, demands for strict administrative fidelity to law have often been advanced too by partisans of executive power. But the paradox by which similar rhetoric has been adapted to opposite purposes is not hard to explain: the same rhetoric is convenient for partisans of many stripes because it remains a convenient way of displacing policy disputes into more compelling language. After all, the rhetoric of strict administrative fidelity to legal mandates can be turned quite as readily against congressional meddling as against presidential meddling. And much of the rhetoric of early twentieth century Progressives was designed precisely to discourage congressional meddling in administration.

If the executive is bound to observe the law as strictly or impartially as the judiciary, the difference between the executive and judicial branches seems to disappear. Government was presented in just that light in the writings of leading Progressive scholars of the early twentieth century. Thus, for example, Frank Goodnow, the founding father of the academic discipline of public administration, insisted that the traditional division of government into three powers was illogical and misconceived. There are only two fundamental powers, Goodnow maintained: a power to declare the will of the state and a power to execute or implement that will. And Goodnow, like a whole generation of Progressive reformers who followed him, was eager to draw out the practical lesson from this seemingly arcane point: "politics" should be kept separate from "administration," as the articulation of the public will is an entirely different function from its implementation.[28]

The practical point of separating "politics" from "administration" was to keep politicians away from administrators—which meant, for the most part, keeping legislators away from executive operations. In state and municipal politics, Progressive Era reformers strove to concentrate administrative authority in the hands of governors and mayors (or, better still, in the hands of nonpartisan "city managers"). At the federal level, Progressive reformers fought for the extension of civil service job protection, largely to prevent the disruptive, wholesale turnover of federal offices, which nineteenth century presidents found necessary to gratify the patronage demands of congressional politicians.[29] Progressive reformers also fought to establish a separate presidential budget office, which was supposed to interpose overall planning priorities between the various federal bureaus and departments and the congressional appropriations committees, with which the bureaus and departments had previously had to deal directly and on their own.

On the whole, Progressive reformers were no more eager for extended judicial interventions into executive affairs than the advocates of congressional supremacy had been in the nineteenth century. The Progressives, too, were generally rather suspicious of (and sometimes quite hostile to) judicial authority, for much the same reason as earlier generations of congressional populists. They saw the courts as too preoccupied with the rights of private property holders and therefore too stinting of the public interest.[30] The Progressives championed administrative authority—more or less in conscious opposition to judicial authority—as a means to ensure that the public interest would receive its due. Progressive reformers sought to appropriate the prestige of judicial neutrality for executive or administrative undertakings, but they certainly did not want such undertakings subordinated to actual courts.

Independent regulatory commissions, which have come to be regarded as a characteristic institutional legacy of the Progressive mentality, may seem an exception to this pattern, for their "independence" seems to distance them from both executive and legislative interference. But the history of the independent commissions since the turn of century is, if anything, the exception that proves the rule. The notion that the commissions should be entirely independent of the president was a late development in their history, and a development eagerly sustained by interest groups that expected to benefit from this notion.

The ICC, prototype of a dozen later commissions, was initially established in 1887 to judge disputes about the fairness of interstate railroad rates; in 1906 it was expressly given independent power to enforce its judgments. The novelty of the commission was precisely its power to constrain or redefine private rights (in individual cases) apart from proceedings in the ordinary courts, as was normally required. From the outset, then, the ICC sought to develop its rulings on the basis of formal, judicialized hearings in order to inspire confidence in its unusual authority, as an administrative body, to exercise powers otherwise reserved to courts. Like all of the later commissions, moreover, the ICC was constituted as a multimember board, somewhat resembling an appellate court. While the commissioners were not given life tenure like actual federal judges, their fixed terms were arranged to expire at staggered intervals; and, by express statutory requirement, no more than half of the commissioners at any one time could be appointed from the same political party. The point of this unusual organizational form (unusual, that is, for an administrative agency) was to make the commissions look particularly trustworthy—and Progressives insisted that courts must share this trust, showing deference to the "expert findings" of the commissions in cases in which the acknowledged rights of regulated firms entitled them to appeal the legality of commission rulings to the courts.

For all of their appearance of judicial impartiality, however, the notable fact about the independent regulatory commissions is that, when they were first established, their form was not questioned by presidents of the day, who included some of our most assertive and ambitious presidents. Woodrow Wilson wholeheartedly supported the establishment of the Federal Trade Commission, the U.S. Shipping Board, and the Federal Reserve Board on the same model as the ICC (as Theodore Roosevelt had actively supported the strengthening of the ICC's powers in 1906). Franklin Roosevelt wholeheartedly supported the establishment of the Securities and Exchange Commission, the Federal Communications Commission, the Federal Power Commission, the Civil Aeronautics Board, as well as other boards and commissions organized along these same lines in the early New Deal years.[31]

By the mid-1930s, a considerable number of other regulatory schemes conferring power to constrain or redefine private rights in particular cases had been lodged in existing Cabinet departments. (As is today required by law, such programs usually allowed affected private parties to contest administrative charges or sanctions before specialized hearing examiners, set apart from ordinary administrative operations, while the department secretary retained ordinary directing authority over investigative and prosecutorial officials and in most cases retained final authority to overturn the rulings of hearing examiners in contested cases.)[32] The reasoning that led Congress to entrust some regulatory powers to executive departments and to assign others to independent commissions was never very clear. But both President Wilson and President Roosevelt seem to have taken it for granted that the commission form would prove no serious threat to their own administrative authority—that it

88

would not, in other words, significantly affect their power to influence or control the broad lines of commission policies. In fact, both were rather free in relaying their own policy views to trusted commissioners.[33]

Near the outset of his first term, President Roosevelt indeed ventured directly to remove a Federal Trade Commissioner over policy disagreements. The assumption of ultimate presidential control was so well established[34] that when the displaced commissioner sued for recovery of his salary and the Supreme Court ruled in his favor, New Dealers took this Court decision *(Humphrey's Executor v. U.S.)* as a willful partisan slap.[35] Roosevelt's closest advisers could find no other explanation for the Supreme Court's insistence on taking the pretense of the commission form altogether literally. Independent regulatory commissioners, the Court insisted, must be protected from presidential control because they "are charged with no policy except the policy of the law." This difference separated them from ordinary executive officials—who, the Court implied, might indeed be expected to temper the law with larger policy considerations, at least if private rights were not at stake. Accordingly, the Court maintained that a commissioner of an independent commission had to be conceived as "an officer who occupies no place in the executive department and who exercises no part of the executive power vested by the Constitution in the President."[36]

Constitutional scholars have continued to find this reasoning rather puzzling,[37] but to Roosevelt's advisers at the time it was infuriating: they could not see that "the law" had any significant meaning apart from sound national policy and could not see the point of separating sound policy from the president's view of sound policy. Only a few years later, therefore, President Roosevelt urged that he be allowed to carry through an ambitious reorganization scheme, which would have had the effect of overturning the Supreme Court's ruling in *Humphrey's Executor* by reconstituting all of the independent commissions as subordinate bureaus in the established executive departments. By then, however, Congress had begun to feel increasingly uneasy about augmentations in the power of an already very powerful president, and to feel correspondingly attached to the Supreme Court's depiction of the independent commission as an "arm of Congress." Most of Roosevelt's reorganization proposals were rejected, and the commissions remained formally independent.[38] The commissions were never independent of Congress, however, at least no more so than any other administrative operations. Their formal independence of presidential control may indeed have encouraged congressional oversight committees to regard them as special preserves for the exercise of congressional influence.[39]

What is certain, at any rate, is that most of the commissions found it easy to identify the public interest with economic controls protecting the market shares and profit margins of regulated firms. The most sophisticated defenders of the commissions in the 1930s presented them as *planning* agencies, imposing "rational" and "stable" patterns of operation in particular industries—a view premised on the assumption that economic development had already reached a stage of maturity that made it feasible to fix industry-wide service standards on a more or less definitive basis.[40] In practice, much economic regulation made this expectation self-fulfilling by acting to resist major changes in service patterns, market shares, or profit levels in the regulated industries. And this situation was not, on the whole, disagreeable for regulated firms, which, if they had to forego some of the wider opportunities of unrestrained competition, gained a good deal of compensating security.

The competitor standing decisions of the interwar years did not, therefore, provoke any great criticism from defenders of the independent regulatory commissions. Although in principle they extended the potential for judicial intervention more broadly, they did so in a way that perfectly complemented the prevailing conception of regulation as the safeguarding of existing market shares among regulated firms. In this respect, the legal and policy biases of the commissions reinforced the natural political bias of congressional oversight, which was also more likely to attend to established business interests than to the potential of business ventures not yet in existence.

In the changed economic and political climate of the postwar world, however, the performance of the commissions looked much more questionable. By the late 1950s, a growing body of scholarly criticism was blaming the sluggishness of regulated industries in adapting to changing conditions on the sluggishness of "judicialized" regulatory patterns within the commissions.[41] James Landis, a New Deal regulator who had been one of the leading defenders of independent commissions in the 1930s, was by 1961 urging President Kennedy to prod the commissions into displaying greater policy initiative and "energy"—in short, to become more executive in character.[42]

In fact, the most dramatic policy innovations during the 1970s occurred in just those rate and route setting regulatory commissions, like the Civil Aeronautics Board and the ICC, which sympathetic New Dealers had expected to develop the most standardized controls. In the 1970s, these commissions began systematically reducing protective controls in order to force regulated firms to adapt to competitive pressures on their own. Many regulated firms protested that this policy was pursued in disregard of existing administrative precedents and accepted interpretations of commission obligations under the law. But deregulatory initiatives in these fields—prominently supported by Presidents Ford, Carter, and Reagan—helped to demonstrate the public benefits of greater competition to skeptics in Congress. In a series of enactments during the late 1970s and early 1980s, Congress itself finally endorsed the removal of most competitive controls on airlines, railroads, trucks, and buses, as well as on the oil and natural gas industries and various financial services.[43]

As it depended on the readiness of regulatory commissioners to look beyond "the policy of the law," deregulation in these fields might have been slowed to a considerable extent if courts had enforced the policy of the law, or rather the restrictive precedents established under earlier interpretations of the law. Legal advisers to the commissions did, in fact, worry much about this possibility, and Alfred Kahn, the reformist chairman of the Civil Aeronautics Board in the late 1970s, boasted that he would never have succeeded in pressing deregulation so far if he had been a lawyer rather than an economist. As it happened, regulated airlines—sensing that the political tide was running against them and recognizing that litigation might be too protracted to be an effective political tactic—did not often invoke competitor standing to block administrative deregulatory initiatives.[44] But the trucking industry complained bitterly about the "lawlessness" of deregulatory initiatives by the ICC and used litigation (and the threat of more litigation) to slow the pace of moves toward greater competition during the 1980s; though here, as elsewhere, litigation was reinforced by the considerable political clout of the trucking industry in Congress.[45] In the end, as in the beginning, the independent commissions did not look very independent, and few were sorry for their reintegration into the broad currents of changing national policy—few, that is, except the special beneficiaries of commission policy in the era when their "independence" was most insistently and perhaps most successfully defended.

The Charm of Expertise

When new environmental, consumer, and "public interest" advocacy groups began to appear in the late 1960s, it was already conventional wisdom (at least among activists) that the existing regulatory commissions had been captured by the industries they were intended to regulate.[46] This charge was, if not the animating cause for the development of these new advocacy groups, at least one of the significant elements in the favorable political climate that developed for them in the late 1960s. In fact, the policy of lifting economic controls on transportation industries in the mid-1970s gained strong support from a number of prominent consumer organizations, such as those associated with Ralph Nader.[47] Like other advocates of deregulation by then, these consumer organizations turned a deaf ear to the protests of regulated industries that reformist commissioners were flouting their statutory responsibilities in pursuing deregulatory initiatives. If statutes gave improper privileges to regulated industries, consumer advocates were content to see such laws go underenforced—and finally repealed.

In most areas, however, public interest advocacy groups thought that the country needed more regulation, not less. In pursuing their own agendas for regulatory action, these groups quickly emulated the tactics of their original targets, those regulated industries which sought to defend regulatory controls favorable to their own interests. So consumer advocates, while welcoming presidential initiatives to reform the older regulatory commissions, persuaded Congress to establish a new Consumer Products Safety Commission as an independent commission in 1972 and, for several years thereafter, waged an ultimately unsuccessful struggle to persuade Congress to establish a larger "consumer advocacy agency" on an independent basis. Environmentalists had to content themselves with a compromise formula establishing the new EPA in 1970 as "an independent agency within the executive branch."

Environmentalists were quite successful, however, in persuading Congress to limit the discretion of EPA regulators by writing quite detailed objectives into new environmental statutes. The statutes sought to ensure impressive results by mandating detailed—and as it turned out, quite unrealistic—pollution reduction targets, to be achieved within specified deadlines.[48] In order to ensure that these statutory directives were implemented, environmentalists also persuaded Congress to authorize any citizen to sue the EPA for failure to comply with any of its duties under the law. Environmentalists, that is, borrowed another leaf from firms regulated by the older independent commissions, by trying to enlist judicial power to ensure that they received every benefit the law might entitle them to receive. In fact, the courts had already begun to offer this opportunity to many other policy advocates, even when Congress had not explicitly authorized it, and read expansive interpretations of standing into a variety of new statutes authorizing judicial review at the behest of "aggrieved" parties.

It is clear enough why environmental, consumer, and other advocacy groups should have wanted to seize every new means of exerting leverage on agency policy that courts might make available to them. It remains a question why the courts were so willing to make this extra leverage so readily available, especially considering the discredited logic of the competitor standing cases of earlier decades. Part of the answer, no doubt, is that many judges in the late 1960s and early 1970s shared strong partisan suspicions of the Nixon administration and simply regarded public interest advocacy groups as "the good guys" who would help keep "the bad guys" in line. No doubt, too, some judges simply conceived it as their duty to ensure that congressional expectations were properly fulfilled; so they opened the courts to a wide range of interest advocates not at all readily encapsulated under the "public interest" rubric.

By the late 1970s, the cooling of partisan passions had deflated a good many earlier delusions. Instead of good guys and bad guys, policy debates were more likely to concede the inevitability of awkward tradeoffs among legitimate, contending concerns. While there were some signs of judicial retrenchment in this calmer climate, the basic outlines of the new judicial role remained in place. And the question again is, why? It begs the question to say that it was necessary to ensure that "the law" was respected. The question is why the "impartial" constructions that the judges might impose on statutes must be respected, when no conventional private rights are at stake. The most candid answer from judges is that broad judicial oversight is necessary to reassure the public about the integrity of administrative decisionmaking.

So, for example, the chief judge of the D.C. Court of Appeals—the court most concerned with appeals against administrative agencies—explained in the early 1980s that "Agencies and courts alike are thrown into areas of ferocious controversy every day and their common function is to discern the path of reasonableness—the agency initially, the court on review."[49] The sentiment sounds unexceptionable. Who favors the path of unreasonableness? But if there is "ferocious controversy," how likely is it that the "ferocious" advocates on either side will accept the agency's or the court's notion of "reasonableness"? And if there is ferocious controversy, why put the emphasis on reasonableness as opposed to, say, compromise or popularity or simply decisiveness, putting an end to the "controversy" one way or another? Of course, courts would not then be very well situated to review the propriety of the agency's decision. But why should that matter, in itself?

The premise of contemporary administrative law, however, is that "only upon a showing of clear and convincing . . . legislative intent [to exclude review] should courts restrict access to judicial review."[50] In other words, the premise is that if people feel "injured"—which may mean as little as feeling upset—they ought to be able to complain to the courts. And then? Courts cannot assure everyone's expectations, of course, but they can, so Judge Wald's formulation suggests, offer the consolation that remaining injuries are justified by the reasonableness of the agency's decision. The more areas of administrative policy making opened to judicial challenge, the more encompassing or expansive this demand for reasonableness or rationality. But what do such phrases really mean?

The most obvious and probably the most frequent approach of reviewing courts is to treat "reasonableness" as the opposite of decisions that are "arbitrary and capricious," which is the term the Administrative Procedure Act employs in authorizing courts to "set aside" agency judgments.[51] But the drafters of the APA, thinking of claims by property owners as the usual context for judicial review, plainly regarded these terms as defined by the statutory standards for particular administrative actions. Even when courts review agency decisions under the more demanding test of "substantial evidence" supporting the result, the evidence can only be judged substantial if the court first determines that it is pertinent to what the court itself judges to be permissible statutory criteria for decision making. This device makes sense, again, when used for protecting property owners, by assuring them that federal officials will not be able to limit their property rights except when authorized to do so by legislative enactment. But why, again, assume that what is not arbitrary (or not supported by substantial evidence) in relation to enacted statutory standards is in itself reasonable? What if the statute is, in itself, somewhat unreasonable or unrealistic in its premises? Does it not constitute a perverse sort of legalism, after all, to insist that statutes be fully enforced or statutory criteria fully observed even when no private rights are involved and both judges and executive officials may regard the statute as unreasonable or unrealistic in the given circumstances? As such legalism is not very appealing, courts often try to conceal misplaced legalism by disguising it as an insistence on technical competence.

Thus Judge Wald concedes that it "would be naive to overlook the fact that most major 'expert' [*sic*] agency decisions are themselves the result of political and pragmatic compromises." But it is only "the legitimate expertise of agencies set up to deal with particular problems," she insists, that is "essential for courts to acknowledge."[52] The point of judicial review, then, is not anything quite so legalistic as enforcing the law at all costs; rather it is to distinguish true "expertise" from spurious political claims masquerading as expertise. But expertise is really little different from legalism—which is why the champions of the independent commissions in the 1930s were so eager to claim expertise for the commissions when they could not claim law.

Expertise (in its modern sense of instrumental rationality) treats all aims and goals as given, requiring only technical calculations about the most effective or efficient way to operate within these accepted parameters. Expertise thus serves precisely the same function as the law in providing an ostensibly neutral authority for decisions, which can then seem to be entirely impersonal: "This is not my opinion," the decision maker piously protests, "but the inescapable conclusion of expertise" or, if he is more old-fashioned, "of law." In other words, expertise is, like law, a device for allowing decision makers to disclaim responsibility for their decisions. And holding executive officials within the bounds of expertise is, in the end, a device for making them more like courts—more like modern courts, at least.

For just this reason, appeals to expertise turn out to be closely related to appeals to law, not just in contemporary judicial fashion but in the history of political thought in the modern world. It is worth a brief excursion into their connections to see how remote such appeals are from the normal presumptions of the American constitutional tradition and how difficult they are to reconcile with the institutional structures of American government.

The View from Europe: Technical Rationality as Moral Authority

The view that so-called "expertise" confers legitimacy and that rationality is equivalent to expertise is most famously associated with the writings of the German sociologist Max Weber. In his most celebrated work, posthumously published in the early 1920s, Weber depicted the growth of bureaucracy as one of the principal manifestations of the increasing "rationalization" of social institutions in the modern world. He presented bureaucracy as a distinct form of social organization: the systematic, hierarchical organization of specialists, each governed by rules and professional norms appropriate to his own delimited sphere of competence and authority. And he compared this form of organization with "precision machinery," yielding a "particularly high degree of calculability of results."[53] Adherence to rules—or to expert norms, conceived as rules—is of the essence: even "the tendency of officials" to adopt "a utilitarian point of view in the interest of those under their authority" is tempered by the compulsion to proceed through "measures which themselves have a formal character and tend to be treated in a formalistic spirit. . . . Otherwise the door would be opened to arbitrariness."[54]

Some scholars have suggested that Weber was excessively reverent or excessively credulous about the particular professional conceits of the old Prussian state bureaucracy.[55] In fact, he expressed great dismay about the overweening power of the state bureaucracies in Wilhelmine Germany and worried much about the spiritually deadening effects of social rationalization and the impersonal, legalistic ethos of a bureaucratized society.[56] These personal misgivings make all the more remarkable his conclusion that the "dominance of a spirit of formalistic impersonality . . . without hatred or passion and hence without affection or enthusiasm" is always most conducive to administrative "efficiency."[57]

In fact, it is not at all clear that this sort of organization is most conducive to "efficiency." Armies do not win victories and business corporations do not win profits by following fixed rules in a "spirit of formalistic impersonality." Even governmental bureaucracies usually depend on more flexibility and inspiration than Weber acknowledges, as is suggested by the phenomenon of the "rule book slowdown," in which public employees, instead of going out on strike, paralyze government operations by fastidiously observing every official rule to the letter. In Weber's account of bureaucracy, questions of motivation, morale, or initiative seem to disappear, leaving managers with no awkward tradeoffs between inspiration and control, between creativity and reliability, between adaptability and predictability.

Weber was quite aware that efficiency must be measured in reference to some desired output and that bureaucracies may measure their own efficiency or effectiveness by merely formal standards, impressive only to the bureaucrats themselves. Nonetheless, Weber's account of bureaucracy frequently blurs the distinction he himself makes between *formal* rationality (conformity of actions or decisions to some fixed, formal standard) and *substantive* rationality (the conduciveness of actions or decisions to ultimate desired ends). Thus Weber sometimes suggests that impersonal devotion to rules and professional norms is a guarantee of superior effectiveness, while often entangling this claim in the rather different notion that impersonal devotion to rules and professional norms is an essential attribute of legitimate authority in the modern world.

The main reason for this ambiguity seems to be that, while Weber often speaks of bureaucracy as a general social phenomenon, he was most preoccupied with its significance as a governmental institution. His most extended analysis of bureaucracy comes in the context of a larger discussion of the (ostensibly) fundamental alternatives for legitimizing political authority. He depicts bureaucracy as the most developed form of authority grounded in "rational-legal norms" and contrasts it to both "traditional authority" (by which people accept a certain ordering of affairs because they have always been ordered that way) and with "charismatic" authority (by which people uncritically accept the directives of a particular leader from a mystical faith in his superhuman power and wisdom).[58]

In this framework, of course, the comparison is all in favor of impersonal norms. Bureaucracy seems to bear the same relation to alternative governing institutions that modern medicine bears to folk remedies or modern chemistry to medieval alchemy. Or, perhaps more aptly, modern bureaucracy seems to bear the same relation to the alternatives that a modern court of law bears to a qadi under a tree. But with judges, as we have noted, devotion to the law—as opposed to the judge's own sense of what is good—serves the logic of private rights. Why should we value the same thing so highly in other governmental officials? Why should we prize a "particularly high degree of calculability of results" more than a high degree of public satisfaction with the results?

Bureaucratic Idealism or Executive Power?

Why indeed suppose that the legitimacy of most governmental operations is more dependent on their adherence to impersonal norms than on their overall effectiveness in achieving desired results? The reason seems to be that adherence to rules or to the tenets of expertise can be fixed with precision, while judgments about results are likely to be disputable, because "results" encompass many effects (or side effects) likely to be differently assessed by differently situated observers. If legitimacy is the primary concern—as it was for Weber—then avoiding disputable conclusions takes on a very high priority.

Quite apart from his particular analyses of bureaucracy, in fact, Weber is much remembered today for his methodological writings, insisting that social scientists must always strive to separate "facts" from "values" in their work and stick only to the facts. Weber's precise reason for condemning the intrusion of the social scientist's values into his analyses was that he conceived values as inevitably personal and arbitrary, rather than objective, demonstrable, and scientific.[59] In other words, Weber tried to make social science into another form of expertise, so he took great pains to protect it from the appearance of being disputable.

If this call for a value free social science no longer has great currency among contemporary scholars, it is only in part because of the powerful philosophical critiques launched against Weber's assumption that facts and values can be neatly separated.[60] It probably has much more to do with the experience that value free research has yielded few interesting findings in itself, because most interesting work requires the interpretation of findings within a framework of analysis that gives them meaning. The appropriateness of different analytical frameworks is almost always a subject of dispute. But most social scientists today would rather do work that is interesting and suggestive, knowing well that their conclusions may be disputed, than work that can stand undisputed, and be dismissed as trivial.

Public policy decisions depend in a similar way not only on a core of factual data that can sometimes be pinned down with a reasonable degree of certainty, but also on a much more disputable framework for assessing the data—or for identifying the factual data that is truly relevant for policy analysis—before reaching a policy conclusion. The more the framework of analysis is taken as fixed and well defined, the more readily policy decisions can be presented as mere technical assessments, following more or less indisputably from the norms of the relevant expert discipline. Weber's account suggests that bureaucratic rationality tends always in this direction, so that bureaucratic determinations seem indisputable; as he notes, even elected Cabinet ministers thus find it nearly impossible to challenge the decisions flowing from the bureaucratic "machine."[61] The initial justification for bureaucracy, as a device for implementing legislative enactments (which may have been quite controversial in themselves when enacted), almost disappears from view in this preoccupation with the legitimizing authority of technical rationality and expertise.

But why should we think that this continual narrowing and formalizing of policy criteria will enhance the legitimacy of bureaucratic decisions? Why suppose that a "machine" will have more appeal than a human government? It is easy to see why bureaucrats (or indeed social scientists) might like to silence their critics by making the technical arguments seem definitive. But why should critics be persuaded by arguments that do rest, in the end, on the disputable assumptions that lie behind all the imposing technical calculations of the experts? It may be that Weber believed that adherence to impersonal norms could confer legitimacy because this is what he actually observed in the behavior of late nineteenth or early twentieth century Germans: a ready willingness to defer to compulsion when it is justified by "expertise" or by "the law."

Still, it is hard to see why people should defer to technical experts with narrow experience as opposed to, say, proven achievers in the wider world of affairs or political figures whose characters inspire personal trust. On the face of things, the suggestion that strict adherence to the impersonal norms of law or expertise will cow people into acceptance seems no more obviously realistic than Weber's suggestion that impersonal, rule-bound behavior is the most efficient or effective way to reach a desired goal. It appears that beneath this supposed realism is a certain idealism—just as Weber's vision of an indisputable science of social affairs seems, in retrospect, less realistic in its disavowal of values than remarkably idealistic in its expectations for science.

Weber's eagerness to associate legitimacy with adherence to impersonal norms may be best understood as a late echo of the much older philosophic tradition of German idealism. At least it is striking how many of Weber's presuppositions about legitimacy in the modern world had already been argued at length by Immanuel Kant, the eighteenth century Prussian philosopher usually regarded as the founder of modern idealist philosophy.[62] Like Weber, Kant contended that moral obligations could not be derived from systematic or scientific observation of nature, even of human nature. Kant was even more insistent than Weber that obligation must be unvarying and indisputable—free of any hint of personal bias or disputable judgment—to be moral, because it might otherwise seem to derive from mere natural prompting or compulsion. Kant accordingly argued that morality must be defined as unwavering adherence to "universal" norms, norms that could be imposed by a "legislator for mankind" and then followed in every case without exception. Because he insisted that the moral authority of these rules could not be grounded in natural patterns of cause and effect, he argued that their moral authority must remain entirely unaffected by their consequences in the real world.[63]

Kant's writings, in fact, devote much more attention to the form of moral rules than to their actual content, just because morality, in Kantian terms, has no concern with consequences. The aim of moral conduct, rather, is to demonstrate one's freedom from selfish or passionate impulses. The truly moral man, according to Kant, will adhere to his universal norms, oblivious to circumstances and consequences in particular cases, no matter how awkward or tragic they might be, lest such considerations provide an opening to be swayed by selfish passions.

Kant thus sought to infuse morality with a highly exaggerated version of the rule bound rigidity we normally associate with judicial decisions. When the rigidity of actual judicial decisions secures boundaries of personal rights or personal control, the rigidity of law can be seen as a bulwark for varying notions of private morality, which may be more or less supple, refined, or spontaneous from one person to the next. Kantian morality, by imposing the legalistic constraints of the judge on every private person, seems to rob private life of its distinctive character. It seems to present the most legalistic jurist—or perhaps still more aptly, the most fastidious bureaucrat—as the archetype of human perfection. And Kant's writings were, in fact, well received in the higher reaches of the Prussian state bureaucracy in the late eighteenth century.[64]

In effacing the distinctiveness of private life, however, Kantian morality also denied the moral distinctiveness of public responsibility. As private persons must never lie, statesmen must never lie; as private persons must never dissemble or conceal, Kant insisted, statesmen must never dissemble or conceal.[65] However edifying this notion may seem, Kant did not flinch from the more grotesque implications of the view that morality means adherence to impersonal norms and morality must apply as much to government officials as to private persons.

So, for example, Kant was an unflinching defender of capital punishment, viewing the imposition of death sentences, when appropriate, as morally obligatory. And he insisted more generally that the laws must always be fully enforced, punishment fully exacted, "and woe to him who rummages around . . . looking for some advantage to be gained in releasing the criminal from punishment or in reducing the amount of it." With a similar sort of legalism, Kant asserted that the state could not properly punish the murder of an illegitimate baby, because the birth of an illegitimate child is not authorized by the marriage laws "and consequently it is also outside the protection of the law. The child has crept surreptitiously into the commonwealth (much like prohibited wares) so that its existence as well as its destruction can be ignored (because by right it ought not to have come into existence in this way)."[66] Officials must do their duty—but, as with private morality, official duty is no

99

more and no less than adherence to the rules. Consequently, "the well-being of the state must not be confused with the welfare or happiness of the citizens of the state."

It is scarcely an exaggeration, then, to say that for Kant, the official's plea that "I was only following orders" is a plea to be rendered in perfectly good conscience, at least if the orders follow the accepted formal pattern. For it is the essence of Kantian morality to free the conscience of its adherent from any qualms—or, as we might say, any sense of responsibility—for the consequences of his actions. This aspect makes it as attractive to the obedient government functionary as to the crusading political idealist, both of whom, in their different ways, are anxious to disclaim personal responsibility for the consequences of what they do.[67]

No doubt both functionaries and idealists are often tempted to conceive their duty in ways that Kant, himself, would not acknowledge as morally valid, because not formulable as consistent "universal" norms of conduct. But the highly formalistic character of Kant's definitions of moral duty make Kantian stances seem all too readily adaptable to a vast range of official and political positions; and there has rarely been a shortage of people in public positions eager to disclaim responsibility and stand upon morality.

Even before the extremist movements of the twentieth century revealed the full potential of such bureaucratic and political idealism when cut free from any meaningful sense of responsibility, thoughtful Americans recognized that this vision of public life was incompatible with the essential premises of constitutional government. In the still relatively innocent era before the end of the First World War, the most prominent constitutional scholar in America at the time published a bitter attack on German idealist philosophy in which he accused Kant's writings of laying rhetorical smoke screens for Prussian authoritarianism.[68] This claim was no doubt unfair to Kant's intentions, but it was not at all off the mark in its perception that bureaucratic idealism is impossible to reconcile with American conceptions of responsible, constitutional government.

The Older American View

It is hardly necessary at this stage to belabor the contrast. The framers of the American Constitution plainly operated on moral and political assumptions quite removed from the idealism that lies behind European celebrations of bureaucratic expertise.[69] *The Federalist* took it for granted that the policy agenda of modern legislation "involves the spirit of party and faction in the necessary and ordinary operations of government."[70] *The Federalist* also took it for granted that government officials would not be exempt from the normal range of human passions and motives. It praised the constitutional scheme for harnessing personal "ambition" and "the interest of the man" in the office to the service of his official duties, thus "supplying, by opposite and rival interests, the defect of better motives."[71]

The framers did not expect that citizens would or should place any great degree of trust in the integrity or good intentions of government officials. They expected that citizens would normally be somewhat skeptical, perhaps even suspicious of government, because they did not try to equate government with morality. They did not blink at the fact that government is primarily "administered by men over men" and consequently "must first enable the government to *control* the governed" (emphasis added).[72] And they did not expect that Americans would ever submit passively or piously to control.

At the same time, the framers did not seek to inflame popular distrust of government by trying to hold it to impossible standards. *The Federalist,* noting that "nations pay little regard to rules and maxims . . . [that] run counter to the necessities of society," concluded that "Wise politicians will be cautious about fettering the government with restrictions that cannot be observed."[73] In fact, *The Federalist* urged a more balanced view: "As there is a degree of depravity in mankind which requires a certain degree of circumspection and distrust, so there are other qualities in human nature which justify a certain portion of esteem and confidence."[74]

The institutional implication of this perspective is that, in its ordinary operations, government need not hide behind technical claims of expertise or the law. It must stand on its record, taking responsibility for its actual decisions and their real consequences. Administration is certainly important because "as a general rule . . . confidence in and obedience to government will commonly be proportioned to the goodness or badness of its administration."[75] But "goodness" or "badness" is not reducible to impartiality or neutral expertise; it refers primarily to popular satisfaction with the results.

This is, no doubt, a more disputable standard of performance than adherence to the law or adherence to the accepted norms of the experts. But the crucial point to notice about the framers of the American Constitution is that they were not overly fearful of dispute. *The Federalist* took it for granted that, "As long as the reason of man continues fallible and he is at liberty to exercise it, different opinions will be formed."[76] The framers did not regard divergences of opinion as fatal to the hopes for republican government, because they did not think governmental responsibility would cease to operate in a context of divided opinion. They did not think governmental responsibility required uniformity of opinion or fixed and uniform expectations by which to measure the conduct of executive officials. On the contrary, *The Federalist* argued that a considerable degree of diversity in opinion and conflict over expectations would be most conducive to genuine responsibility.[77]

The reason for this seeming paradox is that governmental responsibility, as the framers conceived it, is not reducible to the artificial precision of legality. In the American constitutional scheme, the plea that "I was only following orders" (or "only following the rules") is never a sufficient excuse in itself. It may be an adequate *legal* defense when an official is sued by his victims. But it is not an adequate political defense, because responsibility is not reducible to legality. For similar reasons, responsibility is not reducible to obedience. Congress is responsible to the electorate but not subject to its direct control, in the sense that it is never *obliged* to follow the results of a public opinion poll or a popular referendum. So it is with the elected chief executive and his subordinates in the executive branch. If policy decisions have terrible consequences, the decisionmakers cannot escape responsibility for these consequences by pleading that they were only following the dictates of public opinion in deciding as they did.

We may want to say that the executive is obliged to follow the law. But even then it is not the most natural or ordinary construction of the law—and certainly not the construction Congress might want to put on a policy it has enacted into law—that the executive is obligated to follow, at least when private rights are not at stake and judicial interpretations of the law do not intrude. As Alexander Hamilton put it, "He who is to execute the laws must first *judge for himself* of their meaning."[78]

If it were otherwise, and responsibility could indeed be reduced to control, then the plea of "just following orders" would turn out to be an entirely adequate excuse. Responsibility means that officials can be blamed—at least politically—when they passively submit to popular, congressional, or legal pressures instead of adopting what they themselves consider to be the most responsible course under the circumstances. You cannot blame someone for his decision, or hold him responsible for it, if you do not acknowledge that it was *his* decision to make and could have been made otherwise.

Responsibility does not, of course, operate in a vacuum, and the expectations formed around existing laws usually figure quite significantly in the estimations we make about responsible conduct. An official who disregarded all of his duties under the law (or construed them into effectual nullities), merely because he disagreed with the underlying policy of the law, would not usually be viewed as acting responsibly. If the official's disagreements were well founded and widely shared, however, even this conduct might still be regarded as responsible—in those rare circumstances in which well-founded and widely shared objections obtained, but the law involved continued officially in force. In just this way, President Jefferson ordered all federal prosecutors to cease prosecutions under the much derided Sedition Act and proceeded to pardon all of those previously convicted and sentenced for sedition during the previous administration.[79] No doubt, Congress might impeach a president who asserted such prerogatives frequently or in different circumstances in such a way as to show utter disdain for the law. The president's constitutional duty is to "take care that the laws be faithfully executed," which obliges him to assure "good faith" in the discharge of public duties.[80] But "good faith" performance is not necessarily the same as a judge's (much less a congressman's) view of strict legality, because acting in good faith is a matter of acting responsibly, not simply of following rules.

Responsibility, in this extended sense, is the essential purpose behind the constitutional scheme of separated powers. The framers deliberately gave the president a fixed term and devised a separate mode of election for him in order to make the executive more independent of Congress, hence more independently responsible for executing the laws. They viewed the confusion and mismanagement of administrative affairs under the Articles of Confederation as a direct reflection of the absence of any unified, independent executive responsibility in a system in which all of the major administrative officials were directly hired, fired, and managed by separate congressional committees—so that no one was finally in charge or responsible for administrative policy.[81]

But the framers were quite aware that the formal liberation of the executive would also prove liberating for Congress, because it would not have to fear that criticism of the executive would necessarily discredit the dominant party coalition in Congress. In fact, they were quite aware of the emerging patterns of parliamentary or cabinet government in Great Britain. They viewed this pattern with alarm because they saw it as a way of insulating the executive against effectual legislative opposition. The framers therefore wrote into the Constitution an express prohibition against members of Congress holding executive office. They did not want the president to be able to bribe Congress into compliance with seductive offers of office. In other words, instead of seeking to deny or disguise the need for executive discretion, the American framers sought to acknowledge the institutional necessity of executive "energy" without concealing the disputable character of executive choices.[82] Thus they established an executive power both independent and exposed.

It was not merely in the theories of the framers, moreover, or in the practices of our early presidents that executive discretion was accepted as the counterpart of executive responsibility. Some fifty years after the founding, a foreign observer, accustomed to the disciplined administrative structures of Western Europe, was struck by the "arbitrary power" entrusted to American public officials. As Tocqueville saw it, it was precisely the confidence of Americans in the democratic accountability of their officials that explained the fact that "American officials are much freer within the sphere of action by law allotted to them than is any corresponding European official."[83]

To this day American administrative arrangements, following the general outlines of the American constitutional order, do much less on the whole than European systems to conceal the disputable or "political" character of administrative action. In theory, the parliamentary systems of Western Europe go much further in establishing legislative power, as the majority in parliament determines the holders of top ministerial (executive) posts. This theory is reflected in a number of contrasting institutional or legal patterns. In regard to the core executive function of enforcing criminal law, for example, official doctrine in West Germany, France, and other continental states holds that criminal prosecutors must proceed with every case (or at least every felony case), unless there is some explicit, legally sanctioned reason for abandoning the prosecution.[84] In the United States, official doctrine acknowledges virtually unlimited prosecutorial discretion in criminal matters. Federal courts have indeed acknowledged that prosecutorial discretion may turn on such considerations as "the climate of public opinion," even though such discretion is certainly not conferred by statute.[85] But this contrast is only the tip of the iceberg.

In many European countries, governments long ago established special schools for the training of higher civil servants, while in the United States such special academies were established only for the training of military officers. Since the eighteenth century, governments in continental Europe—whether under absolute monarchies, modern parliamentary democracies, or a range of interim regimes—have encouraged the development of elaborate "public law" doctrines and texts, rationalizing and celebrating the distinctive characteristics of service to the state.[86] There is no tradition of such theorizing in America and no effort to train public officials to distinctive public norms.

The most striking difference may be in the relative status and influence of high-ranking civil servants in the United States and in Western Europe. Senior civil servants hold positions of great power and prestige in Western Europe, and it is assumed that the parliamentary ministers of whatever party will want to rely on the same corps of highly experienced, impartially devoted, top career officials. The formation of a new cabinet in Western Europe, therefore, may alter a few dozen top ministerial assignments but does not usually involve an extensive reshuffling of civil service positions. In the United States, by contrast, the organization of a new presidential administration always involves a tremendous turnover in offices, as the president appoints thousands of his own partisan followers to political positions, extending several layers into the bureaucracy in all of the government's administrative departments and agencies.[87] When Europeans speak of *l'administration* (or *Verwaltung*), the term usually conjures a vision of a disciplined, neutral apparatus of the State; when Americans speak of the administration, the term is usually understood as a shorthand for "the president's men"—as in "the Reagan administration."

The Policy Challenges of Politics

Scholars of comparative public policy have disputed whether the greater political vulnerability of American administrators really makes for better policy results. It is clear enough that the American system does little to encourage public respect for administrative officials: below the White House or the Cabinet, officials are generally regarded as bureaucrats, and there is little honor in being a bureaucrat in America, while there is much honor in being a higher civil servant in Western Europe. A number of observers have argued that ingrained American suspicions of government encourage organized interests to approach administrative agencies with intransigent, adversarial postures, which make it particularly difficult to fashion coherent policy compromises.[88]

It is certainly possible that a more trusting, accommodating approach to government by major interest groups would secure better results, even for the groups involved. The problem is that interest advocates who already view government agencies as too responsive to rival interests—as business groups feel about OSHA and its clientele in the labor movement or as public interest safety advocates feel about the FDA and the food and drug industries—cannot be readily persuaded to develop more trust and forebearance. The underlying problem is that the American constitutional scheme tends to encourage rather than discourage controversy and contention.

Much controversy arises, in the first place, from the fact that American regulatory statutes are usually framed in quite broad, sweeping (and, therefore, inherently ambiguous) terms. Underlying differences that Congress has not settled in the enactment of legislative standards are bound to engender continuing dispute about proper standards for implementation. Some scholars, such as Theodore Lowi, have urged that incessant policy wrangling at the administrative level could be avoided if Congress would simply enact more precise legislative standards at the outset.[89] If it did descend to details, however, Congress would likely encounter a whole series of paralyzing objections from affected interest groups, so it is rarely inclined to follow this advice.

In those regulatory measures in which it actually has descended to details, Congress has often found it easier to ignore complicating realities and then contented itself with enacting uncompromising rhetorical postures, which can secure broad support at the time of enactment because few legislators take them quite literally. So the auto emissions standards in the 1970 Clean Air Act, which received nearly unanimous support in Congress, set precise deadlines for precise levels of pollution reduction, imposing targets that were known to be unattainable at the time and have since been relaxed and extended three times without any serious reconsideration of the underlying approach.[90] In any case, detailed standards can hardly assure political consensus or even administrative legality: statutory standards that are unrealistically rigid or overly ambitious simply invite administrative discretion to make them workable, along with the ensuing controversy over where or how to fashion the necessary compromises.

If administrative implementation is to appear to follow in a straight and strict way from statutory standards, statutes must be capable of straight and strict implementation. The easiest way to ensure a sound working match between statutory objectives and implementing capacities is to let those responsible for implementation play the largest role in drafting the statutes. That is just what is done in Western Europe, where the parliamentary system allows the executive ministries to prepare initial legislative proposals in great detail and allows the sitting Cabinet to demand quick parliamentary acquiescence to its legislative proposals. In fact, major regulatory legislation is not simply prescreened by technical bureaucrats but negotiated with major affected interest groups to work out a reasonably acceptable consensus approach. What affected interests have agreed to, they are more likely to comply with in subsequent administrative implementation. In most areas, European governments find it easier to reach such a consensus because they conduct these advance negotiations with a handful of major interests with whom they are accustomed to working. A recent study of regulatory policy in Western Europe describes the process in this way:

> Access to ministerial circles [in Western Europe] tends to be limited to established interest groups with traditionally strong ties to government and a well-defined role in policymaking. Acting in a relatively private arena and in close contact with the bureaucracy, these groups can freely make deals without public justification. In their turn, the ministries for industry, commerce or labor are free to negotiate on behalf of their established clienteles without serious interference from marginal or new coalitions, including most environmental or consumer groups. . . . By limiting participation to "major" interests . . . European governments produce legislative accords that are not easily disturbed by the vagaries of parliamentary politics. Legislation is thus proof against much of the fragility and

incoherence that characterizes the policies emanating from America's more competitive and widely participatory legislative process.

The same study concludes that it "would be unthinkable in Europe" to enact regulatory legislation "with [the] disregard for problems of implementation" that so frequently characterizes American legislation.[91] In the American system, however, there is no reliable institutional mechanism to ensure that legislative deliberations pay heed to executive recommendations or administrative cautions—apart from the presidential veto, which is at best a very crude and blunt instrument of control. Particularly in recent decades, as party ties between the White House and Congress have weakened, Congress has often proceeded to enact major regulatory statutes on its own initiative and according to its own priorities—in an atmosphere in which larger political imperatives were bound to outweigh technical policy calculations.

But statutory standards are only the beginning. Every agency requires budgetary and staff resources to implement its statutory mission. In the parliamentary systems of Western Europe, executive budget requests are almost always ratified by legislatures without any attempt at revision. In the American system, congressional committees frequently revise executive budget requests, punishing disfavored agencies or programs with budget cuts, rewarding others with unrequested increases to please particular constituencies. At the same time, because the American executive cannot secure ready legislative support for statutory changes, budgets are sometimes manipulated as an indirect means of influencing agency operations, a tactic widely charged against the Reagan administration in its early dealings with controversial regulatory agencies.[92]

However they are determined, available agency resources must be meshed with assigned statutory duties in formulating ongoing administrative enforcement or implementation policies. Administrators inevitably face awkward policy tradeoffs in this area. When agencies issue general implementing regulations or interpretive guidelines, they must consider that more rigorous or demanding standards may encounter more resistance and so consume more agency resources in enforcement. But less demanding standards may be regarded as inadequate for achieving desired objectives; and more ambiguous standards, while preserving the agency's maneuvering room, may leave regulated entities in doubt about their actual obligations.

In determining priorities or selecting cases for individual enforcement actions, an agency must consider that going after the largest regulated entities, or the largest sanctions, or the most ambiguous offenses at the borderline of legality may consume a large share of its enforcement resources—and the resulting deterent effect on others may or may not be worth the "price."

Going after clear-cut violations by small, fly-by-night firms may be less of a drain on agency enforcement resources, and going after the clearest offenders first may even appear more equitable; but it risks sending a misleadingly reassuring message to more typical regulatory entities, which may come to regard their own conduct as, by contrast, altogether beyond reproach even if not really in strict compliance with official standards. Even if technical, cost-benefit calculations could determine the proper mix of standards and approaches—a claim much open to dispute on various grounds—agencies rarely have sufficient data or sufficient time and skill to perform such calculations in a very detailed or reliable way.

Faced with a long series of disputable policy choices, administrators must also take the political context or political repercussion of their actions into account. Here too the contrast between European and American patterns is telling. In general, European parliaments have neither the staff resources nor the political incentives to probe administrative implementation policies in any detail. The American Congress has both. In Western Europe, moreover, major affected interest groups, such as industry associations and labor unions, tend to be more fully and more centrally organized, partly because centralized political systems encourage this pattern by giving short shrift to dissident or more isolated groups. By consulting with a few major interests, European administrators can often secure rough political agreement on their implementation standards and policies in the same way that, at an earlier stage, they develop agreement for legislative proposals. In the United States, the rough and tumble of legislative politics carries over into implementation politics. Indeed, it often happens that groups that failed to mobilize early enough to affect the initial legislative battles can mount angry and effective counterattacks on implementation policies at a later stage; and congressmen who seemed to support a certain policy perspective in earlier legislative debate often feel no qualms at all about taking up a rather different view regarding operating programs at the behest of new constituencies.

The more centralized, orderly pattern of regulatory decision making in Western Europe may or may not achieve better overall policy results. Comparative accounts suggest that regulatory officials in the United States are more liable to charges of caving in to regulated interests, or of pursuing grandstanding confrontationalism to please the public, or of pursuing marginal mandates with excessive zeal to please particular constituencies. In many fields, such as health, safety, and environmental regulation, American programs have developed much more rigorous regulatory standards than their European counterparts, though the unevenness of regulatory coverage in the United States and the greater difficulties in securing compliance make many observers question whether American agencies are really achieving better results.[93] There is surely a great deal more wasted motion on all sides in the American system and a great deal more acrimony. But there is also much more political access for a much wider array of advocacy groups and minority interests.

If we wanted to secure more trust in government programs—or to quiet the clamor of dissatisfied interest group advocates—we would have to find some means of centralizing decision making power in the administration of these programs. This change would provide major interest groups with strong incentives to accept policy compromises at an early stage, because they could not thereafter expect to launch successful challenges to established policies. It would also encourage smaller interests to align themselves with those major interest groups with assured access to decision makers. The resulting policy might then be sanctified with the trappings of legality and expertise, and subsequent dissidents might be cowed by the authority of an expert, impartial, legally ordered system of state administration.

What makes this system work in Western Europe is that parliamentary systems force parliamentarians of the governing party to support "their" government and exclude parliamentarians of the opposing party from any significant influence in decisions. What makes such a system impossible in the United States is that Congress has no institutional obligation to support the executive or even to maintain party discipline within its own ranks.

Because they are reluctant to allow challenges to established policies, Western European systems also take the next logical step: they rarely allow courts to challenge administrative policies either, except to safeguard distinct and limited personal or property rights. In the Federal Republic of Germany, where the logic of the system has been applied most methodically, there is simply no standing for judicial challenges to administrative policies or practices, except for those asserting distinct personal or property rights. The system acknowledges that the individual person or the individual firm may require protection against the hasty application of general policies but refuses to allow interest group advocates to challenge general policies; so there are, for example, no special procedural requirements and no direct judicial review for administrative rule making.[94] In France, standing barriers are somewhat more relaxed and general rules are more readily challenged, but all appeals are channeled into the Conseil d'État, which combines judicial functions with a larger role in administrative oversight to ensure that judicial decisions are not overly disruptive to orderly administration.[95] In Britain, standing barriers are more relaxed than elsewhere in Europe, though not so much as in the United States. At the same time, the courts in Britain are also among the most deferential to administrative discretion.[96]

In the American scheme, open access to aggressive courts is the counterpart of ready access to a wide open system of aggressive congressional oversight.

Whatever else it is, this is not a system likely to build trust in administrative decisions. On the contrary, it is a means of encouraging challenge and dispute. In Western Europe, appeals to order and legality help to enhance the State's authority in dealing with dissident interest groups. In the American system, judicial appeals are simply one more way for interest groups to press their claims on government. The current American system thus turns the Weberian vision of rational-legal administration upside down, encouraging appeals to a version of legalism that effectively undermines governmental authority instead of enhancing governmental legitimacy.

Legalism may always be something of a pretense because it implies an indifference to consequences that no government can really indulge. In the end, no one—except Gauleiters and Commissars—wants to live in a Kantian world, where *Fiat justia, pereat mundus* (a favorite Kantian maxim) is an imperative to be taken literally. At the same time, there are certainly advantages to cultivating a vision of governmental administration as a dutiful, impartial instrument of the public will, rather than as a mere tool for the more efficient manipulation of some social interests by others. The more people share the former vision, the less they need to be compelled to comply with government directives by protracted and disruptive coercive proceedings. If associating government operations with legality and order helps to encourage this vision, there may be a good deal to be said for it. But if legalism works well in Western Europe, it is because it operates in a system in which order and legality are managed by powerful, responsible policy elites.

In the American system, where appeals to order and legality have not fared very well historically, they are most unlikely to secure any significant increase in public trust—let alone any significant improvement in results. Ad hoc interventions by well-meaning judges are more likely to provide a further platform for insistent interest groups. Certainly, extended judicial oversight in the 1970s did not generate any notable increase in public trust of government; in the 1980s it did not make public interest advocates and other regulatory constituencies more trusting in their attitudes toward the Reagan administration, but simply encouraged their suspicions. For the very existence of judicial review when no definite rights are at stake implies that executive officials cannot be trusted to pursue the public interest responsibly, or that particular groups ought to have a particular, protected claim on the public interest, which officials cannot be trusted to respect. And when the protests of litigating advocacy groups seem to be endorsed by activist courts, advocacy groups seem less often to be reassured than to feel that their suspicions now have official sanction.

A legalism that encourages the zeal or greed of particular interests in this way is likely to aggravate the policy distortions of interest group liberalism.

When it does not secure interest advocates what they seek and does not even assure them of a fair break—as it often cannot, in view of the limited, ad hoc nature of judicial interventions—it risks becoming legalism for its own sake. Why courts should indulge this risk may be hard to understand. But as we shall see in the next chapter, the faltering justifications for contemporary judicial activism have helped to generate new, reassuring ideological justifications to sustain the ongoing involvement of courts in contemporary public policy.

4

The Rule of Law
or the Mystique of Values?

C ONTEMPORARY administrative law makes little sense as a device for representing interests or for safeguarding regulatory entitlements. As chapter 2 argued, that is so because, even in a democracy, public policy cannot be conceived as a series of discrete obligations to particular constituencies. The fallback defense of contemporary administrative law—that it is merely enforcing the law, quite apart from the interests staking claims under the law—also makes little sense. For as chapter 3 argued, even in a liberal constitutional order, sensible public policy cannot simply be reduced to technical extrapolations from the law. Neither of these arguments is any great novelty. Versions of both arguments were indeed part of the conventional wisdom of the American legal system before the 1960s and still seem to be taken for granted in most other western countries, where judicial involvement in public policy disputes remains essentially limited to conventional legal actions involving traditional private rights.

Nonetheless, general arguments of this kind have plainly failed to persuade most American judges and legal commentators over the past two decades. This fact raises a perfectly fair question: if the theoretical arguments against the current arrangements are so strong, why have these arguments failed to prevail? The simplest answer may be that judges in the late 1960s and early 1970s were carried away with partisan sympathy for the new public interest groups (or with partisan suspicion of the Nixon administration), and the judicial system later sought to legitimize these early ventures, in characteristic judicial fashion, by generalizing the system, extending these new litigational privileges to a whole array of interests and advocates. Then, it might be argued, the system remained entrenched through the 1980s because judges, like politicians, find it difficult to revoke legal privileges previously bestowed.

The difficulty with this explanation, however, is that legal commentary does not generally present contemporary administrative law as an anomalous political concession to the special circumstances of a particular political era. On the contrary, the trends in administrative law have been mirrored by similar patterns in a whole range of other fields. The deeper answer to the question of why these theoretical arguments no longer persuade, then, is that arguments of the kind presented in the preceding chapters have come to seem overly abstract or formalistic in contemporary American legal culture. Thus many judges and commentators, if pressed to make candid responses, might well respond in more or less these terms: "Of course, the claims presented in regulatory litigation cannot really be conceived as 'rights' or as 'representation' in the literal or conventional senses, and of course 'the law' cannot be dispositive of such disputes by itself. But no one expects judges to take these formulas altogether seriously. All that these formulas really mean is that judges will serve as neutral umpires, checking extreme abuse on the part of administrators and assuring some modicum of fair play to concerned constituencies."

The problem with this kind of "realism"—putting faith in the prudence or the good sense of judges rather than in the logic of law—is that, if one thinks about it, it is not at all realistic. If the judge is not actually safeguarding the distinct rights of the litigants or the distinctive requirements of the law, what else could he be doing but managing public policy? And then why is it at all sensible or realistic to suppose that episodic interventions into public policy by unaccountable, amateur policy makers—for all that they wear black robes— will actually improve public policy? In fact, there is no reason to think that judges will improve public policy unless they are adding something distinctive to the policy concerns of the actual, responsible policy makers. For that reason, again, the traditional American scheme, like the legal system that endures in other western countries, refused to sanction judicial intervention when it did not recognize some distinct, legal right on the part of a would-be litigant. The realism of trusting to judges is only as realistic as the rationale for judicial involvement. And the notion that judges are wiser or more well-intentioned or more "neutral" (whatever that means when the public good is at stake) is hardly a realistic rationale.

Conceding the force of this logic, the most sophisticated legal commentators have tried to provide a new rationale for judicial intervention in disputes that do not seem to turn on the distinct rights of individuals. In such cases, it is now argued—at least in leading law reviews—that judges may be understood as safeguarding "public values." This is a sufficiently open and amorphous rationale to cover almost anything a judge may care or dare to attempt. It is also, however, an implicit acknowledgment that much of contemporary public law can hardly be defended as an improvement on public policy in the ordinary sense of assuring better policy outcomes for the public. To put the point bluntly, the most sophisticated commentators have recognized that if the conventional rationales for judicial intervention are discarded as overly formalistic, some other rationale is required; and they have sought to fill this void by the invocation of mystical formulas. In the meantime, judges in the real world continue to tinker with public policy in the name of law and continue to maintain a system that enhances the policy leverage of favored interest groups, depresses administrative initiative, and encourages policy incoherence from a general public perspective. And this system survives because, however tenuous its rationales, it is still eagerly embraced by organized interest groups or their advocates in the gritty world of interest group politics.

Some readers may doubt that these characterizations can be correct. They may remain highly skeptical that the only alternative to the constitutional arguments sketched in the preceding chapters is a flight into "mysticism," covering a series of ad hoc concessions to the clamor of favored interest groups. In the end, there is no easy way to prove that no worthy alternative to these arguments and characterizations can be found. But this chapter may provide, at least, some greater credibility for the characterizations advanced here by viewing the situation of contemporary federal judges in a broader perspective. The argument of this chapter is that contemporary judges have drifted so far from their traditional constitutional role, grounded in the logic of private rights, that they no longer have any clear sense of their role or their capacities in suits against government. In sketching how courts came to operate in the strange, disorienting ideological framework of the present era, this chapter may not finally explain why judges so often embark on strange or foolish enterprises. But it can help to substantiate the larger argument of this book that it is indeed the enterprise of the contemporary public law judiciary that is strange or foolish, when viewed as an ongoing system, and not the traditional constitutional logic that precluded courts from such ventures.

When Rights Did Not Seem Natural

The powers of the three branches of the federal government are set out in succession in the first three articles of the federal Constitution. Article III, which concerns the judicial power, is by far the shortest. It confines "the judicial power" to specified categories of "cases" and "controversies," and it employs these terms without elaboration, as if they already possessed a clearly confined meaning. The famous defense of judicial independence in *The Federalist*, insisting that "the judicial power" will be "the least dangerous," similarly takes for granted that the power to decide "cases" and "controversies" is quite distinct from "the power of the purse" or the power to wield "the sword" of the community.[1]

Although opponents of the federal Constitution did raise questions about the power of the federal judiciary in the course of the ratification debates, there was no great argument about the terms "cases" or "controversies."[2] And decades later, Joseph Story, the most learned and celebrated American legal commentator in the first decades after the founding, still found it unnecessary to devote more than a few lines to this interpretive problem in his multivolume *Commentaries on the Constitution of the United States*. "A case," he explained, "in the sense of this clause of the Constitution, arises when some subject . . . is submitted to the courts by a party who asserts his rights in the form prescribed by law."[3] Well into the twentieth century, the federal courts took it for granted that "the form prescribed by law" imposed limits on the sorts of claims that could be asserted as rights and accordingly on the sorts of claims that could be resolved by courts. The notion that the judicial power stands apart from the general powers of government corresponds to the notion that rights stand apart from the general pattern of political decisions.

But the first notion, regarding judicial independence or judicial limitation, is no more obvious than the second, regarding rights. Thus the Bible describes Moses as "judging the people"—that is, resolving individual complaints and disputes—but he is also described as a legislator (at least as the human vehicle for setting out the divine laws), and he leads the people in battle.[4] The Book of Judges describes subsequent leaders who lay down new rules, lead the people in war, and judge individual disputes, combining (as we would now say) legislative, executive, and judicial powers. So it was in the formative centuries of the legal system inherited by the American Founders. In medieval England, kings issued general edicts and led armies in war, but also judged legal disputes in person—which is why we continue to have the same term, "court," for the place where the king sits and the place where judges sit. In the medieval conception, the royal judges simply acted as agents for the king himself, whose responsibility to "do justice" was regarded as a necessary extension of his power to govern. It was only gradually that judges came to be recognized as a class of officers distinct from those other royal functionaries who acted for the king in nonjudicial or administrative capacities.[5]

Historians trace the origins of the English common law to the system of writs developed by royal judges in the twelfth century, which provided standardized responses—in the form of royal directives or writs—to appeals for royal assistance against certain stereotyped "wrongs." Although new writs were continually improvised, once a writ was well established, the system was supposed to leave "little or nothing . . . to the discretion of the justices" who would be "responsible for nothing beyond an application of iron rules." By the end of the thirteenth century it had thus begun to seem questionable for the king to interfere with the issuing of writs in particular cases by "his" judges.[6] In this sense, petitioners who met the proper conditions for obtaining a writ—because, for example, they had been unlawfully dispossessed of lands by a grasping neighbor—had a right (as we would now say) to receive the proper remedial writ.

But, in form and in theory, all judicial writs for the settlement of private disputes in medieval England were issued on the premise that private wrong-doing violated "the king's peace," so that the king was personally interested in every dispute decided by his judges. In theory, judges were acting for the king even in settling private disputes: the king's authority was thought to be affronted whenever one of his subjects wronged another in a way forbidden by law, so it was the king's responsibility to impose the remedy. "Private law" (as we now call it) was thus not at all clearly distinguished from "public law" or "criminal law" (as now conceived), for the king was always entangled—at least in theory—in every private dispute brought to his courts by contending subjects.[7] At the same time, the pursuit of felons—or "public offenders," as we now conceive them—was not simply the responsibility of the king but a responsibility of all subjects in the vicinity of the crime, and subjects would be punished for failing to pursue wrongdoers. The medieval counterpart of the grand jury was designed not to protect the accused but to compel local communities to identify and accuse wrongdoers before the royal judges. Severe punishment could be inflicted on witnesses or others who failed to come forward with information or accusations.[8]

In the formative centuries of the common law, the feudal land system, under which land holdings were conditioned on pledges of service to higher lords and in turn gave the holder personal authority over others tied to the same land, made it even harder to disentangle ownership from government or private from public. But quite apart from the complications of feudalism, medieval legal thought was disinclined to mark sharp distinctions between public and private because it conceived of law as emanating not from the will of public authority but rather from God or nature, established through cus-tom, which would be binding on all men in any case.[9] Medieval theorists indeed traced the ultimate binding authority of law to its claims on conscience, so they did not sharply distinguish the obligation to obey the law from wider obligations to behave justly or virtuously, whether in private life or in governing. For the same reason, new criminal prohibitions, whether issued by kings in formal edicts or improvised by judges in the context of particular cases, were regarded not as innovations but as elaborations or adaptations of enduring moral obligations. The medieval parliament was seen, in the same way, as a court, merely clarifying or elaborating traditional obligations even when it advised the king to promulgate general statutes in response to new circumstances.[10]

To put the point somewhat crudely, the authority of law was not at all clearly distinguished from the authority of morality or religion, and the king's obligation to "do justice," therefore—for all the formalism of the writ system—was not very clearly distinguished in theory from his wider responsibilities in governing. So, for example, it was taken as a matter of course in medieval times that the obligations of the judges administering the writ system did not extend to persons excommunicated from the Church.[11] Even at the end of the fifteenth century, therefore, when the feudal system of land tenure had almost entirely collapsed, a great English jurist of the era could still compare the common law system to the Law of Moses and affirm that "all laws that are promulgated by man are decreed by God" and that "legal justice is perfect because it eliminates all vice and teaches every virtue."[12]

The English common law, as it was described by Blackstone and practiced by American lawyers in the eighteenth century, was the product of an extensive modernization of the medieval writ system developed in the course of the seventeenth century. It was a system of law that emerged from a century marked by violent but ultimately successful struggles against royal absolutism in England, a century that witnessed the parallel development of modern liberal theories of constitutional government. It was the liberal theory of the seventeenth century that first established the modern conception of a right as a claim to control, seen from the perspective of the right holder. *Ius,* the Latin equivalent (root of *iustitia* or "justice"), was used in a more ambiguous sense in Roman and medieval legal writings to refer to the just disposition of the dispute, as much as to the prevailing party's claim to it—as we still say in English that someone is "in the right" or simply "*is* right" or "righteous," appealing to a conception of just conduct that may have no bearing on whether the person possesses a legal right to act in a certain way.[13] By the end of the seventeenth century, the language of common lawyers was the language of rights.

The shift may seem largely rhetorical, for it is easy enough to shift back and forth from "the rights" of the litigant to "what is right" that he should receive; and medieval litigants, no doubt, were quite as eager to claim what was right for them to receive as modern litigants are eager to claim their own rights. But the modern terminology emphasizes that the litigant's claim is somehow particularly his own, particularly private. And the complete privatization of rights and property implied by modern usage was plainly related to the liberal teaching regarding the private character of conscience: the law that upholds private rights has more modest pretensions than the law that "eliminates every vice and teaches every virtue."[14]

By the time the framers of the American Constitution drafted Article III, English-speaking lawyers had for centuries accepted the notion that judges had to be masters of a technical, routinized system of legal pleadings and should therefore be removed from the fields of government, where "discretion" and "policy" (to use the modern terms) hold sway. When the framers of the Constitution assigned the authority to decide legal "cases, in law and equity" to "the judicial power," however, they understood themselves to be entrusting a rather more modest power to courts because they already took for granted much more modest notions about the proper ends of law.

The Moral Modesty of Rights

In some ways, it is true, the moral perspective of traditional liberalism reduced the power or pretensions of government as a whole more than of judges in particular. Natural rights theories might show that government had no claim to concern itself with the religious salvation of the community or that the ultimate purpose of government was merely to assure the security of private rights. Blackstone's *Commentaries,* the authoritative exposition of the common law in the mid-eighteenth century, could insist that "the principal aim of society" and "the first and primary end of human laws is to maintain and regulate those absolute rights of individuals . . . the right of personal security, the right of personal liberty and the right of private property."[15] It could insist that "the public good" is "in nothing more essentially interested than in the protection of every individual's private rights."[16] But this might well seem to imply that judges, in determining disputes about "private rights," were, after all, performing the essential purpose of government.

And it is certainly true that legal and political thought in the first decades after the founding invested individual rights with a moral aura reserved for "justice" and "virtue" in earlier times. James Madison, for example, in approving Blackstone's definitions of property, could condemn as "immoral" those English statutes, approvingly cited in the *Commentaries,* which limited the freedom of cotton workers to make shrouds of cotton.[17] Early decisions of the Supreme Court could invoke the "first principles of justice" or "natural law" to condemn governmental interference with contractual rights of private persons. After all, the very claim of courts to "disregard" legislative enactments in conflict with the Constitution—a claim advanced by *The Federalist* even before ratification of the Constitution—implied that courts were somehow the guardians of a higher law, with moral claims beyond those of the legislative majority of the moment.[18]

But the moral authority of courts was still sharply limited by the modest pretensions of this "higher law." Judges did not claim responsibility for promoting virtue or for securing the common good. In form, the judicial obligation, even in cases invoking the higher law of the Constitution, was simply an obligation to determine whether individuals had been subject to unlawful coercion. Until well into the twentieth century, even constitutional cases arose from ordinary cases in which an individual asserted his rights against someone who (he claimed) had violated his rights: if the resolution of such cases required courts to apply a statute, and if the courts then judged the statute to be in conflict with the Constitution, the courts would disregard the statute, just as courts would refuse to enforce contract claims grounded on contracts they judged invalid. But no one claimed that courts had a general, ongoing responsibility to ensure that the Constitution was properly respected, any more than courts had a responsibility to roam through the country seeking out and repudiating invalid contracts.

Until recently, this limitation on the judicial role seemed obvious and inescapable. "Nor will a court listen to a constitutional claim by a party whose rights are unaffected" is how Thomas Cooley's late nineteenth century treatise, *Constitutional Limitations,* put it.[19] As late as the 1920s, the Supreme Court insisted that its constitutional rulings did not involve "the exercise of a substantive power to review or nullify acts of Congress for no such power exists. It is simply a necessary concomitant of the power to hear and dispose of a case or controversy properly before the court, to the determination of which must be brought the test and measure of the law."[20]

The notion that courts were simply upholding rights had obvious rhetorical advantages. It suggested that judicial action should be viewed not as an exercise of governmental power but as an external check on governmental power. It suggested that judges should not be held responsible for the consequences of their decisions because they were not making policy for the public: even in the most controversial constitutional cases, courts could insist that the public policy merits of statutes were not at all their concern, that they were simply determining the legal validity of statutes, with reference to the constitutional jurisdiction or power of the enacting legislature. "This court neither approves nor condemns any legislative policy," as the Court explained in a highly controversial decision invalidating a major New Deal measure. Instead, the Court's "office is to ascertain and declare whether the legislation is in accordance with, or in contravention of, the provisions of the Constitution; and, having done that, its duty ends. The question is not what power the federal government ought to have, but what powers in fact have been given by the people [in the Constitution]."[21]

Contemporary scholars may smile at such rhetoric, but the claim that judges were not responsible for making public policy was understood to have some clear limiting implications for judicial power before the 1930s. In private law disputes, federal and state courts were left to elaborate common law rights and remedies with little interference, for judicial action in this sphere—even if it involved a good deal of creativity, as it certainly did, even in the first decades of the nineteenth century—seemed a necessary extension of the judicial responsibility for upholding private rights. But the notion of a common law of crimes was firmly repudiated by federal courts at the outset and quickly abandoned in most of the states, because a power to elaborate new public offenses seemed to amount to a power to make direct judgments about the public good.[22]

So, too, the notion that courts had no responsibility for public policy made Americans reject the notion that the judges could appoint or direct prosecutors on their own authority, even though this traditional practice was accepted in England throughout the nineteenth century, along with a common law of crimes.[23] There were, of course, criminal laws in America, even some (like state laws against blasphemy or Sabbath desecration) that later generations would view as inconsistent with the liberal theory of rights. But while judicial trials might seek to ensure that no one was punished improperly for such offenses, judges disclaimed the authority to conjure the definitions of such offenses from "tradition" or "nature" or "higher law" and disclaimed the responsibility to ensure their effective enforcement.

Judges indeed disclaimed any authority to interfere with executive decisions, as much as with legislative enactments, if private rights were not involved. If executive officials were accused of invading the rights of private property (in the seizure of alleged contraband by customs officials, for example), the injured party could generally demand a full, independent trial of his claims in court. Judges in such cases generally felt entitled to make an entirely independent construction of any statutory authorizations to the executive when such questions entered into the dispute. When, instead, executive officials were acknowledged to have a broad sphere of discretion in interpreting evidence and statutory authorizations—as in issuing licenses or permits according to broad statutory criteria—the courts generally treated the recognition of executive discretion as excluding the recognition of any limiting or countervailing private right. So, for example, through much of the nineteenth century federal law prohibited trade with Indians on the frontier, except for specially licensed agents; and such trading licenses (issued under vague standards, first by the War Department, later by the Interior Department) were regarded as mere privileges, denial of which could not be challenged in court because no protected property right was at stake.[24]

As late as 1903, a Harvard law professor's treatise could summarize the existing law in these unqualified terms:

> The rule . . . is that in all matters that involve the exercise of discretion by a public officer no process of the court will go to control the exercise of that discretion. This must always be the case when the duty in question is one, in the performance of which, the officer must make an investigation and form a judgment. In such a case, the power is a power in the executive department; the judicial department will not therefore be competent to review the evidence before the officer and revise his judgment. That would involve the subordination of a coordinate department.[25]

Such reasoning may seem strained and artificial, but it reflected a determined effort to distinguish judicial decision making—or "law"—from executive decisions on behalf of the public—that is, "public policy." Nineteenth century jurisprudence was anxious to preserve this distinction in order to preserve the legitimacy of judicially enforced limits on public policy in cases concerning private rights. Judges were anxious to deny that in their legal decisions concerning private rights they were simply making public policy along with the rest of government. Here, for example, is the way the Supreme Court explained its refusal to allow judicial review of a mail fraud order (denying mailing privileges for "fraudulent" advertisements) at the turn of the century:

> It is true that the Postmaster General gave notice and a hearing to the persons specially affected by the order and that in making his ruling he may be said to have acted in a quasi-judicial capacity. But the statute was passed primarily for the benefit of the public at large and the order was for them and their protection. That fact gave an administrative quality to the hearing and to the order and was sufficient to prevent it from being subject to [judicial] review.[26]

Such formulas may seem not only stilted and contrived but faintly scandalous to contemporary sensibilities. For by identifying decisions of "an administrative quality" with "the benefit of the public at large," this reasoning seems to imply that ordinary judicial decisions are *not* for "the benefit of the public at large." But that is, in some sense, just what the Court did mean to say. And the sensibility behind such formulas remains rather powerful in the few areas, such as criminal law and criminal procedure, in which contemporary courts still do take private rights very seriously: even today, most lawyers would be shocked at the suggestion that a criminal court should primarily consider "the benefit of the public" and "their protection" in assessing the adequacy of evidence against the accused or the proper construction of the criminal law. Even today, where we still care strongly about rights, we are anxious to draw sharp lines between adjudication and administration.[27]

Cracks in the Edifice

There was always something a bit strained and artificial about the private rights perspective on the judicial role, however, and the most edifying appeals to natural rights or "the first principles of justice" could not entirely conceal the problem. Even Blackstone, in affirming that rights should be constrained "only when the public good requires," implied that those rights left unconstrained *were* compatible with "the public good." Blackstone himself logically maintained that Parliament, as the ultimate guardian of the public good, could not be constrained in its decisions by any prior law or by any subsequent judicial decision.[28]

In seeking to enforce constitutional constraints on legislative determinations of the public good, American courts might claim that they were not substituting their own notions of the public good but simply upholding the legal supremacy of constitutional provisions. But this assertion seemed less and less credible by the end of the nineteenth century as courts drew more and more expansive implications from brief and cryptic constitutional clauses—as when the Fourteenth Amendment guarantee against deprivation of "life, liberty or property without due process of law" was held to prohibit statutory restrictions on minimum wage or maximum hours laws. Indeed, it was scarcely credible that in elaborating common law rules in private litigation, courts expanded or contracted particular rights with no thought at all about the public good.

In truth, even the original seventeenth century theorists of liberalism, such as John Locke, had not based their arguments on disdain for the public good, but rather sought to show that the protection of individual rights would actually be conducive to the common good, by stimulating production, trade, and prosperity, by reducing religious conflict, perhaps even by encouraging more genuine (because more personal) piety. As courts became more active in elaborating new legal doctrines both in private law and in constitutional law during the decades after the Civil War, it was tempting for legal scholars (who first began to assume a professional, academic status in this era) to think about legal doctrines in more or less openly utilitarian terms. So, for example, in *The Common Law*, published in the 1880s, the young Oliver Wendell Holmes tried to show that neither the rules of civil liability nor the criminal law rested on moral notions of blameworthiness apart from what was judged to be of social advantage: "Public policy sacrifices the individual to the general good. . . . Considering this purely external purpose of the law (which is 'only to induce external conformity to rule') together with the fact that it is ready to sacrifice the individual so far as is necessary in order to accomplish that purpose . . . the actual degree of personal guilt involved in any particular transgression cannot be the only element, *if it is an element at all,* in the liability incurred" (emphasis added).[29]

The problem with reducing individual rights to social advantage was that it simultaneously seemed to reduce the public good to an aggregate of private preferences. This situation was comfortable enough for jurists who identified the public good with an untrammeled free market, for they were readily persuaded that the market would be the most efficient means of maximizing the satisfaction of private preferences.[30] But to the extent that economic specialists could show that free markets were not efficient, this same perspective implied that constraints on free exchange were more appropriate. More to the point, the utilitarian perspective suggested that if a majority of voters supported constraints on the market—because they harbored pleasing delusions about the consequences of government controls or because they derived more satisfaction from other concerns than from economic growth or economic efficiency—there was no good reason to deny the majority what it wished. And this was a conclusion with which Holmes, for one, was perfectly comfortable.[31]

It may be a moot point whether battles over the extension of government regulation in the early decades of this century (which displaced the traditional authority of common law courts in many fields) would be better characterized as battles over the utility of the market or as battles over the moral claims of individual rights versus the moral claims of the majority. Advocates of greater government regulation were certainly eager to claim both that administrative regulation could provide more economic benefit overall *and* that the majority was entitled to have its way, in any case; and the latter claim began to be pressed with increasing fervor after the turn of the century, as the distinctiveness of the "public" realm was obscured by claims for broader social controls.[32]

It is certainly true that judicial efforts to maintain common law notions of legal rights threw courts into repeated conflicts with new regulatory authorities. When the ICC was first established in 1887, for example, it was required

123

to go to court for an injunction to enforce each of its individual determinations on fair rail rates. Although the commission reached its determinations after elaborate administrative hearings, the Supreme Court insisted that judges could not issue binding injunctions on behalf of these determinations until they had held their own independent trial proceedings and had independently reconsidered all of the evidence. The Court assumed that only an independent judicial determination could really be a sufficiently fair and lawful determination to justify restrictions on commercial liberty or property rights.[33] Similarly, in a number of states courts struck down early workmen's compensation programs at the turn of the century, on the grounds that such programs allowed the liability of employers to be determined by administrative boards in accord with administrative standards instead of being determined by independent judges according to common law rules of tort liability.[34]

Such resistance did not last very long, however. States amended their constitutions to protect workmen's compensation programs from judicial scruples.[35] At the federal level, Congress amended the Interstate Commerce Act in 1906 to make courts confer at least a presumption of validity on the commission's rate determinations. And the continuing legislative resort to new administrative programs—a Bureau of Food and Drugs in 1906, a Federal Trade Commission in 1914, a Federal Shipping Board in 1916, to cite only a few of the landmarks at the federal level—forced more and more judicial accommodations in further new fields.

Advocates of administrative regulation frequently stressed the potential of administrative boards to provide speedier, cheaper, and more reliable determinations than the ordinary courts, as their professional specialization would allow them to dispense with irrelevant or outdated courtroom rituals and formulas. But there was more at stake than efficiency. Supporters of such regulation usually argued also that administrative agencies—often supplied with large staffs to detect and investigate social and economic problems on their own initiative—would provide a necessary corrective to the passive posture and legalistic detachment of common law courts.

The philosopher John Dewey, for example, urging a rethinking of traditional liberal doctrines, complained in 1906 of the "serious consequences" that had followed from the "fact that the procedures of justice originated as methods of supplying impartial umpires for conflicts waged between individuals": "It has had the undesirable result of limiting the function of the public interest to the somewhat negative one of securing fair play between contentious individuals . . . with the state acting the part of a benevolently neutral umpire."[36] Twenty years later John Dickinson, a young Harvard legal scholar, spelled out the implications of the new understanding of "procedures of justice" in his thoughtful study *Administrative Justice:*

The Rule of Law or the Mystique of Values?

To entrust an administrative agency with the determination of individual rights and interests . . . cannot but make those rights more flexible and more responsive to uncertain factors of discretion than when they are left to be defined by the more rigid processes of a court applying supposedly permanent rules of law. Under the old system of adjudication by courts of law alone, the process of adjudication went on within a separate cell or compartment, as it were, tightly closed off from the sphere of government action. There was thus made possible a single-minded attention to the individual rights of the parties immediately before the court, with only an accidental regard for the interests of the public at large and with a disregard for the exigencies of social policy. . . . The introduction of administrative justice, on the other hand, with the resulting opportunity for policy and discretion to affect the determination of individual rights, is one of the ways in which the newer philosophy of social solidarity has been making its influence felt. It marks the recognition of the fact that in the determination of the rights of individuals, as well as in the conduct of governmental enterprises, the interests of the community as a whole ought to be consulted.[37]

At the same time that apologetic arguments of this sort were mounted on behalf of administrative authority and administrative discretion, other scholars were launching fierce attacks on the ordinary courts. The "legal realism" movement, which first gathered momentum in a few elite law schools in the 1920s, sought to demonstrate that common law adjudication was never so impartial, so rulebound, or so determinate as it was portrayed in judicial opinions and traditional legal scholarship.[38] "Realist" scholars added a few elegant new flourishes in their arguments for such skepticism, but the essential point was hardly new. Oliver Wendell Holmes had said much the same almost half a century earlier in his accounts of the historical development of the common law,[39] and practicing lawyers had surely noticed on their own that judicial practice was not always in accord with judicial pretensions. What made legal realism controversial and inspiring in the 1920s and 1930s was the realist assumption that there were better alternatives to the old-fashioned and "formalistic"—a favorite realist epithet—methods of adjudication by courts. If court decisions were really determined by the judges' hidden prejudices or policy biases, as "realism" taught, why not make the policy implications explicit and ground the decisions in the conclusions of actual policy experts?[40] Legal realists were generally quite enthusiastic about the proliferation of new administrative programs during the 1930s, and a number of the most prominent realists rose to high positions in New Deal administrative service.

Legal realism undoubtedly reinforced the larger trend toward greater judicial deference to administrative rulings. But this was not its only significance. At the same time, "realism"—or, perhaps more accurately, the same intellectual and political atmosphere that nourished realist scholarship—also encouraged judges to show greater flexibility in their own decision making. Just as

John Dickinson could scoff at the "naive individualism of the common law" in defending the more "flexible" decision making of administrative agencies, judges and scholars urged a more realistic approach to judicial decision making in the remaining fields of common law adjudication. In the late 1920's, Judge Benjamin Cardozo, for example, endorsed a mild version of realism in his *The Judicial Process,* which focused attention on the inevitability of discretion in judicial decision making.[41] And as an influential appellate judge in New York State, Cardozo tried to counter the "naive individualism of the common law" by loosening traditional "privity" barriers in contract law (to allow contract beneficiaries to contest breaches of contracts to which they were not themselves parties) and in tort law (to allow consumers injured by defective products to sue the manufacturers, rather than the retailers with whom they had actually dealt). Explicitly utilitarian reasoning became increasingly more common in judicial decisions, and by the 1940s Judge Jerome Frank, a prominent "realist" scholar elevated to the federal bench by President Roosevelt, felt no compunction about soliciting informal advice on policy issues in pending cases from economists and technical experts of his own choosing. Traditional distinctions between adjudication and administration became increasingly blurred.[42]

Judicial Power in the Administrative State

The new perspective was evident in the tangled doctrines of standing that emerged in administrative law during the interwar decades. We have already encountered the most important of the early cases, the 1924 *Chicago Junction* case,[43] in which the Supreme Court ruled that competing railroads should have standing to challenge an ICC order authorizing advantageous new routing arrangements for the New York Central railroad. The Court's opinion by Justice Brandeis emphasized that the ICC had a statutory duty to approve such arrangements only when shown to be in the public interest and read the statute as recognizing a legal interest in competing railroads to be secured against competitive disadvantage from rival routes, except where this disadvantage could be justified by the public interest. Here it is worth noting that the shift in perspective implied by this decision was quite well recognized even at the time. Thus, to an old-fashioned jurist like Justice Sutherland, the Court's new approach made no sense; and he reaffirmed the traditional perspective in a strong dissent: "It is the public not the private interest which is to be considered [by the commission]. The complainants have no standing to vindicate the rights of the public but only to protect and enforce their own rights."[44]

But Justice Brandeis was certainly not hostile or suspicious toward administrative agencies. On the contrary, he was far more sympathetic to administrative authority than were old-fashioned jurists like Sutherland. But in part for this very reason Brandeis was anxious to dispel the notion that the characteristic flexibility of administrative decision making—its openness to a variety of competing interests and policy considerations—made it necessarily as free-wheeling and political as legislative bargaining or ordinary executive discretion. At the same time, Brandeis was open to more flexible or more "realistic" modes of judicial decision making: it was he, after all, who before his appointment to the Supreme Court had pioneered the inclusion of social science evidence in legal briefs—the so-called "Brandeis brief"—in order to encourage judges to look beyond legal formulas in cases with large policy implications. While still a private advocate, he had scored great success in invoking the supposed lessons of modern management "science" in pleading against rate increases before the ICC.[45]

By the early 1940s, Brandeis's disciple Felix Frankfurter, sometimes classified as a "realist" scholar at the Harvard Law School, could articulate the logic of expanded standing with remarkable candor. In a reprise of the *Chicago Junction* case, the Supreme Court divided in the early 1940s on the question of whether competing broadcasters should have standing to challenge the award of new licenses by the FCC. The majority ruled that the Federal Communications Act, in authorizing judicial review of FCC decisions by "any person aggrieved" by a commission decision, could be understood to allow such challenges by competing broadcasters if they could show that the disadvantageous effects of the new competition would not be in the public interest. A strong dissenting opinion, noting that the statute certainly conferred no right on broadcasters to remain free from competition, concluded that the challengers had "no cause of action on the merits" and proceeded to question "how an appeals statute constitutionally could authorize a person who shows no case or controversy to call on the courts to review an order of the commission. . . . The Commission, not the courts, is the ultimate guardian of the public interest under the Act."[46] But Justice Frankfurter's opinion for the majority in *FCC v. Scripps Howard Broadcasting* was quite unapologetic about the premise of expanded standing—that courts could indeed serve as "guardians of the public interest":

> That a court is called upon to enforce public rights does not diminish its power to protect such rights. . . . To do so would stultify the purpose of Congress to utilize the courts as a means for vindicating the public interest. Courts and

administrative agencies are not to be regarded as competitors in the task of safeguarding the public interest. . . . Courts no less than administrative bodies are agencies of government. Both are instruments for realizing public purposes.[47]

Justice Frankfurter was still too much of a realist to take his own rhetoric quite literally, however. He had specialized in administrative law as a professor at Harvard in the 1920s and 1930s, and much of his academic writing cautioned against the danger of imposing rigid judicial formulas on administrative decision making. In his career on the Supreme Court Justice Frankfurter was similarly critical of rigid constitutional formulas, urging his fellow justices instead to attempt a careful balancing of the complex and competing considerations in each case, even in cases involving free speech and other civil liberties. In most constitutional cases during the 1940s and 1950s, Frankfurter's "balancing" analyses concluded that the Court should defer to the balances struck by the legislature.[48] And in most administrative law cases, he was even more insistent on the need for deference to administrative judgment. But there was certainly an underlying theoretical consistency between this usually cautious approach and the unusually candid rationales he offered for expanded standing in administrative law cases: both were premised on the assumption that rights and law—and therefore, finally, courts—had no great distinctiveness in the great stream of public policy decision making. From this perspective, the question was simply who would normally be a better policy maker, and it was not inconsistent for Frankfurter to caution that courts had few comparative advantages as public policy makers.

The judicial activism of later generations began by holding to this premise and then forgetting the cautions tied to it in Frankfurter's day. In time, the rationales for the new judicial activism were driven to deny the premise, while still taking for granted that realist premises had destroyed the structure of the old jurisprudence.

The Jurisprudence of Judicial Activism

The main lines of constitutional doctrine were overthrown in the late 1930s, and this revolution certainly had less to do with changing theoretical perspectives than with brute political force. Traditional doctrines limiting the reach of government regulation in general and federal regulation in particular had presented a barrier to New Deal legislation. After several major programs were struck down by the Supreme Court, President Roosevelt launched a direct attack on the Court's authority and asked Congress to expand the size of the Court to secure a sympathetic majority for the New Deal. The Court avoided this humiliation by abandoning its anti–New Deal doctrines, and subsequent new appointees reinforced the new posture of extreme deference to legislative determinations of the public interest.

No doubt, some such accommodation to an enlarged governmental role was inevitable. No Western country has retained nineteenth century patterns of limited government, and unelected judges could not have been expected to stem the dominant political trends of the twentieth century. Still, it is striking how much the constitutional activism that reemerged in the 1960s reflected an essentially administrative perspective on government and law.

The pattern is clearest in some of the most celebrated constitutional initiatives of the Warren Court, starting with the historic decision against school segregation in *Brown v. Board of Education*. Even in the nineteenth century a few courageous judges, invoking classic private rights doctrines, had insisted that the Fourteenth Amendment should be read as prohibiting race-based restrictions on liberty or property as arbitrary government infringements of private rights.[49] With only a small bit of doctrinal adjustment, the Supreme Court might have used this argument to strike down school segregation laws in the 1950s. But in typical realist fashion, the Court's celebrated decision in *Brown* treated the actual parties to the case—the black schoolgirl arbitrarily excluded from the nearest public school and the school board enforcing this exclusion—as mere legal fictions. Focusing instead on the policy interests of black children as a group, the Court invoked social science evidence purporting to show that segregation had deleterious effects on the education of blacks.[50]

Then, the following year, it "balanced" this group interest against other social interests to conclude that, for all its evident injustice, segregation should not be dismantled at once but only gradually and cautiously, with "all deliberate speed."[51] The recent revelation that Justice Frankfurter secretly consulted with Justice Department attorneys about this formula—before the Court rendered its decision—should not have been surprising.[52] Fifteen years earlier, in one of his first administrative law decisions on the Supreme Court, Frankfurter himself had argued that administrative adjudications could not be treated like actual judicial decisions and could not be held to the same standards of personal detachment by the decision maker.[53] There was no more appropriate place to apply this realist perspective than the Court's barely disguised public policy deliberations in *Brown*.

In essence, the second *Brown* decision depicted desegregation as a long-term federal regulatory venture. As it turned out, the Supreme Court allowed this venture to languish for more than a decade, until Congress finally enacted its own civil rights legislation and established a full-scale regulatory bureaucracy to enforce it. Desegregation gained significant momentum only after 1965, when administrators in the Department of Health, Education, and Welfare began demanding detailed integration plans from all school districts in which segregation had once been the law. For some years thereafter, desegregation suits in the lower federal courts simply piggybacked on the standards and directives of this administrative regulatory program.[54] When Congress sought to restrain this administrative program, courts then imposed elaborate busing plans on their own authority—though often with the expert advice of the same bureaucrats. Whatever the merits of these busing plans as social policy, it certainly was not easy to articulate or to conceive such plans as corresponding to the right of any individual student, white or black, and the Fifth Circuit Court of Appeals was candid enough to acknowledge this point.[55] If there was any right at stake it was essentially a right to have judges rearrange school patterns to encourage improved race relations—a right so vague and open-ended that district judges were still issuing supplementary order upon supplementary order in busing cases into the 1980s, decades after the original victims of deliberate segregation had graduated from the public schools.[56]

A similar regulatory perspective was already apparent in many other fields of constitutional adjudication by the 1960s. Thus in *Baker v. Carr*, the 1962 case in which the Supreme Court first asserted its jurisdiction to review the malapportionment of state legislative districts, the Court dismissed traditional standing limitations with a quick realist shrug. It did not matter whether the challengers had been deprived of liberty or property or any other definite personal right by the population imbalances among legislative districts. It was sufficient, the Court explained, that a challenger had "alleged such a personal stake in the outcome of the controversy as to assure that concrete adverseness upon which the court so largely depends for the illumination of difficult constitutional questions."[57] Within a few years, federal district courts were appointing their own consultants and proceeding to redraw state electoral maps on their own authority, presumably after a nod of thanks to the original litigants for their "illumination" of the need for such administrative undertakings.

Once the plaintiff was understood to be in court simply to provide illumination for the judges, there was really not even much reason to demand a definite personal stake. The Warren Court thereafter found it easier and easier to dispense with such technicalities whenever it decided that it needed illumination on a new set of "difficult constitutional questions." In the field of free speech, for example, the Warren Court was so eager to enforce proper standards on recalcitrant legislatures that it invented the "overbreath doctrine" to bring more cases into the courts. This unique doctrine allowed individuals to protest constraints on free speech on the grounds that, even if their own speech or conduct was not protected by the First Amendment, the statutory language involved might be interpreted to restrict *others*—not before the court—to an improper extent. Communist party members, for example, were allowed to argue that the statute excluding them from work in defense plants would be an infringement of First Amendment rights *if* applied to Democrats or Republicans; and like a typical regulatory agency, seeking to forestall future harms, the Warren Court struck down the statute without waiting to see whether this hypothetical harm would ever actually materialize.[58] By the 1980s, the Supreme Court's eager pursuit of possible First Amendment difficulties had produced a maze of case law so technical and complex that a leading constitutional scholar aptly compared it to the Internal Revenue Code.[59]

In the same way, the Warren Court reached out for Church–State cases, holding in 1968 that taxpayers should have standing to challenge improper government aid to religion, even if the expenditures involved were so marginal that tax obligations would not be at all affected if the expenditures were prohibited by the courts.[60] In subsequent cases, the Court indeed repudiated the notion that mere taxpayers had any inherent right to invoke judicial scrutiny of arguably unconstitutional spending: thus the Court refused, for example, to allow a taxpayer suit arguing, with some plausibility, that the secrecy surrounding the budget of the Central Intelligence Agency violated the constitutional requirement that Congress make a "public statement and account" of all federal expenditures.[61] But Church–State cases were an area in which the Court was happy to have illumination for difficult constitutional questions.

These questions turned out to be exceedingly difficult. In the course of the 1970s, the Court allowed some kinds of government financial subsidy to religious institutions, disallowed others, and then reallowed still others with slight changes.[62] While earlier cases spoke of a "wall of separation between church and state," Chief Justice Burger eventually announced that the Constitution really mandated a "blurred, indistinct and variable barrier."[63] In sum, ideological opponents of government aid to religion do not exactly have a clear right under the First Amendment to prevent such aid. More accurately, they might be described as having a legally recognized interest in the separation of Church and State, an interest sufficient to bring their concerns before a court—rather like the flexible "legal interest" of broadcasters in restricting FCC license awards to their competitors when such awards might not be in the public interest.

With so many new fields of constitutional activism set in train, it was perhaps inevitable that the Supreme Court would begin to endorse similar activist ventures in administrative law. Only a lingering regard for administrative expertise stood between the competitor standing cases of the 1940s and a vast expansion of judicial oversight in administrative affairs. By the late 1960s, with courts already beginning to administer "preferred freedoms" and preferred spending restrictions, managing racial progress and many other special concerns, the judges and justices began to lose much of their earlier reverence for nonjudicial administrators. Thus the barriers to litigation that tumbled in constitutional cases also began to tumble in administrative cases. Like constitutional cases, administrative cases diluted the earlier requirement for a personal stake in the outcome to allow ideological advocacy groups to bring broad-ranging legal challenges to administrative policies. And while the Court had insisted in the 1930s and 1940s that new regulations could only be challenged as applied by administrators in particular cases, the Court sharply relaxed this requirement, too, in the late 1960s.[64] By the early 1970s, new regulations were frequently challenged in litigation on the very day (and sometimes in the very hour) they were promulgated.

Judicial power over administration was extended in other ways. The Administrative Procedure Act, enacted in 1946 as a codification of past judicial doctrine, expressly excludes judicial review of agency decisions when review is prohibited by particular agency statutes or when "agency action is committed to agency discretion by law."[65] The latter provision was an acknowledgment of past judicial decisions recognizing broad areas of administrative or executive discretion as not properly subject to reconsideration by courts.[66] By 1967, however, the Supreme Court could scarcely conceive of any independent reason for courts to restrain themselves and ruled that "only upon a showing of clear and convincing evidence of a contrary legislative intent [i.e., a specific congressional intent to exclude review] should courts restrict access to judicial review."[67] In ensuing years, this formula was quoted over and over by Court decisions reaffirming the "strong presumption of reviewability."[68] One of the principal casualties of this approach was the traditional doctrine that courts ought to refrain from reviewing agency inaction lest such reviews push courts into direct managerial authority over executive officials (as opposed to an external limiting authority over particular agency actions). By the early 1970s, federal courts were demanding that regulatory agencies explain and justify their failure to take action on a whole range of regulatory responsibilities and, in a few cases, were ordering timetables for action.

Inevitably, the standards of review also became far more intense, at least in some areas. Traditionally, when administrative agencies were granted authority to issue general rules by statute, the courts had only sought to verify (and then only when a suitable case arose) that a particular rule was rationally related to the agency's statutory mandate. In the early 1970s, judges on the D.C. Court of Appeals (where most administrative challenges were brought) began to insist that officials prove that they had taken a "hard look" at the evidence and the policy considerations supporting new regulations.[69]

Judges could not ensure a hard look, however, if agencies did not provide extensive records of the evidence and rationales they had actually considered. So the D.C. Circuit began to improvise new procedural requirements for agencies to collect their evidentiary materials in formal "rule making dockets" and then to explain their ultimate rationales for rules in formal opinions. The Supreme Court, after encouraging this trend at the outset, finally chided the D.C. Circuit, in a 1978 case, for imposing more elaborate procedural requirements than Congress had seen fit to require on its own.[70] But this warning was not much heeded, and the Supreme Court itself was not very consistent about enforcing it in subsequent cases.[71] By the early 1980s, then, public interest groups were bringing suits charging that administrative rule making would be "tainted" by informal agency consultations with the White House.[72] And while courts have thus far declined to impose close procedural controls on internal governmental deliberations, a number of court decisions have suggested that such restrictions may be imposed in the future.[73]

Activism Reconsidered

The Supreme Court's second thoughts about the new administrative law after the mid-1970s paralleled its second thoughts in many other fields. But as in other fields, the Burger Court found it very difficult to regain a stable footing. Doctrinal initiatives that had been pressed forward with reckless confidence in earlier years were limited and qualified, but rarely repudiated. This more cautious approach was often characterized by commentators as a tempering of the Warren Court's idealism.[74] In fact, it was often animated by anxiety over the ill-grounded "realism" of earlier decisions. In many areas, the consequence of this unease was not to make jurisprudence more realistic but more self-consciously committed to freestanding ideals.

Prewar legal realists had scoffed at legal forms and urged attention to the social consequences of judicial decisions. And the activist jurisprudence of the postwar decades has been aptly characterized as a jurisprudence of "pragmatic instrumentalism," eagerly manipulating doctrines and forms to achieve desired results.[75] But what were desirable results? Realists of the New Deal era were actually quite vague about this question, placing their confidence in the calculations of expert administrators. As Judith Shklar noted in the mid-1960s, realist polemics, while scorning the formalism of the law, often simply replaced it with formalistic or formulaic appeals to the public interest.[76] If this fact was little noticed before the 1960s, however, the reason was no doubt that New Deal enthusiasts took it for granted that big questions about the public interest were no longer much in doubt.

The Warren Court was buoyed by a similar uncritical enthusiasm, as confident as the New Dealers that it had found the path of progress. In fact, the Warren Court had too many easy cases to worry much about ultimate destinations. Outside the backwaters of the South, few people thought segregation could possibly be a defensible policy in the second half of the twentieth century, just as few people thought grossly malapportioned legislatures were really defensible. When the Court was leading backward states and localities along obvious paths of progress, the justices did not need to worry much about how far they should go.

By the mid-1970s, the Burger Court had to worry, because the paths of progress were no longer so obvious. Doctrinal commitments that had once seemed obviously good policy were seen to have troubling consequences. Such doubts made judges more cautious about their policy making capacity, but they also generated great pressure to defend existing policy ventures by recasting them as principles or ideals, not properly subject to policy evaluation at all. This rhetorical shift was more explicit in scholarly commentary than in judicial opinions. But it perfectly captured the judicial mood of an era in which courts had again become uneasy about activist ventures but remained unwilling to accept the constraints of traditional legal forms and decisional norms.

School busing cases again provide the most dramatic illustration of the new outlook. In the early 1970s, in a last flush of enthusiasm for the policy appeal of systematic integration, the Burger Court had endorsed constitutional demands for busing to correct de facto segregation in northern cities.[77] As political opposition to this policy grew increasingly bitter, however, and evidence for its policy benefits increasingly disputed in the mid-1970s, the Court drew the line against requiring busing into the suburbs.[78] This refusal left district judges to order the continual reshuffling of school assignments in order to achieve "integration" in inner city school districts with fewer and fewer white students. Unwilling to rescue the goal of integration by ordering interdistrict busing, the Supreme Court was equally unwilling to repudiate requirements for integration within the cities, however ritualistic and irrational they might seem in the circumstances. If busing in Boston achieved no discernible good results, its defenders argued, it at least honored a "constitutional principle"—and never mind why that principle had first been discerned in the Constitution, only a few years before.[79]

There was a similar shift from policy to ideals in many other disputed fields. In the early 1960s, for example, the Warren Court ruled that criminal prosecutors could not introduce evidence obtained by illegal searches, and it justified this exclusionary rule on the grounds that it was necessary to deter police misconduct. In the mid-1970s, when empirical studies cast much doubt on the claim that this rule actually did constrain the police, judicial defenders of the rule insisted that it was not after all a utilitarian policy measure, properly judged by its consequences, but an unshakable requirement of "principle."[80] Similar arguments were mounted in the 1970s to defend many other judicial policy innovations of the 1960s, including some with direct implications for administrative procedure.

At the end of the 1960s, for example, the Supreme Court initiated a "due process revolution" by applying the Fourteenth Amendment's due process guarantee to government benefits such as welfare payments. The original decision, in *Goldberg v. Kelly*,[81] stressed that recipients of welfare were so dependent on these payments that they were the functional equivalent of property; hence termination of payments without a full administrative hearing ought to be considered a deprivation of property without due process, in violation of the constitutional prohibition against such deprivations. In short order, the same reasoning was applied to a whole range of government benefits, like driver's licenses and school attendance.[82] But then the Burger Court began to have second thoughts, recognizing that such procedural requirements could often impose considerable cost, delay, and rigidity without much compensating increase in the accuracy of administrative determinations. The Court was unwilling to concede the logical implication of this view, however—that the appropriate level of due process protection for various public benefits is a political policy decision, best left to politically accountable policy makers. Instead, the Court promulgated an elaborate balancing formula, authorizing judges to weigh the likelihood of administrative error against the costs of error to the claimant and the government interest in efficient decision making.[83]

The new doctrine was much criticized by legal commentators, partly because its manipulable formulas did seem to invite lower courts to cut back on procedural protections for benefit claimants. But it was also vulnerable for suggesting that practical policy considerations were the principal determinants of due process protection, while continuing to insist that courts would be the best judges of these policy considerations. Commentators who wanted the Court to extend due process protections more broadly thus insisted that the Court had viewed the whole question too narrowly. Professor Laurence Tribe of the Harvard Law School argued, for example, that it was wrong to take a merely "instrumental approach" to due process, viewing it as a mere mechanical device for "assuring that . . . agreed upon rules of conduct and . . . rules for distributing various benefits are, in fact, accurately and consistently followed." He urged the courts to recognize the spiritual dimension to due process:

> There is intrinsic value in the due process right to be heard since it grants to the individuals or groups against whom government decisions operate the chance to participate in the processes by which those decisions are made, an opportunity to express their dignity as persons. . . . Whatever its outcome, such a hearing represents a valued human interaction in which the affected person experiences at least the satisfaction of participating in the decision that vitally concerns her [*sic*] and perhaps the separate satisfaction of receiving an explanation of why the decision is being made in a certain way. Both the right to be heard from and the right to be told why are analytically distinct from the right to secure a different outcome; these rights to interchange express the elementary idea that to be a *person* rather than a *thing* is at least to be *consulted* about what is done with one [original emphasis].[84]

Tribe did not conceal the implications of this alternative view. If formal interchange with government (through the mediating help of the legal profession) has "intrinsic value" and is altogether "distinct from the right to secure a different outcome," it would hardly matter whether the "right to secure a different outcome"—an "analytically distinct" right—were involved at all. Many public spirited citizens seem to feel that their dignity as persons is affronted when they are helpless to resist government policies or regulations of which they strongly disapprove—as, for example, the licensing of nuclear power plants or the deployment of new weapons systems. Tribe thus noted that groups along with individuals might properly claim the right to a hearing, and that "a hearing may be considered both as a 'mode of politics' and as an expression of the rule of law."[85]

Whether elaborate administrative procedures would actually contribute to more accurate or better results was no longer the only issue, then, even for broad policy or political decisions, like those at stake in the framing of new regulations or general enforcement policies. The lesson was not lost on judges in the D.C. Court of Appeals, who continued to improvise new procedural protections for the public in regulatory rule making, in disregard of the Supreme Court's 1978 counsel that levels of due process in this area really are best left to political judgments.[86]

The very popular and influential writings of legal theorist Ronald Dworkin illustrate a similar—and similarly revealing—trajectory in jurisprudence. In *Taking Rights Seriously,* the 1976 book that established Dworkin's reputation, he defended judicial activism against gathering policy critiques by insisting that rights must be grounded in "arguments of principle," which he sharply distinguished from "arguments of policy" dealing with "collective benefits."[87] The argument was presented as a critique of realist or instrumentalist jurisprudence and seemed to echo traditional notions about the special dignity of rights. But while Dworkin couched his argument in terms of the rights of individuals—above all, in the amorphous right to "equal concern and respect"—a number of acute critics noted from the outset that his account of "principled" judicial decision making had no necessary connection at all with rights or individuals, but was simply an argument for grounding decisions in imaginative reconstructions of precedents rather than calculating projections of possible consequences.[88]

Even in this first book, Dworkin blurred his own categories by insisting that his identification of principles with rights would "not prohibit courts from deciding . . . public law cases . . . on grounds that do not suppose that [any] individual has a right to the decision."[89] By the mid 1980s, Dworkin's reformulation of his position in *Law's Empire* continued to celebrate a vision of principled decision making and legal integrity, conceived entirely as an effort to harmonize past judicial decisions and statutory pronouncements with "the best theory of justice."[90] But his earlier emphatic distinction between "arguments of principle" about rights and "arguments of policy" about collective benefits was silently dropped from the exposition. The demands of integrity— an obligation for legislators and executive officials, as much as judges, in the new version—had swelled to the point that no room was left for mere policy.

Commentators in administrative law had already drawn the implications. Harvard law professor Richard Stewart, in an influential article in the late 1970s, praised activist court decisions for expanding the requirements of the Clean Air Act at the behest of environmentalist public interest groups. Stewart conceded that "conventional statutory analysis would not support the courts' result" in such cases and further that "a constitutional right to environmental quality . . . lacks any foundation in the constitutional text or in [constitutional] history."[91] Still, he defended "quasi-constitutional" judicial activism in this field as a means to "vindicate powerful interests in environmental diversity that can persuasively claim to transcend contingent judgments about economic efficiency or subjective value preferences and that can secure basic values which are implicit in the First Amendment."[92]

In later writings in the mid-1980s, Stewart took great pains to demonstrate that these basic values were altogether distinguishable from the personal policy preferences of affluent environmentalists, who might prefer less economic development and more environmental amenities. Personal preferences should normally be settled by political bargaining, Stewart conceded, citing Dworkin's demand for "equal concern and respect" for all "ways of life." But when courts extend regulatory requirements in ways that "conventional statutory analysis would not support," they should not, Stewart insisted, be seen as aiding the losers in political competition—not, at least, in the environmental field. The basic values in this field transcend mere personal preferences.[93] Stewart, a board member of the Environmental Defense Fund, may even have believed his argument: he certainly had few incentives to question so convenient a theory.

As Stewart saw transcendent values at stake in environmental regulation, Cass Sunstein discerned values in safety regulation, in nondiscrimination regulation, indeed potentially everywhere. Surveying judicial decisions in public interest suits in a wide range of policy fields in the early 1980s, Sunstein claimed to see a broader pattern: "The judicial effort is no longer primarily to protect private rights but instead to facilitate identification and implementation of the values at stake in regulation."[94] And Sunstein saw this pattern pointing toward a truly "independent public law" that would be concerned above all with public values and "would contain no presumption in favor of private ordering [i.e., private control of private property] and would not be primarily designed to protect private interests from government intrusion." Courts would thus devote their energies to ensuring that "the values at stake in regulation" were not distorted by " 'political' considerations that are sometimes illegitimate."[95]

"Political" considerations in this perspective are not opposed to legal considerations: like Stewart, Sunstein concedes that upholding public values often requires courts to reinterpret statutory standards in ways that "conventional statutory analysis would not support."[96] But these unconventional statutory reinterpretations are prompted by values rather than politics—by which Sunstein seems to mean grubby considerations of who gets what, where, and how. Public values seem to exist in a realm transcending all such petty distributional concerns. Indeed, the transcendent character of values seems to insulate them from grubby policy questions about what anyone is getting from them.

This reasoning—or rather the mental atmosphere behind such exhortations—was carried to its logical conclusion in Michael Perry's book *The Constitution, the Courts, and Human Rights,*[97] which was accorded quite respectful notices in law reviews in the mid-1980s. The book belabored the obvious point that almost none of the major, controversial constitutional decisions of the Supreme Court over the past two decades can be traced to "a value judgment . . . constitutionalized by the Framers." But the book then sought to defend this uninhibited constitutional policy making on grounds that Perry himself characterized as "religious": "Such judicial review represents the institutionalization of prophecy. . . . Such review is an enterprise to enable the American polity to live out its commitment to an ever deepening moral understanding and to political practices that harmonize with that understanding."[98]

Some defenders of judicial activism, it is true, were irked by Michael Perry's religion metaphor.[99] But it is, in its way, quite apt. The essence of the public law judiciary is the notion that courts should be free to act even when no claims about rights are involved. In other words, it celebrates a vision of courts free to enforce duties that do not correspond to the rights of anyone in particular. Perhaps the word we most often use to describe such duties—duties owed to no one in particular—is "morality." But the traditional account of moral duties is that they are the duties we owe to God.

The Mystique of Values and the Logic of Courts

At first glance, then, the rhetorical atmosphere of contemporary judicial activism seems to harbor a strange, half-conscious nostalgia for the righteous postures of medieval jurists. It seems to hearken back to a time in which law was inseparable from morals, and both were sanctified by religion. For all its incongruities, however, this posture has a certain logic in the broad context of contemporary legal thought. Contemporary legal culture retains the skepticism of the legal realists regarding "conventional" legal analysis because it retains their suspicions of the property rights that predictable or conventional modes of analysis were designed to protect. But it is no longer very comfortable with pragmatic instrumentalism, because it is no longer very confident that judges are well situated to make pragmatic adjustments in public policy. Accordingly, legal theorists now look to judges to uphold what they call "values" rather than mere policy.

Still this remains a strange way to run a country. It is even a strange way to think about how a country should be run. One can certainly make a serious argument that modern liberal societies suffer from the lack of authoritative moral standards. One can also make a serious argument that liberal individualism and liberal democracy will prove self-destructive without some authoritative check on personal willfulness. If one stands back from the rhetorical imperative of contemporary judicial apologists, however, it is hard to see how such a check can be provided by judicial enforcement of public values.

The strangeness of this approach begins with the very term "public values," a term that betrays a notable degree of squeamishness about authoritative moral judgments. Medieval writers spoke simply of natural law and divine law, of virtue and the common good. Even the drafters of the American Declaration of Independence had no compunction about asserting "self-evident *truths.*" It was not until recently that judges and commentators began to talk about "values." Values sound more substantial than preferences, but the term still conveys a relativistic flavor: our values may differ from their values; our values today may differ from our values in earlier times; but all alike may be values. Talk of public values suggests even more uneasiness about authoritative formulas: *public* values are values attributable to the public, which need not guide any particular citizen in his own private life.

Of course, this very feature may make talk of public values sound less threatening in a liberal democracy. It may seem reassuring to think that when judges find new values in the Constitution, they are simply reflecting changes in "our values"—the values of we the public. More importantly, a system of ever changing values might seem to harmonize rather well with a constitutional scheme in which elected legislators are free to change the laws at will. But if it is all just a matter of what the public wants, why not leave all policy decisions to officials who remain responsible to the public?

If there is any logic in entrusting the care of public values to the most unaccountable of all our officials, the logic must proceed from the premise that values, with all their variability, still remain quite distinguishable from mere choices. And that is indeed the way the term was employed by the writer who first popularized the use of "values" in its modern sense: the German sociologist Max Weber. Weber spoke of values as ultimate goods, as aims or concerns sought without reference to their costs or consequences in relation to other goods.

This is a useful conception for courts, just because courts are so generally ill-equipped to judge the costs or consequences of their policy choices. It remains, nonetheless, a very odd conception, for few people "value" anything in this world in such total isolation from context or consequence. A value in this sense is the mirror image of Weber's notion of a social scientific expertise that is altogether independent of the aims or perspective of the expert: values cut off from consequences are the perfect complement to facts ripped free from interpretive contexts. Weber himself did not hesitate to speak of the champion of "values" in this unworldly sense as the "prophet"—an archetype he carefully distinguished from that of the "statesman," who remains ever mindful of real world consequences.[100]

This separation from the real world is finally what is implied by judicial enforcement of public values. In this sense, public values function as a stand-in for private rights. Americans claiming their rights feel entitled to demand that they get their way, regardless of what others may wish: "It's *my* life, *my* choice, *my* property," says the claimant of rights, "so I *must* be allowed to have my way." Appeals to public values invite the same intransigence, perhaps even intensified because the motive is no longer merely self-interested: "*our* values require that this *must* be done," the advocate of public values insists.

Of course, judges may temporize with claims about public values even as they often temporize with claims about actual rights by disregarding "conventional legal analysis." But it remains the logic of rights that they can be— ought to be—private, in the sense that they can be treated as legally binding apart from broader imperatives of public policy. If courts do not revert to this notion in some form, they will seem to be mere amateurish meddlers in policy decisions about the allocation of public resources. So it is with appeals to values: there is no real logic to judicial intervention on behalf of values unless they can be isolated in some way from the broader complexities of public policy. Thus the logic of judicial enforcement of public values is for judges to reach into complex policy disputes, pluck out one or another policy consideration, and demand that it be fully honored, regardless of the larger consequences.

The problem is that public values still remain quite different from private rights. Private rights are meant to serve the private ends of their claimants. One of the principal reasons that moralism about rights remains powerful in contemporary America (at least in many contexts) is just that a system of legally protected rights often allows us to agree to disagree: within the protected sphere of his own rights, each individual is free to act on his own notions of what is right. Judicial enforcement of private rights might thus be described as safeguarding the "value" of individual freedom, but this remains a very widely shared value precisely because each person may apply it to very different ends in his own life.

When collective decisions must be made, liberal constitutionalism has sought to respect the inevitability of differing views by leaving collective policy decisions to officials who remain directly or indirectly accountable to the electorate, which encompasses a diverse and shifting range of interests and opinions and accordingly presses a diverse and shifting range of expectations on these politically accountable officials. This system may often make it more difficult to satisfy our communal concerns or to realize our various public values; but so does judicial protection for private rights. The logic of judicial enforcement of public values invites judges to leap over political disagreement and policy complexity to insist that public values be served, regardless. Judicially managed conflict thus comes to be afflicted with bouts of ritual extremism, of a sort quite unlikely to emerge from ordinary politics. For example, the Supreme Court insisted in a 1985 ruling that public school reading teachers cannot be allowed to enter parochial school buildings to assist students with special problems—though the same teachers may be allowed to serve the same students if they meet in trailer units supplied by public schools and parked across the street from the forbidden domain of "religion."[101] As rulings of this kind have no connection with the rights of any individual and certainly make no sense in public policy terms, they can only be understood as judicial tributes to public values. Some people no doubt like the results in such cases: after all, organized groups bring them to judicial notice; they do not drop out of the sky. But it is hard to understand why the values espoused by ideological advocacy groups should then be attributed to the public.

The problem is more severe in administrative law, just because the values at stake are not even attributed to the public through the mystical medium of a judicially crafted Constitution over which, for better or worse, the U.S. Supreme Court now exercises essentially exclusive responsibility. In administrative law, courts purport to be the mere instruments of policy choices made elsewhere. But approaching policy questions in terms of values is virtually to guarantee irresponsible policy making. As Martin Shapiro has put it, "the judge enters highly complex ongoing situations just far enough and just long enough to pull out a crucial brick and then scampers away, leaving it to the rest of the political system to somehow make sure that the wall does not fall down."[102] This is literally what is entailed by the enforcement of values.

In some instances, to be sure, we may care as much about the particular brick as about the steadiness of the larger policy structure. For example, we have traditionally been very concerned to ensure that government agencies do not spend money that has not been duly appropriated by Congress, even if particular unauthorized expenditures might be made with good intentions or for good purposes. In today's jargon, this constitutional principle might well be described as a public value. But just because it is a fundamental and strongly held public value, we have never relied on courts to enforce it at the behest of private litigants. Instead, we have always maintained a semiautonomous accounting system to ensure that this principle or value is systematically enforced. If a pattern of illegal expenditures is ever uncovered, we can blame the General Accounting Office for failing in its duty. If we have few officials as systematically insulated from political control as GAO fiscal auditors, that is surely because fiscal integrity is one of the few principles or values we want to insist upon in abstraction from other policy consequences. To put the point more directly, fiscal integrity is one of the few values we have entrusted to a set of officials who remain unaccountable for other, competing concerns—or the concerns of other, competing contituencies.

Allowing courts to enforce public values makes an open-ended range of program goals, operating principles, or administrative concerns into values that *must* be honored in abstraction from the rest of public policy. But, then, still more incongruously, this scheme leaves it to private litigants, in the first instance, to determine which goals, principles, or concerns do qualify for this treatment and to determine when and how they should be so treated. This is a very odd approach to safeguarding the moral integrity of government. But it is a natural consequence of confusing public values with personal rights.

The previous chapter noted that there is something to be said for a more politically insulated bureaucracy on the Western European model. At the same time, it argued that judicial management of the existing administrative scheme in this country is not an approximation of European patterns but rather a complete reversal of the logic in such patterns. If the justification for judicial supervision is not to ensure effective government but to require adherence to moral principle, a similar point still obtains. If a politically insulated bureaucracy is not sufficiently divorced from the exigencies of worldly policy, the logical recourse is not to safeguard public values by allowing courts to interfere with policy at the behest of private advocates. It would be much more plausible to erect an established church. We would face disagreements about which church to establish, but then, outside the law schools, political men have noticed that the country is divided over its public values. With all its faults, the established church of medieval Europe at least was not dependent on the promptings of private litigants.

PART III

DISTORTIONS OF PRACTICE

5

Capture by Court: Civil Rights Advocacy Groups and the Office for Civil Rights

A FTER the first round of the *Adams* litigation against the Office for Civil Rights, government lawyers protested that the suit "virtually places [OCR] in receivership."[1] This characterization proved remarkably apt. The initial decision in the case had effectively certified OCR as a bankrupt agency. Later decisions in the same case would allow one private advocacy group after another to lay privileged claims on the agency's enforcement assets, like so many grasping creditors descending on a failed business firm. And just like the reorganization of a bankrupt firm in judicial receivership, the *Adams* litigation dragged on interminably, continually seeking to appease certified creditors with I.O.U.s that later proved uncollectable and then had to be renegotiated. Launched in 1970, the case was still generating new briefs and new judicial orders at the end of the 1980s, having expanded by then to encompass every facet of the enforcement responsibilities of the defendant agency.

To commentators who noticed the case in its early years, however, *Adams* did not appear to be a legal monstrosity. Rather it was viewed as a striking illustration of the determination of courts, under the new administrative law, to bring agency enforcement operations under the rule of law.[2] And in many ways, *Adams* does indeed offer a striking illustration of what contemporary administrative law implies. Although its duration and scale do make *Adams* somewhat atypical, the same features make it a particularly revealing case.

When courts feel compelled to enter into the management of agency operations in such exceptional detail, on such an exceptional scale, and for such an exceptionally long period, it is natural to suppose that the agency involved must have been particularly delinquent or recalcitrant. Or rather, it is natural to suppose that the relevant statutes spell out the agency's duties in such clear and detailed terms that charges of delinquency (or perhaps we should say insolvency) can be regarded as indisputable.

The truth, however, is that the statutes enforced by the Office for Civil Rights are anything but clear. The agency could be judged delinquent not by the general language of the statutes, but only by the particular expectations of individual advocacy groups. Without any meaningful statutory standard of performance, the litigation proceeded as it had begun: holding the agency to the law meant holding it to standards of performance largely shaped by the advocacy groups (or by privileged bargaining between the advocacy groups and the agency).

The central irony of the litigation, however, is that, with all of the extra leverage it conferred on particular advocacy groups, it never came close to providing the policy results originally desired by these groups—for neither the agency nor the courts had sufficient power to secure these results. In practice, therefore, the *Adams* litigation degenerated into a system in which court sponsored advocacy groups were allowed to help manage a federal agency's response to their own disappointments. Only by the most idiosyncratic definition could this strange arrangement be described as a system for policy making in the public interest. The principal losers seem to have been the people the advocacy groups claimed to be representing, for their actual interests were forgotten rather quickly in the thick fog of legalisms generated by this remarkable litigation. The courts never seriously tried to reach beyond the limited perspective of the advocacy groups involved. And the principal effect of the litigation was to discourage the responsible federal agency itself from attempting to do so.

From Partisan Critique to Legal Maneuver

The Office for Civil Rights (OCR) was organized in the mid-1960s as a separate operating unit within the Department of Health, Education, and Welfare. At the time the *Adams* suit was first filed against OCR, the agency's only statutory responsibility was to enforce Title VI of the 1964 Civil Rights Act.[3] The substantive section of Title VI is a very brief, very general prohibition of racial discrimination in federally funded programs. This is the relevant provision in its entirety: "No person in the United States shall, on the basis of race, color or national origin, be excluded from participation in, be denied the benefits of, or be subjected to discrimination under, any program or activity receiving federal financial assistance."

By the time this measure was enacted, deliberate racial discrimination by governmental entities—such as public school systems—had long been pronounced unconstitutional by the Supreme Court.[4] The significance of Title VI was not that it added new prohibitions but that it authorized a new sanction to enforce them. The statute directs federal funding agencies to "effectuate" its general prohibition on the funding of discriminatory "programs and activities" by "issuing rules, regulations or orders of general applicability" and then authorizes funding agencies to enforce compliance with these regulations "by the termination of, or refusal to grant, or to continue financial assistance to discriminatory programs."

The *Adams* litigation began in the autumn of 1970, when the NAACP Legal Defense Fund (LDF) filed suit against the Secretary of HEW (at the time, Elliot Richardson), ostensibly on behalf of a black student in Mississippi named Kenneth Adams. The suit complained that the public school attended by Kenneth Adams was substantially segregated, yet still receiving federal funds, and insisted that Title VI required HEW to correct this situation immediately. If the suit had been limited to this one school district, however, it would have been much easier for the LDF to sue the local school authorities directly—as civil rights lawyers had indeed been doing throughout the 1960s. But the *Adams* suit, while not officially certified as a class action until 1983,[5] sought to protest and correct what it claimed was a pattern of HEW inaction throughout seventeen southern and border states. By the time the suit was filed, no school district in these states any longer maintained racial segregation as avowed, official policy. But the premise of the *Adams* suit was that previously segregated school districts had an affirmative obligation to assign students by race in order to ensure a relatively even racial balance within each school. And the further premise of the suit was that OCR was obliged by Title VI to terminate federal funding to any school district that did not satisfy this affirmative obligation.

These premises of the original 1970 suit did not, to say the least, rest on an inescapable reading of the actual language in Title VI. They were, moreover, almost directly contrary to the stated purposes of the Congress that enacted Title VI in 1964. In the course of the long and heated congressional debate in 1964, opponents of the measure complained that its key term—discrimination—was not adequately defined and that this ambiguity might be abused by "bigoted bureaucrats."[6] But at the time, the proponents of Title

VI had insisted that the meaning of "discrimination" was obvious and indisputable. So, for example, Senator Hubert Humphrey had assured his colleagues that Title VI would never require the assignment of students to different schools for the sake of "racial balance," because nondiscrimination "does not mean that there must be intermingling of the races in all school districts . . . [but] only that they may not be prevented from intermingling or going to [a neighborhood] school together because of race or color."[7]

Regarding the obligation to terminate federal funding to discriminatory institutions, the record is equally contrary to the assumptions of the *Adams* litigation. The record suggests that Congress did not expect the funding sanction to be at all frequently invoked. Language in Title VI expressly excludes its application to contract and benefit programs involving particular firms or individuals.[8] State and local institutions—the most common remaining category of recipients of federal financial assistance—were already subject to constitutional prohibitions against racial discrimination. Another section of the 1964 Civil Rights Act authorized the Justice Department to bring civil actions to enforce these constitutional limitations, and Title VI itself provides that its substantive prohibition may be enforced either by funding terminations or "by any other means authorized by law." Advocates of Title VI seem to have assumed throughout the debate that federal efforts to reach discrimination would normally be pursued by the Justice Department in civil litigation, so that funding agencies would have little additional obligation.[9]

The implementing provisions in Title VI are plainly designed to discourage resort to funding terminations. Funding agencies are expressly prohibited from resorting to sanctions of any kind until they have "determined that compliance [with nondiscrimination requirements] cannot be secured by voluntary means." Even then, termination of funding is prohibited until the allegedly noncompliant institution is given an opportunity to defend itself in a formal administrative hearing, and until the funding agency has given a full thirty days' notice to "the committees of the House and Senate having legislative jurisdiction over the program or activity involved" with "a full report of the circumstances and the grounds for such action." When funds are finally terminated, recipients are then authorized to seek judicial review of the agency's action. Another provision specifies that any funding termination "shall be limited . . . in its effect to the particular program or part thereof in which such noncompliance has been found."

The point of all these safeguards is obvious. When Congress appropriates funds for subsidy programs, it wants to see the money distributed. Individual congressmen and senators are particularly anxious to ensure unimpeded funding to institutions in their own districts. During the debates in 1964, moreover, the point was often made that cutting off funds to segregated institutions would punish blacks at those institutions as much as whites, without necessarily ending discrimination. Thus the sponsors of the measure took pains to assure their congressional colleagues that "it would be a rare case when funds would actually be cut off."[10] The main reason for including a funding sanction at all seems to have been that such an approach had been urged upon President Kennedy by the U.S. Commission on Civil Rights a few years before and by 1963–64, proponents of a strong civil rights package, both at the White House and in Congress, were anxious to show that no possible approach to desegregation was being overlooked.[11]

The real force of the 1970 *Adams* suit, then, did not derive from any clear implication in the language or legislative history of Title VI. Rather, it derived from the frustration of civil rights advocacy groups with OCR's failure to sustain the expectations generated by an extremely activist administrative policy in the years *following* enactment of the statute. In fact, HEW had given great force to Title VI during the mid-1960s by disregarding or circumventing most of the legal restrictions explicitly written into the statute. The *Adams* suit essentially sought to enshrine this earlier activist phase of implementation as law, while branding the pattern of later years as improper political manipulation. In effect, the suit tried to prevent the Nixon administration from changing earlier policy, on the apparent assumption that changes in policy were principally due to the malevolent influence of a new administration. Subsequent events, however, suggest that this assumption was essentially untrue. The peculiar circumstances of OCR's early years would never return.

The funding sanction in Title VI had proved to be an extremely powerful tool for federal officials in the first years after its enactment for two reasons. The first reason was that enactment of the Civil Rights Act in 1964 opened the way for passage in 1965 of the first large-scale federal subsidy program for elementary and secondary schools. Programs of this kind had previously been resisted by southerners precisely because they feared that large-scale federal funding would undermine local control of public schools. And HEW, the funding agency for these new programs, did in fact move aggressively to exploit this new source of leverage at the outset. In 1965 it simply refused to approve grants to any school district that had not committed itself to ending segregation—even though this action bypassed all of the elaborate safeguards written into the body of Title VI.[12]

The second reason for the early potency of Title VI was that, for a time, the enactment of the 1964 civil rights legislation seemed to ratify a broad national consensus identifying discrimination with southern brutality, and leaving southern representatives in Congress quite isolated politically. This atmosphere could not protect the agency indefinitely, however. Indeed, when HEW made the mistake of using the same tactic of funding deferrals against

the Chicago school system somewhat later, the Illinois congressional delegation quickly secured an amendment to Title VI that specifically prohibited
such funding "deferrals" for more than thirty days.[13] But for a time, OCR
had the political strength to exercise very powerful leverage in the South.

In 1964, a full decade after the Supreme Court's initial ruling against school
segregation, 98 percent of black students in the South were still attending
segregated schools.[14] By the end of 1965, HEW had secured commitments
from almost all school districts in the South to move quickly toward desegregation. Beginning in the summer of 1966, HEW began to apply powerful
pressure against backsliding on these commitments, proceeding to terminate
funding for more than four hundred school districts over the next two years.
It converted funding termination into a particularly powerful sanction, moreover, by interpreting the "pinpoint provision" in the statute in the broadest
possible terms, usually treating the entire school district as "the program
. . . in which . . . noncompliance has been found" in order to cut off the
maximum amount of funding.[15] Many years later, the Supreme Court was to
rule that this approach contravened the statutory language of Title VI.[16] But
in the political climate of the mid-1960s—when defiant segregationists were
still bellowing resistance to all change, and the need for strong federal pressure
seemed very clear—southern school districts met with little success in pressing
such legal claims.

Initial successes quickly encouraged higher ambitions for HEW, which
were pursued by circumventing yet another safeguard in the original statute.
Title VI required that the implementing regulations adopted by federal funding agencies be personally approved and signed by the president, an unusual
requirement that again reflected the high degree of congressional concern
about interference with federal funding. The initial HEW regulations for
Title VI, signed by President Johnson a few months after the measure's
enactment, did not actually define discrimination in much more detail than
the statute, however. When HEW officials refused to release new grants to
segregated school districts in 1965, they assured local school officials that
compliance with the regulations would be satisfied by allowing black students
to attend the nearest public school or any other school of their choice. Without revising the official regulations or returning to the president for a new
signature, HEW officials issued new compliance guidelines in 1966, requiring
that school districts show that at least 20 percent of black students had been
enrolled in previously all-white schools. School officials who thought they had
agreed to comply with one standard raised a storm of protest when the
standard was changed. For a time HEW officials insisted that the 20 percent
requirement was not a fixed quota but a mere "administrative indicator" to
trigger further investigation, lest "freedom of choice" plans be subverted by

hidden pressures. But as the initial controversy subsided, new guidelines were issued in 1967 and again in 1968—again without recourse to the president or to formal rule making procedures—and these guidelines imposed more demanding standards of statistical integration with much less qualification.[17]

HEW's increasingly ambitious approach to school desegregation in the South was endorsed by federal courts in the Fifth Circuit (covering the deep South) in 1967, where judges explicitly invoked HEW's "administrative expertise" in this area as authority for their decisions, even in cases not brought under Title VI.[18] But the policy of assigning students by race to ensure desired racial balances was actually rejected in other circuits, and it was not finally endorsed by the Supreme Court until 1968.[19]

By then, however, the continuing escalation of school intregration requirements had begun to stir misgivings in Congress and greater sympathy for southern protests. Thus, over the sharp objections of top HEW officials, Congress voted a rider to the department's appropriations bill in 1968, requiring that HEW's newly organized Office for Civil Rights apply uniform policies and standards for Title VI throughout the country. Later in that year, Congress voted a rider on a supplemental appropriations bill, requiring that OCR maintain at least as many investigators in northern and western states as in the South. Both measures were implicit endorsements of southern complaints that ambitious desegregation requirements were "picking on the South."[20]

In the presidential campaign of 1968, Republican candidate Nixon sought to appeal to this new mood—and pick up electoral votes in the South—by urging a more "moderate" approach to desegregation. In the first months of the new administration, high officials announced that enforcement of desegregation would no longer rely on funding terminations but instead place more emphasis on civil litigation by the Justice Department. Like much Nixon administration rhetoric seeking to placate southern resentments, this announcement proved somewhat misleading: some one hundred school districts actually had their funding terminated in the course of 1969, no fewer than in 1968, under the last year of the lame-duck Johnson administration.[21] In ill-concealed defiance of the congressional staffing requirements, moreover, OCR "loaned" large numbers of officials assigned to its northern and western regional offices to pursue desegregation efforts in the South. But civil rights advocacy organizations, already alarmed by candidate Nixon's waffling stands in the 1968 elections, remained extremely distrustful.

This distrust was exacerbated in the late spring of 1970 when several hundred school districts, judged to be inadequately desegregated by OCR, were assigned to the Justice Department for legal action, instead of being threatened with funding terminations. Suspicions were further inflamed that summer when Leon Panetta, the Nixon administration's initial appointee to the post of OCR director, was removed from office amid rumors that the White House regarded him as overzealous. A different administration might well have maintained a somewhat more aggressive policy; and Panetta (who was subsequently elected to Congress as a liberal Democrat) insisted that a more aggressive policy should have been maintained.[22] But whatever the intentions of the Nixon administration, it seems unlikely that Congress would have tolerated the continuation of large-scale funding terminations by the 1970s, when the struggle for desegregation no longer involved diehard segregationists but simply disputes over the necessary degree of busing or other remedies to compensate for statistical imbalances in the schools. Resort to large-scale funding terminations seemed all the more unsustainable as the new emphasis on statistical integration threatened school districts outside the South—as it was already beginning to do by 1970.

Still, integration advocates were anxious to believe that the Nixon administration could do more if it really wanted to. And occasional divergences between Justice Department filings and the positions taken by private civil rights groups in individual desegregation suits reinforced suspicions that the new administration was constraining civil rights enforcement simply to please southern voters.[23] In the autumn of 1970, the NAACP Legal Defense Fund wrapped these accumulated suspicions and disappointments into a single, broad-ranging suit against the Nixon administration: *Adams v. Richardson*.

A Policy Judgment in Search of a Policy

Stripped to its essentials, the *Adams* case might have seemed to be little more than a partisan policy dispute dressed up in legal garb. The LDF made little effort to counter or disguise this appearance. Along with Kenneth Adams, the organization recruited a number of other people—described as "black students, citizens, and taxpayers"—to lend their names to a suit demanding judicial intervention to correct OCR's enforcement policies in seventeen southern and border states.[24] Then the LDF secured a prominent Washington lawyer, Joseph Rauh (a past president of the liberal Democratic advocacy organization Americans for Democratic Action), to argue its case. Rauh's initial filings in the U.S. District Court in Washington concentrated on showing that OCR had "defaulted" on its enforcement obligations. The briefs made no serious effort to explain how the handful of citizens and taxpayers named in the suit had been personally injured by this pattern of OCR activity through one-third of the United States. Neither was there any effort in the brief to explain why, if Kenneth Adams had been deprived of some guaranteed right by his local school district in Mississippi, he did not simply sue his own school district to obtain whatever relief he might be entitled to receive.

As it turned out, the judges who heard the case were equally disdainful of these formalities. The initial decision handed down by District Judge John Pratt made no mention of standing; it did not even bother to explain who the ostensible plaintiffs in the case actually were. When the government appealed, the D.C. Court of Appeals also saw no reason to say anything about the standing of the ostensible plaintiffs.[25] Both courts also failed to notice that the case had never been certified as a class action. They treated it as altogether unexceptional that a handful of black "students, citizens, and taxpayers" should be accepted as representing, throughout seventeen states, all other "students, citizens, and taxpayers." Or was it only all other blacks of this description, or only others of this description who disapproved of Nixon administration policies? The courts did not find it necessary to consider *who* was actually being represented in the case, or on *whose behalf*, precisely, the courts were being asked to intervene.

Yet these were not mere pedantic quibbles. In essence, the *Adams* suit demanded that OCR try to force higher levels of statistical integration in southern schools by cutting off more federal subsidies to these schools. Needless to say, not everyone in the South favored this policy and—to say the least—this was not a policy that was ineluctably *required* by the relevant statute. It was not even certain that the majority of black students or parents favored such an emphasis on statistical integration. And it was indeed highly questionable that most blacks would have favored more vigorous enforcement at the cost of reduced federal subsidies for their local schools or reduced support in Congress for other civil rights measures.

As the initial court proceedings were indifferent to the "who" of the case, they were almost as casual about the "what." The original filing submitted by the plaintiffs listed six "causes of action," candidly described as being, "apart from their merits . . . symptoms of a general and calculated default by HEW in enforcement of Title VI."[26] The filing complained that OCR had failed to investigate the adequacy of integration in school districts already covered by separate court orders (following local suits by the Justice Department or civil rights groups) and that it had failed to investigate whether state education departments were channeling federal funds to inadequately integrated school districts. Judge Pratt's 1972 decision acknowledged, however, that OCR was not clearly required to do either of these things under Title VI, and the subsequent decision of the court of appeals endorsed these conclusions.[27] The plaintiffs also complained that OCR was allowing school districts *accused* of discrimination (by the agency itself) to continue to receive federal funds. But on this charge, too, both the district court and the court of appeals demurred, noting that Title VI did not permit OCR to terminate funding before allowing school districts an opportunity to rebut charges in formal hearings. The district court did find merit in the charge that OCR was not taking adequate action against "segregated" systems of higher education, but the court of appeals acknowledged that there were special problems in this area that justified further delays in action by OCR.

Only two charges in the original *Adams* filings, then, met with complete agreement from the courts: a charge that OCR was not taking adequate action against school districts that had defaulted on prior integration plans, and a charge that OCR was not taking adequate action on school districts that remained out of compliance with the latest Supreme Court standards for remedial integration. To remedy these failings, Judge Pratt issued orders—or rather, he ratified orders proposed by LDF lawyers—that set strict deadlines within which OCR must take action against several hundred specified school districts in these two categories: at the end of six months, he directed, the agency must either certify that each of these school districts was in compliance with integration requirements or initiate formal proceedings to terminate their federal funding. The Court of Appeals, in endorsing these orders, affirmed that they were essential to ensure that OCR did not default on its obligations through "interminable delay."[28]

Even here, however, the "default" charge was somewhat misleading. The plaintiffs and the courts were able to identify the noncompliant school districts cited in the court order only because OCR itself had singled them out for attention and had already been seeking to negotiate new integration plans with officials in these districts.[29] The court decisions spoke of bringing school districts into "compliance with Title VI" as if there were some clearly defined standard involved. In fact, there was no clear standard for compliance, because OCR had increased its demands for integration from year to year without ever promulgating definitive standards. Neither of the initial court decisions in *Adams* made any attempt to clarify the precise standards for OCR to apply. Essentially, then, the agency was told that when it did identify a school district as noncompliant with desegregation requirements, the agency could not prolong negotiations with that district for more than a few months before invoking formal sanctions—but the determinations of compliance or noncompliance remained with the agency.

What did the courts expect to achieve by imposing fixed deadlines on OCR's negotiations with noncompliant school districts? Would the court orders result in vast numbers of funding cutoffs; and, if so, how would Congress respond? Or would most school districts agree to ambitious new integration plans rather than lose their funding? How would Congress react in that event, considering the increasing level of public protest against forced busing? Or would OCR simply respond to the deadlines by reducing its demands and diluting its standards in order to make rapid agreements feasible? If so, what would have been achieved by imposing the deadlines?

The Court of Appeals attempted to evade all of the policy dilemmas in the case by falling back on the rhetoric of legalism. Its job, it insisted, was "simply to interpret the statute and see that it is observed."[30] But this claim was, of course, mere rhetoric. The statute did not impose any particular time limit on OCR's authority to "seek compliance by voluntary means"; the courts simply invented this limit and attributed it to the statute. In the abstract, months of bargaining might seem excessive, and the court-ordered deadline of sixty days might seem more reasonable. But why consider the question in the abstract, without any regard to the actual consequences?

The initial court decisions in *Adams* only make sense as a calculated judicial response to a particular set of practical assumptions about OCR's operating conditions. The judges seem to have assumed that OCR officials were capable of devising improved integration plans for the school districts involved; furthermore, the judges seem to have assumed that career officials at the agency were quite eager and ready to impose these plans (or to punish school officials for failing to accept them); finally, the judges seem to have assumed that only the interference of Nixon appointees had prevented the agency from taking decisive action against these districts.[31] All of these assumptions were certainly plausible, and there is no doubt that negotiations between school districts and OCR were complicated by the restraining efforts of the top political appointees at OCR, who were responding in turn to pressure from the White House. A great many of the affected school districts could not have secured further integration without busing programs, and the Nixon White House had expressed open and firm opposition to forced busing.[32]

Even so, it was undeniable that OCR had made much progress in fostering higher levels of integration since the advent of the Nixon administration. In statistical terms the Nixon administration had, in fact, made more progress than its predecessors: in 1968, the proportion of black students in substantially all-black schools in the South was still 68 percent (down from 98 percent three years earlier), but by 1971 the figure had dropped to 9.2 percent. By the time the initial court decisions in *Adams* were handed down, public schools in the affected states were more thoroughly integrated than in any other region of the country.[33] Evidently convinced, however, that OCR could do still more in the South—if only the Nixon administration would cease interfering with the agency—both courts skated over the evidence of past progress and focused on the dramatic falloff in funding terminations after 1970.[34] Along with the LDF lawyers, the judges seem to have assumed that judicial pressure on OCR would encourage the agency to revive its funding sanction and take a more aggressive approach to integration.

The actual results were quite different. In most cases, the pressure of the court-imposed deadlines simply led OCR to reduce its demands on recalcitrant school districts to achieve quick voluntary settlements. The level of statistical integration achieved in the South by 1973—when the Court of Appeals affirmed the initial *Adams* decision—was never significantly improved upon. And there was never any significant return to the sanction of funding terminations by OCR. The forced resignation of President Nixon in the summer of 1974 made no difference. The return of executive authority to a liberal Democratic administration in 1977 made no difference. With respect to the central aims of the original *Adams* litigation, OCR was no more daring or effective at the end of 1970s than it had been at the outset. Neither was there any significant change under the Reagan administration in the 1980s: there was no significant further progress toward integration and no significant increase in the number of funding terminations.[35]

The principal reason was that Congress proved unwilling to maintain an Olympian detachment while the *Adams* litigation wrangled over congressional intentions as expressed in the 1964 Civil Rights Act. Through successive administrations of varying partisan and policy leanings, the responsible executive officials in this area always remained highly sensitive to congressional concerns about the disruption of funding to institutions in their home districts. OCR frequently invoked the *possibility* of funding terminations in bargaining with the institutions it regulated, but after 1970 it rarely went as far as to commence formal administrative proceedings, the necessary prelude to an actual termination of funds. Notwithstanding the pressure of the *Adams* litigation, OCR officials, and their departmental superiors, never lost their fear of what might happen to the agency and its statutory authority if Congress were provoked with massive funding terminations.[36]

With regard to busing for integration, OCR did not have to wait long to find out what would happen if Congress were sufficiently provoked by its actions. Congress was already under tremendous pressure to respond to the widespread bitterness over forced busing when the D.C. Court of Appeals handed down its initial ruling in *Adams*. The pressure on Congress mounted all the higher as lower courts, sometimes with encouragement from OCR experts, began to demand busing to achieve statistical integration in northern cities. In 1974, amid bitter denunciations against federal meddling in local problems, Congress enacted the first of several specific restrictions on OCR's authority to impose busing for racial balance.

Congress intervened in the area in which its own power was most removed from administrative or judicial control—the budget—by specifying that no funds could be expended by HEW to require the busing of public school children to any but the nearest or next-to-nearest public school. Some busing advocates claimed that this ruling still left OCR with maneuvering room to require busing, but Congress enacted a still more emphatic restriction to plug these perceived loopholes in 1976. In 1977, when Carter administration officials claimed to have discovered yet another loophole, allowing OCR to impose some busing requirements, Congress responded with a further restriction.[37]

Through this whole period, however, the Legal Defense Fund persisted in its litigational efforts to force OCR into imposing further integration. A year after their initial victory, the *Adams* lawyers returned to Judge Pratt with evidence that OCR had delayed taking action against several hundred additional school districts, ones that OCR itself had identified as "presumptively out of compliance" with desegregation requirements. Although the named plaintiffs in *Adams* had no greater connection with these districts than with those in the initial suit, the court ordered a new set of deadlines for action in these cases.[38] The following year, the Legal Defense Fund organized a separate suit (again litigated in the D.C. district court by Joseph Rauh), advancing similar charges of delinquency and delay in OCR's handling of desegregation cases in the remaining thirty-three states not covered by *Adams*. This case, originally styled *Brown v. Weinberger*, proceeded to the same mechanical conclusion: "intolerable delays" could not be tolerated, the agency must take "action" within fixed deadlines.[39]

By the end of the 1970s, however, even the judges seemed to have gotten the message. When the *Brown* suit challenged the validity of the 1977 congressional restrictions on desegregation remedies, the D.C. district court rejected the challenge. There could not be any serious objection to these statutory restrictions, the district court ruled, because the Justice Department was still left free to pursue desegregation remedies through civil litigation and this was in no way an inferior remedy.[40] This precise claim had been made by OCR officials in the original *Adams* suit, when they sought to explain that the number of funding termination proceedings had fallen off so dramatically because large numbers of cases had been referred to the Justice Department for enforcement through the courts.[41] The D.C. Court of Appeals, while expressing some skepticism about Justice Department efforts, finally agreed that courts should not intervene on the basis of mere speculation about the relative effectiveness of differing enforcement strategies.[42] In its original *Adams* decision in 1973, the same Court of Appeals had sanctioned judicial intervention on just this basis, but the court seemed to have developed somewhat more caution in the interim.

The Justice Department's Civil Rights Division did not pursue busing suits with any vigor after 1980, when the department passed into the hands of Reagan appointees. But then (as the Court of Appeals had hinted), Justice had not displayed any great commitment to busing even in the late 1970s.[43] At no time, however, did civil rights lawyers make any effort to challenge the litigation policies of the Justice Department, for such a suit seemed most unlikely to succeed against the principle of prosecutorial discretion (the continuing force of which—at least in reference to the Justice Department—had been acknowledged even by the original 1973 appeals court decision in *Adams*).[44] With the handling of desegregation suits by the Justice Department beyond the reach of the *Adams* plaintiffs, OCR had all the more reason to refer its hard cases to Justice and wash its hands of them, regardless of what Justice decided to do thereafter.

In many of the school districts covered by the initial *Adams* orders, OCR did negotiate desegregation settlements on its own. But there were so many such settlements—each with its own complex details—that the *Adams* plaintiffs did not feel it was practical to protest the quality of these settlements to Judge Pratt, however disappointed they might be with their terms. Only in relation to the settlements secured, years later, with entire state systems of higher education (involving only a handful of separate settlements with a mere handful of state systems) was it feasible for the *Adams* lawyers to return to court with charges that OCR had compromised substantive standards too much when certifying compliance. Ironically, when the plaintiffs did try to mount such a challenge in the early 1980s, Judge Pratt (who retained control of the *Adams* litigation throughout), ruled that he had no authority to enter into such questions of detail. This uncharacteristically modest ruling was upheld—over some dissents—by the D.C. Court of Appeals.[45] By the early 1980s, therefore, the judges responsible for the *Adams* litigation had officially conceded that the case was not even supposed to assure any particular level of integration or compliance in any particular public educational system under OCR's jurisdiction.

Perhaps this result was always implicit in the initial Court of Appeals decision of 1973, which had insisted that while OCR might have enforcement discretion "with regard to a few school districts in the course of a generally effective enforcement program," it could not escape judicial review for "a general policy which is in effect an abdication of its statutory duty."[46] This reasoning implied that the plaintiffs were not entitled to have OCR secure any particular result in their own school districts but were simply being allowed to invoke judicial review to ensure that larger or more abstract policies conformed to the court's notion of legality. At least arguably, then, there was a certain perverse consistency in the claim of later decisions that the *Adams* litigation should not descend from the plane of high abstractions to assure any particular outcomes from all of the elaborate procedural and legalistic constraints it eventually entailed. After years of litigation, in other words, the case was acknowledged to be, quite literally, about nothing in particular.

This conclusion is only disorienting, however, if *Adams* is judged by the standards of an ordinary lawsuit. But it never was an ordinary lawsuit. Viewed as a political tactic by a determined advocacy group—not as a genuine case about actual personal rights—the early phases of the litigation may look like a reasonable gamble, which just happened to fail. It was never likely that a federal judge would take over the detailed management of a federal agency. The *Adams* suit always depended, therefore, on the hope that a general nudge from the courts would be sufficient to prompt OCR back into an aggressive integration program. The hope was disappointed because the political obstacles in the path of this strategy proved insurmountable—or at least insurmountable within the limits of the power and daring of the federal courts in the District of Columbia.

If the *Adams* litigation had limited itself to its initial policy aims, and had drawn to a close when it became apparent that these goals could not be achieved, the litigation would not be particularly remarkable. It would simply illustrate the common propensity of contemporary judges to play politics against the odds. At least the failure of the early stages of *Adams* caused no great harm. The truly remarkable fact about the case is that, even after the failure of its initial aims had become apparent, the litigation continued to expand, entangling more and more of the agency's policy prerogatives in its legalistic coils. In these later phases, *Adams* ceased to illustrate the judge as amateur politician. Rather it offered an unusually stark picture of the judge as absentee manager, redelegating remarkable powers to particular advocacy groups. The consequences of this subsequent venture proved quite unfortunate, perhaps most of all for just that portion of the American population which the courts had empowered the NAACP Legal Defense Fund to represent in this sensitive area of federal policy making.

New Rights, New Advocates, New Litigation

The second phase of the *Adams* litigation was launched with a modest, virtually inadvertent maneuver in the spring of 1975, while the LDF lawyers were still largely preoccupied with their efforts to enforce desegregation. Having reactivated the litigation in the previous year with a new list of inadequately desegregated school districts, the *Adams* lawyers complained to

Judge Pratt that they "should not have to return repeatedly to this court with a new list of districts wherein the agency refuses to commence the . . . enforcement activities this court has declared to be mandatory."[47] In addition to imposing deadlines for action against the listed districts (those already in negotiation with OCR), the plaintiffs accordingly urged Judge Pratt to impose a ninety-day deadline for OCR to investigate any "complaint or other information of racial discrimination" which the agency might receive regarding any other school district within the seventeen states covered by the litigation. Although the plaintiffs offered no argument or evidence to justify their choice of this timetable, Judge Pratt imposed it without further modification. At the urging of the plaintiffs, he also imposed a limit of ninety days for the agency to negotiate voluntary compliance whenever it found a complaint to be valid; if negotiations failed to achieve an acceptable result, the order further stipulated that OCR must commence formal enforcement procedures within another thirty days.[48]

Like the previous round of orders, this set of directives had nothing to do with the law. Title VI made no mention of any administrative obligations to private complainants or informants. HEW's 1965 implementing regulations did promise to investigate any "complaint or other information of racial discrimination" received by the department, but made no commitments regarding deadlines for investigation or subsequent follow-up. Even in policy terms, the implications of this new order were quite uncertain. Well into the 1970s, OCR had been largely preoccupied with school desegregation efforts, and information of discrimination in this effort did not have to rely on private informants, because the agency required school districts to report the racial composition of each school in annual surveys. The policy implications of the new requirement would depend, then, on the range and volume of the complaints or information it received in other areas.

On paper, however, OCR had already committed itself to a range of other enforcement obligations by 1975. For example, even though Title VI had expressly excluded employment from its coverage, OCR had asserted jurisdiction over school faculties in the late 1960s on the grounds that it could not assure nondiscriminatory treatment of students if school faculties were not desegregated along with student bodies. By early 1971, it was warning school districts that they must maintain the same black/white ratio for teachers in each school as for the school district as a whole, and must undertake affirmative action to recruit more black teachers if the teacher ratios did not substantially mirror the black/white student ratios for the district.[49] Similarly, in 1972 the agency began to warn school districts that they would be considered in violation of Title VI if they did not maintain equal per capita spending for majority black schools as for majority white schools.[50] In 1975, the agency required all elementary and secondary schools to maintain records on the racial and ethnic backgrounds of students subject to suspension or other disciplinary measures, warning that racial disparities in student discipline patterns would be considered presumptive evidence of discrimination.[51]

Few of these new requirements were spelled out in any detail. All were simply announced as policy guidelines in informal mailings to school authorities rather than as formal amendments to the official Title VI regulations (an approach that allowed OCR to evade the rule making procedures set down by the Administrative Procedure Act and to evade the special requirement in Title VI for express presidential approval of new regulations). For the most part, OCR had invoked these requirements as additional factors to consider in the context of major investigations of school districts targeted by the agency itself. Civil rights organizations had certainly endorsed these efforts (their urgings had helped to convince OCR to adopt many of the new policy guidelines in the early 1970s),[52] but the new orders from Judge Pratt seemed to promise more rigorous enforcement by the agency.

Yet from the outset, the new orders also threatened to shift the initiative in invoking these uncertain requirements from OCR itself to the particular individuals who happened to file a complaint or information. While this change did not trouble the *Adams* lawyers, it worried agency officials considerably. They first sought, unsuccessfully, to persuade Judge Pratt to rescind the order. Then they tried to amend the Title VI regulations to disavow any obligation to proceed with each individual "complaint" received, but the agency subsequently felt compelled to abandon this effort when civil rights groups denounced it as a maneuver to evade its obligations under the *Adams* order and under the law.[53] Over the ensuing years, the agency indeed lost the capacity to shape its own enforcement priorities.

This failure proved particularly unfortunate because racial discrimination was no longer OCR's only enforcement responsibility by the mid-1970s. In 1970, on its own initiative, OCR had warned school districts that they would be considered out of compliance with Title VI if they did not take steps to remedy the English language deficiencies of "national origin-minority group students."[54] In 1974, the Supreme Court's ruling in *Lau v. Nichols* (dealing with Chinese students in San Francisco) emphatically endorsed this policy, suggesting that schools might even be required to provide instruction to non-English speakers in their native languages to avoid discrimination in the provision of educational services.[55]

Still more complicating, from the point of view of enforcement priorities, was the expansion of OCR's jurisdiction by two new statutes enacted in the early 1970s. In Title IX of the Education Amendments of 1972,[56] Congress imposed a ban on sex discrimination in any federally funded "education program or activity" in terms directly parallel to the prohibitions in Title VI of the 1964 Civil Rights Act. In Section 504 of the Rehabilitation Act of 1973,[57] Congress borrowed the same statutory formula to prohibit discrimination on the basis of personal handicap in any federally funded "program or activity." In developing implementing regulations for these new statutes, OCR departed from its previous pattern. Instead of contenting itself with generalities to be supplemented over time, the agency attempted to assert a very detailed and comprehensive jurisdiction under these statutes with its initial regulations. Feminist organizations and organizations of the handicapped urged the agency to this course. In part, it reflected immediate practical concerns: in contrast to traditional civil rights organizations, which had already achieved considerable success in direct litigation under constitutional or other statutory provisions, these new constituencies felt particularly dependent on OCR regulations to provide legal sanction for their claims in private litigation.[58] In part, feminist organizations and organizations of the handicapped clamored for far-reaching initial regulations simply to validate the politically advantageous notion that their own policy preferences were now claims of "right," which the government was simply obliged to respect.[59]

For their part, OCR officials worried that if they failed to provide what these new advocacy groups demanded, the new regulations would quickly be challenged in court as unlawful and improper.[60] Many officials within the agency—though hesitant about committing the agency to altogether new enforcement operations—also seem to have been quite sympathetic to the general ideological claims of the new advocacy groups, which conveniently excused the agency from any hard policy choices by converting policy preferences into obligatory claims of right.[61] At all events, while OCR took several years to put these regulations into final form, when finally promulgated (the Title IX regulations in 1975, the Sec. 504 regulations in 1977) these new regulatory codes suggested a chronic incapacity to decline any of the promptings of its new constituencies. The new regulations also reflected a remarkable willingness to launch new standards with little regard to the political or administrative obstacles likely to be encountered in the course of enforcement.

For example, the Title IX regulations asserted jurisdiction over extracurricular college sports programs and demanded the sexual integration of elementary and secondary school gym classes, even though none of these programs or activities received direct federal funding. They also asserted jurisdiction over school dress codes and "appearance" codes, insisting on unisex requirements in areas in which these were bound to seem ludicrous (as in relation to beard trimming requirements) or extremely presumptuous (as in relation to rules about slacks and dresses).[62] So, too, the Sec. 504 regulations included alcoholics and drug addicts in its definition of persons with a protected handicap.[63]

In their various affirmative action requirements, the regulations sometimes demanded more of recipients of federal funding than the federal government itself was prepared to offer. So the Title IX regulations demanded that school health programs provide funding for student abortions, at a time when the federal government had already acted to prohibit reimbursements for abortions under the Medicaid program and under health benefit programs for federal employees.[64] The Sec. 504 regulations required colleges to install access ramps to make all classes accessible to students in wheelchairs, though the federal government did not then do so in all federal buildings open to the public.[65]

As might have been anticipated, the constituencies that secured these regulations proved no less eager than the *Adams* lawyers to assert control over their enforcement—all the more so as OCR regional offices began turning away complaints from other groups in 1975 on the grounds that all available investigators had to be assigned to race discrimination complaints in order to comply with Judge Pratt's latest order. The first response was a motion to the *Adams* court at the beginning of 1976 from the Mexican-American Legal Defense and Education Fund (MALDEF), seeking to intervene in the suit to protect the claims of its constituents on OCR enforcement resources. As the original plaintiffs in *Adams* did not object, Judge Pratt readily agreed to the motion.[66] As early as 1974, meanwhile, a coalition of feminist organizations, led by the Women's Equity Action League (WEAL), had launched a still more ambitious suit against OCR and another civil rights agency in the Department of Labor. Soon after the MALDEF intervention, WEAL also petitioned to join this suit with *Adams*. This time, Judge Pratt flatly refused, warning that this additional constituency would "overload the boat."[67] But the WEAL plaintiffs appealed this ruling and—with the original *Adams* plaintiffs expressing no objection to their intervention—the D.C. Court of Appeals ruled that the women's groups could not be excluded.[68]

This ruling was the turning point in the case. The following year, the National Federation of the Blind was also admitted to the *Adams* bargaining table to represent persons with handicaps protected by Sec. 504.[69] The *Brown* plaintiffs—representing the black "citizens, taxpayers, and parents" of the thirty-three states not covered by *Adams*—were, of course, implicitly represented in all of the subsequent *Adams* negotiations by having the same lawyers, and every settlement in *Adams* after 1976 was supposed to have national effect. Successive settlements did not settle very much, however. What the various plaintiffs essentially won was the right to bargain with OCR over deadlines, resources, and management priorities in the processing of its cases.

The first grand settlement was negotiated by LDF, WEAL, and MALDEF lawyers, following Judge Pratt's rejection of the agency's plea for the with-drawal of the initial complaint processing order. This agreement, endorsed by Judge Pratt in June 1976, committed OCR to a series of timetables for processing all Title VI and Title IX complaints, while also making other commitments in a new "annual operating plan." But the following year, confessing its inability to comply with the agreement, the agency (this time led by appointees of the new Carter administration) again urged Judge Pratt to vacate the order—and was again refused. A new round of bargaining between agency officials and advocacy group lawyers (now including advocates for the handicapped) resulted in a still more elaborate series of operational commitments from OCR, set out in a fifty-four-page document with eighty-eight separate provisions, which was duly ordered by Judge Pratt in December 1977.[70] But OCR still proved unable to comply with this agreement, as the plaintiffs continually protested in subsequent court appearances over the next four years. The new Reagan appointees, like the new Carter appointees before them, urged Judge Pratt to abandon these complex processing requirements, and endured the same fate: new rounds of bargaining with the various plain-tiffs brought a new set of modified processing agreements, issued by Judge Pratt in March 1983.[71]

Through it all, Judge Pratt refused to relinquish jurisdiction or simply to trust OCR to manage itself. The remarkable endurance of this free-floating case did not, however, reflect a growing sense of confidence on the judge's part regarding his own managerial competence. On the contrary, he freely conceded on several occasions that he had only the foggiest idea of what the wrangling was about: "Yes, I set them up," Judge Pratt exclaimed in an oral hearing in 1982, "but these were time frames that both sides agreed on. . . . I don't know anything about the mechanics of breaking this matter up. That is our problem. . . . We have to rely very extensively on counsel and counsel in that phase of the case did a lot of hard bargaining in good faith. . . . I didn't know whether the time frames should be shorter or longer. I took the informed judgment of the people who were in the best position to know, namely the counsel at that time."[72] At another hearing a few months later, the judge was still more candid: "I think a fair amount of progress has been made and it's been made as a result of the parties getting together and work-ing out their differences because, God knows, we [the judge] don't know enough about the details, or enough about the problems of the [Education] Department."[73]

The initial assumption of the case—that particular civil rights groups should be given a semiofficial role in overseeing OCR operations—simply proved hard for the *Adams* court to abandon. Having launched the litigation on the premise that the Nixon administration was not to be trusted, Judge Pratt could not shake his sense that no subsequent administration could really be trusted, either. As late as 1983 he expressed the conviction that if OCR were "left to its own devices, the manpower [for enforcement] . . . will fade away and the substance of compliance [with statutory duties] will eventually go out the window."[74] When successive administrations displayed the same patterns encountered in the Nixon administration, then, the judge did not reconsider the original partisan premise of the litigation, but simply extended it. No administration could be trusted to operate without the court-sponsored supervision of the advocacy groups.

The Effects of Interest Group Management

For all of the extraordinary scope of Judge Pratt's managerial interventions—or, to put it more accurately, for all of the extraordinary bargaining power conferred on the advocacy groups in *Adams*—there remained substantial limits on what the litigation could accomplish. Courtroom litigation is a very clumsy instrument for managing a government agency, and the ambitions of the judge and the plaintiffs could not change this fact. The court could order its various timetables, but it could not force the agency to comply—and, more often than not in the late 1970s and early 1980s, OCR missed the various processing deadlines it had agreed to meet.[75] The court could order the agency to impose sanctions if accused institutions did not voluntarily agree to correct the agency's findings of noncompliance, but neither the court nor the plaintiffs could monitor the details of the several thousand voluntary settlements negotiated by OCR in the course of resolving complaints. As the scope and scale of the litigation expanded, the court and the plaintiffs necessarily had to operate at greater and greater distance from ground level enforcement realities.

But the litigation unquestionably did have several important consequences for OCR, and the most obvious effects were pleasing to the advocacy groups involved. In 1978, under the pressure of the litigation (and the direct prompting of Judge Pratt), the Carter administration secured a 50 percent increase in the number of OCR investigators.[76] Moreover, the litigation exerted continuing pressure on the agency to improve its management of complaint processing by regional offices. Through most of the 1970s, OCR operations had been very poorly managed, in the most elementary sense that headquarters officials could not reliably track the flow of cases or the day-to-day activities of investigators in regional offices. By the mid-1980s, OCR was a much more professional operation, with a reliable, computerized case tracking system and a detailed set of manuals to guide regional offices in their activities.

Viewed in context, however, even these accomplishments do not seem notably impressive. OCR had already been receiving above-average budget and personnel increases in the mid-1970s.[77] The dramatic further leap in its resources in 1978 proved difficult to digest, and the agency might have avoided significant managerial problems in the late 1970s if the increase had been more gradual. At the same time, it seems most probable that significant managerial improvements would have been made in the late 1970s and early 1980s, even without the pressure of the *Adams* litigation. The Equal Employment Opportunity Commission was even more notorious for managerial incompetence in handling its mounting case load during the mid-1970s and yet had made very substantial and widely acknowledged managerial improvements by the end of the decade without any direct prompting from litigation.[78]

But if managerial improvements of some kind would probably have followed with or without the litigation, *Adams* undoubtedly did made a big difference in the actual pattern of OCR's administrative maturation. In the first place, the litigation forced the agency to devote the bulk of its resources to processing complaints. By the late 1970s, the agency's regional offices expended from 70 to 80 percent of their manpower on the processing of individual complaints, and this proportion rose still higher in the 1980s. Because of the pressures of the *Adams* deadlines, moreover, the scope of complaint investigations had to be narrowed. In earlier years, when the agency followed up complaints at all, it had tended to treat them as "information of discrimination" signaling the need for a general investigation. To comply with the *Adams* deadlines, regional investigators were pressured to adopt a narrow focus on the particular grievances of individual complainants. Thus the litigation forced OCR to become a complaint processing agency, a sort of small claims court for civil rights disputes.

Even by the crudest measures of enforcement efficiency—say, the number of violations corrected for the same expenditure of employee time—this was surely a very inefficient approach. When OCR conducted careful internal operating studies in the late 1970s, the results indeed confirmed its traditional assumption about the relative productivity of complaint investigations as compared with more general, agency initiated compliance reviews: per man-hour expended, these studies showed, compliance reviews secured identifiable institutional changes for twice as many identifiable persons; and unquantified, indirect effects were probably still greater.[79] At the same time, individual discrimination victims who felt their complaints were not adequately pursued by OCR were always free to seek direct relief on their own initiative by hiring a lawyer and launching a civil suit against the alleged perpetrators of their injuries.[80]

As it was, preoccupation with responding to individual complaints proved to have a very considerable influence not just on the efficiency of its enforcement operations but on their substantive distribution. The complaint orientation forced OCR to address most of its resources to those constituencies which were most prolific with complaints, so the share of resources devoted to investigating discrimination against blacks dwindled to less than 10 percent, and the share devoted to non–English speaking minorities (generally poor Hispanics and Asians) dwindled to barely 5 percent in the 1980s. Meanwhile, women claimed one-third of its enforcement efforts, and the handicapped more than half.[81] A very large portion of the complaints about sex discrimination were brought by female college professors protesting unfavorable decisions on tenure, promotion, or employment. The largest portion of complaints regarding discrimination against the handicapped were brought by middle class parents seeking more extensive support services for their children.

Depending on the definitions employed, it may well be that sex discrimination and discrimination against the handicapped were far more prevalent in the 1980s than race discrimination. It can be argued, too, that a reduced emphasis on race discrimination (or discrimination against "national origin minorities") was a sensible way of alerting schools and colleges to their obligations under the newer antidiscrimination regulations. The fact remains that OCR's preoccupation with complaint investigation shifted the great bulk of its efforts to just those constituencies which were already most sophisticated about their rights and already best situated to assert their claims without direct enforcement assistance from OCR. For the ostensible beneficiaries of the original *Adams* suit—blacks in the South—and for others in disadvantaged positions in America, forcing OCR into a complaint processing operation does not seem to have been at all advantageous. But the emphasis on complaint investigation served the litigational interests of the NAACP Legal Defense Fund by allowing it to maintain a united front with the new, politically potent constituency groups in the civil rights field, instead of squabbling with them over relative shares. And the emphasis on complaints also reinforced the continuing premise of *Adams* that OCR could not be allowed to exercise enforcement discretion, because the agency was simply required by law to do everything.[82]

The emphasis on complaint investigation also pleased the advocacy groups by forcing the agency to keep addressing new issues as they were pressed by complainants. In the late 1970s, for example, the pressure of accumulating complaints forced OCR to address a whole series of policy questions relating to sex discrimination in athletic programs, which—considering the unusual degree of controversy surrounding such cases—it might otherwise have chosen to ignore.[83] In the 1980s, the pressure of complaint settling obligations forced the agency, in the same way, to clarify a range of difficult policy questions about the rights of the handicapped to costly educational accommodations—questions that, again, the agency might have preferred to postpone. The Legal Defense Fund had issues that it wanted to force onto the agency's agenda in the same way, such as the legality of class "tracking" schemes that isolated black students within schools.[84]

But here, too, what seemed to be tactical advantages for the plaintiffs proved to have unfortunate implications for OCR operations. The agency was not only inhibited from asserting its own enforcement priorities but diverted from developing any meaningful sense of strategy. In several ways, the litigation robbed the agency of the capacity or incentive to view its responsibilities at all creatively or imaginatively—or responsibly. The pressure of the litigation absorbed a tremendous amount of time and attention from successive OCR directors and their departmental superiors in HEW (and after 1980 in the Department of Education). Managerial energy and initiative came to be focused on speeding up the processing of complaints in order to achieve better compliance with the *Adams* orders, instead of on trying to secure measurable or meaningful benefits in the real world. The great catch phrase in OCR operations in the late 1970s and into the 1980s was "productivity," with an endless stream of memos harping on the need to improve the productivity of regional offices and individual agency investigators. But in a classic example of bureaucratic goal displacement, productivity did not refer to any measure of real-world benefits per man-hour of effort, but simply to the number of complaints that were processed—with whatever outcome—per investigator per month.

In larger terms, *Adams* inhibited serious policy reconsiderations by generating an atmosphere of tension and suspicion, which made successive political appointees especially reluctant to risk controversial initiatives. The feeling was that the agency was already under a cloud and ought not to provoke any new trouble. The lawyers for the plaintiffs developed a network of informants inside the agency, supplementing their extensive access to data, records, and reports as required by successive court orders or mandated by litigational "discovery" demands, which inevitably heightened feelings of suspicion and distrust between successive political appointees at the agency and their career staffs. Political officials within the agency could never be sure what might be held against them in court or what might be subsequently challenged in litigation; and this doubt encouraged a somewhat paranoid atmosphere.[85]

To be sure, not all defensiveness in OCR was the direct result of *Adams*. In the mid-1970s, OCR had incurred a number of bruising shocks from the impulsive actions of regional enforcement officials. In the most notorious case, a regional office ruled that separate mother-daughter and father-son school banquets were in violation of Title IX, and this ruling was promptly reported on the front page of the *Washington Post*—and equally promptly provoked a countermanding order from President Ford and a speedy congressional amendment to Title IX to ensure that such school events would remain forever beyond the reach of federal bureaucrats.[86] But *Adams* plainly aggravated the reluctance of top OCR officials to entrust any real responsibility to regional investigators. Throughout the 1980s, therefore, regional officials were instructed to attempt to satisfy complainants by organizing "conciliation" meetings with the "defendant" institutions. But when such efforts failed, OCR investigators were forbidden to issue findings of discrimination without approval from headquarters in Washington, and headquarters officials scrutinized proposed letters of finding to ensure that they were as narrowly tailored as possible. Top officials put a premium on ensuring that regional officials did not become entangled in controversial cases—so much so that until the summer of 1987, they did not even encourage regional offices to report discrimination issues or problems for subsequent investigation, on the basis of what they might have noticed incidentally in the course of complaint investigations.[87]

By the autumn of 1987, congressional staffers pursuing an oversight study of OCR operations charged that OCR had used the *Adams* timetables as an excuse to confine complaint investigations to the narrowest and most superficial inquiries. The staff of Representative Gus Hawkins's House Education and Labor Committee may not have been the most impartial observers of OCR operations, but there was clearly much evidence for this characterization.[88] There was also all too much logic in this development: by the autumn of 1987, OCR was finally meeting its court ordered timetables on a relatively dependable, routine basis.[89]

In the mid-1970s, OCR launched a series of extremely ambitious compliance reviews of major urban school districts in the North. With their gargantuan data demands—concerning budgetary allocations, school personnel policies, and many other matters—and their potential for arousing fierce political opposition, these reviews proved to be quite beyond the agency's capacity to carry through as originally projected. After much wasted effort, they finally had to be drastically curtailed.[90] By the mid-1980s, OCR was so risk-averse that top officials shied away from anything that they might not be able to wrap up within the *Adams* timetables, which had, of course, come to cover agency initiated compliance reviews along with complaint investigations. This was the central meaning of "improved management."[91]

What made this outcome particularly unfortunate was that race related problems in the United States were not really easing during all the long years of the *Adams* litigation. In crucial respects they were, in fact, worsening.

Civil Rights and the Education of Minorities

OCR's mission came to be so thoroughly preoccupied with satisfying the *Adams* orders that the agency made little effort to assess its effectiveness or even to assess problems in the real world. Agency generated documents make it possible to assess OCR's compliance with court-ordered timetables from month to month (or quarter to quarter) over a ten-year span, but they provide remarkably little hard data with which to measure the impact of its enforcement efforts. One fact, however, is dismayingly clear from other sources. Throughout the 1970s and into the early 1980s, as the *Adams* litigation ground on and on through the legal mills, the educational achievements of black students were, on the average, actually declining. Educational performance for all students declined in the 1970s, but black students fared worse in this period, and the gap between blacks and whites actually expanded. By 1980, an extensive survey of recent high school graduates found that the average white graduate had attained only tenth grade level reading skills, but the average black graduate was reading at only a seventh grade level. Mean SAT scores for college bound white students in 1980 were down considerably from the levels of the 1960s but were still some 30 percent higher than median scores for college bound black students.[92]

By almost any measure, this trend was surely much more deserving of federal attention and concern than possible discrimination against women in college athletics, or any of a vast number of other questions to which OCR's constituency groups and the force of the *Adams* orders diverted the agency's energy and resources. To be sure, not all of the widening disparity in educational performance could be blamed on intentional discrimination. The pattern no doubt reflected neglect more than malice. But then OCR's desegregation efforts in the late 1960s—which the *Adams* litigation tried so hard to reenergize—were not all confined to remedying just those disparities in enrollment patterns attributable to intentional discrimination by school authorities. No doubt there would always be practical limits on what school officials could do to encourage improvements in the education of minority students. The Supreme Court had conceded that, even with busing plans, there were practical limits on what school officials could do to ensure perfect racial balances in school enrollment patterns.[93] For all practical purposes, however, OCR did almost nothing to address the decline in black educational performance, because it did not define this as a "civil rights" issue; and neither its litigious constituents nor its judicial receiver pressed it to do so.

What might the agency have done? Perhaps not very much, in view of the problem's complexity. But two things are clear. First, some things certainly could be done. Declining educational performance (for children of all races) finally had aroused so much concern by the 1980s that governors in many states and officials in the Reagan administration began calling for extensive reforms. In fact, reforms initiated in many states, usually at the insistence of concerned governors, did begin to show results, and by the mid-1980s scores on nationally standardized tests were improving for all students—and faster for blacks than for whites.[94] If there were no magic formulas for securing high levels of educational attainment for all students, there were certainly known methods of improving educational performance by emphasizing accountability standards for teachers and students alike, and by enhancing the authority and responsibility of school principals to enforce accountability. Impressive results were obtained in a number of inner city school districts where focused efforts were made.[95]

The second fact worth noting is that OCR did not actually disclaim jurisdiction over educational results. Its original 1970 guidelines on discrimination against "national origin minority" (i.e., non–English speaking) students had already asserted that school districts would be held in violation of Title VI if they did not take steps to end the disparately low educational performance of such children. In practice, OCR in the mid-1970s pressed schools to adopt bilingual education programs to deal with this problem—which usually involved providing separate instruction in Spanish—even though it was (and remains) much disputed whether bilingual education is an appropriate response, considering its potential to encourage and perpetuate the isolation of non–English speaking children.[96] By the early 1980s, there was so much controversy over bilingual education that top officials in the Reagan Education Department quietly backed away from this program without establishing any clear requirements in its place. But as a matter of law, the approach to Title VI pioneered for non–English speaking children—holding schools responsible for taking measures to assure more equal educational results—had received endorsement from the U.S. Supreme Court; and parallel interpretations for black students, if more thoughtfully conceived, might have been as well received by the courts.

Even in the one aspect of the *Adams* litigation that presented OCR with its most promising opportunities for useful intervention, however, the agency ended up pursuing irrelevant but politically quite inflammatory side issues— because these issues were what the *Adams* plaintiffs demanded. The original *Adams* suit in 1970 had cited, among its other charges, the agency's failure to cut off federal funding to ten inadequately desegregated state systems of higher education identified by OCR itself in 1969 as obliged to take further steps to comply with Title VI. In earlier decades, when segregation was required by law in the South, each of these states had built entirely separate public colleges for whites and for blacks. Admissions had been opened to applicants of all races in all colleges by the late 1960s, but blacks continued to attend traditionally black colleges and whites to attend the traditionally white colleges. The problem was that OCR could not decide what these states ought to do to end this continuing pattern of "racially identifiable institutions" in higher education.

There were, in fact, sharp differences of opinion on proper policy even among organizations claiming to represent blacks. When Judge Pratt's initial 1973 decision imposed a tight deadline for OCR action against these state college systems, an organization of black colleges filed an amicus brief urging the D.C. Court of Appeals to dismiss this aspect of the *Adams* suit altogether.[97] The black colleges feared that the LDF's legal initiative would result in their own destruction, for closing down the traditionally black colleges might have been the quickest and easiest way to ensure the integration of state higher education systems. While these institutions were generally of lower academic quality than their white counterparts, many of the black colleges nonetheless had long, proud histories and loyal, distinguished alumni. The decision of the D.C. Court of Appeals in 1973 was plainly moved by the plea of the black colleges that they be allowed to continue their distinctive, historic role as vehicles for black advancement in the South. The initial opinion of the Court of Appeals thus noted that "black institutions currently fulfill a crucial need and will continue to play an important role in black higher education." It then declared that "the most serious problem" in the higher education systems in these states was not the continuing racial indentifiability of different colleges but "the lack of state-wide planning to provide more and better trained minority group doctors, lawyers and other professionals."[98] Instead of dismissing that portion of the *Adams* suit dealing with higher education, however, the court's decision simply overturned Judge Pratt's deadline for action in this area and directed OCR to take additional time to "carefully assess" proper policy in this field.

OCR responded by negotiating vague agreements with most of the states by which the states promised to undertake affirmative action to recruit more black students to traditionally white colleges, while simultaneously enhancing funding and facilities at the traditionally black colleges. Not satisfied with these agreements, the LDF returned to Judge Pratt in 1976, demanding that OCR impose more specific and demanding requirements to achieve integration in higher education in the affected states. Despite a new protest to the court from the black colleges, Judge Pratt agreed in the spring of 1977 that OCR must do more to "comply with the congressional mandate."[99]

The notion that Congress had issued a "mandate" in 1964 for the statistical integration of southern colleges was, of course, a complete legal fiction. By 1976 these state higher education systems could not be charged with discrimination in any direct or immediate sense. Careful investigations by OCR had determined that by the mid-1970s, "the racial distribution of enrollments," both at predominantly black and at predominantly white colleges in these states, tended "to mirror the distribution of applicants," indicating that student self-selection was the main cause of continuing racial imbalances. Moreover, "the overwhelming majority of the predominantly black colleges currently receive more government appropriations and more total revenue than the average for public four-year institutions in their respective states."[100] This state of affairs certainly did not compensate for decades of underfunding at the black colleges, but there was no ready means to calculate the scale of investment required to achieve retroactive parity. Similarly, the funding patterns of the mid-1970s could not compensate for decades of differing academic standards by which, for example, the black colleges had been allowed to tenure a large proportion of professors without doctoral degrees while the white colleges generally had not. But there was no easy way to undo this history by the mid-1970s without working great hardship and disruption on the faculties in the black colleges.

As all of the states refused to consider eliminating student choice altogether (developing a new system, that is, that would simply assign students to different colleges as they were assigned to different high schools), OCR launched an elaborate regulatory venture to force the states to redesign college offerings to entice students of different races to traditionally one-race campuses.[101] Each of the affected states was required to set various numerical integration goals and come up with a specific, multiyear plan to achieve these goals. The core strategy OCR urged for these plans was for the states to dismantle program duplication between traditionally white and traditionally black campuses. The premise of the strategy was that as individual campuses developed unique programs, students of both races interested in such programs—such as nursing programs or engineering programs or teacher training programs— would be attracted to the campus with such offerings and overlook its traditional racial character. As might have been expected, this effort provoked intense political disputes within the affected states, as different campuses struggled to retain special programs—and special funding allocations—they had previously acquired or had already invested great lobbying efforts in seeking to acquire. Tensions were exacerbated by overall enrollment declines (threatening overall declines in state funding) in the late 1970s and early 1980s. Furthermore, disputes arose about the "educational logic" of placing particular programs on campuses that did (or did not) offer complementary programs or related facilities, and decisions about the funding or placement of new programs were readily interpreted as slights to the prestige or potential of the disappointed campuses.[102]

Political feuding and jockeying within state higher education systems quickly extended to state legislators and then to congressmen and senators in Washington—often alumni of one or another campus and eager to lend a hand to the alma mater.[103] At the climax of OCR's regulatory efforts in North Carolina in the late 1970s, the political furor in the state reached such a pitch that President Carter felt it necessary to make a personal intervention in the negotiations between state officials and the Secretary of Health, Education, and Welfare. But the plaintiffs in *Adams* kept up their pressure, returning to court in 1981 to challenge the adequacy of the agreement finally negotiated by OCR with North Carolina. It was at this point that Judge Pratt suddenly disclaimed any authority to review the substance of particular settlements.[104] But in 1983, in response to a new motion from the plaintiffs, he nonetheless turned around and ordered OCR to negotiate new integration plans with state systems that had not made adequate progress under their earlier plans.[105] OCR thus continued an ongoing cycle of tense negotiations, extended monitoring of performance, and renegotiation of new agreements, amid charges of unreasonableness and bad faith on both sides.

As far as the original goal of integration was concerned, not much was achieved in the end. The traditionally black colleges continued to be overwhelmingly black and the traditionally white campuses overwhelmingly white. Many black campuses received extra funding for alluring new programs, then faced intense financial strains when these programs failed to attract many students. Many traditionally white campuses instituted ambitious remedial education programs to entice anxious black students, but the dropout rate for black students on these campuses nonetheless proved alarmingly high. And black enrollments in the white colleges, having risen significantly in the early 1970s (before the *Adams* litigation forced OCR to become more involved), began to decline thereafter, despite all of the regulatory pressures from OCR. Still more discouragingly, throughout the 1980s the overall proportion of black high school graduates going on to college in these states—as throughout the country—remained significantly lower than it had been in the mid-1970s.[106]

If the aim was to increase statistical integration at the college level, this aspect of *Adams*—like the earlier phases involving elementary and secondary education—was largely a failure. But it was never at all clear why integration in itself should have become the focus of OCR's efforts, in view of the fact that continuing racial imbalances by the mid-1970s reflected voluntary student choices. Neither OCR nor the major civil rights advocacy groups profess to see any problem with the fact that Howard University in Washington, D.C. has remained almost totally black.[107] No one objects, either, when traditionally Catholic or traditionally Jewish colleges continue to serve disproportionately large numbers of Catholics or Jews. But the history of discrimination against blacks, as against Catholics and Jews in earlier times, undoubtedly figures to some degree in the explanation for all of these anamolous enrollment patterns today.

If, however, OCR's policy goal was to obtain "more and better trained . . . minority group professionals," as the D.C. Court of Appeals had suggested in 1973, the *Adams* litigation still failed to achieve any significant results in the affected states. But as a practical matter the ongoing litigation never really directed OCR back to this goal. The principal cause of high college dropout rates among black students and continuing college enrollment declines, in the *Adams* states as elsewhere, was the lack of adequate preparation for college in elementary and secondary schools.[108] But the agency directed almost no attention at all to this problem. The disproportionately poor performance of black students in public schools was no more remote from the congressional mandate than the lack of racial balance in various southern colleges. Pressuring for changes in elementary and secondary education would surely have aroused outraged protests about federal meddling and threats to academic autonomy; but OCR provoked outraged protests of this kind anyway in seeking to rearrange program offerings on different college campuses in the *Adams* states. And the agency's financial leverage remained potentially quite as potent in elementary and secondary education as in higher education. The educational reform movement in the 1980s was stimulated by governors and other high level officials at the state level, and OCR might have held up grants channeled through state agencies to prod backward states into following the example of the leading states in this movement. Certainly, in states with a history of segregation in higher education OCR had an immediate and quite plausible opening to exert such pressure.

In fact, one state made the connection on its own. In the course of negotiating a new plan to encourage desegregation of the state higher education system, officials in Virginia offered in the mid-1980s to include proposals for improving college preparation in high schools. OCR accepted the proposal and, at a time when Education Secretary William Bennett was publicly emphasizing the need to improve elementary and secondary school education in the inner cities, there was some thought given in the department to including such provisions in all of the other state plans that had to be renegotiated. But the idea was quickly abandoned for fear that such provisions would be difficult to enforce, as long as the agency was still under fire from the *Adams* plaintiffs for not adequately ensuring that the affected states honored a variety of other commitments in their plans.[109] Characteristically, this particular failure of nerve was never raised in the *Adams* litigation.

Parting Assessments

Whatever its other failings, the Reagan administration at least put up more of a struggle against the *Adams* litigation than its predecessor. The Carter appointees had urged Judge Pratt to terminate the suit but then resigned themselves to bargaining with the plaintiffs when the judge refused to do so. Although the Reagan appointees failed in their turn and had to submit to similar bargaining sessions, they pressed forward with an appeal, questioning— for the first time since 1970—how the named plaintiffs in *Adams* could really have standing to pursue such an ambitious set of policy complaints through a lawsuit. And in 1984, the D.C. Court of Appeals, citing a recent decision of the Supreme Court denying standing to "black citizens, taxpayers, and parents" in a somewhat similar suit against the Internal Revenue Service, agreed that Judge Pratt should reconsider the matter.[110]

After years of chiding OCR for "interminable delay" and "taking its own sweet time" to make decisions,[111] Judge Pratt proceeded to sit on this question for more than three years, issuing no decision at all despite repeated promptings from the Justice Department. While the judge delayed, his past orders remained in effect. On December 11, 1987 the judge finally washed his hands of the case with a rather tortured thirty-page opinion purporting to explain why none of the various plaintiffs could any longer have standing to pursue the litigation. The opinion stressed that "the original order of 1973 stemmed from defendants' abdication of their statutory responsibility in pursuing a conscious policy of non-enforcement" and suggested that it was only the subsequent orders that "intrude on the functions of the Executive branch and violate the doctrine of the separation of powers, which is the basic core of standing." But the opinion also claimed that the plaintiffs lacked standing because "the injury claimed in the instant case is the right [*sic*] to be educated in a racially integrated institution or in an environment which is free from discrimination based on race," and this injury was neither caused by OCR nor clearly redressable by the agency.[112] If this was so, the plaintiffs should never have had standing. But this conclusion might readily have been avoided by holding—as the *Adams* lawyers had indeed argued in 1970—that the federal government had perpetrated a separate and distinct injury by channeling federal funds to discriminatory institutions.

The most obvious and natural basis for questioning the standing of the *Adams* plaintiffs was never considered at all in Judge Pratt's opinion: namely, that whatever injury had been done to Kenneth Adams, it could not give him (or rather his LDF lawyers) any claim to speak for millions of other students throughout the nation. This objection would not have been a technical one. It was the heart of the difficulty with the *Adams* litigation from the beginning. By the time Judge Pratt took his leave of the case, OCR had become, to a very large extent, what the pressures of the litigation—that is to say, the pressures brought to bear by the LDF—had made it. The question that should have been asked, legally as much as politically, was why the NAACP Legal Defense Fund was ever entitled to assert this kind of privileged influence on the development of a very important federal regulatory program.

What the LDF gained through the litigation was never anything guaranteed by the law—unless "law" is defined as anything a judge says it is. If the law in this case had been interpreted in accord with the intentions of the enacting Congress, its intended effect had been substantially achieved some years before *Adams* was ever filed. But neither the top officials in OCR nor the dominant political opinion in Congress by 1970 would have been satisfied to rest with the original modest understanding of discrimination. One way or another, the agency was bound to continue in a rather activist direction. The question was how and where the agency would choose to exert its leverage. The *Adams* litigation gave the LDF a remarkably large say in developing the answer.

It is surely misleading to compare actual agency performance with some idealized, hypothetical alternative and then to suppose that the alternative would have been realized but for some particular factor in the agency's actual operating conditions. OCR by the mid-1970s was an agency with high ambitions, limited resources, and almost no sense of strategy. Constituency groups were continually urging it to pursue still higher ambitions without supplying it much of an increase in its political resources or much of a strategic focus. The agency was bound to be something of a mess. But the *Adams* case forced the agency to work its way through the mess along particular lines that were certainly not inevitable; and they were lines that served the institutional interests of the LDF far more than the interests of minority students.

In view of OCR's activist traditions, it is most unlikely that it would have allowed the bulk of its resources to be committed to processing complaints at the behest of middle class women or middle class parents of handicapped children. It was the *Adams* litigation that forced the agency in this direction.

Even when it became clear that the litigation was pushing race discrimination issues to the margins in OCR's operations, however, the LDF refused to reconsider its position. The essential reason seems to be that the organization was unwilling to disrupt its coalition with women's groups and with advocates for the handicapped: "We never considered doing anything else," a top LDF strategist recently acknowledged.[113] In congressional politics, traditional civil rights groups have held onto the coalition with women's groups even when doing so has hurt their own immediate objectives.[114] And perhaps this strategy is sensible for traditional civil rights groups. But the political strategy of civil rights groups need not have determined the operating policy of a public regulatory program.

It may be that if OCR had retained more freedom of action, it would still have squandered its resources on unproductive efforts. The fact remains that LDF lawyers forced the agency to devote a good deal of time and effort—and a great deal of political capital—to a highly questionable program for securing statistical integration in higher education, to the neglect of improving actual educational performance among blacks. And in this regard the *Adams* litigation has mirrored the general priorities of the LDF and other prominent civil rights advocacy groups.

LDF strategist Phyllis McClure claims that the organization has always been concerned about the quality of education for minority students at the elementary and secondary level. It was unable to pursue this concern very directly in the 1970s, she says, because there was then so little available data breaking down educational performance by race.[115] But before 1968, there was also a lack of data on the racial breakdown of school enrollment patterns: such data became readily available for schools and colleges throughout the country because organizations like the LDF insisted that OCR collect such data. Neither the LDF nor any other major civil rights organization has pressed OCR to collect data on actual educational performance.[116]

What civil rights organizations like the LDF actually did in the 1970s was to press OCR to monitor school discipline patterns in order to ensure that black students would not be suspended or disciplined in other ways in disproportion to their numbers.[117] In other words, they focused on threats to equality instead of threats to order—at a time when many inner city schools had become too disorderly for effective teaching. Eventually, mounting evidence of educational failure stimulated several states to press for educational reform by imposing basic competency standards for graduation. The LDF challenged competency testing in several states on the grounds that such tests placed a disproportionate burden on minority students—as if minority students had less of a stake in the maintenance of educational standards than others.[118]

As the educational reform movement caught the attention of Washington policy makers and received at least strong verbal encouragement, first from Reagan Education Secretary Terrell Bell and then from his successor William Bennett, the LDF made no effort to urge Education Department officials to incorporate reform concerns into their civil rights enforcement activities.[119] Instead, the LDF continued to harp on the slow pace of desegregation in the higher education systems of the South. So, for example, at hearings before a sympathetic House subcommittee, first in 1985, then again in 1987, LDF officials emphasized OCR's deficiencies in complying with *Adams.* They said nothing about the challenge of improving public education for minority students at the elementary and secondary levels.[120]

At the end of 1988, LDF lawyers were preoccupied with efforts to appeal Judge Pratt's dismissal of the case. Their other major effort in relation to education was a litigation campaign to establish the constitutional principle that states must guarantee equal per capita funding for all public schools.[121] In the mid-1970s the Supreme Court rejected such a claim, in part because there was no good evidence that educational expenditures were closely correlated with educational performance. There is still no good evidence to this effect. But LDF lawyers insist that the statistical equalization of school funding is the contemporary complement of earlier campaigns for the statistical integration of school enrollment patterns. In its way, the LDF's funding equalization campaign may indeed be the natural counterpart to its earlier efforts: as it has traditionally focused not on the training of minds, but on the moving of bodies, it now seeks to focus on the moving of dollars. If the Court of Appeals does not reinstate *Adams,* there is at least some hope that OCR may avoid being drawn into this latest ill-considered diversion from the most pressing problems of minority students.

Like many other enthusiasts of federal regulation in quite disparate fields, civil rights organizations have urged external, mechanical solutions that would not demand any significant effort from the ostensible beneficiaries. In this respect, the regulatory agenda of civil rights organizations invites comparison with that of consumer safety advocates, who demand outright product bans instead of warning labels, or that of workplace safety advocates, who demand elaborate engineering controls instead of protective gear for exposed workers. Political and organizational imperatives, as much as force of habit, might explain this priority within the leading advocacy organizations: it is easier to focus on objects than on people, more inspiring to think of big programs than modest steps, more encouraging to imagine that problems can be solved with one-step mechanical solutions than with long-term prodding and pleading. But the imperatives of advocacy organizations need not be the imperatives of public policy.

6

Reinforcing Bureaucratic Inertia: The Case of the Food and Drug Administration

T HE FDA has unusually strong regulatory powers because its regulatory responsibilities involve matters of particularly direct public concern: the control of health hazards in pharmaceutical drugs, food additives, and cosmetics. Oversimplifying a bit, one might describe the central mission of the Food and Drug Administration as protecting people against inadvertent poisoning. And people seem to feel a peculiar, primal horror at the thought that what they take into their bodies may be poisoning them.

Thus the FDA's regulatory powers were successively enlarged by several major congressional enactments in the course of this century. Each enactment followed a flurry of excited publicity over fatal or deforming accidents traced to particular drugs or food additives.[1] Americans casually accept a great many other hazards of modern life with relative complacency, such as the the risk of automobile accidents, which take many more lives each year.[2] Perhaps people feel they have less control over hazards in this area. Or perhaps they feel that it is more sinister for business to profit from "poison" than from products such as cars that are known to pose some risk of injury to the user. At any rate, regulation in this area is far older, tighter, and more securely established than in other fields of safety regulation. And from the outset, advocates of tighter regulation in this domain have played on public suspicions of deception by unscrupulous businessmen.

Reinforcing Bureaucratic Inertia

Food and drug regulation might thus seem to be an area in which public interest advocates could not very plausibly claim to represent interests that would be otherwise unrepresented. At regular intervals in earlier decades and almost continually since the late 1950s, congressional committees have devoted much attention to this field of regulation, which so readily rouses the public's attention. Nonetheless, public interest advocates, attracted by the same ready limelight, have also devoted much attention to the FDA from the outset of the modern "public interest" movement in the late 1960s. In their eagerness to influence FDA policies, public interest advocates have frequently resorted to the courts, and the courts in turn have frequently lent additional influence to these advocates.

But regulatory policy can err not only by undue laxity, but also by excessive stringency. And there is much reason to think that, on the whole, the FDA has more often erred on the side of excessive stringency in recent decades, to an extent that has needlessly limited consumer choice and dangerously restricted the quality of American medical care. This was certainly the view of high officials in the Reagan administration in the 1980s. From the outset of the new administration, the President's Taskforce on Regulatory Reform pointed to the FDA as an agency in which reform was particularly urgent; and this view was publicly and emphatically endorsed by successive Reagan appointees at the Department of Health and Human Services and at the FDA itself. Although a number of valuable reforms were eventually instituted in the mid-1980s, hopes for decisive change were generally disappointed. So, for example, the drawn-out process for securing FDA approval of new drugs—a particular target of reform advocates—actually became more drawn out for most new drugs in the 1980s.[3]

Consumer advocacy groups, most notably Ralph Nader's Public Citizen, were fiercely critical of Reagan administration reform efforts and continued to insist that the FDA was required by law to maintain very restrictive regulatory approaches. Their efforts to enforce this view through the courts were certainly not the main reason for the slow pace of change at the FDA during the 1980s. Reform efforts had to contend with entrenched policy perspectives within the agency and with a good deal of suspicion and resistance to change in Congress. Nonetheless, the targets of public interest litigation against the FDA during the 1980s became increasingly removed from serious public health issues. The main aim of the various suits seems to have been to reinforce policy commitments and perspectives developed in the previous decade and to reinforce the general premise that highly restrictive regulatory approaches were indeed required by the law. Some recent litigation has actually had no other conceivable purpose than to vindicate the abstract principle that extreme stringency is required by the law. For the most part, judges have readily lent their authority to these symbolic crusades, even though the policies at stake had much less to do with actual statutory requirements than with policies developed by the FDA itself in earlier years.

The Setting: Remote Laws and Immediate Biases

The FDA's initial statutory charter, the Food and Drugs Act of 1906,[4] was largely aimed at "adulterated" food products. Its most important drug provisions, aimed more at punishing deception than at assuring safety, simply authorized the agency to act against fraudulent or misleading labeling of packaged products, and left the FDA with the burden of proving in individual court actions that contested labels actually should be considered "false and fraudulent." The Food, Drug, and Cosmetics Act of 1938,[5] enacted after a hundred people had died from the use of a faulty new drug product, focused more directly on safety concerns. It gave the FDA for the first time a direct licensing authority: no "new drug" (or food additive)—defined as a chemical entity not already "generally recognized as safe"—could be marketed without FDA approval.

In the late 1950s, a series of amendments to the food and cosmetic portions of the act—amendments popularly known as "the Delaney clause" (though there are actually three different versions)—prohibited the use of any food additive or cosmetic agent shown to "induce cancer in animals or in man." In 1962, the drug portion of the act was amended to require that new drugs be proved "effective," as well as "safe."[6] In contrast to the Delaney clauses, the 1962 drug amendments were rather controversial at the time of their enactment; and the new drug law indeed proved to have much more dramatic and troubling consequences within its first decade of operation.

In the late 1950s, it seemed quite plausible to adopt a "zero risk" cancer policy for chemical additives in food and cosmetics. Few substances had yet been identified as carcinogens, and it was easy to suppose that the suppression of proved carcinogens would be an altogether unmixed blessing for consumers. By the 1970s, events required the reconsideration of this pleasing assumption, as we shall see in the last section of this chapter. For the present, it is more important to notice that therapeutic drugs were always understood to be a different matter. Few drugs in modern pharmacology are altogether risk-free. Nonetheless, for people with serious health problems it is often worthwhile to run the risk of dangerous side effects if a drug promises significant therapeutic benefits.

Even under the 1938 law, therefore, the FDA had routinely considered the promised therapeutic effects of new drugs before deciding whether to approve them as safe for particular indicated uses. But *effectiveness* is a relative concept, quite as much as safety. Many drugs have only a limited effect on most people and no effect on others. Because the actual biochemical operation of most drugs is poorly understood, determinations of effectiveness are often simply a matter of inference. Just as a dangerous drug might be the safest treatment for a still more dangerous health problem, a drug of doubtful effectiveness might still be the best hope for otherwise untreatable conditions. Before 1962, the FDA had generally been willing to rely on the clinical impressions of physicians in assessing the therapeutic value of new drugs. Amending the law to require more conclusive evidence of effectiveness was likely to mean tighter controls all around.

For just this reason, a separate effectiveness requirement was opposed not only by drug companies but also by the American Medical Association, which feared that it would reduce the range of treatment options available to practicing physicians.[7] To placate the opposition, Congress adopted compromise language in the 1962 drug law. Instead of requiring a "preponderance of evidence" for the efficacy of new drugs, the law required only that drugs show "substantial evidence" of effectiveness for their proposed uses. The statute defined "substantial evidence" as "evidence consisting of adequate and well-controlled investigations, including clinical investigations, by experts qualified by scientific training and experience to evaluate the effectiveness of the drug involved"; but even the lobbyists for the Pharmaceutical Manufacturers Association accepted this wording as a less demanding standard than "preponderance of the evidence."[8] The Senate Judiciary Committee, which sponsored the final language, emphasized the latitudinarian implications of the "substantial evidence" formula in its final report on the 1962 amendments. In "the difficult area of drugs testing and evaluation," the committee report noted, "differences of opinion frequently arise," but "such a difference in opinion should not result in disapproval of a claim of effectiveness." The committee also rejected a proposed requirement for a showing of relative effectiveness, indicating that drugs should still be approved even if other, seemingly more effective drugs were available.[9]

The FDA continually tightened its regulatory approach to these new standards in the course of the 1960s, however, until there was finally no difference between the FDA's working approach and the more stringent approach Congress seemed to have rejected quite deliberately in 1962. By the 1970s, the FDA's effectual standard was more stringent than anything even contemplated in 1962. At the end of the 1970s, for example, the director of the FDA's Bureau of Drugs candidly explained to a congressional committee that "the words 'substantial evidence' connote a certain quality of evidence to lawyers and I think that that connotation is incorrect. Operationally the amount of evidence needed to support the effectiveness of a drug [before the FDA] is closer to the legal standard of 'beyond a reasonable doubt.' "[10] Similarly, as a practical matter, the FDA gave much attention to the "relative efficacy" of new drugs, compared to existing drugs designed for similar purposes. The agency tended to be very cautious about approving new drugs when drugs for similar conditions were already on the market.

Testing standards were not applied consistently, and probably they could not have been under any reasonable system. As William Wardell, a leading scholar of drug approval procedures, has observed, "the perfect clinical trial has never been achieved."[11] In theory, the most conclusive test is a "double-blind" test in which two large samples of patients with the same condition receive exactly the same treatment, except that one sample also receives the drug under study and the other does not—and not even the doctors and nurses involved know which is which. In practice, it is very difficult to maintain strictly uniform treatment for large groups of people who are seriously ill, because doctors feel bound to respond to changes in the condition of individual patients as they occur. Patients who are not so seriously ill as to require hospitalization present different testing problems, because they do not always adhere to prescribed regimens. And for a variety of reasons, it is difficult to maintain complete secrecy about what is being prescribed to different patients under the test. Thus it is almost always possible to question test results on the grounds that human samples were not sufficiently comparable or sufficiently controlled or sufficiently large to provide conclusive results. While FDA practice varied from case to case, the overall tendency was toward more and more stringency in accepting test results, and in authorizing testing protocols at early stages.[12]

The consequences of this new stringency were strikingly evident by the 1970s. While documentary submissions of a few dozen pages had been common in the early 1960s, a decade later the typical application for a new drug approval had soared to a hundred thousand pages. The testing costs of seeing a drug through to final approval, estimated at $3 to $4 million in the early 1960s, had soared to $50 to $70 million by the mid-1970s.[13] While the 1962 drug amendments specified that FDA should approve a new drug application within 180 days of submission, actual approval times by the early 1970s had stretched to almost three years for the average submission.[14] And the reality was even worse, because additional delays—often stretching to several years—were imposed by the FDA before authorizing the preliminary testing of drugs on human subjects (an essential step in securing ultimate approval).

The ultimate consequences for medical care were quite troubling. The rate at which new drugs came onto the American market slowed considerably between the mid 1960s and the mid-1970s. In some important fields, like the treatment of heart conditions, no new drugs at all were approved for more than a decade. Dozens of drugs approved for routine use in Western Europe remained long unavailable to American medicine. American drug companies began to transfer an increasingly large share of their testing and marketing operations to foreign countries, where they encountered less regulatory obstruction. Four times as many new drugs were pioneered in Great Britain during the 1970s as in the United States.[15]

The result was not merely a loss of profits or productivity or marginal therapeutic gains. In many cases, the loss could be measured in human lives. Medical researchers estimated, for example, that some "breakthrough" heart drugs of the 1970s, withheld from the American market by the FDA, might have saved up to twenty thousand lives a year, if available here as early as in Western Europe.[16] This was one of the more dramatic examples, but by no means an isolated or atypical one. Drugs for the treatment of neurological disorders and many other crippling or life-threatening conditions were also delayed for disturbingly long intervals in the 1970s.[17]

For a time, the FDA's performance principally aroused concern among a small group of medical and pharmacological specialists. By the late 1970s, this "drug lag" finally gained the sustained attention of a congressional subcommittee, chaired by Representative James Scheuer. Hearings of the subcommittee developed a good deal of evidence about the extent of the problem and publicized a number of outrageous cases of bureaucratic myopia and obstruction—like the heart drug intended for patients whose life expectancy might otherwise be limited to weeks or months that was withheld by the FDA because animal studies suggested it might prove carcinogenic if taken continuously by the same patient over several decades.[18] Scheuer's subcommittee, in turn, commissioned a careful three-year study of the FDA's drug approval process by the General Accounting Office, which documented sluggish management and misguided policy in considerable detail.[19] When the Reagan administration took charge in 1981, it promised, as part of its "regulatory reform" effort, to devote special attention to speeding up FDA drug approvals, at least for important new drugs; and it was warmly applauded for these good intentions by the Scheuer subcommittee.[20]

But in retrospect, it is hardly surprising that the FDA developed the policy bias that it did in this area, or that efforts to reform the agency proved frustratingly difficult. To begin with, it seems to be a natural human tendency to be more upset about direct actions that go awry—like mishaps with a new drug—than lost opportunities for improvement. This was certainly the way congressional committees read the public mood or the opportunities for commanding public attention during the 1960s and 1970s and to a large extent in the 1980s, as well. Various subcommittees, most notably the House subcommittee chaired by Representative H. L. Fountain, held periodic hearings to highlight this or that threat to public health from FDA negligence. Almost invariably the subcommittees posed as champions of the people against the reckless greed of the drug companies. Until the Scheuer hearings at the end of the 1970s, the FDA was never taken to task by a congressional committee for refusing to approve a valuable new drug.[21] Representative Fountain's subcommittee indeed continued its traditional pattern thereafter, calling immediate hearings in 1982, for example, to find out why the FDA approved a new drug ("oraflex") that subsequently was found to have fatal reactions in a few cases and had to be withdrawn from the market.[22] Throughout the 1980s, Representatives Ted Weiss (who succeeded to the chairmanship of the Fountain subcommittee) and Henry Waxman (chairing another powerful oversight subcommittee) continued to hold hearings berating the FDA for its laxness and coziness with industry. Staffers on both of these subcommittees denied that the "drug lag" had ever been a serious health issue, and both subcommittees continued to focus attention on the need for tighter controls on the drug industry.[23]

As a matter of fact, the drug industry itself did not fight very hard against the FDA's imposition of increasingly stringent controls on new drugs. At one hearing in the late 1970s, Representative Scheuer wondered whether the major drug companies were developing "an Uncle Tom attitude toward the FDA," giving in to its bureaucratic obstruction without struggle.[24] Under the 1962 drug law, applicants for a new drug approval were authorized to seek judicial relief if the FDA delayed a decision for more than 180 days. But instead of forcing speedier FDA decisions in this way, major drug companies meekly submitted to FDA demands for more testing or more documentation, allowing the approval process to stretch out for years and years.

Drug companies certainly had reason to fear that if pressed to a quick decision, the FDA would simply say no and reviewing courts would defer to the agency's "expert discretion." But there is also reason to question the incentives of the major drug companies to force speedups in the approval process. Delays in the approval of innovative new drugs served, after all, to protect the market share of already established drugs, cushioning the major companies against unsettling competition from newer products. In at least one celebrated case in the mid-1980s, the Pharmaceutical Manufacturers Association, the trade association of the major companies, urged the FDA to withhold approval for an extremely promising new drug for the treatment of heart disease.[25] The drug happened to be the product of a small, new firm specializing in the new field of bioengineering, and the firm happened not to be a member of the PMA. For some years previously, the PMA had also persuaded the FDA to require elaborate new drug approval proceedings for companies wishing to market exact copies of well-established products for which the patents had already expired.[26]

If there was a single, serious consumer or public interest not adequately represented in the atmosphere of FDA policy making in the 1960s and 1970s, then, it was surely the interest in speeding approval of valuable new drugs. Self-styled public interest champions filed no suits in this area, however. They did not even participate in the Scheuer hearings. Instead, working closely with the Waxman and Weiss subcommittees, they continued to agitate the need for tighter FDA controls. And on the whole, they were quite sympathetically received in the courts.

Old Drugs and Odd Categories

The 1938 drug law essentially established a licensing scheme for new drugs. If a drug was not already "generally recognized as safe," a manufacturer wishing to market the product had to submit a "new drug application" (NDA) and have the application approved by the FDA. The 1962 efficacy amendments did not change the underlying structure of this scheme, but considerably tightened the standards for approving NDAs. While urging the FDA to maintain very close scrutiny of all NDA applications, consumer advocates never launched direct litigation to challenge any particular NDA approval. But in this area, the FDA hardly needed to be pushed by litigation. Public interest suits focused instead on the FDA's handling of drugs already on the market. Here, too, though, it is highly questionable whether the FDA really needed to be pushed by litigation. The main effect of the litigation was to reinforce the FDA's own commitment to applying its strict new standards as broadly as possible.

Just as the licensing provisions of the 1938 law had exempted drugs already "generally recognized as safe," the 1962 drug amendments included a similar grandfather clause exempting drugs already "generally recognized as safe and effective," if they were not "covered by an NDA." At a minimum, this wording implied that drugs that had entered the market before 1938—before, that is, manufacturers had been required to submit NDAs—would still be exempted from licensing and testing requirements. But the drug industry read this provision as also exempting post-1938 products, if they had been in use for so long that they had come to be "generally recognized as safe and effective" by the medical community. The industry maintained that in such cases, even if a manufacturer had once submitted material for an NDA, the drug was no longer "covered" by the NDA because it was no longer in need of such special licensing approval. Drug companies also argued that the grandfather clause exempted "me-too" drugs—identical formulations of older drugs for which the patents had expired—because the manufacturers had never submitted separate NDAs for these non-"new" drugs.

From the outset, however, the FDA took the uncompromising position that the 1962 amendments must apply to *all* formulations that had ever been "covered by an NDA." It insisted on extending its new licensing authority—its authority to deny marketing approval to drugs not proved effective—to every product that had entered the market between 1938 and 1962. It was not even certain that the law permitted this expansive approach, much less that it was required by the 1962 amendments. In ensuing litigation, some lower courts actually upheld drug industry challenges to the FDA's assertion of renewed licensing authority over long established products. Eventually, the Supreme Court resolved all of the issues in favor of maximum jurisdiction for the FDA—though not until 1973.[27] In the meantime, the FDA had committed itself to an enormous undertaking. Simply in administrative terms, it was an enormous undertaking to reassess the efficacy of the more than four thousand separate drug products launched between 1938 and 1962. In an era in which the FDA was falling two to three years behind in processing NDAs for some two hundred new drugs each year, the retrospective efficacy review threatened to swamp the agency's capacities.

In its first approach to the problem, in 1964, the FDA simply asked drug manufacturers to supply it with evidence of effectiveness for all of their 1938–1962 products that they still wished to market. Along with obstructive lawsuits, this request brought an avalanche of paper. To help sort through the claims, the FDA signed an agreement in 1966 with the research arm of the National Academy of Sciences, the National Research Council (NAS-NRC). The NRC in turn recruited some two hundred medical experts, usually from academic institutions, and organized them into thirty separate panels to review different categories of drugs. Over the next two years, these panels submitted evaluative reports on more than 3,700 drug formulations and some 16,000 individual efficacy claims (because many drugs claimed to be effective for multiple uses). Even with this massive research assistance, however, the FDA itself was still left with the responsibility for making—and defending—its own decisions on each product. This undertaking seemed likely to be an enormous one, considering the already evident determination of manufacturers to fight FDA efforts to withdraw approval for established products.

The scale of the undertaking could have been dramatically reduced, however, if the FDA had adopted a more modest approach. Of the 3,700 drug formulations involved, only 7 percent were rated by NRC panels as "ineffective" for all of their therapeutic claims; overall, of the 16,000 therapeutic claims reviewed, still only 14 percent were rated "ineffective." But the agency refused to limit its attention to these drugs or these claims. For under the classification system worked out with the FDA in 1966, the NRC panels had classified only some 19 percent of these 16,000 claims as simply "effective." The vast bulk of the claims were rated somewhere between: "probably effective" (7.3 percent); "possibly effective" (34.9 percent); "effective, but . . ." [meaning that the dosage or combination of ingredients did not clearly add anything to smaller or simpler formulations] (24.0 percent).[28] While it might have limited its attention to the few thousand drug claims judged "ineffective," the FDA chose instead to take responsibility for all but the few thousand drug claims judged "effective," thus multiplying its task fivefold over what it might have been.

This decision was remarkable for several reasons. First, the FDA was required by law to offer manufacturers an opportunity to defend their claims in a formal administrative hearing before taking action against a drug already on the market. But the agency had only two hearing examiners in the late 1960s and a comparably small legal staff to defend the agency's proposed actions in formal hearings. If manufacturers demanded hearings for even a fraction of these thousands of disputed efficacy claims, the agency's procedural machinery would have been altogether overwhelmed. Yet manufacturers had every incentive to demand hearings and avail themselves of every procedural protection, because their products could normally stay on the market until the hearings were concluded, which might take months or years.

Even if the FDA could find some means to expand and so speed up its hearing procedures, though, it had to consider the likely reaction if it suddenly withdrew a very large portion of existing drugs from the American market. Massive cancellations of NDA approvals would provoke bitter protests not only from the drug industry but also from practicing physicians, suddenly deprived of accustomed pharmaceutical treatments. In these circumstances, there would be great pressure on Congress to alter or relax the 1962 drug law, to which the FDA was already quite committed. This result might have been averted, in turn, if drug companies had been given time to supply new evidence for the efficacy of disputed products. For most of the disputes reflected the failure of the companies to pursue carefully controlled efficacy tests in the past—when they had not been required to do so—and further testing could clearly save many of the claims. But such testing would have required a vast diversion of financial and medical resources, which would surely be better devoted to the development of new drugs. New drugs, after all, were generally better drugs (which is why profit-oriented drug companies invested the time and effort in developing them) and could be expected to stay on the market much longer than these disputed pre-1962 drugs.

Nevertheless the FDA still insisted that it must hold pre-1962 drugs to the highest standards of evidence for efficacy and order their withdrawal from the market when they could not meet these standards. In a 1970 *Federal Register* notice codifying its stringent efficacy testing standards, the FDA claimed that it simply had no choice in the matter: "Congress has provided that drugs introduced before 1962 shall meet the same standards of proof of efficacy as are applicable to newly developed drugs. A different and lesser standard of effectiveness is impermissible legally."[29]

This claim was not strictly true. To begin with, the statutory language was sufficiently ambiguous that, at the time this notice was issued, federal courts were still divided on the extent of the FDA's jurisdiction over pre-1962 drugs. More importantly, the statutory language was quite vague about "standards of proof of efficacy," and it was the FDA, not Congress, that read the provision for "adequate and well-controlled investigations" to require the elaborate, costly, and time-consuming testing protocols required by the FDA by the end of the 1960s. Finally and perhaps most tellingly, the FDA itself did not, in practice, always require pre-1962 drugs to meet "the same standards of proof of efficacy as are applicable to newly developed drugs."

The same *Federal Register* notice, for example, explained that the FDA would not "require new trials of drugs . . . evaluated by the NAS-NRC as effective." But it is clear that NRC panels did not reserve their "effective" ratings for drugs that could meet the same standards of proof of efficacy as the FDA had made applicable to new drugs. When the panels were organized they were instructed to consider data available in the scientific literature, along with further data supplied by the FDA and the manufacturers. But they were also advised that "The informed judgment and experience of the members of the panels is valid evidence contributory to the final decision on the efficacy of a drug." "In some cases," according to William Wardell, "the panels obviously accepted drugs as effective on this basis and on this basis alone. Antibiotics experts, for instance, would be entitled to few authoritative statements if they were to limit themselves to the data generated by modern controlled trials. Such trials have not been traditional in infectious disease research."[30] Even the final report of the NAS-NRC project conceded that different panels had applied differing standards in developing their ratings. In later years, the FDA itself upgraded the lower ratings of many drugs in the study to "effective" without demanding the same standards of proof of efficacy as it required for new drugs.[31]

Why, then, did the FDA continue to maintain, at least in its formal pronouncements, that it had no choice about the standards to apply? The central reason was that the agency did not want to acknowledge any significant degree of discretion in the standards it applied to drug approvals, because it feared that such an acknowledgement would invite pressure to make exceptions from its general standards. And it was particularly anxious to maintain its general standards as fixed obligations by the early 1970s, as its very stringent testing requirements began to encounter serious criticism from medical researchers. As an official in the FDA General Counsel's Office put it, "As soon as we admitted we could apply a different standard in one case, we'd have people demanding the same exemption for their own favorite product."[32] The agency faced pressure and made exceptions, anyway. But it continued to pretend that it had no significant discretion on the substance of policy.

What the agency finally did to accommodate such severe standards for older drugs was simply to delay their implementation. At the outset, however, when the first NRC panel reports were being delivered to the FDA in the spring of 1968, the agency announced that it would proceed expeditiously. Once it had assessed the reports, it would give manufacturers one year to provide further evidence of effectiveness for drugs rated "probably effective" but only six months for drugs rated "possibly effective" and only thirty days for drugs rated "ineffective" or "effective, but." If adequate further evidence were not forthcoming in these intervals, the agency would send the manufacturer a formal "notice of opportunity for hearing" (NOH) and immediately proceed to withdraw approval for the drug if no hearing was requested.

When the agency's first efforts to apply these rules made it clear that manufacturers would exploit hearing procedures to create maximum delay, the FDA announced in 1969 that it would not allow a hearing unless the manufacturer could show that it had some new evidence with which to challenge the agency's assessment. This approach was quickly challenged by drug companies as a violation of due process. It was ultimately confirmed by the Supreme Court, though the Court insisted on some extra due process safeguards designed to make such hearing denials more difficult.[33] In the meantime, the FDA proceeded rather slowly in assessing and implementing the NRC recommendations. By the end of 1970, it had still failed to complete initial assessments for more than half of the reports it had received from the panels.

It was at this point that the agency received its first public interest challenge in the courts, a suit demanding prompt action against non-"effective" pre-1962 drugs. The suit was filed in 1970, officially in the name of the American Public Health Association (APHA).[34] But it was actually engineered by the then recently formed Center for Law and Social Policy, whose director, Charles Halperin, had testified to a congressional committee in 1970 that his group sought to counter the one-sided pressures of regulated businesses on regulatory agencies—regarding which, he claimed, "Certainly there is no worse example than the Food and Drug Administration, an agency that has steady pressure from the major drug companies and virtually no countervailing pressure from any other interests in society."[35] Animated by this remarkably one-sided view of the political climate of drug regulation, the suit was fought to a successful judgment in the U.S. District Court in Washington in the summer of 1972.

Two things are most striking about the outcome. The first is the sloppiness of Judge William Bryant's opinion, explaining his ruling for the plaintiffs. The judge felt it appropriate to mention a recent article in the *Washington Post*—on an unrelated matter—that "dramatically evidenced [sic] . . . the type of intolerable procrastination" he thought he saw in this case.[36] Yet he gave no figures at all to indicate how much of the FDA's retrospective drug review was still to be completed at the time of his decision, which was ostensibly the whole point of the case. And he did not bother to consider any of the actual policy difficulties in ordering the immediate withdrawal of hundreds of widely used drugs. Instead, his opinion depicted the entire case as if it were a simple confrontation between corporate profits and consumer interests. The opinion made no effort to explain why the nominal plaintiffs in this case should have standing to speak for all consumers. It did not even explain who the nominal plaintiffs were. And on the central point in dispute, the opinion misquoted the relevant statutory provision to reach the erroneous and irrelevant conclusion that "the Secretary [of HEW] *must* begin procedures to withdraw a drug when he concludes there is no substantial evidence of efficacy."[37] The delays at issue in this case followed staff assessments of NRC reports, which could not be taken as "conclusions" of "the Secretary" (or of his delegate, the FDA Commissioner).

The second thing that is striking about this decision is that, with all its defects, it was not appealed by the government. Judge Bryant's August 1972 opinion, while using quite uncompromising language about the FDA's obligations under the law, had not imposed any specific directives for the agency's future conduct but instead appealed to "the parties" to present him with proposed remedial orders. Instead of appealing the case, the FDA simply drafted a court order it thought it could accommodate and then persuaded the public interest lawyers to accept it.[38] In practice, this order negated the essential premise of Judge Bryant's opinion, for it provided for a phased plan of operations, allowing the FDA up to four more years to take action on many of the drugs involved. The order also provided a catch-all exemption to defer action on "medically necessary drugs," which the FDA was left to designate at its own discretion. With both the plaintiffs and the government supporting this order, Judge Bryant endorsed it without any changes.[39]

In general terms, then, the *APHA* case confirmed what the FDA was actually quite eager to have confirmed—that it was *obliged* to move forward with the review of all drugs rated less than "effective" by the NRC panels. And the case did so a year before the Supreme Court confirmed (in suits brought by manufacturers) that the agency actually did have the legal authority to make such reviews. At the same time, the order committed the agency to very little that it was not already planning to do.

As it turned out, moreover, many of the commitments the FDA made in order to settle this lawsuit—agreeing to process various categories of drugs within specified deadlines—it did not keep. After the Center for Law and Social Policy lost interest in the case, it was reactivated in 1979 by Ralph Nader's Public Citizen. The Nader lawyers had no difficulty demonstrating that the FDA had failed to act as it had promised, as some five hundred drugs (more than a quarter of those covered by the 1972 order) still remained to be reclassified or withdrawn from the market. The FDA accordingly negotiated a new settlement, approved by the court in 1980, promising a phased completion of the remaining efficacy reviews over the next four years.[40] Then it failed, in turn, to live up to this set of commitments. Several dozen drugs remained to be acted upon at the end of 1988, and the Nader lawyers threatened further litigation—though this course seemed unlikely, in view of the dwindling number of products remaining and the poor results achieved through past prodding in the courts.[41]

The pressure of the litigation probably did help to speed up the review process by securing additional resources for it within the FDA.[42] It can certainly be questioned, though, whether this was a sensible priority at a time when the agency was falling farther and farther behind in the processing of NDAs for genuinely new drugs, many of which promised important therapeutic gains. Moreover, by pressing the FDA to move more quickly, the litigation also put pressure on drug companies to do more rapid testing of old products, which may have slowed the development of new products.

The compensating benefit for consumers was not particularly great. Some three-quarters of the drugs involved were finally reclassified as "effective," though in many cases the manufacturers were obliged to relabel the products to settle disputes about particular indicated uses.[43] The majority of the drugs finally suppressed by the FDA were not "ineffective" but rather drugs rated "effective, but" by the NRC panels, meaning that questions were raised about the dosages or the combinations of ingredients involved. In many cases, manufacturers agreed that the products should be removed from the market because they offered no clear compensating benefits, relative to newer products, for their particular associated hazards.[44] But even in this regard the balancing of risk and gain was rarely clear-cut. The FDA initially concentrated on what it regarded as the most clear-cut cases, and by November 1970 had taken action on 369 such drugs. When Britain's Committee on the Safety of Medicines (the British counterpart to the FDA) reviewed this list of suppressed products and the official rationales for their withdrawal in the United States, it decided not to suppress even a single one of these drugs in Britain.[45]

Pursuing Larger Efforts for Smaller Hazards

Perhaps the main significance of this litigation, however, was to reinforce the FDA's entrenched operating perspective on testing standards for new drugs. The FDA had insisted all along that it could not deviate from its very stringent testing standards, even for long established and widely used products; and the APHA litigation insisted that the agency must hold to this course. It is difficult to say how much it may have helped to entrench the FDA's determination to maintain very stringent standards in reviewing new drugs. But it is certain that the FDA's inclinations to stringency remained unchanged. A number of "breakthrough" drugs were approved with record speed in the early 1980s—showing what could be done—but the mean approval time for NDAs actually increased from 34.5 months in 1980 to 39.9 months in 1984. Efforts to alter established operating routines within the agency were accompanied by a considerable number of resignations and retirements from senior career officials, which provoked charges that the agency was being overly politicized.[46] In this climate, promised procedural reforms in the new drug approval process were continually deferred. Major procedural reforms promised by Reagan officials in the early 1980s were not actually implemented until 1987, and long-time observers of the agency remained skeptical of their effectiveness, even then.[47]

There are certainly risks in an overly accommodating stance regarding approval of new drugs, as there are risks in excessive stringency. But efforts to strike a better balance were bitterly denounced by consumer advocates, who insisted that corporate profits were the sole consideration in these efforts. So, for example, Dr. Sidney Wolfe of Ralph Nader's Health Research Group insisted that FDA Commissioner Frank Young was making the FDA into "a plaything for industry" instead of "a law enforcement agency." Then he drew the inevitable conclusion that "Ronald Reagan's FDA cares more" about drug company profits than "it cares about the lives and health of the citizens it is supposed to protect."[48] In fact, before coming to the FDA Young had served as dean of the University of Rochester Medical School, which became a center for research on the problem of "drug lag" in American medicine during the 1970s. He was in no way plausibly described as a mere drug industry patsy.

The most charitable interpretation of such strident rhetoric is that consumer advocates see it as a necessary counterweight to the pressures of the drug industry, which certainly does deploy considerable lobbying resources in Washington. It might be argued, in other words, that the more the FDA relaxes its controls for good purposes, the more it will be open to pressure to compromise its standards for bad purposes; and that the best way to head off this risk is by decrying, with moralistic fervor, any possible signs of reduced stringency that emerge to public view. Of course, the obvious risk in this strategy it is that it may push the FDA farther along the path of unreasonable restrictiveness. Private advocacy groups certainly cannot be restrained from adopting the political strategy they deem most appropriate or most convenient. Still, it is hard to see why courts should be helping to prop up such a dubious course.

In fact, courts have enabled public interest advocacy groups to pursue their strategy even in areas quite remote from genuine safety issues. The pattern is most evident in relation to FDA regulation of food and cosmetics. But before turning to those cases, it is worth noticing the manner in which Ralph Nader's Public Citizen replayed the litigation over the retrospective drug efficacy review in a parallel round of wrangling over the FDA's review of "over-the-counter" (OTC) drugs.

Over-the-counter drugs are products that can be purchased by consumers without a doctor's prescription. They are products, in other words, that the consumer may prescribe for himself based on his own "diagnosis" of what is wrong. Most of the conditions they seek to treat—head colds, hemorrhoids, indigestion, itchy rashes, and so on—are indeed rather readily diagnosed by those who suffer from them. By the same token, the ordinary consumer would seem to be rather well situated to judge whether these self-prescribed products are truly effective. These products are allowed to be sold OTC, however, because their active ingredients are considered so relatively harmless that consumers will be taking little risk in employing them for self-treatment, whether or not the chosen product is the most appropriate treatment.[49]

In 1972, with its efficacy review of prescription drugs already well along, the FDA announced a still more ambitious program to review the efficacy of OTC products. Here it faced not several thousand but several hundred thousand individual products. For the bulk of these products, manufacturers had never applied for NDA approval. Most OTC products were slight variations on long established formulas (often in use long before 1938), and the manufacturers accordingly assumed that they were "generally recognized as safe and effective." By invoking the branding provisions of the original Food and Drugs Act of 1906, the FDA could still prosecute a manufacturer for making false or misleading efficacy claims about a particular product. But if it sought to bring a misbranding suit, the FDA was required by law to bear the burden of proof in making its case. And because of its limited resources, the agency could not possibly hope to prepare such cases for tens of thousands of separate enforcement actions.

To make its review of OTC drugs administratively feasible, therefore, the FDA determined not to proceed product by product as it had with pre-1962 prescription drugs. Instead, it arranged for panels of medical experts to survey the active ingredients and the basic chemical formulas employed in several dozen categories of products (antacids, decongestants, cough suppressants, and the like) and then to prepare general reports or monographs distinguishing effective from ineffective (or not yet proved to be effective) ingredient formulas within each category. The FDA then proposed to assess and refine these monographs and finally promulgate them as binding rules, which would specify permissible labeling standards along with permissible formulation standards.[50] When any OTC product did not conform to these rules or marketing "conditions," the FDA then proposed to treat its manufacturer as per se in violation of the original drug law. The agency asserted, that is, that if it took court action against such a violator, it would be sufficient to prove that the manufacturer had not conformed to the required conditions, without having to make a separate case against the particular product. In effect, the FDA's OTC review proposed to transform a mixed prosecutorial and licensing enforcement scheme into a general rule making regulatory system—the focus of which would now shift from safety concerns to concerns about consumer value.

Few of these products posed any real safety risk unless grossly misused, and the FDA had no means to control gross misuse by individual consumers. If the expert panels did raise serious safety questions about individual products, the FDA took direct action to suppress the product (or reclassify it as requiring a prescription) without waiting for the promulgation of the final monograph setting out marketing conditions for the entire relevant category of products.[51] For the most part, then, the rationale for suppressing ineffective OTC products would have to stress protecting consumers against wasting their money, not against risking their health. Consumers convinced of the efficacy of particular products from their own experience might not even be grateful for this degree of protection.

Despite the marginal value of the OTC review, consumer advocacy groups returned repeatedly to court to force the FDA to pursue this review more speedily and more rigorously. The essential difficulty from the outset was the rigor imposed by the expert panels. Most OTC producers had readily cooperated with the program at the outset; and the Proprietary Association, the trade association of major OTC producers, even praised the program for promising to enhance consumer confidence. The major producers had obvious reasons to welcome a program to standardize product quality in a field in which most producers did not actually belong to the industry trade association or subscribe to its guidelines.[52] To the surprise and chagrin of the major manufacturers, however, the expert panels ended up classifying between one-quarter and one-third of ingredient formulas in Category III, meaning that the reviewers found insufficient evidence to support an efficacy claim, though they were not prepared to declare the formula "ineffective." In effect, the expert panels often applied the same standards for proof of efficacy for OTC preparations as for prescription drugs. Then the FDA rule drafters became much more insistent on labeling limitations than the major manufacturers had expected.[53]

As the first monograph moved toward final adoption, the FDA received so many requests for exceptions, clarifications, and modifications that the agency amended its rules. It announced in 1977 that any product still classified in Category III in the final monograph could continue to be marketed, if the manufacturer requested extra time to pursue scientific studies to demonstrate the product's effectiveness.[54] In effect, the FDA was bidding for voluntary cooperation with an ambitious program it was not at all anxious to pursue through the courts.

The Health Research Group of Ralph Nader's Public Citizen went after this compromise as soon as it was announced. The subsequent proceedings did not exactly elicit models of judicial craftsmanship. At the outset, D.C. District Judge John Sirica fastidiously denied standing to the Health Research Group itself—on the grounds that it could not fairly represent nonvoting members of Public Citizen—but then immediately allowed the suit to be reactivated as a suit on behalf of three "consumers of various OTC drugs" who just happened to want Public Citizen attorneys to represent them in "their own" suit.[55] The subsequent opinion in the case made no effort to explain why the Health Research Group could not be trusted to represent ideological sympathizers but these three individual consumers *could* be trusted to represent all other consumers in America. Judge Sirica then ruled that consumers had been wronged by the FDA rule authorizing the continued marketing of Category III OTC products; but they could not demand that the FDA take action against these products because the agency must retain prosecutorial discretion. The challenged rule might make "eminently good sense" as a means to "encourage continued testing of safe drugs which are capable of being shown effective," the judge conceded, and overturning the rule might "simply permit the agency to accomplish informally and indirectly what it cannot accomplish in a formal order. But that is the system Congress created."[56]

Distortions of Practice

Not at all displeased at having its own program attributed to Congress, the FDA did not appeal. It simply revised its regulations to provide that products not classified as acceptable could not be lawfully marketed after a final monograph was issued—but henceforth no final monograph would be issued for at least twelve months following the publication of a "tentative final monograph" to assure adequate time for further testing and reporting efforts by manufacturers. Even this assurance was somewhat academic for most products: two years after Judge Sirica's ruling, the FDA had not yet issued even tentative monographs for some 90 percent of the product categories for which monographs had been promised.[57] The Nader lawyers accordingly returned to court in 1981 to protest both the twelve-month official delay provision and the slow pace of the overall program.

This time their suit was rejected in its entirety by a different district judge,[58] so plaintiff Cutler (a self-avowed user of "OTC cold and headache drugs") appealed to the D.C. Court of Appeals. After hearing oral arguments in 1983, that court proceeded to sit on the case for almost five full years—despite repeated pleas from both Justice Department and Nader lawyers for a decision. Perhaps the appellate judges were simply waiting to see how much progress the FDA would actually make. (They do not seem to have been watching the FDA too closely, however, for the opinion they finally rendered continued to style the suit as an action against an FDA commissioner who had actually resigned his position a full three years earlier.)[59] Without offering any apology or explanation for its own remarkable delay in deciding this case, the D.C. Court of Appeals finally handed down a decision in the autumn of 1987, and directed the district court to consider carefully whether the FDA might be guilty of "unreasonable delay" in the processing of twenty-eight complex rule making procedures.[60]

The D.C. Court of Appeals rebuked the district judge for characterizing the OTC review as "voluntary," though it never explained what statutory enactment actually required the FDA to undertake this enormous project. Apart from "the law," however, the appellate judges seemed quite unsure about the policy logic of proceeding at one pace or another. The court acknowledged that the official policy of delaying final monographs for at least one year was not actually unlawful, and that "as an agency with limited resources, FDA reasonably may assign enforcement of a statutory requirement designed to prevent unnecessary consumer expense to a lower priority than that accorded ... threats to human life." But then the same opinion expressly directed the district court to take account of the "legal" standard that "[d]elays ... are less tolerable when human lives are at stake"[61]—suggesting that the Court of Appeals thought life or death questions might, after all, be at stake in the FDA's review of hemorrhoid remedies and other OTC products.

The Nader lawyers immediately proceeded to arrange a cross-examination of top FDA managers in a private deposition, which "discovered" the fact that the agency was only devoting some twenty-five man-years of effort to this program each year, or barely one-fifth of the internal resources devoted to the prescription drug review at a seemingly comparable stage of its operation.[62] Whether the district court would finally decide that the OTC drug review should have received more manpower and attention because it was more than one-fifth as important (or more than one-fifth as demanding) remained to be seen at the end of 1988.

Two questions of considerable interest were entirely neglected in the "discovery" proceedings by the Nader lawyers, however. The first was the amount of legal manpower that the FDA had to devote to preparing briefs and documentation for this litigation. This was an interesting question because, according to officials in the general counsel's office, legal resource limitations imposed delays in many areas, even in the OTC review. It also prevented the agency from pursuing as many enforcement actions against unsafe manufacturing or marketing practices as it would have liked.[63] Ironically, the considerable falloff in such actions during the 1980s had earlier been a major theme of complaint from Public Citizen's Health Research Group.[64]

Perhaps the more interesting question—one frequently raised by OTC manufacturers in the 1980s—was why the FDA insisted on running the OTC review through normal review channels in its Center for Drugs and why the agency refused to consider industry proposals to delegate more decisional authority to a separate division for OTC products. The effect of this choice was to divert resources from new drug approvals while simultaneously slowing the pace of the OTC review. It also implied that efficacy questions about OTC products should be treated with the seriousness of safety questions about new prescription drugs—but this seems to have been the point.[65]

Pursuing the *de minimis* in Food and Cosmetics Regulation

Just as with drug regulation, the FDA's regulatory authority over food and cosmetics has been continually expanded by successive statutory additions and amendments. In contrast to drug regulation, however, statutory controls in these other areas make no reference to the effectiveness or value of food or cosmetic products. This distinction no doubt reflects the general assumption that consumers should be left to judge the value of such products for themselves. The exclusive legislative focus on "safety" in these areas has tended to encourage a particularly restrictive regulatory approach, especially in recent decades.

Despite this inherent bias, the legislative framework in this area does not actually provide for a consistent system of safety controls. Rather, the current statutory scheme has been well described by a leading scholar as "a patchwork of divergent . . . often offhand, legislative policies which invite inconsistent treatment of comparable risks."[66] Most food additives (and cosmetic coloring agents) are subject to particularly tight control, for example, while non-"added" food constituents (and noncoloring agents in cosmetics) are subject to much more casual or accommodating control standards and procedures. The differences are further complicated by the fact that statutory language leaves much ambiguity regarding the boundary lines of different categories (such as when a substance should be considered "added") and the operation of different enforcement procedures. All of these factors have helped to make regulatory law in this area a particularly arcane legal speciality.

The most celebrated and controversial provision in this scheme is the so-called "Delaney clause" (after its initial sponsor, Representative James Delaney), which prohibits the use of any food additive "if it is found to induce cancer when ingested by man or animal, or if it is found, after tests which are appropriate for the evaluation of the safety of food additives, to induce cancer in man or animal." The Delaney clause was first adopted as an amendment from the floor to the Food Additives Amendment of 1958, which strengthened the FDA's licensing control over certain kinds of food additives (while introducing a new set of ambiguous distinctions by exempting substances already "sanctioned" for food use before 1958 and substances "generally recognized as safe by qualified experts").[67] Very similar Delaney clause provisions were then incorporated into the 1960 Color Additives Amendments[68] and the 1968 Animal Drug Amendments,[69] each of which established tighter FDA controls in specialized areas, but subject to further ambiguous qualifications and exceptions.

Though relatively uncontroversial when initially adopted, these Delaney provisions ultimately dragged the FDA into a good deal of conflict. The most heated public controversy was unloosed on the agency—and on Congress—in 1977, when the FDA invoked the original Delaney clause in support of its decision to ban saccharine (a widely used, low calorie sweetener, which for most dieters was at the time the main available alternative to sugar). There was so much public outcry against the decision that Congress, in one of the rare instances of direct legislative intervention in the regulatory process, enacted an appropriations rider prohibiting the FDA from implementing the saccharine ban. Instead of revising the Delaney language or reshaping the statutory framework for safety regulation in this area, however, Congress simply commissioned "studies" of the advisability of statutory changes.[70]

Although various official studies did urge reconsideration of the statutory framework in this area, Congress took no direct action at all over the next decade, beyond ritually reextending its anomalous stay of the saccharine ban. The underlying difficulty seemed to be congressional reluctance to go on record on behalf of a more relaxed approach to cancer. But there was also much disagreement about what precise changes to make. Many consumer and public interest advocates, in fact, opposed any change in the original Delaney formulas, insisting that the zero-risk policy was a valuable ideal for public policy and a necessary safeguard against industry pressures to "gamble with public health."[71]

Even before the saccharine controversy, however, the FDA was beginning to realize that changing circumstances made a literal approach to the Delaney provisions no longer a tenable policy. In the first place, extensive testing through the 1960s and 1970s had turned up more and more suspected carcinogens, until cancer inducing substances had come to seem ubiquitous. In 1958, only four human carcinogens had been firmly identified. By 1978 laboratory studies—generally involving the forced feeding of rats or mice with vastly inflated dosages of suspected substances—had identified some five hundred substances as animal carcinogens and, by a literal reading, the Delaney clause indicated that all must equally be considered human carcinogens. In the same two decades, moreover, the sensitivity of analytical detection techniques increased at an even more dramatic rate. As the power to detect minute impurities increased, allowing analysts by the late 1970s to find traces one million times smaller than the smallest traces detectable in the late 1950s, the challenge of removing "all traces" of carcinogens from the food supply increased accordingly.[72]

Under the impact of these developments, other federal agencies with responsibility for regulating carcinogenic hazards, most notably the Environmental Protection Agency and the Occupational Safety and Health Administration, had already by the mid-1970s started to develop methods for quantitative risk assessment, in recognition that zero-risk approaches in this area would not be feasible. Despite the seemingly unyielding language of the Delaney provisions, the FDA had several powerful reasons to follow in their path. First, a literal approach to the Delaney provisions would seem to preclude the use of a disturbingly large range of valuable food additives—including Vitamin D, Vitamin C, proteins, and many other essential nutrients found to induce cancer in laboratory animals fed grotesquely exaggerated dosages. The net result of a literal enforcement approach to the Delaney provisions would not assure absolute safety, then, but in many instances could significantly increase the risk of other dietary hazards (such as vitamin or protein insufficiencies) in exchange for minuscule reductions in already minuscule (and possibly nonexistent) cancer risks.[73] Second, if the FDA demanded the recall of too many familiar consumer products under a literal reading of the Delaney provisions, it risked encouraging an unwarranted public hysteria about the scale of the cancer menace, or a despairing apathy as people came to think that "everything causes cancer"; neither of these outcomes would be likely to promote sound health habits.[74]

Even when the suppression of additives (like coloring agents) might pose no risk to health, it was certain to raise costs for consumers in many instances. This concern could not be considered negligible, in view of the effort expended on programs like the OTC review for the purpose of saving unwarranted consumer expense; and considering the altogether meaningless safety gains for some applications of the Delaney provisions, *any* cost to consumers would be hard to describe as warranted. In many other cases, of course, the cancer risk might seem significant enough to warrant stringent controls, even if such controls would raise costs to consumers, limit the availability of essential nutrients, or exacerbate public anxieties. A final reason for avoiding a literal approach to the Delaney provisions was that, as long as the agency pretended to be bound by this literal reading, it would as a practical matter have to seek increasingly devious means to avoid their application, making overall policy in this area much more ad hoc and inconsistent than it needed to be.

The FDA did, in fact, pursue inconsistent approaches to the various Delaney provisions in the course of the 1970s. In dealing with carcinogenic animal drugs, for example, the agency managed to avoid invoking the relevant Delaney provision against a widely used cattle drug in 1973, despite clear evidence of its carcinogenic properties. Instead, the FDA invoked a statutory exemption allowing the use of hazardous substances in animal feed if no residue of the substance would remain in the animal parts destined for human consumption. To ensure that this exemption could be employed, the FDA deliberately decided not to require that meat testing use the most powerful detection techniques then available. Instead, it merely required the use of detection techniques that were powerful enough to detect the smallest remaining residues that the FDA judged to be potentially carcinogenic in human consumption, allowing smaller traces of residue to remain officially undetected and hence unregulated.[75]

In other cases the FDA took a much more inflexible approach, so inflexible that it finally encountered judicial resistance to its position. In 1977, to cite the leading example, the agency sought to ban the sale of beverages in plastic bottles on the ground that minuscule but still detectable traces of acrylonitrile (a component of plastic bottles recently discovered to have carcinogenic properties) would inevitably "migrate" from the bottle to become an "added" ingredient of the beverage. When the Monsanto Company appealed this ruling to the D.C. Court of Appeals, the Court refused to allow the ban to go into effect until the FDA could demonstrate some actual health risks from such microscopic traces of acrylonitrile "additives." Some applications of statutory language, the court maintained in its 1979 decision, are so utterly trivial (or *de minimis*) that they cannot reasonably be ascribed to the intention of Congress, whatever the literal words of a statute.[76] Under this prompting, the FDA gave up its plan to ban the use of plastic bottles.

Nonetheless, the FDA still remained very cautious about openly asserting an authority to disregard *de minimis* cancer risks under the Delaney provisions. The *Monsanto* decision, like earlier evasions, focused on whether a carcinogenic substance was meaningfully present at all, thereby skirting the ultimate question of whether the substance was meaningfully carcinogenic. The latter question was one the agency was arguably prohibited from raising because, under the most literal reading of the Delaney provisions, any evidence at all that a substance induces cancer in animals would be sufficient to trigger the statutory prohibitions. When it was unwilling to evade this problem by relying on deliberately less sensitive detection methods, the FDA looked for other means of postponing ultimate decisions on the force of the Delaney provisions.

So, for example, in 1983 the agency developed another evasion when it ruled that a particular color additive should not be prohibited under the Delaney clause of the Color Additives Amendment, because only a constituent element of this dye was found to induce cancer in animals but not the coloring formula as a whole. This ruling was upheld when challenged in federal court.[77] Other dodges—delaying action on other color additives pending further study, avoiding the promulgation of formal standards on minute traces of carcinogenic mold residues on corn in favor of informal "action levels" (twenty parts per billion)—brought further rounds of public interest litigation. But this litigation, focusing on procedural issues for the most part, brought no conclusive results.[78]

In fact, important officials within the FDA were eager to avoid an open embrace of a *de minimis* exception to the Delaney provisions on several grounds. First, there seem to have been lingering reservations among FDA scientists about the techniques of quantitative risk assessment for carcinogens, even though the agency had itself employed such techniques in other contexts. Any effort to extrapolate human risks from experiments with laboratory animals must make a great many disputable assumptions about the potency of carcinogens revealed in animal studies and the way these substances would affect human beings at various dosage levels. Risk assessment in this area is thus inevitably somewhat conjectural. The principal justification for such an approach is that, by adopting extremely conservative assumptions at each stage of such an analysis, scientists can at least project a rough estimate of the order of magnitude of a particular risk in order to facilitate rough comparisons with other risks. In practice, therefore, calculated risks of more than one in one million are often regarded, in regulatory decision making, not as predictions that one person in every million will contract cancer under the stated level of exposure but that, in all likelihood, no one will. While this technique has come to be widely employed by researchers, it remains true—as other specialists have emphasized—that scientific investigation has not determined that there is a threshold of exposure to proved carcinogens below which carcinogenic effects simply *cannot* occur.[79]

This objection might seem to be altogether academic in view of the fact that the FDA had already begun to adopt carcinogenic risk assessments in other contexts. But the FDA had never committed itself to a general definition of *de minimis* risk, and there was no consensus among FDA officials on where it should be set. By continuing to rely on indirect or informal approaches, some officials concluded, the agency would preserve more discretion on such matters. Perhaps the ultimate reason for caution was expressed by the director of the FDA's Bureau of Foods in a 1983 internal memorandum: "a decision to adopt a [direct] *de minimis* exception to Delaney would require changing an interpretation that is 25 years old. Furthermore, an approval would be seen as a political decision that would likely be challenged. A successful challenge *would be extremely embarrassing and could also threaten our related policies*" (emphasis added).[80]

But top officials of the FDA were continually prodded by officials in the Office of Management and Budget, by an interagency risk management group, and by several trade organizations to reconsider their official no-risk approach to the Delaney provisions, and after years of hesitation the FDA finally acknowledged its authority to make *de minimis* exceptions in cases otherwise directly covered by Delaney provisions. In December 1985, the FDA approved the continued use of methylene chloride to decaffeinate coffee, in spite of the fact that methylene chloride had recently been identified as an animal carcinogen and some residue of this substance would remain in the coffee. At the same time, the agency acknowledged the carcinogenic properties of methylene chloride by banning its use in hair spray, where it calculated the cancer risk of exposure at somewhat larger than one in one million, hence considerably greater than the risk presented by decaffeinated coffee.[81] Six months later the FDA took the somewhat bolder step of authorizing the continued use of two coloring additives used in cosmetics, when both dyes had been identified as animal carcinogens in laboratory tests and neither could be excused as merely trace elements in cosmetic products.

As expected, both sets of decisions were promptly challenged by Public Citizen. In the meantime, the agency's decisions on the coloring additives were subject to intensive scrutiny by Representative Weiss's subcommittee, which raked over the evidence of internal disagreement on this policy within the agency and within the Reagan administration generally, and then produced a scathing report accusing the FDA of disregarding its duty under the law—an openly partisan report, from which thirteen of the fifteen Republican members of the committee dissented.[82] For some reason, the D.C. Court of Appeals delayed making a decision on the earlier methylene chloride suit but did hand down a decision on the cosmetic dyes within weeks after the publication of the critical House report. And like the House report, the Court of Appeals concluded that the FDA had violated the law in approving the use of these carcinogenic dyes.[83]

Unlike the House report, however, the court did not conceal the tiny level of the risk presented by these dyes, calculated at one in nine million for one and one in nineteen billion for the other. To put these risks in perspective, the court offered two examples of carcinogenic risks calculated at one in one million. One was the risk posed by eating one peanut every 250 days, with the degree of carcinogenic impurities (from naturally occurring molds) tolerated by FDA policy in this area. The other was the risk involved in spending one day each year in the city of Denver—with its higher elevation and consequently greater exposure to potentially carcinogenic cosmic radiation—rather than in the District of Columbia. The first dye approved by the FDA, as the court noted, was calculated to be nine times less risky than these very trivial risks, and the other was calculated to be nineteen thousand times less risky.

Without questioning the validity of these estimates, the court nonetheless insisted that Congress had not authorized the FDA to consider such risk assessments and accordingly ruled that the FDA must impose a total ban on the use of these dyes in cosmetic (and food) products. The court did not even try to defend this decision in policy terms, but simply insisted—like the Democratic majority on the House Government Operations Committee the month before—that this result was inescapably required by the Delaney clause of the 1960 Color Additives Amendment. Before the New Deal, federal courts would surely have questioned whether Congress had the constitutional power to prohibit multimillion dollar business ventures for no other reason than that they posed a one in nineteen billion risk of inducing cancer. But the D.C. Court of Appeals simply took it for granted that once the will of Congress is determined, no result is too arbitrary or absurd to question.

This ruling may appear to be the reductio ad absurdum of contemporary administrative law, in which Congress is treated like some ancient oriental potentate, whose orders must be followed without question, whether they are rational or not, whether they are seriously intended or not. In fact, the case was handled in highly legalistic terms. The public interest plaintiffs in the case treated the issue in these terms, declining to challenge the validity of the FDA's risk estimates and resting their whole argument on technical legal grounds. At least two very knowledgeable lawyers (both of whom had served as general counsel for the FDA in the 1970s) had published articles over the previous two years arguing that the Delaney clause would compel this result, however inappropriate it might appear in policy terms.[84] Like most such abstract legal arguments, this one had a perfectly plausible legal counterargument; and a powerful defense of the FDA's action was indeed submitted on behalf of the cosmetics industry in this case by another former FDA general counsel, who has since come to be widely acknowledged as one of the leading scholars of food and drug law.[85] But the Court of Appeals chose to discount these arguments and maintain that it simply had no choice.

The surface legalism of this whole episode is undoubtedly misleading, however. Even the Court of Appeals was not entirely indifferent to the consequences of its insistence on "the law." The court did acknowledge the danger that an equally literal application of the Delaney clause in other contexts might restrict access to essential nutrients and pose other disturbing risks for public health. But the court consoled itself with the vague suggestion that this decision, because it dealt with the Delaney clause in the Color Additives Amendment, did not necessarily "foreordain" a similarly restrictive approach to the parallel language in the Delaney clause of the Food Additives Amendment. And if dangerous consequences did ensue, "we suppose that . . . Congress would respond."[86] Perhaps the court actually hoped that its decision in this case would encourage congressional reconsideration of the Delaney provisions, as had been urged by many studies since the controversy over the saccharine ban a decade earlier.

If this was the court's aim, however, it did not seem likely to succeed. A few weeks earlier, the Republican dissenters to the House Government Operations Committee Report had indeed described the Delaney clause as "a terribly outmoded and inflexible law" and expressed the hope that "if the court rules against the FDA . . . Congress would act with due speed to revise the Delaney Clause."[87] But according to the chief counsel of the Weiss subcommittee, Democratic members saw the court's decision as confirmation of their charge that the FDA had "disregarded a clear statutory duty" and after this experience would be less inclined than ever to entrust greater discretion to the FDA.[88]

In fact, no one regards the banning of a few cosmetic dyes, considering their extraordinarily trivial risk to consumers, as a meaningful contribution to public health. At the same time, no one wants the FDA to restrict sharply the availability of essential nutrients in the American food supply. Neither does anyone seriously object to many FDA policies that evade the force of the Delaney clause in order to avoid this result. Public interest advocates had indeed argued in the early 1980s that revisions of the Delaney clause were unnecessary because the FDA could rely on the *Monsanto* decision and other precedents to avoid having to invoke the clause in most situations in which it might seem dangerous to do so.[89] The Weiss subcommittee seems to have focused its attention on cosmetic dyes—a subject on which it held several earlier hearings and released an earlier critical report, while ignoring the FDA's handling of food additives under the Delaney clause—precisely because insistence on a "zero-risk" approach is much more plausible in relation to cosmetics than to food. Apart from its partisan eagerness to embarrass a Republican administration, the committee's insistence on holding the FDA to the law in this connection may be understood as simply one chapter in a larger, ongoing struggle over federal cancer policy.[90] Everyone understands that federal policy in this area will never secure "zero risk" or ever be mechanically driven by the law: rhetoric to this effect is simply a means of pressing toward a more restrictive policy.

From this point of view, the litigation campaign fought by Public Citizen was not necessarily a sign of fanaticism or sectarianism, though there is no doubt that Public Citizen's Health Research Group generally does take a much more alarmist view of health threats—and a much more dismissive view of compensating consumer benefits, such as a wider choice of cosmetic colors—than most other informed observers of federal regulatory policy.[91] Still, it is not necessary to take an absurdly extreme view on safety issues to think that "the law" may be a useful slogan in pressing for more cautious or risk averse policies than might otherwise obtain.

But there remains the stubborn fact that policy must deal with many kinds of risks. In a larger perspective, it is not at all certain that the "zero-risk" slogan actually will press policy toward the genuinely least risky course in dealing with carcinogens, especially as it forces the FDA to disguise the actual risks involved in many cases in order to avoid invoking an unacceptable "zero-risk" standard. It is even less obvious that, assuming they could get their way, Public Citizen or Congressman Weiss of Manhattan would impose the standards of risk management that were truly the most appropriate. It seems far more likely that the FDA's historic aversion to the acceptance of risk—especially in the regulation of pharmaceuticals—has actually been quite damaging to public health. To the extent that public interest litigation has helped to entrench the FDA's historic approach, it has undoubtedly served the public quite poorly.

7

A Judicially Nurtured
Policy Stalemate:
The Case of Occupational
Health Standards

FEW federal regulatory agencies have generated as much controversy as the Occupational Safety and Health Administration (OSHA). The underlying reasons for this controversy are not hard to discern. On the one hand, OSHA's health and safety concerns involve it in policy questions that are sometimes, quite literally, of life or death significance. At least in some areas, regulation can indeed reduce workplace hazards—including some fatal hazards—and there is no doubt that the public in general, and the organized labor movement in particular, regard such regulation as morally compelling. On the other hand, the cost of compliance with OSHA health and safety standards is often extremely high. Compliance costs for some standards may run into the billions of dollars. And for all this cost, the effectiveness of particular standards, in terms of injuries prevented or lives saved, usually cannot be demonstrated with any degree of confidence or precision.

In this setting, it might seem inescapable that courts would come to play a large mediating role. And so they have. Regulated business has sought judicial relief from what it regards as arbitrary or unjustified standards and has succeeded in securing significant limitations on OSHA regulatory power. At the same time, labor and safety advocates have turned to the courts to secure what they regard as statutorily assured rights to adequate health and safety standards. In the past decade, such advocates, too, have often won favorable responses from the the courts.

Almost no one is pleased with the results, however, which are not, in fact, anything approaching a sensible compromise. On the one hand, OSHA continues to provoke business hostility with a large number of picayune and apparently quite ineffectual safety rules and a small number of extremely costly health standards. On the other hand, it has failed to set adequate standards on several dozen carcinogens, and has failed to take any action on several dozen known chemical hazards of other kinds, despite widespread agreement that the agency might make a significant difference if it acted in these areas. This perverse pattern was not directly imposed by judicial "mediators"; nonetheless, judicial action has done much to exacerbate the political and policy cross-pressures that have brought OSHA to this quite perverse—but, so far, quite enduring—"compromise" of the contending interests in occupational health policy.

The Setting: OSHA and Its Clientele

OSHA was established in 1970 by the Occupational Safety and Health Act. The enactment of this measure reflected bipartisan support for regulation in this field, but not much clarity about its proper scale.[1] Like many regulatory measures, the OSH Act was, in fact, the product of compromise and haste. Thus the statute grandly declares its intention "to assure so far as possible" that "every working man and woman in the Nation" will have "safe and healthful working conditions." But it also includes significant softening language, most notably in its direction that health standards be set at that level "which most adequately assures, *to the extent feasible,* on the basis of best available evidence, that no employee will suffer material impairment of health" (emphasis added).[2]

Basic operating procedures under the OSH Act also display this pattern. While the Nixon administration had proposed vesting standard setting authority in an independent technical authority, the OSH Act actually vests standard setting authority in the Secretary of Labor. Leaders of organized labor had urged Congress to entrust this power to the Labor Department in the expectation that the department would be more sympathetic to their concerns in this field, as in others.[3] At the same time, the OSH Act seems to reflect a certain distrust of the department, for it directs courts to uphold challenged standards only if they are supported by "substantial evidence"—a technical term usually reserved for adjudicatory proceedings generating a formal record on the basis of which reviewing courts might judge the supporting "evidence."[4] What Congress actually meant to achieve by designating this review standard is uncertain, however, because the statute does not actually require that standards be based on evidence developed in formal proceedings.

In later years, judges were to complain about such ambiguities.[5] But Congress's resort to evasive formulas in the OSH Act is neither particularly surprising nor perhaps—viewed in realistic terms—particularly deplorable. The federal government had had little prior experience with occupational safety regulation in 1970. Even the existing state programs in this field were still relatively modest and cautious. Systematic epidemiological study of occupational hazards, such as exposure to carcinogenic substances, was much less developed than it was to become over the next decade, as federal involvement began to generate much more interest (and much more funding) for such studies. Even private advisory organizations—like the American National Standards Institute, which had already developed thousands of particular safety recommendations over the preceding decades—did not claim to have any precise methodology or well-developed philosophy to determine the most appropriate or feasible level of stringency for these recommended safety standards.[6]

If Congress, then, sidestepped many issues at the outset that would later prove very contentious—like the precise relation between feasibility and cost effectiveness—it was hardly alone. If Congress in 1970 had actually tried to provide detailed guidance for OSHA standard setting, it is doubtful it would have offered very sensible or appropriate guidance, considering the existing state of knowledge and experience in the field at that time. Almost two decades later, with the benefit of vastly greater experience and much more extensive data, there is still no consensus in Congress for a different, more detailed approach.[7] And the basic provisions of the OSH Act have never, in fact, been amended.

If Congress left a good deal of discretion to the Labor Department, the department certainly did not feel it could exercise this discretion with disdain for the expectations of unions and safety advocates. On the contrary, OSHA's first major policy decisions seem, above all, to have reflected its fear of antagonizing its principal constituencies, who were from the outset somewhat suspicious of Republican appointees at the Labor Department. OSHA's eagerness to conciliate major constituencies may be the principal explanation for several early policy decisions that, at least in retrospect, must be regarded as great strategic blunders.

The first major decision dealt directly with standards. To help OSHA make a quick start, the OSH Act authorized the Labor Department to adopt all "consensus" standards already recommended by health and safety advisory organizations like the American National Standards Institute. Yet the statute explicitly authorized the Secretary of Labor to exclude any existing standard if "he determines that the promulgation of such a standard [for OSHA enforcement] would not result in improved safety or health for specifically designated employees." And the statute allowed the Secretary of Labor to take up to two years to determine which of these existing consensus standards to put into effect. Instead, in its first month in operation, OSHA promulgated all existing standards at one stroke in a *Federal Register* announcement running to three hundred pages of fine print and encompassing more than four thousand separate standards.[8]

This step proved to have very unfortunate consequences. While some of these standards had already been legally binding under existing state or federal programs, few had been seriously enforced before. Most of the standards involved had actually been designed as recommendations, not as fully binding rules. It soon became apparent that many of them were too vague or contradictory for a serious enforcement program. Many others were too petty or pointless for a politically sustainable program. OSHA thus provoked a great deal of ridicule and resentment, which it might readily have avoided if it had taken the time to adopt existing standards selectively and by gradual stages in its first two years. A careful scholarly study of OSHA's early years suggests that the agency rejected gradualism and caution in its initial approach because "this strategy would have demanded a willingness on OSHA's part to risk enlarging the rift between the agency and organized labor," and OSHA was unwilling to take this risk.[9]

This initial mistake was then compounded by the overly rigid character of OSHA's enforcement policies. At the insistence of labor leaders, the OSH Act authorized OSHA inspectors to impose immediate fines of up to $1,000 for "nonserious" violations of agency standards and up to $10,000 for "serious" violations detected in the course of on-site inspections. The statute makes provision for business firms to appeal these fines—technically, "proposed penalties"—to the independent Occupational Safety and Health Reviewing Authority; but the fine is binding unless the firm assumes the burden of bringing such an appeal.[10] Most fines actually imposed by the agency in its early years (as in later years) were quite small, however—averaging only $25 per violation in the early 1970s and rising to barely more than $100 at the end of the 1970s.[11] Like policemen writing speeding or parking tickets—who know that most people will simply pay the fine, whether they feel they have been fairly ticketed or not—OSHA inspectors had an easy time imposing fines.

But just as with traffic tickets, what was not formally challenged could still be greatly resented. And business resentment against OSHA's inspection system was greatly exacerbated by the system's preoccupation with petty or technical violations, which were, of course, hard for workplace managers to avoid, because of the scale and character of OSHA's initial standards. Quite apart from the resentment stirred among businessmen, moreover, OSHA's failure to target inspections on serious problems meant that it was squandering its enforcement resources. Yet as late as 1976, after several years of experience with the defects of this approach, OSHA inspectors issued citations for some 380,000 separate citations for violations, 96.7 percent of which were classified as "nonserious."[12] The same study of OSHA's early years attributed the perpetuation of this perverse pattern to the fact that "legislative and union leaders have been unwilling to give up the policies that are responsible. . . . Unions fear that inspectors will use discretion to weaken enforcement against serious as well as minor hazards. . . . Consequently OSHA . . . requires strict enforcement of all regulations . . . citing all the violations detected, even if they are trivial."[13]

As might have been expected, the combination of petty requirements and rigid enforcement policies generated a tremendous amount of opposition from business. In its first year in operation, OSHA provoked so much bitter criticism, particularly from small businessmen, that more than one hundred bills for amending or repealing the OSH Act were introduced in Congress. Amendments exempting small employers from OSHA's jurisdiction were actually passed by the House of Representatives in 1972, 1973, and 1974, though the measures were finally defeated each time, as union leaders rallied Senate support for the agency's original mandate. A congressional conference committee report at the end of 1975 urged OSHA to eliminate "nuisance" regulations, simplify other requirements, and do a better job of targeting its enforcement efforts.[14] The agency did make serious efforts to comply with such promptings during the Carter administration, but by then it was very difficult for the agency to shake off its reputation for intolerable heavy-handedness.[15]

But the high level of continuing opposition from business groups also seems to have intensified the suspicions and the vigilance of safety advocates in and out of organized labor. This watchfulness in turn put pressure on Carter administration appointees in the Labor Department to show that, though OSHA might be cutting back on "Mickey Mouse" safety rules, it would be all the more firm in dealing with serious health hazards.

In principle, OSHA's increasing emphasis on health hazards in the late 1970s was quite appropriate. In the mid-1970s, several careful studies attempted to determine the impact of OSHA's enforcement efforts on the frequency of workplace accidents. None of these studies was able to verify any significant reduction in workplace injuries that could reasonably be attributed to OSHA regulation (except in a few particular areas, such as the handling of explosive materials).[16] In retrospect, this finding should not have been surprising. Most workplace accidents do not result from failure to observe OSHA safety standards. Back muscles are strained by the wrong kind of lifting; fingers or toes are smashed by falling objects; workers trip and injure limbs. No set of rules can ensure that such common workplace accidents will not occur, for the causes are far too numerous and complex to regulate.[17]

In relation to health hazards, however, even many of OSHA's most severe critics conceded that the agency could make a genuine contribution.[18] OSHA's regulatory potential seemed especially promising in dealing with those occupational diseases traced to long-term exposure to particular toxic substances. In contrast to ordinary safety hazards, which may often be quickly recognized and avoided by those most affected, such long-term health threats are far less likely to be noticed by either workers or employers. Whereas the causes of many ordinary accidents can never be adequately regulated, scientific testing may often help to determine dangerous exposure levels to particular substances, which can then be regulated accordingly.

The force of these arguments was not lost on OSHA's political supporters. While still strongly defending continued enforcement of safety rules, labor and safety advocates became much more interested in long-term health hazards in the course of the 1970s.[19] The difficulty was in determining proper standards. The initial consensus standards adopted by OSHA in 1971 included exposure limitations on some four hundred toxic or hazardous substances, most recommended by the American Conference of Governmental Industrial Hygienists (ACGIH), another private advisory body. But these standards were already three years old at the time. New research was continually monitored and encouraged by the National Institute of Occupational Safety and Health (NIOSH), which had been created by the OSH Act to advise OSHA on the need for new standards. As evidence of new hazards accumulated, the ACGIH itself took repeated action to update and expand its recommendations in this field.[20]

For OSHA, however, devising new standards was more difficult. The OSH Act only authorized the agency to promulgate consensus standards during its first two years of operation. Thereafter, it was required to demonstrate that its standards were supported by "substantial evidence" and in conformity with the statutory directive to set "the standard which most adequately assures, to the extent feasible, . . . that no employee will suffer material impairment of health or functional capacity even if such employee has regular exposure to the hazard . . . for the period of his working life." Of course, this wording still gave OSHA very broad regulatory power, whenever it could marshal evidence to support new standards. But stringent new standards would be costly for business and would be likely therefore to encounter challenge and resistance.

Even in its early years, OSHA did worry about business opposition to new standards. But as OSHA was taking its first steps toward revising its health standards, labor and safety advocates worried about OSHA, especially that the agency might compromise new health and safety standards to appease business protests. And from the outset, they took these worries to the courts. OSHA's initial experience with such litigation encouraged just those inclinations within the agency which, in later years, were virtually to paralyze its standard setting operations.

The First Phase of Judicial Management

OSHA promulgated its first new health standard in 1972, dealing with exposure to asbestos. As soon as the new standard was promulgated, it was challenged in court, not by industry, but by labor and by Ralph Nader's Health Research Group. The resulting 1974 decision of the D.C. Court of Appeals in *Industrial Union Department, AFL-CIO v. Hodgson,* [21] expressed a good deal of caution about judicial competence to review the technical bases for OSHA decisions. It expressed no caution at all, however, about the propriety of unions or safety advocates suing OSHA to demand tighter regulation.

Amid considerable evidence that workers exposed to high levels of asbestos faced higher than average risks of cancer, OSHA had issued a "temporary emergency standard" for asbestos exposure in 1971. This standard limited permissible exposure levels for airborne asbestos dust to 5 fibers per cubic centimeter of air. On the basis of new evidence, NIOSH then recommended that OSHA reduce this exposure limit to 2 fibers/cc, though it also suggested that OSHA give industry two years to adapt before this new standard was put into effect. A study commissioned by OSHA, after polling a variety of doctors and industrial asbestos users, concluded that compliance with a 5 fiber/cc standard would achieve 99 percent of the health benefits to be expected from the 2 fibers/cc standard, while costing industry only half as much.[22] At a public hearing on the issue at the Labor Department, a variety of technical specialists presented evidence for a variety of "safe levels" of exposure. Different witnesses urged standards as permissive as 12 fibers/cc and as restrictive as 0 fibers/cc. Reviewing this testimony and more than a thousand pages of other documentation, the Court of Appeals judged it "fair to say that the evidence did not establish any one position as clearly correct."[23]

The challengers in *I.U.D. v. Hodgson* did not, however, protest OSHA's final decision setting the exposure limit at 2 fibers/cc, as NIOSH had recommended; and the Court of Appeals made no suggestion that there was any impropriety in choosing a far more costly standard with no clear evidence of greater health benefits. The court's decision indeed dwelled at some length on the incongruity of the OSH Act asking courts to determine whether there was "substantial evidence" to justify a challenged rule. The statute did not require OSHA to develop facts in a formal trial procedure and, the court noted, Congress must have anticipated that the Secretary of Labor would exercise considerable legislative discretion in settling on particular standards: "where the decision making vested in the Secretary is legislative in character, there are areas where explicit factual findings are not possible, and the act of decision is essentially a prediction based upon pure legislative judgment, as when a Congressman decides to vote for or against a particular bill." The court thus concluded that it must "approach our reviewing task with a flexibility informed and shaped by sensitivity to the diverse origins of the determinations that enter into a legislative judgment."[24]

Language of this kind seemed to acknowledge that the court would not hold OSHA to a constraining interpretion of the the statutory requirement that standard setting decisions be based on the "best available evidence."[25] At the least, the court's language implied that it would not dispute OSHA's identification of the "best available evidence" in relation to disputed medical findings. Even in regard to strictly scientific evidence regarding health risks, this deferential inclination was certainly understandable. Particularly in relation to carcinogens, where the underlying physiological operation of cancer "causing" substances is still very poorly understood, scientific evidence rarely provides clear evidence about safe exposure levels. Controlled experiments with rats or other laboratory animals may provide reliable indications of carcinogenic effects for particular substances. But for a variety of reasons, it is difficult to extrapolate from laboratory studies to reliably safe exposure levels for human beings. Epidemiological studies of disease rates in human populations provide more pertinent evidence, but that evidence is often difficult to interpret because small effects may only be recognizable in large samples and large samples are difficult to control for research purposes. It is difficult, that is, for researchers to establish the precise levels of exposure to the pertinent substance when they are dealing with a large, diverse sample; and it may be still more difficult in such samples to determine the cross-cutting influences of other factors, to which various individuals in the sample were variously exposed.[26]

In relation to asbestos itself, there was doubt in the early 1970s about how to interpret studies of workers exposed to very high levels of asbestos dust many years earlier. While neither industry nor labor chose to litigate OSHA's decision to impose a 2 fiber/cc standard in 1972, evidence compiled in subsequent years cast much doubt even on the safety of this relatively low exposure level. By 1980 the American Conference of Governmental Industrial Hygienists (ACGIH), which generally tries to develop recommendations acceptable to industry, was urging that asbestos exposure levels be cut to 0.2 fibers/cc—or one-tenth of what NIOSH researchers had proposed for the OSHA standard only a few years earlier.[27] OSHA itself finally adopted this much more stringent standard for exposure to asbestos in 1986.

The striking fact, however, about the litigation over OSHA's initial asbestos rule in *I.U.D. v. Hodgson* was that it scarcely dealt at all with the scientific or medical evidence. The principal complaint of the AFL-CIO and the Nader lawyers was that OSHA had agreed to allow industry up to four years to come into compliance with its new 2 fiber/cc exposure standard. The court expressly rejected the challenger's claim that OSHA was legally obliged to adopt the recommendation of NIOSH in setting its binding standards. The court also acknowledged that "on the basis of the conflicting testimony in the record" it could not "say" that the Secretary of Labor had "erred in his prediction" of the minimal "health effect of the four year delay." The principal question, then, was whether the Labor Department was justified in regarding this delay as necessary to make the new 2 fiber/cc standard feasible. Because the OSH Act directed OSHA to adopt the most protective health standard "to the extent feasible"—without at all defining the term "feasible"—Congress would seem to have delegated very broad discretion to OSHA in its final choice of standards. Since all regulatory programs require a good deal of cooperation from regulated interests to operate effectively, OSHA's discretion to define the "feasible" in this context might have seemed precisely the sort of political judgment—the judgment about how far to push—that the court itself had in mind when it spoke, rather delicately, about the need for "sensitivity to the diverse origins of the determinations that enter into a legislative judgment."[28]

Yet on just this sort of legislative judgment, the court set itself up as the judge of OSHA's integrity. The court acknowledged that on such questions "judicial review inevitably runs the risk of becoming arbitrary supervision and revision of the Secretary's efforts to effectuate the legislative purposes," and this "in an area where variant responses might each be legitimate in the sight of Congress." The court explicitly acknowledged, moreover, that if OSHA's standard in this case had "been made in the first instance by Congress itself and embodied in the statute, its vulnerability to judicial scrutiny would have been dubious indeed."[29] Yet with all of these disclaimers, the court nonetheless went ahead and tried to supervise OSHA's exercise of legislative discretion. Rejecting the challenger's contention that cost considerations should not enter into OSHA's standard setting decisions, the court ruled that "Congress does not appear to have intended to protect employees by putting their employers out of business." But then it cautioned that what was economically feasible for most employers in an industry might still be "consistent with the purposes of the [OSH] Act" even if individual firms were put out of business by the costs of a particular standard.[30] And the court's final ruling, while not striking down OSHA's four-year "transition" period, "remanded" this aspect of the new standard for OSHA to provide further explanation to the court of why such an extension could not be limited to the particular industries most in need of it, rather than extended to all.

With all of its disclaimers, then, the decision in *I.U.D. v. Hodgson* clearly asserted a judicial responsibility to hold OSHA within bounds in determining when health standards might be feasible. To be sure, the court did not go very far in this case in defining the bounds of the feasible. But the court plainly invited challengers to come forward with further charges about whether OSHA had stretched the definition of the feasible too far with any particular standard. In this very case, the court underscored its eagerness to hold OSHA in bounds—whatever they might be—by ordering the agency to gather new evidence and present new arguments in defense of its extended compliance deadline for all industrial users of asbestos. OSHA's own initial deadline would have run out within two years of the court's decision and, considering the usual pace of administrative and judicial proceedings, the further proceedings ordered by the court might well have consumed most or all of this period. But if the D.C. Court of Appeals had any doubt about the utility of further litigation over the difference between a few months more or less in the imposition of a permanent deadline, it certainly gave no indication of it.

More significantly for the future, the decision in *I.U.D. v. Hodgson* suggested that the courts would raise no question at all about the legal standing of those seeking to invoke this kind of judicial supervision. The OSH Act provides that "[a]ny person who may be adversely affected by a standard" promulgated under its terms may "file a petition challenging the validity of such standard in the U.S. court of appeals for the circuit wherein such person resides or has his principal place of business."[31] The decision in *I.U.D. v. Hodgson* simply noted in one sentence that the petitioners in the case were "unions whose members are affected by the health hazards of asbestos dust," as if nothing more needed to be said. The court of appeals did not question whether it was the court of proper jurisdiction for the case or whether Washington, D.C. was "the principal place of business" for the unions, evidently taking it for granted that their business was political lobbying.

The court did not inquire whether these unions actually qualified as a "person . . . adversely affected" within the meaning of the OSH Act. The court did not even bother to inquire into the meaning of this phrase in the context of the OSH Act, much less seek to identify the precise manner in which the petitioners in this case actually were adversely affected. It did not say a word about who else might be adversely affected by the contested OSHA policy in this case. It did not seem to matter to the court whether the unions represented the vast majority or a merely a small minority of workers exposed to asbestos, or whether the unions might have special interests conflicting with the interests of other OSHA constituencies, or whether or how its decision in this case might have affected other, ongoing OSHA programs and responsibilities. Following the already well-established conventions in administrative law, the court simply took it for granted that a powerful interest group ought to be allowed to come to court to demand judicial scrutiny of a particular administrative policy decision in complete abstraction from the larger policy or program responsibilities of the agency involved.[32]

In this respect, *I.U.D. v. Hodgson* set a decisive precedent. As it did not question the standing of the AFL-CIO, the D.C. Court of Appeals would never thereafter question the standing of any other advocacy group seeking to secure more stringent regulation from OSHA. There was, indeed, quick confirmation that *I.U.D. v. Hodgson* was not a fluke in this respect. OSHA's next major standard setting effort, following the initial asbestos standard, was a rule relaxing an American National Standards Institute consensus safety standard on hand guards on mechanical power presses, which had been adopted in 1971 with thousands of other ANSI standards and which OSHA proposed to relax in accordance with a new ANSI recommendation. The new standard was also immediately challenged by the AFL-CIO, and, as with the asbestos rule, the 1975 court of appeals decision in this case *(AFL-CIO v. Brennan)* resulted in an order to OSHA to explain why it had failed to consider various possible alternatives to the standard finally proposed.[33] OSHA was henceforth entitled to assume that it would be dragged into court any time it promulgated a new standard that did not satisfy an advocacy group demanding tighter standards.

By and large, this assumption proved to be correct. The agency could not be sure how severely courts would scrutinize its new standards, but it was put on warning that compromises with the recommendations of health and safety specialists would be questioned by the courts. By the same token, OSHA might have been justified in assuming, after its first major encounter with judicial review of its health standards, that the courts would not inquire too carefully into the scientific basis for its standards, at least when they were endorsed by government specialists in NIOSH. This assumption proved to be wrong.

Judicial Ambivalence and Administrative Paralysis

In the short term, it may be that OSHA would have pursued essentially the same course as it did over the next several years, quite apart from the influence of these initial court decisions. Steven Kelman's studies of OSHA's perform-ance in the 1970s have emphasized the great extent to which the agency's approach was influenced by the outlook of public health professionals, eager to protect life and health at all costs.[34] Other scholars have placed more emphasis on the political pressures brought to bear by unions and safety advocates. But in the relevant respects, both the perfectionist impulses of health professionals and these political pressures from well-connected constitu-encies largely paralleled the most evident policy implications of the decision in *I.U.D. v. Hodgson.* Over the next several years, OSHA indeed behaved in a manner that was quite consistent with the initial signals it received from the courts.

In the months following the decision in *I.U.D. v. Hodgson,* OSHA issued two new health standards, one specifying work practices for the handling of fourteen well-established carcinogens (which did not involve new exposure limits) and one imposing new exposure limits for the handling of vinyl chlo-ride. The new work practices rule did not arouse great controversy, but the vinyl chloride standard did. To avoid any doubt about safety, the vinyl chloride standard set a maximum exposure level at what was then viewed as the very lowest possible level: for practical purposes, it required no detectable level of exposure. OSHA chose this standard even though it had no firm evidence that somewhat higher levels would really pose any significantly greater degree of risk. With available technology, moreover, the cost of compliance with this standard was projected to be quite heavy, so heavy that OSHA itself conceded that plastics manufacturers "will not be able to attain" the required exposure limits "for all job classifications in the near future." The courts upheld this rule, however, and industry as it turned out was able to adapt to it with only a few plant closings.[35] The following year, OSHA accordingly began work on a dozen new health standards, all of which promised to be very stringent and very costly.[36]

By 1975, the immense potential compliance costs of OSHA health stan-dards had begun to attract the attention and concern of White House econo-mists. As part of its general effort to contain inflationary pressures on the economy, the Ford White House had initiated in 1975 a general program requiring regulatory agencies to assess the relative costs and benefits of major new regulatory proposals. With "major" proposals defined as those imposing annual costs greater than $100 million, economists at the White House

Council of Wage and Price Stability (CWPS) felt entitled to demand that OSHA undertake careful consideration of the relative costs and benefits of each one of the new health standards it was then considering. This requirement slowed down OSHA's standard setting operations without, however, making the agency much more flexible in its conception of proper standards. The CWPS economic assessment program was bitterly criticized by labor and safety advocates; and fortified by the protests of its leading constituencies, OSHA itself—alone among major regulatory agencies—refused to make any direct economic assessment of the benefits to be secured by its new proposals, insisting that it would be wrong to "put a price tag on the lives of workers."[37]

Nonetheless, OSHA did gather data to illuminate the financial costs and the expected health benefits of its new proposals. And these data suggest a remarkable determination to press forward with new standards in defiance of economic logic. Over the protests of White House economists, for example, OSHA went ahead in 1976 and issued a new standard limiting exposure to various substances emitted by coke ovens in the highly unionized steel industry. Compliance costs were estimated to be quite high, with some estimates ranging as high as $1.28 billion per year. At the same time, OSHA estimated that even with perfect compliance—which was not at all certain to occur—the standard would probably avert somewhere between eight and thirty-six fatal cancers a year. These numbers were less than one-third of the annual death toll of persons struck by lightning—a cause of death long proverbial for its rarity. The estimated risk factor from work with coke ovens under existing conditions (comparing the number of fatalities to the number of those exposed to the hazard) was about one-tenth of that borne by cigarette smokers.[38]

Here, as elsewhere, protests from CWPS were disregarded by OSHA. The Carter administration, which developed a similar regulatory review program staffed by CWPS economists, also pressed OSHA to consider the cost effectiveness of its new standards. For the most part, these appeals were also disregarded. In 1978, OSHA issued six new health standards, most again threatening very substantial compliance costs for rather limited additional gains.

What White House pressures could not avert, however, the courts finally proved unwilling to accept. Different industry organizations challenged every one of the new standards, trying their luck in different courts of appeal around the country while avoiding the proregulatory D.C. Court of Appeals. The American Petroleum Institute, suing on behalf of member companies in the oil refining industry, was the first to win a decisive victory. Its challenge to OSHA's new benzene exposure standard was endorsed by the Court of Appeals for the Fifth Circuit (covering the oil states of Texas and Louisiana, among others), which ruled that OSHA must demonstrate that new standards would actually be cost effective.[39] The Labor Department regarded this ruling as a serious blow to OSHA's entire standard setting program and promptly appealed to the Supreme Court. But the Supreme Court, too, sided with the challengers.

The Supreme Court's 1980 decision in the benzene case did not quite say that the OSH Act required cost-benefit analysis. But it emphasized that when a more stringent exposure standard involved very considerable extra compliance costs, OSHA must provide evidence that the additional cost would secure some "significant" additional health benefit, which was "at least more likely than not" to follow from the imposition of the additional cost. If the OSH Act were not read as imposing this check, the Court warned, any "[e]xpert testimony that a substance is probably a human carcinogen . . . would [by itself be taken as sufficient evidence to] justify the conclusions that the substance poses some risk of serious harm no matter how minute the exposure and no matter how many experts testified that they regarded the risk as insignificant. . . . In light of the fact that there are literally thousands of substances used in the workplace that have been identified as carcinogens or suspected carcinogens, [this] theory [about how to interpret the OSH Act] would give OSHA power to impose enormous costs that might produce little, if any, discernible benefit."[40]

Four justices, however, signed an angry dissenting opinion by Justice Marshall, which characterized this decision as "both extraordinarily arrogant and extraordinarily unfair." Comparing the decision to judicial attacks on early labor legislation at the turn of the century, the dissenters predicted that the Court's decision in this case would soon "come to be regarded as an extreme reaction to a regulatory scheme that, as [the Court] perceived it, imposed an unduly harsh burden on regulated industries." The dissent then insisted that it was not the Court's "responsibility . . . to strike its own balance between the costs and benefits of occupational safety standards." But the dissenters plainly did not mean this to be a generic appeal for judicial restraint. In an artful footnote, Justice Marshall acknowledged that there should be "room for especially rigorous judicial scrutiny of agency decisionmaking" on certain kinds of questions; and he illustrated his meaning by citing three prominent cases in which courts had struck down administrative findings at the behest of environmental advocacy groups.[41]

A year later, when the Supreme Court accepted an appeal of another new OSHA standard—this one limiting the exposure of textile workers to cotton dust—the dissenters in the benzene case were able to speak for the majority. And they did not speak with hesitation or restraint. Writing for a bare majority of his colleagues, Justice Brennan's opinion in *American Textile Manufacturers Institute v. Donovan* insisted that "Congress itself defined the basic relationship between costs and benefits, by placing the 'benefit' of worker health above all other considerations save those making attainment of this 'benefit' una-chievable. Any standard based on a balancing of costs and benefits by the Secretary [of Labor] that strikes a different balance than that struck by Con-gress would be inconsistent with the command set forth" in the OSH Act.[42]

Yet the majority opinion in the cotton dust case did not expressly repudiate the decision in the benzene case and indeed purported to be consistent with it. In effect, the different factions on the Court had come to rest on a compromise formula requiring OSHA to show "significant risk" before pro-ceeding to regulate—but then forbidding the agency to consider costs, unless the costs were so steep as to shut down entire industries. Perhaps this formula struck the Court's new majority as a Solomonic compromise or perhaps it was simply an artifact of intracourt bargaining, a concession wrung from the dissenters in the benzene case to secure the additional vote they needed to make this a majority decision.

The results, at any rate, left OSHA exposed to serious challenge from both sides. If its standards imposed heavy costs on particular industries, they were virtually certain to be challenged by industry, which would demand "substan-tial evidence" that the stringency of a particular standard was justified by "significant" health gains. If courts showed any sympathy for this demand, as they did in the benzene case, OSHA might find it rather difficult to provide the necessary evidence, considering the paucity and ambiguity of most scien-tific evidence regarding particular dosage or exposure levels. To be sure, OSHA might seek to avoid such challenges by compromising its standards in order to cut down on associated compliance costs—as it managed to escape industry challenges in the courts with its initial asbestos standard and its 1978 exposure standard on acrylonitrile, two of its least costly rules.[43] But if the agency were at all open about these compromises, it was likely to sued by unions—as it was in the asbestos case—and might be forced to gather more evidence about feasibility of compliance or more evidence to demonstrate the relative safety of proposed compromises. Even when it had a good deal of scientific evidence and had tried to assess cost considerations with some care so as to respond to objections from both sides, OSHA might very well encounter litigational challenges from both business and labor advocates—as it did with its 1978 health standard on lead. After an extremely complex round of litigation, the D.C. Court of Appeals upheld most of the standard but still remanded several crucial issues for further clarification from OSHA.[44]

The problem posed for OSHA officials by these burdens was partly a matter of specialized staff resources. The agency had a relatively small number of officials in its office of standards development, and the heavier the evidentiary burden it faced, the more burden was laid on this small office.[45] Even though most of its evidence was compiled by outside research contractors, it required specialized technical staff to negotiate these contracts, assess the resulting reports, organize testimony for public hearings, and package all of the evidence for official rule making purposes. When the agency needed to commission new toxicological studies to supplement existing evidence, as the Supreme Court had demanded in the benzene case, still further delays would occur.

OSHA feared the blow to its credibility if inadequately defended standards were overturned in the courts. It also had to worry about training inspectors to enforce compliance with more technically complex and disputable exposure standards (some of which involved "time-weighted average" exposure limitations and other requirements that were difficult to measure with confidence).[46] OSHA was therefore particularly reluctant to commit enforcement resources and staff work to any new standard if it could not be sure the standard would survive judicial scrutiny.

The result of these inhibiting pressures was apparent even before the Supreme Court issued its ruling in the benzene case. In the course of 1978, OSHA promulgated six new health standards and was known to be at work on half a dozen more. Work lagged on the other standards as OSHA waited to see whether the Supreme Court would save it from the lower court's ruling against its benzene standard. After the Supreme Court's benzene ruling, "OSHA was completely paralyzed."[47] No new standards were issued through the rest of the Carter administration, or in the first three years of the Reagan administration. OSHA did not promulgate another new health standard until 1984, and then it produced only one—which was immediately entangled in further litigation. Although several other health standards were proposed, only one had been promulgated by the end of 1986; another was added in 1987 and one more in 1988. In all, OSHA promulgated nine new health standards in the six years before 1978, though litigation prevented some of them from going into effect; in the eleven succeeding years, OSHA promulgated only another four health standards.[48]

After 1981, OSHA faced a new source of delay as the Reagan administration tried to tighten White House review of major new regulations. Instead of authorizing CWPS economists simply to lobby regulatory agencies for better economic analysis, as had been the practice in the Ford and Carter administrations, the Reagan administration sought to put more force into its requirement for such cost-benefit analysis by requiring agencies to submit their proposed regulations for advance clearance with a regulatory analysis staff at the Office of Management and Budget. Under an executive order issued at the outset of the Reagan administration, OMB was authorized to demand further analysis before permitting publication of regulatory proposals or final rules in the *Federal Register*, which at least gave OMB the power to impose delays and in practice often afforded some leverage in pressing for actual revisions in regulatory proposals.[49]

The Supreme Court's 1981 decision in the cotton dust case might have been expected to constrain White House oversight of this kind, insofar as the Court's ruling denied OSHA's legal authority to engage in cost-benefit balancing, once the costs of a significant health benefit were classified as feasible. In fact, the ruling seems actually to have intensified White House determination to keep a close eye on OSHA. For in inviting sharper legal challenges by advocates of tighter OSHA standards, the cotton dust decision made it all the more crucial to pin down actual costs (to bolster arguments about feasibility) and to pin down actual benefits (to bolster arguments that additional benefits would not be significant). As the analyses on which these estimates were based usually involved a great many disputable assumptions, OMB officials were determined to scrutinize the assumptions involved in OSHA analyses before they became fixed in litigation as "facts."[50]

Union officials and safety advocates charged throughout the early 1980s that OMB was deliberately seeking excuses to delay the promulgation of new OSHA standards, and there appears to be some truth in these charges.[51] OMB officials certainly wanted to discourage OSHA from issuing new standards that they regarded as wildly out of line with reasonable notions of cost effectiveness. But the fact remains that OSHA's paralysis began three years before the Reagan administration's OMB review program. Even from the standpoint of controlling regulatory costs, moreover, it was never a plausible strategy for OMB to seek to thwart the issuance of all new OSHA health standards over a four-year (much less an eight-year) period. Regulatory review operations by OMB were continually under attack in Congress during the early 1980s and could not have survived at all if exercised in such total disregard for a powerful congressional constituency.[52] As it was, the standards that did finally emerge from OSHA during the 1980s—with OMB's grudging consent—were very far from what OMB officials would have liked.

By the same token, once new OSHA standards were in place, it was bound to take a good deal of time and effort to revise them. This fact gave the Reagan administration very considerable incentives to press for the adoption of new standards while it could still be done under its own cost-conscious auspices. But OSHA, citing the Supreme Court's cotton dust ruling, remained extremely resistant to pressures to issue more modest standards. Regulatory analysts at OMB thus saw the courts as a crucial factor: "As a result of the court decisions, OSHA adopts many fewer new standards, but each one it does issue is more complicated, more stringent and takes longer to complete."[53]

By the mid-1980s, courts were expressing open exasperation with the extreme slowness of OSHA's standard setting activities. But judicial efforts to prod OSHA into speedier action had only limited success and had some further troubling consequences. Public interest litigation proved a weak tool for undoing a logjam it had done so much to nurture in the first place. Before turning to these difficulties, however, it is worth stepping back to assess the larger costs imposed by the legal pressures on OSHA to maintain the most protective health standards feasible.

The Hazards of Excessive Caution

In 1974, the D.C. Court of Appeals thought it worthwhile to question OSHA's authority to extend the application of its more stringent asbestos standard for a mere two years. In retrospect, the court's concern looks particularly ironic. While worrying over a one- or two-year delay in the effective date of one standard, the court encouraged a pattern of legal wrangling that was to induce many times greater delay for many more standards. In relation to asbestos dust itself, for example, an expert consensus about the inadequacy of OSHA's 1972 exposure standard began to form in the mid-1970s, but OSHA did not promulgate a new standard until 1986. A decade after its 1978 standards for benzene exposure were called into question, the agency still had not settled on alternative standards.

Focusing on delays in the development of individual standards misses the larger point, however. This point has been nicely illustrated by John Mendeloff's comparison of OSHA health standards with the recommendations of the American Conference of Governmental Industrial Hygienists.[54] OSHA's original list of consensus standards, adopted in 1971, incorporated all standards for exposure to toxic substances on a list of health recommendations compiled by ACGIH in 1968. ACGIH, a private organization, consults continually with industry representatives and develops new recommendations through a "balancing of risks with the practicality of reductions," but does try to keep abreast of new scientific findings on health hazards. By the mid-1980s, ACGIH had lowered exposure limits for more than one hundred of the hazards on its 1968 list and developed new recommendations for two hundred additional chemicals.

OSHA, in this same period, promulgated lower exposure limits for only ten hazards on ACGIH's 1968 list. When OSHA did make changes, it usually tried to set considerably lower exposure levels than those proposed in new ACGIH recommendations; but it was able to consider only a small fraction of ACGIH recommendations. Mendeloff estimates that at least one million workers face exposure levels well above those now recommended by ACGIH, but below those required by existing OSHA standards (promulgated, with a handful of exceptions, in 1971). On the basis of current risk data, Mendeloff concludes that rapid adoption of ACGIH's current recommendations by OSHA—for all that they might not satisfy the most protective health advocates—could prevent several hundred cancers a year.[55] The actual OSHA standards promulgated between 1976 and 1986 that survived judicial scrutiny were estimated to avert about fifty cancers a year.[56]

By insisting on maximum feasible protection in the few standards it has promulgated, OSHA has limited its capacity to regulate more broadly or effectively. Mendeloff describes this trend as overregulation in a few areas leading to more pervasive underregulation. This policy would be perverse even if health benefits (or risk reductions) were generally proportionate to compliance costs, so that a standard costing five times as much yielded five times the health benefits or saved five times as many lives. But this is not the general pattern. Rather, the cost of reducing exposures typically rises dramatically at the margin, where whole new technologies may be required to achieve the last increment of reduction—so that, for example, reducing exposure levels by 95 percent is not fractionally more costly than reducing exposure levels by 80 percent but many times more costly. The relation between exposure reductions and health benefits, by contrast, generally seems to be directly proportional. If there are any cases in which a slight reduction in exposure generates a dramatic reduction in disease rates, they have not been documented in the scientific literature. And it is precisely these marginal reductions, threatening enormous compliance costs for limited health gains, that have generated so much controversy and litigation about OSHA standard setting.[57] To the extent that OSHA's insistence on maximum feasible standards has prevented it from promulgating more new standards more rapidly, the tradeoff has not been between a little more here and a little less there. In overview, it appears to have been a much more perverse tradeoff between insisting on a tiny benefit here and foregoing a vastly greater benefit there.

This conclusion, moreover, does not require one to believe that OSHA could have enacted all ACGIH recommendations without resistance or delay if it had simply agreed to take ACGIH's generally more modest approach to individual standards. As a private advisory body with no power to enforce its recommendations, ACGIH can certainly move more quickly than a government agency. Still, OSHA has been "dramatically slower" in setting new standards than its counterparts in other countries, as the congressional Office of Technology Assessment noted in an impressively detailed 1985 study of OSHA operations.[58] In Sweden, to cite the most dramatic counterexample, occupational health authorities completed a systematic revision of health standards in 1981 and then, over the following three years, added twenty-two new substances to these standards and revised existing standards for eighteen other substances already regulated, promulgating four times as many new standards in three years as OSHA had in the previous thirteen years. Because Sweden places considerable emphasis on occupational health and safety and has a long tradition of consensual negotiation among business, labor, and government on such regulatory efforts, this example may also be an unrealistic illustration of OSHA's potential. In the United States, there is no assurance that even more modest health standards, designed to be broadly acceptable to most regulated firms, would not be challenged in court by a dissident firm or industry, thus dragging the whole process back through time consuming, data crunching formalities.

Still, it is quite plausible to suppose that less demanding standards would be less often challenged by regulated businesses. And it is still more plausible to suppose that challenges to less demanding standards would less often succeed in the courts.[59] The change would not need to be total to have very helpful consequences for OSHA standard setting. OSHA's effectiveness could still be vastly improved even if it never became anywhere nearly as swift in promulgating new standards as ACGIH or the Swedish occupational safety authorities. Whatever the scale of the effect, the relation seems clear: if OSHA did not have to worry so much about legal challenges to its new standards, it could proceed more quickly and promulgate more standards. If OMB did not fear OSHA's disregard of costs, moreover, it would have less need to impose time consuming data demands or demands for analytical reassessment.

What prevented OSHA from speeding up its standard setting was its insistence on adopting the most protective standards feasible—a disposition, reinforced by court decisions and advocacy groups, that continued throughout the 1980s. OSHA's proposed exposure standards for EDB (1983) and formaldehyde (1985) were the least efficient health standards ever proposed by the agency—with projected costs of $15.6 billion and $72 billion, respectively, per life saved—and both have predictably remained under reconsideration for years since initially being proposed.[60] If OSHA was already strongly disposed to such perverse policy approaches, it hardly needed to be encouraged by the courts to continue in this direction.

In fact, OSHA did seem to be trying a new approach in January 1989, in the last weeks of the Reagan administration, when it promulgated a package of new standards for several dozen substances. But it was quite uncertain whether the agency would have the chance to prove the merits of this approach: many of the new standards were immediately denounced by unions and health advocacy groups and seemed almost certain to be entangled in complex litigation for years to come. It seemed likely that only a new attitude in the courts would allow OSHA to persevere in this new approach.

It is not hard to understand, however, why past court decisions continually pressed OSHA to disregard systematic cost-benefit considerations. The trade-off between the stringency of individual standards and the extensiveness of overall standard setting only appears in sharp relief when one views OSHA's operations from an overall policy perspective. This is just the perspective that is least likely to emerge in litigational battles over any particular standard. The normal perspective of litigation is insular—as it is supposed to be. The regulated firm, claiming that its rights have been infringed without statutory warrant, does not care to hear about the exigencies of overall policy. It insists on a black and white ruling on whether government does or does not have the legal authority to coerce the firm in the particular case at hand. When advocates of stiffer regulation are admitted to court, they operate in the same artificial legal context, demanding a black and white ruling on whether a regulatory agency does or does not have the legal authority to withhold the particular regulatory standard the advocates seek. The regulated firm need not care if, in winning a favorable decision, it deranges the agency's overall operations. A favorable decision for regulatory advocates loses a good deal of its savor if it proves to have such deleterious effects on the whole regulatory program.[61] But contemporary administrative law abstracts from this difference, pretending that the cases are quite parallel. In a word, it pretends that judges can enforce a right to adequate regulation without taking on the management of the regulatory agency. So courts make what are in reality important managerial decisions, with one eye steadfastly closed to managerial realities.

Even if judges must be half blind, why do unions and safety advocates pursue such a self-defeating course? Perhaps the most important reason is that, from the beginning of OSHA's operations in the early 1970s, unions and safety advocates have been strongly committed to the position that cost considerations should not matter—or, as one union official put it, that it is not "possible to equitably balance economic considerations with the paramount consideration of life."[62] Economists have responded for more than a decade that the "paramount consideration of life" makes it all the more inexcusable for OSHA to pursue inefficient or ineffective regulatory strategies that end up saving many fewer lives than might have been saved under better conceived alternatives.[63] But union officials and safety advocates have feared that cost-benefit analysis will become an excuse for OSHA to pursue not more efficient strategies but simply less costly strategies, so they have attached great importance to the symbolism of denying that costs matter. Whether or not disregard for costs is a sound strategy, they insist, "The bottom line here is we have a law and we must live with it. New standards must be consistent with the OSH Act itself."[64]

The political calculation underlying this premise—the assumption that

OSHA would face no significant pressure to improve health and safety once it was acknowledged to have room for compromise on very costly standards—does not appear very realistic in light of the actual history of OSHA operations, which have repeatedly frustrated White House promptings to pursue different balances. Efforts to cut back on punitive fines at the outset of the Reagan administration were also substantially reversed, as the result of pressure from Congress.[65] Even if there remains some possibility that the worst fears of safety advocates would be realized in the absence of judicial interference, the question remains why courts should be drawn into political maneuvers based on worst-case fears.

This question becomes all the more pressing when one considers the actual stake of union officials and safety advocates in OSHA performance. Improving levels of workplace health and safety are unlikely to be noticed by workers, for even under the most optimistic projections, the margins for improvement are statistically small. Nothing prevents unions from seeking higher health and safety standards in collective bargaining agreements, but—to the disappointment of many health and safety analysts—they have rarely done so. In actual bargaining over particular contracts, union officials (and presumably the workers they represent) seem to place a rather low priority on the upgrading of health standards.[66] So if the strategy pursued by labor or safety advocates in Washington (including their litigation strategy) does not secure significant gains, they are not likely to feel any great pressure from their constituencies to find more effective alternatives. In the internal politics of the labor movement, or the world of consumer advocacy, there may even be strong incentives for striking defiant or intransigent postures against government agencies, which are quite as strong whether the posturing influences government for the better or not.[67] Thus it is less surprising than it might at first appear that the counterproductiveness of the strategy pursued by union and safety litigators has not forced reconsiderations within their own ranks.

For all of that, unions and safety advocates have certainly been very critical of the pace of OSHA standard setting. Some labor spokesmen have urged in recent years that Congress amend the OSH Act to allow OSHA again to adopt ACGIH consensus standards on a wholesale basis, as it was authorized to do in 1971. Bills to this effect have gone nowhere, however, because business remains strongly opposed to any wholesale increase in OSHA's standard setting powers.[68] And business has no reason to lessen its opposition as long as it cannot trust OSHA to apply ACGIH standards with flexibility. In fact, its experience in the 1970s was that OSHA's efforts to relax major consensus standards were challenged in the courts by unions.[69] So the underlying stalemate has endured. And efforts to break this stalemate through further litigation offer little reason to expect significant improvements in the future.

Litigational Agenda Forcing

Before the 1980s, the principal bias introduced into OSHA standard setting by public interest litigation was a bias toward the stringency of individual standards. This bias pressed OSHA toward stricter but fewer standards. By the 1980s, public interest litigants sought to correct this emphasis by also demanding more and speedier standard setting, without abandoning earlier efforts to press for more stringent standards. On the whole, this strategy has had limited effectiveness because courts cannot supply OSHA the resources it needs to process standards more rapidly, a fact of which judges are well aware. Nonetheless, suspicious of delay and eager to prod the agency toward activism, courts have tried to press it for faster standard setting.

This litigation has reinforced a different managerial bias in OSHA operations, one that again parallels existing pressures on OSHA. This is a bias toward regulating newly discovered hazards at the expense of long recognized but still inadequately regulated hazards. The reasons for the preexisting bias in this direction are easy to explain. The discovery of new hazards generates excitement, attention, and research efforts. By contrast with the hazards of automobile driving or cigarette smoking, for example, which are by now too well known to arouse great public excitement, there is a rush of publicity whenever a new substance is found to be carcinogenic—though the risks involved are invariably very much lower than those involved in driving or smoking. This high profile means that politicians have special incentives to focus on newly discovered risks and to press safety regulators to demonstrate responsiveness to the problem. It also means that health researchers have more incentive to discover new hazards than to refine our understanding of long recognized hazards.[70]

The thrust of agenda forcing litigation in relation to OSHA has been precisely in this direction. The leading example is litigation over ethylene oxide (EtO), litigation spearheaded by Ralph Nader's Public Citizen. Under the consensus standards adopted in 1971, average workday exposure to EtO was limited to 50 parts per million. At the time the standard was adopted, EtO was not known to be a carcinogen. In 1981, citing newly discovered evidence that EtO might be both carcinogenic and mutagenic (inducing chromosomal abnormality), Public Citizen petitioned OSHA to issue an emergency temporary standard, reducing permissible exposure limits to 1 ppm. OSHA rejected the petition on the ground that large numbers of employers were already voluntarily reducing EtO exposure, and there was no clear evidence that the situation constituted an emergency.

In fact, OSHA's past experience with emergency standards—it had tried to issue several in the early 1970s—was that they were immediately appealed and often struck down by courts unless the agency could show a very compelling reason for not proceeding through the ordinarily prescribed route for adopting new standards.[71] The agency did acknowledge that a permanent new standard for EtO should be adopted, however, and promised to commence the rule making process within a few months. But Public Citizen proceeded to sue the agency to demand the immediate promulgation of an emergency standard, and it persuaded a federal district court judge in Washington to order the agency to do so.[72] This order was overturned by the D.C. Court of Appeals,[73] which somewhat grudgingly acknowledged that available evidence did not support the district court's finding that OSHA's refusal to issue an emergency standard was "irrational" or "an abuse of discretion." Nonetheless, the court of appeals insisted that it was "not tolerable" for OSHA to take longer than another year to issue a final rule in this matter—all the more so, as the court explained, because its "command" requiring OSHA "to expedite the EtO rulemaking . . . would [not] seriously disrupt other rulemakings of higher or competing priority."[74]

This confident managerial projection turned out to be wrong. In explaining why the EtO rule would not compete with "other rulemakings," the Court of Appeals noted that OSHA's efforts to formulate a tighter asbestos standard were already so far along that a formal proposal would be shortly forthcoming, in any case. OSHA's EtO standard was completed within the year. The formal proposal on asbestos was not published for another three years. It was estimated that the new asbestos standard might save seventy-five lives each year, and that the EtO rule might save three to five lives each year.[75] EtO was pressed forward more quickly because it happened to be singled out for special treatment by public interest litigants.

And this was not the end of the matter. The EtO standard promulgated by OSHA in 1984 did provide for a stringent 1 ppm daily average exposure limit, but did not adopt a separate short-term exposure limit, as the agency had originally contemplated. The extra cost of a short-term exposure limit would have been dramatic, and the benefits to be secured for this extra cost had been sharply questioned by regulatory analysts in OMB.[76] In a new round of litigation, the D.C. Court of Appeals rejected all challenges to the rule from the Association of Ethylene Oxide Users on the grounds that OSHA did not have to produce "definitive evidence" or even a single study that was "a model of textbook scientific evidence" because "incomplete proof is inevitable when the agency regulates on the frontiers of scientific knowledge."[77] But the court then turned around and upheld a challenge, pursued simultaneously by Public Citizen, that OSHA had not provided sufficient evidence to justify its omission of a short-term exposure limit. OSHA then proceeded to commission more studies to determine whether this decision was appropriate, resulting in another lawsuit from Public Citizen and another reprimand from the D.C. Court of Appeals, which exhorted that "when lives are at stake . . . OSHA must press forward with energy and perseverance."[78]

The court's concern about "lives hanging in the balance" may be understandable; but it is also quite misleading. There are lives at stake not only when OSHA takes time in developing a particular standard, but also when it decides to develop one standard rather than another. OSHA began to pursue a new standard for EtO because an advocacy group—with backing from the courts—insisted on it. Would more lives have been saved if the agency had devoted the same effort to setting new standards for different carcinogens? The Court of Appeals had no way of knowing, because this issue was not argued before the court. OSHA itself does not have very good data on the subject, because developing risk estimates is costly and time consuming, and the agency rarely commissions intensive studies until after it has already made a tentative decision to set a new standard.

The evidence that is currently available, however, suggests that OSHA's choice of which carcinogens to pursue has been highly questionable. The point is well made in the following table, recently published by John Mendeloff,[79] using data developed by the Carcinogenic Assessment Group of the EPA. The table shows the annual number of cancer cases that may be attributed to workplace exposure to various carcinogens at the levels of exposure prevailing before the promulgation of a new standard by OSHA.

The numbers in this table rest on a series of disputable assumptions and may

Workplace Carcinogen	Annual Cancer Cases (at pre-OSHA exposure levels)
Substances covered by new standard (as of 12/87)	
Arsenic	6–27
Asbestos (manufacturing only)	9–32
Benzene	11–36
Coke oven emissions	5
Ethylene Oxide	4–6
Formaldehyde	3–23
Substances without new standards (as of 12/87)	
Chromium	450
Perchloroethylene	547
Trichloroethylene	2,444

SOURCE: John M. Mendeloff, *The Dilemma of Toxic Substance Regulation* (Cambridge, Mass.: M.I.T. Press, 1988), p. 98, table 4.8. Copyright © Massachusetts Institute of Technology. Used with permission. All rights reserved.

be misleading in several respects. But as the same assumptions were employed in each estimate, they do offer a reasonable basis for comparing relative risks. And the comparisons, needless to say, do not inspire great confidence in OSHA's priorities.

Without the pressure of advocacy groups, OSHA might not have gone after the much more serious risks listed in the lower part of this table, anyway. Throughout its history, OSHA has done poorly in setting sensible priorities. But the strongest argument for the risk assessment efforts demanded by White House officials since the mid-1970s is precisely that without some rough sense of the relative scale of risk posed by various occupational hazards, OSHA will never do much better in setting rational priorities. The priorities pursued by the agency in standard setting are largely a reflection of the priorities demanded by advocacy groups. And instead of helping to remedy this problem by checking the pressures of special interest groups, courts have exacerbated the problem by extending the leverage of particular groups. Thus, following the EtO litigation, OSHA devoted its attention to a new rule for formaldehyde when formaldehyde was discovered to have carcinogenic properties—because advocacy groups, including Public Citizen, demanded that the agency take action on formaldehyde, though no one disputes that many other substances pose far greater risks.[80] AFL-CIO officials insist that they are not opposed to having OSHA set priorities, but they justify agenda forcing litigation on the grounds that the agency might end up doing nothing at all if not subject to such pressures.[81] Once again this worst-case assumption is strongly disputed by officials at OMB, who argue that they might have been able to prod the agency to take up more severe hazards—and therefore, generally more cost effective standards—if OSHA's standard setting resources were not preempted by litigation.[82]

What is certain, at any rate, is that the AFL-CIO is not organized to help OSHA improve its priorities. On some of the most severe hazards, it has not pressed OSHA for action, apparently because the workers most affected are not generally unionized. In relation to chromium, which is estimated to be one hundred times more hazardous than EtO, the AFL-CIO did petition OSHA for a new standard in the 1970s. But EtO was pressed forward earlier in litigation because health care unions, eager to expand unionization in a traditionally nonunionized filed, have placed special emphasis on job safety questions (hospital sterilization devices are a major source of EtO exposure). The health care unions were not interested in chromium exposure because it did not affect hospital workers. And the AFL-CIO "has interests across the labor movement and can't ignore the concerns of particular unions."[83] Neither has Public Citizen proved much of a corrective or much of a device for "representing unrepresented interests." It has instead closely coordinated its litigation efforts with those of unions, which have actually carried most of the burden of presenting evidence at OSHA hearings—as was true with the EtO case, in which the health care unions were represented by the very large and powerful American Federation of State, County, and Municipal Employees.[84]

But even if the pattern of litigational pressures were less imbalanced, the underlying problem would remain. In seeking to force particular rules onto OSHA's agenda, judges ritually disclaim any intention to take over the management of the agency. In one sense, such disclaimers are quite valid. The judges do not know—and, consoled by their legalistic formulas, may disclaim any need to know—what effects their decisions may have on the agency's overall management. To put the point more directly, the judges do not know what interests they are displacing when they press a particular litigious constituency to the head of the agency's priorities list, and they act as if the law ceases to make it an important question. There are obvious reasons why OSHA officials do not want to consider such questions very carefully themselves. But judicial intervention simply affords one more powerful excuse for failing to consider questions of priorities in a sober and serious way.

What seems at first to be the exception to this pattern in the history of OSHA litigation is, in fact, the exception that proves the rule—or at least illustrates the difficulties in sorting out political and policy priorities in a sensible manner. This case is the fourteen-year history of litigation concerning sanitary provisions for farmworkers. The workers to be served by a standard in this area are largely migrant workers, many of whom are Hispanics or Haitians. Poor, poorly organized, often ineligible for the vote, these people might seem to be at a tremendous disadvantage in the political process. And this disadvantage may seem to be reflected in OSHA's response to this constituency. For all that, it would be hard to regard judicial intervention in this case as a vindication of public interest litigation.

In 1972, the National Congress of Hispanic American Citizens (El Congreso) petitioned OSHA for the promulgation of a field sanitation standard requiring access to drinking water, handwashing facilities, and portable toilets. When no action was taken, El Congreso then brought a suit to compel such action. The Labor Department finally sought advice from an advisory committee, which did recommend a standard. When OSHA failed to proceed with this recommendation, El Congreso reactivated its suit and won a court order directing OSHA to promulgate the standard within a few months.[85] In 1977, the D.C. Court of Appeals reversed this ruling, however, finding that nothing in the OSH Act excluded the "traditional agency discretion to alter priorities and defer action due to legitimate statutory considerations."[86] But the court also directed OSHA to make regular status reports, explaining further delays to the district court. And the appellate judges instructed the district court, if it doubted the sincerity of these explanations, to "take such action as the circumstances require."

This ruling set the stage for another decade of wrangling, punctuated by periodic *Federal Register* notices and periodic reactivations of the litigation, as OSHA first promised to issue the standard within a particular deadline, then changed its mind, then renewed the promise. In fact, OSHA had reason to hesitate. The principal health hazard that might be remedied by such a field sanitation standard was the higher incidence of certain infections among farm workers which often produced diarrhea and other digestive disorders but were not fatal. Even advocates of the standard often stressed that the absence of adequate toilet facilities threatened the dignity of farm workers as much as their health.[87] At the same time, OSHA feared that a standard requiring farms to set up portable, temporary toilet facilities, for the few weeks each year in which large numbers of employees would be active in distant fields, would be difficult to enforce, just because it did not require heavy, fixed investments in equipment. With no other reason to inspect outlying farms, OSHA officials were reluctant to divert inspectors to ensure that the sanitation standard was fully enforced.[88]

There was also a larger problem. When OSHA had first begun to address safety measures for farmworkers in the mid-1970s, it had aroused a great deal of ridicule and a great deal of opposition. Congress had responded by limiting OSHA's jurisdiction to farms with more than ten employees.[89] A decade later this restriction was still in effect, and OSHA calculated that it would exclude action against the farms employing some 65 percent of farm workers. Fortunately, however, some of the states with the largest number of farmworkers had already adopted field sanitary standards on their own, and such state regulatory programs were estimated to cover some 75 percent of farmworkers. After changing its mind several times under the impact of litigation, the Labor Department finally announced in 1985 that it would promulgate a federal standard in this area within two years unless a sufficient number of states took action on their own. Pressuring the states to take further action in this way might not succeed, but if it gained any success it might turn out to be the most satisfactory approach: with the continuing restrictions on OSHA's jurisdiction, direct action by the agency would leave most farmworkers unprotected (and under the circumstances, even a direct federal supplement to existing state programs would only increase coverage of farmworkers by an additional 4 to 9 percent).[90]

The D.C. Court of Appeals simply lost its patience, however, and in a split decision at the beginning of 1987 ordered OSHA to promulgate a binding standard in this area within thirty days.[91] The decision was a characteristic blend of moral indignation against OSHA's record and legalistic arguments to support judicial intervention. Its central argument of "law" was that, as Congress had excluded farms with fewer than eleven employees from OSHA's jurisdiction, the agency could not properly delay further for the sake of pressuring more states to take action on behalf of farms with fewer than eleven employees. As the dissenting opinion noted, this reasoning "reads the restrictive appropriations riders as manifesting unqualified congressional indifference to the welfare of two-thirds of the nation's farmworkers." Moreover, as the dissent protested, the decision "commits" OSHA "enforcement resources to the nation's farms, at the expense of enforcement against lethal hazards elsewhere, without so much as allowing [the agency] an opportunity to review the situation under the majority's view of the law."[92]

With all of these policy complications, it is not even so clear that judicial intervention in this case was really a necessary assist to an otherwise underrepresented constituency. Although the litigation was conducted by lawyers from a small public interest group, the Migrant Action Program, evidentiary submissions for OSHA hearings were developed by the AFL-CIO on behalf of the United Farmworkers. The proposed standard also received strong support from an OSHA oversight subcommittee in the House.[93] It is not at all clear, then, that OSHA's reluctance to act in this area simply reflected the political weakness of those advocating the new standard. OSHA's hesitations might very plausibly be seen as a considered response to the weakness of their policy claims.

Responsible national policy certainly does not require that everything possible be done to reduce avoidable cancer threats to industrial workers before anything is done to reduce the lesser health hazards of farmworkers. In this sense, the policy decision made by two judges of the D.C. Court of Appeals might well have been made by a responsible policy maker. But it is foolish to pretend that decisions of this kind are in themselves exercises in responsible policy making. The court simply manipulated legal formulas to "demonstrate" that its own preferred outcome was "required" by "the law"—and then insisted that "the law" made all contrary policy considerations irrelevant. The court's hunch about what will best serve farmworkers may or may not be correct. Its hunch that farmworkers had earned priority attention by 1987—though they had not deserved it in 1977—may or may not be plausible. But the judges were considerably less honest than OSHA officials about the actual rationales for their decision.

Perhaps integrity is merely a fetish of academic lawyers in any case. And perhaps the play of political forces will always end up steering OSHA away from the optimal allocation of its powers, energies, and resources, from the standpoint of saving human life. But ill-informed judges, viewing particular disputes in isolation from larger policy concerns and retaining neither power nor responsibility for larger policy, are most unlikely to improve the agency's priorities. And whatever the consequences of judicial intervention on behalf of farmworkers, the larger pattern of which it is a piece has undoubtedly made OSHA a much less effective agency. If there is any defense at all for this state of affairs, it cannot be that "lives are at stake."

PART IV

CONCLUSION

8

The Constitutional Choice: Responsible Government or Administrative Legalism

THIS BOOK has emphasized the ways in which contemporary administrative law extends the policy leverage of particular interest groups or advocacy groups and ends up, in this way, aggravating the maladies of interest group politics. It has also focused on the ways in which, once judges depart from the logic of private rights and seek to manage the claims of contending interest groups, they end up retreating into legal formulas that are far more formalistic than those associated with the logic of private rights and which finally seem a retreat into sheer mysticism. Taken together, these characterizations may suggest that contemporary administrative law reflects the workings of some dark political conspiracy—or some inexplicable institutional pyschosis.

Of course, this is not so. Rather, the current system has evolved from haphazard adjustments in a disoriented legal culture. This disorientation reflects not simply the obfuscations of visionary law professors or the confusions of impulsive judges, but the underlying ambivalence in modern American liberalism. To put it most simply, administrative law has sought to accommodate the desire for increasingly large government programs capable of rearranging society to serve consciously formulated plans, while at the same time seeking to accommodate deep-rooted suspicions of "big government" or of centralized administrative power. It might be said, without sarcasm, that administrative law has reflected the changing moods of a political outlook much attracted to social democratic programs and perspectives but ever skittish about socialism.

If this larger political background helps to explain the confusions in contemporary public law, however, it hardly excuses them. The system of legal controls on administration that has developed in the past two decades remains a very confused and dysfunctional one.

Private Rights and Government Power

Socialist thinkers of the nineteenth century, beginning with Marx and Engels, were disdainful of "law" and dismissive of "rights," seeing them as mere ideological masks for the social control of the propertied classes. In the 1920s, the Soviet legal theorist E. B. Pashukanis drew out the logical conclusion of the socialist perspective. Where there is no private property (because everything is owned and controlled by society as a whole), there cannot, he argued, be any need for law: systems of law and rights will, therefore, be replaced by systems of management and technical administration.[1]

As it has turned out, even Communist regimes have found it useful to retain certain institutional trappings of law and legality. But these have usually proved to be empty pretenses, because state officials have been unable to conceive any reason to let law stand in their way. In Western Europe, however, even periods of rule by avowedly socialist parties have not threatened the continued operation of independent courts, imposing some genuine constraints on official action. And this situation probably reflects the force of the original socialist insight about law: socialist parties in Western Europe have not sought to destroy all law and rights because they have not sought to "socialize" all private activity. Hence socialist parties did not threaten the civil law system for adjudicating disputes between private parties or the highly legalized systems of administrative law, developed in France and Germany and other European states in the nineteenth century, to assure relatively stable and predictable dealings between governmental administrators and private firms.[2]

Still, the success of socialist parties in Western Europe reflects a more trusting popular attitude about governmental power, a consequence, no doubt, of long traditions of centralized governmental power. When socialist governments nationalized previously private industries, therefore, they (and their more conservative successors) assumed that these nationalized or socialized industries could be operated with few more legal constraints than those applying to private owners. They did not imagine that earlier systems of administrative law—designed to protect the rights of private owners—should be extended to safeguard "social interests" in the conduct of new government enterprises.[3]

In the United States, there was no recognized system of administrative law at all in the nineteenth century, because there were so few programs involving direct administrative control of private property or personal liberty. It was assumed that if government sought to impose such controls, it must allow private owners or private persons recourse to the ordinary courts to contest the validity of such coercive orders or sanctions in any particular case. The development of a separate system of administrative law was largely prompted by American unwillingness to follow even modest European steps toward social control of the economy. Industries that had historically been established by European states or taken under state control in the twentieth century under socialist initiative—railroads, telegraph and telephone, electric power generation, coal mining, oil and natural gas pipelines, broadcasting, and so on—were left under private ownership in the United States and simply subjected to specialized forms of regulation. And the meshing of these regulatory powers with the traditional system of legal controls on government was a source of considerable controversy as late as the 1930s.

Almost from the outset, the law applied by regulatory commissions was understood to be necessarily less formal or rule bound than the law applied by ordinary courts, because in setting prices and allocating routes (or service sectors or market shares), the commissions were not simply attempting to prohibit certain determinate types of bad conduct: they were inevitably involved in economic management and were therefore accorded some of the flexibility of business managers, even when issuing coercive orders, from case to case. Formal hearings and judicial review for contested decisions were supposed to protect private ownership by ensuring that regulatory constraints would be well considered or well grounded or nonarbitrary in nature—in sum, no more intrusive or burdensome than necessary.

On the whole, the American experience with the regulation of individual industries by specialized commissions has proved disappointing. Much of the problem may be the operation of political pressures on the regulatory commissions to protect regulated industries from the normal economic imperatives of a changing economy. In many industries—most notably the railroads, regulated by the ICC—such protection may well have hastened the long-term decline of the industry as a whole.[4] Still, many of the nationalized industries of Western Europe, such as steel and coal, do not have a much better record; and the trend toward deregulation of economic controls in the United States over the past decade has therefore been paralleled by a similar trend toward privatization of nationalized industries in Western Europe. When the aim is simply to satisfy private or consumer preferences most efficiently, government planners rarely seem to have enough information, enough flexibility, enough incentive to improve on the performance of competitive markets.

Yet there continues to be much demand for regulation—in the United States as in all other western countries—because few people are content simply to purchase or consume goods that can be privately traded. For one thing, people may place a very high value on some things—like clean air or pleasing natural settings—that cannot be privately purchased, so there remains a need for government regulatory programs to protect such public goods. Then there are a variety of regulatory programs pursuing less obvious or less perfect public goods, exemplified by the case studies in this book.

Government asserts collective control over many kinds of consumer decisions, for example, that do involve the private consumption of goods by individuals, but in circumstances in which it is thought that people are too ill-informed to evaluate the risks involved—as with pharmaceutical drugs. Regulation will continue to be maintained when general controls seem cheaper and easier than efforts to convey all of the available technical information to each potential consumer. In other areas, protecting people from hazardous personal choices seems to be a way of compensating for inequalities in income: without regulation, it is feared, financial pressures might induce some people to accept more remunerative but more physically hazardous employment and so incur more risk (or more injury) than the rest of society thinks appropriate. This rationale for safety regulation may be the only justification for much that is done by OSHA and by the Consumer Products Safety Commission (the latter protecting consumers against cheaper but more hazardous products).[5] Such regulatory programs may be described as paternalistic. But they might be more appropriately described as "communalistic." Like direct government financial assistance to the poor or disabled, regulatory programs of this kind assert the community's concern for the well-being of fellow citizens. This communal concern may be more obvious in various moral constraints imposed by the criminal law—such as laws against gambling or prostitution—but it is also a large element in the justification for civil rights regulation, which seeks to assure people respectful treatment by fellow citizens or to encourage their social integration into the community.

It may be said that the ultimate public motivation for such measures is not entirely altruistic, because measures designed to improve the condition of particular groups—whether industrial workers, racial minorities, or others—are implicit efforts to placate the clamor of such groups and buy their loyalty and cooperation. But the classical liberal argument for public protection of property rights was also couched in terms of *buying* loyalty: that is the effectual meaning of tracing the origins of public authority to a *contract.* At some level, politics in a liberal society or a free country is always preoccupied with renegotiating the terms on which citizens will adhere to communal norms or collective decisions, so it almost always appeals to complex combinations of public spiritedness and selfish calculation. It remains true that what the community offers must be understood to reflect a public or communal judgment on what citizens may expect, as expressed through appropriate public or communal authorities.

Contemporary administrative law tries to make such public policies as much subject to private control as actual private property or private rights. The result is that, in most respects, administrative action in the United States has come to be subject to much more elaborate and pervasive procedural and judicial controls than administrative action in Western Europe.[6] This result may be understandable, in view of the historic American distrust of governmental authority. But it is not sensible, especially in the context of the actual constitutional structures built up in the past in this country to satisfy this distrust of government.

The Limits of Legality

Law is a device for limiting power. It is, by the same token, a device for securing power. As law limits the power of others to interfere with my plans, it secures my own power to pursue those plans. But power is not everything. It may be a consolation that I was free to "do it my way"; this consolation may be rather small if my way ends up making me wretched. Similarly, others may be forced to concede my right to pursue my own self-ruin; they may still think me a wretch for actually doing so. Rights do not guarantee pleasing results. A right merely confirms the personal responsibility of the right holder for what he does with it.

Up to a point, the same is true of government. Law limits the power of government to coerce private persons and, by the same token, confirms the power of government to act within these limits. But again, power is not everything. Neither is legality. Legal power can still be exercised prudently or foolishly, helpfully or destructively. When governmental power is involved, however, responsibility for legal choices takes on a different meaning. Even wretches may have rights, but we do not want them exercising public authority. That is why, in free countries, there is political accountability for government, not merely legal constraint.

There would be no need for political accountability, any more than for law, if everyone agreed on what government should do. And just as classical Marxists looked forward to the abolition of law, they also expected an ultimate abolition of politics, for essentially the same reason: they supposed that the abolition of private property would put an end to serious disagreement.[7] But the abolition of politics now seems even more visionary than the abolition of markets. Those regimes which have gone farthest in seeking the elimination of private property and free commerce have also felt obliged to go farthest in applying brutal police measures to suppress disagreement (or mere evidence of dissatisfaction) with existing government policies. It now seems quite obvious that people may sharply disagree about public policy even when they no longer have different economic stakes in government policy. Stated another way, it now seems obvious that abolishing private property does not eliminate differing stakes, economic or otherwise, in government policy.

Free countries find disagreement less threatening, in part because they do not have such utopian expectations. Limiting the reach of government means that we do not have to reach agreement on everything, because in most areas we are free to go our different ways. And when the reach of government is limited, the stakes, even in the remaining sphere of public activity, are correspondingly reduced. But we still have disagreements about public policy, that is to say, disagreements about the choices made by public officials.

If people can claim legal rights against government, they can demand to have government choices confined by legal limits. The more people can pursue legal claims against government, the wider is the range of government decisions that will have to be fixed by legal norms. The more government is accountable to private litigants, then, the less it can be accountable to anyone else. In sum, limiting the choices of government officials limits their responsibility, for they cannot be responsible for choices they are not allowed to make. Of course, such restriction is part of what is involved in reducing the stakes in public policy: governmental responsibility for much of private life is sharply limited in free countries. People who invoke their rights are insisting that what they do with their liberty or property is their own affair and not the responsibility of government officials. But people who invoke their own rights are not claiming to act on behalf of the public. Contemporary public law rests on a blurring of lines between private rights and public claims, so that people who are not asserting their own personal rights—rights to control something distinctly their own—may still remove questions of public policy from governmental responsibility.

In fact, all western governments are rather eager to limit the choices of public officials or to claim that their choices are limited. They do so in part because it is administratively convenient to follow standard operating routines and limit occasions for policy reconsideration. They also do it to deflect responsibility for policy choices by denying the range of choice actually available. The difference in America is that a more open political system leaves officials much more exposed to criticism and prompting from a broad range of political constituencies. In some circumstances, this situation makes officials simply treat the demands of powerful interest groups or of well-connected advocates as binding law. Contemporary administrative law is less a corrective to this pattern than a formalization of it, for it is essentially about fixing authoritative claims on public policy at the behest of private advocacy groups.

So in the *Adams* case, litigation converted administrative policy decisions by the Office for Civil Rights into guarantees that advocacy groups could insist upon: not Congress, but the agency and its constituencies—along with a rather confused district judge—decided that federal investigators should be devoting their energies to complaints about sex discrimination in high school sports programs in a period in which minority students were falling farther and farther behind in obtaining basic education from public schools. Not Congress but the FDA has determined that the United States should restrict access to new medical drugs more tightly than any other country in the world, but distracted courts and strident advocacy groups have helped to entrench this policy as law. Not Congress but OSHA has determined that occupational health policy should impose the most stringent exposure standards with almost no regard for cost, but courts and advocacy groups have again entrenched this counterproductive policy as law.

The formal logic of contemporary administrative law is to focus responsibility for public policy back on Congress, by treating administrative policy as properly a more or less technical extrapolation from legislative mandates. In another words, it rests on a systematic reduction of executive responsibility along with a systematic inflation of legislative authority. It is certainly true that the vast scale of contemporary federal programs has been made possible by the repudiation of any significant, substantive constitutional limitations on Congress. Since the constitutional revolution of the 1930s, responsibility for the scale of federal undertakings is squarely fixed on Congress in the sense that no court will limit congressional power to preempt state or local authority with federal operations or enforce any significant constitutional limitations on federal control of private activity.

But Congress still operates within the framework of the traditional constitutional scheme in other respects. And the enduring features of the traditional constitutional scheme continue to work at odds with the notion that Congress may serve as an ultimate, authoritative voice of the people, leaving executive officials with no responsibility but to obey.[8] Given the actual operating character of the American constitutional scheme, it continues to be more plausible to think that responsible government overall is not served by allowing executive responsibility to be drained away by litigating advocacy groups and their judicial patrons.

The Logic of Separated Powers

The American Constitution does not provide for an ultimate sovereign authority. Its most distinctive feature is its provision for an institutionally grounded separation of powers. This scheme of separated powers only makes sense on a certain understanding of private rights as rights not to be coerced—or not to have one's property taken—except in accord with a general rule. This view of rights is almost entirely formal or negative, in the sense that it simply promises the claimant of rights what will *not* happen: he will not have his liberty constrained or his property taken except when such incursions are authorized by a general rule.

One consequence of this principle is familiar and obvious even today: we separate courts from the rest of government in order to ensure that individual applications of coercion do correspond to a fair reading of what the relevant general rule permits. We want courts to view individual cases without regard to consequences. We want courts, that is, to view the relevant rule in relatively formal terms, so that coercion will be confined, in the particular case, to law and will not merely reflect the exigencies of policy. We do so in order to assure individuals that they can confidently conduct their own affairs as they choose, if they stay within the rules. There may not be a great deal of security in this formal guarantee—for it says little about the content of rules—but it remains a broadly accepted notion in all western countries that private activity should receive at least this much protection from the exigencies of public policy or the ambitions of public authorities.[9]

But the original argument for the separation of powers, as we find it in Locke and other seventeenth century English writers, was an argument not so much for the independence of the judiciary as for the limitation of the legislature. The original argument stressed that the legislative power to lay down new rules for private conduct must be separated from the power to enforce these rules in particular cases, so as to ensure that rules are conceived with general concerns in mind, and to emphasize that only such general concerns, formulated in rules, can be invoked to justify coercion.[10] It was plainly with this view of the legislative power in mind that the framers of the American Constitution included a distinct prohibition on bills of attainder— the legislative imposition of punishments on particular individuals. The same perspective led the Supreme Court to hold in the nineteenth century—and indeed in a number of cases in recent decades—that legislative enactments that are overly particularized or invidious in their terms (even if they do not go so far as to single out particular individuals) may deny "due process of law."[11]

From this traditional perspective, the executive cannot be subordinate to the legislative power any more than the judiciary is. The whole point of the separation of powers in this view is to forestall direct legislative control of the enforcement or implementation of laws. James Madison indeed argued at the constitutional convention that securing the independence of the executive from legislative control was even more important than securing the independence of the judiciary. The formal character of judicial decision making, he argued, would make legislative interference with judicial decisions immediately obvious; with the executive, by contrast, "much greater latitude is left to opinion and discretion" because "the collective interest & security were much more in the power belonging to the executive," so legislative manipulations of executive decisions could not be so easily detected.[12] With the legislative power limited to the enactment of general rules and the judiciary confined to formal reasoning from these rules, the executive was the one power left to think strategically or tactically, setting priorities among individual cases in order to serve larger aims. The separate election of the chief executive, retaining exclusive power of removal over administrative officials, was designed to ensure that this strategic discretion would be exercised at some distance from the promptings of the legislators in Congress.

The American system never quite worked in this way. The framers themselves were not entirely consistent about insulating the executive from legislative interference; and considering their own understanding of executive power, perhaps they could not have been. So, for example, while prohibiting reductions in the salary of the chief executive, the framers left Congress in control of appropriations for all other administrative undertakings. They were well aware, from the history of the English House of Commons, that the power of the purse was a formidable engine of control, but they were not willing to let the executive branch make independent claims on the public treasury.[13] And almost from the outset, Congress organized itself into specialized committees to extend the powers of control expressly granted in the Constitution.[14]

Still, it is plain that the framers did not regard the relation between executive officials and Congress as a simple managerial hierarchy, because they thought of Congress primarily as a *legislative* body—primarily responsible, that is, for formulating general laws that would be binding on private citizens. Even in the early nineteenth century constitutional doctrine, as declared by the courts, conceded that Congress could give directly enforceable orders to the executive when Congress sought to confer particular benefits on particular individuals, as in the award of cash payments.[15] For the rest, until well into this century the legal force of congressional directives to the executive was essentially left to political bargaining between Congress and the president (or between congressional committees and presidentially appointed department secretaries) and could not be determined by clear legal rulings of the courts.[16] A rather different or more definite view has been encouraged, however, in the course of this century as the most important or most characteristic work of Congress has come to be associated with the establishment of ambitious administrative programs. As long as Congress seems to be more concerned with formulating policy aims or goals for administrative agencies than with directly establishing rules for private conduct, it may seem natural to think of Congress as the ultimate directing power in a managerial hierarchy.

This view of legislative authority is still much more plausible in Western Europe, where long traditions of centralized state power, dating to the era of absolute monarchies in the seventeenth and eighteenth centuries, have sustained the notion of an ultimate directing power in society. The conventions of parliamentary government reinforce this notion by making the leading executive ministers directly responsible to the parliamentary majority. European courts (or administrative courts) may still require that coercion of individuals rest on some more or less direct statutory warrant, but whether the reality of modern party government is that parliament controls "the government" (the leading executive ministers) or that the government controls parliament is essentially irrelevant for legal purposes. Policy seems to flow downward from a unified political authority at the top, and the bureaucracy can thus be viewed as an entirely subordinate instrument for implementing the policy of the state, in accord with irreproachably nonpolitical, technical norms of administrative action. Studies of policy making in Western Europe make plain that the actual relations between political ministers and their bureaucratic "subordinates" are usually a good deal more complex.[17] But the conventions of parliamentary government assign responsibility to the handful of political ministers at the top of the hierarchy, who remain responsible both for guiding new statutory policies through parliament and for deciding major policy questions that arise in the course of their implementation.

In its actual operation, the American administrative system institutionalizes not political unity but political competition. The president appoints not merely a handful of department secretaries but several hundred partisan followers to positions reaching rather deeply into the bureaucracy. Congress does not merely confirm a few top appointees, but exercises continual oversight of administrative operations through dozens of subcommittees and thousands of specialized staff assistants. In itself, this much more heavily or openly political atmosphere of administrative operations in the United States would make it implausible to think of administrative policy as a mere technical extrapolation from statutory policy: these elaborate political controls are not, after all, the hidden background but the deliberately constructed, official foreground of administrative policy making, which plainly rests on the premise that administrative implementation cannot and should not be trusted to proceed in accord with the technical, nonpolitical judgments of professional administrators.

But there is a larger reason why it is highly implausible to regard Congress as the ultimate authority in the policy making hierarchy: namely, that Congress as a whole does not have the capacity to respond to policy challenges in the prompt, direct manner of an ultimate policy manager. The legislative process remains awkward and cumbersome, as the framers of the Constitution designed it to be. And as the framers hoped and expected, Congress remains so riven with competing factions that it is extremely difficult to reach agreement on new statutory measures, even when it is clear that previously enacted policies no longer provide adequate or relevant guidance for executive operations (if they ever did).

In taking statutory enactments as binding statements of contemporary policy, then, administrative law moves into a world of legal fiction that becomes more and more strained the more it demands adherence to the so-called "policy." Each of the case studies in the preceding chapters offers different examples of the perversities that arise from this situation. So, for example, a statutory prohibition on race discrimination in federally funded programs—enacted in 1964, when discrimination was still assumed to mean simply differing treatment by race and when federal funding of education programs was, in any event, quite limited—is treated in the *Adams* case as a meaningful guide to policy for the sizable regulatory bureaucracy that has grown up in the intervening decades. A 1962 statute aimed at the regulation of new drugs is made to say what the Food and Drug Administration should be doing more than twenty-five years later in relation to products that Congress was not sure how to handle even in 1962. Even earlier prohibitions on additives that "induce cancer" are given literal effect in the 1980s, when advances in detection technology have made this policy seem absurd. The vague provisions of the 1970 Occupational Safety and Health Act—enacted when Congress had no meaningful conception at all of the costs or difficulties of reducing health hazards from toxic substances—is supposed to guide the very awkward policy tradeoffs encountered in this field a decade and more later. In all of these cases, Congress has failed to update the underlying statutes (as it has failed to reconsider dozens of other major regulatory statutes) because it cannot agree on what to do, and advocates of tighter controls fear that opening the statutes to reconsideration might open the door to advocates of other policy perspectives to introduce what they view as weakening amendments.[18] In the meantime, policies actually developed by the agencies are retroactively attributed to Congress in order to maintain the pretense that the statutes settle all of the issues.

Political deadlocks do not undermine the logic of the traditional judicial role in protecting private rights from unauthorized administrative intrusion. There is not even any necessary resort to legal fiction in holding administrative agencies within the limits authorized by statute—however old or outdated the relevant statute may be. It may be regrettable that Congress has not authorized wider action to accommodate new concerns, but when courts refuse to read such accommodations into existing measures, they are not, after all, primarily acting to implement the congressional policy vision. They are simply upholding constitutional protection for private rights, by ensuring that private rights are not constrained except as authorized by a legislative process deliberately designed to be slow-moving and cumbersome. When courts intervene to enforce claims to regulatory action, by contrast, they must fall back on the fiction that they are enforcing the policy mandate of Congress, as if Congress were actually in a position to offer ongoing policy directives. Courts are driven to this fiction because they are supposed to enforce law and not policy. In fact, they have no particular competence to make policy, so courts tend to churn out rigid, formal rulings that do, after all, often function with all the clumsiness of law.

There would be no need for these efforts if courts could simply acknowledge that, as long as they do not interfere with particular private rights, executive operations need not be so closely bound by law—or need not be held to formal, judicial conceptions of what the law requires. There would be no need for strained legal fictions, that is, if courts could concede what everyone knows—that the implementation of congressional directives is a matter of political judgment as much as of "law." The obvious inference from this fact, however, is that the implementation of congressional directives is therefore unsuitable for judicial management. Contemporary administrative law is very reluctant to concede this point, because it does not want to acknowledge that the diluted protections for regulated interests under judicial review of administrative decisions are somewhat less protection than the rule of law as traditionally conceived. Having come to accept administrative decisions as law in some contexts, it is now loath to acknowledge that they should ever be less than law in this quasi-managerial sense. It does not want to acknowledge that the disappointments of private interest advocates may stem from nothing more authoritative than the disputable policy judgments of public officials. Putting the matter most directly, contemporary administrative law is reluctant to concede that implementation is largely a political matter, because this admission would imply that disappointed private policy advocates have no claim to bring suits against the policies that disappoint them.

The Logic of Distinctive Powers

The traditional constitutional scheme of separated powers is grounded on the assumption that the different powers should have not only different tasks, but characteristically different perspectives on those tasks. It assumes, for example, that in formulating standing laws, the legislative power will be preoccupied with balancing the claims of competing constituencies. The framers of the American Constitution sought to separate the executive power from the legislative power just because they assumed—quite correctly, as it has turned out—that elected legislators would retain this "representational" or "constituency-minded" perspective in assessing executive enforcement operations; and they saw this perspective as interfering with the fair and effective enforcement or implementation of public measures. In its immediate decisions, the judiciary was most removed from the other powers in order to ensure that private rights would be most protected against the pressures of politics and policy.

In thrusting the judiciary back into politics and policy, contemporary administrative law inevitably forces judges to assume the responsibilities of the other powers and accordingly to claim their special virtues. But all this dress-up play (this institutional transvestism, as we might call it) does not change the underlying nature of the various constitutional actors. It simply perverts their relations in unnatural ways. So in opening the courthouse doors to claimants seeking more or better regulation, contemporary administrative law effectively makes the judges responsible for the implementation of public measures. They are responsible in the sense that they do not merely prompt or criticize, like congressional committees, but hand down binding orders, which executive officials are required to follow. Judges may speak of a "partnership" between courts and administrative agencies, but the judges are plainly the senior partners, at least in legal terms: in the extreme, judges assert the power to sentence executive officials to jail (without so much as a jury trial) for defying their directives, while executive officials can do nothing to protest judicial orders except appeal them to another set of judges.[19] As judges assert the power to review a wider and wider range of executive operations, they make themselves responsible for more and more executive policy.

But, of course, judges cannot be responsible in the ordinary sense of the word. They are not responsible to the voters because they do not stand for reelection. They are not responsible to the president because they cannot be removed by the president even when their decisions prove to have harmful or unpopular consequences. They are not even responsible to Congress (in the sense in which executive officials are) because they are never compelled to come forward and justify their decisions to congressional committees, and neither their budgets nor even their statutory authorizations are put at risk in congressional appropriations.

So judges try to disclaim responsibility at the same time as they assert powers that seem to demand it. They do so by insisting that they are simply upholding the law, not making policy, even when they decide cases demanding more aggressive or effective executive performance. Responsibility is then displaced or concealed by legalism. This is what courts always do, of course. It is what they are supposed to do. Courts provide legal protection for private rights by disclaiming any responsibility for determining what any claimant of a right ultimately deserves or what would most benefit the public to have him do or receive. Courts insist they must simply give the claimant what is his due under the law—and in such cases the executive, too, must honor the judicial construction of the law because claims about rights should be altogether removed from the pressures of mere policy. However much pretense or disingenuousness there may be in this depiction, it remains the characteristic way in which courts describe their tasks; and most people want courts to view their tasks in this way (certainly when their own rights are at stake). Allowing courts to impose their views of the law on wider and wider spheres of executive operations, then, displaces this legalistic perspective into executive operations. To this extent, it undermines executive responsibility.

Judges are certainly aware that legalism is not really appropriate for the conduct of executive operations, so contemporary administrative law continually concedes the need to respect the "lawful" or "legitimate" discretion of administrative agencies. Or, viewing the matter in more realistic terms from the other side, judges are certainly aware that they are not equipped to serve as ultimate managers of executive policy, so contemporary administrative law continually concedes the need for courts to defer to the "reasoned conclusions" or "expert findings" of administrative agencies. But despite all of these concessions, contemporary administrative law can never shake off its unworldly legalism because its central concern is to provide the same legal protection for claims to regulatory benefits as for private property. And there is no way to affect this false symmetry without recourse to obfuscating legalism.

The symmetry is inherently false because the claims are not comparable. The regulated firm seeks to defend its own property rights before a court; that is to say, it seeks to defend what is by definition its own. Some people may think the nation would be better off if less economic or social activity were in private hands, but as long as we seek to maintain a free market economy and a free society, we will maintain legal guarantees for private ownership or private control, that is, fairly reliable guarantees against unauthorized interference. Advocates for more regulation seek what is by definition *not* their own—because public policy cannot be under the control of particular private persons in the manner of private property.

Contemporary administrative law seeks to disguise this asymmetry by viewing regulatory benefits as already guaranteed by statutory enactments, so that any claimant may insist that these benefits are already rightfully his own. But claiming that the litigating advocate is already entitled to receive some regulatory benefit means that he ought to be the judge of whether the benefit has been adequately delivered or should be further secured—as the ordinary property owner may waive his own rights when he finds it convenient to do so. To get around this difficulty, contemporary administrative law is always abstracting from the character of the particular claimant for regulatory benefits, reverting to an unworldly legalism in which it does not matter who actually has advanced the claim or for what purpose.

For this reason, even while administrative law may seem to be animated by the recognition of contending interests at stake in regulatory policy, it characteristically drifts away from the particular interests of particular claimants to focus on more general questions about statutory policy. At the extreme, environmental statutes authorize "any citizen" to come before the courts to challenge decisions of the Environmental Protection Agency, on the assumption that any citizen has as much claim to protest EPA policy as any other. If these suits are conceived as enforcing rights, then the rights in question no longer serve to protect the distinctions between citizens—each holding or claiming something distinctly his own—but rather assert the perfect socialization of the citizenry, so that each citizen is interchangeable with any other for purposes of pursuing his interest.

Environmental statutes are the extreme case, but much of contemporary administrative law pursues the same dreamy vision, that the law can do what the elimination of private property was supposed to do under socialism: eliminate differences between citizens. Courts thus talk about "standing" to litigate rather than about "rights" as if it does not really matter whether the particular litigant is personally entitled to what he seeks. Courts thus talk about "the law" rather than about actual policy benefits or policy beneficiaries, as if we could all agree on the former without regard to the latter. And the academic apologists for contemporary administrative law talk about regulation as a device for affirming "public values," not as a device for securing actual consequences. In sum, contemporary administrative law makes a legalistic indiffer-ence to consequences into a virtue—as it makes a virtue of the lack of responsi-bility inherent in legalism.

If we step back from particular cases and view regulatory operations in larger terms, it is easy to see that even with a good deal of litigation, regulatory agencies still do not operate with legalistic detachment, in mechanical, rule bound fashion. In this larger, more realistic perspective, judicial interventions are merely one element—perhaps not even the most important—in an array of influences at work in the formulation of regulatory policy. Even for regu-lated firms or institutions, litigation is the exception; more often firms seek to influence administrative policy through participation in administrative hear-ings or through informal bargaining with agency officials. They may also pursue efforts to lobby higher level officials in the executive branch or in Congress and to appeal to citizens at large through public relations. Much of this latter activity is not even pursued by individual firms, moreover, but by a variety of trade associations and organizations representing various business interests. At this level their political activities are not much different from the parallel efforts of consumer advocates, or environmental advocates, or many other organizations seeking to advance the interests of their constituencies.

In this broader perspective, litigation may appear to be simply one more tool for gaining marginal advantage in a system characterized by ongoing political competition and policy maneuver. This view makes it plausible to think of public law litigation as simply a device to enhance the strength of underrepre-sented interests in a process that remains, after all, largely political. Adopting this perspective, some commentators have celebrated public interest litigation as a vehicle for enhancing citizen participation in government decision mak-ing. In this perspective, courts are not so much surrogate policy managers, ensuring Weberian conformity to the hierarchical authority of the statute makers; rather they function as surrogates for legislative oversight, ensuring administrative sensitivity to the concerns of various political constituencies that would normally be nurtured by the representative concerns of Congress.

The problem with this view is that Congress remains quite involved in legislative oversight whatever the courts may do. Moreover, judicial oversight does not act in the same way as congressional oversight. Congressional over-sight may prompt, criticize, pressure, but nothing that is done by congressional subcommittees or by individual members or staff members in Congress has the force of law. Administrators are not bound to obey, even if they find it difficult to disregard, these promptings and pressures. Because Congress has an ongo-ing relation both with constituency groups and with the agency, and because congressmen also remain at some level accountable to other and perhaps broader constituencies, the tendency of congressional oversight is to highlight concerns or perspectives rather than to articulate precise rules of conduct. To the extent that congressional factions seek responsiveness, that is, they measure this responsiveness in general terms, so that particular incidents or episodes are weighed in a larger pattern. This arrangement may leave administrators with more maneuvering room. It certainly leaves them with more independent responsibility.

Because courts can rarely escape their characteristic legalism, however, citizen participation through litigation has a different logic. In principle, it is not the logic of citizen participation or political advocacy but its opposite, because it seeks to reduce political advocacy to legally binding claims. It may seem realistic to view litigation as merely one of many tactics that regulated firms employ to assert or defend their interests. But once they do come to court, the legal system cannot view regulated firms (or disgruntled taxpayers, or government contractors, or any of the multitude of traditional litigants who come before the courts to protect their own rights) as merely engaging in citizen participation or political advocacy, for this interpretation would reduce their rights to mere hopes, with no necessary legal force. When litigants come forward to assert their rights, they are allowed—they are indeed encouraged—to come forward with a special degree of insistent self-assertion: they are asserting their own rights, after all, claims that are uniquely their own, private claims that are by definition no one else's business.

Allowing interest group or policy advocates to come forward as litigants encourages (or, rather, ratifies) the transference of this perspective to public policy. It implies that citizens—or self-styled "public citizens"—may come forward as owners of some piece of public policy, demanding what is due them as if it were a private matter, not properly subject to objection or protest from anyone else. This is not citizen participation but its opposite, for it negates the notion of the citizen as a member of the public—as a part of a larger community—whose advocacy proceeds on the premise that the entire public or community may have a stake in the outcome. The expression of this reversal is the notion that citizen participation may be secured through the judiciary, the least politically accountable—in fact, the least political, because most legalistic and formalistic—branch of government.

The ultimate difficulty with citizen participation through litigation is not that it encourages extreme policies—though that may sometimes be the result. The ultimate difficulty is that it invites deadlock and perversity in the conduct of public policy. The interest advocates who come to court to demand what the law has ostensibly assured them cannot actually secure most of the policy benefits they seek through litigation. Courts simply do not have enough power or enough expertise to supply the ultimate policy benefits that interest advocates seek. What courts can (and often do) deliver instead is a legalistic parody of what they provide to ordinary property owners: the satisfaction of having a particular rule enforced in a particular corner of administrative operations. Even if the rule is important, even if many rules are affected, interest advocates and courts can rarely secure sufficient managerial control to direct effective operations and produce desirable results—assuming they had the patience, understanding, and goodwill to seek this end. Even if one thinks that executive officials have bad motives, such interventions are as likely to provide further excuses for poor performance as they are to compel good performance. If one thinks executive officials are, for the most part, conscientiously struggling with genuine difficulties, there is much reason to fear that such interventions undermine a sense of responsibility as they limit necessary maneuvering room—and so discourage appropriate initiatives.

The case studies in this book provide vivid illustrations of the way in which judicial interventions inhibit and discourage sensible policy making. Seventeen years of management by litigating groups forced the Office for Civil Rights to devote a great deal of attention to a great many secondary, marginal issues, irritating and exasperating school officials around the country at the behest of civil rights advocacy groups demanding their rights—while the agency has done little to enhance educational opportunities for racial or ethnic minorities. The Food and Drug Administration has been pressed to squander its resources on peripheral "efficacy" issues, diverting its attention and resources from more serious safety issues. The Occupational Safety and Health Administration has been pressed to adopt extremely severe and costly exposure standards in relation to a handful of dangerous substances, provoking a great deal of powerful resistance, while leaving the bulk of serious hazards substantially underregulated.

In all of these cases, litigating advocacy groups were convinced that intransigent insistence on previous policies was an appropriate strategy to counter competing pressures and policy obstacles faced by regulatory officials. In none of these cases does this opinion seem to have been borne out by events. But judicial intervention made it much more difficult for the responsible executive officials to deviate from this operating premise of private advocacy groups. The physical and moral pressures of the law made it difficult for officials to pursue their own sense of good strategy. Both physically and morally, executive officials were made less responsible for the conduct of executive policy.

If one wanted to adopt the sensationalist rhetoric of public interest advocacy groups, one might speculate that hundreds of thousands of Americans have actually lost their lives and millions received less adequate schooling because of these misguided judicial interventions.[20] Whether the full consequences ought to be assessed as still more severe or perhaps as more modest, it is certain, at any rate, that no one can be held responsible. In the legalistic world of contemporary administrative law, no one is clearly responsible for the management of public programs, which are supposed to proceed with technical correctness from "congressional mandates" that Congress itself does not feel responsible for reconsidering even after decades of demonstrated difficulty.

Policy Without Legalism

Would regulatory policy outcomes be dramatically altered, then, if courts simply abandoned the role they have come to play over the past two decades? Probably not. All of the same advocacy groups that take to the courts to press their demands on regulatory agencies would continue to press their demands through political advocacy and no doubt remain a continuing intimidating presence. Agency officials would continue to find it easiest to accommodate powerful pressures from different sources and defer to prevailing routines, even when this course resulted in perverse or ineffectual policies. Still, it is reasonable to think that without the pressure of litigation, agency officials would have somewhat greater maneuvering room and perhaps a somewhat livelier sense of responsibility, which might sometimes allow for significantly better results.

The ultimate effects are uncertain. But this much is clear: we cannot gauge the full consequences of withdrawing judicial protection for the claims of advocacy groups simply by studying the immediate effects of judicial interventions in particular cases under the current dispensation. It is a mistake to think of administrative law as *merely* a vehicle for interest group politics, as it is a mistake to think of regulatory policy outcomes as no more than the summation of interest group pressures. Law appeals to opinion as much as to force and fear. It is for that reason that organizations like the American Civil Liberties Union go to the trouble of litigating such seemingly marginal issues as the placement of a Christmas crèche in a public park: they expect to reinforce the lesson that resisting "entanglements" between religion and government is a matter of high urgency and "principle"—and with a sizable constituency (including many public officials) they seem to have been quite effective in cultivating and strengthening this attitude.[21]

Courts might well teach a different and more helpful lesson by withdrawing from their current role in managing regulatory disputes. They might, that is, help to reinforce the lesson that most claims about administrative obligations to "the congressional mandate" combine large elements of partisan posturing, misguided idealism, and crass selfishness—along with their share of plausible and reasonable objections or suggestions—and ought, therefore, to be taken with a large grain of salt, as we usually apply a good deal of skepticism to other political arguments and appeals for public action. Encouraging such a climate might do much more to restore maneuvering room to administrative policy making than the mere withdrawal of direct judicial constraints.

Would this climate encourage executive agencies to feel that they could disregard legal mandates—or the legal arguments of advocacy groups—at will? In general, the most convenient course for executive officials is precisely to wrap themselves in congressional mandates instead of troubling to think through the requisites of sound policy. When there is strong political pressure behind a mandate, complete disregard is particularly dangerous for executive officials and not at all common. Disputes center on whether executive officials have complied as Congress intended.

It may well be that when advocacy groups can no longer resort to the courts, the arguments and evidence they present to administrative agencies in support of their favored policy approaches will be considered less attentively by those agencies. The testimony and evidence introduced in hearings before congressional committees are not always taken very seriously by congressmen. But the political constituencies behind such evidence are taken quite seriously in Congress and surely would continue to be taken seriously by administrative agencies. No one charges that it is grossly unfair or unacceptable that advocates for greater government intervention cannot sue Congress when it fails to enact their favored policies, because it is taken for granted that a political voice, rather than a judicially supervised claim to fair consideration, is all that is appropriate. When pursuing their policy preferences with established administrative agencies, such advocates tend to have more strength than they would in Congress, because they loom larger in the smaller arena of agency politics. In major regulatory fields it is implausible to suppose that the political strength of such advocates—with a corps of sympathetic patrons in Congress standing behind them—would melt away to insignificance if they did not have the chance to reinforce their arguments through litigation.

Similarly, there is not much reason to think that access to the courts allows self-styled public interest advocates to provide an effective voice for claims not already well represented in the political process. Ralph Nader's Public Citizen, as we have seen, essentially duplicates the advocacy stances of labor unions in its litigation against OSHA, and in litigation against the FDA simply reinforces regulatory perspectives already very powerful in Congress. If the concerns of racial minorities are poorly served by OCR, that state of affairs reflects not the limited clout of civil rights advocacy organizations so much as their own misguided tactics and priorities.

When there is no great political constituency for a strict adherence to statutory obligations, the executive may assume much greater freedom of action. This is, of course, what happens even now—at least when there is so little support for strict adherence to statutory norms that no one bothers to litigate departures from the law or judges are unreceptive to such claims.[22] If no one is complaining very loudly or effectively, such "lawlessness" may be a perfectly good thing. The risks and benefits of withdrawing judicial control will come into focus in those disputes in which aroused, but not overwhelmingly powerful, political constituencies think administrative policies are neglecting the law—and care very much about this problem.

Without the opportunity to obtain judicial endorsement for such claims, advocates may press them less stridently or be heard with less sympathy in Congress. In some cases it may be that the absence of a judicial arbiter to resolve—or at least to channel—politico-legal controversies will simply exacerbate conflict, spurring rival constituencies and perhaps administrative officials themselves to dismiss opposing arguments as hysterical rhetoric. It is hard to see why a few episodes of this sort should be unbearable or why they should not be cheerfully accepted as the price paid for allowing more freedom of action to administrative policy. All free politics presumes a willingness to accept a considerable degree of conflict, and the American scheme of separated powers plainly builds a certain degree of ongoing tension and conflict into the heart of the governing system. The American political system surely can live with a great deal of conflict and disappointment for particular advocacy or interest groups. The question ought to be whether public policy can live with a legal system designed to assure all such groups that their interests will never be neglected or denied their day in court.

Prospects and Possibilities

Are such changes in administrative law and administrative policy making at all likely over the next decade? Contemporary administrative law has flourished in a political context in which national political parties have been particularly weak and in which shifting or indecisive electoral outcomes have encouraged an unusual degree of tension between Congress and the White House. Congress has been particularly reluctant to clarify or update unworkable regulatory statutes in this context; it has also been content to allow courts to work out their own supervisory role in administrative affairs. A decisive electoral shift, delivering the White House to a party with relatively cohesive majorities in both houses of Congress, might alter the entire context of administrative policy making and might even allow for a systematic readjustment of administrative law through a fundamental revision of basic statutes like the Administrative Procedure Act. Such a dramatic transformation in the broader political context, however, does not appear to be likely in the near future.[23]

In principle, courts do not need to await congressional action to withdraw from the extended supervisory role they have developed over the past two decades. As that role was essentially developed through independent judicial improvisation, it might readily be cut back in the same way. Even when particular congressional enactments purport to confer jurisdiction to review administrative policy at the behest of mere interest group advocates—or of "any citizen"—courts need not accept such jurisdiction. The Constitution indeed specifies that federal courts may only hear actual "cases" or "controversies," and the Supreme Court has continued to affirm that this limitation is constitutionally binding, regardless of what Congress might wish. The Court could make this limitation meaningful again by returning to the traditional doctrine that a legal argument only presents a "case" or "controversy" within the meaning of Article III if it relates to a claim about rights—and that only distinct claims held by individuals can be considered rights. Even if the Court were unwilling to return entirely to this traditional understanding of the judicial power, it could still insist on the limiting force of the nondelegation doctrine, barring Congress from delegating to private parties the executive power to coerce other persons (or to demand the coercion of other persons) when these others have done no injury to their own rights.[24]

Returning to these traditional limitations would upset many established legal practices. But then the Supreme Court has been quite willing to overturn widely established practices when persuaded that the Constitution so required. In its 1983 ruling in the *Chadha* case, for example, the Court invalidated the legislative veto device, which Congress had inserted into dozens and dozens of legislative enactments over the preceding fifty years. The Court's decision in the *Marathon* case the same year, invalidating the authority of court appointed masters in federal bankruptcy proceedings, placed a cloud over several hundred bankruptcy cases then in progress.[25] But it remains much in doubt whether the Court will have the courage or the self-discipline to invoke these constitutional limitations against judicial authority.

Several major court decisions in the past decade have certainly shown signs of uneasiness—on the Supreme Court and in some appellate courts—about overextending the role of courts in supervising administrative policy. Limitations on standing articulated in the mid-1970s have been applied with more bite in some cases, and there have been signs of greater resistance to judicial improvisation beyond the clear implications of statutory language.[26] But the clearest trend toward retrenchment, at least in the influential D.C. Court of Appeals, has focused not on the substance of the legal claims presented by challengers, but rather on the kind of executive discretion they have sought to challenge.[27] In other words, the trend has been to acknowledge greater limitations on the managerial capacity of courts without challenging the underlying premise of contemporary administrative law, that particular advocacy groups may advance preemptive claims on the conduct of public policy.

It is encouraging, by contrast, that courts have thus far declined to impose direct limitations on the review of regulatory agency operations by officials in the Office of Management and Budget apart from insisting that OMB not prevent agencies from implementing (what courts conceive to be) their congressional mandates.[28] But there has been great resistance in Congress to the notion of greater White House supervision of regulatory policy making. In the summer of 1986, the House of Representatives tried to eliminate systematic or institutionalized White House oversight altogether by voting to defund the Office of Information and Regulatory Affairs in OMB, which had been responsible for routine oversight activities. The Senate restored funding, but only after OMB officials agreed to make all of their written communications to regulatory agency officials available for public inspection in the future. This requirement may inhibit candid exchanges and so weaken the potential of OMB oversight. But even in earlier years, OMB leverage was much limited by the sensitivity of department secretaries to congressional pressures; and when department secretaries pressed disputes with OMB to President Reagan and his cabinet, OMB was rarely the winner. In practice, moreover, OMB concentrated most of its efforts on forcing agencies to give more thought to the costs of proposed new regulations instead of prodding agencies to reconsider already established rules and practices, because OMB officials expected to have most leverage on policies not yet settled.[29] Whatever the future course of OMB's regulatory oversight efforts, there is no chance that the sprawling regulatory bureaucracy, entangled with many contending interests and many alert factions in Congress, will soon become a disciplined instrument of the presidential will. If the White House retains a serious interest in regulatory reform, however, it might do much in the future to prod various agencies to reconsider outdated policy approaches and strengthen the independence of agencies from constituency pressures. The White House might do more, that is, if courts will permit it.

CONCLUSION

Paradoxes and Promises

The paradox of contemporary administrative law is that it seems, from one perspective, extremely democratic, allowing for an unusually direct and effective form of citizen participation in public policy making. Yet at the same time, it seems rather strangely authoritarian, appealing to unelected judges to enforce the law, appealing to constraining formal procedures, appealing to the policy sanction of technical expertise. This paradox is related to the frequently paradoxical outcomes of public law litigation. On the one hand, it allows advocacy groups to make direct, preemptive demands on public policy, while on the other it contributes to a wider policy paralysis, frustrating many of the underlying policy goals of these very same advocacy groups. The connection is obvious: public law litigation gives leverage to advocacy groups but not enough control to get what they want—or what anyone actually wants.

All of these paradoxes present a curious mirror image of paradoxes associated with the traditional conception of executive authority. There is, first, the paradox that decisive leadership often proves more effective than do cautious or methodical efforts to accommodate existing expectations. In the words of The Federalist, "energy in the executive" may be "essential" even "to the steady administration of the laws." Then there is the larger paradox that decisiveness—though it may require a readiness to antagonize and disappoint—is often the condition for ultimate popularity or ultimate popular satisfaction with the results. Thus it is, as the The Federalist argued, a "very crude notion" to "regard the servile pliancy of the executive to a prevailing current, either in the community or in the legislature, as its best recommendation," for even very democratic people sometimes leave "lasting monuments of gratitude to the men who had courage and magnanimity enough to serve them at the peril of their displeasure."[30]

Legalism, which is the central characteristic of contemporary administrative law, is above all a device for escaping "the peril of displeasure," while disclaiming any larger responsibility that might oblige officials to risk this "peril." The problem with reducing executive responsibility to legalism, then, is not merely that it often does mask a "servile pliancy" to interest group pressures or to anticipated congressional reactions. At a more fundamental level, the objection to legalism is that it undermines the capacity for "energy in the executive." Legalism appeals to a wholly unrealistic model of policy making, in which administrative implementation appears to follow as a mere matter of technical deduction from legislatively given ends. Legalism seeks assurances that everything is proceeding properly and correctly; and such assurances are bound to be misleading. Effective policy making is bound to be a good deal

266

more opportunistic, continually adjusting goals to meet available capacities, because it is hard to say what government can or should do in a world of changing circumstances and changing expectations.[31] Perhaps the underlying paradox in *The Federalist*'s conception of executive power is that "energy" is not in this view the enemy of responsible government but a necessary ingredient in responsibility.

At its best, energetic policy making allows the executive to anticipate new wants, trusting to vindication from opinions not yet fully established, from constituencies not yet fully formed. The natural result is that energetic policy making is often controversial, for it appeals beyond existing expectations or constituencies. Initiative is always risky, and in the American constitutional scheme there is a standing institutional check on executive initiative from the pressure of congressional representatives, who are likely to be much more attentive to existing constituencies and existing expectations, just because they have so little opportunity to claim direct credit for successful administrative initiatives. Often this restriction may be just as well, for new ideas may be bad ones. The question is whether we should really seek to reinforce the inertial pressures of congressional oversight and the ongoing temptations of legalism with a new layer of legalistic constraints from the courts.

Withdrawing judicial protection for interest advocates might well reduce the influence of particular advocacy groups and sharpen their sense of disappointment and frustration. But the potential for improving the conduct of public policy might offer compensating advantages, even to many of the same constituencies. Public policy is not usually a zero sum game. It tends to look like one only when particular policy goals become reified as legal entitlements, so that a claimant of policy benefits may, like the owner of private property, calculate precisely what he has lost or retained from what was due him. It may be in the nature of organized advocacy groups—or of any intensely committed advocate—to focus in this way on short-term goals to the detriment of larger aims. But this is just the tendency that contemporary administrative law encourages and reinforces.

Even without broad access to the courts, specialized advocacy groups would no doubt continue to urge specialized causes through political channels. The Sierra Club and the Urban League provided strong advocacy for their causes long before such causes could be widely pursued through litigation, just as antiabortion and antipornography advocates have achieved considerable policy influence over the past decade, even though their causes have largely been denied the privilege of asserting influence through private litigation. But every organization must adapt to its environment and adjust its strategy and tactics to available opportunities. And it is at least a reasonable hope that advocacy groups would not direct so much of their efforts into narrow and legalistic claims if litigation did not provide so many opportunities to do so. It seems unlikely, for example, that the NAACP Legal Defense Fund would have continued to devote so much effort to achieving statistical integration in public schools systems or in state systems of higher education—at a time when blacks were falling distressingly behind in so many more substantial indicators of educational and economic progress—except for the fact that courts had already provided legal leverage to go after the former, highly formalistic criterion of black advancement. Similarly, it seems unlikely that consumer safety advocates like Ralph Nader's Public Citizen would have focused attention on color additives or food additives posing absurdly tiny risks—when so many more substantial health risks, even so many more substantial carcinogens, remain unregulated or underregulated—except for the fact that the Delaney clause happened to provide an easy legal claim against the former. A system that offers easy victories by appealing to legalistic criteria of good policy is bound to encourage even serious advocacy groups to end up defining their policy aims in legalistic terms.

Viewing the operation of this system from the other side of the bench, one can still say, of course, that judges retain some latitude to reject overly legalistic or overly formalistic policy appeals and to limit their interventions instead to more serious complaints about the substance of policy. Contemporary administrative law cases are indeed filled with acknowledgments of the need for judicial deference to legitimate administrative discretion. But as this book has argued throughout, it is unrealistic to suppose that judges can detach themselves from the dynamic of litigation and assume a sensible, overall public policy perspective in advocacy litigation, merely because the subject of the litigation, as viewed by realists, is nothing more than the proper course for public policy. Once an advocacy group is allowed to press its claims before the courts, the claim gains additional force by that fact alone. The issue is no longer why the agency should heed this group's policy promptings over a hundred other suggestions in the larger constellation of policy options. Instead, the issue becomes whether the agency has a sufficiently good excuse for disappointing *this* advocacy group (when it happens to have latched onto a plausible legal argument). Judges may say that they are merely forcing the agency to consider all of the options carefully—to take a hard look before deciding—but this process inevitably comes to be defined in terms of what will satisfy the claims of the advocacy group standing before the court, rather than the claims of the larger public outside the courtroom.

Each of the case studies presented in this book offers dramatic examples of this dynamic. Anyone might find much ground for complaint in the initial performance of all of these agencies. But it is absurd to claim that OCR, even under the Nixon administration, was simply disdainful of civil rights concerns or that the FDA and OSHA have ever been cavalier and dismissive toward their own safety missions. In none of the cases could the policies pursued by the agencies—whatever their other defects—fairly be characterized as clear-cut violations of statutory standards. Rather, in all of the cases in which the agencies lost, they lost because judges decided to endorse the particular arguments or constructions advanced by the private advocacy groups before them.

It is true that in insisting on their own views, or on those of the advocacy groups, the judges did not thereby assume complete managerial control of the agencies involved. Even the extremely elaborate and intrusive directives of the *Adams* litigation did still leave a great deal of discretion to OCR in coping with its general responsibilities. But that is just the point. Public law litigation does not force the judges—much less the litigating advocacy groups—to assume responsibility for the broader management or the overall performance of administrative agencies. The judges (or the advocacy groups they empower) simply seize on some corner or criterion of agency policy and demand that the agency meet their expectations in this area. Because they do not accept responsibility for the agency's management or its overall performance, neither the judges nor the advocacy groups are under any obligation to view their particular preoccupations of the moment in any larger context. The whole dynamic of litigation, providing preemptive attention to the claims of the particular litigating party before the court, indeed discourages them from doing so. In this setting, to say that judges will limit their interventions to the "extreme" or "clear" cases of abuse is simply to say that judges may allow advocacy groups to swallow some disappointments but not to have their particular expectations disappointed in an "extreme" way.

In a wider perspective, the notion that courts can find just the right level of legal control on executive discretion can be viewed as the latest episode in a long but discredited tradition in regulatory law. It is the contemporary counterpart of the older belief in administrative law that regulatory agencies—with backup prompting from courts—could determine just the right distribution of market shares and profit margins for industries subject to rate and service controls. Few people now think such controls serve the long-term interests of the public or even of the regulated industries: competitive risk is now more accepted as the inevitable counterpart of economic dynamism. The increasingly well-accepted paradox about economic development is that relatively secure private rights, protected by relatively fixed legal standards, are the counterparts of great economic dynamism. The relatively greater dynamism of the American economy in the 1980s, compared with most of Western Europe, suggests that even government sponsored corporatist arrangements, if they often make for smoother cooperation between major social sectors, yet smother a great deal of valuable initiative and development.[32]

Conclusion

In those areas where we are determined to maintain regulatory programs for particular social purposes—to enhance safety or equality, or whatever may be the aim—we cannot pretend that economic and social forces remain fixed and constant simply because regulatory action would be easier if they did. Congressional factions, attentive to the pleas of existing constituencies, may often resist change, and there may sometimes be a social or political logic to cushioning abrupt change. But just to the extent that we welcome and accept change, we should recognize that executive energy is the natural complement of a changing society. In the American governmental scheme, in which extensive political competition makes it much more difficult to reach agreement on new measures, it is all the more important to protect the remaining potential for executive energy. Energy may, after all, be most vital in such fields as safety regulation and civil rights, where support for continuing effort is most solid and performance in recent decades so disappointing.

Allowing room for executive energy, however, means allowing more room for disputable decisions that may turn out to be mistaken. It certainly means leaving a wider range of decisions open to criticism. If we cannot trust presidentially accountable officials to make acceptable decisions—or cannot tolerate the clamor of organized advocacy groups when policy decisions disappoint them—then we should consider fundamental constitutional reforms to insulate administrative agencies from political influence and political criticism. Under a different constitutional scheme, we might then seek to build up the trappings of administrative legalism, as is done in Western Europe, to help insulate administrative agencies from improper influence or inhibiting controversy.

But in the contemporary American system, courts can only insulate policies in pieces, and then not for the benefit of the general public but for the satisfaction of particular interest or advocacy groups. This system leaves administrative agencies widely exposed to the promptings and complaints of competing advocacy and interest groups, and then allows the same groups to invoke legalistic rationales to protect their preferred policies from reconsideration or adjustment over time. For well-situated advocacy groups, preoccupied with immediate agendas, this situation may seem like the best of both worlds. For the general public it more often seems to deliver the costs of legalism with few of the benefits. By any criteria, judicial compulsion cannot be responsible execution. What animates the compulsions of judges is sheer constitutional confusion.

NOTES

Chapter 1

1. For a review of the political rhetoric of that era, see Michael McCann, *Taking Reform Seriously: Perspectives on Public Interest Liberalism* (Ithaca, N.Y.: Cornell University Press, 1986).

2. The Administrative Office of the United States Courts characteristically maintains no statistics that would enable one to infer the proportion of cases of this "new" kind. The figures cited in the text were derived from a hand count of published opinions by the D.C. Court of Appeals in cases dealing with federal government agencies, from a list generated through a computer search service. Excluding criminal cases, cases by government employees, information requests, and other cases not directly concerned with regulatory policy *per se*, there were eighty-six regulatory decisions decided by the D.C. Court of Appeals with full opinions in 1985; thirty of these (or some 35 percent) involved suits seeking to impose or intensify regulatory controls on third parties; of these thirty, the challengers—those seeking to goad the regulators to further effort—were successful in seventeen (or some 57 percent). In 1987, cases seeking to extend or intensify regulatory controls on third parties accounted for 80 of 201 relevant cases (or 42 percent) and 36 of these (or some 45 percent) were successful or at least partially successful.

3. See, e.g., the symposium in the 1986 *Duke Law Journal*, where all of the articles take issue with the claim that administrative decision making has become "over judicialized."

4. See, e.g., Richard Stewart and Cass Sunstein, "Public Programs and Private Rights," *Harvard Law Review* 95 (1982): 1193.

5. The leading entries in the hagiographic literature are Abram Chayes, "The Role of the Judge in Public Law Litigation," *Harvard Law Review* 89 (1976): 1281 and Owen Fiss, *The Civil Rights Injunction* (Bloomington, Ind.: Indiana University Press, 1978). Similar arguments are developed in R. A. L. Gambitta, M. L. May, and J. C. Foster, *Governing Through Courts* (Beverly Hills, Calif.: Sage Publications, 1981).

6. The leading critical study is Donald Horowitz, *The Courts and Social Policy* (Washington, D.C.: Brookings Institution, 1977). Gambitta, May, and Foster, *Governing Through Courts* reviews other versions of the argument.

7. Of course, prison and hospital reform cases look rather different if one focuses on the wider effects on the public of judicial pressures to release inmates into the community to relieve overcrowding or "unnecessary" confinement. But these cases are, after all, about the rights of the inmates, not about the best course for public policy in some larger public perspective.

8. *The Federalist* 70, C. Rossiter, ed. (New York: New American Library, 1961), p. 423.

9. *Marbury v. Madison*, 1 Cranch 137 (1803) at 170.

10. *Amalgamated Utility Workers (CIO) v. Consolidated Edison Co. of New York*, 309 U.S. 261 (1940).

11. See McCann, *Taking Reform Seriously*.

12. Richard Stewart, "The Reformation of American Administrative Law," *Harvard Law Review* 88 (1975): 1669 presented extended judicial controls as a response to the demise of the nondelegation doctrine. Similar arguments were advanced in J. Skelly Wright, "Beyond Discretionary Justice," *Yale Law Journal* 81 (1970): 575 and Kenneth C. Davis, *Discretionary Justice* (Champaign-Urbana: University of Illinois Press, 1971). More recently, Judge Carl McGowan of the D.C. Court of Appeals has emphasized the judicial role in precisely these terms: "What purpose does judicial review of agency action serve? The answer to this question is simple and clear. Judicial review serves as a check on the power of administrative agencies" ("A Reply to

271

Notes

Judicialization," *Duke Law Journal* [1986]: 222). Put in these terms, one might wonder why the D.C. Court of Appeals does not extend its checks to the operations of the U.S. Navy, which surely deploys more power than the typical regulatory agency.

13. Stewart, "The Reformation," 1675, describes administrative agencies as "transmission belts" for the legislature. This conception assumes that administrative authority is as closely bound to the law as judicial policy, that administrators merely add technical expertise. It assumes, in other words, that executive power is not a separate constitutional category. But as Stewart himself notes, this idea can be traced at least as far back as the writings of prominent scholars of the Progressive Era, such as Frank Goodnow.

14. R. Cushman, *The Independent Regulatory Commissions* (New York: Oxford University Press, 1941), pp. 74–78, 189–96 offers useful overviews of the initial uncertainties about the meaning of these statutes.

15. See, e.g., Martin Shapiro, "The APA: Past, Present, and Future," *Virginia Law Review* 72 (1986): 271.

16. Clean Air Act Amendments of 1970, 42 U.S.C.A. §1857h-2; Federal Water Pollution Control Act of 1972, 33 U.S.C.A. §1365; Noise Control Act, 42 U.S.C.A. §4911; Marine Protection, Research and Sanctuaries Act, 33 U.S.C.A. §1415(g). The Consumer Product Safety Act, 15 U.S.C.A. §2073 originally had a more limited provision for "citizen suits" regarding petitions for particular new standards, which has since been substantially revised.

17. See, e.g., the symposium on "court stripping" proposals in the *Harvard Journal of Law and Public Policy* 7 (Winter 1984), surveying a variety of proposals to cut back federal court jurisdiction, all of which deal with controversial constitutional rulings. Indeed, Congress gave serious consideration instead to the Bumpers amendment, directing courts to give no presumption of validity to administrative findings in contested decisions—an amendment to the APA first proposed in the late 1970s by Senator Dale Bumpers, as a concession to business protests against administrative excess, though it would plainly also have given courts a freer hand in suits demanding more extensive regulation. See *Administrative Procedure Act Amendments of 1976*, Hearings Before the Subcommittee on Administrative Practice and Procedure, Committee on the Judiciary, U.S. Senate 94th Congress (1976), pp. 151–52. See also the exasperated comment on continuing support for this measure among congressional conservatives into the early 1980s: Antonin Scalia, "Regulatory Reform—The Game Has Changed," *Regulation* (Jan.–Feb. 1981): 13–14. Nonetheless, the Bumpers Amendment, then S. 1080, passed the Republican-controlled Senate in 1982, though (as expected) it was allowed to die in the House.

18. Robert Lichter and Stanley Rothman, "What Interests the Public and What Interests the Public Interests," *Public Opinion* (April–May 1983).

19. C. H. Pritchett, *The Roosevelt Court: A Study in Judicial Politics and Values, 1937-1947* (New York: Macmillan, 1948) pp. 71–90.

20. See, e.g., Roscoe Pound, "Administrative Law: Its Growth, Procedure and Significance," *University of Pittsburgh Law Review* 7 (1941), attacking administrative regulation as an expression of "Marxist" thinking.

21. Richard Epstein, "The Social Consequences of Common Law Rules," *Harvard Law Review* 95 (1982): 1717.

22. Louis Jaffe, *Judicial Control of Administrative Action* (Boston: Little, Brown, 1965).

23. *Office of Communication of the United Church of Christ v. FCC*, 359 F2d. 994 (D.C. Cir., 1966).

24. *Scenic Hudson Preservation Conference v. FPC*, 354 F.2d 608 (1965).

25. *Environmental Defense Fund v. Hardin*, 428 F.2d 1098 (1970), ordering the Agriculture Department to explain why it was not taking action to ban use of the pesticide DDT. *EDF v. Ruckelshaus*, 439 F.2d 584 (1971), the follow-up case, rejected the explanations offered and demanded speedy administrative action against DDT—over a dissenting opinion, which stated the obvious fact that "the court is undertaking to manage the Department of Agriculture."

26. The general "notice and comment" rule making provision in the Administrative Procedure Act now appears at 5 U.S.C. §553. Provisions for "formal" decision making procedures, requiring decisions to be grounded "on the record," that is, developed in a formal hearing, are set out at 5 U.S.C. §§556, 557 but only apply where "required by statute" for the particular decision making power granted by statute. The new approach to rule making in the 1970s was encouraged in a few instances by statutory provisions for particular agencies requiring that rules be supported by "substantial evidence" (as in the Occupational Safety and Health Act) or even that they be supported by evidence in the record, implying that the rule must be formulated through formal

hearings (as in the 1975 Magnusson-Moss Act authorizing broader rule making powers for the FTC). But the courts have imposed relatively formal procedures for rule making even when rule making is simply covered by the APA "arbitrary and capricious" requirement. "Since the mid-1960s, many courts have declared that in reviewing rules they will review the sufficiency of factual evidence and act as a partner to the agency in evaluating the factual issues. These courts could not undertake this task, however, until they had invented a practice that clearly is not in the APA, namely the rulemaking record" (Shapiro, "APA," p. 477).

27. 448 U.S. 607 (1980).

28. See, e.g., Joseph Vining, *Legal Identity: The Coming of Age of Public Law* (New Haven: Yale University Press, 1978); Louis Jaffe, "The Citizen as Litigant in Public Actions," *University of Pennsylvania Law Review* 116 (1968): 1033; Henry P. Monaghan, "Constitutional Adjudication: The Who and the When," *Yale Law Journal* 82 (1973): 1363.

29. Cass Sunstein, "Interest Groups in American Public Law," *Stanford Law Review* 38 (1985): 29.

30. While the "hard look" doctrine has come to be associated with environmental and safety regulation, the first important case announcing this approach actually involved a policy question as seemingly inconsequential—and as inevitably rather arbitrary—as the award of a television broadcasting license by the FCC. D.C. Circuit Judge Harold Leventhal, the pioneer of the doctrine, explained in *Greater Boston Television Corp. v. FCC*, 444 F.2d 841 (1969) at 851: "Its supervisory function calls on the court to intervene not merely in the case of procedural inadequacies, or bypassing of the mandate in the legislative charter, but more broadly if the court becomes aware, from a combination of danger signals, that the agency has not really taken a 'hard look' at the salient problems, and has not genuinely engaged in reasoned decision-making." This statement comes very close to saying that the reviewing court should reconsider all arguments and evidence considered by the agency to determine if it has actually made the correct decision. And Judge Leventhal indeed proclaimed that under this approach, "The court is in a real sense part of the total administrative process" (852).

31. Jeremy Rabkin and Neal Devins, "Averting Government by Consent Decree," *Stanford Law Review* 40 (1987): 203, reviews several examples from the 1980s.

32. When litigants seek financial damages, lawyers may pursue the case on a "contingency fee" basis—that is, they may agree to represent the claimant for a share of the ultimate proceeds without demanding payment from the start. This arrangement is not possible with public interest litigation seeking to alter policy rather than to collect sums of cash. Public interest groups have accordingly pressed Congress and the courts—and with general success—to widen their opportunities to collect attorneys' fees for successful litigational policy challenges. But attorneys' fees may not cover all costs, and in any case are not usually available unless the lawsuit succeeds. Few public interest groups receive more than a small portion of their operating income from attorneys' fees, therefore, and most largely rely on support from private donations—which are hard to secure, in turn, without an established operation.

33. Marc Gallanter, "Why the Haves Come Out Ahead," *Law and Society Review* 9 (1974): 95.

34. See n. 39 below.

35. Lettie McSpadden Wenner of Northwestern University has surveyed all published environmental cases from federal courts in the 1980s and established that environmental groups won more cases than businesses in every one of these years: "The Reagan Era in Environmental Litigation," unpublished paper presented at the 1988 American Political Science Association Convention. For similar tabulations of relative outcomes in the 1970s, see Wenner, *The Environmental Decade in Court* (Bloomington, Ind.: Indiana University Press, 1982).

36. The litigation culminated in *FCC v. WNCN Listeners Guild*, 450 U.S. 582 (1981), where the Supreme Court firmly repudiated efforts by the D.C. Court of Appeals to force the FCC to identify the "public interest" with the "preservation of a format [that] would otherwise disappear." More revealing than the Supreme Court's decision, however, was the FCC's resistance to such promptings by the Court of Appeals, evidenced, among other things, by its willingness to fight the issue up to the Supreme Court. For an account of earlier FCC resistance, see "Reversing the D.C. Circuit at the F.C.C.," *Regulation* (May–June 1981): 11–14.

37. Joel Handler, *Social Movements and the Legal System* (New York: Academic Press, 1979).

38. See *National Black Media Coalition v. FCC*, 791 F.2d 1016 (1986), for the judicial response when the FCC finally tried to change this policy.

39. The Administrative Office of the United States Courts keeps no separate tabulation of "public interest" filings; neither does the Justice Department or any other government agency.

Notes

I tried to secure a rough map of pattern of filings through a computer search of federal court decisions between 1970 and 1985, selecting for the names of public interest groups listed with the "Alliance for Justice," an umbrella organization in Washington that has tried to develop a fairly complete listing. This search brought up 530 cases in which self-declared "public interest" groups were involved. It is not a complete sample, because groups may be extensively involved in litigation without being mentioned in the resulting judicial opinions, even when their lawyers are listed by name in the headnotes, and many suits never get to a formal judicial opinion. Still, it probably provides a fairly good overview of the pattern: Of the 530 cases, 299—or some 56 percent—were accounted for by eight frequent targets of public interest litigation: EPA (92), Interior (66), HEW/HHS (39), Transportation (35), Nuclear Regulatory Commission (20), Energy (17), Corps of Engineers (17), Labor (13). Interestingly, these suits brought favorable results in 48.4 percent of the cases, which is an extremely impressive record. For a rough comparison, one might note that appeals against administrative agencies decided in the U.S. Courts of Appeals in 1985, a not untypical year, brought favorable results to the challengers in only 11.2 percent of the cases overall. Public interest litigators seem to be unusually skillful in picking their targets—or perhaps the agencies they sue do not resist as much as they might.

40. See $n39$ above and chapter 3, $n47$ below.

41. James Q. Wilson, *Political Organizations* (New York: Basic Books, 1973), pp. 331–32.

42. "Taking a Dive at CPSC," *Regulation* (July–August 1981): 7.

43. "Sudden and profound alterations in an agency's policy constitute 'danger signals' that the will of Congress is being ignored" (*State Farm Mutual Automobile Insurance Co. v. Department of Transportation*, 680 F.2d 206 [1982]).

44. *Motor Vehicle Manufacturers Assn. v. State Farm Mutual Automobile Ins. Co.*, 463 U.S. 29 (1983). The Transportation Department did not restore the rule but substituted in its place a commitment (or threat) to impose the airbags requirement unless a sufficient number of states imposed mandatory seat belt laws by 1990. According to Christopher DeMuth, then director of the OMB Office of Information and Regulatory Affairs, White House officials pressed DoT to provide better documentation to justify abandoning the rule altogether, but Secretary Elizabeth Dole insisted that the Supreme Court's decision required the department to do more than merely explain itself; and Transportation regulators urging some regulatory response accordingly carried the day (DeMuth, personal interview, April 1987).

45. *International Ladies Garment Workers Union v. Donovan*, 722 F.2d 795 (D.C. Cir., 1983).

46. *Griswold v. Connecticut*, 381 U.S. 479 (1965). Guido Calabresi has described this decision as "interring . . . a legislative anachronism" despite his acknowledgment that "the constitutional basis" for the decision "was tenuous to say the least" (*A Common Law for the Age of Statutes* [Cambridge, Mass: Harvard University Press, 1985], pp. 8–9). The book as a whole urges courts to take a much more active, forthright role in dealing with "anachronistic" statutes on the somewhat curious assumption that only courts will be capable of breaking legislative logjams.

47. Aaron Wildavsky and Mary T. Douglas, *Risk and Culture: An Essay on Selection of Risk and Environmental Dangers* (Berkeley: University of California Press, 1982).

48. R.L. Stanfield "The Nuclear Option," *National Journal* (July 5, 1986): 1646–52, reviews the fate of the nuclear power industry during the 1980s, noting the reviving interest in nuclear energy—and the continuing resistance by safety advocates.

49. Burt Solomon "Ganging Up," *National Journal* (July 19, 1986): 1778–81, and R.L. Stanfield "Paying for Nothing," *National Journal* (April 4, 1987): 812–14, review the politics of FERC efforts to deregulate natural gas pipelines.

50. R. Shep Melnick, *Regulation and the Courts* (Washington, D.C.: Brookings Institution, 1983).

Chapter 2

1. On the role of public law in enforcing regulatory entitlements, see Joseph Vining, *Legal Identity: The Coming of Age of Public Law* (New Haven: Yale University Press, 1978) and Richard Stewart and Cass Sunstein, "Public Programs and Private Rights," *Harvard Law Review* 95 (1982): 1193. Stewart and Sunstein acknowledge several of the characteristic difficulties with entitlements to regulatory benefits but, like Vining, try to escape the difficulties by appealing to "public values" to which private individuals are unaccountably allowed to stake a preemptive claim against actual public officials.

Notes

2. *The Federalist* 10, C. Rossiter, ed. (New York: New American Library, 1961), p. 80.

3. Ibid., p. 78.

4. Friedrich A. Hayek, *Law, Legislation and Liberty*, vol. 2: *The Mirage of Social Justice* (Chicago: University of Chicago Press, 1976), p. 63.

5. Stephen C. Yeazell, *From Medieval Group Litigation to the Modern Class Action* (New Haven: Yale University Press, 1987), describes the medieval attitudes that allowed courts to hear claims from unincorporated "groups"—like the people of a village or town—but also notes that such proceedings had become incomprehensible to courts by the seventeenth century because judges could no longer recognize such groups as having a single common interest.

6. "As late as the time of Elizabeth, the law reports reveal that the current legal attitude toward statutes and enactments was that they were not innovations, but fresh definitions of already existing rules. Despite the fact that considerable law was actually made by parliament in the Middle Ages, and that considerably more was made in the Tudor and Stuart periods, the early idea that statutes were affirmations of existing law persisted long after that theory no longer described the facts" (G. L. Haskins, *The Growth of English Representative Government* [Philadelphia: University of Pennsylvania Press, 1948], pp. 100–101).

7. In fact, this assumption is rather misleading. Its pervasiveness in contemporary social science seems to derive from Max Weber's oft-cited definition of the state as that entity which "successfully upholds a claim to the monopoly of the legitimate use of physical force in the enforcement of its order" (*The Theory of Social and Economic Organization*, A.M. Henderson and Talcott Parsons, trans. [New York: Oxford University Press, 1947] p. 154). Weber justified this definition on the grounds that, through the course of history, actual states have pursued so many varied and differing ends that "it is possible to define the 'political' character of a corporate group only in terms of the means peculiar to it, the use of force" (p. 155). This is not the classical liberal view. Locke was quite explicit and emphatic that individuals retain the moral right to use force when necessary for self-defense (or the defense of private property), and no government may properly deny this right (see The Second Treatise of Government ¶19 in *Two Treatises of Government*, Peter Laslett, ed. [New York: Mentor, 1965]). The common law indeed acknowledged this as a legal right—so that "self-defense" is a valid defense to charges arising from private resort to force (see Sir William Blackstone, *Commentaries on the Laws of England*, facsimile of the first edition of 1765 [Chicago: University of Chicago Press, 1979], 1.126). Locke (and the common law) assumed that this exception to the public monopoly of force was necessary to serve the ultimate end of government—the preservation of individual rights. The Weberian view overlooks this exception because it is so eager to avoid any intrusion of moral theories into its definition.

8. But some scholars *are* willfully perverse. The preceding is merely a rough summary of the initial presentation in William Landes and Richard Posner, "The Private Enforcement of Law," *Journal of Legal Studies* 4 (1975): 1. Posner's "economic" approach to law tries to reduce all legal decisions to calculations about what will maximize overall social wealth, and from this perspective rights are indeed mere instruments of social utility. Posner attempts a systematic moral defense of this perspective in *The Economics of Justice* (Cambridge, Mass.: Harvard University Press, 1982). It is only fair to add that in this, as in most of his writings, Posner's efforts are as brilliant and provocative as they are willfully perverse.

9. *Marbury v. Madison*, 1 Cranch 137 (1803) at 170. Among other things, Article III, §2 of the Constitution provides that "the judicial power" shall also "extend" to "controversies between two or more states" or "between a State . . . and foreign states." Is a state, then, a "person"? The answer is emphatically yes, just as a corporation is a "person" for many legal purposes. When the state comes to court in its corporate capacity, it must be conceived as the holder of rights that it can decide to deploy or not for its own "personal" ends. The Supreme Court traditionally restricted "standing" for states in just the same way as it did for private individuals: states could seek judicial relief for "rights actually invaded or [imminently] threatened" but could not bring suit in federal court over "abstract questions of political power, of sovereignty, of government" (see *Massachusetts v. Mellon*, 262 U.S. 447 [1923] at 484).

10. *Massachusetts v. Mellon*, 262 U.S. 447 (1923) at 484, citing *Cherokee Nation v. Georgia*, 5 Pet 1 (1831) at 75.

11. It is worth noting that product liability suits of this kind are a twentieth century innovation, just because nineteenth century courts found it too disorienting—or too impractical or too unfair—to attribute liability to complete strangers. In a general way, the trend in modern tort litigation has indeed paralleled legal trends elsewhere, so that commentators speak of the emergence of a "new tort law" since the 1960s, as of a "new administrative law." The novelty in both

areas has been to extend actionable claims beyond the traditionally recognized boundaries of private control, so that modern product liability claims, involving thousands of claimants against several manufacturers, are described by some commentators as "public torts." See, e.g., Peter Huber, "The Hazards of Public Risk Management in the Courts," *Columbia Law Review* 85 (1985): 277. Punitive damages may also seem to make the tort plaintiff into a representative figure or a "private attorney general" for those he protects through the deterrent effects assumed to follow from punitive damages. In fact, the device was controversial as late as the 1930s. Still, private litigation has retained more of a connection with private rights, at least in form: no one suggests that a plaintiff may file a public tort action or demand punitive damages when not himself a victim. And in contrast to the pattern in administrative law cases, the Supreme Court has insisted that lawyers seeking to organize a "class action" tort claim must secure the written consent of every member of the class they claim to speak for and must demonstrate that every such class member had the requisite financial claim to file such a suit on his own. In sum, tort lawyers cannot operate as self-appointed spokesmen for a merely conjectural class—though this is exactly what public interest lawyers are allowed to do in administrative cases, seeking injunctive relief.

12. Blackstone, *Commentaries*, Chicago facsimile edition, 3.2.

13. The classical perspective assumed that security could never be absolute and efforts to make it so would simply generate new risks of injury and oppression. Locke argued, for example, that in the absence of government, everyone would have a right not only to repel and punish assaults on himself but also to punish (even with capital punishment) those who attacked strangers in order to "terrifie others [i.e., other would-be assailants or thieves] from doing the like" (Second Treatise ¶12 [Laslett, ed., p. 315]). But in agreeing to form a "political society," each person "wholly gives up" this "right" to ensure that crime is adequately deterred (¶130, p.398). Locke argues that everyone will be more secure under such arrangements—which is certainly believable—but does not conceal that the greater security afforded by "political society" depends on each person's trusting to a large extent in "society" and renouncing any general claim of *"doing whatsoever he thought fit for the preservation of himself"* (¶129, p. 397, original emphasis). What remains is the "distinct right" of "taking reparation, which belongs only to the injured party" (¶11, p. 314).

14. For the best known and most readily accessible examples, see Richard Esptein, *Takings, Private Property and the Power of Eminent Domain* (Cambridge, Mass.: Harvard University Press, 1985) and Ronald Dworkin, *Taking Rights Seriously* (Cambridge, Mass.: Harvard University Press, 1976).

15. State of the Union Address by Franklin D. Roosevelt, H.R. Doc. No. 377, 78th Cong., 2d Sess. 2 (1944).

16. Henry Shue, *Basic Rights, Subsistence, Affluence, and U.S. Foreign Policy* (Princeton: Princeton University Press, 1983). In fact, Shue's reasoning is more radical and also more dubious than that of the classical liberal tradition. The purpose of rights, in the classical liberal perspective, is not autonomy but personal security. The state of nature metaphor indicates that, in consenting to the establishment of government, the individual indeed sacrifices some of his primal autonomy for the sake of security. Shue argues that even the classical negative rights—life, liberty, and property—require "affirmative government" action through the police and are therefore not different from positive or "welfare" rights. But the amount of police protection available to most citizens in England and America before the late nineteenth century was quite minimal. And no one ever supposed that a citizen, merely by invoking his negative rights, could get courts to appropriate more money for more police without legislative consent. Even today, it is certainly not obvious that the traditional view is outdated or mistaken—at least if the alternative view, emphasizing government's obligation to assure minimal welfare rights, is taken (like the traditional view of property rights) to imply that such rights must be respected, regardless of legislative consent. This situation would leave a great deal of governmental power removed from effective political control, and so much uncontrolled power does not rest very comfortably with personal security.

17. Laurence H. Tribe, *American Constitutional Law* (Mineola, N.Y.: Foundation Press, 1978), p. 574.

18. Even in the first edition of his treatise, Tribe noted the refusal of courts to go far in this direction: ibid., pp. 1127–36. The second edition of Tribe's treatise (1988) affirms the same pattern, pp. 1663–65.

19. In Locke's account, it is precisely the renunciation of the right to exercise force—except in immediate self-defense against violence—that constitutes "political society": "there and only

there is *Political Society*, where . . . *all private judgement* of every particular Member *being excluded, the Community comes to be Umpire*, by settled standing Rules, indifferent and the same to all Parties; and *by the Men having Authority from the Community, for the execution of those Rules"* (emphasis added; *Second Treatise* ¶87 [Laslett, ed., p. 367]).

20. See *Fletcher v. Peck*, 6 Cranch 87 (1810), land grants; *New Jersey v. Wilson*, 7 Cranch 164 (1812), tax exemption; *Dartmouth College v. Woodward*, 4 Wheaton 517 (1819), corporate charter.

21. *Stone v. Mississippi*, 101 U.S. 814 (1879) at 817. Leading Supreme Court decisions to the same effect are *Atlantic Coast Line R.R. v. City of Goldsboro*, 232 U.S. 548 (1914); *Minneapolis & St.L.Ry. v. Emmons*, 149 U.S. 364 (1893); *Butcher's Union Slaughter-House v. Crescent City Live-Stock Landing and Slaughter-House Co.*, 111 U.S. 746 (1884).

22. *Schechter Poultry Corp. v. U.S.*, 295 U.S. 495 (1935) at 225, describing the legislative scheme authorizing private "trade or industrial associations . . . to enact the laws they deem to be wise" as "utterly inconsistent with the constitutional prerogatives and duties of Congress." *Carter v. Carter Coal Co.*, 298 U.S. 238 (1936) at 311, reaffirmed that "delegation . . . to private persons" is "legislative delegation in its most obnoxious form."

23. It is misleading to say that the legislature must always act in general terms in the constitutional scheme or that it may never give direct, binding orders to the executive in cases involving individuals. There is no difficulty with such direct orders when they do not involve coercion of private parties, as when the executive is directed, by legislative action, to make a payment from the treasury to a particular individual. In *Kendall v. Stokes*, 12 Pet. 524 (1838), the court insisted that the executive was obliged to comply with such a legislative directive regarding financial payments. This decision is sometimes cited, however, to establish that any congressional directive to the executive must be binding, which is clearly wrong; and the fact that modern commentators must reach back for such an inapt case illustrates the paucity of truly relevant traditional precedents for the claim that the "will of Congress" is simply binding on the executive. Conversely, even in its rather strained 1988 decision in *Morrison v. Olson*, 108 s.ct. 2597, endorsing the special prosecutor provisions in the Ethics in Government Act, the Supreme Court was anxious to emphasize that the attorney general retains significant discretion to decline to seek the appointment of a special prosecutor to pursue any particular case.

24. The traditional doctrine was that writs of mandamus or mandatory injunctions—that is, direct orders to government officials to act in a certain way—should only be issued in relation to "mandatory" as opposed to "discretionary" duties, so that courts would not be controlling executive discretion but merely enforcing those duties already prescribed in precise detail by legislation; see Edwin W. Patterson, "Ministerial and Discretionary Official Acts," *Michigan Law Review* 20 (1922): 848. This rule could be readily manipulated, of course, by the simple device of declaring that whatever the court wanted an official to do was a "mandatory" duty. To cope with this problem, the Supreme Court insisted that statutory duties should not be controlled by mandamus whenever an official's duty under the statute was "not free from doubt" or not "beyond peradventure clear." *Wilbur v. U.S. ex rel. Kadrie*, 281 U.S. 206 (1930); *U.S. ex rel. Chicago Great Western R. Co. v. ICC*, 294 U.S. 50 (1935).

25. Traditionally, federal courts allowed taxpayers to challenge the constitutional validity of spending programs only when financed by taxes that imposed measurable financial burdens on the taxpayer—as when special programs were financed by special taxes—so the taxpayer could indeed be conceived as complaining about *his own* property; see, for example, *Bailey v. Drexel Furniture*, 259 U.S. 20 (1922) or *U.S. v. Butler*, 297 U.S. 1 (1936). Local taxpayers could more readily object to local spending programs just because the spending might have a direct, measurable impact on their tax bills. See cases described in Louis Jaffe, *Judicial Control of Administrative Action* (Boston: Little, Brown, 1965), pp. 470–71. When a general taxpayer sought to challenge the validity of a federal spending program financed from general revenues, the suit was firmly repudiated by the Supreme Court on the ground that the individual taxpayer's stake was "comparatively minute and indeterminable," hence "essentially a matter of public not of individual concern" (*Frothingham v. Mellon*, 262 U.S. 447 [1923]).

26. For this reason the nineteenth century version of the citizen suit was altogether different. To cut down on government expenditures, a number of public measures in the nineteenth century authorized private enforcement and even provided incentives to private enforcers by according them a percentage of the financial proceeds in such suits on behalf of the government. The "informer action" was usually authorized for action against private violators of public measures (such as smugglers) but was sometimes also authorized for the correction of misconduct or

Notes

misappropriation by low-level public officials. It was the litigational equivalent of bounty hunting and, like bounty hunting, remained under ultimate executive control: no enterprising informer had a right to take the matter to court if executive officials determined that it was not in the public interest to do so. See the ruling to this effect and the background history of the procedure in *The Confiscation Cases*, 7 Wall 454 (1868). A somewhat similar arrangement survives in England and some other common law countries, by which private citizens are allowed to initiate enforcement suits *ex relatione* or "on the relation of" the attorney general. But the attorney general, acting for the government, may refuse his consent to such action, and the private citizen then has no right of his own to continue with the suit. For a survey of provisions for relator actions in common law countries, see M. Cappelletti and J. A. Jolowicz, *Public Interest Parties and the Active Role of the Judge in Civil Litigation* (Dobbs Ferry, N.Y.: Oceana Publications, 1973), pp. 101–6. Contemporary public interest suits in the United States, in which citizens are authorized to act as "private attorneys general"—over the objections of the actual attorney general—have as much in common with these publicly controlled actions as citizen posses or citizen arrests have in common with lynch mobs.

27. Vining, *Legal Identity*, p. 55. It is revealing that, according to Vining, the earliest consistent use of the term seems to be in English parliamentary inquiries, in which directly affected individuals were given standing to testify in political or governmental proceedings understood to be quite different from courtroom litigation (p. 56).

28. A useful collection of studies, covering several different agencies, is James C. Miller, ed., *Perspectives on Federal Transportation Policy* (Washington, D.C.: American Enterprise Institute, 1975). An extensive bibliography of earlier studies is offered in Paul Joskow and Roger Noll, "Regulation in Theory and Practice: An Overview," in *Studies in Public Regulation*, Gary Fromm, ed. (Cambridge, Mass: M.I.T. Press, 1981).

29. *The Chicago Junction Case* 264 U.S. 258 (1924).

30. *FCC v. Sanders Brothers Radio Station,* 309 U.S. 470 (1940).

31. Louis Jaffe offers a useful (and not at all unsympathetic) summary of the squishy, sublegal "law" advanced by these decisions: "Congress has seen fit to command the ICC to consider as relevant to decision a complex of complementary and conflicting interests. . . . It is not possible to formulate these interests in traditional right-duty terms. But . . . because there can be no rights—no 'legal injury' in the traditional sense—we are [not necessarily] driven to the opposite pole that there is only a 'public interest.' Where the legislature has recognized a certain 'interest' as one which must be heeded, it is such a 'legally protected interest' as warrants standing to complain of its disregard" (*Judicial Control,* pp. 507–8). In other words, competing firms were given not a definite private right but a privileged claim on administrative determinations of the public interest.

32. The original Senate bill (S. 7) had provided that judicial review should be available to "any person affected by an agency action" and the subsequent adoption of the phrase "any person suffering legal wrong" was "used as [a term] of limitation," extended by the following phrase ("adversely affected or aggrieved within the meaning of any relevant statute") only to encompass agencies with this phrase in their own statutory charters: U.S. Department of Justice, *Attorney General's Manual on the Administrative Procedure Act* (1947), p. 96, summarizing a construction that was "not questioned or contradicted in the legislative history." For a more extensive account, see Note, *University of Pennsylvania Law Review* 104 (1956): 843ff., esp. 858. The Supreme Court's 1970 interpretation of the APA thus restored the expansive view of standing that had been expressly rejected by Congress when the APA was enacted.

33. *Association of Data Processing Service Organizations v. Camp,* 397 U.S. 150 (1970).

34. K. C. Davis, *Administrative Law of the 1970s* (Rochester, N.Y.: Lawyers Cooperative Publishing Co., 1976), pp. 509–10.

35. For example, Monaghan, "Constitutional Adjudication: The Who and the When," *Yale Law Journal* 82 (1973): 1363; and Louis Jaffe, "The Citizen as Litigant in Public Actions," *University of Pennsylvania Law Review* 116 (1968): 1033.

36. The most scholarly effort was that of Louis Jaffe in a chapter on "Public Actions" in *Judicial Control,* which rehearsed examples of taxpayer or citizen suits in state courts, mostly in the nineteenth century and mostly for the purpose of controlling fiscal irregularities in municipal government. Jaffe conceded, however, that there was "little authority" for bringing such taxpayer or citizen challenges to local government actions in federal courts (p. 473). As it is, he fails to mention that the elected judges in the states—particularly in the nineteenth century—were often allowed to render advisory opinions, to assume administrative responsibilities in connection with

tax assessments and maintenance of public works, and to act in a variety of other nonjudicial capacities. The unelected federal judiciary has always been held to a higher standard of impartiality and observed a greater degree of limitation on its activities. Raoul Berger, in "Standing to Sue in Public Actions," *Yale Law Journal* 78 (1969): 816, sought to show that nineteenth century informer actions were a solid precedent for public actions, but he overlooked the constitutional limitations on such suits. See n. 26, supra.

37. *Flast v. Cohen,* 392 U.S. 83 (1968). *Flast* insisted that taxpayers could only have standing to contest alleged violations of those constitutional provisions designed for the special protection of taxpayers—a formula designed to preclude challenges to federal spending under the Tenth Amendment. The Court then solemnly announced in a subsequent case that the constitutional provision requiring "a regular statement of account" for federal expenditures was not designed for the special benefit of taxpayers, though it freely conceded that if it was not for the special benefit of taxpayers, it might prove to be for the special benefit of no one: *U.S. v. Richardson,* 418 U.S. 166 (1974). Similarly, in *Schlesinger v. Reservists,* 418 U.S. 208 (1974), the Court insisted that the provision prohibiting members of Congress from holding executive office was not for the special benefit of taxpayers—and so denied standing to taxpayers making the very plausible charge that congressmen were being seduced into voting higher defense appropriations by the offer of honorary commissions in the National Guard. Justice Powell, in a concurring opinion in *Richardson,* had the honesty to acknowledge that the *Flast* test was devoid of "real meaning and of principled content," because standing to challenge expenditures for alleged violations of the First Amendment never had any real connection with distinctive rights of taxpayers.

38. Paul Bator, Paul Mishkin, David Shapiro, and Herbert Wechsler, *Hart & Wechsler's The Federal Courts* (Mineola, N.Y.: Foundation Press, 1973), p. 156. The text goes on to suggest that even viewed in terms of "representation," the question of standing "becomes inextricably bound up with the whole law of rights and remedies, does it not?" Putting the question this way, however, acknowledges that standing is merely "bound up with" but not reducible to "the whole law of rights and remedies."

39. For a striking recent example, see *Bob Jones University v. U.S.,* 461 U.S. 574 (1983), in which the IRS agreed with Bob Jones University that it was entitled to a tax exemption under existing law, and the Supreme Court on its own initiative appointed a private advocate to argue the contrary. The case might thus more accurately have been styled *Bob Jones University v. U.S. Supreme Court*—except, of course, that this would have made it uncomfortably obvious that the Court was not an impartial judge, but rather an active policy maker with interests adverse to those of the private party. As it was, after appointing its own advocate to hear the argument it wanted to hear, the Supreme Court pretended that it could judge this argument with unbiased detachment. To no one's surprise, the resulting decision came down squarely on the side of the advocate appointed by the Court, although the legal reasoning is highly questionable.

40. *Sierra Club v. Morton,* 405 U.S. 727 (1972).

41. *Citizens to Preserve Overton Park v. Volpe,* 401 U.S. 402 (1971), concerning the proper considerations for the routing of federally financed highways under the Federal Aid-Highway Act of 1968, 82 Stat. 823, which most assuredly makes no provision for citizen suits.

42. *Eastern Kentucky Welfare Rights Organization v. Simon,* 426 U.S. 26 (1976).

43. See *Wright v. Regan,* 656 F.2d 820 (1982), a notable example because it does try hard to reconcile the grant of standing with past Supreme Court decisions denying standing. This ruling was overturned by the Supreme Court in *Allen v. Wright,* 468 U.S. 737 (1984), ostensibly on standing grounds. But the Supreme Court's ruling did not prevent two lower courts from subsequently granting standing (and ruling in favor of) abortion advocates demanding withdrawal of tax exempt status for the Catholic Bishops Conference, on the grounds that this "subsidy" of right-to-life advocates injured the business of abortion clinics: *Abortion Rights Mobilization v. Regan,* 603 F. Supp. 970 (S.D.N.Y., 1985), aff'd., *In re U.S. Catholic Conference,* 824 F.2d 156 (2d Cir., 1987).

44. See, e.g., *Industrial Union Department, A.F.L.-C.I.O. v. American Petroleum Institute,* 448 U.S. 607 (1980) and the recent D.C. Court of Appeals decision in *Farmworkers Justice Fund v. Brock,* 811 F.2d 613 (D.C. Cir., 1987) described in chapter 7 of this study.

45. A considerable list of such commentaries is offered in Gene R. Nichol, Jr. "Rethinking Standing," *California Law Review* 72 (1984): 68 n. 3

46. *Center for Science in the Public Interest v. U.S. Treasury Department,* 789 F.2d 995 (D.C. Cir., 1983).

47. *American Trucking Association v. ICC,* 659 F.2d 452 (5th Cir., 1982); *Port Norris Express Co. v. ICC,* 751 F.2d 1280 (D.C. Cir., 1985).

48. *ILGWU v. Donovan,* 772 F.2d 795 (1983).

49. *Farmers Union Central Exchange v. FERC,* 734 F.2d 1486 (D.C. Cir., 1984).

50. See, e.g., *National Small Shipments Traffic Conference v. CAB,* 618 F.2d 819 (D.C. Cir., 1980). See also decisions demanding the imposition of protective tariffs or other trade constraints by the International Trade Commission at the behest of American competitors—and to the obvious detriment of American consumers: e.g., *Bingham & Taylor, Div. v. U.S.,* 627 F. Supp. 793 (CIT 1986); *Carlisle Tire & Rubber Co. v. U.S.,* 622 F. Supp. 1071 (CIT 1985); *American Grape Growers Alliance for Fair Trade v. U.S.,* 615 F. Supp. 603 (CIT 1985); *Republic Steel Corp. v. U.S.,* 591 F. Supp. 640 (CIT 1984). In this area, Congress has established a special court (the Court of International Trade) to ensure that the International Trade Commission does not fail to deliver as much "protection" as American competitors of foreign firms are "entitled" to receive. But this is only a special case of a larger pattern.

51. So, for example, R. Shep Melnick notes in his study of environmentalist suits against the EPA: "What is surprising . . . is how seldom the two sides that most disagree—industry and environmentalists—have come before the same court at the same time" (*Regulation and the Courts* [Washington, D.C.: Brookings Institution, 1977], p. 361).

52. This point was brought home to me most vividly when I sought to obtain copies of the pleadings and evidentiary documents in a suit between Ralph Nader's Public Citizen and the FDA. These papers were unavailable in the docket room of the U.S. District Court in Washington because the judge in the case had kept them in his chambers for further study. When I pursued the papers to the judge's chambers, a nervous clerk relayed my request to the astonished judge with the explanation that, "This gentleman is here from . . . the public." It seemed to all of us that I was somehow playing the part of a snoop or a busybody in trying to discover details of Mr. Nader's litigation with the FDA—which had by then come to seem as much his own private affair as a divorce proceeding or a tax adjustment suit. Although the judge did not refuse my request for the documents outright, he insisted that I submit a formal request for access to the papers, explaining my reasons for wanting to peruse them. I have made several dozen similar document requests to executive agencies and congressional committees, and have never once encountered this sort of suspicion or resistance.

53. *The Federalist* 10, Rossiter, ed., p. 78.

54. *The Federalist* 71, Rossiter, ed., p. 433. See also Madison's warning in no. 48: "in a representative republic where the executive magistracy is carefully limited . . . and the legislative power is exercised by an assembly, which is inspired by a supposed influence over the people . . . it is against the enterprising ambition of this [legislative department] that the people ought to indulge all their jealousy" (p. 309).

55. *The Federalist* 72, Rossiter, ed., p. 436. Madison made much the same point in the first Congress in 1789 in the course of the famous removal power debate, where he urged that the Constitution must be read as giving the president the power to remove administrative appointees, for otherwise he could not bear "responsibility" for their performance.

56. Charles Thach, *The Creation of the Presidency, 1775–1789,* Johns Hopkins University Historical Studies 40 (Baltimore: The Johns Hopkins University Press, 1922), pp. 55–75. See also Benjamin Wright, "Origins of the Separation of Powers in America," *Economica* 13 (May 1933).

57. *The Federalist* 70, Rossiter, ed., p. 427.

58. *The Federalist* 70, Rossiter, ed., p. 423.

59. *INS v. Chadha,* 462 U.S. 919 (1983).

60. For a relatively dispassionate overview of the "subgovernment phenomenon" emphasizing the congressional role, see Harold Seidman, *Politics, Position and Power: The Dynamics of Federal Organization,* 3d ed. (New York: Oxford University Press, 1980).

61. Cass Sunstein, "Faction and the APA," *Virginia Law Review* 72 (1986).

62. See U.S. Department of Justice, *Sourcebook of Criminal Justice Statistics* (1986), p. 125, summarizing *New York Times*/CBS News polls in the mid-1980s asking, "What do you think is the most important problem facing the community you live in?": 3 percent say "environment, pollution" while 8 percent say "crime" (among black respondents the figures are 0 percent and 10 percent, respectively).

63. John Morrall, "A Review of the Record," *Regulation* (Nov.–Dec. 1986): 26–27, using data from the National Center for Health Statistics and the National Safety Council for 1979, reports

Notes

22,500 deaths from homicide; 11,200 deaths directly attributable to workplace hazards. Both figures have declined during the 1980s.

64. See Robert L. Rabin, "Agency Criminal Referrals," *Stanford Law Review* 24 (1972): 1036, for examples of how changing public opinion indirectly affects U.S. attorneys in their exercise of prosecutorial discretion.

65. *Ex parte Grossman,* 267 U.S. 87 (1925) at 121.

66. *U.S. v. Nixon,* 418 U.S. 683 (1974) at 693.

67. *Smith v. U.S.,* 375 F.2d 243 (1967) at 247–48.

68. *U.S. v. Empresa de Viacao Aerea Rio Grandense (VARIG Airlines),* 104 S.Ct. 2755 (1984).

69. The Tort Claims Act excludes government liability for "Any claim . . . based upon the exercise or performance or the failure to exercise or perform a discretionary function or duty on the part of a federal agency or an employee of the Government, whether or not the discretion involved be abused," 28 U.S.C. §2680(a). For further background on government tort liability in comparison with administrative law jurisdiction, see Jeremy Rabkin, "Where the Lines Have Held: Tort Claims Against the Federal Government," in Walter Olson, *New Directions in Liability Law* (New York: Academy of Political Science, 1988), pp. 112–25.

70. The APA precludes judicial review when "agency action is committed to agency discretion by law," 551 U.S.C. §701(a)(2). The Senate Judiciary Committee explained this exclusion as applying whenever "the matter is discretionary." See *Administrative Procedure Act, Legislative History,* Sen. Doc. 248, 79th Cong., 2d Sess. (1946), p. 36.

71. *Heckler v. Chaney,* 470 U.S. 821 (1985). Justice Rehnquist's opinion does mention that "when an agency refuses to act it generally does not exercise its *coercive* power over an individual's liberty or property rights, and thus does not infringe upon areas that courts are often called upon to protect" (832, original emphasis). But even here, the decision treats what courts "are often called upon to protect" as an indication of judicial competence, not as a consequence of an underlying principle that limits access to the courts to those claiming individual rights.

72. Justice Marshall's opinion (at 840) was technically a concurrence, as it did not object to the result in this case, but it took strong exception to the reasoning. The lower court opinion, at 718 F.2d 1184, is of particular interest because of the strong dissenting opinion by Judge Scalia, then serving on the D.C. Court of Appeals. On the face of things, Mr. Chaney might have seemed to have had an unusually personal and distinct interest in the FDA policy in this case: condemned to capital punishment in a state relying on lethal injections for executions, Chaney complained that the FDA had not certified the compound to be used as "safe and effective." In fact, it is not logic chopping to argue that if Chaney had a right to be free from unsafe or ineffective methods of execution (!), this right should have been invoked against the state under the Eighth Amendment. The suit against the FDA, as even Justice Marshall acknowledged, was simply a desperate tactic, undertaken only because the claim Chaney would have liked to have made against state prison officials had no chance of succeeding. He had no separate right at stake in FDA policy in this area.

73. See Food and Drugs Act, 21 U.S.C. §355(h), authorizing appeals from denial of marketing approval by the FDA.

74. See *Cutler v. Hayes,* 818 F.2d 879 (D.C. Cir., 1987), discussed in chapter 7.

75. For example, *Farmworkers Justice Fund v. Brock,* 811 F.2d 613 (D.C. Cir., 1987), discussed in chapter 7.

76. *U.S. v. Jefferson County Board of Education,* 372 F.2d 836 (5th Cir., 1966) at 864.

77. Michael S. Greve, "Terminating School Desegregation Lawsuits," *Harvard Journal of Law and Public Policy* 7 (1984): 303.

78. Gerald M. Pomper, ed., *The Election of 1984* (Chatham, N.J.: Chatham House, 1985), p. 67, reports projections from exit poll data indicating that 43 percent of union households voted for Reagan in 1980 and 45 percent in 1984 (as against 48 percent for Carter in 1980, 53 percent for Mondale in 1984).

Chapter 3

1. There are at least three a priori reasons for supposing that judges are more prone to arrogance, bias, negligence, and other defects of character than are executive appointees. First, for all practical purposes, judges cannot be removed from office, directly inconvenienced, or even

Notes

effectively censured, so they have few meaningful external incentives to conduct themselves conscientiously. The normal assumption in liberal democratic societies, of course, is that people in these circumstances cannot be relied upon to make major public decisions responsibly. Second, the pretense that decisions are determined not by the judge but by the law may insulate judges from the reproaches of their own consciences, a point often stressed by legal realists, who urge that judges would be more conscientious if they were more honest about what they are doing. This advice has rarely been adopted, but the insight may remain all the more valid for that. Finally, judges are more socially insulated from those their decisions affect—even compared with executive appointees, who usually feel obliged to do a good deal of traveling and meeting with constituencies. Judges deal rather with lawyers, who are required to address them at all times in respectful, even deferential terms (such as "your honor," a term not even used with the president). In this regard, judges most resemble eighteenth century princes attended by obsequious courtiers, and the atmosphere of court life is now regarded as inevitably corrupting. Perhaps none of these considerations is decisive, but together they may raise enough doubts to rid us of any presumption that judges will more often display good character than executive appointees.

2. Lloyd L. Weinreb, *Denial of Justice: Criminal Process in the United States* (New York: Free Press, 1977), p. 71, estimates that criminal charges are settled by plea bargain rather than by trial in "eight or nine cases out of ten."

3. *U.S. v. Richardson*, 418 U.S. 166 (1974).

4. The leading cases limiting congressional power under the Tenth Amendment are *Hammer v. Dagenhart*, 247 U.S. 251 (1918), prohibiting congressional regulation of "local" production; *Bailey v. Drexel Furniture*, 259 U.S. 20 (1922), prohibiting taxation for purposes of controlling local production; and *U.S. v. Butler*, 297 U.S. 1 (1936), prohibiting spending for nonfederal purposes. The leading "substantive due process" cases limiting congressional power under the Fifth Amendment are *Adair v. U.S.*, 208 U.S. 161 (1908), invalidating a congressional prohibition on antiunion contracts for abridging freedom of contract; and *Adkins v. Children's Hospital*, 262 U.S. 525 (1923), invalidating the congressional imposition of a minimum wage law.

5. *Schechter Poultry Corp. v. U.S.*, 295 U.S. 495 (1935); *Carter v. Carter Coal*, 298 U.S. 238 (·936).

6. *Buckley v. Valeo*, 424 U.S. 1 (1976), invalidating a provision allowing members of Congress to appoint commissioners of the Federal Election Commission; *INS v. Chadha*, 462 U.S. 919 (1983), invalidating a legislative veto provision; and *Bowsher v. Synar*, 106 S.Ct. 3181 (1986), invalidating the delegation of budget cutting powers to an official removable by Congress.

7. See, e.g., R. Shep Melnick, "The Politics of Partnership," *Public Administration Review* 45 (1985): 653–660 at 654.

8. *Chevron, U.S.A. v. Natural Resources Defense Council*, 467 U.S. 837 (1984) at 842–43 and n. 9: "If the intent of Congress is clear, that is the end of the matter; for the court, as well as the agency must give effect to the unambiguously expressed intent of Congress. . . . The judiciary is the final authority on issues of statutory constructions and must reject administrative constructions which are contrary to clear congressional intent."

9. *INS v. Chadha*, 462 U.S. 919 (1983) at 953, n. 16: "Executive action is always subject to check by the terms of the legislation that authorized it; and if that authority is exceeded it is open to judicial review."

10. *TVA v. Hill*, 437 U.S. 153 (1978). In this case, as the Court may have anticipated, Congress amended the statute to prevent further decisions of this kind by establishing an administrative review board with power to grant exemptions.

11. See, e.g., the speech of Patrick Henry on June 5, 1788 at the Virginia ratification convention, warning that "your president may easily become a king" (H. Storing, *The Antifederalists*, M. Dry, ed. [Chicago: University of Chicago Press, 1985], p. 310).

12. See Richard Buel, *Securing the Revolution: Ideology in American Politics, 1789–1815* (Ithaca, N.Y.: Cornell University Press, 1972); and Lance Banning, *The Jeffersonian Persuasion: Evolution of a Party Ideology* (Ithaca, N.Y.: Cornell University Press, 1978), both stressing the degree to which the "Republican" opposition associated nationalism and centralization with executive supremacy.

13. So, for example, Henry Clay denounced Jackson's assertion of presidential control over the treasury secretary as "a revolution . . . a total change of the pure republican character of our government" (W. E. Binkley, *President and Congress*, 3d ed. [New York: Vintage Books, 1962], p. 96).

14. Arthur Schlesinger, Jr., *The Imperial Presidency* (Boston: Houghton Mifflin, 1973).

Notes

15. See Thomas Hobbes, *Leviathan*, chaps. 2–10, 26, 29, and *Dialogue Between a Philosopher and a Student of the Common Laws of England*, Joseph Cropsey, ed. (Chicago: University of Chicago Press, 1979).

16. *United Steelworkers v. Weber*, 443 U.S. 193 (1979), endorsed racial quotas as consistent with Title VII of the 1964 Civil Rights Act when designed to benefit minorities. The vehement dissenting opinion by Justice Rehnquist (joined by Chief Justice Burger) offers a sampling of the overwhelming evidence that Congress had not meant to authorize such "benign discrimination" in 1964 but had rather meant to prohibit racial discrimination of all kinds.

17. 443 U.S. 193 (1979) at 209: "While I share some of the misgivings expressed by Mr. Justice Rehnquist's dissent, concerning the extent to which the legislative history of Title VII clearly supports the result the Court reaches today, I believe that additional considerations, practical and equitable, only partially perceived, if perceived at all by the 88th Congress [in 1964], support the conclusion reached by the Court today and I therefore join its opinion as well as its judgment." The opinion does not actually cite any "additional considerations" that could not have been "perceived" in 1964: it simply concludes that "the bargain struck in 1964" should "not be construed" to stand in the way of affirmative action programs thought desirable in 1979. Justice Stevens acknowledged with similar candor that the Court's decision to permit employment preferences for women over men was "at odds with my understanding of the actual intent of the authors of [Title VII]" and he then went on to "conclude without hesitation" that the Court's construction should now be preferred to "the actual intent" of Congress: *Johnson v. Santa Clara Transportation Agency* 107 S.Ct. 1442 (1987) at 1459.

18. Judge Patricia M. Wald, now Chief Judge of the D.C. Court of Appeals, recently summed up the court's role as "one of ensuring the [defendant] agency's fidelity to the intent of . . . the Congress that passed the legislation that the agency was now deregulating. . . . we were, if you will, a trustee for the ghosts of Congresses past" ("The Contribution of the D.C. Circuit to Administrative Law," *Administrative Law Review* [Fall 1988]: 40: 507 at 522).

19. *Farmers Union Central Exchange v. FERC*, 734 F.1486 (D.C. Cir., 1984).

20. On the hostility of Jeffersonian Republicans to unelected judges, see Richard Ellis, *The Jeffersonian Crisis* (New York: Oxford University Press, 1971). Of their post–Civil War namesakes, it may be sufficient to note that after voting to impeach President Johnson, Republicans in the House of Representatives passed a measure denying effect to any Supreme Court judgment holding an act of Congress unconstitutional, unless affirmed by two-thirds of the justices. When the Senate failed to approve this measure, Republican Radicals put through a measure denying jurisdiction to the Supreme Court in an upcoming case expected to test the constitutionality of the Reconstruction laws: see Bernard Schwartz, *From Confederation to Nation: The American Constitution, 1835–1877* (Baltimore: The Johns Hopkins University Press, 1973), p. 186. The latter maneuver was accepted by the Supreme Court in *Ex parte McCardle*, 6 Wall. 318 (1868).

21. "To assist Congress in appraising the administration of the laws and in developing such amendments or related legislation as it may deem necessary, each standing committee of the Senate and the House of Representatives shall exercise continuous watchfulness of the execution by the administrative agencies concerned of any laws, the subject matter of which is within the jurisdiction of such committees": §136, 60 Stat. 832 (1946).

22. See, e.g., Roger Davidson, "Subcommittee Government: New Channels for Policy Making," in *The New Congress*, Thomas E. Mann and Norman J. Ornstein, eds. (Washington, D.C.: American Enterprise Institute, 1981), pp. 99–133.

23. Congressional preference for informal policy making at the behest of particular constituencies over formal legislation has been stressed most forcefully by Morris Fiorina, *Congress: Keystone of the Washington Establishment* (New Haven: Yale University Press, 1977) and David R. Mayhew, *Congress: The Electoral Connection* (New Haven: Yale University Press, 1974).

24. Barry Weingast and Mark Moran, in "Bureaucratic Discretion or Congressional Control: Regulatory Policymaking by the Federal Trade Commission," *Journal of Political Economy* 91 (1983): 756, demonstrate that changes in the composition of congressional oversight committees correlate almost perfectly with changes in policy at the FTC, though the correlation may be less perfect with executive agencies.

25. For an overview of the American Bar Association campaign that led up to the enactment of the Walter Logan Act, see the relevant section ("The Special Committee on Administrative Law of the ABA") in Louis Jaffe, "Invective and Investigation in Administrative Law," *Harvard Law Review* 52 (1939): 1201.

26. Like most special interest measures, the first citizen standing provision, the one contained

Notes

in the Clean Air Act of 1970, was slipped into the bill in the course of redrafting by committee staffers, after all public hearings on the rest of the bill had already been completed. In floor debate in the Senate (where the provision was first introduced), Senator Griffin protested "that this far reaching provision was included in the bill without any testimony from the Judicial Conference, the Department of Justice or the Office of Management and Budget concerning the possible impact this might have." But the objection was ignored in the rush of enthusiasm for quick action on the environment. Senate floor debate, September 21, 1970, reprinted in *Legislative History of the Clean Air Amendments of 1970* (Washington, D.C.: Congressional Research Service, 1974), p. 350. To trace Senator Muskie's stealthy insertion of this provision, see *Air Pollution— 1970: Hearings on S. 3229, S. 3466, S. 3546*, Subcommittee on Air and Water Pollution, 91st Congress (1970). Public hearings were concluded in May, while the first appearance of the provision for citizen suits against the EPA was in an unnumbered draft bill dated August 25. Subsequent comments by the Automobile Manufacturers Association, printed as an appendix beginning at p. 1576, complained about "time schedules which did not permit open hearings on new and important provisions in the bill."

27. At the urging of Ralph Nader, who protested that "the way the law of standing is now interpreted, it prevents 215 million Americans from obtaining review in the courts of their claims that the Government is acting unlawfully in particular instances . . . [and] that amounts to a declaration of tyranny," Senator Edward Kennedy introduced a bill to amend the APA to authorize citizen suits against all federal agencies. At hearings on the bill in the spring of 1976, however, Kennedy himself questioned whether "this reform would shift in a major way the balance between the legislative and judicial branches . . . which exists and has been established by the Founding Fathers." While evidently agreeing with Nader's implicit equation of executive discretion with tyranny, Kennedy wondered whether it would not be "more effective to hold the Federal Government accountable to the public through the legislative branch rather than . . . in a vague and haphazard manner through the courts" (*Administrative Procedure Act Amendments of 1976*, Hearings before the Subcommittee on Administrative Practice and Procedure, U.S. Senate Judiciary Committee, 94th Congress, [1976], p. 5).

28. Frank Goodnow, *Politics and Administration: A Study of Government* (New York: Macmillan, 1900), chap. 1.

29. The principal impetus for civil service reform in the decades after the Civil War was not to ensure the impartial performance of administrative officials but to reduce the corruption of politics by reducing the volume of government jobs available for political patronage: see Leonard White, *The Republican Era, 1865–1901: A Study in Administrative History* (New York: Macmillan, 1959), pp. 278–304, for a useful overview.

30. "It was freely charged that the courts were . . . using the economic theories of generations past to block the adoption of new policies designed to meet new industrial conditions. It was contended that the power of the judiciary was being employed to protect property against persons and defeat regulative measures in the interest of the many as against the privileged position of the few. . . . Even where the judges were personally honest, it was said that their class prejudices led to decisions against the commonwealth or that their *devotion to precedent made their reasoning processes inadequate to solve modern problems*" (emphasis added; Charles E. Merriam, *American Political Ideas: Studies in the Development of American Political Thought, 1865–1917* [New York: Macmillan, 1927], pp. 188–89, summarizing the Progressive criticism of courts). In the election of 1912, the presidential candidate of the new Progressive Party, Theodore Roosevelt, proposed that federal judges be made subject to popular recall and that judicial decisions overturning statutes on constitutional grounds be made subject to reconsideration in popular referendums, lest the people be "victims of perfunctory legalism" (ibid., pp. 189–92).

31. Robert Cushman, *The Independent Regulatory Commissions* (New York: Oxford University Press, 1941) pp. 69–70, 185–87, 331, 341, 373, 379, and 394–96.

32. *The Final Report of the Attorney General's Committee on Administrative Procedure* (1941) offers an extensive survey of existing regulatory programs in chapter 1, including several in the Agriculture Department, Interior Department, and the Labor Department. The discussion of "Problems of Procedure" in chapter 5 notably does not distinguish between independent commissions and regulatory programs lodged in executive departments.

33. Roosevelt seems to have maintained a close, ongoing relationship, for example, with James Landis, first during his service at the FTC, then at the SEC, as is well described in Thomas McGraw, *Prophets of Regulation* (Cambridge, Mass.: Harvard University Press, 1984), pp. 160–203.

284

Notes

34. The assumption of ultimate presidential control over administration seemed well established by the early 1930s because it had been emphatically endorsed in a constitutional ruling of the Supreme Court a decade earlier. In *Myers v. U.S.*, 272 U.S. 52 (1926), the Court seemed to have put an emphatic end to a long debate on the subject by ruling that when the president had power to appoint officials (outside the judiciary), he must be understood to retain an unqualified power of removal. After an extensive review of the arguments advanced on this matter by James Madison and other leading figures at the founding, the Court concluded that the presidential removal power must be unlimited in order to allow the president to control the conduct of executive officials so as to secure "that unitary and uniform execution of the laws which Article II of the Constitution evidently contemplated in vesting general executive power in the President alone" (at 135).

35. *Humphrey's Executor v. U.S.*, 295 U.S. 602 (1935). On the reaction of New Dealers to this decision, see Robert Jackson, *The Struggle for Judicial Supremacy* (New York: Alfred A. Knopf, 1949), p. 109: "Within the [Roosevelt] administration there was a profound feeling that the opinion of the Court [in *Humphrey's Executor*] was written with a design to give the impression that the President had flouted the Constitution rather than that the Court had simply changed its mind. . . . the Court was applying to President Roosevelt rules different from those it had applied to his predecessors."

36. 295 U.S. 602 (1935) at 624, 628.

37. One of the earliest critical analyses of the decision was offered by Cushman, *Independent Regulatory Commissions*, pp. 455–67. One of the most recent and emphatic is Geoffrey Miller, "Independent Agencies," *Supreme Court Review* (1986): 41.

38. R. Polenberg, *Reorganizing Roosevelt's Government* (Cambridge, Mass.: Harvard University Press, 1966), pp. 55–78.

39. Harold Seidman and Robert Gilmour, in *Politics, Position and Power*, 4th ed. (New York: Oxford University Press, 1986), pp. 278–80, review efforts by Congress to exclude closer presidential control over the commissions into the current era.

40. See Ellis Hawley, *The New Deal and the Problem of Monopoly* (Princeton: Princeton University Press, 1966), pp. 205–69, 53–90.

41. See, e.g., Marver Bernstein, *Regulating Business by Independent Commission* (Princeton: Princeton University Press, 1955).

42. James Landis, *Report on Regulatory Agencies to the President-Elect*, December 1960.

43. For a useful overview, see M. Derthick and P. Quirk, *The Politics of Deregulation* (Washington, D.C.: The Brookings Institution, 1985) pp. 97–102.

44. Bradley Behrman, "Civil Aeronautics Board," in *The Politics of Regulation*, James Q. Wilson, ed. (New York: Basic Books, 1980), pp. 116, 416 (n. 183), 118.

45. See, e.g., *American Trucking Associations, Inc. v. ICC*, 659 F.2d 452 (5th Cir., 1981); *American Trucking Associations, Inc. v. ICC*, 751 F.2d 957 (5th Cir., 1982); *Port Norris Express Co. v. ICC*, 757 F.2d 58 (3d Cir., 1985).

46. Robert C. Fellmeth, *The Interstate Commerce Omission* (New York: Grossman Publishers, 1970) is the leading Naderite version of the story. Others are reviewed in Derthick and Quirk, *Politics of Deregulation*, pp. 42–43.

47. Derthick and Quirk, *Politics of Deregulation*, p. 122, which notes that only Ralph Nader's "Transportation Consumer Action Project" devoted extensive lobbying effort to this area, though a wide range of other consumer oriented public interest groups endorsed deregulation of trucking and airlines.

48. R. Shep Melnick, in "Pollution Deadlines and the Coalition for Failure," *The Public Interest* 75 (Spring 1984), argues that the setting of impossible deadlines has become a deliberate strategy of environmental advocates.

49. Judge Patricia M. Wald, "Judicial Review of Complex Administrative Agency Decisions," *Annals of the American Academy of Polical and Social Science* (July 1982), special issue on "The American Judiciary: Critical Issues," A. L. Leven and R. R. Wheeler, eds., p. 77.

50. *Abbott Laboratories v. Gardner*, 387 U.S. 136 (1967) at 141.

51. 5 U.S.C. §706: "The reviewing court shall—. . . (2) hold unlawful and set aside agency action, findings, and conclusions found to be—(A) arbitrary, capricious, an abuse of discretion or otherwise not in accordance with law." It should be recalled, however, that agency rules, which were to be judged under this standard, were allowed to be promulgated under the APA without any formal evidentiary proceeding, so that courts were essentially obliged to accept the agency's own claims regarding the evidence supporting new rules.

Notes

52. Wald, "Judicial Review," p. 75: "It is, of course, essential for courts to acknowledge the legitimate expertise of agencies. . . . But it is also important to recall that Congress, itself an assembly of generalists, has assigned courts the task of ensuring that those agencies are faithful to its mandates." In this perspective, courts and congressmen, as fellow "generalists," work together to assure civilian control of expert policy making. Judge Wald's account leaves no room for (and makes no mention of) the president—perhaps because he is regarded as a mere politician, not as a policy making generalist, or perhaps because, as commander in chief, he does not qualify as a true civilian generalist.

53. Max Weber, *The Theory of Social and Economic Organizations*, T. Parsons, ed. and trans. (New York: Oxford University Press, 1947), pp. 337, 339–40.

54. Ibid., p. 340.

55. See, e.g., Carl Friedrich, "Some Observations on Weber's Analysis of Bureaucracy," in *Reader in Bureaucracy*, Robert K. Merton, ed. (New York: Free Press, 1952).

56. Weber's personal and political reservations about the spirit of bureaucracy in general, and the state bureaucracies in his own Wilhelmine Germany in particular, are reviewed in J. G. Merquior, *Rousseau and Weber: Two Studies in the Theory of Legitimacy* (London: Routledge & Kegan Paul, 1980), pp. 117–21.

57. Weber, *Theory of Social and Economic Organizations*, p. 340.

58. Ibid. at pp. 328–29, 338–39, 341–45, 358–63.

59. Weber's fullest discussion of this matter appears in a paper on scientific method, originally delivered in 1913, which is translated as "Value-Judgments in Social Science," in *Max Weber: Selections in Translation*, W. G. Runciman, ed. (London: Cambridge University Press, 1978). Better known and similar is Weber's postwar lecture "Science as a Vocation," available in English in *From Max Weber: Essays in Sociology*, H. H. Gerth and C. W. Mills, trans. and eds. (New York: Oxford University Press, 1946).

60. One of the earliest and still most powerful is L. Strauss, *Natural Right and History* (Chicago: University of Chicago Press, 1953), pp. 36–78.

61. Weber, *Theory of Social and Economic Organization*, p. 338.

62. Strauss, *Natural Right*, p. 60 n. 22, describes Weber's insistence that moral values cannot be derived from the physical world as "neo-Kantian," identifying it, at least to this extent, with the revival of Kantian epistemology in late nineteenth century German thought. Some neo-Kantians, like Hermann Cohen, also sought to revive the prestige of Kantian formulas in moral thought, and there seems to be more than a trace of them also in Weber's understanding of values as concerns pursued without regard to consequences (or in Kantian terms as "nonheteronomous" ends).

63. "an action done from duty must altogether exclude the influence of inclination and therefore every object [or goal] of the will . . . the moral worth of an action does not lie in the effect expected" (Immanuel Kant, "Grounding for the Metaphysics of Morals," J. W. Ellington, trans., *Ethical Philosophy* [Indianapolis: Hackett Publishing, 1981], p. 13).

64. Hans Rosenberg, *Bureaucracy, Aristocracy and Autocracy* (Boston: Beacon Press, 1966), p. 189.

65. Immanuel Kant, "Perpetual Peace," in Beck, ed., *Kant On History*, Lewis Beck, ed. and trans. (Indianapolis: Bobbs-Merrill, 1963), p. 129.

66. Immanuel Kant, *The Metaphysical Elements of Justice*, John Ladd, trans. (Indianapolis: Bobbs-Merrill, 1965), pp. 100, 106.

67. The history of totalitarian regimes in this century demonstrates that the revolutionary and the functionary are not, after all, so far apart, but may well represent the same monstrous individual. For both, as Solzhenitsyn has eloquently warned, an ideology is necessary that "gives evildoing its long-sought justification and gives the evildoer the necessary steadfastness and determination. That is the social theory which helps to make his acts seem good instead of bad in his own and others' eyes, so that he won't hear reproaches and curses but will receive praise and honors" (*Gulag Archipelago*, trans. Thomas P. Whitney [New York: Harper & Row, 1973], 1. 174.

68. W. W. Willoughby, *Prussian Political Philosophy* (New York: D. Appleton, 1918), pp. 56–59.

69. Kant himself credited Rousseau for inspiring his moral philosophy, and one might plausibly trace much of the European statist tradition—at least in its modern intellectual rationales—back to the argument in Rousseau's *Social Contract* that the only legitimate public authority is that based on a "general will," which is derived in turn from a complete identification on the part of each citizen with the community. Rousseau then drew the logical conclusion that the citizens

who determine the general will must have no involvement with the government that executes it in detail, lest this contact corrupt the citizen's proper preoccupation with the generality or the community as a whole. What is said in the text about the distance from *The Federalist* of the Kantian or Weberian conceptions might be said just as well about Rousseau's conception. It is sufficient to note, in this respect, the matter-of-fact claim in *The Federalist* that "giving to every citizen the same opinions, the same passions, and the same interest" would be altogether "impracticable": "As long as the reason of man continues fallible and he is at liberty to exercise it, different opinions will be formed" (*The Federalist* 10, C. Rossiter, ed. [New York: New American Library, 1961], p. 78).

70. *The Federalist* 10, Rossiter, ed., p. 79.
71. *The Federalist* 51, Rossiter, ed., p. 322.
72. Ibid.
73. *The Federalist* 25, Rossiter, ed., p. 167.
74. *The Federalist* 55, Rossiter, ed., p. 346.
75. *The Federalist* 27, Rossiter, ed., p. 174.
76. *The Federalist* 10, Rossiter, ed., p. 78.

77. The famous argument in *The Federalist* 10 regarding the advantages of a self-canceling multitude of factions in a large republic presumes that government will behave more responsibly if more removed from homogeneous clamor. Hence the argument in no. 63 that the extended terms of senators will make them more rather than less responsible. A contemporary version of this argument has been well put by Eugene Bardach and Robert A. Kagan in *Going by the Book: The Problem of Regulatory Unreasonableness* (Philadelphia: Temple University Press, 1982), p. 321: "We can define responsibility as doing what one judges to be right in a problematic situation involving someone else's welfare and accepting the moral blame for any harms that flow from one's judgement. Accountability, on the other hand, implies doing what an outside reviewing party, not immediately present in the situation, will subsequently judge not to have been wrong. ... These ... might overlap. If they do not, and if a course of action [that would meet the relevant accountability requirements] is chosen, one can say that *accountability displaces responsibility*" (original emphasis).

78. Alexander Hamilton, "Pacificus, No.1" in *Works of Alexander Hamilton*, J. C. Hamilton, ed., 7 vols. (New York: Charles S. Rancis, 1850), 7. 14.

79. This episode is described in Norman J. Small, *Some Presidential Interpretations of the Presidency*, Johns Hopkins University Studies in Historical and Political Science 50 (Baltimore: The Johns Hopkins University Press, 1932), pp. 20–22.

80. *The Federalist* 77, Rossiter, ed., p. 463 speaks of the "powers of the executive . . . in faithfully executing the law," taking it for granted that this is a grant of power, not simply a fixed duty. As Harvey Mansfield, Jr. has pointed out, the presidential oath, prescribed in Article II, pledges the president to "faithfully execute *the office* of President" rather than simply to execute the laws, thus emphasizing the independent source of responsibility and discretion inhering in the office ("The Ambivalence of Executive Power," in *The Presidency in the Constitutional Order*, Joseph Bessette and Jeffrey Tulis, eds. [Baton Rouge: Louisiana State University Press, 1981], p. 317).

81. Charles Thach, *The Creation of the Presidency, 1775–1789*, Johns Hopkins University Historical Studies 40 (Baltimore: The Johns Hopkins University Press, 1922), pp. 55–75.

82. A number of recent historical studies have stressed the influence on late eighteenth century American thought of the ideas of the so-called "country party" opposition to Walpole's government in England decades earlier; the central theme of the attacks on Walpole was the danger of overweening executive power gained through the bribery or "corruption" of Parliament with offers of jobs and patronage. A useful study tracing the influence of this ideology into the nineteenth century is Lance Banning, *The Jeffersonian Persuasion: Evolution of a Party Ideology* (Ithaca: Cornell University Press, 1978).

83. Alexis de Tocqueville, *Democracy in America*, G. Lawrence, trans., J. P. Mayer, ed. (New York: Anchor Books, 1969), p. 206.

84. In practice some discretion inevitably remains, but the point is that it is concealed: see Abraham S. Goldstein and Martin Marcus, "The Myth of Judicial Supervision in Three 'Inquisitorial' Systems: France, Italy and Germany," *Yale Law Journal* 87 (1977): 240.

85. *Pugach v. Klein*, 193 F. Supp. 630 (S.D.N.Y., 1961) at 635.

86. See Kenneth Dyson, *The State Tradition in Western Europe* (New York: Oxford University Press, 1980).

Notes

87. One recent study estimates that a "new administration" in Britain is "entitled to choose afresh . . . approximately 100 top officials" and in France about 360, but that 85 percent of them are drawn from the civil service. "The United States outdoes all other modern democracies in its provision for change when party control of the executive shifts. About 1600 higher positions are filled by political appointment. . . . In the Department of Commerce, 93 high political incumbents can be displaced; in the Department of Agriculture, 65" (James W. Fesler, "Politics, Policy and Bureaucracy at the Top," *Annals of the American Academy of Political and Social Science* 466 [March 1983]: 24–25).

88. E.g., David Vogel, "The Public Interest Movement and the American Reform Tradition," *Political Science Quarterly* 95 (1980): 607.

89. Theodore Lowi, *The End of Liberalism* (New York: W. W. Norton, 1969).

90. R. Shep Melnick, "Pollution Deadlines and the Coalition for Failure," *The Public Interest* 75 (Spring 1984).

91. R. Brickman, S. Jasanoff, and T. Ilgen, *Controlling Chemicals: The Politics of Regulation in Europe and the United States* (Ithaca, N.Y.: Cornell University Press, 1985), pp. 64, 72.

92. See, e.g., Martin Tolchin and Susan Tolchin, *Dismantling America* (Boston: Houghton-Mifflin, 1983) p. 25.

93. For a thoughtful effort to assess the balance, see David Vogel, *National Styles of Regulation: Environmental Policy in Great Britain and the United States* (Ithaca, N.Y.: Cornell University Press, 1986).

94. A useful English language summary of German standing limitations is provided in Eckard Rehbinder, "Private Recourse for Environmental Harm: Federal Republic of Germany," in *Environmental Pollution and Individual Rights: An International Symposium*, S. McCaffrey and R. Lutz, eds. (Deventer, The Netherlands: Kluwer, 1978). See also Michael Greve, "The Non-Reformation of German Administrative Law: Standing to Sue and Public Interest Litigation in West German Environmental Law," *Cornell International Law Journal* 22 (1989).

95. A useful English language summary of French standing limitations is provided in Michel Prieur, "The Rights of Associations for the Protection of Nature and the Environment in France," in *Environmental Pollution*, McCaffrey and Lutz, eds. See, more generally, L. N. Brown and J. F. Garner, *French Administrative Law* (London: Butterworths, 1973).

96. W. H. R. Wade, *Administrative Law* (Oxford: Clarendon Press, 1985).

Chapter 4

1. *The Federalist* 78, C. Rossiter, ed. (New York: New American Library, 1961), p. 465.

2. H. Storing, in *What the Antifederalists Were For* (Chicago: University of Chicago Press, 1981), notes that "the broadest reaches of the judiciary . . . were seldom canvassed during the ratification debates." One of the exceptions, the Antifederalist writer "Brutus," expressed great alarm about the powers that might be exercised by the Supreme Court in interpreting the Constitution and warned that the Court would give an expansive interpretation to congressional power at the expense of the states. But regarding the provision in Article III that "extends [judicial] authority to all cases in law and equity arising under the laws of the United States," he acknowledged that "this power as I understand it is a proper one," and raised no questions about the meaning of the term "cases" ("Letters of Brutus" 13 [February 21, 1788]; see Storing, *The Antifederalist: Writings by the Opponents of the Constitution*, M. Dry, ed. [Chicago: University of Chicago Press, 1985], p. 173).

3. Joseph Story, *Commentaries on the Constitution of the United States*, 3 vols. (Boston: Hilliard, Gray, 1833), 3. 507.

4. See, e.g., Exodus 18:13, 16 (Moses "sat to judge the people," acting as "judge between one and another"); Deuteronomy 4:1 (Moses urges the people to "hearken . . . unto the statutes . . . which I teach you"); Numbers 31:3, 6 ("Moses spake unto the people, saying, 'Arm some of yourselves unto the war.' . . . And Moses sent them to the war, a thousand of every tribe"): King James Version. Of course, it is not surprising that Moses exercises these diverse powers as the special instrument of God. God's power to do justice—to *judge* man—is not confined by liberal conceptions of due process: by turns, God decides disputes between individuals (Genesis 16:5: "The Lord judge [*y'shpot*] between me and thee"); executes judgment on the guilty (Exodus 12:12: "I will smite all the firstborn in the land of Egypt . . . I will execute judgment [*sh'fatim*]");

Notes

and hands down "judgments" in the form of general, prospective laws (Leviticus 18:4: "Ye shall do my judgments [*msh'patai*] and keep mine ordinances, to walk therein." The same root word can be used to describe these divine acts, because with God, it seems, there is no difference between judgment and willfulness.

5. Until late in the thirteenth century, the royal justiciar served as chief judge, chief administrative officer, and chief policy adviser to the king. When this office was abolished, the chief judges had no administrative superior; but the chancellor, the administrative and political successor to the justiciar, continued to exercise judicial functions through the court of chancery (or "equity"). See F. W. Maitland, *The Constitutional History of England*, H. A. L. Fisher, ed. (Cambridge: Cambridge University Press, 1974; orig. 1908), pp. 133–36. County courts continued to transact fiscal and administrative business long thereafter, for "in the middle ages [judicial] jurisdiction is never very clearly separated from government" F. Pollock and F. W. Maitland, *The History of English Law Before the Time of Edward I*, S. F. C. Milsom, ed. (Cambridge: Cambridge University Press, 1968; repr. of 2d ed., 1898), 1. 554–55.

6. Pollock and Maitland, *History of English Law*, 2.563. As late as the mid-thirteenth century, English kings still decided "private" suits in person, and the legal "theory of the time saw no harm in this." By the fifteenth century it "had become unlawful for [the king] to meddle with the ordinary course of justice," but the king still retained the legal authority to dismiss any judge at will until after the revolution of 1689 (Maitland, *Constitutional History*, pp. 134, 195).

7. Pollock and Maitland, *History of English Law*, p. 572.

8. Ibid., p. 648.

9. "It was not conceived that the state could alter law; law was not a matter of will but of knowledge" (G. L. Haskins, *The Growth of English Representative Government* [Philadelphia: University of Pennsylvania Press, 1948], p. 100).

10. Ibid.

11. Pollock and Maitland, *History of English Law*, p. 478.

12. Sir John Fortescue, *De laudibus legum Angliae*, S. B. Chrimes, ed. and trans. (Cambridge: Cambridge University Press, 1942), p. 10.

13. Richard Tuck, in *Natural Rights Theories, Their Origin and Development* (Cambridge: Cambridge University Press, 1979), argues that the conventional wisdom on this point overstates the contrast because, whatever the ambiguity in the term *ius*, the Latin term *dominium* ("lordship" or "ownership") had already come to be used in the modern sense of "a right" in some late medieval writings on law (pp. 24–30). But even Tuck's revisionist account acknowledges that the modern conception of rights in the sense of powers of personal control was deeply influenced by the writings of seventeenth century natural rights theorists, and the latter accordingly receive the bulk of his attention in this study.

14. Courts of equity or chancery were supposed to have somewhat more discretion to ensure that their inherently more intrusive remedies—direct orders rather than money payments—would fit the circumstances of the particular case. But questions of jurisdiction and the merits of suits were already governed by an elaborate stock of rules and precedents by the eighteenth century.

15. Sir William Blackstone, *Commentaries on the Laws of England*, 4 vols., facsimile of the first edition of 1765 (Chicago: University of Chicago Press, 1979), 1.119.

16. Ibid., p. 135.

17. James Madison, "Property," *National Gazette* (March 29, 1792), repr. in *The Mind of the Founder: Sources of the Political Thought of James Madison*, Marvin Meyers, ed., rev. ed. (Hanover, N.H.: University Press of New England, 1981), p. 187. The English statute requiring all shrouds to be made of wool is described and defended in a famous passage in Blackstone, *Commentaries*, 1.122.

18. *The Federalist* 78, Rossiter, ed., p. 465. See Edward S. Corwin, *The Higher Law Background of American Constitutional Law* (repr. Ithaca, N.Y.: Cornell University Press, 1981).

19. Thomas M. Cooley, *A Treatise on the Constitutional Limitations on the Legislative Power of the States of the American Union*, 2d ed. (Boston: Little, Brown, 1871), p. 172.

20. *Adkins v. Children's Hospital*, 261 U.S. 525 (1923) at 544.

21. *U.S. v. Butler*, 297 U.S. 1 (1936) at 63.

22. Randall Bridwell and Ralph Witten, *The Constitution and the Common Law* (Lexington, Mass.: D. C. Heath, 1977), pp. 35–51.

23. See R. M. Jackson, *The Machinery of Justice in England*, 4th ed. (Cambridge: Cambridge University Press, 1966), pp. 120–22. Even in this system, however, the attorney general—a

cabinet official responsible to Parliament—retains absolute authority to block any attempted "private prosecution" at will.

24. Leonard White, in *The Federalists: A Study in Administrative History* (New York: Macmillan, 1948), describes the operation of this licensing scheme in the chapter on "Government in the Wilderness."

25. Bruce Wyman, *Principles of the Administrative Law Governing the Relations of Public Officers* (St. Paul, Minn.: Keefe-Davidson, 1903), p. 139.

26. *Degge v. Hitchcock,* 229 U.S. 162 (1913).

27. The connection remains apparent if one views rights in the traditional way: Lon Fuller, who offered a powerful defense of rights as safeguards of individual autonomy in *The Morality of Law* (New Haven: Yale University Press, 1967), argued in his last published work that "polycentric disputes"—disputes involving the legitimate interests of several competing claimants—could not be resolved by courts, because they could not be settled by appeal to fixed rules. See Fuller, "The Forms and Limits of Adjudication," *Harvard Law Review* 92 (1978): 353.

28. Blackstone, *Commentaries,* 1.91.

29. Oliver Wendell Holmes, Jr., *The Common Law* (Boston: Little, Brown, 1881), pp. 48–49. On Holmes' utilitarianism, see H. L. Pohlman, *Justice Oliver Wendell Holmes and Utilitarian Jurisprudence* (Cambridge, Mass.: Harvard University Press, 1984).

30. See, e.g., James Barr Ames, "Law and Morals," *Harvard Law Review* 22 (1908): 97.

31. Bentham himself urged that all power in the British government be vested in the House of Commons, so that the will of the popular majority could be readily translated into law. And "Holmes consistently and early defended the utilitarian doctrine of judicial deference to the sovereign" (Pohlman, *Justice Oliver Wendell Holmes,* p. 155).

32. "The jurist of today . . . seeks to discover and to ponder the actual social effects of legal institutions and legal doctrines. He views them as instruments of social engineering" (Roscoe Pound, "The Administrative Application of Legal Standards," Report of the 42d Meeting of the American Bar Association, 1919). During the 1930s, Pound himself seemed to abandon at least the more extreme versions of this perspective in his anxiety to defend "the rule of law."

33. See, e.g., *ICC v. Cincinnati, New Orleans and Texas Pacific RR. Co.,* 167 U.S. 479 (1897).

34. F. J. Port, *Administrative Law* (New York: Longmans, Green, 1929), pp. 282–84.

35. Ibid., p. 283.

36. John Dewey and James Tufts, *Ethics* (New York: Henry Holt, 1908) p. 404.

37. John Dickinson, *Administrative Justice and the Supremacy of Law in the United States* (New York: Russell & Russell, 1927), pp. 29–30.

38. The connection between legal realism and enthusiasm for administration has recently been stressed by Bruce Ackerman, *Reconstructing American Law* (Cambridge, Mass.: Harvard University Press, 1983), pp. 6–22.

39. "Holmes' ideal judge was neither a mathematician nor an idealist but an empirical social scientist, whose feet were firmly planted in reality" (Pohlman, *Justice Holmes and Utilitarian Jurisprudence,* p. 151).

40. The most visionary and enthusiastic version of this view was offered by a junior disciple of the realists some years later: Myres S. McDougal, "The Law School of the Future: From Legal Realism to Policy Science in a World Community," *Yale Law Journal* 56 (1947): 1345.

41. Benjamin Cardozo, *The Nature of the Judicial Process* (New Haven: Yale University Press, 1921).

42. Robert Glennon, *The Iconoclast Reformer: Jerome Frank's Influence on American Law* (Ithaca, N.Y.: Cornell University Press, 1985).

43. *The Chicago Junction Case,* 264 U.S. 258 (1924).

44. Ibid. at 271.

45. See Thomas McGraw, *Prophets of Regulation* (Cambridge, Mass.: Harvard University Press, 1984), pp. 80–142, stressing Brandeis's eagerness to protect small firms from uncontrolled competition and his "litigator's" eagerness to defend their claims in terms not readily squared with economic rationality. See also G. Edward White, "Allocating Power Between Agencies and Courts: The Legacy of Justice Brandeis," *Duke Law Journal* (April 1974), stressing the distinctions Brandeis sought to draw between regulatory commissions and "executive" agencies.

46. *FCC v. Scripps Howard Broadcasting,* 316 U.S. 4 (1942), dissenting opinion of Justice Douglas at p. 21.

47. Ibid. at 15.

48. Frankfurter's reluctance to see courts play more of a role in checking administrative

discretion can be traced to his outlook as a professor of administrative law at Harvard in the 1920s and 1930s, according to William C. Chase, *The American Law School and the Rise of Administrative Government* (Madison: University of Wisconsin Press, 1982). For the continuities in Frankfurter's outlook on the Supreme Court, see the deferential view of administrative fact finding urged in his opinion in *Universal Camera v. NLRB*, 340 U.S. 474 (1951). On Frankfurter's devotion to "balancing" in civil liberties cases, see Mark Silverstein, *Constitutional Faiths* (Ithaca, N.Y.: Cornell University Press, 1984), pp. 176–206.

49. The most celebrated example is the dissent by Justice Harlan in *Plessy v. Ferguson*, 113 U.S. 537 (1896). Although Harlan's insistence that "Our Constitution is colorblind" has become famous, it is less often remembered that his objection to racial segregation was premised on a devotion to liberty, not equality: "The *fundamental* objection . . . to the statute is that it interferes with the personal freedom of citizens" (emphasis added). See also the dissenting opinion in *Berea College v. Kentucky*, 211 U.S. 54 (1908).

50. *Brown v. Board of Education*, 347 U.S. 483 (1954).

51. *Brown v. Board of Education II.* This criticism is elaborated in Lino Graglia, *Disaster by Decree* (Ithaca, N.Y.: Cornell University Press, 1977), pp. 37–45.

52. Philip Ellman, interviewed by Norman Silber, "The Solicitor General, Justice Frankfurter and Civil Rights Litigation, 1946–1960," *Harvard Law Review* 100 (1987): 817.

53. See *U.S. v. Morgan*, 313 U.S. 409 (1941), known as "Morgan IV" because it was the fourth go-round for the Supreme Court on essentially the same case, and this final round sought to preclude further litigation of the same kind by insisting that courts should not "probe the mental processes" of "responsible" administrators by seeking to assess their personal understanding of decisions made in their name.

54. Note, "The Courts, HEW and Southern School Desegregation," *Yale Law Journal* 77 (1967): 321.

55. *U.S. v. Jefferson County Board of Education*, 372 F2d 836 (5th Cir., 1968).

56. See Michael Greve, "Terminating School Desegregation Lawsuits," *Harvard Journal of Law and Public Policy* 7 (1984): 303.

57. *Baker v. Carr*, 369 U.S. 186 (1962) at 204.

58. *U.S. v. Robel*, 389 U.S. 258 (1967).

59. Frederick Schauer, "Codifying the First Amendment," *Supreme Court Review* (1982): 285.

60. *Flast v. Cohen*, 392 U.S. 83 (1968).

61. *U.S. v. Richardson*, 418 U.S. 166 (1974).

62. Compare *Board of Education v. Allen*, 392 U.S. 236 (1968), allowing loan of state textbooks to parochial schools; *Wolman v. Walter*, 433 U.S. 299 (1977), prohibiting state loans of maps, magazines, and other materials to parochial schools; *Levitt v. Committee for Public Education*, 413 U.S. 417 (1973), prohibiting reimbursement of parochial schools for administering state required tests; *Committee for Public Education v. Regan*, 444 U.S. 646 (1980), allowing reimbursement of parochial schools for administering state required tests when tests are prepared by state officials; *Lemon v. Kurtzman*, 403 U.S. 602 (1971), prohibiting state financial grants to parochial schools; and *Mueller v. Allen*, 463 U.S. 388 (1983), allowing special state tax benefits to parents of children in parochial schools to offset tuition costs.

63. *Lemon v. Kurtzman*, 403 U.S. 602 (1971).

64. In 1939, reviewing the American Bar Association proposals for wider judicial control on administrative decision making, Louis Jaffe singled out the proposal for immediate review of new rules as among the most ill-conceived. He also questioned the constitutionality of such a proposal, as a rule by itself would not involve a "case or controversy" in the sense of Article III: see his "Invective and Investigation in Administrative Law," *Harvard Law Review* 52 (1939): 1201. Arguments of this sort prevailed in the 1930s. By the mid-1970s, however, ripeness notions had been so thoroughly forgotten that contending interests often engaged in a competitive "race to the courthouse," rushing to file challenges to new rules within minutes of their official promulgation (sometimes with the aid of two-way radios and special runners) so as to establish jurisdiction for the challenge in the most favorable circuit, before rivals could establish jurisdiction in a different circuit. The pattern for OSHA rules is described in Steven Kelman, *Regulating America, Regulating Sweden* (Cambridge, Mass.: M.I.T. Press, 1981), pp. 133–46.

65. Originally $10, later codified at 5 U.S.C. 701(a).

66. Six years before the enactment of the APA, President Roosevelt vetoed the more far-ranging and constraining Walter-Logan administrative procedure bill and instead commissioned

the attorney general to organize a careful study of the whole issue. The resulting *Final Report of the Attorney General's Committee on Administrative Procedure* (1941) is usually regarded as the principal influence in the drafting of the APA. In its analysis of the accumulated case law on judicial review of administrative decision making, the *Final Report* described a residual category of discretionary decisions, immune to judicial review, in these terms (p. 15): "Finally there is the category of cases in which judicial review is denied because it is thought that the cases deal with matters which are more fittingly lodged in the exclusive discretion of the administrative branch, subject to controls other than judicial review. It relates of course to matters which do not involve private rights." And this seems to have been precisely the category of cases Congress had in mind in enacting the APA's preclusion of judicial review for matters "committed to agency discretion": "The introductory exceptions," explained a Senate Committee Report on the APA bill in 1946, "state the two present general or basic situations in which judicial review is excluded—where (1) *the matter is discretionary* or (2) statutes withhold judicial powers" (emphasis added): Senate Comparative Print, p. 18, cited in *Attorney General's Manual on the Administrative Procedure Act* (Leavenworth, Kans.: Federal Prison Industries Press, 1947), p. 95 n. 5. In the original understanding of the APA, then, consistent with the traditional understanding of constitutional categories, the exclusion of judicial review from matters "committed to agency discretion" was a very broad exclusion.

67. *Abbott Laboratories v. Gardner*, 386 U.S. 171 (1967) at 182.

68. K. C. Davis, *Administrative Law of the 1970s* (Rochester, N.Y.: Lawyers Cooperative Publishing, 1976), p. 631 provides many citations along with criticism of the Court's failure to follow the formula consistently.

69. The doctrine is most closely associated with the late Judge Harold Leventhal of the D.C. Circuit Court of Appeals, who defended it at length in "Environmental Decisionmaking and the Role of the Courts," *University of Pennsylvania Law Review* 122 (1974): 509.

70. *Vermont Yankee Power v. NRDC*, 435 U.S. 519 (1978).

71. See, e.g., Cass Sunstein, "Deregulation and the Hard Look Doctrine," *Supreme Court Review* (1983) at 184, citing *State Farm* as at least a partial repudiation of *Vermont Yankee*.

72. *Sierra Club v. Costle*, 657 F.2d 298 (D.C. Cir., 1981).

73. See, e.g., *Public Citizen v. Tyson* 796 F.2d 1479 (D.C. Cir.; 1986).

74. See, e.g., the recent collection of essays in Herman Schwartz, ed., *The Burger Years: Rights and Wrongs in the Supreme Court 1968–1986* (New York: Viking, 1987).

75. R. S. Summers, *Instrumentalism and American Legal Theory* (Ithaca, N.Y.: Cornell University Press, 1982).

76. Judith Shklar, *Legalism* (Cambridge, Mass.: Harvard University Press, 1967), pp. 97–98.

77. *Keyes v. School District No. 1, Denver, Colo.*, 413 U.S. 189 (1973).

78. *Milliken v. Bradley*, 418 U.S. 717 (1974).

79. See Lino Graglia, *Disaster by Decree: The Supreme Court Decisions on Race and the Schools* (Ithaca, N.Y.: Cornell University Press, 1976), chap. 10: "Busing to Achieve Racial Balance Though the Whites Have Left."

80. See, e.g., the dissenting opinion of Justice Brennan in *U.S. v. Calandra*, 414 U.S. 338 (1974).

81. *Goldberg v. Kelly*, 397 U.S. 254 (1970).

82. *Bell v. Burson*, 402 U.S. 535 (1971), revocation of driver's license; *Morrisey v. Brewer*, 408 U.S. 471 (1972), revocation of parole; and *Goss v. Lopez*, 419 U.S. 565 (1975), suspension from school.

83. *Mathews v. Eldridge*, 424 U.S. 319 (1976).

84. Laurence Tribe, *American Constitutional Law* (Mineola, N.Y.: Foundation Press, 1978), pp. 502–3.

85. Ibid., p. 503.

86. See Antonin Scalia, *"Vermont Yankee:* The APA, the D.C. Circuit, and the Supreme Court," *Supreme Court Review* (1978): 345.

87. Ronald Dworkin, *Taking Rights Seriously* (Cambridge, Mass.: Harvard University Press, 1976).

88. See, for example, Stanley Brubaker, "Taking Dworkin Seriously," *Review of Politics* (January 1985): 50–51.

89. Dworkin, *Taking Rights*, p. 345.

90. "What is law? . . . Law's empire is defined by attitude, not territory or power or process. . . . It is an interpretive self-reflective attitude addressed to politics in the broadest sense. It is

a protestant attitude that makes each citizen responsible for imagining what his society's public commitments to principle are, and what these commitments require in new circumstances. . . . It is finally a fraternal attitude, an expression of how we are united in community" (Ronald Dworkin, *Law's Empire* [Cambridge, Mass.: Harvard University Press, 1986], p. 413).

91. Richard Stewart, "The Development of Administrative and Quasi-Constitutional Law in Judicial Review of Environmental Decisionmaking," *Iowa Law Review* 62 (1977): 714–15.

92. Ibid., p. 756.

93. Ibid.

94. Sunstein, "Deregulation and the Hard Look Doctrine," p. 178.

95. Ibid., p. 213.

96. Ibid.

97. Michael Perry, *The Constitution, the Courts, and Human Rights: An Inquiry into the Legitimacy of Constitutional Policymaking by the Judiciary* (New Haven: Yale University Press, 1982).

98. Ibid., pp. 97, 99.

99. For example, note the dismissive comment on Perry's religion metaphor in Ronald Dworkin, *A Matter of Principle* (Cambridge, Mass.: Harvard University Press, 1985), p. 71.

100. Max Weber, "Politics as a Vocation," *From Max Weber: Essays in Sociology*, H. H. Gerth and C. W. Mills, trans. and eds. (New York: Oxford University Press, 1946).

101. *Aguilar v. Felton*, 105 S.Ct. 3232 (1985).

102. Martin Shapiro, "Judicial Activism," in *The Third Century: America as a Post-Industrial Society*, S. M. Lipset, ed. (Stanford: Hoover Institution Press, 1979), p. 129.

Chapter 5

1. *Adams v. Richardson*, 480 F.2d 1159 (D. C. Cir., 1973).

2. One of the most flattering was Note, "Judicial Control of Systematic Inadequacies in Federal Administrative Enforcement," *Yale Law Journal* 88 (1978): 407.

3. Codified at 42 U.S.C. §2000(d).

4. While the decision in *Brown v. Board of Education*, 347 U.S. 483 (1954), purported to be based on the importance of education, subsequent decisions applied the ruling to all other state entities.

5. The failure to certify *Adams* as a class action at the outset went unnoticed until the early 1980s, when the Justice Department renewed efforts to have the suit dismissed. At that point, government attorneys called attention to the fact that Kenneth Adams had already graduated from public school. To get around this problem, Judge Pratt finally did certify the case as a class action in 1983.

6. Bernard Schwartz, ed., *Statutory History of the United States—Civil Rights* (New York: Chelsea House, 1970) digests the debates on the 1964 Civil Rights Act to a manageable few hundred pages from the thousands of filibustering pages—the longest congressional debate on record—in the *Congressional Record.* The speech by Senator Richard Russell (D-Ga.), complaining that the measure would "leave the definition [of discrimination] up to any one of an army of bigoted bureaucrats," appears at pp. 1147–48. A useful overview of the debates is offered in Gary Orfield, *The Reconstruction of Southern Education* (New York: John Wiley, 1969), pp. 33–47.

7. Orfield, *Reconstruction*, pp. 1343–46. The words quoted in the text appear at *Congressional Record*, perm. ed., 89th Cong., 2d Sess., p. 22337.

8. "Nothing in this title shall add to or detract from any existing authority with respect to any program or activity under which Federal financial assistance is extended by way of a contract or insurance of guaranty." A separate provision also excludes coverage of employment discrimination "except where a primary objective of the federal financial assistance is to provide employment." The stated purpose of both exclusions was to focus nondiscrimination guarantees on "participants" in federal programs or the immediately intended beneficiaries.

9. At one point, for example, Senator Hubert Humphrey ridiculed charges that the civil rights bill as a whole would "produce a gigantic Federal bureaucracy, when in fact it will result in creating about four hundred permanent new Federal jobs" (Schwartz, ed., *Statutory History*, p. 1236). This estimate was apparently meant to cover all personnel in the Equal Employment

Notes

Opportunity Commission, new personnel in the Justice Department responsible for civil rights concerns in other sections of the bill, and then all officials in federal funding agencies responsible for enforcing Title VI. Ten years later, OCR alone had more than eight hundred full-time personnel, and this figure nearly doubled over the next five years.

10. Schwartz, ed., *Statutory History*, p. 1285. Orfield, in *Reconstruction*, notes that briefing papers prepared for defenders of the bill by the Johnson administration contained explicit assurances that Title VI would generally be enforced by the Justice Department in civil suits instead of through funding terminations by federal funding agencies.

11. In the spring of 1963, when the prospects for civil rights legislation seemed rather dismal, the U.S. Commission on Civil Rights urged President Kennedy to issue an executive order denying federal funds to segregated institutions—an order that would not require enabling legislation, in the commission's view. While the executive order proposal was explicitly rejected by President Kennedy at the time, a similar measure was included in the package of civil rights proposals sent to Congress by the Kennedy administration later that spring, following a shocking police assault on civil rights marchers in Birmingham, Alabama. After the highly successful civil rights "March on Washington"—at which Martin Luther King, Jr. delivered his celebrated "I Have a Dream" speech at the Lincoln Memorial—the House Judiciary Committee strengthened the Kennedy funding withholding provision, converting an optional sanction into the separate guarantee against discrimination that became Title VI.

12. This approach not only denied school districts any form of due process to rebut discrimination charges but also penalized entire districts for discrimination in particular programs, contrary to the pinpoint provision in the statute.

13. The episode is described in detail in Orfield, *Reconstruction*, pp. 151–207. The restriction on funding deferrals appears at 80 Stat. 1209, now codified at 42 U.S.C. §2000d-5.

14. Orfield, in *Reconstruction*, pp. 18–22, provides a useful overview of the cautious—or indulgent—view of desegregation taken by federal courts before 1964.

15. In 1969, the Fifth Circuit did insist that discrimination findings and funding terminations must be confined to particular programs instead of entire school districts (*Taylor v. Finch*, 414 F.2d 1073), but allowed terminations to apply to programs that were fiscally interdependent with the culprits; and OCR exploited this exception to continue to threaten funding terminations for entire school districts until the Supreme Court reaffirmed the limited reach of the program language in the statute in its 1984 decision in *Grove City College v. Bell*.

16. *Grove City College v. Bell*, 464 U.S. 555 (1984), arose under the parallel language in Title IX, but neither the Court nor any of the litigants suggested that the implications of the decision for Title VI would be any different.

17. See Orfield, *Reconstruction*, pp. 220–23 and the background explanations at pp. 135–47.

18. Note, "The Courts, HEW and Southern School Desegregation," *Yale Law Journal* 77 (1967): 321.

19. *Green v. County School Board of New Kent County*, 391 U.S. 430 (1968). Lino Graglia, in *Disaster by Decree: The Supreme Court Decisions on Race and the Schools* (Ithaca, N.Y.: Cornell University Press, 1976), offers a useful analysis of the decision and its significance as a break with previous constitutional rulings in the chapter aptly titled "The Second Revolution."

20. P.L. 91-230, codified at 42 U.S.C. §2000d-6(a) and P.L. 90-557 (see 1 U.S. Code Cong. & Admin. News, 1147 [1968]). Both measures were vigorously opposed at the time by HEW.

21. The precise number of termination proceedings is actually quite difficult to pin down, reflecting OCR's continuing reluctance to publicize such data, its chronic administrative disarray, as well as, it seems, ambiguity over how to count cases settled before or during the opening phases of the hearing process. The most reliable count was made by OCR's Office of Administration and Management in the mid-1970s: an internal HEW Memorandum, dated August 23, 1978, from Don Vernon, chief of OA&M, reports that a total of 605 school districts had faced at least the opening phases of administrative proceedings for funding termination by the end of 1971, 98 of them in 1968 and the same number again by early 1971.

22. Leon Panetta and Peter Gall, in *Bring Us Together: The Nixon Team and the Civil Rights Retreat* (Philadelphia: J. B. Lippincott, 1971), record Panetta's assessments soon after his dismissal.

23. Gary Orfield, in *Must We Bus? Segregated Schools and National Policy* (Washington, D.C.: Brookings Institution, 1978), pp. 242, 286–87, describes these episodes from the point of view of civil rights advocacy groups.

24. There were fewer than seventeen plaintiffs named in the initial brief.

Notes

25. The original district court decision in *Adams v. Richardson* simply noted in one sentence that "Plaintiffs have standing to bring this action on behalf of themselves and others similarly situated." As it provides no explanation of who the plaintiffs are, it offers no clue as to the identity of those "others similarly situated": 351 F. Supp. 636 (1972) at 640. The affirming decision by the D.C. Court of Appeals, 480 F.2d 1159 (1973), is no more enlightening.

26. *Adams v. Richardson*, "Complaint for Declaratory and Other Relief," filed October 19, 1970, D.C. District Court, p. 5.

27. When the original charge against state education agencies was limited to a protest against discrimination in specific special-purpose schools run directly by the states (such as schools for the deaf or the blind), Judge Pratt approved this complaint and issued a corresponding order, subsequent to his initial decision; see 356 F. Supp. 92 (1973) at 98. At this stage, Judge Pratt also agreed that to "the extent that their resources permit [OCR officials] have the duty to monitor school districts under court order and to bring their findings to the attention of the court concerned." But the court emphasized that "responsibility for compliance by a school district . . . under court order rests upon the court issuing said order": 356 F. Supp. 92 (1973) at 99. The Court of Appeals affirmed that this did not "require close surveillance by HEW of all court-order districts, nor that HEW shall be accountable for more than the resources available to it from time to time permit in the good faith performance of its general obligation not to allow federal funds to be supportive of illegal discrimination": 480 F.2d 1159 (1973) at 1166.

28. The Court of Appeals described judicial orders in this case as an effort to ensure that "the agency properly construes its statutory obligations and that the policies it adopts and implements are consistent with those duties and not a negation of them": 480 F.2d 1159 (1973) at 1164.

29. The original briefs did not specify school districts: districts named in Judge Pratt's initial decision two years later were "uncovered" through "discovery" proceedings in the course of the litigation.

30. 480 F.2d 1159 (1973) at 1162.

31. See Judge Pratt's contemptuous reference to "benign neglect," 351 F. Supp. 636 (1972) at 642.

32. By the time the initial decision in *Adams* was handed down, President Nixon had already publicly announced his support for legislative measures to curb compulsory busing programs. The largest number of school districts named in the initial *Adams* decree were under investigation for failure to comply with the Supreme Court's decision in *Swann v. Charlotte-Mecklenburg Board of Education*, 402 U.S. 1 (1971), which suggested that busing might be required in some cases to achieve desegregation.

33. "HEW News," Press Release of Thursday, January 13, 1972, which also reported that an "estimated 35.6 per cent of Negro pupils in the U.S. are in majority white schools, 27.8 per cent in the North and West, 43.9 per cent in the eleven state South."

34. Judge Pratt did mention this fact in his initial opinion, 351 F. Supp. 636 (1972) at 640, acknowledging that "despite defendants' reluctance or failure to employ enforcement proceedings terminating funds, substantial progress toward compliance with Title VI has been made." The Court of Appeals made no mention of the fact. In fact, OCR deserves the bulk of the credit for what was accomplished in the South. Court orders resulting from suits by the Justice Department or by private litigants affected little more than 150 school districts by the early 1970s. OCR had "investigated, negotiated and arm twisted" more than 3,000 school districts by this time; Jennifer Hochschild, *The New American Dilemma: Liberal Democracy and School Segregation* (New Haven: Yale University Press, 1984), p. 28.

35. According to the Vernon memorandum (see n. 21 above), OCR initiated an average of twelve proceedings a year between 1974 and 1978. When the *Adams* litigation was reopened in 1981, the plaintiffs again complained about the failure to initiate funding termination proceedings, and the pressure of the litigation may have moved the agency to invoke formal sanctions somewhat more readily—but not much more readily. In 1985, the Assistant Secretary of Education for Civil Rights reported to a House subcommittee that "since 1981" the agency had "initiated formal enforcement proceedings seeking fund termination in 26 cases" (statement of Harry M. Singleton before House Committee on Government Operations, Subcommittee on Intergovernmental Relations and Human Resources, printed in *Investigation of Civil Rights Enforcement by the Department of Education, Committee on Government Operations*, 99th Cong., 1st Sess., p. 100). Regarding actual progress toward statistical integration, the crucial facts are conveniently summarized in Gary Orfield, *Public School Desegregation in the United States, 1968–1980* (Washington, D.C.: Joint Center for Political Studies, 1983), p. 4: taking the percent-

age of black students in schools with more than one-half minority students as the measure of desegregation, Orfield reports that the figure for the South was 80.9 percent in 1968; 55.3 percent in 1972; 54.9 percent in 1976; and 57.1 percent in 1980. In other words, an improvement of 0.4 percent in the four years following *Adams* was itself followed by a regression over the next four years, which left overall segregation higher than in 1972, when Judge Pratt issued his first order. Orfield's figures show greater improvements in what he describes as "Border States" (from 71.6 percent in 1968 and 67.2 percent in 1972, down to 60.1 percent in 1976 and 59.2 percent in 1980), but these data include more than the six additional states added to the eleven-state "old South" in *Adams,* and the general pattern through the rest of the nation showed most change concentrated between 1972 and 1976. After 1976—the year that the LDF's *Brown* suit took effect—change in integration levels through the rest of the nation was also limited (less than 1 percent reduction in segregation in the West and Midwest, while in the Northeast, segregation—by this statistical measure—increased by almost 8 percent).

36. Even LDF officials subsequently conceded the intensity of congressional opposition to funding terminations: "There has been bipartisan anathema to employing even the threat of fund termination by initiating the administrative enforcement process when voluntary negotiations fail": Testimony of Julius Chambers, Director-Counsel, NAACP Legal Defense and Education Fund, July 18, 1985, reprinted in *Investigation of Civil Rights Enforcement by the Department of Education,* Hearings Before a Subcommittee of the Committee on Government Operations, 99th Cong., 1st Sess., p. 11.

37. The initial restriction, known as the Esch amendment, appears at 88 Stat. 517 (1974); the so-called Byrd amendments of 1975 and 1976 appear at 90 Stat. 22 and 1434. The Eagleton-Biden amendment, added in 1977, is the most restrictive and appears at 91 Stat. 1460. Orfield, *Must We Bus?* describes the congressional debate on the early measures at pp. 264–68 and 312–13 and on the later amendment at pp. 317–18.

38. *Adams v. Weinberger,* 391 F.Supp. 269 (1975).

39. *Brown v. Mathews,* Doc. No. 75-1068, D.C.D.C., "Memorandum and Order," July 20, 1976.

40. *Brown v. Califano,* 455 F. Supp. 837 (1978).

41. Affadavit of J. Stanley Pottinger, Director of OCR, filed December 10, 1970, paragraphs 8 and 11.

42. *Brown v. Califano,* 627 F.2d 1221 (1980).

43. See, e.g., the implied rebuke to the Justice Department in the concluding recommendations of U.S. Commission on Civil Rights, *Desegregating the Nation's Public Schools* (Feb. 1979).

44. "It is one thing to say that the Justice Department lacks the resources necessary to locate and prosecute every civil rights violator; it is quite another to say HEW may affirmatively continue to channel federal funds to defaulting institutions": 480 F.2d 1159 (1973) at 1162.

45. *Adams v. Bell,* Order of June 25, 1981, aff'd. 711 F.2d 161 (1983).

46. ". . . this suit is not brought to challenge HEW's decisions with regard to a few school districts in the course of a generally effective enforcement program. To the contrary, appellants allege that HEW has consciously and expressly adopted a general policy which is in effect abdication of its statutory duty": 480 F.2d 1159 (1973) at 1162.

47. "Motion for Further Relief and Points and Authority in Support Thereof," filed May 30, 1974, p. 21.

48. The "modified order" covering complaint investigations was issued on March 14, 1975.

49. The policy was announced in a letter to school superintendents across the country, dated January 14, 1971. Interpretive guidelines for Title VI, issued in 1968, had already asserted jurisdiction over discrimination in "recruiting, hiring, assigning, promoting, paying, demoting and dismissing . . . professional staff," on the legal theory that the exclusion of employment discrimination in Title VI did not apply to discrimination that affected "participants" or "beneficiaries" of funded programs, and OCR maintained that discrimination against teachers would necessarily affect the quality of education afforded to students.

50. OCR Memorandum to state and local education officials, entitled "Equal Educational Services," dated July 1976.

51. "Student Discipline," an HEW Fact Sheet (mimeographed circular produced by HEW for release to the press), dated September 1975, stressing that lack of intent to discriminate would not excuse findings of racial disparities in the imposition of school disciplinary sanctions.

52. Personal interview with Martin Gerry, OCR Director, July 1976.

53. OCR actually went so far as to publish proposed new procedural regulations in the Federal

Notes

Register in the early part of 1976, but then withdrew the proposal in response to the protests of constituency groups.

54. The policy was originally announced in a policy statement to school officials dated May 25, 1970. According to Martin Gerry, the new policy was initiated within the agency as a means of developing regulatory responsibilities outside the increasingly controversial area of school desegregation (personal interview, July 1976).

55. *Lau v. Nichols*, 414 U.S. 563 (1974).

56. Title IX of the Education Amendments of 1972 is now codified at 20 U.S.C. §1681.

57. Section 504 of the Rehabilitation Act of 1973 is now codified at 29 U.S.C. §706.

58. Private rights of action for both statutes were subsequently confirmed by the Supreme Court, as the advocacy groups had expected. See n80, below.

59. See Jeremy Rabkin, "Office for Civil Rights," in *The Politics of Regulation*, J. Q. Wilson, ed. (New York: Basic Books, 1980), for further analysis of this political stance and its appeal both to the agency and to its constituents in the 1970s.

60. Interview with Martin Gerry, July 1976.

61. In the first instance, it was officials at OCR who persuaded the White House and Congress that Sec. 504, an ambiguous one-sentence provision as originally enacted, ought to be treated as a mandate for a general regulatory program. See Robert A. Katzmann, *Institutional Disability: The Saga of Transportation Policy for the Disabled* (Washington, D.C.: The Brookings Institution, 1986), pp. 50–55. Thereafter in formulating implementing regulations, OCR officials took a very sympathetic view of claims by organizations of the handicapped to receive special affirmative protections: interview with John Wodatch, principal coordinator for the Sec. 504 regulation drafting process, December 1979.

62. Secretary Califano proposed to eliminate the dress code requirement from Title IX in 1978, but the proposal was shelved after protests from women's groups. The proposed deletion was finally adopted in 1981.

63. An exchange of documents with the Justice Department in 1979, prior to final publication of the Sec. 504 regulations, brought an official legal interpretation from lawyers in the Justice Department that the statute must apply to alcoholics and drug addicts to comport with "legislative intent," and this requirement was agreed to. The statute, as adopted in 1973, is one sentence long and was adopted without debate.

64. 40 Fed. Reg. 24129 (June 4, 1975).

65. 44 Fed. Reg. 71413 (December 11, 1979).

66. "Motion for Intervention," filed January 22, 1976 on behalf of "Jimmy Martinez, Ben G. Salazar . . . and others similarly situated."

67. "Motion for Intervention as Plaintiffs," filed March 17, 1976.

68. The "order" of the Court of Appeals was handed down on May 7, 1976, with a five-page memorandum stressing that the other parties had not objected.

69. The intervention was again unopposed.

70. The consent decree was issued by Judge Pratt on December 29, 1981, but never published.

71. Order of March 11, 1983, allowing OCR to postpone a certain portion of complaints from the regular "time-frames" under special circumstances.

72. *Adams v. Bell*, hearing before Judge Pratt on March 15, 1982, official transcript, p. 16.

73. Chambers conference with Judge Pratt on July 13, 1982, official transcript, p. 11.

74. Statement at 1983 hearing in *Adams v. Bell*, quoted by Marcia Greenberger, National Women's Law Center, in testimony before U.S. House of Representatives, Subcommittee of the Committee on Government Operations, April 23, 1987, printed in *Civil Rights Enforcement by the Department of Education*, p. 60.

75. Data supplied to the plaintiffs in the autumn of 1979 showed OCR missing its deadlines for complaint investigation only 13 percent of the time in one regional office and as much as 54 percent of the time in another, with most regional offices closer to the high figure: unsigned, undated manuscript headed "Complaints Summary (July to Sept. 1979)," prepared for William Taylor, Center for National Policy Review, Catholic University Law School. Taylor frequently consulted with the *Adams* lawyers from the outset of the litigation.

76. "Order" of October 26, 1977, ¶4, directing OCR to seek higher appropriation recommendations from the Office of Management and Budget.

77. Orfield, *Must We Bus?* p. 297 summarizes OCR's expansion in a convenient table: authorized staff positions climbed from 326 in 1969 to 1,054 in fiscal year 1977; appropriations jumped from $5.4 million in 1969 to $31.3 million in fiscal year 1977.

297

78. See U.S. Commission on Civil Rights, *Federal Enforcement of Equal Employment Opportunity Requirements,* July 1987, pp. 11–13 for figures on the EEOC's improvement in case processing during the late 1970s.

79. These results were reported to HEW Secretary Joseph Califano in an internal memorandum from OCR Director David Tatel, "Recent Management Achievements for the Office for Civil Rights," dated October 17, 1979, at p. 7.

80. A private right of action under Title IX was officially recognized by the Supreme Court in *Cannon v. University of Chicago,* 441 U.S. 677 (1979) and was assumed to exist for Title VI in *Regents of University of California v. Bakke,* 438 U.S. 265 (1978) and *Lau v. Nichols,* 414 U.S. 563 (1974). For Sec. 504, see *Davis v. Southeastern Community College,* 442 U.S. 397 (1979).

81. "Office for Civil Rights, Sixth Annual Report, F.Y. 1986" (unpublished agency document), p. 18.

82. "It is simply not legal for HEW to provide funds to school districts beyond the scope of its ability to assure protection of the civil rights of their students and teachers": "Memorandum of Plaintiff-Intervenors in Opposition to Defendant's Motion to Modify Order," filed September 30, 1977, p. 4.

83. Complaints about discrimination in athletic programs became so numerous at one point in the late 1970s that OCR's policy development office devoted nearly all of its time to this issue for nearly a year.

84. A particular complaint regarding racial discrimination in school tracking programs, for example, forced OCR to wrestle over its policy in this area for two years before it finally moved to initiate formal enforcement proceedings against the South Carolina school district involved.

85. Personal interviews, Martin Gerry and David Tatel (OCR Director 1977–79), January 1982.

86. The incident is described in somewhat greater detail in Rabkin, "Office for Civil Rights," p. 335.

87. Interview with Terence Pell, Deputy Assistant Secretary of Education for Civil Rights, July 1987.

88. Interview with Shirley Wilshire, committee staff, House Education and Labor Committee, January 1988. The committee was preparing a major report on a months-long investigation at the time of the interview.

89. Interview with Terence Pell, January 1988.

90. OCR's frustrating experience with its extremely ambitious investigation of the New York City public school system is analyzed in Michael Rebell and Arthur Block, *Equality and Education: Federal Civil Rights Enforcement in the New York City School System* (Princeton: Princeton University Press, 1985).

91. The agency's fear of awkward commitments may account for the fact that half of its compliance reviews in the mid-1980s have been entirely untargeted; that is, they pick school districts at random, focusing on no particular problem area—a deployment of resources that certainly seems highly questionable.

92. These figures and similar ones are reported by Charles Murray, *Losing Ground: American Social Policy, 1950–1980* (New York: Basic Books, 1984), pp. 104–7.

93. "An objection to transportation of students may have validity when the time or distance of travel is so great as to either risk the health of the children or significantly impinge on the educational process": *Swann v. Charlotte-Mecklenburg Board of Education,* 402 U.S. 1 (1972) at 30.

94. For example, reading ability scores on a national survey showed black seventeen-year-olds improved their average score from 244.0 in 1974–75 to 263.5 in 1983–84, an improvement of nearly 10 percent. White scores improved much more modestly from 290.7 in 1974 to 294.6 in 1983–84; but the gap between white and black performance remains too large to be significantly affected by the relatively higher rate of improvement among blacks; see U.S. Department of Education, *Digest of Educational Statistics* (1987), p. 87. SAT scores for college-bound students display a similar pattern: combined math and verbal scores averaged 690 (out of a possible 1,600) for blacks in 1980–81 and rose to 730 in 1985–86. Average combined scores for white students increased much more modestly from 890 to 906, but the gap again remains too large for the greater pace of black improvement to make much of a difference.

95. Summaries of research findings by the U.S. Department of Education have been published in a departmental pamphlet entitled "First Lessons: A Report on Elementary Education in America" (1986).

96. For a useful survey of the problems in this field, see Noel Epstein, *Language, Ethnicity and the Schools: Policy Alternatives for Bilingual-Bicultural Education* (Washington, D.C.: George Washington University Press, 1977).

97. The amicus brief was submitted by the "National Association for Equal Opportunity in Higher Education," claiming to represent the presidents of 110 traditionally black colleges, both state-supported and private. Of a subsequent brief filed by this organization, Judge Pratt said, it "is not so much of a legal document, but it is a real cry from the soul": Transcript, Oral Hearing, June 14, 1976, p. 27.

98. 480 F.2d 1159 (1973) at 1165.

99. *Adams v. Califano*, 430 F.Supp. 118 (1977).

100. "Discrimination in Postsecondary Education: Analyses and Recommendations," unpublished internal memorandum for HEW Secretary Joseph Califano by Secretary's Work Group on *Adams* Criteria, 1977.

101. 43 Fed.Reg. 6358 (February 15, 1978).

102. Q. Whitfield Ayres, "Desegregating or Debilitating Higher Education?" *The Public Interest* 69 (Fall 1982): 100–116.

103. Francesta Farmer, "Selling the *Adams* Criteria: The Response of OCR to Political Intervention in *Adams v. Califano,*" *Howard Law Journal* 22 (1979): 422 ("congressional interest in the outcome of the *Adams* negotiations . . . was often an emotional interest in protecting the integrity and educational 'quality' of the *alma mater*").

104. See *Adams v. Bell*, 711 F.2d 161 (D.C. Cir., 1983), approving Judge Pratt's refusal to intervene in the settlement accepted with North Carolina.

105. Order of March 11, 1983.

106. Data presented by the LDF to a House subcommittee in the spring of 1987 showed, for example, that in Georgia the percentage of black high school graduates going on to college declined from 17.5 percent in 1978 to 16.9 percent in 1985, while the comparable figure for white high school graduates in Georgia climbed from 34.3 percent in 1979 to 44.0 percent in 1985. The percentage of black high school graduates going on to traditionally white institutions of higher education in the Georgia state system remained essentially stable, however, suggesting that the state colleges were making some effort to resist the broader negative trend; the percentage of black faculty members at these state colleges also showed a small but steady increase: see *Civil Rights Enforcement by the Department of Education*, Hearings Before a Subcommittee of the Committee on Government Operations, 100th Cong., 1st Sess., 1987, pp. 40–42. Similar findings are reported for Oklahoma (pp. 5–7), Arkansas (p. 302), Virginia (p. 369), and South Carolina (p. 385). More impressive progress in all states was secured between 1970 and 1978—that is, before the *Adams* litigation finally forced OCR to apply significant pressure. See the comparison of 1970 and 1978 enrollment figures presented by Q. Whitfield Ayres, "Racial Desegregation in Higher Education," in *Implementation of Civil Rights*, Charles S. Bullock and Charles M. Lamb, eds. (Monterey, Calif.: Brooks/Cole Publishing, 1984), pp. 123–25.

107. See, e.g., the exchange between Rep. E. L. Konnyu and Julius Chambers of the LDF on the fact that Howard University in Washington, D.C. has an undergraduate enrollment that is 99.5 percent black: "I don't condemn Howard at all," said Mr. Chambers; *Civil Rights Enforcement by the Department of Education*, House Government Operations Committee Hearing (1987), pp. 260–61. Chambers made the point that Howard was more integrated in its graduate programs, but virtually all of the data and discussion presented by the LDF at this hearing focused on undergraduate enrollment patterns in formerly segregated state higher education systems in the South.

108. According to surveys conducted in 1986 by the U.S. Department of Education as part of the National Assessment of Educational Progress, black and Hispanic students at age seventeen are reading, on the average, only slightly better than the average for whites at age thirteen: see Office of Educational Research and Improvement, U.S. Department of Education, *Digest of Educational Statistics* (1987), p. 32.

109. Personal interview with Terence Pell, July 1987.

110. *Allen v. Wright*, 468 U.S. 737 (1984).

111. The HEW secretary, as Judge Pratt noted early in the litigation, "has a basic responsibility to enforce the law and he can't kiss it off on the ground that in his own good time he decided not to do anything about it"; cited in "Supplemental Memorandum for Plaintiffs," filed February 1, 1971, p. 2 (citing "Transcript of Oral Hearing," undated, p. 22).

Notes

112. *Adams v. Bennett*, "Memorandum Opinion and Order," December 11, 1987, pp. 10, 17, 20, 27.

113. Interview with Phyllis McClure, January 1987.

114. The most recent example concerned political maneuvering over a bill to restore institutionwide coverage to all of the statutes prohibiting discrimination in "programs or activities receiving federal financial assistance," following the Supreme Court's *Grove City* ruling that limited the application of the phrase to particular programs. A bill proposed by Senator Edward Kennedy in 1984 was expected to receive ready passage when right-to-life advocates urged an amendment to the measure, pledging that it would not restore OCR's Title IX rule on abortion services. As this rule seems to have been rarely if ever enforced, this concession might have seemed a small sacrifice to restore broader coverage for all other OCR regulations and requirements. Women's groups indignantly opposed the right-to-life "abortion neutral" amendment, however, and the bill was consequently stalled over this dispute until the end of 1987. The stake of the black civil rights organizations in supporting the unyielding position of women's groups was, to say the least, not obvious. But they did not publicly oppose the women's groups' position, and they did not call for a separate compromise approach. For three and one-half years, the traditional civil rights groups waited patiently while women's organizations fought to prevent any direct legislative compromise on the abortion services issue.

115. Interview with Phyllis McClure, January 1987.

116. Interviews with John Walters, Special Assistant to the Secretary, and Terence Pell, January 1988.

117. Surveys of school discipline patterns were successfully urged on OCR in the mid-1970s by the Children's Defense Fund, a well-established civil rights advocacy organization that has worked closely with the LDF on many projects in the past; personal interview, Martin Gerry, July 1976.

118. See *Debra P. v. Turlington*, 474 F.Supp. 244 (M.D. Fla., 1979); reversed in part, on other grounds, 644 F.2d 397 (5th Cir., 1981), enjoining use of a high school graduation competency test until blacks have attended integrated schools for twelve years. See also *Larry P. v. Riles*, 495 F.Supp. 926 (N.D.Cal., 1979), enjoining use of intelligence tests for black students in California public schools, though the tests may still be used to help white students. LDF's opposition to college graduation competency examinations in Georgia is described in *Investigation of Civil Rights Enforcement by the Department of Education*, Hearings Before a Subcommittee of the Committee on Government Operations, U.S. House of Representatives, 99th Cong., 1st Sess. (1985), pp. 36–37.

119. Personal interview with John Walters, December 1987.

120. *Investigation of Civil Rights Enforcement by the Department of Education* (1985) and *Civil Rights Enforcement by the Department of Education* (1987), both conducted by the Subcommittee on Human Resources and Intergovernmental Relations, House Committee on Government Operations, chaired by Representative Ted Weiss of New York.

121. Terence Pell, "After Busing What? A Not So Good Idea Makes Its Move," *New Perspectives* (Fall, 1987).

Chapter 6

1. A useful summary is offered in Paul Quirk, "The Food and Drug Administration," in *The Politics of Regulation*, James Q. Wilson, ed. (New York: Basic Books, 1980).

2. Using figures from the National Center for Health Statistics and Accident Facts, *Monthly Vital Statistics* (1982) and the National Safety Council, *Accident Facts* (1983), John Morrall sets the annual deaths from car accidents in the early 1980s at 53,500 and from poisoning at 4,600: "A Review of the Record," *Regulation* (November–December 1986), p. 26.

3. Linda E. Demkovich, "Playing the FDA Waiting Game," *National Journal* (March 3, 1984): 411.

4. 34 Stat. §7468.

5. 52 Stat. §1041–42.

6. 76 Stat. §780, codified at 21 U.S.C. §301–81.

7. William Wardell and Louis Lasagna, *Regulation and Drug Development* (Washington, D.C.: American Enterprise Institute, 1975), pp. 14–16.

Notes

8. Sen. Rep. no. 1744, 87th Cong., 2d Sess. (1962), p. 6.

9. Ibid., p. 16.

10. *Drug Regulation Reform—Oversight*, vol. 1: *New Drug Approval Process*, Hearings Before the Subcommittee on Health and Environment of the Committee on Interstate and Foreign Commerce, U.S. House of Representatives, 96th Cong., 2d Sess. (1980), p. 13.

11. Wardell and Lasagna, *Regulation and Drug Development*, p. 37.

12. Ibid.

13. *FDA's Process for Approving New Drugs*, Hearings Before the Subcommittee on Science, Research and Technology, U.S. House of Representatives, 96th Cong., 1st Sess. (1979), p. 10 (reporting results of GAO study).

14. Ibid.

15. Ibid. See also Wardell and Lasagna, *Regulation and Drug Development*, pp. 55–78, describing the results of this study in some detail.

16. *FDA's Process for Approving New Drugs*, 1979 hearings, pp. 67, 279. Between 1963 and 1973, when cardiovascular disease was the leading cause of death in America, the FDA refused to approve a single new drug that treated this illness.

17. On the consequences of delay in approval of drugs for the treatment of neurological disorders, see the testimony of Dr. Paul Dyken in *Drug Lag*, Hearing Before the Subcommittee on Natural Resources, Agriculture, Research and Environment, Committee on Science and Technology, U.S. House of Representatives, 97th Cong., 1st Sess. (1981), pp. 15–17.

18. *FDA's Process for Approving New Drugs*, 1979 hearings, p. 284.

19. The GAO subsequently organized a formal commission of outside experts in pharmacology to assess its findings: See Commission on the Federal Drug Approval Process, "Final Report," Subcommittee on Natural Resources, Agricultural Research and Environment, Committee on Science and Technology, U.S. House of Representatives, 97th Cong., 2d Sess. (October 1982).

20. See remarks of Chairman Scheuer ("I have met several times with the [FDA] Commissioner and Vice President Bush and I'm enormously encouraged at their acceptance of the challenge to make the . . . new drug approval process more responsive to the needs of the American people"), *Drug Lag*, 1981 hearing, p. 3.

21. Quirk, "Food and Drug Administration," in *Politics of Regulation*, Wilson, ed., p. 216. FDA Commissioner Alexander Schmidt told a congressional subcommittee in 1974, "By far the greatest pressure that the Bureau of Drugs or the Food and Drug Administration receives with respect to the new drug approval process is brought to bear through congressional hearings. In all our history, we are unable to find one instance where a congressional hearing investigated the failure of FDA to approve a new drug. . . . The message could not be clearer": *Regulation of New Drug R&D by the Food and Drug Administration*, Hearings Before the Committee on Labor and Public Welfare and the Committee on the Judiciary, U.S. Senate, 93d Cong., 2d Sess. (1974), p. 207.

22. *The Regulation of New Drugs by the Food and Drug Administration: The New Drug Review Process*, Hearings Before a Subcommittee of the Committee on Government Operations, 97th Cong., 2d Sess. (1982).

23. Personal interview, Daniel Sigelman, Counsel, Subcommittee on Human Resources and Intergovernmental Relations, House Committee on Government Operations, December 1987. Chairman Fountain, "without expressing an opinion" on "those interests [which] allege the existence of a 'drug lag' in the United States as compared with other countries," noted that "whether or not new drugs are approved more quickly in other countries is not FDA's concern" because "the American people, as a matter of policy, have chosen to apply the world's highest standards for the approval of new drugs": *Regulation of New Drugs by the FDA*, 1982 hearings, pp. 1–2.

24. *FDA's Process for Approving New Drugs*, 1979 House hearings, p. 284.

25. "Drug Lag Defenders," *Wall Street Journal* (May 15, 1987): 14.

26. A compromise was eventually worked out in Congress allowing an abbreviated, accelerated approval process for generic drugs if patents on the original product had expired, in return for which patent protection for new drug products would be extended to ensure at least ten years of patent protection after FDA approval: see Demkovich "Playing the FDA Waiting Game," p. 412. Consumer advocacy groups strongly supported accelerated approval for generic drugs as a means of lowering prices. It is notable that Congress intervened to ensure speedy approval for these cheaper products but has taken no action to help speed the approval of genuinely new products, even when they may have lifesaving importance. These congressional priorities have not

gone unnoticed at the FDA, which has indeed used the new procedures to reduce approval time for generic products to less than six months: interview with Bruce Artim, Special Assistant to the Assistant Secretary for Health, Department of Health and Human Services, July 1987.

27. The drug industry claim that the FDA had no authority to ban a pre-1962 drug merely by withdrawing approval for its NDA was upheld in *Bentex Pharmaceuticals v. Richardson,* 463 F.2d 363 (4th Cir., 1972) but was finally rejected by the Supreme Court in *USV Pharmaceuticals v. Weinberger,* 412 U.S. 655 (1973). The industry's claim that the FDA could not withdraw NDA approval for a pre-1962 drug without a separate administrative hearing was upheld by *Hynson, Wescott and Dunning, Inc. v. Richardson,* 461 F.2d 215 (4th Cir., 1972) and *USV Pharmaceutical Corp. v. Secretary of HEW,* 466 F.2d 455 (D.C. Cir., 1972), but rejected—with some qualifications—by the Supreme Court in *Weinberger v. Hynson, Westcott and Dunning, Inc.,* 412 U.S. 609 (1973).

28. A useful account of the entire review process is provided in Note, "Drug Efficacy and the 1962 Drug Amendments," *Georgetown Law Journal* 60 (1971): 185. The breakdown in the text appears at p. 210 n. 160.

29. 35 Fed.Reg. 7251.

30. Wardell and Lasagna, *Regulation and Drug Development,* p. 18.

31. National Academy of Sciences, *Drug Efficacy Study, Final Report to the Commissioner of Food and Drugs* (1968), p. 7.

32. Interview with Jeffrey Springer, Deputy Associate General Counsel, FDA, July 1987.

33. *Weinberger v. Hynson, Wescott and Dunning, Inc.,* 412 U.S. 609 (1973).

34. APHA, with headquarters in Washington, engages in lobbying on a wide range of health issues, but it did not take an active role in the suit after agreeing to lend its name. Interview with Michael Harper, formerly of the Center for Law and Social Policy, July 1981.

35. *Public Counsel Corporation,* Hearings Before the Subcommittee on Administrative Practice and Procedures of the Committee on the Judiciary, U.S. Senate, 91st Cong., 2d Sess. (1970), p. 97.

36. *APHA v. Veneman,* 349 F.Supp. 1311 (1972) at 1317 n. 19, citing a recent article in *Washington Post* about over-the-counter drugs, which the NRC had only just begun to study.

37. 349 F.Supp. 1311 (1972) at 1315. Judge Bryant's opinion quotes the statute as saying "The Secretary *shall* [judge's emphasis] . . . withdraw approval" of any NDA when "the Secretary finds . . . that there is a lack of substantial evidence that the drug will have the effect it purports or is represented to have." The unedited version of the statute actually says: "The Secretary shall, *after due notice and opportunity for hearing to the applicant* [my emphasis], withdraw approval. . . ." Plainly this provision could not apply to the drugs in dispute in the APHA case, for the manufacturers had not yet been given "due notice and opportunity for hearing."

38. Interview with Jeffrey Springer, November 1981.

39. The court order was never published, but it was filed with the U.S. District Court in Washington on October 11, 1972.

40. *APHA v. Veneman,* unpublished "Order," dated September 24, 1980.

41. Interview with Jeffrey Springer, December 1987.

42. This result seems likely, though the effect may not have been great. Figures published in 1978 indicate that the drug efficacy review jumped from 10 to 68 man-years of work within the Bureau of Drugs between 1969 and 1971, then climbed to 112 man-years the following year, before the APHA suit was concluded. Thereafter there was only a slight increase in resources committed to the project. But it may be that the threat of the litigation encouraged the agency to take the project more seriously even before the court orders were negotiated, near the end of 1972. The figures are printed in *Competitive Problems in the Drug Industry, Fixed-Dose Combination Antibiotic Drugs,* Summary and Analysis, Congressional Research Service (for Select Committee on Small Business), 1979, p. 53.

43. Interview with Jeffrey Springer, July 1987.

44. Ibid.

45. Rita Ricardo Campbell, *Drug Lag: Federal Government Decisionmaking* (Stanford: Hoover Institution Press, 1976).

46. Linda Demkovich, "Critics Fear the FDA is Going Too Far in Cutting Industry's Regulatory Load," *National Journal* (July 17, 1982): 1249, 1250.

47. Julie Kosterlitz, "Drugs for Sale," *National Journal* (April 4, 1987): 850; "A New Era for New Drugs," *Wall Street Journal* (March 13, 1987): 24.

48. "Still No FDA Ban on Color Dyes," *Public Citizen* (July–August 1985): 6; "FDA Nixes Feldene Ban," *Public Citizen* (October 1986): 10.

49. The distinction between prescription and nonprescription or OTC drugs is an artifact of FDA regulatory practice. The 1938 Food, Drug and Cosmetics Act said nothing about the matter, but the FDA, on its own initiative, issued a regulation soon after it assumed its new licensing powers under the 1938 act, specifying that some drugs would be approved for use only if their retail sale were made contingent on the approval of state licensed "prescribers": see *U.S. v. El-O-Pathic Pharmacy*, 192 F.2d 62 (9th Cir., 1951), upholding application of this rule on the grounds that labeling for certain products would be "false or misleading"—within the terms of the 1906 act—unless handled by a licensed prescriber qualified to comprehend all of the implications of the product's use. This approach was codified in the 1951 Durham-Humphrey amendment to the FD&C Act.

50. The scheme is explained in some detail in Linda Demkovich, "Do Over-the-Counter Drugs Work? FDA is Still Looking for the Answer," *National Journal* (March 22, 1980): 484.

51. Kenneth Baumgartner "A Historical Examination of the FDA's Review of the Safety and Effectiveness of OTC Drugs," *Food Drug Cosmetic Law Journal*, Vol. 43 (1988): 482–83.

52. Beyond the appeal of standardizing the market—which was not urgent for Proprietary Association members, because they already accounted for the overwhelming bulk of OTC sales—the OTC review provided an opportunity for drug companies to have prescription products reclassified for OTC use. In some cases, companies simply switched their marketing practices and submitted data to the panels in the expectation that the panels would confirm the product's ingredients "safe and effective" for OTC use. As the review progressed, OTC producers became increasingly enthusiastic about the potential for expanding the OTC market in this way: see Gregory Fisher, "Legal Aspects of Rx/OTC Switches," paper presented at the Regulatory Affairs Professional Society Annual Meeting, September 16, 1987, distributed by the Proprietary Association. On the industry's enthusiasm for the switching potential, see H. I. Silverman, "What Lies Ahead for Rx-to-OTC Switches," *Drug and Cosmetic Industry* (August 1987).

53. For example, Proprietary Association officials protested the FDA's insistence on using clinical rather than colloquial terms ("emetic" rather than "vomiting") for fear that most consumers would not understand the clinical terms: interview with William Bradley, Director of Scientific Services, Proprietary Association, December 1987. In general, moreover, drug companies resisted FDA's demand that labels carry word-for-word the "indications" approved in the monograph. The FDA relaxed this requirement in 1985, without objection as it turned out, from the public interest lawyers. See Baumgartner, "Historical Examination," pp. 487–88.

54. 42 Fed.Reg. 12137, amending 21 C.F.R. §330.10(a).

55. *Health Research Group v. Kennedy*, 82 F.R.D. 21 (1979). At p. 23 n. 3, Judge Sirica's opinion notes the revealing fact that the Justice Department raised questions about the standing of the HRG, though "the client agency" (i.e., the FDA) had "previously requested the issue not be raised." At that time, the FDA does not seem to have been very unhappy about being sued—hence its failure to seek an appeal, when the suit went forward and the agency "lost."

56. *Cutler v. Kennedy*, 475 F. Supp. 838 (D.D.C., 1979).

57. Baumgartner, "Historical Examination," p. 480.

58. *Cutler v. Hayes*, 549 F.Supp. 1341 (1982).

59. *Cutler v. Hayes*, 818 F.2d 879 (D.C. Cir., 1987). Arthur Hayes was succeeded as FDA Commissioner by Frank Young in 1984.

60. The court was not embarrassed to quote an earlier decision on the harm done by "excessive delay": "Quite simply, excessive delay saps the public confidence in an agency's ability to discharge its responsibilities and creates uncertainties for the parties." Perhaps the court supposed that shoring up public confidence was more vital for the FDA officials than for judges. Perhaps the court supposed that plaintiff Cutler as a "representative" of some 200 million consumers of OTC drugs was not really a "party" to FDA's policy in this area, but in this case was merely an escort for the issue being considered by the D.C. Court of Appeals.

61. 818 F.2d at 898, quoting from a previous decision of the D.C. Court of Appeals dealing with an OSHA standard to limit exposure to a recently discovered carcinogen.

62. This information was "discovered" in depositions taken by Public Citizen attorney William Schultz from officials in the FDA in December 1987.

63. Interview with Kenneth Baumgartner, December 1987.

64. Demkovich, "Critics Fear the FDA is Going Too Far," p. 1249, citing report by Public Citizen, Health Research Group.

Notes

65. The Proprietary Association urged the FDA to upgrade the OTD division to avoid bottle-necks in the Bureau of Drugs (subsequently renamed the Center for Drug Evaluation and Research), and presumably to discourage nitpicking evaluations: interview with William Bradley, Director of Scientific Studies, Proprietary Association, December 1987. But the Bureau of Drugs insisted that the OTC review ought to be run in the same manner as reviews of new drugs. Thus the director of the Bureau of Drugs told a journalist: "I know some individuals who say that a 'quick and dirty' study should suffice, but I don't believe we're going to accept that ... our people are going to be certain [the data on OTC drugs] meet 1980 [approval] standards": Demkovich, "Do Over-the-Counter Drugs Work?" p. 486.

66. Richard A. Merrill, "Regulating Carcinogens in Food: A Legislator's Guide to the Food Safety Provisions of the Federal Food, Drug and Cosmetic Act," *Michigan Law Review* 77 (1978): 173.

67. 72 Stat. 1785 (codified at 21 U.S.C. §348).

68. 74 Stat. 399 (codified at 21 U.S.C. §376).

69. 82 Stat. 343 (codified at 21 U.S.C. §360b).

70. Saccharine Study and Labeling Act, 91 Stat. 1451 (1977).

71. See Demkovich "Critics Fear the FDA is Going Too Far," pp. 1251–52, for a sampling of strongly supportive remarks about the Delaney clause from consumer advocates.

72. R. Wilson, "Risks Caused by Low Levels of Pollution," *Yale Journal of Biology and Medicine* 51 (1978): 48.

73. R. J. Scheuplein et al., "New Approaches to the Regulation of Carcinogens in Foods," in Harry Milman and Elizabeth Weisburger, eds. (Parkridge, N.J.: Noyes Publications, 1985), p. 643. Among the food substances already identified as animal carcinogens are essential nutrients, like protein, calcium, vitamin C, and vitamin D; basic agricultural commodities, like eggs and black pepper; and inherent constituents of raw agricultural commodities, like nitrite and tannic acid.

74. Public interest advocates are not altogether indifferent to warnings that the public will cease to take cancer warnings seriously if they become too frequent. Thus when FDA Commissioner Hayes testified before Congress that even vinegar has been shown to have carcinogenic properties, Bruce Silverglade of the Center for Science in the Public Interest sent him a sharp letter of protest, pointing out that vinegar is not a food "additive" and is not therefore covered by the Delaney clause.

75. 38 Fed.Reg. 19,226 (1973) and 42 Fed.Reg. 10,412 (1977), described in Richard A. Merrill and Peter Barton Hutt, *Food and Drug Law: Cases and Materials* (Mineola, N.Y.: Foundation Press, 1980), pp. 496–97.

76. *Monsanto v. Kennedy,* 613 F.2d 947 (D.C. Cir., 1979).

77. *Scott v. FDA,* 738 F.2d 322 (6th Cir., 1984).

78. Public Citizen sought a court order to speed up FDA decision making on the carcinogenic status of various color additives, but the suit was ultimately rejected as an improper interference with agency discretion in *McIlwain v. Hayes,* 690 F.2d 1041 (1982), in an opinion by Judge Robert Bork from which Judge Abner Mikva vigorously dissented. A different litigational campaign, sponsored by the Center for Science in the Public Interest and several other public interest organizations, sought to force the FDA to set formal tolerance standards for afflatoxins—naturally occurring molds known to be carcinogenic—on corn. After an initial success in the D.C. Court of Appeals, the plaintiffs were set back by the Supreme Court in *Young v. Community Nutrition Institute,* 106 S.Ct. 2360 (1986), holding that the FDA was not required by law to set formal standards in this area. In the ensuing round, the Court of Appeals plunged ahead with a demand for the FDA to explain and justify its "informal" policy in this area: *Community Nutrition Institute v. Young,* 818 F.2d 943 (D.C. Cir., 1987).

79. Government demands for risk assessment have generated a body of professional, technically trained risk assessors with their own professional journal. The risk assessments on color additives, commissioned by the FDA, were eventually printed in this journal with full explanations of the methodology employed: R. Hart et al., "Final Report of the Color Additive Scientific Review Panel," *Risk Analysis* 6 (1986): 117.

80. Department of Health and Human Services Memorandum, from Director, Bureau of Foods, to FDA Commissioner, "Carcinogenic Color Additives" August 12, 1983), p. 4. Reprinted in *Regulation by the Department of Health and Human Services of Carcinogenic Color Additives,* Hearing Before a Subcommittee of the Committee on Government Operations, 98th Cong., 2d Sess. (1984), p. 641.

Notes

81. 50 Fed.Reg. 51,551 (1985). The suit was dismissed in November 1987 on the grounds that the FDA's order was not yet "final," hence not yet "ripe" for review; *Public Citizen v. Bowen*, 833 F.2d 364 (D.C. Cir., 1987).

82. *FDA Continues to Permit the Illegal Marketing of Carcinogenic Additives*, Twenty-fifth Report by the Committee on Government Operations (October 9, 1987).

83. *Public Citizen v. Young*, 831 F.2d 1108 (D.C. Cir., 1987) at 1120.

84. Richard M. Cooper, "Stretching Delaney Till It Breaks," *Regulation* (November–December 1985); Richard A. Merrill, "FDA's 'Erasure' of the Delaney Clause: A Study in Statutory Interpretation," *Association of Food and Drug Officials, Quarterly Bulletin* 50.4 (October 1986).

85. Peter Barton Hutt, "Brief for Intervenor-Respondent, The Cosmetic, Toiletry and Fragrance Ass'n. in Public Citizen v. Young, No. 86-1548," reprinted in *FDA's Regulation of Carcinogenic Additives*, Hearing Before a Subcommittee of the Committee on Government Operations, House of Representatives, 100th Congress, 1st Sess. (1987), p. 175. Hutt is the coauthor of *Food and Drug Law: Cases and Materials*.

86. *Public Citizen v. Young*, 831 F.2d 1108 (D.C. Cir., 1987).

87. *FDA Continues to Permit the Illegal Marketing of Carcinogenic Additives*, "Additional Views," pp. 36–37.

88. Personal interview, Daniel Sigelman, Counsel to the Human Resources and Intergovernmental Affairs Subcommittee, House Committee on Government Operations, December 1987.

89. Memorandum from Chief Counsel to FDA Commissioner, "Reaching a Decision on Color Additives" (June 21, 1983), p. 3 n. 3, reprinted in *Regulation by the DHHS of Carcinogenic Color Additives*, Hearings (1984), p. 637, summarizing "statement" submitted to the FDA by William Schultz, Public Citizen Health Research Group.

90. For a useful overview, see Jane Stein, "Reagan's Cancer Wars," *National Journal* (February 26, 1983): 456.

91. See, e.g., "Melt in Your Mouth, Sicken in Your System," *Public Citizen* (June 1987): 7, warning that "red M&Ms aren't safe" because the red dye involved is "carcinogenic." According to Kathy Baker, editor of *Public Citizen*, PC litigators do not seek publicity for their work in PC, but rather regard the magazine as a separate service for contributors to the organization. This story, for example, was chosen by the editor on her own initiative: personal interview, January 1987.

Chapter 7

1. Steven Kelman, "Occupational Safety and Health Administration," in *The Politics of Regulation*, James Q. Wilson, ed. (New York: Basic Books, 1980) offers concise legislative history.

2. 29 U.S.C. §651 et seq.

3. Kelman, "OSHA," in *Politics of Regulation*, Wilson, ed., p. 241.

4. Under the APA provisions for judicial review, which would govern in the absence of special statutory provisions for a particular program (as here), courts would be authorized to set aside an administrative standard only if "arbitrary and capricious," presumably a much harder charge to prove than the lack of "substantial evidence."

5. The most important is the concurring opinion filed by Justice Rehnquist in *Industrial Union Department, AFL-CIO v. American Petroleum Institute*, 448 U.S. 607 (1980), insisting that the legislation was so vague on the crucial question of feasibility limits on the stringency of standards that it had no genuinely ascertainable meaning and ought therefore to be struck down as an unconstitutional delegation of legislative power.

6. John Mendeloff, *Regulating Safety: An Economic and Political Analysis of Occupational Safety and Health Policy* (Cambridge, Mass: M.I.T. Press, 1979).

7. A modest set of alternative proposals that might go far in speeding up OSHA standard setting operations is advanced in John Mendeloff, "Regulatory Reform and OSHA Policy," *Journal of Policy Analysis and Management Science* 5.3 (1986): 440–68, but the same article explains why there is little support for such compromise formulas.

8. *Federal Register* (May 29, 1971).

9. Mendeloff, *Regulating Safety*, p. 40.

10. For an overview, see Steven Kelman, "Enforcement of Occupational Safety and Health

Regulation," in *Enforcing Regulation*, Keith Hawkins and John Thomas, eds. (Boston: Kluwer-Nijhoff Publishing, 1984).

11. Charles Noble, *Liberalism at Work: The Rise and Fall of OSHA* (Philadelphia: Temple University Press, 1986), p. 183.

12. Ibid.

13. Mendeloff, *Regulating Safety*, p. 41.

14. Kelman, "OSHA," in *Politics of Regulation*, Wilson, ed., pp. 260–61.

15. See F. J. Thompson, "Deregulation by the Bureaucracy: OSHA and the Augean Quest for Error Correction," *Public Administration Review* (May–June 1982) for an account of the difficulties encountered in the Carter administration's effort to cut back on unnecessary regulations.

16. Various studies are reviewed in Noble, *Liberalism at Work*, pp. 202–5. Studies from data in the mid-1970s are analyzed most thoroughly in Robert Smith, "Impact of OSHA Inspections on Manufacturing Injury Rates," *Journal of Human Resources*, 14 (1979): 145–70 and David McCaffrey, "An Assessment of OSHA's Recent Effects On Injury Rates," *Journal of Human Resources* 18 (1983): 131–46.

17. Mendeloff, *Regulating Safety*, pp. 14, 85–87.

18. See, e.g., Albert Nichols and Richard Zeckhauser, "The Perils of Prudence," *Regulation* (November–December 1986); K. Viscusi, *Risk by Choice* (Cambridge, Mass.: Harvard University Press, 1983), p. 78.

19. Noble, *Liberalism*, pp. 128–30.

20. ACGIH's approach is described in Mendeloff, "Regulatory Reform and OSHA Policy," pp. 463–64.

21. *Industrial Union Department (I.U.D.), AFL-CIO v. Hodgson*, 499 F.2d 467 (1974).

22. Mendeloff, *Regulating Safety*, pp. 61–65.

23. *I.U.D. v. Hodgson*, 499 F.2d 467 (1974).

24. Ibid. at 478–79.

25. 29 U.S.C. §655(b)(5).

26. A concise account of the difficulties in this field of research is offered in Kelman, "OSHA," pp. 249–51. For a more extensive and up-to-date but still quite accessible account, see John Mendeloff, *The Dilemma of Toxic Substance Regulation* (Cambridge, Mass.: M.I.T. Press, 1988), chap. 4.

27. Mendeloff, "Regulatory Reform and OSHA Policy," p. 441.

28. 499 F.2d 467 (1974) at 475.

29. Ibid. at 488.

30. Ibid. at 478. The court also remanded for further explanation OSHA's decision to require employers to maintain health records for monitoring purposes for no more than three years, a duration the court believed might be too short.

31. 29 U.S.C. §655(f).

32. Some excuse for the court's inattention to the standing question may be drawn from the fact that Justice Department briefs in the case did not pursue the question either. But a court's obligation to stay within its proper jurisdiction is not dependent on the preferences of the parties, which is why "friendly suits" or "feigned cases" remain improper. In fact, courts have not taken the position that anyone at all may challenge OSHA standards: in *Fire Equipment Mnfrs. v. Marshall*, 679 F.2d 679 (7th Cir., 1982) the court denied standing to manufacturers of fire equipment demanding tighter standards regarding fire safety equipment. Only the intended beneficiaries of OSHA standards could make such a demand, the court insisted, though it is hard to see why a manufacturer likely to benefit from regulatory requirements is a less suitable "private attorney general" than Ralph Nader's Public Citizen.

33. *AFL-CIO v. Brennan*, 530 F.2d 109 (3d Cir., 1975).

34. Steven Kelman emphasizes the ideology of health professionals in his most extended study, *Regulating America, Regulating Sweden: A Comparative Study of Occupational Safety and Health Policy* (Cambridge, Mass.: M.I.T. Press, 1981), which suggests that this factor may account for many similarities in approaches to standards in the two countries, despite many other contextual differences.

35. The episode is described in Mendeloff, *Regulating Safety*, pp. 52–56.

36. Noble, *Liberalism*, p. 186.

37. Noble, *Liberalism*, p. 172.

38. The CWPS analysis of the data appears in *Occupational Safety & Health Reporter* (May 13, 1976): 1796.

Notes

39. *American Petroleum Institute v. OSHA,* 581 F.2d 493 (1978).
40. *Industrial Union Dept., AFL-CIO v. American Petroleum Institute,* 448 U.S. 607 (1980) at 645.
41. 448 U.S. 607 (1980) at 695 n. 9.
42. *American Textile Manufacturers Institute v. Donovan,* 452 U.S. 490 (1981).
43. Mendeloff, "Does Overregulation Cause Underregulation? The Case of Toxic Substances," *Regulation* (September–October 1981): 51.
44. *United Steelworkers of America v. Marshall,* 647 F.2d 1189 (1980).
45. Mendeloff, "Does Overregulation Cause Underregulation?" p. 51 suggests that even a doubling or tripling of resources devoted to standard setting would by no means leave idle hands.
46. Mendeloff, *Regulating Safety,* pp. 42–43.
47. Interview with John Morall, OMB regulatory economist, Office of Information and Regulatory Affairs, OMB, July 1987.
48. OSHA also promulgated a major new regulation in 1988 dealing with communication of health hazards to workers—but even this was promptly entangled in litigation from unions demanding more stringent record keeping requirements.
49. OMB's coordinating authority was extended by a new executive order, issued in January 1985, requiring agencies to submit annual "calendars" of regulations they would be working on in the future for OMB approval. Although OMB seems rarely to have tested the limits of its authority in seeking to alter agency agendas, OSHA was regarded as an obvious target for such a trial—except for its continual entanglement in litigation: interview with Scott Jacobs, OIRA analyst, December 1987.
50. OMB officials worried that data reported in official OSHA documents in the *Federal Register* would be fixed as the law—in the sense that courts would respond very negatively if the government later sought to change particular figures—and this fear made them all the more determined to scrutinize OSHA figures: interview with Robert Damus, Deputy General Counsel, OMB, July 1987.
51. A particularly partisan sampling is collected between covers in Susan Tolchin and Martin Tolchin, *Dismantling America: The Rush to Deregulate* (New York: Oxford University Press, 1985), pp. 72–95.
52. A sense of the wrath OMB courted by imposing excessive delays can be readily gleaned from *EPA's Asbestos Regulations,* Hearing Before the Subcommittee on Oversight and Investigations, Committee on Energy and Commerce, House of Representatives, 99th Congress, 1st Sess. (1985), subtitled *A Case Study of Interference in Environmental Protection Agency Rulemaking by the Office of Management and Budget.*
53. Interview with John Morall, July 1987.
54. Mendeloff, "Regulatory Reform and OSHA Policy."
55. Ibid., p. 442.
56. Morall, "A Review of the Record," p. 30.
57. Mendeloff, "Does Overregulation Cause Underregulation?" p. 48.
58. Office of Technology Assessment, *Preventing Illness and Injury in the Workplace* (Washington: U.S. Congress, 1985), p. 261.
59. Even a single resistant firm, it is true, might try to challenge a compromise standard accepted by most other firms, and if it brought the challenge outside the D.C. Circuit—as it likely would do—the court might not be well informed or particularly sympathetic to the larger compromise program. Still, OSHA could probably improve its chances of success in such a suit by demonstrating that the challenged standard was far more cost effective—or far more reasonable, in the sense of not being indifferent to compliance costs—than others already upheld by reviewing courts.
60. Morall, "Review of the Record," p. 30.
61. Of course, particular advocates for stronger regulation may not care about the overall effectiveness of the program, but may be preoccupied instead with the few standards most directly relevant to their own industry or their own circumstances. But then the question is why such parochial advocates should be allowed to settle policies with direct implications for the entire program, or why they should be given priority over other beneficiaries.
62. Sheldon Samuels, Director of Health and Safety, Industrial Union Department, AFL-CIO, quoted in Mendeloff, *Regulating Safety,* p. 47.
63. E.g., Richard Zeckhauser, "Procedures for Valuing Lives," *Public Policy* 23 (1975): 419.

Notes

64. Interview with Margaret Seminario, Industrial Union Department, AFL-CIO, December 1987.

65. For example, annual OSHA inspection fines, which had averaged $14.8 million per year in the Carter administration, fell to $5.5 million in 1982 but had risen back to $9.2 million in 1985 (Noble, *Liberalism*, p. 183). For a detailed account of early congressional pressures on Reagan OSHA appointees for a tougher stand, and the growing signs of responsiveness to this pressure by 1983, see Michael Wines, "Auchter's Record at OSHA Leaves Labor Outraged, Business Satisfied," *National Journal* (October 1, 1983): 2008.

66. Noble, *Liberalism*, pp. 136–42.

67. Appearing to take an uncompromising position may impress constituents or contributors as well as the other side in bargaining situations. But there may also be more specialized incentives in this case, at least for labor unions, because safety is only a small part of their agenda—with employers as with the Labor Department. Mendeloff, in *Regulating Safety*, p. 77, notes that unions may use the threat of OSHA sanctions for bargaining leverage; but this tactic is only possible when firms find it difficult to achieve full compliance. For legal advocates like Public Citizen, it may not be overly cynical to wonder where they would turn their energies if they had to acknowledge that previous targets of litigation where now running smoothly and effectively.

68. A proposal sponsored by Representative Henry Jefferts would allow OSHA to impose any "threshold limit value" for exposure to hazardous substances that has already been accepted by ACGIH, without having to undertake a separate rule making proceeding. In spite of its obvious advantages, the proposal has encountered so much opposition that it has not even been aired in a formal committee hearing.

69. F. J. Thompson, "Deregulation by the Bureaucracy," *Public Administration Review* (1982): 202 notes that OSHA had to retreat from a number of proposed reductions in consensus standards in the late 1970s under pressure from union advocates.

70. See Mendeloff, *Dilemma of Toxic Substance Regulation*, chap. 4 for a fuller discussion of the research biases and limitations.

71. *Florida Peach Growers Ass'n. v. Dept. of Labor*, 489 F.2d 120 (5th Cir., 1974); *Dry Color Mnfrs. Ass'n. v. Dept. of Labor*, 486 F.2d 98 (3d Cir., 1973).

72. *Public Citizen Health Research Group v. Auchter*, 554 F. Supp. 242 (1983).

73. *Public Citizen Health Research Group v. Auchter*, 702 F.2d 1150 (1983).

74. Ibid. at 1158.

75. Morall, "A Review of the Record," p. 30.

76. OMB's strong objections to the short-term exposure limit led OSHA to abandon its own previous proposal for such a limit—and Public Citizen accordingly argued that OMB had improperly interfered with the rule making.

77. *Public Citizen Health Research Group v. Tyson*, 796 F.2d 1479 (D.C. Cir., 1986).

78. Ibid. at 1490. See also the acknowledgment at 1491: "OSHA recognized the equivocal nature of this evidence. The agency never stated that this particular evidence conclusively established the harmful health effects of EtO. Rather, the agency stated that the evidence ... *supported* [original emphasis] its conclusion that EtO is a carcinogen." In the summer of 1987, Public Citizen won a new directive from the court of appeals, demanding rapid action on the short-term exposure limit standard. See *Public Citizen Health Research Group v. Brock*, 823 F.2d 626 (D.C. Cir., 1987), conceding that "we should avoid if possible any direct judicial meddling with the details of OSHA's rulemaking schedule" (at 629)—and then proceeding to meddle, on the grounds that "the public health, as defined by Congress, requires that we set a clear end point to the regulatory snarl that is the EtO short-term exposure limit rulemaking." The decision nowhere explains where the relevant standard of public health has been "defined by Congress," but quite obviously it did not have in mind 29 U.S.C. §655(g): "In determining the priority for establishing standards under this section, the Secretary shall give due regard to the urgency of the need for mandatory safety and health standards." By this criterion, the EtO short-term exposure limit was hardly a matter of highest urgency, considering the much more serious health hazards already documented but not yet covered by any new OSHA standard.

79. Mendeloff, *Dilemma of Toxic Substance Regulation*, p. 98.

80. The proposed standard on formaldehyde has been in litigation since 1985, with both business and labor attacking OSHA's proposal, which was spurred by a separate AFL-CIO action.

81. Interview with Margaret Seminario, December 1987.

82. Interview with Scott Jacobs, regulatory analyst, Office of Information and Regulatory Affairs, OMB, December 1987.

Notes

83. Interview with Margaret Seminario, December 1987.

84. Public Citizen's Health Research Group, with only one medical specialist, has generally specialized in litigation, relying on unions to provide evidence and testimony at OSHA hearings as new standards are being developed. In the EtO case, the American Federation of State, County, and Municipal Employees took the lead in developing the administrative record on behalf of health care unions. The only instance in which Public Citizen has acted independently of the unions has been with its recent petition urging OSHA to promulgate a new standard prohibiting smoking in the workplace—a policy with which unions do not agree: interview with Margaret Seminario, December 1987.

85. *National Congress of Hispanic American Citizens (El Congreso) v. Dunlop*, 425 F. Supp. 900 (D.D.C., 1975).

86. *National Congress of Hispanic American Citizens v. Usery*, 554 F.2d 1196 (D.C. Cir., 1977) at 1200.

87. See *OSHA's Failure to Establish a Field Sanitation Standard*, Hearing Before a Subcommittee of the Committee on Government Operations, U.S. House of Representatives, 99th Cong., 1st Sess. (1985), pp. 7, 37, 157–64.

88. See the explanation of this view in OSHA's *Federal Register* announcement of April 16, 1985, 50 Fed.Reg. 15,088.

89. Kelman, "OSHA," in *Politics of Regulation*, Wilson, ed., offers a concise account of the episode, pp. 260–61.

90. 50 Fed.Reg. 15,092 (April 16, 1985). This estimate was not disputed in the subsequent litigation.

91. *Farmworkers Justice Fund v. Brock*, 811 F.2d 613 (D.C. Cir., 1987).

92. 811 F.2d 613 (D.C. Cir., 1987) at 642–43. It may not be altogether irrelevant to note that the majority opinion was written by Chief Judge Patricia Wald, a Carter appointee and former public interest lawyer, while the dissent was filed by Judge Stephen Williams, a Reagan appointee. It is also noteworthy that Judge Williams, while expressing much more sympathy for the reasoning of Reagan appointees at the Labor Department, expressly accepts Judge Wald's premise that the Labor Department's policy decision not to issue a standard in this case ought to be subject to judicial review at the behest of the Farmworkers Justice Fund.

93. See *OSHA's Failure to Establish a Field Sanitation Standard*, Hearing Before a Subcommittee of the Committee on Government Operations, House of Representatives, 99th Cong., 1st Sess. (1985), illustrating strong support for the standard by the subcommittee chairman, Representative Barney Frank (D-Mass.), who actually prepared a bill to impose the standard directly but found little support for it.

Chapter 8

1. See E. B. Pashukanis, *Law and Marxism: A General Theory*, B. Einhorn, trans., C. Arthur, ed. (London: Ink Links, 1978). Pashukanis held a particular fascination for Lon Fuller: see *The Morality of Law*, rev. ed. (New Haven: Yale University Press, 1969), pp. 24–27, and somewhat earlier for Roscoe Pound: see *Administrative Law: Its Growth, Procedure, and Significance* (Pittsburgh: University of Pittsburgh Press, 1942), pp. 3, 127, because both recognized much validity in Pashukanis's characterizations of Western law. Pound could not refrain from noting that Pashukanis's theories fell from favor in the Kremlin in the mid-1930s, perhaps due to the new rhetorical needs of "popular front" diplomacy, and Pashukanis "did not move fast enough in his teaching to conform to the doctrinal exigencies of the new order. If there had been law instead of only administrative orders [in Soviet Russia] it might have been possible for [Pashukanis] to lose his job without losing his life."

2. European notions of "legality" may have faced less challenge from socialists in this century because, even in the nineteenth century, they were much more positivistic and state oriented—less bound up, that is, with a "higher law" tradition of individual rights—than the traditional American versions; see Gottfried Dietze, *Two Concepts of the Rule of Law* (Indianapolis: Liberty Fund, 1973). For example, under the Vichy government, the French Conseil d'État labored diligently to assure the forms of legality to the most extreme and illiberal policies, including the policy of cooperation with the mass murder program of the Germans: Margherita Rendel, *The Administrative Functions of the Conseil d'État* (London: Weidenfeld & Nicholson, 1970), p. 116.

Notes

3. Of course, state business enterprises in Europe are subject to different forms of control than private firms; there would be no point in public ownership if they were not. But in public enterprises, special protections for particular interest group beneficiaries are typically built into governing schemes—as by representation on corporate boards—instead of being secured by legal guarantees, enforceable in the courts. For a useful survey of the French system, see F. Ridley and J. Blondel, *Public Administration in France* (London: Routledge & Kegan Paul, 1964), pp. 233–55.

4. See Richard C. Levin, "Regulation, Barriers to Exit, and Investment Behavior of Railroads," in *Studies in Public Regulation*, Gary Fromm, ed. (Cambridge, Mass.: M.I.T. Press, 1981), tracing the decline of rail freight traffic not to excessively severe rate limitations, as some economists had previously argued, but to route controls that prevent railroads from concentrating on the most efficient hauls, where they would be most competitive with trucking.

5. For an economist's criticism of such paternalism, see W. K. Viscusi, *Risk by Choice* (Cambridge, Mass.: Harvard University Press, 1981). For a thoughtful defense, see Steven Kelman, "Regulation and Paternalism," in *Rights and Regulation: Ethical, Political and Economic Issues*, Tibor Machan and Bruce Johnson, eds. (San Francisco: Pacific Institute for Public Policy Research, 1983).

6. "The uniqueness of the American approach to regulation is the one finding on which every cross-national study of regulation is in agreement. The American system of regulation is distinctive in the degree of oversight exercised by the judiciary and the national legislature, in the formality of its rulemaking and enforcement process, in its reliance on prosecution" (David Vogel, *National Styles of Regulation* [Ithaca, N.Y.: Cornell University Press, 1986], p. 267). A sympathetic French visitor to the United States in the late 1970s thus expressed astonishment at the extent to which public policy had become legalized and proceduralized, a trend he he termed "due process delirium": Michel Crozier, *The Trouble with America* (Berkeley: University of California Press, 1984).

7. After "taking possession of the means of production in the name of society . . . [the] interference of the state power becomes superfluous in one sphere after another and then ceases of itself. The government of persons is replaced by the administration of things": Engels, *Anti-During*, trans. Emile Burns (New York: International Publishers, 1939), p. 307.

8. This vision of ultimate congressional sovereignty remains an appealing notion to some political scientists, perhaps partly out of partisan loyalties in an era in which Congress has been almost continually in the hands of one party and the White House frequently in the hands of the other party. But the vision of congressional supremacy also seems to appeal to those who take a Rousseauan view of the moral authority of "the people" and accordingly suppose that anything that deflects the will of "the people" as pronounced by Congress must be illegitimate. Theodore Lowi, *The End of Liberalism* (New York: Norton, 1969), a work much more preoccupied with "legitimacy" than with policy outcomes, is the outstanding example. Quite apart from the complications of bicameralism, this is a remarkably romantic view of the national legislature, in which, after all, there is a lower turnover rate for incumbents than in high administrative posts, apparently because congressional incumbents have become so adept at pandering to specialized constituencies.

9. P. S. Atiyah and R. S. Summers, *Form and Substance in Anglo-American Law: A Comparative Study in Legal Reasoning, Legal Theory and Legal Institutions* (Oxford: Clarendon Press, 1987) emphasizes the much greater degree of formalism even in contemporary English law—a reflection, as the authors suggest, not of greater judicial regard for property or personal rights in England but of greater deference to the political or policy making authority of government.

10. Theories recommending a balance of powers in government are at least as old as Aristotle. The modern theory is distinctive in locating an ultimate power to make and unmake the laws in a separate legislature. The more clearly this notion was embraced, the more eager theorists were to insist that this legislative power was still somehow limited. Hence Locke and others insisted that "those who hold this [legislative] authority should make only general rules. They are to govern by promulgated established Laws, not to be varied in particular cases": M. J. C. Vile, *Constitutionalism and the Separation of Powers* (London: Oxford University Press, 1967), p. 63. W. B. Gwyn calls this the "rule of law" argument for the separation of powers. While he identifies other arguments for a separation of powers in seventeenth century English writers, the others do not seem to require any particular division between legislative and executive powers: see W. B. Gwyn, *The Meaning of the Separation of Powers*, Tulane Studies in Political Science, vol. 9 (New Orleans: Tulane University, 1965).

Notes

11. In this respect, due process limitations are a generalization of the particular prohibition on bills of attainder. That prohibition has been restricted to punitive measures, but the logic of due process protests against overly particular measures also appeals to the notion of protection against invidious distinctions. For example, in *U.S. Deparatment of Agriculture v. Moreno*, 413 U.S. 528 (1973), the Supreme Court invoked the due process clause to invalidate a legislative amendment to the food stamp program, which had sought to exclude households of unrelated individuals from participating in the program.

12. Max Farrand, ed., *The Records of the Federal Convention of 1787* (New Haven: Yale University Press, 1911), 2. 34.

13. See, e.g., *The Federalist* 58, C. Rossiter, ed. (New York: New American Library, 1961), p. 359, noting "the continual triumph of the British House of Commons over the other branches of the government, whenever the engine of a money bill has been employed." But this was one reason that the framers were eager for a workable executive veto on legislative appropriation measures.

14. In fact—and it is a revealing fact—the committee system was not established at the very outset but was, like "party" organization, seen as a temporary expediency when first urged by the Republican opposition in the mid-1790s. The committee system did not become accepted as a routine and appropriate means of conducting legislative business until some years into the nineteenth century: see Ralph Volney Harlow, *Legislative Methods in the Period Before 1825* (New Haven: Yale University Press, 1917).

15. The leading example is *Kendall v. Stokes*, 37 U.S. (12 Pet.) 524 (1838).

16. Even when cases did come before the Supreme Court in the nineteenth century, the Court displayed considerable reluctance to interpose its own formal pronouncements into ongoing disputes between Congress and the executive. For example, prior to the *Myers* decision in 1926, the Supreme Court "contrived to side-step every occasion for a decisive pronouncement regarding the removal power, its extent and location": Edward C. Corwin, *The Presidency, Office and Powers*, 4th ed. (New York: New York University Press, 1957), p. 85.

17. See, e.g., J. D. Aberbach, R. D. Putnam, and B. A. Rockman, *Bureaucrats and Politicians in Western Democracies* (Cambridge, Mass.: Harvard University Press, 1981), emphasizing the degree to which bureaucrats have come to accept an avowedly political role in advancing and defending various policies in internal government debate.

18. The Civil Rights Restoration Act, which sought to amend Title VI and other statutes enforced by OCR in response to the Supreme Court's *Grove City* decision limiting their reach, is the exception that proves the rule. Originally introduced in 1984, the measure was stalled for four years because the sponsors refused to consider amendments. In the Senate, the rules of procedure could not prevent a successful amendment dealing with abortion from being (successfully) moved from the floor when the bill was finally put to a floor vote at the beginning of 1988. In the House, special rules of procedure were finally adopted to limit critics of the bill to a single amendment, which was then voted down. In neither house were committee hearings permitted after 1984, lest they provide opportunities for the development of distracting criticism and proposals for change.

19. *Ex parte Grossman*, 267 U.S. 87 (1925) held that even the presidential pardon power does not extend to punishments imposed by judges for civil contempt—that is, failure to obey judicial directives. Sentence and judgment are handed down by the judge who is defied; this remarkable power is thought necessary to assure the authority of judicial directives. In practice, of course, judges do not dare to send Cabinet officials to jail for contempt of court, but their formal power to do so illustrates the official conception of their relations: whereas executive officials must obey judicial directives, courts need not take any account of executive orders or executive directives, because the executive has no power to enforce compliance on the courts.

20. It would not be hard to demonstrate that a less restrictive policy on new drugs over the past two decades could have averted tens of thousands, perhaps even hundreds of thousands of premature deaths, because comparisons with European policies and results can be made. It would only be somewhat more difficult to demonstrate that a different set of priorities at OSHA over the past fifteen years would have reduced cancer fatalities in many industries, though the number of lives at stake is considerably smaller. Again it would not be overly difficult to demonstrate from available evidence that different school policies would have contributed to better educational performance. The crucial difficulty in all of these cases would be to demonstrate that better policies would indeed have occurred *but for the intervention of the courts*. This sort of claim is necessarily speculative. But it is precisely the sort of claim on which contemporary administrative

Notes

law rests: interest group or advocacy group standing claims almost always rest on speculative claims about how diffuse constituencies *might* be better off if different policies were followed.

21. H. McCloskey and Alida Brill, in *Dimensions of Tolerance: What Americans Believe About Civil Liberties* (New York: Russell Sage Foundation, 1983), document through extensive opinion surveys that, on most civil liberty issues, "elite opinion" tends to be more in accord with prevailing doctrines of the Supreme Court than "mass opinion." The authors attribute this finding to the greater exposure of "elites" to reporting on Supreme Court opinions—though it may also be that the Supreme Court itself enforces views that are more congenial to "elites" than to the majority of Americans.

22. An amusing catalog of such "illegalities" was compiled in the mid-1970s by Jethro Lieberman, *How Government Breaks the Law* (New York: Stein & Day, 1972). Despite some earnest efforts, the author is unable to sustain a tone of indignation—perhaps because so many of the "laws" involved made so little sense to begin with.

23. The point is not that one party must sweep both houses of Congress along with the White House in order to have the political strength to amend the APA. Rather, it is a question of political incentives. A more unified government would be more resentful of political intrusion from the courts, just as the parliamentary governments of Western Europe refuse to tolerate any significant degree of political interference from the courts. From this point of view, the chance fortunes of any one election are not likely to make a serious difference. The question is whether a larger realignment will persuade Congress to develop sufficient internal discipline to protect, if not the executive, then at least its own leading committee chairmen from the centrifugal tugs of litigating advocacy groups.

24. The traditional jurisprudence limiting jurisdiction to claims about personal rights would face great objections from interest groups, which rely on access to the courts to enforce their own favored policies on so-called "Church-State" issues. If the Supreme Court finds it impossible to abandon this constituency, it might still declare this area a unique exception—as Justice Powell indeed urged in his concurring opinion in *U.S. v. Richardson*, 418 U.S. 166 (1974). If the Court is unwilling to acknowledge that it has carved out a single arbitrary exception in relation to "religion," it might still distinguish the religion cases on the grounds that they deal almost entirely with expenditures by government entities, rather than coercion of third parties in the private sector. And the court might still insist that while the Constitution allows authority over public expenditures to be shared with privileged advocacy groups, it does not permit public coercive authority to be delegated to private parties.

25. *Northern Pipeline Construction Co. v. Marathon Pipeline Co.*, 102 S.Ct. 2858 (1982).

26. The leading Supreme Court decision on standing in recent years is *Allen v. Wright*, 468 U.S. 737 (1984), denying standing to black parents seeking to compel the IRS to adopt more vigorous enforcement of nondiscrimination requirements for tax exempt private schools. The notable fact about the decision, as critics have emphasized, is that it approaches standing not as a question about the particular plaintiff's claim but as a general question about the appropriateness of judicial review ("the law of Art. III standing is built on a single basic idea—the idea of separation of powers"). In other words, even the very case most associated with a restrictive view of standing confirms the Court's general inclination to disregard the question of who precisely is bringing the case—and this inclination is, of course, the very thing that has eroded standing barriers over the past two decades. When Reagan appointees on the D.C. Court of Appeals have tried to limit standing still further in recent years, they have sometimes been rebuffed by the Supreme Court for going too far: see, e.g., *Clarke v. Securities Industry Ass'n.*, 107 S.Ct. 750 (1987); *UAW v. Brock*, 106 S.Ct. 2523 (1986).

27. See, e.g., *International Union, United Automobile, Aerospace & Agricultural Implement Workers of America v. Brock*, 783 F.2d 237 (1986), refusing to review the Labor Department's failure to bring enforcement action for noncompliance with the Labor-Management Reporting and Disclosure Act; *Community Nutrition Institute v. Young*, 818 F. 2nd 943 (1987), refusing to review the FDA's failure to initiate seizure actions against certain blended corn products.

28. See, e.g., *Public Citizen v. Tyson*, 796 F.2d 1479 (1986), in which the D.C. Court of Appeals took note of OMB's opposition to a short-term exposure limit in reviewing the adequacy of OSHA's ethylene oxide standard, declined to say whether OMB interference was improper, but demanded that OSHA provide further evidence and an explanation for adopting the position favored by OMB.

29. Interview with Christopher DeMuth, former director of the Office of Information and Regulatory Affairs, OMB, July 1987. The leading example of the problems in reconsidering

Notes

established rules is the Reagan administration's experience with OSHA's cotton dust standard, which was issued over the objections of the Carter White House in 1978 and targeted for immediate reconsideration by the President's Taskforce on Regulatory Relief in the new Reagan administration. Critics had urged that the standard be modified to allow companies to cut down on cotton dust exposure by providing workers with breathing masks instead of having to install very costly engineering controls. When it came under consideration in 1981–82, however, the existing standard was staunchly—and in the end, successfully—defended by Reagan appointees at the Labor Department. One of the principal reasons for retaining the standard seems to have been that firms that had already invested heavily in engineering controls lobbied hard for retention, lest their competitors, having delayed on these investments, gain a competitive advantage.

30. *The Federalist* 71, Rossiter, ed., p. 432.

31. The reasons have been well explained in Aaron Wildavsky's trenchant critique of "program based budgeting," a policy fashion in the mid-1960s, which supposed that budgeting decisions could be deduced from first principles of policy—much the way that contemporary administrative law supposes that implementation policy can be deduced from a fixed set of statutory guidelines for each program: see *The Politics of the Budgetary Process*, 3d ed. (Boston: Little, Brown, 1979), pp. 198–202, for one version of the argument.

32. ". . . just as, in some sense, Britain's dismal economic performance may be the price it pays for its relatively successful system of regulation, America's adversarial style of regulation may be the price it pays for the relative competitiveness of much of its industry" (Vogel, *National Styles of Regulation*, p. 287). By contrast, Peter Katzenstein's *Corporatism and Social Change: Austria, Switzerland, and the Politics of Industry* (Ithaca, N.Y.: Cornell University Press, 1984) still suggests that small corporatist states like Austria and Switzerland may provide "something of a model" (p. 9) even for larger and freer countries like the United States. The verbal argument, however, may be less impressive to many people than the actual figures, which the author supplies in a table on p. 21: increase in total employment during the 1970s was 3.4 percent in Austria, -4.9 percent in Switzerland, -1.4 percent in West Germany, and 22.2 percent in the United States, nearly three times greater than the next well-performing industrial country (Japan, at 8.6 percent).

INDEX

Index

Carter, Jimmy, 12–13, 90; *Adams v. Richardson* and, 166, 167, 176, 178; Occupational Safety and Health Administration and, 214, 225

Carter v. Carter Coal Co., 277n22

Center for Law and Social Policy, *APHA* case and, 193–96

Checks and balances, 32–33; *see also* Separation of powers

Chevron, U.S.A. v. Natural Resources Defense Council, 81, 282n8

Chicago Junction case, 57, 126, 127

Church-State issues, Supreme Court and, 131, 141–42

Citizens to Preserve Overton Park v. Volpe, 279n41

Citizen standing provisions, 283–84n26

Civil Aeronautics Board, 88, 90, 91

Civil Rights, *Adams v. Richardson* and, 147–81

Civil Rights Act of 1964: Supreme Court and, 83–84; Title VI and *Adams* case, 148–52, 153, 155, 156, 158, 162–63, 164, 166, 173

Civil rights advocacy groups, *Adams v. Richardson* and, 147–81

Civil Rights Restoration Act, 311n18

Clarke v. Securities Industry Ass'n, 312n26

Clean Air Act of 1970, 81, 106, 137, 284n26

Coke ovens, Occupational Safety and Health Administration and, 222

College integration, *Adams v. Richardson* and, 173–78

Color additives, Delaney clause and, 205

Color Additives Amendments of 1960, 202, 205, 207

Commerce Act of 1906, 15–16

Commissions, *see* Independent commissions; *names of specific commissions*

Committee for Public Education v. Regan, 291n62

Common law, 115–17, 120, 122, 123–24, 125, 126, 275n7

Community Nutrition Institute v. Young, 304n78, 312n27

Competitor standing cases, 58, 132

Confiscation Cases, The, 278n26

Congress: *Adams v. Richardson* and, 156–57, 158–59; committee system, 311n14; courts without legalism and, 262, 263; desegregation and, 129–30, 154; Food and Drug Administration and, 183, 185–86, 187, 188, 189, 191, 199–201, 202–3, 205, 207–8, 209; independent commissions and, 89, 91; Interstate Commerce Commission and, 15–16; judicial controls over, 85–86; new administrative law and, 249–50; Office for Civil Rights and, 153; Occupational Safety and Health Administration and, 211, 212, 214, 218–19, 231, 237, 238; oversight by, 25–26, 33, 68, 85, 89, 90, 258–59, 267; regulatory statutes and controversy from, 105–7, 109; responsibility of, 102, 103; separation of powers and, 103, 251–55; supremacy of, 80–86, 310n8; Supreme Court and, 80–81; *see also specific legislation*

Congressional oversight, 25–26, 33, 68, 85, 89, 90, 258–59, 267

Constitution, 6–11; Congress and, 51, 68, 80–86, 253; courts and, 114–18, 119, 120, 264; due process and, 22–23, 56, 135–36, 311n11; as enduring, 69–75; executive and, 66–68, 100–103; new administrative law and, 31–33; rights and, 41–44; school integration and, 73; separation of powers in, 13, 52, 65, 66, 68, 80–81, 103, 250–55, 310n10

Consumer Products Safety Commission, 92, 246

Contemporary administrative law, *see* New administrative law

Cooley, Thomas, 119

Cosmetics, Food and Drug Administration and, 201–9

Cotton dust, Occupational Safety and Health Administration and, 223–24, 226, 312–13n29

Council of Wage and Price Stability (CWPS), Occupational Safety and Health Administration and, 222

Courts, 11–15; administrative rulings and, 16, 123–33; character of judges and, 281–82n1; Clean Air Act and, 137–38; common law and, 115–18; Congress and, 12–13; constitutional basis for power of, 114–18, 119, 120; control by, 19–23, 31; European versus American, 109–10; Food and Drug Administration and, 189, 190, 192, 197; interest groups and, 17–18, 39–40, 43–44, 259–61, 267–70; Interstate Commerce Commission and, 56–57, 58; judicial review, 18, 22, 32, 71, 72, 84, 85–86, 92–94, 109–11, 132–33, 245; law and, 8; Law of Moses and, 115, 117; new administrative law and, 5–6, 112–13, 133–34, 255–63; Occupational Safety and Health Administration and, 210–11; 212, 216–27, 230, 232, 236–39; Office of Management and Budget and, 265; private rights and 44–48, 119–22, 254, 255; Progressivism and, 87; public policy and, 7–8, 113–14, 119–26; public values and, 113–14, 138, 139–43, 257–58; regulatory benefits and, 71; separation of powers and, 250–51, 252, 254, 255; standing and, 126–28, 257; without legalism, 261–65; *see also* D.C. Court of Appeals; Supreme Court

Court stripping proposals, 272n17

Criminal law, Constitution and, 69–70

316

Index

Debra P. v. Turlington, 300n118
Delaney, James, 202
Delaney clause, 184, 202–9
De minimus risk, Food and Drug Administration and, 205–6
Deregulation, 27, 91, 245
Desegregation: Adams v. Richardson and, 147–81; Supreme Court and, 129–30, 134
Dewey, John, 124
Dickinson, John, 124–25, 126
D.C. Court of Appeals, 4, 271–72n12; Adams v. Richardson and, 155, 157, 158, 160, 165, 174, 177, 178, 181; Agriculture Department and, 17; airbags and, 27; Chaney case and, 72; due process and, 136; environmental statutes and, 81; Food and Drug Administration and, 199, 200, 205, 207–8; Garment Workers Union and, 27, 30; judicial review and, 93, 133; natural gas pipeline rates and, 84; Occupational Safety and Health Administration and, 216–20, 227, 233–34, 236, 237–38; prosecution policy and, 70–71; retrenchment by, 265; tax exemptions for private schools and, 62
Douglas, Mary T., 29
Due process, 22–23, 56, 135–36, 311n11
Dworkin, Ronald, 48, 136–37

EDF v. Ruckelshaus, 272n25
Education Amendments of 1972 (Title IX), Adams v. Richardson and, 163–65, 166, 171
Education and Labor Committee (House), Office of Civil Rights and, 171
Education of minorities, Adams v. Richardson and, 147–81
Efficacy amendment, of Food and Drug Administration, 185, 188, 189, 190, 191–92, 195
Endangered Species Act, 81
Energy Regulatory Commission, natural gas pipelines and, 31, 63
Enforcement, tradeoffs in, 107–8
England: Committee on the Safety of Medicines, 196; common law of, 115–17, 120, 122, 123–24, 125, 126
Environmental Defense Fund v. Hardin, 272n25
Environmentalists: citizen standing provisions and, 85; Clean Air Act and, 137–38; D.C. Court of Appeals and, 81; litigation of, 24; offshore oil drilling and, 31
Environmental Protection Agency (EPA), 25, 55, 92
Epstein, Richard, 48

Equal Employment Opportunity Commission, 168
Esch amendment, 296n37
Ethylene oxide, Occupational Safety and Health Administration and, 232–34, 235, 236
Europe, see Western Europe
Exclusionary rule, Supreme Court and, 135
Executive: congressional oversight of, 68; The Federalist and, 8, 33, 66–67, 100–102, 266, 267; paradoxes of, 266–67; prosecution policy and, 70; responsibility of, 66–68, 100–105; separation of powers and, 251, 252, 255; third parties and, 53–54
Ex parte Grossman, 311n19
Expertise: appeals to law as, 91–95; as rationality, 95–98

Factions, The Federalist and, 41, 43, 65, 115
Farmworkers, Occupational Safety and Health Administration and, 236–39
Federal Communications Act, 127
Federal Communications Commission, 88; classical music radio programming and, 24, 25; competing broadcasters and, 57; NAACP and, 25; new licensing by, 127; television licensing and, 17
FCC v. Scripps Howard Broadcasting, 127–28
FCC v. WNCN Listeners Guild, 273n36
Federal Energy Regulatory Commission, natural gas pipeline rates and, 31, 63, 84
Federalist, The, 280n54, 280n55, 287n69, 287n77, 287n80, 311n13; courts and, 119; executive and, 8, 33, 66–67, 100–102, 266, 267; factions and, 41, 43, 65, 115
Federal Power Commission, 17, 88
Federal Reserve Board, 88
Federal Shipping Board, 124
Federal Tort Claims Act, 71
Federal Trade Commission, 88, 124
Federal Trade Commission Act of 1914, 12
Feminism, see Women's issues
Fifth Circuit Court of Appeals, school integration and, 73
Fire Equipment Mnfrs. v. Marshall, 306n32
First Amendment, Warren Court and, 130–31
Flast v. Cohen, 279n37
Food additives, Food and Drug Administration and, 203–209
Food Additives Amendment of 1958, 202, 208
Food and Drug Administration, 182–209, 249, 253, 260, 280n52; APHA case and, 193–96; Chaney case and, 72; foods and cosmetics and, 201–209; old drugs and, 189–96; over-the-counter drugs and, 197–201; stringency of, 184–89, 196

317

Index

Index

Kelman, Steven, 220
Kendall v. Stokes, 277*n*23
Kennedy, John F., 90, 151, 294*n*11
King, Martin Luther, Jr., 294*n*11

Labor Department: Garment Workers Union and, 27, 30, 63; Occupational Safety and Health Administration and, 211, 212, 213, 216, 223, 236, 237
Landes, William, 275*n*8
Landis, James, 90
Larry P. v. Riles, 300*n*118
Lau v. Nichols, 163
Law: bureaucracy adhering to the, 95–98; expertise and, 91–95; independent commissions and, 86–91; moral authority of, 98–100; responsibility versus, 102–103; rule of, 15, 19, *see also* Legalism; New administrative law
Legal Defense Fund, *Adams v. Richardson* and, 149, 154, 156, 157, 159, 161–62, 165, 169, 170, 174, 179, 180, 181
Legal formalism, 64
Legal interest cases, 17, 18
Legalism, 110–11, 266–67; courts and, 256–59, 261–65; interest groups and, 3–35; judicial review and, 109–11
Legality, limits of, 247–50
Legal realism, 125–26, 133
Legislative supremacy, constitutionalism and, 80–86; *see also* Congress
Legitimacy, expertise conferring, 95–98
Lemon v. Kurtzman, 291*n*62
Leventhal, Harold, 273*n*30
Levitt v. Committee for Public Education, 291*n*62
Liberal constitutionalism, 41–44
Litigation, effectiveness of, 23–26
Locke, John, 41, 52, 122, 275*n*7, 276–77*n*19, 310*n*10
Lowi, Theodore, 105, 310*n*8

McClure, Phyllis, 180
Madison, James, 118, 251
Marathon case, 264
Marbury v. Madison, 13, 51, 275*n*9
Marshall, John, 8, 51, 72
McIlwain v. Hayes, 304*n*78
Melnick, Shep, 34, 280*n*51
Mendeloff, John, 227–28, 234
Methylene chloride, Food and Drug Administration and, 207
Mexican-American Legal Defense and Education Fund (MALDEF), 165

Migrant Action Program, 238
Mikva, Abner, 304*n*78
Minority education, *Adams v. Richardson* and, 147–81
Monsanto Company, Food and Drug Administration and, 205
Monsanto v. Kennedy, 209
Moral authority, of the law, 98–100
Morrison v. Olson, 277*n*23
Moses, Law of, 115, 117
Motor Vehicle Manufacturers Assn. v. State Farm Mutual Automobile Ins. Co., 274*n*44
Myers v. U.S., 285*n*34, 311*n*16

NAACP, Federal Communications Commission and, 25; *see also* Legal Defense Fund
Nader, Ralph, 68, 79, 85, 91, 280*n*52, 284*n*27; *see also* Health Research Group; Public Citizen
National Congress of Hispanic American Citizens (El Congreso), Occupational Safety and Health Administration and, 236
National Federation of the Blind, *Adams v. Richardson* and, 165
National Institute of Occupational Safety and Health, Occupational Safety and Health Administration and, 215, 218, 220
National Labor Relations Board, Supreme Court and, 10–11
National Research Council, Food and Drug Administration and, 190–91, 192, 193, 194, 195
Natural gas pipeline pricing, 31, 63, 84
New administrative law, 4, 12–13, 18–19, 78, 243–44, 252–55; administrators and, 71; bureaucratic inertia and, 26–28; claims and, 15; Congress and, 80–86, 249–50; constitutional government and, 43–44; courts and, 6, 21–22, 93, 112–13, 133–39, 255–63; equality and, 64–69; interest groups and, 4–5, 20, 23–26, 34–40, 73; interests in isolation and, 69–75; law and, 76–80; legalism and, 261–63, 266–67; paradox of, 266; private control and, 247; public policy privatization and, 31–33, 79; Supreme Court and, 71–72
New Deal, 16, 125, 133; Congress and, 12; private rights and, 49–52; Supreme Court and, 119–20, 128–29
New drug application (NDA), Food and Drug Administration and, 189, 190, 191, 195, 196, 197
Nixon, Richard, 12, 92; *Adams v. Richardson* and, 151, 153–54, 155, 157, 158, 166, 167; Occupational Safety and Health Administration and, 211

319

Index

Index

Roosevelt, Theodore, 88, 284n30
Rousseau, Jean Jacques, 286–87n69, 310n8

Saccharine, Food and Drug Administration and, 202–203
Schecter Poultry Corp. v. U.S., 277n22
Scheuer, James, 187, 189
Schlesinger, Arthur, Jr., 82
Schlesinger v. Reservists, 279n37
School desegregation, *Adams v. Richardson* and, 147–81
Securities and Exchange Commission, 88
Sedition Act, 103
Sex discrimination, *see* Women's issues
Shapiro, Martin, 142, 272n15
Shklar, Judith, 134
Shue, Henry, 49–50, 276n16
Sierra Club, Supreme Court and, 61
Sirica, John, 199
Social welfare, private rights and, 49–51
Standing, 55–59, 78, 257, 284n27, 312n26; *Adams v. Richardson* and, 178–79; in administrative law, 126–28; advocacy groups and, 311–12n20; competitor standing cases and, 58, 132; evasions of, 60–64
State, definition of, 275n7
Stewart, Richard, 137–38
Story, Joseph, 115
Substantive due process, 56, 282n4
Sunstein, Cass, 138, 271n4, 273n29
Supreme Court: *Adams v. Richardson*, 156; *American Textile Manufacturers Institute v. Donovan*, 223–24, 226; *Association of Data Processing Service Organization v. Camp*, 58–59; *Baker v. Carr*, 130; bilingual education and, 173; *Bowsher v. Synar*, 80–81; *Brown v. Board of Education*, 129–30; Burger Court, 131, 133, 134, 135; *Chevron, U.S.A. v. Natural Resources Defense Council*, 81; *Chicago Junction* case, 57, 126, 127; Church-State issues and, 131, 141–42; Civil Rights Act of 1964 and, 83–84; Congress and, 68, 80–81; Constitution and, 264; desegregation and, 134, 152, 172; due process and, 135–36; Endangered Species Act and, 81; exclusionary rule, 135; *FCC v. Scripps Howard Broadcasting*, 127–28; federal aid to parochial schools and, 60; Federal Communication Commission and, 57; Food and Drug Administration and, 190, 193, 195; free speech and, 130–31; *Goldberg v. Kelly*, 135; *Griswold* case, 28; *Heckler v. Chaney*, 71–72; hospital tax exemption and, 62; *Humphrey's Executor v. U.S.*, 89; independent commissions and, 89; *INS v. Chadha*, 80, 264, 282n6, 282n9; Interstate Commerce Commission and, 124; judicial

intervention barrier and, 71; judicial review and, 132–33; *Lau v. Nichols*, 163; *Marathon* case, 264; *Marbury v. Madison*, 13; Marshall Court, 8, 51, 72; National Labor Relations Board and, 10–11; New Deal and, 52, 119–20, 125; Occupational Safety and Health Administration and, 62, 223–24, 225; prosecution policy, 70; rights and, 45, 118–19, 121; separation of powers and, 80–81; Sierra Club and, 61; standing and, 60–64, 78, 132, 312n26; Warren Court, 129–31, 134, 135
Sutherland, George, 126
Swann v. Charlotte-Mecklenburg Board of Education, 295n32

Taft, William H., 70
Taxation, 50–51, 62
Taylor v. Finch, 294n15
Tenth Amendment, 282n4
Third parties: at administrative hearings, 17; executive enforcement and, 53–54
Title VI of 1964 Civil Rights Act, *Adams v. Richardson* and, 148–52, 153, 155, 156, 158, 162–63, 164, 166, 173
Title IX of Education Amendments of 1972, *Adams v. Richardson* and, 163–65, 166, 171
Tocqueville, Alexis de, 104
Tort Claims Act, 281n69
Tort liability, 71
Transportation Department, airbags and, 27
Tribe, Laurence, 50, 135–36
Trucking companies, suits by, 63
TVA v. Hill, 282n10

UAW v. Brock, 312n26
Unions, Occupational Safety and Health Administration and, 230, 231, 235–36, 238
U.S. v. Butler, 277n25, 282n4
U.S. Commission on Civil Rights, 151, 294n11
U.S. Court of Appeals for the District of Columbia Circuit, *see* D.C. Court of Appeals
U.S. ex. rel. Chicago Great Western R. Co. v. ICC, 277n24
U.S. District Court, *APHA* case and, 193–96
U.S. v. El-O-Pathic Pharmacy, 303n49
U.S. v. Morgan, 291n53
U.S. v. Richardson, 279n37, 312n24
U.S. Shipping Board, 88
United Steelworkers v. Weber, 283n16
USV Pharmaceutical Corp. v. Secretary of HEW, 302n27
USV Pharmaceuticals v. Weinberger, 302n27

321

Index

the
lyre
of
Science

Richard Minadeo is assistant professor of
Greek and Latin at Wayne State University.
He received his B.A. from Syracuse Univer-
sity (1951), and his M.S. and Ph.D. from the
University of Wisconsin (1956, 1965). Pro-
fessor Minadeo has published articles on
Lucretius in *Arion* and *Classical Journal*. He
is a member of the American Philological
Association, Classical Association of the Mid-
west and South, and the Detroit Classical
Association.

the
lyre
of
Science

FORM AND MEANING
IN LUCRETIUS'

De Rerum Natura

by RICHARD MINADEO

WAYNE STATE UNIVERSITY

Wayne State University Press

1969 *Detroit, Michigan*

for my parents
in memoriam

CONTENTS

Preface

The work that follows represents a somewhat revised version
of my doctoral dissertation accepted at the University of Wisconsin
in 1964. The main portion of Chapter II appeared in the autumn
1965 edition of *Arion* under the title, "The Formal Design of *De
Rerum Natura*," while sundry footnotes have been collected into
a paper entitled "Three Textual Problems in Lucretius," which is
available in the March 1968 issue of *The Classical Journal*. I
wish to thank the editors of both journals for their permission to
republish these materials.

With the understanding that all of its shortcomings and errors
are entirely my own responsibility, I should like to thank the following friends and scholars for their assistance in bringing the
present study to light: my dissertation director, Professor Paul L.
MacKendrick, who guided my researches with exquisite wisdom
and patience; Professor Ernest A. Fredricksmeyer of the University of Colorado, who read the revised M.S. with great care and

offered many invaluable suggestions; Professors Jacob E. Nyenhuis of Wayne State University and Herbert M. Howe, J. P. Heironimus, Paul C. Plass and Barbara H. Fowler of the University of Wisconsin, all of whom read the work at one stage or another of its development and offered valuable comment. I acknowledge special gratitude also to Mrs. Louise Hemsing of the Wayne State University Press for her painstaking editing of the text and, finally, for her unstinting enthusiasm, encouragement and assistance, *optimae uxori,* Dianna.

The prose translations appended to quoted passages are my own and are intended strictly as an aid to the Latinless reader. For the best poetic version of Lucretius available in English I refer the reader to W. E. Leonard's rendition in Everyman's Library.

R. M.

Detroit, Michigan
March 1968

I

The Leitmotif

The body of writing on *De Rerum Natura* which might reasonably be called literary criticism is small. Within it, no nearly thorough study of the work's positive art has ever been attempted. Indeed, despite its evident contribution to the understanding of, among others, Homer, Sophocles and Vergil in recent times, Lucretian scholars have remained all but indifferent to this manner of criticism. As a result, the form of the poem has been only barely and inadequately recovered and, where recovered, largely ignored. As for its meaning, by which I wish to imply its intended poetic import, not merely the aggregate factual significance of the scientific data which it contains, we have been brought nowhere near appreciating the fullness and finality with which it lies molded in the poem.

Instead, almost without exception where judgment is passed, we read grave imputations of poetic failure. Regenbogen, for instance, daring to invoke Lucretius' most open admirerer, contrasts the

"Erfüllung" of the *Georgics* to the *"Anlauf"* and *"Aufbruch"* of *De Rerum Natura,* a general lurching which, he says, is the product of its "uneven, jagged, jerky execution."[1] Schoder's criticism is fuller:

> The work is too spotty and uneven, its blend of magnificent poetic bursts with long arid tracts of lumbering prose (however resonant and pounding) too patently a mixture or even a colloid rather than a compound. The work is not a living whole animated throughout and to the depths of its being by a pervasive soul or spirit that is inherently *poetic.*[2]

He concludes with a suggestion that would perhaps be less puzzling if we possessed some other work or two by Lucretius: though *De Rerum Natura* is not a great poem, its author is yet a great poet. Even Sellar, for all the appreciation he otherwise brings to the poem, cannot grant it the stature of a thoroughly realized work of art: "If it be the condition of a great poem to produce the purest and noblest pleasure by its whole conception and execution, the poem of Lucretius fails to satisfy this condition."[3]

No confident dissent has arisen to this strain of criticism.[4] It prevails. Yet, clearly, it is hardly blameless. First, it presents at best a difficult view of the poet: he has about him a definite greatness; yet, his effectiveness is another matter; he can treat us to some of the most finely wrought poetry in Latin literature; but his art is inept: in the poem, the parts take their own disparate expression, the whole goes its own jagged way. Verses he could put together, then, but not verse. It should give us pause to recall that Cicero spoke highly of Lucretius' art.

Next, this criticism has contributed nothing of note to the advancement of Lucretian scholarship, not even on a matter so consistent with literary interest as the text. Lucretius' nineteenth century editors, because they found scant logical sequence in the poem as it stands, transposed its parts with an insouciance that is far to seek in classical scholarship.[5] No account was taken of poetic sequence. Unfortunately, our literary critics, since they have given no more positive thought to the matter of poetic texture than did the editors, have offered nothing to discourage their sort of textual license. Meanwhile, those studies which have availed to throw tolerable light on Lucretius' logic owe nothing to our critics.[6]

The final and most serious deficiency is a matter of method. These critics do not pretend that their findings are anything more than impressionistic. By every fair standard, therefore, they have succeeded only in raising the question of poetic unity and fulfillment. They have not solved it. Nor can it be said that they have investigated it in any fundamental way. First and foremost this would have required an open search of the entire poem for any and all positive traces of formative art and, as already noted, just this approach has been lacking.

It ought therefore not be very surprising that, once encountered on its own terms, the poetry invalidates all of the criticisms just noticed. It discloses an extraordinary concert of conception and execution, acquires an all-infusing poetic spirit of wonderful significance and even manages to turn to its own advantage those traces of jerkiness or jaggedness with which it may seem to be flawed. Finally, it produces pleasure indeed, but pleasure subordinated to the end for which it was specifically designed: instruction.

All of which is to say that *De Rerum Natura* is a fully realized poem of its own genre. Detailed proof can be adduced only gradually; a moment will suffice, however, to show the means by which Lucretius gathered the massive work into significant unity. Beginning with its hymn to Venus as the creative force in nature and closing with a long description of the Athenian plague, the work quite evidently sketches at its terminal points the cycle of creation and destruction in nature. Here is no small matter. It is precisely in an understanding of that cycle's relation to the poetry that Lucretius' plan, purpose and meaning come finally to light.

Lucretius is himself nearly explicit about the cycle's importance for his work. In lines 146–148 of Book I[7] (thus, at that very point where he expounds the poem's thesis) the poet states that the terror and ignorance of mind previously described is to be dispersed by *naturae species ratioque*. Implied is a unique capacity of this "outer form and inner law of nature" to bring such relief. He follows immediately with the declaration *principium cuius hinc nobis exordia sumet / nullam rem e nilo gigni divinitus umquam.* The proposition, then, that nothing ever arises from nothing by divine power is to be intimately construed with *naturae species ratioque* as part of its "first rule" or "principle"—*not* as part of the principle of *natura* alone, nor of *naturae ratio* alone, but of the full proposition: the outer form and inner law of nature.[8] Also to be stressed is that we have so far been given only a first installment (*exordia* gives the clue) on the *principium*. As an *exordium* on the paramount law of *ratio*, the proposition makes eminent sense. Its relation to *species*, however, remains obscure. The solution comes with line 215f. and the completion of the *principium: huc accedit uti quidque in sua corpora rursum / dissolvat natura neque ad nilum interemat res.* In the first proposition, I suggest, the crucial word is *gigni,* in the second *interemat;* the two propositions together, keyed as they are to birth and death, sketch the cycle of creation and destruction in nature, which plainly recommends itself as the fundamental principle of nature's *species* or "outer form."

Or, if this cycle does not constitute the *principium* of nature's *species* for Lucretius, what, then, does? The question resolves itself into a requirement that we find the outer form of nature otherwise and better represented in the two laws just quoted. It cannot be done. Accordingly, Lucretius discloses that, as the principle of *species,* the cycle has an important place in the poem's design.

A little thought shows that its promise for the work has two definable aspects. *Naturae species* itself can only denote nature in all of its observable details. This notion when placed side by side with *ratio* easily recalls a most fundamental Epicurean concept. The canonical Epicurean method for the investigation of nature proceeded from sensible natural phenomena to the unseen laws underlying them. *Species* and *ratio* fit the two ends of the process with more than reasonable clarity. At 146ff., therefore, Lucretius discloses that the method of natural investigation which he intends to use alone can illuminate reality. It follows that, since the cycle is the principle of *species,* its role in the poem's process of argument from the seen to the unseen must be very large. It obviously is. The very postulation of an atomic universe, after all, is unthinkable except on the basis of the observed occurrence of creation and destruction in nature.[9]

Significant as this function of the cycle may be, however, there is another implied in the same lines that is poetically far more important. First, it will be necessary to show that the cycle may reasonably have a function outside its part in the process of natural investigation. The likelihood is seen when we examine the two laws stated in the *principium*. They combine to establish the doctrine of the "conservation of matter" in nature. Surely, the centrality of this principle for the poem does not subsist merely in its being derived from observed phenomena. It is the foundation of the work's whole science. Similarly, the cycle is free to become, if it can, the work's fundamental poetry.

And, finally, does not Lucretius confirm it as such at 146ff.? When he discloses that *species* and *ratio* alone will dispel ignorance and fear, he perforce stipulates in the two terms the work's organic theme and subject.[10] *The work is poetry.* The two terms must therefore somehow predicate its organic poetry. On this side, *ratio* by itself surely offers nothing, and neither does the canonical method of natural investigation just noticed promise anything that is fundamentally poetic. This leaves only *species* and its basic principle, the cycle. In truth, it leaves essentially the cycle. For, obviously, the work's organic poetry starts not with line 146, but with the poem's beginning. Here the reader has found Venus, creation and (l. 10) the *species* of Spring: the first surge of the poem's first cycle. The cycle that the *principium* adumbrates, therefore, tends distinctly to confirm the Venus *exordium* already experienced as the deliberate first movement of the work's organic poetry.

Considered with care, then, Lucretius' very thesis yields the poem's deliberate design. Nor is this the whole of its content. By the poet's declaration, it is *species* together with *ratio* that will solve man's ignorance and fear. At first, the role of *species* in the process of natural investigation may appear to account sufficiently for its contribution to the poem's final doctrine. It is perilously easy, however, to underrate the doctrinal possibilities of nature's "outer form." Given the Epicurean view of the universe, it is clear that *ratio* can be reached through *species* only because the latter is a direct and inevitable result of the former. Indeed, this is the fundamental relation between the two. One (*species*), then, is the direct natural expression of the other and, in terms of doctrinal value, can be expected to carry precisely an *expressive* force. That is to say, the lessons which nature's laws have to teach will express themselves inevitably in phenomenal, sensible nature. Didactically, this is of the utmost advantage. Theory (*ratio*) becomes practice (*species*), and the theory's didactic content is made available through the senses at every turn in daily life. *Species,* then, is nothing less than the doctrinal completion of *ratio* and, as such, wonderfully justifies the high place which Lucretius accords it in the poem's didactic scheme. It follows that the cycle as the poetically dominant principle of *species*—as, in fact, that visible product of *ratio* which subsumes and orders all of *species* in its unending flow—is offered a potentially momentous role in the poem's didactic process. Such a development, it is clear, would make for an impressive concert of form and meaning. We shall later see that precisely this is what develops.

Much of course depends on the extent to which Lucretius implants the cycle in the poem. It is everywhere. Aside from the great circle which, starting with Venus, closes in the plague, the same creative Venus gives way to those *quorum tellus complectitur ossa* (l. 135) at the close of the first proem and to a *destructive* Venus at the termination of the fourth book. Besides, the first, second and third books end on notes, however different, of destruction, while, if we but look, we will readily detect that Books III, IV, V, and VI begin, like Book I, on the formal theme of creation. As for the body of the poem, we need merely wait a bit to see how a nearly unbroken series of the same cycle of birth and death runs through it all—dogma and polemic, eulogy and satire, metaphor and image —from beginning to end.

To sum up, then, a signal clue to the form of *De Rerum Natura* lies in the specific meaning of its very thesis. On Lucretius' own testimony, the clue to the form provides a fundamental key to the poem's meaning as well, for, by his declaration, it is *species* (and, therefore, principally the cycle) together with *ratio* that will solve

14

man's ignorance and dissolve his fears. The cycle, which is, of course, the poem's formative principle, is thus intimately fused with the work's science; more, it is in its own right a definite part —as we shall later see, a most important part—of the science.

There is one thing further, and this we are already in a position to see. The work itself, since it contains as its own internal substance the dynamic inner processes of nature and wears nature's own dynamic outer form—since it therefore imitates *naturae species ratioque* in operative process—becomes, in effect, nature herself. *In effect*. But it is the effect that matters.

So much, I trust, is enough to suggest that the poem shows a high degree of order and integrity and that, in missing the whole of it, Regenbogen, Schoder and Sellar have radically failed poet and reader alike. If we were to inquire which school of criticism has done the least justice to Lucretius, however, we would find that Sellar and Schoder, at any rate, have been surpassed in their failure. These scholars have had the virtue of accepting the poem as it is and of treating it as an entity. As a result, though they have failed to uncover its essential design, they have at least responded intelligently or obtusely enough to the actual poetry to incite others to fuller and better efforts. I submit, for example, that no one can read Sellar without acquiring a deeper appreciation of how majestically nature comes to life beneath Lucretius' descriptive genius. Once possessed of this grandeur, which we must recognize as a deliberate effect of the poetry, we need merely probe for the technical sources and controls of its expression to come into the poem's vital center. Schoder, meanwhile, wakens us to the poem's greatness by very means of his rare insensibility. "Lumbering prose" indeed. These critics, then, have lent their modest parts to a final sound critical estimate of the work, and we ought not begrudge them their contribution.

But another mode of criticism has arisen to distort the body of the poem into a grotesque dissemblance of its true self, and to this we owe only our astonishment. I speak of the search for an *"Urlukrez,"* a quest for the sequence of composition of the poem's various books and, thereupon, an earlier, substantially different plan of the work. It is true that this sort of study has shown lofty results in connection with works of various authorship composed over an extended period of time. The purpose it was meant to achieve in regard to Lucretius, however, is difficult to guess.[11] Plainly, he did write *De Rerum Natura,* and that within his own lifetime. Moreover, in the absence of any clear understanding of the poem's plan as it stands, what intelligent end is served by the discovery of a more ancient, abandoned one? Surely we cannot assume that the rejected plan would have determined the new? But anyone who has even scanned this literature is aware that its authors are little interested in any plan of the work, past or present, if we define the word as a proposed meaningful poetic entity. In fact, the poetry itself plays almost no part in their investigations. Rather, it is the number of enjambments, the bald sum of backward references, the presence or absence of Memmius or of passages of logical transition—in a word, statistics—that are made to possess the secrets of art. The final objection to their approach is that, assuming the poet had any proper prospectus in mind for his work at all, the order of composition need not in the least reflect the intended sequence of books within the plan. That is, Lucretius may have written the sixth book first and the first last without dreaming of allowing the last to appear first in the published poem. But the main objection is our initial one. The present plan and the principle behind it is the only important matter. Indeed, if these scholars had found the principle, they would have discovered that Lucretius never entertained any intention except to execute the poem on the lines of the cycle of creation and destruction in nature. Given this, the order of composition signifies nothing, while any sound evidence of an intended different arrangement of the books is meaningful only insofar as a rejected ordering of the cycle's poetic evolution can have meaning. Be this little or much, the poem as it is ought not to have been abandoned for a course of analysis that would never have attained it.[12]

There are four writers who may be said to have brought some essential illumination to the poem as we have it. The first, but least is the Italian scholar Alfredo Menzione.[13] One of Menzione's leading merits is his boldness to assert that the key to Lucretius lies in the form, or, as he prefers to style it, the "physiognomy" of the poem. As it happens, his margin of error in estimating the form is at once hair-thin and immeasurable. He can, for instance, close his study with the exhilirating assertion that the essence of the poem consists in the continuity of a flowing (*"fluire"*) which reproduces the flux of existence itself, without having at all proven the point according to the actual movement of the poetry. As we shall see, however, the cause of his spectacular miss was not itself spectacular; his point of departure, his very inspiration were not impartial; his analysis was not strictly formal.

Menzione is aware of the cycles of birth and death in the poem, but only where they are most explicit (he too complains of "desert tracts" in Lucretius), and those of which he is aware are not allowed to stand by themselves as structural elements. Instead, they are miscalled a flow or rhythm of life (rather than birth) and death and, so mistaken, absorbed into a higher scheme of an alternating flow between optimism and pessimism, which, Menzione asserts, constitutes the poem's true physiognomy.[14]

Now, in terms of their formal potential for this poem, the difference between an anthithesis of birth and death and one of life and death is enormous. The first pair stand as the simple, if awesome, terminal facts of life. As such, they of course inspire emotions, but emotions controlled by a rational appreciation of the process of which they are parts. Add to this emotional governance the great store of rhythm inherent in the process, and we have formative elements of supreme poetic potential. But life and death, forming, as they ultimately do, a static and imponderable antithesis, cannot perform such rhythmical and rational work. Where in our imaginative experience, we may ask, is that "flow" between life and death which Menzione so easily asserts? If we presume to see it in the constant rise and fall of things, we are, like Menzione, giving this process a wrong name. Otherwise, we are soon left with the strict propositions of existence and nonexistence, and between these there is no sensible reciprocal movement, no ready music. As for the rational side, the one cannot be placed over against the other without the intrusion of mystery, or even of the tremendous —hence, even of fear. As such, of course, the pair crucially enter the poem, but, plainly, as influences needing formation and control, rather than as formative, controlling forces. Hence, though Menzione may serve his own thesis well by his use of life and death (one *can* affirm by life and deny by death) he asks us to believe, in effect, that Lucretius set out to control his poem by means of those very human failings which the poem itself seeks to govern and even eradicate.

Very much the same objection holds true for the higher business of optimism and pessimism. Clearly, these casts of mind alternating to no set design throughout the work could only viciously serve Epicureanism and its promised *ataraxia*. If death is pessimism and the poem ends in horrendous plague, where are we, the readers, made to end? What new rational apprehension of the *omne* have we attained? Numerous further objections are ready at hand against such an interpretation of Lucretius' design. I shall bring just one. We have already seen that this optimism-pessimism conplex can hardly govern the poem. The next question is whether Lucretius governed it or it him. Menzione does not answer. We shall learn in a minute that he had no means of answering well. Nor, indeed, would we need to trouble ourselves to answer for him were it not our place to defend any just claim the poet might have had to philosophical competence. Such extremes of emotional and intellectual response to the processes of the universe—such mere moods and infantile changes of mood—cannot but reflect an unstable, distracted, even pathetically overmastered vision of things, a condition certainly lethal to philosophy and poetry alike. In the end, therefore, Menzione brings us not a whit closer to an understanding of the true Lucretius than we had been before.

Ironically, the blame for his misfathoming the work's actual *"fluire"* lies with the very inspiration without which he would not have detected one at all. The matter, though we digress, will be worth our pursuit, since it will lead to yet another mode of deficient criticism and so complete our melancholy tableau of the responses that have for so long failed Lucretius' poetic genius.

Toward the end of his work, where he undertakes an apologetic analysis of the poetry's "inner form," Otto Regenbogen, the same whom we earlier met, sets down a series of tensions or conflicts which he discerns both in Lucretius and in his poetry.[15] A few examples are internal tensions between Homer and Epicurus, *ratio* and *amor*, anti-religion and religiosity. Optimism and pessimism as such are not included; yet, we may be sure from his numerous admiring citations of that scholar that Menzione's chief inspiritor was Regenbogen. It is not surprising, therefore, that he failed to penetrate to the essential *De Rerum Natura*.[16]

For these "tensions," far from connecting with anything inward in the poem, are gleaned effortlessly from its topmost level and, if judged rightly, reflect more on the man than on his work. They are, if anything, impediments of personality or of persuasion which stand between the man and the execution of his purpose, and the critic's task, if he feels he must treat them, is to demonstrate how the poet overcomes their hindrance to emerge with his purpose fulfilled: the finished work, the ingredient impulses resolved in a harmony of meaning. Else, he must show how he fails. What is more, it is imperative especially in regard to this work, if we seem to detect such conflicts, to seek the executed design first. For, besides the failure of his poetry, every one implies a failure of the poet's own Epicureanism.[17] This being so, nothing could be more unjust than to entertain them as the end, rather than the occasion of critical labors. Yet, precisely this has happened again and again. A still celebrated, but misleading work, for instance, is Patin's *Anti-Lucrèce Chez Lucrèce,* where the poet is represented to be in dubious conflict with Epicurean theological principles. Even Klingner[18] cannot explain Lucretius without recourse to a second, darker, tenaciously resisting side. And what handbook does not speak of his pervasive melancholy or of his pessimism, or his morbidity or violence, of one or all, although every one is an imputation of failure? *Nequiquam,* as our poet would say. There is a design to this work, delicately considered and beautifully implemented, which makes mirages of them all.

But to have finally done with Menzione, he has surpassed the rest by suggesting the presence of a meaningful new rhythm in the poem. This is the sum of his contribution; and, in sum, he was entirely right and all wrong.

The next two writers are men of a decidedly different inclination.

One reason for the relative insufficiency of work done on Lucretius' poetry is the fact that *De Rerum Natura* happens to be our chief source for the content of the Epicurean philosophy. Yet (to state an ambivalent case) we have as a result of this circumstance gained in philosophy fully as much as we have lost in poetry. The gain derives largely from the efforts of the poem's various editors. Invited to occupy themselves predominantly with the poem's philosophical substance, they have gone about the task with admirable acumen and patience, with the result that for the student who wants a detailed exposition of the system, along with a judicious estimate of its relation to other ancient philosophies, their works remain the indispensable point of departure. Still, in the hands of these scholars the philosophy remains merely a skein of systematic thought—complete, orderly and detailed enough, but conspicuously lacking that urgent, vision-breeding inner spirit that alone can turn philosophy into superior poetry. Such a spirit inheres in the philosophy nonetheless, and, as the event would suggest, it perhaps eluded our editors because they were not philosophers in their own right. At any rate, the two students of Lucretius who have detected it can both lay just claim to that title. Both are able to present the philosophy as a living entity; and it is in great part due to their insight that we may now discern a thorough harmony of philosophic and poetic impulses in the poem.

The pair, Henri Bergson and George Santayana,[19] each in a study of Epicurean physics and ethics as they figure in Lucretius, arrive at closely related conclusions as to the core inspiration that the poet found in Epicureanism. As seen by both, it is intimately and necessarily connected with the cycle of creation and destruction in nature. To Bergson the absolute rigidity of the laws underlying the cycle (in Lucretius' terms, *ratio*) appears the dominant element:

> Everything consists and has always consisted solely of atoms, and changes in the arrangement of atoms; atoms move on, eternally and inexorably; definite, changeless laws must govern the birth, growth and decay of things caught up and squeezed from every direction by the tight bond of necessity. And inspired by what he assumes to be

the basic idea of Epicureanism, Lucretius discovers that while natural phenomena appear to follow no set plan, their infinite variety actually masks the movement of atoms in predetermined directions and the uniform force of immutable laws.[20]

Santayana rather emphasizes the cycle (*species*) itself:

This double experience of mutation and recurrence [death and birth], an experience at once sentimental and scientific, soon brought with it a very great thought, perhaps the greatest thought that mankind has ever hit upon, and which was the chief inspiration of Lucretius. It is that all we observe about us, and ourselves also, may be so many passing forms of a permanent substance. This substance, while remaining the same in quantity and inward quality, is constantly redistributed; in its redistribution it forms those aggregates which we call things, and which we find constantly disappearing and reappearing. All things are dust and to dust they return; a dust, however, eternally fertile, and destined to fall perpetually into new, and doubtless beautiful forms.[21]

When we place the two views together (for thus, surely, they belong) and so grasp the full revelation that Epicurean physics held for Lucretius—the vision of eternal substance eternally modifying its distribution in response to timeless, unchanging laws—we find the exact point where the philosophy becomes poetry. After this point which, as we have seen, is Lucretius' point of departure, the two never diverge. There is no poetry without philosophy in the work, no philosophy without poetry. There is only *naturae species ratioque,* the poetry and the philosophy, unfolding smoothly to their promised end.

In a general way, Bergson recognizes the poetic potential in the philosophical insight he describes:

. . . the indisputable fact is that the theory of atoms offers a poetic conception of the universe . . . Countless atoms that by virtue of immutable laws regularly move across boundless space, worlds that are constantly being shaped and destroyed, vast streams that are created by the calm and measured

21

course of events determined by inexorable natural laws—
all that is certainly enough to capture and enslave an
imagination even less vivid than his.[22]

This, no doubt, is a detailed enough exposition of the poetry to suit
the purposes of his study, but it withholds all the specifics of
Lucretius' art, and it is in these, as I have implied, that the full
impact of the work, including, of course, its philosophy, takes
shape.

Santayana, ranging further, even briefly gets down to questions
of form. Where he does so, however, he becomes, after a sound
start, effeminate and superficial. His suggested ending for the
poem gives the key to his general approach:

> If the poem had ever been finished, and Lucretius had
> wished to make the end chime with the beginning, and
> represent, as it were, one great cycle of the world, it is
> conceivable that he might have placed at the close a mythical
> passage to match that at the beginning; and we might have
> seen Mars aroused from his luxurious lethargy, reasserting
> his immortal nature, and rushing, firebrand in hand, from
> the palace of love to spread destruction throughout the
> universe, till all things should burn fiercely, and be consumed
> together.[23]

The language here is guarded enough to suggest that Santayana
was not confident of such an ending; but this item aside, the very
fact that he offers it for our consideration discloses serious flaws in
his understanding of Lucretius' art.

The comment has virtue too, however, and we ought to recognize this first. Since Santayana views Mars as the central symbol of
destruction in *De Rerum Natura*,[24] such an ending as he suggests
would fit the fundamental design of the poem. He has therefore
been the first to imply that the natural cycle of creation and
destruction is the work's logical organic formal motif; the implication, as we can see, derives directly from his observations on the
philosophy and thus, so far, his analysis has been brilliantly conceived.

Henceforth, however, he fails us. As we shall later observe, there is no possible different ending for the poem than the one we have. The reason is that, given the commitments and objectives of Lucretius' art, no ending chimes better with the beginning—and with every other element and segment of the poem—than the present one. We have not yet seen enough of the art's objectives to cite them as evidence; its commitments, however, should already be sufficiently clear to point the error of Santayana's formal concept. The essence of that nature which Lucretius was bound to portray is raw, wild, full of violent motion and furious change. The technique required to represent it had, first of all, of course, to accommodate these qualities; more, since the vehicle was poetry, it had to effect a dramatic movement of the whole. Now, since by the poet's admission it is precisely elemental nature herself who is to teach us, the dramatic movement must be nature's own; or, stated more fully, the revelation and evolution of her own energies within the poem must themselves provide a dramatic development toward a didactic end. This could only be accomplished by an increasingly more intense revelation of the significance of nature's brute inner energies for mankind, the whole culminating in the sum of her might in human terms and the sum of its moral significance. Just this is what happens in the poem. I present it, however, not as what happens but as what had to happen, given Lucretius' formal needs and commitments. At the very least, then, the work's entire formal concept demanded a progressive, compelling accumulation of inner power toward a *natural* denouement. Hence, on principles of form, the insistence throughout on vivid, sometimes violent and tortured, preludes and cadenzas, each a movement of *naturae species,* all mounting inexorably toward the consummate natural and human horror of the plague; hence the dearth of apposite, matching sketches, quiet equipoise, rigid symmetries; and hence the impossibility of Santayana's suggested close. It chains the end to the beginning with silken fetters. Removed from nature and man, looking backward, it culminates nothing that is essential, teaches nothing climactic.[25] It is a sheer formality. Santayana, rather than a gruelling exploration of the mortal condition, offers us in *De Rerum Natura* almost a pastoral idyll.

We must remember, nonetheless, that neither he nor Bergson was principally concerned with the work's poetic lines. Their central interest and contribution was philosophical; and the fact that, coming this way, they, and Santayana in particular, approached as closely as they did to the genuine poetry redounds impressively to their credit. Even more so, of course, the credit is Lucretius', since it was he who blended poetry and science so perfectly together.

Only one critic, Elizabeth M. McLeod, has caught sight of both the poem's formative principle and its relation to Lucretius' didactic purpose.[26] On either side, it is true, Miss McLeod's analysis is sketchy. Her study itself is curiously uneven, beginning with an aimless series of definitions of some ordinary poetic tropes and closing with a sudden burst of insight into the poem's essential movement. The last, however, is enough to make it the most revealing critique of the poem yet published.

Let us first clear the way of its flaws. Miss McLeod has not demonstrated significantly more of the cycle's actual presence than Santayana. Except for the first, she entirely misses the creation theme in the proems; she has not discerned the implication of *naturae species ratioque;* and the evolution of the cycle within the several books goes all unnoticed.

She does detect the theme of destruction at the end of Books I, II, III, IV and VI, however, and from the Venus-plague cycle she draws conclusions of deep import. Foremost, she has the sense to declare the poem completed with the scene of the plague. Her reasons have weight. On the side of form, it is true, she does no better than to note the "artistic balance" which the scene establishes over against *Venus creatrix;* but let us hear her observations on Lucretius' motives: "The final impact of the plague is the inevitability of death for all created things . . . ";[27] and, "It is Lucretius' final appeal to his reader's sensibilities. For if they refuse to accept the Epicurean explanation of the fact of inescapable death with every fiber of their being, all the preparation and instruction for achieving human happiness, so painstakingly presented in the body of the poem, will go for nought."[28] Though these statements capture but a corner of the plague's mighty significance and are, at that, only its negative expression, their suggestion that the work's poetry—its cycle—itself has moment for the central theme of the dread of death represents something spectacularly new in Lucretian criticism. They are the first reasoned hint of a crucial harmony between the poem's design and its philosophical argument, its form and meaning. It is the start of a true criticism.

More fully perhaps than anything else, our survey has disclosed a failure on the part of Lucretius' critics to discern the nexus of internal cycles in the poem. Meanwhile, beyond indicating the poet's implied promise to deliver them as part of *naturae species,* I have not myself furnished definite evidence of their existence. The time is appropriate, then, for a reasoned proof. Lines 615–23 of Book III offer the occasion:

> Denique cur animi numquam mens consiliumque
> gignitur in capite aut pedibus manibusve, sed unis
> sedibus et certis regionibus omnibus haeret,
> si non certa loca ad nascendum reddita cuique
> sunt, et ubi quicquid possit durare creatum
> atque ita multimodis partitis artubus esse,
> membrorum ut numquam exsistat praeposterus ordo?
> usque adeo sequitur res rem neque flamma creari
> fluminibus solitast neque in igni gignier algor.

> Moreover, why do the intellect and judgment never come into being in the head, hands or feet, but remain fixed for all men in particular seats and places determined, if not because precise locations are allotted to all things for their birth, places where each, once created, may endure and have its several components so ordered that their arrangement is never haphazard? To such a degree does the law of harmony maintain in things, nor is flame customarily generated in running water nor ice born of fire.

This passage, which we must take to represent a self-contained proof for the mortality of the soul, has long troubled scholars and will be found bracketed in some texts. Bailey sums up its difficulties by observing that it interrupts the sequence of thought and lacks a formal conclusion. Both charges can be extenuated. First, the passage is a part of a long section (ll. 548–669) keyed to the structural connection of body and soul; hence, there is at least a thematic sequence. Besides, though the implication of the lines—that the mind's proper seat is the human breast—is not expressly stated, it is easily inferred from the theme itself. There is therefore no doubt as to the completeness of the thought. But even if, supplying a further inference, we understand the passage to mean that the mind, since it is tied to the body, cannot exist apart from it and is therefore mortal, we have not come up with anything new in the way of a proof for its mortality. Rather, after all our free construal, the passage remains merely an echo of the whole section and in some ways even of the whole book. Since Lucretius nowhere else works us so hard for such trivial profit, we shall do well to seek the passage's essential purpose outside of the specific argument which it carries.

Book III furnished Lucretius a peculiar formal problem in that its substance, the case for the soul's mortality, was by nature parsimonious of the creation theme. At no point is the difficulty so apparent as in this section. For the space of more than one-hundred-and-fifty lines prior to our passage there is no firm representation of the theme; nor does it again appear till forty-seven lines thereafter. Over two-hundred vacant lines, on the basis of its frequency elsewhere, would have made for an unparalleled suspension of theme. Now, seeing that the present passage contains no less than five thematic words (*gignitur, nascendum, creatum, creari, gignier*) and cannot justify itself on other grounds, can we doubt that its principal *raison d'être* was to feed these words to the reader's senses and so renew the thematic flow? Granting this, we must allow that there is an internal scheme of cycles.

Only at this point in the poem will the reader discover a forcible imposition of form on substance—or, if you will, a "purple patch." True, we shall find in a few other places that the substance has refused to submit to force, but the results are nowhere serious. Such nearly flawless execution is foremost a testimony to the poet's skill; it testifies also, however, to the work's great felicity of form, the propriety of its design to its substance. Of that propriety's many aspects we have already glimpsed two of the highest importance. It allows the poem of nature to wear nature's own dress, and it permits a smooth fusion of poetry and philosophy. One more, perhaps the most significant of all, awaits our notice. *De Rerum Natura* is nothing if not a didactic poem, and, clearly, when Lucretius imparts that the natural cycle shall itself be our teacher, he makes a high claim for its didactic aptness. Where does this aptness lie?

Poetry that is meant to be didactic must be first of all poetic. Accordingly, if the cycle is to instruct us it needs intrinsic poetic virtue. This it has. We have previously noted the strong sense of movement that it imparts; within the movement, also, there arises a spontaneous feeling of measure; further, its store of imagery is as unlimited as the *omne* itself; and in the measured movement of the imagery which, building and unbuilding worlds and men, orders the sensuous response, there inheres a compelling dramatic appeal; man being the dramatic center, there is emotional force; finally, given the spontaneous dramatic rhythm as a fostering over-theme, the skillful poet can hardly fail to create in the sound and measure of the verse a rich and abundant music. In short, such poetry as the cycle allows is not only worthy of the name; it may well be the secret cadence of all poetry.

Next, all that is good for the poetry—the movement, the drama, the rhythm—is good for its didactic function. Being moved and involved, we attend to our lesson. Nor is the fact of the cycle an abstruse or indifferent matter; it is immediate, familiar and enormously pertinent. Every pedagogue knows the value of the next quality. There is reiteration; and, happily, since this continuous regathering of force works as keenly for the poetry as for its didactic burden, there is no risk of boredom. Even the indispensable Epicurean requirement that all truth must enter through the senses is perfectly served by the cycle, since its whole poetic and didactic force springs from its appeal to our senses. Completing all, the fact of the cycle carries the supreme didactic bonus of intellectual conviction. To paraphrase Santayana, it comprises perhaps the greatest truth ever discovered; and to teach from truth is superlative felicity.

The poem's moment of genesis, then, would seem to have been that instant when Lucretius first found the cycle lying ready at hand in the philosophy itself as his work's logical formal-didactic principle. If it were so, no case for original genius could be more convincing. It is probably not so, however. The fragments of Empedocles disclose evidence too striking to dismiss that he used the cycle in much the same formal manner as Lucretius.[29] In view of Lucretius' reverential familiarity with the works of Empedocles, therefore, we cannot but suspect that he derived the formal concept from his predecessor.

If such borrowing appears to diminish Lucretius' glory as an original poet, it fully redeems the loss by recommending him more than ever as an original philosopher. Epicurus, as far as we can make out, did not anywhere employ the cycle as a principle of doctrine. In his extant writings it does not figure at all. For Lucretius, as we shall see, it provides half the doctrine. As a result the philosophy in his hands is not only more vivid, but transfigured, new; and, since we have descried a source for the cycle other than Epicurus, it becomes all the more likely that the Epicureanism which Lucretius expounds is his own philosophical construct—not one in any way inconsistent with the master's doctrine, but nevertheless a materially expanded version. Its author, then, may certainly be considered a philosopher in his own right.

The poetic reflections of Empedocles raise the question of Lucretius' own influence. It is a matter of some importance. If adaptations of the poem's fundamental design can reasonably be discerned in the works of Lucretius' Roman successors, the case for the design itself becomes all the more convincing. We need look no further, I think, than to Lucretius' two greatest successors in Roman letters.

Ode I, 4 of Horace begins with references to Spring and Venus and ends with moral reflections on the inevitability of death. What is more notable is that, as Commager explains, it is precisely and exclusively the ode's implicit play on the cycle of creation and destruction that gives it poetic unity.[30] Horace's moral inferences, of course, are very different from Lucretius', but the poetic matrix is strikingly the same.

If this were the place for a detailed study of a second lengthy didactic masterpiece, an even stronger case could be made for the formal influence of *De Rerum Natura* on Vergil's *Georgics*. In any event, the citation of a few eminent structural similarities may recommend the likelihood. The climactic image in the *Georgics*— bees generated spontaneously from putrefying carcasses—unmistakably suggests an essential reflex in the Lucretian cycle: from death birth naturally proceeds. Earlier, and especially in Book III, there are evidences of the cycle even more Lucretian. The third book opens with Vergil's self-celebration as creator. This, as we shall soon see, is exactly the note on which Lucretius commences the second half of his own poem.[31] Later (ll. 242–88) comes a passage describing the destructive force of *amor,* and the book ends with a description of plague. The two themes are used by Lucretius to close, respectively, Books IV and VI.

At beginning and end, then, Book III of *Georgics* conforms to the pattern of the cycle. So, in structural design, does the whole poem. Its first words, *quid faciat laetas segetes,* evoke the creative potential of nature—the same note upon which the poem ends. Then, after the invocation of numerous fostering deities (among them *alma Ceres* and *inventrix Minerva* instantly recall Lucretius' *alma Venus genetrix*), Augustus is addressed, to be hinted at as a kind of fosterer of harvests in his own right (l. 27). Immediately thereupon *materna myrto* calls forth Venus herself. Finally, as the introduction draws to a close, a switch of attention to Tartarus, as to Orcus and Acheron in *De Rerum Natura* (ll. 115, 120) completes the poem's first great structural cycle. Vergil's opening words after the introduction (*vere . . . novo,* l. 44) starts the movement anew. Book I ends on the theme of Rome's civil war, not merely a motif of destruction, but one chosen with obvious care to counterbalance the opening theme. Book II commences with an invocation of Bacchus (*pater* his thematic epithet), another fostering deity, and closes once again (ll. 539–40) on the note of war. The last book begins less distinctly than the others on the motif of creation, but Mackail has surely captured the burden of the first words in translating, "Now I will advance to heaven-born honey, the gift of air." All four books, then, begin and close on thematic hints of the cycle.

Vastly more of the theme lies within the poem, but all of this we must forego. Let it suffice to say, pending the reader's own verification, that there is enough of the cycle in the *Georgics* to postulate an organic movement similar to that of *De Rerum Natura*. Nor would it all be a matter merely of form. For, whatever the symbolism of the last book may be otherwise, the climactic image of rebirth must surely signify the regeneration of Augustan Rome from the ruin of civil war.[32] Given an internal pattern of the cycle, this emblematic deliverance becomes as never before the climactic expression of the work's organic trend.[33]

II

The Great Design

The biographical tradition on Titus Lucretius Carus is meager indeed, and those notices that are at all striking are both late in source and so compromising as to seem the work of a master ironist. As the result of a love potion, the tradition runs, the poet went insane, composed *De Rerum Natura* during intervals of lucidity and ultimately committed suicide. Save for the miracle of the poem itself, there is plainly nothing here that reflects the promised fruits of the Epicurean ethical life; and the fact that the poem was written, it must be stressed, is the one item in the story for which we have any evidence except the biographer's word. I shall not be the first to suggest that the tradition is suspicious enough to demand the most careful circumspection.

Yet, surely, nothing has more impeded critical progress on *De Rerum Natura* than these few scraps of biographical data. First, predictably enough, they have distracted a great deal of scholarly interest from poem to poet, which is rarely a promising circumstance. But their deeper bane has been something more subtle. Most of the small body of criticism that has come forth on Lucretius speaks ever and again of antimony, discontinuity, conflict and confusion. I submit that the biographical tradition more than anything else has inspired this obvious critical preoccupation with impressions of disorder. Here the entire question of Lucretius' private life will be given a wide berth. It is after all irrelevant enough. Now as ever, only his art can finally illuminate his poetry.

This study, in concerning itself with the form of *De Rerum Natura,* aims at revealing not only the chief traits of Lucretius' art, but also the work, proximate and ultimate, performed by the art. It aims, that is, at recovering the poem's meaning as defined, through the medium of its art, by its form. The present chapter will deal first with the work's over-all design and then with a few of the techniques employed by the poet to implement that same design throughout the body of the poem. Book by book, the succeeding chapter will reveal and analyze the design thus implemented. So much will furnish a working familiarity with the poem's form and thereby prepare us for the final chapter, a statement of its meaning as established by the form.

If we may for the moment assume, and later prove, a point that is in grave doubt, namely, that *De Rerum Natura* leaves off quite where Lucretius intended it to close, the problem of winning our way to the poem's grand design will be considerably facilitated. Such an approach may appear to place last things first; but a moment's reflection will show that, even if the poem's intended ending were our primary concern, we could not establish it except on the basis of the poem's intended design. Hence, besides all justification, there is urgent need to penetrate to the design as simply and directly as possible.

Book I of our poem begins with an invocation of Venus as the creative force in nature; Book VI, the poem's last, closes with a lengthy description of the ruinous Athenian plague. The two passages together, aided, to be sure, by a slight dash of imagination, clearly describe the cycle of creation and destruction in nature. This cycle of creation and destruction, supported by numerous others of parallel figure, provides the poem with its formal design.

Reasonably careful study will show that the proems and closes of almost all the individual books conform to the cyclical pattern of the whole. In addition to Book VI, Books I, II, III and IV close pointedly on the theme of destruction; meanwhile, Books III, IV, V and VI, though not so manifestly as Book I in this respect, start on the theme of creation. Thus, only the beginning of II and the close of V fail to participate in the leitmotif—for such it is—of the cycle. The reasons for these omissions, significant reasons indeed, will be more feasibly treated later on.

Let us get some of these passages before us; first, as a matter of convenience, those dealing with death or destruction. Book I, cutting thereby a nice antithesis with its Venus invocation, closes with a portrait of universal cataclysm. Unfortunately, a lacuna of eight lines bars us from seeing how the passage was introduced and may even purloin a part of the description. Even as they stand, however, the verses deliver their formal burden with magnificent finality:

> ne volucri ritu flammarum moenia mundi
> diffugiant subito magnum per inane soluta
> et ne cetera consimili ratione sequantur
> neve ruant caeli tonitralia templa superne
> terraque se pedibus raptim subducat et omnis
> inter permixtas rerum caelique ruinas
> corpora solventis abeat per inane profundum,
> temporis ut puncto nil extet reliquiarum
> desertum praeter spatium et primordia caeca.
> nam quacumque prius de parti corpora desse
> constitues, haec rebus erit pars ianua leti.
> hac se turba feras dabit omnis materiai.

$$(I, 1102–13)^1$$

. . . lest, swift as flame, the walls of the world fall apart, suddenly dissolved through the vast void, and all else follow in the same manner, and lest the thundering tracts of sky collapse and the land, swooning beneath our feet, vanish through the deep void amid the murderous wrack of earth and sky, so that in an instant nothing remain behind besides space and the invisible atoms. For wherever you suppose the bodies of matter are first insufficient, this side will be the door of death for things. Here will the whole mass of matter rush forth.

Book II closes on the more famous, more fatalistic, *grandis arator* passage. The passage's theme (decline and death) is clinched, and Venus once more antithesized, in the last two verses by a grim reminder on the sure mortality of things.

> iamque caput quassans grandis suspirat arator
> crebrius, incassum magnos cecidisse labores,
> et cum tempora temporibus praesentia confert
> praeteritis, laudat fortunas saepe parentis.
> tristis item vetulae vitis sator atque vietae
> temporis incusat momen saeclumque fatigat,
> et crepat, antiquum genus ut pietate repletum
> perfacile angustis tolerarit finibus aevum,
> cum minor esset agri multo modus ante viritim.
> nec tenet omnia paulatim tabescere et ire
> ad capulum spatio aetatis defessa vetusto.
>
> (II, 1164–74)[2]

Now the aged farmer, shaking his head, sighs again and again that his mighty labors have perished emptily, and when he compares the present times with days gone by, he often lauds his father's blessings. And, too, the planter of the gnarled, ancestral vine assails the trend of the times, condemns the age and mutters to reflect how the good men of old, when each man's acreage was much smaller than now, made an easy living from a tiny plot. But he does not comprehend that everything is decaying bit by bit and proceeds to the grave, done in by its failing lease on life.

The close of Book III—the *nil igitur mors est ad nos* section (ll. 830–1094)—fits so clearly into the pattern of the cycle as to need no citation. We should note before passing, however, the careful progression made in these three terminal passages from the abstract notice of destruction at the close of Book I, through II's more personalized, though yet ruminative recollection of mortality to the utterly direct confrontation with death in the great cadenza[3] of Book III. It is a definitely climactic progression,[4] and, on the one side, as we are led to expect by its deadly pursuit of the individual, it climaxes with the triumph of mortality over man. This conquest is made explicit several times within the cadenza, but nowhere more distinctly than at its close:

> nec prorsum vitam ducendo demimus hilum
> tempore de mortis nec delibare valemus,
> quo minus esse diu possimus forte perempti.
> proinde licet quot vis vivendo condere saecla;
> mors aeterna tamen nilo minus illa manebit,
> nec minus ille diu iam non erit, ex hodierno
> lumine qui finem vitai fecit, et ille,
> mensibus atque annis qui multis occidit ante.

> We take away not an instant from the duration of death by prolonging life, nor can we diminish its span a trice, so as to be less long dead. So put behind you as many generations as you like. Death everlasting will await you all the same. Nor will the man who expires with this day's light more briefly cease to be than he who died many months and years ago.

This resolution, however, contains its own counter-resolution; for it is precisely because death triumphs over the individual that the individual triumphs over the superstitious fear of death; hence, when Lucretius says "death therefore is nothing to us," the *igitur* rests both upon the proofs of the soul's mortality set forth in the body of Book III and upon the force of the progression in the terminal passages under study. To put this last even more precisely, the whole weight of the poem's cyclical movement up to this point, by stressing the unavoidable onset of mortality, builds toward this peculiar triumph of man in III's close. By any standard, it is all scrupulously well made, and, considering besides the art the magnitude of the triumph itself (*nil . . . mors est ad nos*) as it pertains both to the philosophy and to the doctrinal objectives of the poem, we may well mistake this climax in III as the poem's truest. But the remarkable truth is that a yet more forceful and triumphant climax remains, destined to arrive, as we should expect, with the close of Book VI. Meanwhile, however, the poet has closed down the first half of the poem with all the exquisite might that is its due.

Only at the end of Book IV does Lucretius permit himself to become elegantly subtle—and then for the sake neither of elegance or subtlety—in the main tracery of the destruction motif. Venus, who entered the poem as the sublime strength of all creation, reappears here to turn common destroyer. The formative antithesis is thus adroitly turned, and, in large part, while depicting the ravages of love, Lucretius himself turns to his wrier side: the hopeless lover anointing the "haughty" doorstep; the catalogue of graces with which women are blindly attributed; and then, to cap all, the fork-tongued final couplet with its ironic twist of phallic wit:

> nonne vides etiam guttas in saxa cadentis
> umoris longo in spatio pertundere saxa?[5]

> Do you not see also how drops of water falling on rocks
> bore through the rocks over a long stretch of time?

The main elegance, however, is not of wit, but of form. That Venus should antithesize herself so neatly—that we should finish Book IV precisely where we started the poem and yet completely opposite that start and still experience exquisite formal perfection —is the most delicate of elegances. Charmed, we smile and prepare to pass on.

But we have missed almost everything. For, these graces aside, a profound doctrinal irony clings to the split role of Venus; the fact that creative and destructive forces are, at their base, totally indistinguishable. More than a fact, this is a fundamental Epicurean law of the universe, for, amid the milling sea of atoms (and, therefore, everywhere) that force which has gone to create one composite has necessarily lent to the destruction of another, and that which destroys one lends necessarily to the creation of another. Our ambivalent Venus, then, turns out to be nothing other than this ambivalence dramatized, and, it need scarcely be added, she assumes an infinitely firmer place in the fabric of the poem by having thus entered *quam maxime* also into its doctrinal substance. Such felicitous capitalization on her qualities, beyond all considerations of elegance or subtlety is, I submit, supreme art.

As we have noticed, Book V alone does not end on the theme of destruction; as for Book VI's close, we need at this point only notice that its denouement reiterates the theme once and for all.

Before turning to evidences of the creation theme at the commencements of the several books after Book I, we would do well to glance at the proem of I as a unit. It is scarcely open to question that, from the standpoint of form, no portion of a literary work of art is of more critical importance than its beginning. Here, in some manner at least, the author must establish the pattern of things to come. If he makes his beginning with so conscious an overture as a proem, we may reasonably expect this piece to be a miniature of the whole. From Lucretius, then, if he plans to form his work on the cycle of creation and destruction in nature, we may certainly expect a bold delineation of that cycle in the first proem, one configured ideally at its terminal points. To be brief, these expectations are met almost to the letter. The proem's great cycle begins, of course, with Venus and comes to a close with the section 80–135 (ending, thus, just ten lines short of the proem's own end), where death and the superstitious fear of death are insistently recurring themes down to the section's last line and its reminder of those *quorum tellus amplectitur ossa.* When we note further that this verse is preceded by the phrase *somnoque sepultis* and, later on, that practically the last lines of the poem itself (VI, 1278–81) are,

nec mos ille *sepulturae* remanebat in urbe
quo prius hic populus semper consuerat *humari;*
perturbatus enim totus trepidabat, et unus
quisque suum pro re ⟨compostum⟩ maestus humabat

Nor did those ceremonies of burial endure in the city with which this people had ever been accustomed to be buried. For the entire populace was in panic confusion and each and all mournfully interred his dead as circumstances offered, we discover that the cycle of the first poem is deliberately moulded to the cycle of the whole. Hence, another specific evidence of the poem's grand design.[6]

Except for the first poem, the theme of creation in the *exordia* of the several books is considerably more recondite than that of destruction in their closing passages.[7] Once its terms are understood, however, the theme emerges distinctly and performs its functions with something precious to spare. Meanwhile, the devices themselves introduce us to yet another facet of Lucretius' rare sense of craft.

Properly enough, the main device emerges amid the first lines of the poem, where its relation to the cycle motif seems, however, only tributary and incidental. This from the first proem (ll. 62–79):

> Humana ante oculos foede cum vita iaceret
> in terris oppressa gravi sub religione
> quae caput a caeli regionibus ostendebat
> horribili super aspectu mortalibus instans
> primum Graius homo mortalis tollere contra
> est oculos ausus primusque obsistere contra
> quem neque fama deum nec fulmina nec minitanti
> murmure compressit caelum, sed eo magis acrem
> irritat animi virtutem, effringere ut arta
> naturae primus portarum claustra cupiret.
> ergo vivida vis animi pervicit, et extra
> processit longe flammantia moenia mundi
> atque omne immensum peragravit mente animoque,
> unde refert nobis victor quid possit oriri,
> quid nequeat, finita potestas denique cuique
> quanam sit ratione atque alte terminus haerens.
> quare religio pedibus subiecta vicissim
> obteritur, nos exaequat victoria caelo.

When human life lay cowering for all to see upon the earth, ground beneath the heel of religion, which, showing its head from celestial regions, lorded it over mortals with chilling mein, a mortal man of Greece first dared to raise his eyes in defiance and take up a stand; neither the tales of the gods nor thunderbolts nor heaven itself with its menacing rumblings cowed him, but all the more spurred his boldness of mind to be the first to force the gates of nature. And so his puissant mind prevailed and he coursed out far beyond the fiery battlements of the world and in intellect and spirit explored the boundless whole, whence, victorious, he brings back to us report of all that can come into being, all that cannot, the law by which each thing has its power limited and its deep-driven boundary stone. Thus is religion in turn tumbled beneath our feet and victory makes us peers of heaven.

If, on the side of form, there are any key words in this passage, they are *primum* (1. 66), *primusque* (1. 67), and, again, the repeated *primus* (1. 71). These are equivalent to establishing Epicurus, as indeed he is later literally established (III, 9), as *inventor rerum* and (in the same line) as *pater*.[8] In fine, they prepare us for meeting him as creator and then, by degrees, even as a divine creator. As such, he—or, where he is absent, the same devices which make him such—supplies the creation theme for the beginnings of Books III, IV, V, and VI; theme and eulogy are thus wedded, and, as Lucretius no doubt desired, Epicurus enters the essential poetry (the cycle) of the work.

But the art of it is not realized until we comprehend the full significance of Epicurus' designation as, of all things, a god. On the one hand, it is a piece of rhetorical hyperbole designed to confer the ultimate in praise. It succeeds, of course; but this is the least of its effects. A more important one is that this fiction of his deity, since it palpably associates him with the great goddess of the first proem, imparts something of her own magical grandeur to his role as creator and so immensely strengthens the formal impact of the proems in which he appears. This, an impressive gain, becomes all the more so when we realize that the poet has all but purloined it from a directly opposite tendency in the very same poetry. For, surely, however much he wanted its illusion, Lucretius could not allow even the smallest positive suggestion of true divinity to cling to his *Venus genetrix;* and, accordingly, perhaps beyond all other intentions, he meant his deification of Epicurus to act as a *reductio ad absurdum* not only, indeed, of her own godhood, but of that also of any but the authentic Epicurean gods.[9]

To appreciate fully how this comes about, we must first recall the results of the Cybele passage in Book II (ll. 592ff.)—a point, incidentally, prior to the first intimations of Epicurus' divinity. Cybele, though, of course, she is not the same as *Venus genetrix,* resembles her closely enough so that conclusions which bear on the divinity of the one must also bear intrinsically on that of the other. Now, the conclusion on Cybele's divinity is that she is not divine at all. In fact, Lucretius not only goes to toilsome lengths to rationalize every aspect of her worship, but ends with a statement of the true nature of the gods[10] and then subjoins the reflection that, if one likes to call the sea "Neptune," the grain "Ceres," etc., he is free to do so, provided only he does not corrupt his mind with religious superstition. All of which involves Venus; and then, with this denial for a precedent, her divinity is left to gradual but complete corrosion as we learn that a mere mortal—his very death is stressed in the close of III (ll. 1042ff.) and again in the last proem —has, in fact, a sounder claim than any Roman deity to godhood. But the gradualness and seemingly incidental manner of her rejection must be appreciated. It is in particular important to note that, though always implicated in the poet's denials, Venus is herself never directly impugned; for the result of this strict abstinence toward her is that Lucretius is able all the while he subverts her divinity to retain and even intensify the lovely fiction of its reality, so that she subsists, indeed as *if* a goddess (and thus far more than a bare symbol) as the awesome central *persona* of the poem, the all-radiant mask through which creation speaks and is celebrated. Meanwhile, for all that he is the agent of her destruction, such a *persona* also is Epicurus-*deus,* and, as we have noticed, the two as such have momentous formal commerce in the elaboration of the creation theme.[11]

But let us have a closer look at these proems. Except for the faint and perhaps fortuitous recall of *Venus genetrix* in lines 32–33 (*praesertim cum tempestas arridet et anni/tempora conspergunt viridantis floribus herbas*) the proem to Book II contains nothing direct on the creation theme at all. This is as we have already noticed. There are, however, two important links to the Epicurus-creator device that will provide the theme in succeeding proems. The first comes in lines 14ff.:

> o miseras hominum mentis, o pectora caeca!
> qualibus in tenebris vitae quantisque periclis
> degitur hoc aevi quodcumquest!

> O wretched minds, o blind hearts of men, in what existential darkness, in what dangers do you spend your paltry sum of days!

The second appears in line 54:

> omnis cum in tenebris praesertim vita laboret.

> Especially since all of life is a toiling in darkness.

These *tenebrae vitae* consist, of course, in ignorance of Epicurus' precepts and are offset in the first two verses of Book III by the *tam clarum lumen* which Epicurus first (*primus*) availed to raise, revealing thereby the *commoda vitae*. Proem, then, leads to proem and motif to motif.

The entire body of motifs on the creation theme comes together for the first time in III's proem. Here, as we have just seen, the thematic word *primus* bobs up again; here Epicurus becomes *inventor rerum;* here light, the symbol of creation,[12] is intimately attached to the master; here emerge the first hints of his divinity and here he first comes into the epithet *pater.* That epithet deserves special notice. Coupled with *tu patria nobis suppeditas praecepta,* it is aimed directly at the Roman's patriarchal feelings, and so would have been even more keenly felt by Lucretius' primary audience than it can be by us.

A tranquil air of celebration pervades the thematic matter in the proem of Book IV. It may at first seem strange that, after the tremendous, death-filled close of Book III, Lucretius should have resumed the leitmotif and, into the bargain, began the whole second half of the poem with so delicate a hand. There is perfect justification, however. First, as we have seen, the close of III laid stress on death as vanquished rather than, as normally hitherto, triumphant, and, hence, the proem's joyful little "dawn song" becomes, more than admissable, exquisitely right. Second, as Bailey shows, the poem's subject matter breaks naturally into three parts as well as, according to Barra, two;[13] accordingly, Lucretius takes no serious formal risk in commencing Book IV as quietly as he does. The proem required merely some representation of the theme, not necessarily a bold one.

Its poetry makes such use of established motifs that, in a firm yet unobtrusive way, the poet allows himself a share in his master's creative achievement.[14] The opening lines are most significant:

> Avia Pieridum peragro loca nullius ante
> trita solo. iuvat integros accedere fontis
> atque haurire, iuvatque novos decerpere flores
> insignemque meo capiti petere inde coronam
> unde prius nulli velarint tempora musae.

> I explore the virgin haunts of the Pierides never once trodden
> by the foot of man. I exult to discover fresh fountains, to
> drink their waters down. I exult to pluck new flowers and
> weave them into a chaplet of fame for my brow, blooms with
> which the muses have graced the temples of none before.

The verses immediately establish a correlation (without, however, once repeating the word itself) with the *primus* motif in the Epicurus-proems. No less than four times does the notion arise: *avia . . . loca nullius ante trita solo; integros fontis; novos flores* and *unde prius nulli velarint tempora musae.* We should notice the arrangement of these allusions to the word—two direct ones enclosing two metaphors. Noteworthy, too, if only as a delicacy, is the way Lucretius sharpens the distinction between the two pairs by his distributions of *nullius* and *nulli, iuvat* and *iuvatque.* With such modesty and charm does he inform us that he too is a creator. Finally, there is the force of *avia . . . loca.* The words correspond (with, alas, the intrusion of some unintended bathetic comicality) to the *extra longe flammantia moenia mundi* of the first proem, thus linking Lucretius even closer to Epicurus in the creation theme.[15]

The reentry of an image of light in line 8 (*deinde quod obscura de re tam lucida pango/ carmina*) represents an attempt to establish a further such connection, but it achieves only a very qualified success. Insofar as the image *does* occur and, therefore, *does* keep a pattern which runs also through proems III, V, and VI, we can grant Lucretius some formal advantage. But the image flounders in contradiction. First of all, the philosophy which was earlier *tam clarum lumen* now infelicitously becomes *obscura;* there is thus a complete turnabout in imagery. More serious is a parallel contradiction in symbolism. For, just as light is the poem's symbol for birth and creation, so, inevitably, darkness symbolizes death and destruction.[16] In the present use of the image, accordingly, the philosophy becomes associated with destruction—an unhappy contradiction indeed.[17]

But if we are nonetheless willing to grant *lucida* at least a strained and arbitrary symbolism, the *carmina* of Lucretius become life-giving, and we are thus led smoothly into the long metaphor that closes the proem. The metaphor's true inner burden is this: just as the physician with his healing potion revives the ailing child, so Lucretius with his healing verses restores the ailing man. The effect of his verses, that is, is to show the profit (*utilitatem*) of knowing the nature of things, which profit is nothing less than salvation. "Poetry" as the "trick" which brings it all off, far from showing Lucretius' actual concept of his art, is a mere piece of poetic expediency.[18] *Recreata,* the key word of the metaphor—and, indeed, of the whole proem—points to his true view: art, *his* art, at any rate, is life-bearing.[19]

Despite its blemish, then, the proem delicately succeeds in celebrating Lucretius as both colleague and agent of Epicurus in the presentation of a new way of life. It is the poet's own little proem, his buoyant and beautiful self-eulogy.

Book V's proem nicely explicates the established pattern of motifs on the creation theme. Two little thematic hints, *parta* (l. 5) and *cretus* (l. 6), lead into the motifs. Then (l. 8) arises one broached in the proem of III: . . . *deus ille fuit, deus* . . . *;* and immediately therafter the *primus* sequence further unfolds in the word *princeps*. Once again, therefore, Epicurus is made to share, by plundering, Venus' creative powers and once again he becomes *rerum inventor* and, thereby, creator. On the heels of this (ll. 11f.) arrives the familiar darkness-light symbolism, this time legitimate, and then, to come full turn, a reversion to the *deus* motif with *divina . . . reperta* (l. 13).[20] This motif persists, occurring again at line 19 and then once more, to sum up the proem, at lines 49ff. Its prevalence has two connected purposes, the main drift of which we have already seen. First, as a rational absurdity, it mocks and magnifies the absurdities of religious beliefs in general;[21] thus, while yet playing on the creation theme, it prepares us for the principal matter of the book: false (superstitious) and true (Epicurean) notions on the origin and development of the universe. Second, still as a rational absurdity, it squeezes *Venus genetrix* finally dry of every trace of actual divinity. After this proem, indeed, all that remains where once were the Olympian gods is that sublime aura of creation borrowed artfully from a fictive Venus for a fictive Epicurus all in the cause of form. But the form is everything, the hint of creation everything, these particular gods nothing.[22]

Although the primary formal significance of VI's proem happens not to lie in its internal order, we had yet best attend first to its arrangement, and so complete our most immediate business, the analysis of the proems' creation theme. On this, we meet more of the established and familiar. The *primus* motif rounds itself off with the double occurrence of *primae* (ll. 1, 4). (The coupling of the word with Athens is a deliberate means of emphasizing that city which, as we shall presently see, is in every way the main player in this proem.) The *deus* motif subsides as quietly as it first arose in *divina reperta* (l. 7). As for light imagery and its symbolism, this very subtly comes forth in *praeclaro nomine* and quite as delicately, but with a sharper metaphorical force, expires in the word *extincti*. We ought not miss a peculiar bit of appropriateness in the use of the two images: here, in the last proem, they at last delineate the little life cycle of the master himself: his birth with its attendant glow, his death and ensuing darkness.

So much for the formal pattern. Standing outside of it but lending an inestimable force to the theme is the characteristically Lucretian phrase *frugiparos fetus* (1. 1). It contains no less than three hints of the creation theme. Also without the pattern is the familiar thematic word *recreaverunt* (1. 3). Both notions attach to Athens and help thrust the city forward as the proem's emphatic agent of creation.

Even if that were the whole of it, we could agree that Lucretius met the proem's formal demands with admirable grace and style. But Athens blooms into prominence here for purposes that reach far beyond the proem itself. Indeed, we need merely leaf back a page in the text to find a signal hint of broader intentions. The entire close of Book V, it will be recalled, described man's gradual rise from primeval savagery to civilization and culture; the book closes with the lines:

> sic unumquicquid paulatim protrahit aetas
> in medium ratioque in luminis erigit oras.
> namque alid ex alio clarescere corde videbant,
> artibus ad summum donec venere cacumen.

> Thus, little by little, time reveals everything and reason lifts it into the shores of light. For men saw one thing after another crystallize in their minds until they reached the very pinnacle of arts.

Note that *cacumen,* otherwise emphasized by *summum,* is the last word of Book V. Where was this "utmost pinnacle of culture" attained? Surely, at Athens. Hence, we cannot but suspect a calculated formal purpose behind the city's large prominence in the verses that immediately follow. Now that we know Lucretius' methods, the obvious next step is to look to the end of Book VI: Athens again, but this time in the grip of destruction. These few pointed associations reveal perhaps the greatest masterstroke in the poem's design. First, Athens as the home of creation and Athens as the place of destruction provide a superlative cyclical frame for Book VI itself. More important, the city's place as the goal of Book VI tends to make a formal unity of the entire segment of the poem that stretches from V, 925 through to the end of VI. For, the beginnings of man described at V, 925ff. together with the whole story of man's gradual cultural progress itself forms an immense cycle, clearly pointed up by the closing lines of V, with the description of the plague at Athens.[23] Most important of all, this gigantic arch, subsuming as it does the whole history of man's upward struggle to glory, the brief glory itself, and then, symbolically in the plague, the pathetic, death-stained lapse from glory—all this provides the poem with a magnificent dramatic close.

And the drama has a quintessential appropriateness. Its design, to begin with, is of the whole; it is of the poem's own nature.[24] Furthermore, it keeps for the last and proper place the most meaningful distillation in human terms of everything that the poem has through its nature and design thus far taught. We have seen but little of that all; extensive and compelling as it is, however, it is merely preparatory to this ultimate affirmation of the cycle. Here the poem finally lays hands on the reader. The abstract Venus, threats of universal collapse, the ebb and flow of *other* things, even the inspired mixture of reason and passion in III's close he could assent to without real self-commitment. But to stand aloof from this encroachment of human history itself would require, as it turns out, dissociation from both past and future and from the very human condition. By narrowing, then, the compass of the cycle has become too large; each man, each individual effort is swept up by forces which are seen to govern all men and all efforts. Yet they are not unkind forces. They are, in fact, absolutely neutral, being the way of the ancient universe itself and of its "outer form and inner law."[25]

Perhaps we have already sufficiently uncovered the actual lines of force in the poem to discern that, in the reader's thus absorbing the exact personal significance of the omnipresent *naturae species ratioque,* the whole of the poem's experience, aesthetic, didactic, and philosophical comes intimately home to him. If not, we have here at least caught a precious first glimpse of that point where form releases perfected meaning. But even this lies beyond our immediate concern, which is merely the poem's over-all design, whose various threads we may now pause to draw together.

Counting the proem and close of each book as distinct units, we find twelve main structural segments in the poem's design.[26] Of these, ten, five proems and five closes, are built on the creation-destruction leitmotif. Since we have regarded it as a formal microcosm of the whole we may take the proem of I also into account and note once again that it is both formed on the leitmotif and shows at its close a very evident anticipation of the poem's own final verses. Though each has certain functional connections, only two units of the above-mentioned twelve, the proem of II and the close of V, fail to figure directly in the leitmotif. In effect, we have already detected the cause of the motif's absence at the end of V; its intrusion would have fatally disturbed the blending of that book's close with the proem of VI. The theme's interruption in the proem of II, meanwhile, is to be explained as a symmetric compensation for the interruption at the end of V, symmetric since, among the twelve units of the poem, the second proem stands third from the start of the poem, the close of V third from its end. There is, accordingly, no trace of disorder on the score of the interruptions.

It is also worth noting that these intermissions occur at the only two points in the poem where a suspension of the leitmotif is feasible. Again, according to the findings of Bailey and Barra,[27] the poem breaks structurally both into thirds and halves. These considerations taken together would have necessitated a representation of the leitmotif at the beginnings of Books I, III, IV, and V and at the closes of II, III, IV, and VI. Add to this the requirement of thematic stuff also at the close of I and the beginning of VI—since these books are, as the terminal segments of the poem, fundamental structural units—and only the commencement of II and the close of V are left to the poet to deal with as he would.

More important, of course, is the extreme compactness which these thematic *exordia* and closes bring to the poem's structure. Venus and the plague draw all of the structural components tightly together and, at the same time, each is made itself separately compact by its own cyclical configuration. Meanwhile they are interlaced one with another; for Venus starts a cycle that closes not only with the description of the plague, but with the thematic matter at the closes also of I, II, III and IV. Similarly, each proem begins a cycle that is resolved in every subsequent close (the beginning of II and the close of V, of course, omitted) and, as a corollary, every close resolves the cycle commenced in each preceding proem. Viewed thus, the poem already begins to disclose a complicated network of inner bonds. As the next chapter will show, there is a great deal more to that network.

Such, then, is the design of *De Rerum Natura* and also its structure. Together they propound a definite and deliberate unity which, once recognized, automatically settles the question earlier left unanswered. Obviously, the poem was quite intended to end where it ends.[28]

But, before we leave the subject of over-all architecture, what is to be said of the poem's incomparable music? I would like nothing better than to be able to confirm this too as an organic component of its design. To furnish clear proof of intent on this matter, however, would require considerably more space and skill than I have at my disposal. For, unless I mistake its nature, the full rhythm—this organic music—of Lucretius springs not alone from the meter, but from the sound-pattern as well and also, as I suspect, from the vocabulary, imagery and even in part from the very sense and tone of the verses.[29] Meanwhile, beneath all, enabling all to come to form, is the nature of the subject itself. Clearly, to analyze all of these together with such sure discernment as to recover anything like the deliberate acts of synthesis by which they became objective pattern (all of which would be requisite for an adequate proof) would require, besides a rare critical acumen, an elaborately technical, full-length study of its own. To indicate a *de facto* harmony between rhythm and design, however, and to show such desirability in that harmony as would surely have made it an object of conscious art will not be at all impossible even in a short space, provided we can only agree on a certain eminent feature of the rhythm.

Leonard leads the way when, at the beginning of his lucid introduction to the poem, he cites the "long roll" of its opening hexameter. That sort of roll, I suggest, does not cease with the first line but continues prominently on, as voluptuous as it is grave, throughout the seven thousand and more that follow. For those who will not hear it, we may suggest that Lucretius' fondness for multisyllabic words and for frequent correspondence of ictus and word accent, since these tend to impart a protracted and even, while firmly stressed, fluency to the hexameter, conduce to just such an undulation as Leonard mentions. More, even supposing that the roll were not there as a special effect of Lucretius' art, it would inevitably come, as I think all will agree, with the very nature of the hexameter. What Latin hexameters, after all, do not roll? Add to this the long, liquid explication of such random but oft-occurring words as *corrumpere, dissolvere,* the enormous sense of grandeur in phrases like *immensum profundum, magnum per inane,* or even in words, themselves ordinary, *longe, omnia, vaste, summa,* which by their frequency create the same image and feeling—words and phrases which, like their numerous counterparts, arise almost spontaneously out of the subject matter itself—and we see that, even had he wished, Lucretius could hardly have avoided an expansive surge and fall in the general sensory impact of his verses.

The next thing to see is that he had every reason to woo this quality. For, in terms of rhythm, this constant roll is to poetry precisely what the explicit verbal cycle is in terms of idea. Or, that is the way we are forced to put it analytically. In our actual experience of the poetry, provided only that we hear and feel this steady roll, both merge in a single rhythm, itself also idea, which is the poem's whole concept and vital force and, once appreciated, its very essence.

If all of this is true, then there indeed exists a *de facto* harmony between rhythm and design that was worth the poet's most careful attention. I am aware I have not properly proved the harmony; much less have I proved that Lucretius deliberately instilled it; but I am also certain that any reader who misses profound sensuous involvement in this music's solemn rise and fall misses half the poem's formal might and, given all that this deficiency presumes, practically its entire effective meaning.

We may conclude this chapter with a notice of some of the other means—other, that is, than the music's suggested effect—by which the cycle is implemented in the internal stretches of the poem. It should be cautioned, however, that, though it has general relevance, our survey will lead to only a comparative few of the most essential interior cycles, since the construction of but few will submit to out-of-context description.

The first device, the symbolic use of imagery, we have already touched upon. We have, in fact, treated it fully enough to ascertain that Lucretius was not fastidious in his employment of it. The critical purists among us will no doubt discover further grounds for the same conclusion. Yet I think that we shall all largely agree that he turned this sort of imagery which, it is fair to say, would have found its way into his poem whether he liked its arduous formal demands or not, to very good advantage.

Those occasional images that are drawn by some peculiar symbolism or other into the nexus of the cycles must await their appearance for their exposition. Here we are primarily interested in those recurring pairs of images whose members bear both an antithetical relationship to each other and corresponding hints of birth and death. Where such images occur (the familiar ones of light and darkness are obvious prototypes), we may safely attribute symbolic suggestions of creation and destruction. So it is with images of warmth and cold, starting and stopping, awakening and sleeping. The pairs, however, are not always quite so regular. At times, by extension, a symbolism, or at least a part in the symbolic play, is transferred to images which cannot themselves lay claim to it. Whiteness and blackness, for instance, paralleling light and dark, play on the master theme even though the quality of whiteness has no clear suggestive connection of its own with birth. Or, again, in other instances where but one member of an antithesis carries a distinct thematic hint, the poet may employ it to the complete exclusion of its opposite. Plainly, such a technique can apply only where the specific image carries a compelling symbolic force, as with stillness, for example, to symbolize death.[30]

So much will serve to give a notion of the device. We shall avoid exaggerating its importance to the full scheme of the cycles by quietly passing on.

Next is the device of repetition. In itself, repetition is, of course, indispensable to the poem's cyclical movement and to the rhythm of that movement. Apart from its indispensability, however, it makes decisive independent contributions to the movement's sensory and emotional impact. It is in the repetition that the rhythm becomes huge, the movement immense. Through the repetition too, and particularly through its endlessness, the movement acquires its final emotional significance for the poem. The emotion can hardly be named in its own terms; it amounts, rather, to a solemn knowledge—grown solemn in the repetition—of the rhythm itself. In any case, since it underlies the final emotion, the repetition underlies the cycle's poetry as well and, therein, the poem's whole formal concept.

It should be made clear, however, that the effective formative-poetic force of repetition is not limited to the recurrence of the explicit cycle alone. For just as cyclical movement is impossible without repetition, so is it impossible for either prolonged or widespread repetition in poetry not to impart a feeling of cyclical movement.[31] This would be so even in poems where such movement and its rhythmic burden is not, as in ours, the whole informing aesthetic. In *De Rerum Natura* it only becomes significantly the more so. Clearly then, all of the poem's innumerable repetitions, since they participate in the reiterative, cyclical rhythm of the whole, assume a definite voice in its formal poetry.

Hence, when the poet introduces Book IV with a passage already perused in Book I, he elaborates the poem's design according to its prescribed formative principle. The same occurs not only in the repetition of other lyrical passages, long and short, but also in the reiteration of the poem's various maxims and formulas and, in fact, once the device takes hold, everywhere that the language gives definite reminiscence of earlier language. Instances of the last cannot be catalogued to every reader's satisfaction; yet, every reader must agree that they are practically omnipresent in the poem. We may now see that, in proportion to their presence, the steadying influence of form is present.

A noteworthy result is that, owing to his poem's design, Lucretius was promised greater, not less, aesthetic force as a result of fixity in the patterns of his language—even of his barest, most technical language. When we realize that, despite its threat of monotony, just such fixity was urged by didactic and dialectical as well as by scientific-expository considerations, that, in short, the whole nature of the poem's content made it the only feasible mode of exposition, we can hardly estimate how reassuring this congruence of form and substance must have been.

We can, however, even better appreciate the felicity of it all when we grasp that the influence of design (that one true and infallible muse of the poem) extends so far as to stir the very skeletons of the arguments and expositions into poetic life. Again and again, as every reader knows, the declarations roll out in the sequel *principio, praeterea, denique, postremo,* with variations and additions, of course, but always keeping a recognizably recurrent pattern. Once more the feeling, through the force of repetition, is distinctly cyclical and, therefore, in this work, part of the essential poetic flow.

We must nonetheless be careful not to exaggerate the role of repetition; for, despite its harmony with the poetry's central aesthetic, the device does not figure essentially in the formation of the work's internal cycles. To Lucretius (and here we can see his caution) the literal cycle was all but exclusively fit for that kind of service. As the next chapter will reveal, he relied on the force of the device to supplement and corroborate, perhaps even to deepen, the work of the literal cycle, but almost never—if, indeed, ever at all—to assume its place. In fact, the final analysis will possibly establish the device as one of the many elements of the poem's music.

Finally, there are those methods and mannerisms in the poetry which fix the setting, spatial, temporal and psychological, of the cycle's operation. In its fundamentals, the complete setting is provided in the first two books, where Lucretius introduces us to the spectacular world of the atoms. Nothing about that world is more significant to the poetry than its vastness and volatility, or more exactly, than the spectacle of the eternally seething intercourse of matter within infinity that its description evokes. This is the milieu within which things, all save the imperishable divine, rise into and pass out of being, the medium within which the poetry's—which is to say, the cycle's—fullest drama evolves and will evolve.

There is, of course, nothing novel in designating the boundless, changing universe as the poetry's true setting. Entirely absent until now, however, has been anything near a right estimate of the setting's psychological function and of the relation of this to the true poetry. By any standard, the whole of Lucretius is meant to draw the reader irrevocably out of his shriveled world of self-absorption.[32] The grandeur of his universe, made palpable by our constant immersion in its infinite store of milling matter, is the poet's chief means of effecting—we may even say, of forcing—that self-release. Inevitably, the reader shrinks in self-importance as the universe burgeons sensibly larger, and by the end of the first two books this removal has proceeded to the ultimate degree possible. If the reader has not by then learned his place beneath the aspects of infinite space and time, he never will; and if he has not by then acquired a proper humility, he has not learned. Now, since, as we shall later see, the final and most momentous didactic effect of the poem's cycle is precisely to refine that sense of humility, so engendered, by giving it ethical direction, the cycle's setting, specifically in its psychological aspect, becomes as intrinsic to the poetry's evolution and goal as the cycle itself.

If this is so, we must take notice of how the setting is kept before us throughout the length of the work. After Book II, the surface dimensions narrow, drastically in III and IV, where Lucretius turns to analyze atomic processes that reside chiefly in the individual himself, and, meanwhile, the broadening of scope in the final two books never quite reattains the literal universal compass of I and II. Yet, as far as art can provide, the universal setting is nowhere submerged. For, just as we have elsewhere found artistic and didactic purposes to blend as one, so here also it is art quite as much as pedagogy that insures the constant reemergence of those primary conditions that maintain in the universe: the atoms and the void, motion, collision and change—and particularly, always and everywhere, the atoms, the atoms, the atoms. Behind these the universe itself sensibly lurks, omniform, omnipresent.

But vastness and volatility are a very mood of the poem, and, as there is hardly anything in Lucretius which does not somehow contribute to that mood, the setting is in this way too made immediate. A confused antagonist *"longe aberrat a vera ratione"*;

time passes amid "innumerable lustrations of the circling sun"; death is *"immortalis"*; or, open the poem almost anywhere and you are likely to learn that *". . . quapropter simulacra pari ratione necessest / immemorabile per spatium transcurrere posse . . ."*; and so, in its countless figures, images and epithets, the poem ever broods on the grand dimensions of things. Meanwhile, its rapid pace and urgent tone, coupled with the sinuous intricacy of its composition, create an atmosphere of electric mobility—the volatility of mood corresponding to the vastness just noticed. A constant eagerness to get on with things (*"nunc age,"* thunders the poet), a tendency to race the reader through arguments, to build a crescendo of arguments, to cross-refer the arguments, to enfold one or more within another and, finally, even the seemingly counter tendency of breaking off abruptly into a digression—all of these mannerisms inject a tumultuous vitality into the poem that seems to mimic and finally even become the vital tumult of the atoms themselves as they race through the boundless void.

Yet, clearly, all of this swirling immensity would amount only to the magnificent disorder that its critics have seen in the poem were it not for the secret transfiguration effected by the cycle. Under its influence, the turbulence takes on dramatic design, furious haste is transmuted into a solemn rhythm, imponderable vastness becomes functional milieu. Order, unity, control, proportion set in, spontaneously in part, and yet so evidently solicited by the conscious hand of the poet that we can at last seize the superlative truth in Cicero's little remark: *". . . multis luminibus ingeni, multae tamen artis. . . ."*

III

The Cycles

Even on the basis of the cycle's poetic effect so far noticed *De Rerum Natura* must appear sufficiently ordered and integrated to suit any standard of good form. Yet, Lucretius provides us with a great deal more of the cycle, as much more, indeed, as his interest in it exceeded its architectonic function alone. His aim, expressly didactic and philosophical as well as artistic and aesthetic, is not merely to impress its rhythm further upon our senses, nor only to establish it—the cycle and the rhythm —as a fundamental condition of human existence, but to instill an acceptance of it as a *sine qua non* of conscious being. Nothing less would have sufficed for his final didactic purpose. For, as we shall later see, it is directly by means of our total personal submission to the cycle and its rhythm that the course of action which the philosophy implores attains its final conviction.

Such conclusions, however, are the business of the following chapter. Here our objective is principally to catalogue the cycle's movement within the poem. Since all that is new in the way of method will readily explain itself as the work unfolds, no further analysis is required on these matters. Suffice it to say that, at the least, Lucretius demands a bare appearance of the ideas of creation and destruction in alternating succession and that, at his best, he uses the movements of nature herself.

BOOK I

Little need be added to the observations previously made on the cycle in the first proem. The main division between the themes of creation and destruction comes at line 84. Previously, the only important hints of destruction, besides the symbolism of Mars,[1] are *resolvat* (l. 57) and the reminders of mortality (ll. 76f.) in *finita potestas* and *alte terminus haerens*. It is to be noted that in each place the hints describe a cycle together with the preceding verse. The result is a cycling within a larger movement of the cycle, a frequently employed technique. Similarly, after the proem turns to the motif of destruction, the words *parentem, patrio . . . nomine, parentis* (ll. 89, 94, 99) revive the theme of creation; and then, more in keeping with the earlier technique, *nata* and *nascentibus* (l. 113) and the implication of rebirth in *insinuet se* (l. 116) perform with the two intervening lines a rapid cycling within the movement of destruction. The effect will only seem unnatural if death in the Spring or birth in Winter, which are the obviously implied analogies in nature, appear unnatural.

All together, the proem offers a very powerful representation of the cycle; the same strength persists through the next hundred-odd lines, where Lucretius unravels the poem's *principium*, the first principle of nature's outward form and inner law. The cycle, as we have discovered, inheres in the divisions of the *principium* itself; but the whole section feels its pulsing movement. After a brief restatement of the theme at line 155 and the repetition of the thematic word *creari* at 157, the poet launches himself into a long argument (ll. 159–214) supporting his law, wherein the fact of creation lies throughout on the very surface:

Nam si de nilo *fierent,* ex omnibu' rebus
omne genus *nasci* posset, nil *semine* egeret.
e mare primum homines, e terra posset *oriri*
squamigerum genus et volucres *erumpere* caelo; *etc.*[2]

For if things *came into being* out of nothing every kind of thing would be able to be *born* from every thing and would require no *seed*. First, men could *arise* from the sea, fish from the earth and birds might *spring forth* from the sky.

No more of the argument need be quoted, I think, to convince the reader of the theme's presence. We should notice, however, that, besides the idea of birth, the poet manages to weave in also the idea of increase (ll. 184–91):

nec porro augendis rebus spatio foret usus
seminis ad coitum, si e nilo crescere possent.
nam fierent iuvenes subito ex infantibu' parvis
e terraque exorta repente arbusta salirent.
quorum nil fieri manifestum est, omnia quando
paulatim crescunt, ut par est semine certo,
crescentesque genus servant; ut noscere possis
quidque sua de materia grandescere alique.

Besides, for the growth of things no time would be needed for the coming together of the seed, if they were able to grow from nothing. For tiny infants would immediately become adolescents and trees would leap up whole, suddenly burst from the earth. It is plain to see that none of this happens, since everything grows gradually, as is natural from a specific seed, and, growing, maintains its kind. Thus you can know that each thing grows to adulthood and is nourished out of its own substance.

Finally, it is notable, particularly in regard to Lucretius' formal prospectus of his poem at this point, that the *grandis arator,* who closes Book II, is already prefigured at the end of this section (ll. 208–14). An intimation, then, of decay and death.

And, indeed, immediately after our taste of creation and increase, the poet introduces the second part of his *principium,* whose theme is destruction. The theme prevails for only twelve lines, however (ll. 215–26), whereupon, just as abruptly, creation reenters; and then, six lines further on (l. 232), the motif of destruction resumes, persisting with only one swift interruption by its counterpart (l. 235) down to line 252, where creation once more blooms (nowhere more beautifully in the entire poem), the whole section closing with a three-line recapitulation (ll. 262–64), the first verse restating the second law of the *principium,* thereby returning us to the theme of destruction, the second and third describing in so many words the cycle itself:

> haud igitur penitus pereunt quaecumque videntur, quando
> alid ex alio reficit natura nec ullam rem gigni patitur nisi
> morte adiuta aliena.[3]

> Scarcely, then, does anything that is seen perish entirely, since nature builds one thing anew from another, nor does she allow anything to be born unless aided by the death of a separate thing.

I shall attempt only a few discrete comments on the artistic handling of the *principium.* The cycles are all cleanly contiguous. Since we are at the commencement of the poem's main body, there is a proper overbalance on the side of creation and yet not the least retardation of the cycle's full movement. Echoes from the first proem[4] produce a voluptuous feeling of concert in the poem's *exordium;* and also on the side of the familiar there appears in the second half of the *principium* a constant cycling within the cycle. But perhaps best of all is the exquisite turn into the last great movement of the theme (ll. 250f.) before the final summing up:

> postremo pereunt imbres, ubi eos pater aether
> in gremium matris terrai praecipitavit;
> at nitidae surgunt fruges ramique virescunt
> arboribus, crescunt ipsae fetuque gravantur; . . .

Finally the rains perish when the sky-father has poured them
into the lap of mother earth, but the glistening crops surge
up and the boughs turn green on the trees, which, themselves
increasing, grow weighted with fruit.

If not yet finally till this point, nature here engulfs us in her primal
rhythm. Most important of all is the way Lucretius sets the entire
universe in motion in these few score lines. The laws that nothing
arises from nothing and that nothing perishes into nothing postulate, of course, the principle of the indestructibility of matter.
Nature's whole store of matter is thereby evoked—a summoning
everywhere aided by the poet's allusion to primordial bodies—and
the matter together with the moving cycle calls into being the full,
living *omne*. The poem's central image is thus established at the
very beginning; more, we have been ingeniously primed for the
long and detailed technical treatment of matter and void and of
the atom and its properties, which constitutes the principal doctrinal substance of the book (ll. 265–634).

We have already noticed the heavier weight given to creation in
the *principium*. Lucretius now sets out, as it were, to restore the
balance of things. After a quick, recapitulative cycle at lines 265f.,
the theme of destruction introduced by *ad nil revocari* is hugely
extended by a description of the wind's ruinous power (ll. 271–94).
I shall quote only the beginning:

principio venti vis verberat incita pontum
ingentisque ruit navis et nubila differt,
interdum rapido percurrens turbine campos
arboribus magnis sternit montisque supremos
silvifragis vexat flabris: ita perfurit acri
cum fremitu saevitque minaci murmure ventus.

First the onslaught of the wakened wind flogs the ocean and
scuttles great ships and tears the clouds to tatters; at times
sweeping over the plains in swift tornado it litters all with
huge trees and harasses the mountaintops with forest-slaying
blasts; with such piercing moans does the wind rant, with
such menacing murmur does it roar.

Throughout, the passage gives superlative evidence of Lucretius' ability to execute theme and argument simultaneously.

Toward the end of the paragraph (ll. 311ff.), the theme of destruction gives way to that of decay, which, after passing through several figures,[5] is resolved in a full representation of the principle of growth and decay (ll. 322–27):

> postremo quaecumque dies naturaque rebus
> paulatim tribuit, moderatim crescere cogens,
> nulla potest oculorum acies contenta tueri;
> nec porro quaecumque aevo macieque senescunt,
> nec, mare quae impendent, vesco sale saxa peresa
> quid quoque amittant in tempore cernere possis.

> Finally, strain as it will, the sight of the eyes cannot at all discern what time and nature gradually add to things, inducing them gradually to grow; moreover, you may never see what is lost moment by moment from things that age through time and disease or from rocks which overhang the sea and are gnawed to nothing by its mordant salt.

This principle, which maintains the cycle's rhythm without quite comprising the cycle itself, marks a deliberate diminution in the theme. After nearly three hundred lines of restless ebb and flow, the abatement is both welcome and appropriate. The senses have been seized and mastered. The rest, for a while at least, need be only gentle reminder.

Accordingly, the cyclical figures for more than a hundred lines henceforth are sparse and, compared to those we have seen, faintly traced. The first arrives at lines 344f. with *genita* and *quiesset*, the latter evoking an eerily dead universe. Next, there is *fetus . . . fundunt* at line 351, coupled with *rigidum permanat frigus ad ossa* (l. 355), whose figurative suggestion of death is more than sufficient to carry the motif. Then, after a kind of thematic diminuendo within which *natura*, l. 363,[6] *primum*, ll. 383, 389, and *fiat*, l. 386 alone represent the movement, there appears one of the poem's miniature showpieces (ll. 410–17), where, much as in the proem to IV, the process of poetic invention itself blends with the creation theme:

quod si pigraris paulumve recesseris ab re,
hoc tibi de plano possum promittere, Memmi:
usque adeo largos haustus e fontibu' magnis
lingua meo suavis diti de pectore fundet,
ut verear ne tarda prius per membra senectus
serpat et in nobis vitai claustra resolvat,
quam tibi de quavis una re versibus omnis
argumentorum sit copia missa per auris.

But if you grow torpid or draw back even a little from the
task, Memmius, I can promise you plainly: my sweet tongue
will pour forth such copious draughts from the vast founts
of my fertile breast that I fear that slow old age will coil
through my members and undo the bonds of my life before
the entire fund of proofs on any one point should be sped to
your ears by my verses.

Next we meet a dim and highly contingent, but probably not
unintended, cycle in *prima . . . fundata* and *occultis* (ll. 423f.).

With line 449 the movement begins to deepen. The expansive
phrase *quaecumque cluent,* since it evokes all of creation, touches
off the theme, the resolution appearing two lines later with *permitiali discidio.* In line 457, *adventu* and *abituque* trace another cycle.
The latter word's suggestion is faintly extended by *placidaque
quiete* in line 463, and thereupon creation immediately reenters
with *Tyndaridem, Troiugenas gentis* and *saecla hominum,* all
suggesting generation, all erased by *abstulerit* (l. 468). An ingenious cycle follows (ll. 473ff.), where *ignis,* born in *conflatus,* wreaks
its destruction in *accendisset*—words of the same meaning, but
opposite burden. Nor do the fires subside. In the next lines *partu
. . . Graiugenarum* gives way to *inflammasset.* Both cycles, as often
in Lucretius, sketch out creative movements with destructive ends;
in the first, the end is mere result, in the second, purpose; both
ends, but the second only where mind is at work,[7] are parts of
nature; and both serve to remind us of the near indistinguishability
of nature's creative and destructive forces.

Creation returns with *primordia, constant* and *principiorum* (ll.
483ff.) at the beginning of the next paragraph; then (ll. 486)

destruction in *stinguere,* followed by an expansion on the theme in line 489. The next several verses, though they do not all explicitly indicate destruction, also manage to swell the theme through their imagery: *labefactatus . . . solvitur, devicta liquescit, penetraleque frigus.* At the paragraph's close, *primordiaque* and *creata* renew the cycle.

By this point, the poem has reached its exposition of the atoms themselves. Lucretius seizes the occasion to step up the cyclical movement, thereby building afresh the changing universe, the poem's central image.

Together with the last words quoted above, *genitis* (l. 511) provides the new creation motif. Touched off by *dissoluantur*[8] (l. 519), a great shower of thematic words signifying destruction then appear (ll. 528–37), including the indeed inclusive phrase *quibus omnia conficiuntur.* Subsequently, creation barely peeps through in *corpora prima* (l. 538); as for the rest, the reader may see for himself how smoothly it spirals down to the paragraph's end (ll. 540–50):

> praeterea, nisi materies aeterna fuisset,
> antehac ad nilum penitus res quaeque redissent
> de niloque renata forent quaecumque videmus.
> at quoniam supra docui nil posse creari
> de nilo neque quod genitum est ad nil revocari,
> esse immortali primordia corpore debent,
> dissolui quo quaeque supremo tempore possint,
> materies ut suppeditet rebus reparandis.
> sunt igitur solida primordia simplicitate
> nec ratione queunt alia servata per aevum
> ex infinito iam tempore res reparare.

Besides, if matter were not eternal, all things would have returned utterly to nothing before this, and everything we see would have been born again from nothing. But since I have taught above that nothing can be born of nothing and that nothing once born can be recalled to nothing, primordial bodies must be of immortal substance, into which each thing can be dissolved on its final day, so that matter be available for the restoration of things. The primordial bodies, therefore, are solid and whole, nor can they in any other way, preserved through the ages from all eternity, go on restoring things.

I shall add just two comments on the passage: the recollection of the *principium,* through the feeling it imparts of renewal and return, itself adds a kind of cyclical rhythm; the phrase *res reparare* at the end denotes the cycle itself and thus again accords it prominent explicit statement.

The cycles continue. The next paragraph, since the last broke off with creation, commences on the note of destruction: *frangendis* (l. 552) and *frangente* (l. 553). For the next nine lines, the movement is rapid: *conceptum; summum aetatis . . . finem* and *dissolvi; refici; fregissit* and *dissoluensque; reparari; frangendi; refici.* Starting with the last word, one cycle reaches through the remainder of the paragraph: *fiunt* (l. 567) and *creari* (l. 571), extending the force of *refici,* give way in line 577 to *frangendis,* the same thematic word with which the paragraph began.

In the subsequent paragraph, *finis . . . vitam tenendi* (ll. 584f.) restates the destruction motif, and then *primordia* (l. 592), *revicta, oriri* and *finita potestas* along with *alte terminus haerens* yield two quick turns of the cycle, which itself receives a nearly explicit statement in the final two lines.

Of extreme aesthetic importance in these last two paragraphs is Lucretius' steady insistence on order and limit in things, and especially on the limit set to natural growth (ll. 555, 564, 585). In concert with the leitmotif, these themes effect a plenitude and neatness of movement that is rarely matched in the entire book.

Even in the ensuing, extremely technical paragraph, the poet manages a sensible evolution of the theme. The motif of destruction makes a bold entrance with *revelli* (l. 608); then creation with *primordia* (l. 609) and *conciliata* (l. 611), destruction with *avelli* (l. 613), creation with *semina* (l. 614), the whole section on the atom cycling to an appropriate close with another open allusion to the universal ebb and flow (ll. 628–34):

denique si minimas in partis cuncta resolvi
cogere consuesset rerum natura creatrix,
iam nil ex illis eadem reparare valeret
propterea quia, quae nullis sunt partibus aucta,
non possunt ea quae debet genitalis habere
materies, varios conexus pondera plagas
concursus motus, per quae res quaeque geruntur.

Besides, if nature, the universal creatress, had been accustomed
to force all things to be resolved into their minimal parts,
then she would not now be able to restore any of them,
since that which does not have sufficient bulk to possess parts
cannot attain to those faculties which must belong to progenitive matter—various fastenings, weights, blows, meetings,
motions—by which all things are carried on.

If Lucretius' success in turning the exposition on the atom into
an abundant flow of poetry seems greatly attributable to the substance he had at hand, we need merely glance into the subsequent,
materially far different, refutation of rival philosophies (ll. 635–
920) to gather that his resources for elaborating his theme owed
their depth and facility principally to his superior imagination. It is
true that, in places, his devices are a bit more mechanical than before. Still, the cycles roll on, majestic as ever, and, after all, their
quality is the only real measure we have of the resistance he found
in their progenitive material.

Creation first enters by implication with *consistere* (l. 636). The
conjunction of *primus, clarus* and *obscuram,* familiar from the
proems, then reenters;[9] *creatae* (l. 646) and *fieri . . . variantia
rerum* (ll. 652f.) follow in quick order to reestablish the creation
theme, which yields to a regular cycling in lines 665–74:

quod si forte alia credunt ratione potesse
ignis in coetu stingui mutareque corpus,
scilicet ex nulla facere id si parte reparcent,
occidet ad nilum nimirum funditus ardor
omnis et ⟨e⟩ nilo fient quaecumque creantur.
nam quodcumque suis mutatum finibus exit,
continuo hoc mors est illius quod fuit ante.

proinde aliquid superare necesse est incolume ollis,
ne tibi res redeant ad nilum funditus omnes
de niloque renata vigescat copia rerum.

But if they believe that fire can in any other way be extin-
guished in union and transform its body, then, to be sure,
if they do not relent at some point, heat will perish absolutely
into nothing and everything will come into being out of
nothing. For whatever changes and transgresses its boundaries,
this instantaneously spells the death of that which existed
before. Accordingly, some portion of those fires must survive,
lest you find all things returning utterly to nothing and then,
reborn from nothing, all of variegated nature thriving anew.

The rest of the paragraph, while continuing the argument against
Heraclitus and shifting it fully to an Epicurean basis, gives us the
most explicit presentation so far of the universal ebb and flow.

After the perfunctory *labefactat* (l. 694) and *naturam* (l. 702),
the cycle takes on a broader flourish. Indeed, since we have reached
the revered Empedocles, we are treated to something of a minor
proem. In lines 705–17, *consistere, gignundis, fingere, creare, primordia, procrescere, primis* and *gessit* combine in a strong creation
movement. Through the ensuing eight lines with their picture of
the gnawing Ionian sea, *vasta Charybdis,* and wrathful Aetna, the
opposite theme supervenes. Thence to the end of the paragraph,
the *deus* motif of the proems together with *creatus* (l. 733), fill all
once more with the feeling of creation. The *deus* motif extends the
theme into the next paragraph till lines 740f. and *ruinas* and *magno
cecidere . . . casu.* Then, the very next line brings *primum,* which,
faint as its proper force may be, effects along with suggestions of
generation in line 744, another turn of the creation motif, itself
giving way in lines 746f. to a more powerful impulse of destruction.
Finally, starting with line 753 a regular cycling along familiar lines
carries us to the paragraph's end.

At lines 763f. *creantur* and *dissoluuntur* describe another cycle.
Thereupon, creation takes hold over several lines (ll. 765–89), keyed
principally by *primordia* (l. 765), *gignuntur* (l. 767), *creata* (l. 773),
creatur (l. 781), *gigni* and *creari* (l. 784) and *primordia* (l. 789).
Again, familiar formulas bring the destruction theme (ll. 791–93).

Then, besides continuing the thematic cycle, the present paragraph comes to a close with another direct representation of the natural cycle itself.

Nothing, not even lacunae, stops the movement from here on down to the section's end: *crescere alique, crescere* (ll. 804ff.)—*vita . . . exsoluantur* (ll. 810f.); *primordia, primordia, constituunt, primordia, creari, gigni, creari, consistere, concrescere, esse* (ll. 815–41) —*secandis* (l. 844); *primordia, primordia* (ll. 847f.); *pereunt, exitio, mortem, leti, mortalis, victa perire, reccidere* (ll. 850–57); *crescere, auget, alitque, crescunt, exoriuntur, exoriuntur* (ll. 858–73)— *franguntur, friatis, praefracta* (ll. 882, 888, 892);[10] *semina* (l. 895) —*flammai fulserunt* (l. 900); *semina, creant* (ll. 902f.)—*incendia silvis,*[11] *conficerent, cremarent* (ll. 903, 906); *primordia, creare, primordia* (ll. 908, 911, 918)—*pereunt* (l. 918).

Glancing briefly back, then, the whole middle expanse of the book (ll. 483–920) is one continuous flow of cycles. Previously, if we remember, we detected a diminishment of the theme. In the book's closing section, Lucretius employs the technique at least once again.

The finale opens with a proper movement of the creation theme (ll. 926–50), a group of verses already familiar to us from our study of proem IV. From this point up to line 1015 in the text as we have it, however, there is small trace of the leitmotif. The only figures approaching an explicit cycle are *finitum constituatur* (l. 968) and *consisteret . . . finitumque* (ll. 985f.).[12] Otherwise, in lines 984–97, the poet alternately depicts conditions of eternal lifelessness and eternal life in the universe, the last affording us another precious glimpse of the moving *omne,* but none of this, despite the suggestive juxtaposition of *requies* and *principiorum* in line 992, gives the actual cycle. There is perhaps but one deliberate implication of it, very covert and beautiful, in the entire section: the thunderbolt's futile little rise and fall within the wide tracts of infinity (ll. 1002–1007). In any case, the meagerness of the theme gives no cause for concern, since the passage's very evocation of infinity produces as much of formal value (see Chapter II) as might have been gained by any representation of the cycle.

The resumption is an exquisite formal recapitulation and climax of the entire book (ll. 1015–51). I shall only mark off the cyclical turns; first, it seems likely that the lacuna after line 1013 gave some hint of creation to start the movement; as for the rest: destruction (ll. 1015–18); creation (l. 1019); destruction (l. 1020); creation and increase (ll. 1021–27); decay and destruction (ll. 1028–41); creation (ll. 1042–45); destruction (ll. 1045–48); creation (l. 1049); destruction (l. 1055).[13]

Aside from the great urgency of its movement, the passage's most important formal contribution is its direct depiction of *naturae species ratioque* in full operative harmony. Formally, indeed, through its intermittent revelations of one or another aspect of the actual *omne,* the whole book has been tending toward just this realization of the *principium.* The book revisits its start; but in a stronger sense we are already in Book II.

Defects in the manuscript obviate any certain conclusions as to the quality of thematic movement in lines 1052–1093ff. As the text stands, light-darkness imagery (*solem,* 1065; *noctis,* 1065, *noctes,* 1067; *diebus,* 1067; *signis,* 1089; *solis,* 1090) provides the main impetus up to line 1090. Then *frondescere* (l. 1092) touches the literal theme. It is all rather faint, but, without doubt, the missing lines (*post* 1093) would have furnished substantially more before releasing us to the portrait of universal collapse (ll. 1102–13) that brings the book to its thematic close.[14]

In sum, we have detected at least three aspects of cyclical rhythm in Book I, all of which the reader may expect to reappear later on. Fundamentally, there is the undulation of the cycles themselves. Next, especially toward the book's beginning, there is the surge of the cycle within the cycle. And, last, in a process important to Book I, since it is here that the theme must be established, there is a continually recurrent impulse toward explicit statement of the inner and outer aspects of the *omne,* culminating in the climactic passage (ll. 1014–55) just noticed. Nor is this the entire tale. For, within and above the rest, moulding the theme to its own rich cadence, the poem's music interminably voices the same rise and fall.

BOOK II

The chief formal difference between Books I and II is a marked thematic overbalance in II on the side of creation. The disproportion, I think, is not to be explained either by any wish on Lucretius' part to promote the theme for its own sake or by any seeming freer adaptability of II's material to creation. Of the book's four great divisions, the first and fourth (atomic movements, the infinite number of worlds) are clearly suitable to either, while the middle two (atomic forms, secondary qualities of atoms) are equally indifferent to both. Meanwhile, as we shall see, the stress on creation often precludes the even flow to which the first book's cycles have accustomed our senses, and this is not a result that Lucretius would seem likely to have encouraged without some compensatory profit.

The most reasonable supposition, then, is that II's stress on creation had a function to perform in the poem as a whole. As the work stands, such a function is indeed executed, principally through the book's thematic relation to III. What it might have consisted of at the time of II's composition is a different matter, however, since definite evidence exists that Book IV, and not III, was meant to succeed II in the poet's original plan.[15] Seeing that III's preponderance in the mood of destruction, along with IV's thematic neutrality and a stress in II on creation would have allowed a first-half emphasis on creation and a second-half stress on destruction in the earlier order of I, II, IV, III, V, VI, my own notion is that a solicitude for the poem's general movement determined both II's thematic mood and the earlier sequence of books itself. Other considerations may have affected the latter. Book IV's close, for instance, makes such a formal nicety in combination with I's proem, that Lucretius might at first have favored this more elegant commencement and ending for the first half of his poem. In any case, it is clear that the present sequence won out. I suggest that, though it is but one of the several advantages realized,[16] the resulting relation between II and III was an important factor in the poet's decision to make the change.

The placing of III after II self-evidently effects a powerful cycle from creation to destruction within the whole final two-thirds of the poem's first half. Moreover, coming as it does after the regular thematic flow of I, this sudden and prolonged swell in the movement instills a dramatic gathering of force that obviously involves the thematic energies of the poem's entire first half. These formal advantages might in themselves have seemed justification enough for the transposition of IV and III. But the actual gain is even greater. Book III's close, we will remember, is the first of the poem's two major climaxes. It is here that we first begin to learn the poem's concrete meaning, and, if the cycle indeed has a voice in the doctrine on mortality, the present enormous movement from the depths of II makes an intrinsic contribution to the III's final significance.

After the proem which, as we have seen, is almost free of the regular introductory motifs, Lucretius restores briefly the same sort of balanced cyclical flow that characterized Book I. First, a clear cycle in lines 62–3; then, from line 68, at which point the destruction motif picks up where line 63 leaves off, a fluent exchange of themes extends to line 79, the whole affording an explicit statement of the cycle of animate things. The beauty and force of the final image speak for themselves.

There is every reason to believe that a fuller representation of the cycle than the text shows was woven into the section 80–166. At lines 62f., we will note, Lucretius promises to explain by what movements the atoms beget various bodies and break up those that are begotten. Immediately thereafter he promises to discourse on the cause and velocity of atomic movement. All of these topics are treated in the ensuing division on atomic movement save the manner of dissolution of created bodies.[17] Bailey, following Giussani and Diels, supposes that the subject was taken up in the lacuna after line 164, which he considers an extensive one.[18] Surely, these editors are correct—all the more so in that it is precisely a movement of destruction that is poetically wanting in the section.

The note of creation is struck immediately with *primordia* (l. 80) and *progignere* (l. 81); *primordia* (l. 84) extends it till the hintful intrusion of death in *quies* (l. 95). Creation returns in the very next verse with *corporibus primis,* and then in lines 98 to 108 the described creation of things adds depth to the movement. The theme, punctuated by only faint entrances of destruction, persists all the way to line 164 and the lacuna, carried not so much by the literal verbal motif (on this side, principally, we have *primordia* three times, ll. 121, 133, 157 and *conciliatu* in line 134, along with two appearances of the *principia,* ll. 135, 138), but by the extensive use of sun imagery, which, as line 211 clearly reveals, signifies creation. The imagery enters quietly in line 108, more definitely in line 114 (here accompanied, as so often with images of light, by an antithetical image of darkness), fades after line 126, is announced once more in line 140 and then opens radiantly at lines 144ff. into a full portrait of dawn with subtle recollections of the first proem. Here the verb *spargit* prepares us for *conserit* in line 211 and so helps clinch the symbolism of creation; also, *novo . . . lumine* suggests a resumption rather than a prolongation of the earlier sun imagery, thus yielding a putative night in between and a deeper feeling of cyclical rhythm;[19] finally, the images of heat (*vapor,* 150; *corpuscula . . . vaporis,* 153), in combination with the change of the light's quality from *serenum* (l. 150) to the suggestions of *fulgura* (l. 164), imply the ripening day, which leads us to suspect a resolution in night in the lost lines, and this, together with the expected description of atomic dissolution, would have applied high polish to a skillful explication of the cycle.[20] Even on the strength of the explanation alone, however, the cycle would have achieved satisfactory configurations.

The technique in this section and especially the technical contrast to the methods of Book I is worth our notice. There, as was fitting at the poem's outset, the poet's sketches of the cycle were almost always direct and literal, so that the movement rarely depended on symbolism or anticipation of further movement for its effect. In the section just traversed, of course, the latter devices become an essential medium of the leitmotif. The poet's indulgence in greater technical freedom at this point will, I think, surprise no one. What may prove surprising, however, is how little license he permitted himself in the long run. It is certainly safe to say that the poem's music aside, the leitmotif is executed throughout mainly by means of the literal verbal cycle. So fundamental was the poet's wish to communicate the theme.

Another evidence that the lacuna after line 164 contained a strong representation of the destruction motif is the self-conscious formality of the thematic resumption in lines 170ff. Venus herself enters, along with other unmistakable tokens of the first proem. Nonetheless, the poet keeps up the full cycle: *creare* (l. 170); *mortalis* (l. 171); *Veneris . . . propagent* (l. 173); *occidat* (l. 174); *primordia* and *creatam* (ll. 177, 180). The cycle, indeed, is in the very sense of the lines. And the movement perseveres. The surge of creation, *gignuntur* and *crescunt* (ll. 188f.), gives way to destruction and gore in lines 192, 195. Next, the image of night (ll. 206ff.), which symbolically maintains the latter motif and presents its own little portrait of fiery destruction in line 209, yields to the sun and the previously noticed *conserit arva* (l. 211), which itself is superseded by the thunderbolt's *vis flammea* (l. 215).[21]

The next great cycle, like the one configured in lines 80 to 164ff., gives disproportionate weight to creation—a characteristic, as noted, of Book II as a whole. The cycle, with some secondary internal movement, stretches from verse 223 to verse 306. I shall list first the main verbal allusions to creation: *natus* and *creata* (l. 223); *principiis* and *creasset* (l. 224); *gignere* and *genitalis* (l. 228); *gignere* (l. 241); the implication of *natura gerat res* in line 242; and of *exoritur* (l. 252); *primordia* (l. 253); *exstat* (l. 256); *creari* (l. 269); *seminibus* (l. 284); *innata* (l. 286); *fieri* (l. 287); *fiant* (l. 288); *principiorum* (l. 292); *adaugescit* (l. 296); *principiorum* (l. 297); *gigni* and *gignentur* (l. 300). Signs of destruction in the same section lie in the symbolism of *quietum* in line 238, *deperit* in 296 and, of course, the cycle's close (ll. 303–307):

nec rerum summam commutare ulla potest vis;
nam neque, quo possit genus ullum materiai

effugere ex omni, quicquam est ⟨extra⟩, neque in omne
unde coorta queat nova vis irrumpere et omnem
naturam rerum mutare et vertere motus.

Nor can any force transform the sum of things: for there is
nothing outside whither any kind of matter can escape from
the universe, nor whence a new force, springing up, might
burst in and change the entire nature of things, confounding
its motions.

Though I describe this cycle as great more because of its expanse
than its depth or power, it yet shows tokens of Lucretius' highest
art. Its beginning and close, first of all, show a nice coordination in
that both are rooted in the *omne,* and this, in turn, produces a
satisfying harmony of form and substance. The subjects treated in
the section are the swerve of the atom and the conservation of
matter and motion. How more suitably than with the universal
cycle might these essential ingredients of its cause have been
moulded?

As often in Lucretius, the section also contains a secondary
movement which, taken together with the poem's other energies,
must effect a cyclical feeling. Frequently this sort of play on the
theme is too liable to individual differences of sensibility to admit
of ready analysis, or, if analyzed, is better recommended in a study
of the poem's music. Here, however (ll. 251–93), the poet makes his
intentions entirely plain. Our feeling of cyclical motion arises
through a deliberate play on the starting and stoppage of willed
activity. The central movement (ll. 261–76) will give the clue to the
whole. The first important word is *principium* (l. 262). Its relation
to the thematic *primus* and use as a name for the atom establish its
creative associations, while its linkage to willed motion makes
formal bond between that impulse and the creation motif.[22] By
inference, then, the checking of willed activity must give a derivative movement of the destruction theme. Admittedly, this would
all be of questionable formal value were it not for the modulated
rush of power lent by the poetry. In the present figure, for instance,
the cycling gets off with *principium* and *carceribus,* which is the
first implication of the "destruction" motif; and so far we have

next to nothing; but a long, intense poetic swell finally gives the will and the motion a bursting release, which then subsides in *refrenavit* (l. 276).[23] Subsequently, *obstare* in line 280, carrying the same literal significance as the preceding *refrenavit,* closes a further movement, *refrenatur* in line 283 still another and *prohibet* in 288 yet one more. Earlier, meanwhile, the whole series takes its rise in 254, where *fati foedera,* the Stoic argument, looms as the master motif of obstruction.[24] It is a fragile poetry, and the lines of force subtly shift; but, unquestionably, the paragraph's final rhythm is made into that of the central ebb and flow.

Both Book II's stress on the creation theme and its tendency, already sighted, toward extended movements of the cycle become more pronounced from this point forward. As before, the poet's ordinary stratagem is to let the creation motif run on, punctuated lightly by hints of destruction, until a sharp, usually quick resolution and then to resume along the same lines. Accordingly, the next major resolution comes not till lines 551ff.; however, in so arriving, we will note, it gives a perfect cyclical configuration to the whole section on atomic shapes (ll. 333–580).

To clear up a small piece of unfinished business first, we will note that lines 308–332 gently enter the cyclical movement by means of *primordia* and *quiete* (ll. 309f.). The major movement, however, begins with not unconscious aptness in line 333 on *exordia.* Creation becomes more vivid at 341ff. as the first proem is once more strikingly recalled. Then generation itself is strongly marked by *matrem, mater* and *prolem* (ll. 349f.). Destruction makes its first entry in *mactatus* (l. 353) and the gory line that follows. In line 358 *fetum* reestablishes the main motif, which persists formally till the paragraph's end. By implication, destruction enters again in line 382 with the familiar figure of the thunderbolt. In the next line, *ortus* brings back the creation motif, and then *ortus* again (l. 387), strengthened by *creatus* in the same line and followed by *almus* (l. 390) and *primordia* (l. 396), extends it until a figurative appearance of the antithetical motif in *rescindere* and *perrumpere* (ll. 406f.). Soon after, *perfecta* (l. 409) and *primordia* (l. 414) give way to *cadavera* (l. 415).

Here, to be sure, the sketching of the cycle is highly formal. No worlds are being made and unmade, and for the moment we are even out of the atomic swirl. Indeed, one might even be tempted to speak of a diminution of the movement were it not for the exceptional impress of the music. Throughout lines 380–477 troop upon troop of antithetical images induce a rhythmical swim of the senses, which, fused with the unremitting undulation of the meter, gives all the thematic effect that is needed, and more.

Meanwhile, the verbal leitmotif continues to evolve. Line 423, with *principiali* and *creatast* is the next main entry; *gelidamque pruinam* (l. 431) symbolically carries the destruction theme, and then, after Venus reappears (l. 437), lines 455ff., where a tenuous sketch of natural destruction once more enters, carries the movement yet further forward. For more than thirty lines hereafter only a scattering of the *primordia* represents the literal theme, but with line 496 the verse begins to cycle on the idea of changing fashions in an impossible universe, breaking at 507 toward the principle of the *alte terminus haerens*—the fixed limit in things—which restores the natural world and, at the same time, the natural frame of the cycle. I shall comment only on how the exquisite cyclical implication in 515f. is made to disappear in 519ff., where, though the same figure is retained, *creata* and *infesta* transact the cyclical business and where, without losing the point of the hither and thither limit in things, Lucretius, by his use of *infesta,* restores the earlier insinuation of the *alte terminus haerens,* which is mortality. The whole passage from 496 to 521, I would venture to say, shows the poet at once at his most subtle and most extravagant in his execution of the leitmotif.

Nonetheless, he keeps the poem under perfect control. The emergence of the natural world with its inherent laws just now noticed deftly prepares us for the doctrine of *isonomia* (the universal equilibrium, among other things, of creation and destruction) which insinuates itself into the discourse a bit further on (ll. 531–40). Little by little, then, the theme rises to the surface, and by line 569, as we shall see, it will achieve one of its most limpid expressions in the poem.

After the manifestation of *isonomia,* where the stress is on the maintenance of the sum of things and, hence, creation, that theme is extended powerfully to line 550, whereupon, by the strategic use of analogy, the destruction motif at last breaks decisively through in the form of a sonorous shipwreck. There follows still more on creation and increase (ll. 560–68), leading us into a passage which, for as long as it lasts, must be the finest piece of formal poetry in *De Rerum Natura* (l. 569–80):

Nec superare queunt motus itaque exitiales
perpetuo neque in aeternum sepelire salutem,
nec porro rerum genitales auctificique
motus perpetuo possunt servare creata.
sic aequo geritur certamine principiorum
ex infinito contractum tempore bellum.
nunc hic nunc illic superant vitalia rerum
et superantur item. miscetur funere vagor
quem pueri tollunt visentes luminis oras;
nec nox ulla diem neque noctem aurora secutast
quae non audierit mixtos vagitibus aegris
ploratus mortis comites et funeris atri.

And so, neither can the moments of destruction prevail and bury life in a timeless tomb, nor can the motions of generation and growth preserve creation forever. Thus a combat of atoms continues on from time immemorial, without victory, without defeat. Now here, now there the powers of birth prevail and are overcome in turn. The wails which infants raise when they look upon the shores of light mingles with the funeral. No night has followed day nor any dawn the night which has not heard, mixed with the melancholy birthing cry, the dirge that companions death and the black funeral.

So ends a turn of the cycle extending as far back as line 332, and, surely, whatever the movement may seem to have withheld in resolution and power along the way is fully infused at the close.

Next, lines 581ff. get immediately back to the business of creation and increase, pausing once (ll. 592f.) for a reminder of fire and destruction. The verses serve to introduce, in *Magna Mater*, one of the book's most decisive surges of the creation theme. In her section (ll. 598–660), the only hints of mortality are the perfunctory *mortalis* (l. 625) and the allusion to Saturn's projected ingestion of the infant Jupiter (l. 638). They are perhaps sufficient to arouse at least a formal trace of the cycle within the cycle.

The creation movement does not cease where the Great Mother recedes; rather, lines 661ff. carry us clearly back to the theme as given at the commencement of the previous cycle (especially lines 367ff.) and thence to the first proem. Destruction, again by the agency of fire, does enter, however, at line 673. After much mention of the primordial bodies, the creation theme takes solid hold once again in lines 698f. and then burgeons out in the next paragraph where, after a brief interlude amidst unnatural creatures (one breathing flame and destruction), Lucretius firmly traces the fixed principles of birth, growth and preservation of kind (707–09):

> quorum nil fieri manifestum est, omnia quando
> seminibus certis certa genitrice creata
> conservare genus crescentia posse videmus.

> But obviously, none of these things come into being, since we see that all things are born from fixed seeds and a specific parent and are able to grow and preserve their kind.

Were we in Book I, we should now expect an imminent resolution in the destruction motif. Here, however, the purposes being different, creation carries on. In lines 721f., *genitae* and *principiorum* prolong the theme, which then even cuts across the demarcation between the third and fourth divisions of the book, appearing principally in *nata* (l. 733) and *caecigeni* (l. 741) before extinction in a well-used Lucretian formula (l. 751–54).

The appearance of blackness-whiteness and light-darkness imagery in lines 731, 733, 741 and 746 is important. These introduce a series of like antithetical images, which, through their symbolism and rhythmic sequence, lend great force to the cyclical evolution for more than a hundred lines. They subside, indeed, precisely with the next major entrance of the destruction motif (l. 826).

As before in the midst of such play, the literal theme runs on, the major verbal entries being *gignunt* (l. 759), *creantur* (l. 790), *exorientur* (l. 792), *nata* (l. 793), *gignuntur* (l. 808). In line 790, meanwhile, *occidit* brings a covert reminder of destruction, while *addita demptaque* (l. 770) injects a notice of the cycle itself. The imagistic play mostly carries the movement from line 810 up to the thematic denouement (ll. 826ff.) which, it will be noted, skillfully executes the dissolution of the section's very subject: color. The cycle has elegance.[25]

At line 833, *semina*—the shred of destruction that contains inevitable new life—revives the creation motif; *constare* (l. 838), *corpora prima* (l. 843) and *facere* (l. 849) carry it forward till *perdere* (l. 853), and then *gignundis* (l. 855), *mortalia constent* (l. 859) and the whole of line 864 key a perfect cyclical turn within the remainder of the paragraph.

Though an outward stress remains on creation throughout the rest of this division of the poem (up to line 991), the inner thematic movement becomes generally more even and, therefore, more conspicuous. *Principiis constare* (l. 867), *gigni* (l. 870) and *exsistere* (l. 871) start a new cycle; *putorem* (l. 872) momentarily introduces destruction; then, shifting his attack for the space of six lines (874-79), the poet openly mulls over the transformation of things, whereupon the explicit verbal leitmotif, returning in *procreat* and *flammas* (ll. 880, 882), gathers new momentum: *gigni* (l. 888), *creant* (l. 892), *gigni* (l. 893); *putrefacta* (l. 898); *pariunt* (l. 899); *antiquis ex ordinibus permota* (l. 900); *gigni* (l. 901), *creari* (l. 902); *mortali . . . corpore* (l. 906); *creta* (l. 906); *secreta* (l. 912); *primordia* (l. 917); *leti* (l. 918), *mortalibus* (l. 919); *facient* (l. 921); *gignere* (l. 923); *dimittunt* (l. 924); *capiunt, attribui* (l. 925); *detrahitur* (l. 926); *effervere* (l. 928); *putor* (l. 929); *gigni* (l. 930). I give only the bare skeleton, but even from this the reader will sense the powerful draught of the rhythm.

In lines 931–43, only the creation motif appears, itself resolved in the following paragraph, which lingers on the theme of death. Within that movement, however, starting at 954, a secondary theme of revival takes shape and proceeds into the subsequent paragraph, giving a subtle new impetus to the creation theme. It is formally extended by *primordia* (l. 967), *principiorum* (l. 969), *almae* (l. 971), the whole of line 975, which brings the race of men to implicit birth, and by *primordia* again in line 979. A brief entrance of destruction is then made with *mortalibus* (l. 980) before the double occurrence of *seminibus* (ll. 988, 990), prefiguring the beautiful image of 991, prepares us for the book's final division and a magnificent new surge of cyclical rhythm.

Lines 991–1022, bring the cycle once more completely to the surface and present the most precise description so far of the mere exchange of matter that constitutes the processes of creation and destruction. Meanwhile, as is evident, the thematic movement progresses throughout the whole. A nearly total suspension of the leitmotif, though not of its setting (infinity), ensues till line 1054, whence the creation theme, interrupted only by the *vitae depactus terminus alte* in 1087, extends to line 1090. Lines 1101–03 duly bring destruction and then, having preserved for the close a subject that offered a rare harmony of argument and leitmotif, the poet negotiates two flawless and profound turns of the cycle, steering us with the final couplet straight into Book III.[26]

The close as a whole (ll. 1023–1174) is an adroit didactic climax and summary of the first two books. As in the closing division of I, Lucretius diverts our attention to the infinite deep. There infinity itself was the subject; here he fills the boundless tracts of space with innumerable worlds and applies to the result the name *nova species rerum* (l. 1025). But if the *species* is new, its principle is not. Since, as lines 1067–89 clearly imply, 1023–90 must be taken intimately with 1105–74, we are given to know that the same principle of birth, growth, decay and death which governs in our world operates also in the infinity of others. The image with which Book II leaves us, then, is stupendous: an infinite number of universes in endless transmutation, truly universal ebb and flow. Being now apprized also of the laws that underlie the plenitude and the change, we emerge with the broadest apprehension possible of the poem's didactic principle, *naturae species ratioque*.

BOOK III

After the creation motifs already noticed get Book III under way, *Acherusia templa* (l. 25) lightly raises the theme of mortality. Following the reentrance of creation (ll. 31–4), the same motif, entering in lines 37 and 86, then begins and ends the first great movement of the destruction theme.

No book shows a more manifest unity of purpose than the third. Its whole doctrinal aim is to reason the fear of death from men's minds. Appropriately, therefore, we now find reiterated the principle by which all terror and ignorance is to be dispersed, *naturae species ratioque* (l. 93).

Nowhere, also, does nature's *ratio* rise to more relevant expression. In III, its pertinence comprises not only the fact of an immutable complex of laws, all thoroughly determinable, underlying all things, but also the practical application of those laws to a critical human concern, the fact of death. Yet, as ever, the *ratio* represents but one of the two didactic means by which all doctrine unfolds; *species* remains, and, as before, its principle, the cycle, evolves continuously throughout the book and beyond. We should therefore not expect any final teaching on mortality or any other matter until *ratio* and *species* have together reached their final goal.[27]

I have suggested earlier that, because of the unavoidable weight of destruction in the present book, Lucretius at least at one point was forced to consciously promote the creation theme. It is a measure of his art that, despite the evident resistence of the material, the thematic flow in III is, over all, reasonably even and, in the book's second half, as smooth as in any other part of the poem. The book's weight, however, in both subject and theme remains on mortality, and, again, this emphasis, coupled with the stress on creation in II, produces a long movement of the cycle that has happy effect on the close of III.

The first main instance of the creation theme after the proem comes at line 97 with *exstant* (Bailey translates "are created"); *faciat . . . vivere* (ll. 100f.) lends its suggestive force and then, after several images involving sickness and loss of limb trace the downward path, the cycle closes with *relinquit* in line 123. *Semina* (l. 127) and *moribundos* (l. 129) give another cyclical turn before the paragraph's close.

The next notice of creation, *unam naturam conficere ex se* (l. 137), is technically important. Strictly, the words translate as "form of themselves a single nature." They might just as well be rendered, however, "form a single created entity." In any case, the phrase tends to bring forth the etymological hint of birth in the word *natura,* as does also—for just one of several other examples— line 167, *corporea natura animum constare animamque.* By such means the word, which has that inclination even without the poet's prodding, is fully initiated among the motifs that carry the creation theme.[28] Even with the help of the motif, however, the present paragraph does not generate much thematic movement. There is a probably intended secondary play of *exsistere* (l. 154) over against *infringi, aboriri, caligare, succidere* and *concidere* in the following verses, but, unless we go into musical elements, nothing more.

The next paragraph is a bit stronger; *naturam* (l. 161) and *natura* together with *constare* (l. 167) evoke the creation theme, and then the finely woven vignette of violence starting at line 170, though it studiously avoids death, manages to impart a sensible thematic rhythm through the sequence of *disclusis intus, petitus, gignitur, exsurgendi* and *naturam.*

With line 176, Lucretius begins a discourse on the precise constitution of the mind, and the thematic movement, helped by the subject, begins to settle into a more regular pattern that persists till the end of the book's first division (l. 416). Creation, coming forth first in *unde constiterit* (ll. 177f.) and *factum constare* (l. 180), is extended by numerous thematic words, most vividly by *creata* (l. 190), before dissolution in *leti . . . quies* and other notices of death in lines 211ff. Within that very movement of destruction *natura* raises the opposite theme, and subsequently a light, but steady cyclical flow is established by the train of *seminibus* (l. 217), *evanuit* (l. 221), *creatam* (l. 229), *fugiens* (l. 230), *natura* (l. 231), *moribundos* (l. 232).

Broader and more complicated movements ensue. Between lines 235 and 239, *natura, primordia, creandum* and *creare* present a new creation theme based on the rise of sensation. Lines 246–50 trace the full course of sense-bearing movements, ending (ll. 251–55) with those that bring death. It is the tidiest cycle so far in Book III. Another extended but more perfunctory movement, keyed principally to *creant . . . naturam* (l. 270) and *diductaque solvant* (l. 287), transpires in the first half of the following paragraph. A rhythmical imagistic sequence (heat and cold) then provides some secondary thematic play before the literal creation theme emerges once more at the paragraph's close (ll. 316ff.).

The next paragraph, which has been adjudged, in my opinion mistakenly, "certainly one of the least closely knit in the whole poem,"[29] deserves full quotation for the richness and excellence of its thematic texture:

> Haec igitur *natura* tenetur corpore ab omni
> ipsaque corporis est custos et causa salutis;
> nam communibus inter se *radicibus* haerent
> nec sine *pernicie divelli* posse videntur.
> quod genus e thuris glaebis *evellere* odorem
> haud facile est quin *intereat natura* quoque eius;
> sic animi atque animae *naturam* corpore toto
> extrahere haud facile est quin omnia *dissoluantur*.
> implexis ita *principiis ab origine prima*
> inter se *fiunt* consorti praedita vita
> nec sibi quaeque sine alterius vi posse videtur
> corporis atque animi sorsum sentire potestas,
> sed communibus inter eas *conflatur* utrimque
> motibus *accensus* nobis per viscera sensus.
> praeterea corpus per se nec *gignitur* umquam
> nec *crescit* neque post *mortem* durare videtur.
> non enim, ut umor aquae dimittit saepe vaporem
> qui datus est, neque ea causa *convellitur* ipse,
> sed manet incolumis, non, inquam, sic animai

discidium possunt artus perferre relicti,
sed penitus *pereunt convulsi conque putrescunt.*
ex ineunte aevo sic corporis atque animai
mutua vitalis discunt contagia motus
maternis etiam membris *alvoque* reposta,
discidium ut nequeat fieri sine *peste maloque*
ut videas, quoniam coniunctast causa salutis,
coniunctam quoque *naturam* consistere eorum.

This *nature* of the soul, then, is protected by the whole body
and is itself custodian of the body and the source of its life;
for they cling one to the other with common *roots,* and it is
clear that they cannot be *torn apart* without *destruction.*
Just as it is not easy to *tear away* the odor from a lump of
frankincense without *destroying* its *nature* as well, so is it not
easy to extract the *nature* of mind and soul from the entire
body without *dissolving* everything together. With *primordial*
parts so bound together from their very *origin* do they *come
into being* and enjoy mutual life; nor, as is plain, can the force
of body or mind, either one without the might of the other,
experience sensation separately, but sense is *kindled* for us and
breathed throughout our innards by their mutual and reciprocal motions. Besides, the body is neither *born* alone nor grows
alone nor, plainly, does it endure after *death.* For unlike the
moisture of water, which can lose the heat given to it and
yet not be *disintegrated* for that reason, the *abandoned limbs
of a man,* I say, cannot endure the *shattering* of the soul, but
they go *utterly to ruin, perish utterly* and *rot utterly away.* So
from the *beginning* of their life body and soul experience life-
giving motions by means of common contact, even while
yet reposing in the *mother's* limbs, and *womb,* so that no
sundering can occur without *calamity* and *ruin.* Hence you
may see that, since the source of their life is common, so must
their *natures* also be common.

Since the paragraph leaves off on a motif of creation, the next
movement (ll. 356–8) is of destruction. The theme is extended by
the half-playful *reductio ad absurdum* at 367ff. Meanwhile, however, the whole paragraph 359–69 cannot but be intended to prefigure lines 408–15, which, returning our attention to the human eye

and its destruction, brings the poem's first division to a close. In its art, the sequence is quite serious.

The division's final cycle begins with the vivid image of creation in 372f. and closes with the whole of the following paragraph (ll. 396–416), which dwells throughout on destruction. We are thereupon directed to a long chain of proofs for the mortality of the soul. To the nimble reader, the subject is anything but new or surprising. Through its participation in the thematic movement up to this point, the soul's formation and dissolution has already become a part of the book's own pulse.

The words *nativos* and *mortalis* (l. 417) yield the first cycle of the new division. In the next paragraph, *principiis factam* (l. 427), *discedit* (l. 436), *perire* (l. 437), *corpora prima* (l. 438) and *conquassatum* (l. 441) key the thematic movement. A powerful cycle, leading man from birth and childhood to old age and death (ll. 445–54) follows, and then *gigni,* occurring in a recapitulation of the same cycle in ll. 457f., affords the last definitive movement of the creation theme for more than a hundred and fifty lines.[30]

As we have observed,[31] this ensuing stretch of III marks the one clearly discernible spot in *De Rerum Natura* where Lucretius found himself in formal difficulty. Still, since lines 459–614 represent a brooding concentration on death and destruction, the question of sequence in thematic movement is not involved. It is only the section's effect on the book's cyclical cadence that is formally dubious.

Verses 615–23 reintroduce creation, but then over the space of forty-five lines only *naturam* (l. 641) interrupts a new flood of the destruction theme.[32]

Discounting the book's closing division, whose formal stress had to be on destruction, III's thematic over-balance on that side may definitely be located between lines 459 and 623. For, from the latter point right on to line 830, where the final division begins, as if to compensate for the retarded movement in the book's middle section,[33] the poet sees to an admirably even alternation of the opposite motifs.

The strong thematic words *nascentibus, leto* and *creatam* pull lines 671–78 into form. Even the topical references of the next two paragraphs, the first concerning the body at birth, the second the body at death, help give us the cycle. Within, meanwhile, the movement continues; *gignimur* (l. 681) and *originis* (l. 686) prolong the creation theme till *leti* in line 687. Then, after a short respite, the cycling becomes more intense. Hardly a line between 698 and 712 fails to communicate some thematic word or other, and from 703 onward the cycle rises to the literal surface,[34] subtly reminding how mortals *inter se mutua vivunt*. Nor should the calm, almost reassuring formality of the final couplet be missed.

In the following paragraph, Lucretius continues the *mutua vivere* motif by depicting the birth of vermin in the putrefying cadaver. The cyclical turns are keyed principally to *semina* (l. 713), *exanimo* (l. 714) *cadavera* (l. 719), *exspirant* (l. 720), *perfluctuat* (l. 721), *conveniant* and *recesserit* (l. 725), *fabricentur* (l. 728), *facere* (l. 735) and *faciunt* (l. 737). The creation theme laps over into the ensuing passage, sustained by *generascunt* (l. 745), and does not finally disappear until *dissolvitur* and *interit* (l. 756); *ire* (l. 761) and *mortalem* (l. 767) next sketch a light cycle before Lucretius yet again traces the full course of human birth, growth, decay and death in 769–75.

In quick succession thereafter, Venus returns and is offset by *mortalia* (l. 778), which swiftly gives way to the rise of the division's final cycle in *prima . . . insinuetur* (l. 780). Creation persists till line 797 and *genique,* whereupon *interiit* and *periisse* (l. 798) introduce a fading movement (*mortale,* 800; *mortale,* 804; *dissoluique,* 815; *dissolvere,* 818) as the division draws to its end.[35]

Within the great closing movement of destruction, the creation theme continues to emerge, giving the effect of the cycle within the cycle. Perfunctory appearances, whether implied or literal, occur at lines 884, 895, 916, 924, 925, 929, 931, 951, 1003, 1006, 1028, 1034, 1036, 1043, 1044, 1072, and 1081. More significant is its contribution to the stupendous prospect on the cycle that begins to develop immediately after the division's opening couplet and reaches its fullest dimensions in lines 854–58. But its most important entrance is as part of the direct statement of the cycle in lines 964–77, which, in turn, marks the cycle's most revealing appearance so far in the poem. It constitutes the first—and, indeed, the only—use of the cycle as an explicit argument against the fear of death. Form and purpose have become officially one. More, the statement gathers to itself the entire force of the poem's prior cyclical movement and then delivers it to the book's final lines, where mortality closes over the reader like a shroud.[36]

But, despite its predominantly oppressive effect within the poem's first half, the rhythm's final force in the work's assault on the fear of death is, as we can already begin to see, a blend of compulsion and reconciliation. With its every return as it circles through the poem, death looms larger—birth's inevitable partner in a solemn process which, crowding ever in upon the reader, compels him to accept his mortality. But the process is at the same time impersonal and death only a reflex within its impersonality. The sum of all things at any moment is but this majestic rhythm of the universe, reflecting a shift of atoms. One submits indeed because one must, but also, reassured by the impersonality and schooled to the grandeur, because one will. One is reconciled by his very act of submission, which is only an act of perfected understanding.

The final submission and reconciliation, then, is not directly to death but to the process which comprises it. And the perfected understanding, it must be stressed, is a poetic entity. It takes place only in the presence and as an effect of the rhythm and is, in the end, precisely the intimate apprehension of the process—and of its greatness—as rhythm. Finally, therefore, *species* offers something beyond *ratio* in regard to death precisely in that the cycle, having become the felt rhythm of the universe, affords something more than a rational apprehension of death's place in the nature of things.[37]

Given the staggering task that Lucretius set before himself, it is well that it is so. For the Epicurean, physics alone—and all the reasoned proofs of Book III—can finally convince the reader of nothing more than that the condition of death is not to be feared.[38] In III's close, however, Lucretius attempts a great deal more.[39] He argues the folly of attachment to life, even the folly of lamentation over the dead, and, surely, these instinctive emotions will not dissolve beneath the mere rational arguments that he can bring to bear. Nor is it for any single reader to say that they are ever removed; but half the cycle's work remains to be performed; fuller dimensions will appear; and, before the poem's end, the reader, instructed by the rhythm, will experience a yet higher perspective on both these and all other matters pertinent to mortality.

Meanwhile, we may note that the closing section's tendency to lay brutally bare and so magnify, even while assuaging, the poignancy of death tends to magnify also the process of which death is a simple part.

BOOK IV

Practically throughout, the fourth book maintains the same sort of thematic subtlety that marks its proem and close. In large part, it attains their artistic delicacy as well. Nowhere, for instance, does Lucretius more rely on imagery, symbolism and imagistic movement to produce the thematic flow, and nowhere more successfully. The result, once we recognize the techniques and capture the rhythms, is a cyclical evolution fully as distinct as that of the first three books, though not as strong. Of the earlier violent and tortured emotional involvement there is, save in the Venus-close, none.

The book's formal-aesthetic product in the poem as a whole is a gradual and quiet, but definite channeling of cyclical energies into the surging movement of V, which itself does not abate till the final encroachment of the plague. The book is a re-introduction, light but fateful.

In the syllabus, *natura* with *compta* (ll. 26f.), followed by *distracta, ordia prima* (l. 28) and *luce carentum* (l. 35) give two quick turns of the cycle before a lingering in death (ll. 36–40) and an ultimate return to creation with *natura* and *primordia* (ll. 40f.). The suggestions of *diffusa solute* (l. 55), *fumum* and *vaporem* (l. 56) reintroduce the destruction theme, giving way to *nascentes* in line 60; *cadant* and *recedant* (l. 65), since they suggest atomic dissolution, have force enough to close out the cycle.

A short abatement follows, the theme resuming in lines 91–95 with *diffusae, ortae, scinduntur* and *coortae*. Since the thematic movement of the book's first half depends greatly on light-darkness imagery, however, the intervening passage has importance. In lines 75–83 Lucretius broaches the imagistic play. Though it remains indistinct within these verses, their floating, muted modulation of shadow and light is the seed of refulgence and darkness to come.

An influx of primordial bodies and other tried motifs give the creation theme in the first dozen lines of the next paragraph, whereupon pungent and bitter olfactory images lead to a lacuna (l. 127), wherein, if we follow Bailey's suggestion as to the intended sense, at least a slight image of destruction appears. Next, creation, emerging distinctly again in *gignuntur* (l. 131), is strengthened by *concrescere* (l. 134); a highly suggestive change of *species* ensues, involving light and dark, serenity and implied violence, a hint of destruction in the unexpected *avulsa* (l. 138); then *liquentia* (l. 141), dissolving all, steals a superlative scene away.

A superb cyclical movement permeates the following paragraph as well. In *genantur* (l. 143), *scinditur* (l. 149), *constant* (l. 150) and *scindi* (l. 153) two cycles appear; *genuntur* and *origo* (ll. 159f.), stimulate a fresh movement, which darkness, Acheron and night bring to a close. And yet, not quite; *coorta* (l. 172), signifying creation, allows yet one last impulse, which carrying over into the next paragraph, is resolved in the suggestive song of the swan.

Symbolic and explicit themes continue to move on interwoven lines. The sequence of *factas* (l. 184), *solis lux* (l. 185), *facta* (l. 186), *lumine lumen* (l. 189), *fulgere fulgur* (l. 190), *textura* (l. 196), *lux* (l. 200), *lumina* (l. 208) returns the creation theme. Night, evoked in lines 212f., *sole* (l. 218), *exesor* (l. 220), the suggestions of *dimittitur* and *requies* (ll. 226f.), *tenebris* (l. 231), *luce et claro candore* (l. 232), *tenebris* and *luci* (l. 235) then generate a rapid thematic exchange.

Next, for more than eighty lines (239–323) the poet maintains a rather severe thematic *diminuendo*.[40] Thereupon, as deeper movement commences, the opening words of the first two paragraphs (*Splendida, E tenebris,* ll. 324, 337) candidly confess its direction. In the first paragraph, *turbantia, adurit, semina, gignunt* and *semina* manage to rekindle the explicit theme within the imagistic surge, but in lines 337–52 the movement is all of the imagery—darkness and light in stringently regular alternation. Coupling with the darkness image that closed the previous paragraph's movement, *perit* pulls lines 353–63 into form, and then, after once more releasing us to darkness-light motifs, Lucretius effects an exquisite new tie with the explicit theme in line 375f.:

> semper enim nova se radiorum lumina fundunt
> primaque dispereunt, quasi in ignem lana trahatur.

I shall not attempt to dissect the pageant of imagery which follows (ll. 379–468). If there were nothing else, the glittering sunrise at 404ff., together with the ultimate onset of night and sleep (ll. 453ff.) would be sufficient to give it thematic form. But moon and stars also rise and set, images of water, sky, mountains and the columned abodes of men keep succeeding each other in rhythmic alternation and even seem to reproduce themselves in dream (ll. 456f.), antithetical comparisons swing thought and senses steadily to and fro and the twinkling light in the darkness with which the stream of images begins and closes appears again and again in between. In a sense, the whole passage is a fabulous day's journey amidst—not nature's landscapes, but her mightiest primal rhythms.

With this passage, fittingly, the high thematic reliance on imagistic play ends. In line 476, *crearit,* subsequently extended by *creatam* (l. 478) the double incidence of *orta* (ll. 483f.) and *nascuntur* (l. 495), touches off a new and decisive creation theme, which is matched in vigor by the warning of destruction in lines 505–8. As the paragraph closes, the repetition of its main thematic motifs—*ruantque* (l. 518) and *ortast* (l. 521)—extends the movement.

Motifs light and heavy, and more than usually disparate, combine to instill a steady cyclical rhythm in the ensuing paragraph:

constare (l. 526); *radit* (l. 528); *coorta* and *primordia* (ll. 530f.); *raditur* (l. 532); *constent* (l. 533); *laedere, auferat, detrahat, nigrai noctis* (ll. 534ff.); *aurorae* (l. 538), *constare* (l. 540); *amittit* (l. 541); *fit, principiorum, creatur, primordia* (ll. 542ff.); and the closing swan song. A tidier movement is provided next by *exprimimus* and *daedala* (ll. 550f.), *conturbari* (l. 559), *diffugit* (l. 566) and *perit* (l. 569), which trace the course of sound from first expression to final dissolution. Thereupon, the filmy evocation of woodland deities and their fictive melodies amid the dark, solitary silence (the imagistic sequel, after the lonely echoes of 570ff., of *perit*) effects a fragile movement of the creation theme at 580ff.[41] The sinewy *perscinduntur* (l. 601) follows, and soon thereafter *gignuntur* and *exorta* (ll. 604f.) are resolved in *obtunditur* (l. 613). At line 625, *lacerantque coorta* trace a faint, self-contained cycle; *disperit* (l. 639) extends the destruction motif; a preoccupation with primordial bodies (l. 643–62) gives rise to creation; disease and disturbance of bodily texture (ll. 664ff.) imply destruction, and then *progignere* (l. 670) starts a new cycle. The movement, rather perfunctory since line 615, is awarded a touch of subtlety at 679f.: bees with their procreative and vultures with their funereal associations. *Romulidarum* (l. 683) evokes a whole race of mortals; *perit* (l. 692) and *collabefacta* (l. 697), followed immediately by *creatum* (l. 698), enter the thematic flow, as does further darkness-light imagery at 710f. and, gently, *semina* and *interfodiunt* at 715f.

At 715ff., we have to do with the origin of things that stir the understanding; hence, the creation theme is pervasive. Chief among the paragraph's thematic words are *iunguntur* (l. 726), *fiunt* (l. 736), *confiunt* (l. 738), *fit* (l. 739), *natura* (l. 740), and *creantur* (l. 744). Even within their movement, however, destruction raises its head (l. 734). In the subsequent paragraph, *fieri* (l. 751) protracts the creation theme till, announced by *somnus* (l. 757), death crowds in at line 761; *natura* (l. 762) gives way to *mortis letique* (l. 766) and *perit* (l. 771), but then *nata* instantaneously reasserts creation. The series rolls on: *creat natura* (l. 785); *perit* and *nata* (l. 800); *pereunt* (l. 804); *fit* (l. 806).

Verses 823–57, displaying the greatest thematic density of any passage so far in the book, afford two vigorous surges of creation, sundered (ll. 843f.) by an arresting reference to strife and gore. The second impulse is checked by *fluere atque recedere* (l. 860), and then *recreet* (l. 868) and *restinguit* (l. 873) sketch yet another turn of the leitmotif.

Between *primum* at line 881 and *quietem* at 907—between, that is, the first, unconscious impulse to movement and the abatement of movement—an implied cycle transpires. Throughout the section on sleep, too, the cycles remain for the most part secondary and implicit. After another allusion to swansong (l. 910), *fit* (l. 916) strikes the creation theme. Then, since, as lines 920–24 emphatically reveal, sleep is as a partial death, the words *distracta* (l. 916), *eiecta* (l. 917) *dissoluuntur* and *fluunt* (l. 919) become forceful enough to move the destruction motif. These are supported by the unequivocal *leti* (l. 924). Given their precedent, *reconflari* (l. 927), *confiat* (l. 929), *perturbari* and *languescere* (l. 930), *elementaque prima* (l. 941), *ruina* (l. 942), *principiorum* (l. 943), *eiciatur* (l. 945), *distracta* (l. 946), *natura* (l. 948), *languescuntque* (l. 951), *cadunt* (l. 952), *resolvunt* (l. 953), *eiectus* (l. 960) and *divisior* with *distractior* (l. 961) execute more subtle thematic movement. Further, the revealed physical resemblance of sleep to death deepens the mortal symbolic suggestion of *quies* (l. 907), so that the whole inner flow of lines 907–61 is felt as a delicate cyclical tide within a larger, if relatively light, movement of the cycle.[42]

Starting with line 990, where an image of commenced motion has plainly been lost, the section on dreams generates a sensible thematic activity with the sequence *quiete* (l. 991), *expergefactique* (l. 995), *propago* (l. 998), *seminiorum* (l. 1005), *iugulentur* (l. 1014), *mortem* (l. 1020), *semen* and *creavit* (l. 1031) and *semine* (l. 1034). Save for the images of destruction clustered about line 1049, paragraph 1037–57 is thematically all creation and then, metamorphosed at *frigida cura* (l. 1060), *Venus creatrix* becomes *Venus destructrix* as the book's close begins. As usual, however, the thematic mood of the close is not absolute. The original Venus and creation return at 1209ff. with a lengthy discourse on genetics and conception, so forcibly, indeed, that only the varicolored image of destruction in the book's final couplet precludes a false, or, at best, equivocal ending.[43]

BOOK V

No book can quite match V's definiteness and power of cyclical evolution. The strength is needed, since here the long approach to the poem's final, all-resolving cycle of human culture—an approach already quickened by the emotional impact of the Venus-close—must attain the most intense consummation possible. The strength is therefore functional and, certainly, deliberate.

After the proem, the leitmotif crowds immediately in with *creata* (l. 56), *nativo* (l. 60), *vita reliquit* (l. 63), *exstiterint* and *natae* (l. 70), *augendas* (l. 80) and the mortal implication of *alte terminus haerens* (l. 90). Extending the force of the last, a vivid movement of destruction ensues at 93–96, is reasserted at line 109 and, then, though the factors change, the theme persists till line 120 and *restinguere*. At line 132, the opposite theme vigorously reenters (*oriri*) and dominates throughout the remainder of the paragraph and beyond; *natura* (l. 148) introduces even the gods into the flow of creation; creation being the subject of paragraph 156–94, it teems with the motif, with only *evertere* (l. 163) and the hints of *quietos* (l. 168),[44] *veteres* (l. 171) and *tenebris* (l. 175) interrupting the movement. At its start, the following paragraph continues on the theme, but lines 204–5 reassert destruction, as do lines 215–17 and 219–21, while the rest of the paragraph is all creation.

At lines 235f., Lucretius gathers the four elements and straightaway commences a deep cyclical rhythm: *nativo ac mortali* (l. 238), *nativo ac mortalibus* (l. 241), *mortalia* (l. 242), *nativa* (l. 243), *consumpta regigni* (l. 244), *principiale . . . tempus clademque futuram* (l. 246), *mortalia* (l. 248), *perire* (l. 249), *gigni* (l. 250), *dispergunt* (l. 254), *rodunt* (l. 256), *alit* (l. 257), *redditur* (l. 258), *omniparens* and *sepulcrum* (l. 259), *libatur* and *recrescit* (l. 260). Nor do I cite every thematic word.

As the poet next unravels the proof for the constant diminishment and renewal of the earth's supply of water, *umore novo* (l. 261), *tollitur* (l. 265), *deminuunt* (l. 267) and *remanat* (l. 269) mainly transact the cyclical business; *fluit* (l. 275), *retribuat* and *recreetque* (l. 277), *resoluta* (l. 278), *gigni* (l. 279) and *fluere* (l. 280) spontaneously join the flow.

For the fusion of symbolic imagery and explicit theme, paragraph 281–305 is the poem's greatest showpiece. Its texture, which will only be disturbed by analysis, explains why Lucretius here chose to treat the element of fire predominantly in terms of light.

Building onto *perdere* (l. 304), the subsequent paragraph is practically all destruction; and then the tight cycling resumes (ll. 318–23):

> Denique iam tuere hoc, circum supraque quod omnem
> continet amplexu terram: si procreat ex se
> omnia, quod quidam memorant, recipitque perempta,
> totum nativo ac mortali corpore constat.
> nam quodcumque alias ex se res auget alitque,
> deminui debet, recreari cum recipit res.

> Now look up up at this sky which, above and all around us,
> holds the whole earth in its embrace: if, as some men say,
> it generates all things from itself and receives them back when
> dead, it consists entirely of body that suffers birth and death.
> For whatever increases and feeds other things out of its own
> substance must be diminished and then reconstituted when
> it takes them back.

After *genitalis origo* (l. 324) and *funera* (l. 326) with *cecidere* (l. 328) have described another swift cycle, an extended movement of creation (ll. 330–37) is followed by a vast surge of destruction (ll. 338–75), whereupon (ll. 376–7) another quick cycle supersedes. The section on the world's mortality then comes to an end (ll. 380–414) amidst a series of images of ruin (ll. 387, 390, 396, 401, 410), punctuated, however, by *recreavit* (l. 404) and rhythmically relieved by the described alternate ascendency of the various elements as things evolve cyclically toward ultimate dissolution.

The section, technically one of the most effective in the poem, builds the universe quite as fully as it dissolves it and so represents as never so skillfully before the cycle within a movement of the cycle. Withal, there is just enough emphasis on destruction to relieve the long ascent to the book's close that begins just ahead.[45]

With line 416, Lucretius commences on his description of the world's formation. Throughout the introduction we hear a familiar patter of thematic words (e.g., *fundarit*, l. 417; *creare*, l. 426), but, being unneeded in the depicted throes of universal birth, they abruptly taper off. The great impulse of creation lasts till line 509.

Verses 495–508 establish an important motif. The ether glides, keeping *unum tenorem*. Next, the motions of the stars, which are set in this same undulating ether,[46] are called forth; and throughout the treatment of astronomical phenomena (ll. 509–771) evocations of such natural rhythms, often by means of well-tried imagery, greatly help provide the thematic movement. In paragraph 509–33, for instance, *vertitur* (l. 510), *volvenda* (l. 514), *ferantur* (l. 518), *versantur* (l. 520) and *volvunt* (l. 521), evoking the measured rhythms of the universe, unmistakably add to the poem's seminal flow.

The explicit theme is also at work. The powerful *creatis* (l. 528) gives way to *evanescere* and *decrescere* (l. 535), *naturam* (l. 536), *ex ineunte aevo* (l. 537) and *prima concepta ab origine* (l. 548) to the loud hint of destruction in lines 550f., *ex ineunte aevo* (l. 555) to the thematic burden of *libant* and *contractior* (ll. 568f.).

By this point, however, another thematic thread, light imagery, has entered the weave. It grows strikingly definite at 571 with *fulgent* and persists through the paragraph, though the moon's entry (l. 575) and, by implication, that of other nocturnal heavenly bodies (ll. 586f.) also awaken the image of night.[47] The *lumina* pour in with a new surge in paragraph 592–613; and, within, the explicit theme (*fontem* etc., ll. 598ff. and *accidere . . . incendia*, l. 609) resumes. Sun, moon and stars roll through paragraph 614–649, instilling the rhythm of their own revolutions and stirring the rhythm of the seasons (ll. 614–17; 637–42), while the light imagery proper fades into the full bloom of night (l. 650), itself dissolving into dawn and another fresh flood of radiance in lines 656f. The new paragraph contains more movement of the seasons (ll. 675ff.) and a vigorous execution of the literal theme: *gigni* (l. 662), *conficere* (l. 665), *reparare* (l. 668), *florescunt* (l. 670); *dimittunt* (l. 671), *cadere* (l. 672); *pubescere* (l. 673), *fiunt* (l. 676), *exordia prima* (l. 677), *origine prima* (l. 678). Then, the beautifully implied rhythms of the seasons and of the revolving heavenly bodies, the light-darkness imagery and the explicit theme all coalesce in two innocent lines (ll. 680f.):

> Crescere itemque dies licet et tabescere noctes,
> et minui luces, cum sumant augmina noctes, . . .

> And perhaps days lengthen and nights diminish,
> and daylight wanes when night increases . . .

The heavenly revolutions, the change of the seasons and light-darkness imagery continue their rhythmical work in the rest of the paragraph and on into the next, where the literal theme again joins on (*oriens obitus*, l. 709, made explicit by *creari*, l. 731, *aborisci* and *creata*, l. 733, *reparari*, l. 734, *creari*, l. 736, *gignitur*, l. 749 and *deletur* in the same line). In the treatment of eclipses (ll. 750–71) all of the same forces remain in evidence (the explicit theme anchored by *recreareque*, l. 759, and *perire*, l. 761), save the procession of the seasons, which motif reached perfect resolution in lines 737–47.

In sum, though the explicit leitmotif is perhaps scarcer in 509–771 than in any other passage of equal length so far treated, Lucretius has nowhere better succeeded in summoning the rhythm of *naturae species*.

The "quarters of the world" now formed, the poet addresses the generation of living things, and, after a final movement of darkness-light imagery (ll. 774–80), the explicit theme aggressively returns. Till line 826 only the twice-occurring *mortalia* (ll. 791, 805) and an allusion to destructive agents (818f.) serve to interrupt a huge swell of creation. Then, earth grows effete, and destruction and change (the cycle of things) ensue till 836. Creation blossoms again in the same line, is cut off at 846f. but reemerges to prevail through the rest of the paragraph. After the definitive *interiisse* (l. 855), it dominates in the following paragraph as well, but the resolution (ll. 871–77) brings the destruction motif again. In much the same foiling manner, destruction coils also through paragraph 878–914, appearing at lines 886f., 896 and 901f., but the creation theme, surging on, bursts the divide into the book's closing section (l. 925) and meets no significant resistance till line 971, where an influx of light-darkness imagery evolves toward the *dulcia lumina vitae* of 989 and a profound movement of destruction (ll. 988–1010) which firmly restores thematic balance.

Through the remainder of Lucretius' "anthropology"—which, we must not forget, is itself a long thematic swell of capital importance—the movement is often quieter, but no less definite. In paragraph 1011–27, *creatam* (l. 1013) and *peremptum* (l. 1026) mark the cyclical turn. A subsurface development from infancy to old age (*infantia*, l. 1031; *catuli, scymni*, l. 1036; *florenti aetate*, l. 1074; *vetusta*, l. 1084) plus *nata* (l. 1034) and *creati* (l. 1038), along with the symbolic suggestions of *cornicum* and *corvorum* (ll. 1084f.) give the right configuration to 1028–90. In ll. 1091–1103, speculations as to the birth of fire, giving way to a suggestion of fire's destructive force (*victa*, l. 1104), produce the same effect.

Turning next to political and cultural development and change —or, better, revolution—the poet comes suggestively close to the ethical drift of the poem's whole great closing cycle. The foundation of monarchial power (ll. 1109ff.) and its fate cue the central movement. The shift from beauty and strength to wealth as the distinguishing mark of honor (ll. 1110ff.) imputes an incidental cyclical configuration in cultural change—for we cannot have gotten this far in Lucretius without understanding that the day must again come when strength and beauty will prevail. Then the ethical "digression" (ll. 1123ff.) ushers in the crucial destruction motif. It is the heights (the kings of the creation motif), says the poet, that lie most open to destruction, and he expands on the foolishness and futility of political ambition. With lines 1140ff. we are in the heart of the destruction movement. The kings perish, their emblems trampled and defiled. But the key word is *Ergo* (l. 1136) with its burden of inevitability. In part, it refers us back to the preceding observation on envy: the kings *must* perish because others are covetous of their power. Far more, it refers us to the natural cycle of things, which endures the indefinite duration of nothing created.[48] Thus, it marks the first occasion where human institutions and human values are brought pointedly into the tide of the cycle. Though this is only a foretaste of things to come, it is imperative to note that the cycle already begins to close in on man in a much different way than in the development that led to the close of III, that the ethics are organically associated with the new tensions and, above all, that the movement, since man and his works are so intimately involved, more keenly than ever realizes the depth and grandeur of a universal rhythm.

Line 1143 introduces a new impulse of creation, but, right off (ll. 1145–50) the poet revisits the destruction theme that had preceded, thus underscoring the bitter arduousness of a cultural evolution that will only end in the encroachment of plague. The minuscule cycle within the cycle finally comes to a close with *morbo* (l. 1159), the movement's prefiguration of the pestilence itself.

Lines 1105–60 declare a shift in the poem's dramatic course already tacitly made with the beginning of the "anthropology." Formerly the individual, the dramatic protagonist has become the whole of mankind. And, clearly, the broadening of scope entails a certain foreboding in that the central dramatic event remains grandly the same: the inevitable course of the universe. In consequence, ultimate ruin moves tangibly closer. It is one of the crowning strokes of Lucretius' art that it should be made to do so while the reader is yet struggling up the difficult path *artibus ad summum cacumen.*

The implied creation of divine powers (ll. 1161f.) gives rise to a new movement; *mortalibus* (l. 1165) and *mortalia* (l. 1169) foreshadow the cycle's close in *mortis* (l. 1180), and then the recaptured rhythms of the universe and more darkness-light imagery sustain the theme till the paragraph's end. Thereupon, *peperere* (l. 1197), *sanguine* (l. 1201), *genitalis origo* (l. 1212) and *finis* (l. 1213) give formally onto the deep swell of destruction that commences with 1218, wherein the mention of trembling kings, trampled rods and axes and ruined cities allow us both to recollect and freshly experience the cycle's ethical relevance. So indeed does also the *vis abdita quaedam*, itself nothing more or less than the principle of destruction in the universe,[49] which wears away *res humanas* (l. 1233).

With line 1241, the rhythm becomes more technical, the tensions more subtle. The discovery of metals, an event all-progenitive to culture, gives a fresh rise to the creation theme; the wasting force of fire (ll. 1243f.) brings destruction; *pandere agros, interficere, ortum* and *exederat* maintain the formal rhythm through lines 1248-53; then, a play on the changing form of the metals, involving their physical dissolution and reformation and issuing in the creation of weapons and tools, furthers the movement till 1271, where *victa,* after providing the required destruction motif, broaches a discussion of the changing fashions of things, which carries the cycle to the paragraph's close.

The opposing motifs of plough and sword with their obvious thematic suggestions provide the chief movement in the ensuing paragraph. In paragraph 1297-1307, the themes become ironically mixed as the discovery of new skills and techniques are depicted exclusively in connection with their use in war, the irony heightened by *peperit discordia* (l. 1305) and then magnificently, if, on the surface, curiously, spun out to the fullness of its inner absurdity in the grim movement of destruction that ensues (ll. 1308-40).[50] *Creatis* (l. 1345) and *perire* (l. 1348) yield another cycle.

As is predictable after so wild a scene of devastation as that of 1308-40, creation now forces an emphatic reentry. Awakened by *gigni* in line 1352, the movement swells gorgeously out in the next paragraph's portrait of agricultural bounty (the plough succeeding the sword) and is extended by the following description of the discovery of song, its instruments and its solace. Destruction (l. 1415), death (l. 1420) and blood (l. 1421) interrupt, and then the creation theme arises once more, briefly, in line 1427 before the paragraph's final, climactic couplet, steeped in destruction and returning war, again brings the cycle full turn.[51] In lines 1423-35, we detect further definite associations between the Epicurean ethics and the theme—further Lucretian hints that the two are becoming indissoluble.

Next (ll. 1436-39), after so much struggle against the countercurrents of civilized progress, the poet returns us momentarily to the huge, impersonal rhythms of the universe. The superb effect, inadequately described, is a sense of relief mixed with a presentiment of deeper pressures to come. In any case, no other verses in this place could have at the same time more deftly broken the reader's preoccupation with human toils and yet so surely urged him on, through the pinnacle of arts, to the mortal toils that lie ahead.

BOOK VI

It would seem evident that, save for proem and close, wherein the poem's climactic cycle is traced to resolution and the work of *species* perfected, the sixth book demanded no representation of the explicit theme whatever. Indeed, its avoidance in the body of the book might even appear the wiser course artistically, since the cultural cycle would thereby stand out in more emphatic relief and so effect a greater sense of finality; more, it would seem clear that, if, in the absence of the literal theme, some formal continuance of the rhythm were yet felt necessary, the poem's omnipresent music would have amply fulfilled the need.

All of this Lucretius saw otherwise. The explicit cycle perseveres steadily throughout the book, the only technical difference of any consequence between its evolution here and earlier being a fairly marked decrease in the incidence of the more ordinary thematic words (*creare, perire,* etc.). This in itself becomes quite reasonable if we but grant that even the most vigorous promotion of such words at this point would have been as useless to those who have not yet discerned the theme as it is undoubtedly needless for those who have. A little reflection clarifies also Lucretius' refusal to dispense with the literal theme. The plague and its full context, the cycle of culture, as remarked earlier, acquire their climactic point as being the culmination in moral terms of all that the energies themselves of nature have to teach mankind. It is all important, then, that they be understood as part of the natural rhythm of things. By maintaining the by now overwhelming rhythm of the literal theme within the movement of this cultural cycle—or, better, by thus representing the cycle of culture as a subordinate and even incidental part of the greater movement—the poet keeps us better reminded than otherwise of the participation of the one in the other. Moreover, he intensifies the moral lesson to be learned from the course of cultural evolution by having gathered the full previous energies of the natural rhythm more intrinsically and far more forcibly into its expression. These are advantages which no convenience of thematic suspension in VI could have induced him to forego.

The first paragraph after the proem opens on familiar cyclical lines and closes (ll. 85–89) with images of the coming and going of thunderbolts, depicting meanwhile their destructive career. The rhythm is of the cycle's own nature. In line 94, *requies,* occurring in a verse that must recall the poem's first, and standing in a place there held by *genetrix,* tells its own elegant little formal tale.

The next paragraph contains little in the way of thematic words, but, as it obviously deals with the source of thunder, the subject itself gives the creation theme. Lines 121–23 bring the destruction motif. Creation, since the subject of thunder's origin is constant, immediately supersedes and prevails till line 136, where images of destruction, some violent, some frail, begin a domination of the movement through line 159, even though the fundamental subject remains creation.

The ambivalence, itself by no means obstructive, is formally broken in the next line, as *semina* clarifies the theme; and then the succession of *caedere* (l. 167), *natus* (l. 172), *liquescit* (l. 179) with *perscidit* (l. 180), *semina . . . faciunt* (l. 182), *sepultis* (l. 193) and *semina* (l. 201) reminds us of the thematic rhythm of earlier books. All the while however, the creation theme is dominant, and it becomes even more so in the ensuing verses, being only lightly interrupted by *dissoluitque* in line 216 before 223–4 finally introduce a definite mood of destruction, which, immediately after the formal *gignantur* in 239, swells into the most penetrating movement of the theme thus far.

More of the earlier books' formality ensues with *gignier* (l. 246) and *Acherunta* (l. 251). Lines 256–60 depict the birth of the thunderbolt amidst the Hades-like dark, and then 261–68 return unrelieved darkness and release flood and destruction. Creation reenters firmly at 269ff., but its course is just as stoutly checked in 285–94 especially by *displosa . . . opprimere* (ll. 285f.) and the reinforced motif of deluge (recalling line 267) in line 292. From 295 to 356 is all one cycle; lines 295–322, as it were, forge the thunderbolt, lines 322–47 trace its course from origin to destination while the rest hints at all that it may spare and all that it destroys.

Perhaps more than anything else in the following paragraph it is the suggested cycle of the seasons that gives the thematic rhythm. In line 379 *naturam* awakens the literal theme anew. Lines 383–86, partially familiar from 87–89 and producing the same organic rhythm, then give onto an extended movement of destruction, wherein, with all archpoetic ease, the poet concurrently argues an important theological point and even manages in the last two lines (ll. 421f.), which distinctly recall V, 1125–30, a reminder of the tie between ethics and theme.

Next, *missi veniant* (l. 425), a most compressed reflection of the earlier course of the thunderbolt from sky to earth, carries a petite cyclical configuration of its own; matched with it—the intention made clear by the repetition of the verb—is *veniant . . . periclum* (l. 430), which suggests the "fiery prester's" destructive force and so also carries us back to the earlier figure. Again, therefore, but delicately, the development is from origin to destination and destruction. In 435, *discidit* ironically generates both the themes of creation and destruction, and then *semina* (l. 444) and *dissoluitque* (l. 446) key a further cyclical turn.

Another extensive turn of the cycle transpires between 451 and 526. The movement has several facets. On the one side, it is the development of the rainstorm from origin to extinction that is depicted; on another, it is the water cycle. Woven in besides is a hint of the storm's destructive force, and it is perhaps in the handling of this element that the passage's poetic impress is most deeply made. The movement begins imagistically with the slow gathering of innocent clouds; *caligine* (ll. 461, 479) gives the first hints of things to come; at line 482, the *nubila* become *nimbis,* and by line 491 darkness and the ripening storm lour over all; *imber* (l. 496) is the predictable next suggestion and at this point, since we now know the poet's methods, we confidently await the storm's explosion and the harvest of destruction which must inevitably follow. But the poet most tantalizingly retards climax and resolution, adding, as it were, still more moisture to the already swollen deck of clouds (ll. 495–507). Then we hear two reasons why the rain *must* burst forth before, at last, the storm is allowed to break, furiously indeed (*vehemens . . . vehementer,* l. 517), but with only the slightest sequel of destruction—the consequence, not even mentioned, of extended rains (themselves at ll. 519ff.). Where we should expect more, we get—a luminous rainbow. The storm is over, the cycle finished; and, formally, it is a good and sufficient cycle even as it stands, but an exquisite one if, as was surely intended, the tableau of destruction which the reader is so charmingly denied has worked its way into the poetry by anticipation.

After a very formal recommencement of the movement (*creantur,* l. 527; *fiant* and *creentur,* l. 533), earthquake ensues for more than seventy lines. The formality of paragraph 527–36 is no doubt much due to the heavy accent on destruction in the ensuing section, especially at lines 546f., 565ff., 585ff. and 596ff. Even here, however, the creation motif is not utterly dormant. In connection with two of the destruction movements (ll. 565, 598) the word *natura* reoccurs to remind us of the earth's creation; also, each cause for earthquakes adduced in the section, since it concerns their generation, can be felt to sit with the creation theme.

Paragraph 608–38 smoothly enters the general movement by its play on the process of addition and subtraction which keeps the volume of the sea constant. The cycle is of the water particles themselves, with the paragraph beginning and ending on the idea of increase. With a bold transition then the poet strikes the literal theme of destruction in the following paragraph as he turns to the subject of volcanic eruptions.

But on the side of form Lucretius at this point becomes as busily occupied with the task of preparing for his poem's close as with the further evolution of the cycle. In the last line of the present paragraph (*moliretur*) he evokes the whole gamut of awesome change of which nature is capable; immediately thereafter, for the first time in direct physical comparison to the earth and man, he reminds us of the universe's infinite size. Change represents the cycle of things and infinity its setting. As stated earlier, the two work together throughout the poem toward a specific ethical lesson that centers on man's insignificant place within the sum of things. The lines thus are an open preparation for the ultimate moral lesson. And there is yet further anticipation of things final in the paragraph as a whole. Between lines 656 and 664, helped by the highly thematic *febrim* and *morbi* (thrice), we get an unmistakable foretaste of the plague. More, the paragraph's central argument forcibly reminds us that in all sensible phenomena—in an individual's sensation of fever as in, perchance, the collapse of a whole universe—the fundamental cause is always the same: the natural interworking of atoms in the void. The paragraph's express motive is to underscore the naturalness of all grand physical phenomena, but, along the way, the poet firmly establishes the same quality also in fever and disease, which, as we shall see, he takes great pains to assert once more, and to very good purpose, before the tremendous finale.

As for the thematic movement, *natura* (l. 646) touches the creation and lines 655–63, especially with their anticipatory effect, the destruction motif. Even before these verses have run their course, however, creation glimmers once in *semina* (l. 662). Then a reversion to Aetna (l. 669) recalls destruction before *semina* (l. 672) modifies the theme once again. Where we come finally to the volcanic eruptions themselves, their causes (ll. 682–89, 694–99) mainly carry the creation theme,[52] while lines 690–92 and 700 touch the destructive result.

Images express and implied of heat and cold manage the cyclical business in the passage (ll. 712–34) on the mystery of the Nile: the opening *aestas* yields to the hint of cold in *aquilones* (l. 715); *gelidis ab stellis axis* (l. 720) solidifies the suggestion just before *aestifera* with its explicit verbal force of creation and other images switch the motif; *aquilonum* (l. 730) next is reversed by *mediam regionem . . . diei* (l. 732), and then the final two lines generate both heat and cold, *tabificis* throwing their stress on the side of destruction.

After *natura* (l. 739) and death (ll. 743f.) start the movement in the long treatment of Avernian places, a brilliant thread in the poem's formal weave appears. At line 750 Athena becomes *"alma,"* and the epithet carries us both subtly backward through the proem of the present book to the all-fostering goddess of the poem's first lines and forward, though ironically, to the scene of the plague. But even this indwelling irony is made to lend unity, instructing us once more in the near affinity of all creative and destructive forces.[53] The thematic words *natura* (l. 755), *mactata* (l. 759), *naturali* with *origo* (ll. 760f.) and *Orci* with *Acheruntis* (ll. 763f.) cue the remainder of the thematic movement in the section's opening paragraph. For the rest, a steady preoccupation with things noxious and deadly, together building an oblique presentiment of the plague (*morbos* l. 771, *morbo,* l. 793 and *febris,* l. 804, add their explicit sense) sustains the theme of destruction, which flowers into a pervasive encroachment of death in lines 818–39. Concurrently, *vitalia* (l. 771), *naturam* (l. 775), *primasque figuras* (l. 776), *semina* (l. 789) and *gignier* (l. 807) keep the creation motif alive.

An extensive play on images of light and dark and cold and heat (already evident in ll. 840–47), the elements of which touch nearly every line, furnishes the main thematic rhythm in paragraph 848–78; and, though the incidence of thematic words lessens, the same rhythm persists also through the ensuing paragraph.

There is thematic matter to be found in the lengthy section on the magnet as well (ll. 906–1089), but here Lucretius' chief poetic concern clearly lies elsewhere. This section focuses our attention as never before in Book VI on fundamental nature—matter, its sensible properties, and void. As a result, it serves incidentally as a brief epitome of the philosophy's whole physical theory, but its main formal function is to reinforce from lines 639ff. the notice of the natural atomic basis of all sensible phenomena. The poet's manifest purpose is to sweep the reader into the climactic passage on the plague with his senses thoroughly absorbed in primal nature, thereby reminding him as fully as art might that plague too is nothing more than a natural result of natural atomic processes. As a prelude to the Athenian plague proper, Lucretius expressly asserts this very position (ll. 1090–1137), but how much more forceful these verses are after the careful conditioning of 906–1089 the reader himself can easily determine.

Since its most significant formal work has already been noted and the whole matter of its relation to the central meaning belongs properly to the following chapter, little need be remarked here concerning the poem's close. Two details, however, are well worth our notice. At line 1209, magnifying a detail in Thucydides, Lucretius writes *ferro privati parte virili* and in 1256–58 he expands Thucydides' version with a pathetic portrait of generation heaped on generation in death. The alterations are not idle. Each in its own way, the two details spell the end of generation.[54] Thus subsides the poem's creation theme.

In another sense, however, poem and cycle never end, but, upon the fading of the plague, we pass "through unknown, remembered gates" back into the radiance of Venus and creation, back into nature's unending rhythm. The poem's every element of form compels it.

In this chapter, however, I have by no means attempted to bring to light every such element, but only the principal trend of the thematic movement. Many a contributing image and incidental thematic word has been passed over without citation—this and perhaps a great deal more that will lie on the surface for a sharper eye than mine.[55] Principally, however, almost every ingredient of the poem's superlative music remains unsought, and, again, not before each and all are recovered and made known will we have the fundamental guide to Lucretius' achievement.

IV

Form & Meaning

The question of poetic meaning in *De Rerum Natura*, far from having ever been solved by the students of Lucretius, has scarcely been raised. Rather, the abiding assumption has been that the poet's entire purpose was his apparent achievement: a lucid exposition of the Epicurean system in verse, with a preponderant stress on the physics and scant inclusion of the ethics. I have earlier suggested that Lucretius' real intention was his reader's moral salvation. We are now on the point of seeing that the process by which this is attained, if attained it is, admits the ethics absolutely into the poem as its true end and meaning. That process, of course, is the fused evolution of *naturae species ratioque*. Since *De Rerum Natura* is a poem, the element of the two more expressive of its final meaning is, not curiously, *species* and particularly its poetic *principium*, the natural cycle of creation and destruction. Indeed, so true is this that, if one were to describe the poetic argument and meaning in a single sentence, it would be to say that the only true way of life—the Epicurean—is written visibly on the face of nature.[1]

It is crucial for the comprehension of Lucretius to understand that neither birth nor death as each figures in the poem tells a significant story of itself. In particular, the emotions that attach to either, whether deliberately implanted by the poet or arising spontaneously from the reader's predisposition or prejudice, are not to be conceived of as intended final experiences. None lie at the heart of the poem. Here there is only process and rhythm, an all-commanding movement that subsumes every emotion to its ordered flow. And, the attendant emotions aside, birth and death, of course, are merely balanced reflexes within the process. Neither is more significant than the other or significant at all without the other. Death, then, does not exist for the poem without reference to birth. Accordingly, even the *vis abdita quaedam,* the principle of destruction in nature by means of which the poet warns against contempt of her moral admonitions, is in reality no more a manifestation of her destructive than her creative energies. The process is all. Accordingly, too, when the plague spreads its might in the work's final lines, Lucretius cannot intend merely to express the ultimate horror of nature's potential for destruction. His aim can only relate to the poem's organic natural process whose force for destruction has its fount nowhere else than in a reciprocal balance with its creative might. In effect, therefore, to finish with absolute feelings of the poem's violence, morbidity or burden of pain or to end in despair is to see in its opening lines the intention of a perverse and malevolent Venus. It is a fatal misapprehension of all that Lucretius set out to teach.[2]

With these principles in mind we may proceed to the poem's meaning. There is but one proviso. The meaning *is* the form, and just as the form, which is the poetry harmonized in all its elements, cannot be realized by any amount of analysis, so the meaning cannot be transmitted by any quantity of pointing or description. It must be experienced. What follows, therefore, is offered only as a directive to some of the most important work of the poetry. At that, the greatest interest by far will be concentrated on the poem's climax and its intended effect.

To this, however, must be added an important reminder. With Lucretius we are given a special advantage in estimating deliberate poetic effect. Unquestionably, his fundamental motive was to elucidate the content and worth of the Epicurean philosophy. The philosophy's essentials we possess also from other sources. We therefore have considerable objective knowledge of whither the poet was tending. Where the poetry produces distinct effects that are typically and essentially Epicurean, then, there can be scant doubt that these were its premeditated aim.

The rich, solemn cadence of the poem's first line, far from ever wavering at any subsequent point, only grows larger, inevitably so, since, after its conjunction with the rhythm of the literal cycle, it becomes fleshed with deep human significance. The task of Lucretius' art is precisely to control and define the significance. From this point forward, the rhythm is so handled as to evolve an implicit poetic argument of its own, bearing, as promised, on the dissolution of human ignorance and fear. As the first book unfolds, the rhythm becomes understood as the very principle of the human condition. The reader gathers not only that his separate life is a rhythm, but one in keeping with the smooth, irresistable permutations of the universe. Thus, together with nature's *ratio,* the rhythm contends the inevitability of death, and, as we have seen, this part of the argument is completed by the end of Book III. It is, however, not yet consummated. For it is the reader's reasoned submission to the fact of death and even his serene reconciliation to it that Lucretius most desires to win by the rhythm, and, surely, this cannot be effected by the harrowing cyclical pressures of the first three books.

His method, however, is not to relent. In the poem's tremendous final cycle, the reader gathers that not merely the individual human but each movement of civilization and the finest accomplishments of man in community must pass within the universe's impersonal exchange of atoms. These perish, as it were, consumed with pestilence. It is the very magnitude of this outcome that compels logical submission and reconciliation to the fact of death. If ever, the individual's resistance to his own mortality must now crumble before the natural process that has been shown to govern and bring low all of human kind and its works. If ever, therefore, he must now grasp that it is precisely this process of change which governs in the universe. And, finally, he must comprehend that it rules only as an absolute unity: that, being founded in the simple universal shift of atoms, the process is in its essence neither the force of destruction nor any combination of birth and death conceived as true natural entitites, but nothing more or less than a great cadence of the universe as it undergoes its lawful mutations.

Ranged against such comprehension, fear of death must logically subside with the last hope of indefinite life. For it is now apparent that, if a proper object for such dread exists, it is not death, but the very process of universal change. Accordingly, if death, then birth too must reasonably be an object of dread. Nay, life itself. Not only is fear of death exposed as irrational, but the calm acceptance of nature's governing process becomes an absolute dictate of reason. One makes his peace with mortality as an impartial reflex in the lawful movement of the universe. Thus the poem's close perfects the close of III.

As we shall soon observe, the ultimate perfection extends even beyond this, but the rhythm's significance for the poem is by no means exhausted by any relation it bears to the question of death. It relates intensely also to life and its conduct, and herein, as I have implied, *De Rerum Natura* reaches its fullest meaning. In attaining it, the rhythm's mode of instruction remains implicit argument, so that this aspect of meaning also comes forth as a logical conclusion. As in the argument on mortality, the conclusion is unvoiced, but, if anything, it is even more accessible. As there also, the argument's course, at first oppressive, terminates in reconciliation.

With the poem's closing cycle, there comes to bear importunately upon the reader a movement that argues nothing if not the impermanence of human glory and the hazards of human ambition. Hard reminders of the hazards—slaughtered kings, trampled rods and axes, death at sea, and more—are the contributions of the close of V. All, the reader gathers, are expressions of the *vis abdita quaedam,* the hidden force of destruction that moves inevitably in the rhythm of things. In the plague, he is subjected to its ultimate expression, expanded to its widest cultural relevance possible. He has known the bitter human struggle to reach the pinnacle of culture, the brief, fragile bloom of Athens, and now he knows her ruin and passage into the irrevocable past. The moral is unmistakable: if the supreme in human glory and the flower of innumerable human ambitions so vanish within the governing rhythm of things, what genuine glory is there for a single mortal to seek? What glory especially since that same rhythm which humbled a mighty city is omnipresent, working as surely in the trivial as in the great? Better to conform to the movement of nature, expose oneself the least possible to the resources of ruin: better to live, unnoticed, the hard life of Epicurean pleasure.

Described apart from the poetry, the moral conclusion has scant impact. But in the grip of the plague, in the final toils of the music, at the final funeral pyre, amid its mixed feelings of helplessness and shame—all of this after a thousand gruelling revolutions in the endless ebb and flow—it comes forth with all of the spontaneous power that poetry can produce.

It was not Lucretius' intention, however, merely to crowd the reader to the Epicurean side by disclosing the peril and vanity of the non-Epicurean life. Imperative as well was that he express the compensation and reward of the life that he had to offer in its stead. These inhere in the same poetry.

For, again, the process that has led the reader inevitably on to the poem's final moral is the absolute expression *naturae ratio*—nature's inner law. Being so, being particularly that beyond which there is no expression of justice in the natural universe, it looms as all just, making no claims beyond the clear necessity of its own evolution. Once comprehended, then, its very impersonal movement becomes the absolute universal justice. In another sense, it becomes the justification of the plague and all other forms of natural perdition. This understood, all sense of oppression in the rhythm's movement must dissolve, and the reader is at last open to Lucretius' definition of true piety (V, 1203): "To be able to regard all that is with a mind at peace." Now fortified to yield serenely all that is the rhythm's own, he can as a matter of course concede in peace all that, *fortuna gubernante,* it has shown to be perilous in human affairs. In short, then, the rhythm offers a mind to shun all that is potentially hazardous in human affairs out of a tranquil conviction of cosmic justice. It is at once Lucretius' offer of moral salvation and perhaps the richest expression possible of the Epicurean ethical life.

What is more important for us is that it is all a sheer product of poetry. Indeed, the exigencies of analysis have forced an imperfect description of the poetry's actual effect. Plainly, the argument on mortality and the moral argument are not separate. Not only does the same poetry produce them, but both together form the poem's moral reward. Though late, then, we must stress the unity of the work's poetic effect and, above all, the oneness of its resolving agent. This surely is the apprehension of cosmic justice which the rhythmic movement, itself the expression of cosmic law, brings into being. On the question of death—which, we must remember, is the poem's central problem—it remains to be seen that it has yet further conciliatory potential.

In the close of III, as we recall, Lucretius stimulated and left unresolved certain instinctive agonies associated with death, and one in particular. His most bold—because most moving—gesture in this direction was his evocation of the anguish of bereavement (III, 894ff.). It is apparent that, if resolution is to come, it must subsist in the work's final poetic effect. And it may be claimed at least that the final poetry does offer the means, if not the capacity, to accommodate this most fundamental of human agonies. Imbuing the reader in the essence of *mortales mutua vivunt,* the rhythm proclaims once for all that death is the equitable toll of birth. Necessarily, then, it denies all reasonable sting of injustice in the occasion of one's losses, and, this removed, it leaves no place to turn for the assuagement of grief save to reason itself. Once again, therefore, the rhythm opens the way to the resources of reason, the philosophical mind.[3]

Lucretius' ultimate aim in *De Rerum Natura* may now be seen to have been a persuasive formulation in Epicurean terms of the moral reason that the natural stresses of the universe urge upon mankind. The ethical results are impressive. Humility becomes the natural basis and moderation the natural principle of all human action.[4] If we hope to measure the poet's achievement against his aim, however, it becomes necessary to ask whether even so much can compensate for the sacrifice of meaningful belief in the divine which the philosophy necessitated. The answer, of course, need only be attempted in relation to Lucretius' own time; and if, given that context, we limit our concept of religious value to its highest aspect, the spiritual, it is affirmative.

It is not necessary to the proof to argue that the Roman religion was then in a moribund state, for it is doubtful whether that religion even in its prime offered the breadth and depth of spiritual experience subsisting in a true comprehension of Lucretius' rhythmical universe. Again, "to be able to regard all that is with a mind at peace" is the spiritual reward and the assurance of inherent universal justice its never failing fount of renewal. Even this side of its moral guidance, then, the poem offers in a spiritual way the continuing sense of a deep, just and serene personal harmony with all universal powers. Nor ought the spiritual content of the moral teachings pass unnoticed. If the great Greek religious doctrine of *hybris* and *ate* may be said to have possessed spiritual might, then a kindred value accrues also to the content of *De Rerum Natura*. For what else is Lucretius' *vis abdita quaedam* than *ate* transformed into a purely physical reflex in the nature of things and what else the excessive ambition that flies in its face than an adumbration of *hybris?*[5]

It is not all for nothing, then, that numerous critics have caught sight of a spiritual greatness somehow religious in our poet. Only the source and definition have been mistaken. He found the universe itself an abundant home of the spirit.

A last crucial strand of the cycle's work must be collected before we close. The poem's two professed major problems are the fear of death and fear of the gods. Lucretius early gives a pair of connected notices as to how he intends to deal with the latter. Immediately as he starts upon the poem's *principium* (I, 151ff.), he proclaims that the *ratio* of creation will help remove fear of the gods. Earlier (107ff.), he had disclosed with equal clarity that the *ratio* of destruction would contribute toward the same end. These are his only pronouncements on methodology, and, as is his wont with matters of large importance, both are intrinsically tied to the poem's thesis and *principium*. In sum, Lucretius argues that a true grasp of the atomic causes of creation and destruction will eliminate all possible suspicion of divine agency in the operations of the universe, and, thereby, all reasonable mistrust of the gods. Once again, of course, *ratio* is the foundation of doctrine; but if this study has established anything, it is that the poetic process of the cycle expresses the *ratio* of birth and death with a fullness and finality that *ratio* alone cannot attain. It can be claimed, therefore, that every beat of the poem's organic rhythm contributes directly to the dissolution of holy dread. Thus, no aspect of the work's purpose lies outside the scope and function of its essential poetry.

Notes

CHAPTER I

1. Otto Regenbogen, *Lukrez, seine Gestalt in seinem Gedicht,* (Leipzig, 1932), p. 87.
2. R. V. Schoder, "Lucretius' Problem," *The Classical Journal,* XLV (1950), 180.
3. W. Sellar, *The Roman Poets of the Republic* (Oxford, 1905), p. 386.
4. Such dissent, however, has made at least a tacit appearance in a recent article by Elizabeth M. McLeod, "Lucretius' *carmen dignum,*" *The Classical Journal,* LVIII (1963), 145–56. Though roughly, the author has revealed the cycle of creation and destruction in nature to be the poem's unifying formal element. For some reason, however, she has not noted how this discovery reverses a pernicious critical tendency to find only symptoms of disorder in the work. The article will be treated in some detail later on.
5. Giussani's edition, for example, though a great landmark in the elucidation of Lucretius' science, thoroughly misuses the poetry through its radical indulgence in transposition.
6. See Karl Büchner, "Beobachtungen über Vers und Gedankengang bei Lukrez" (*Hermes, Einzelschriften,* Heft I, 1936, Kap. III, 47–103) and C. Bailey, "The Mind of Lucretius," *American Journal of Philology,* LXI (1940), 278–91.
7. All references will be to the text of Cyril Bailey, *Lucretius, De Rerum Natura,* 3 vols. (Oxford, 1947).
8. Bailey, *op. cit.,* II, 625.
9. It is apparent, moreover, that Lucretius largely bases his arguments for the *principium* itself (I, 159–264) on the observed occurrence of the cycle. The arguments, depending heavily on what is not seen to be born and perish in nature, are ultimately founded on that which is observed to be created and destroyed.
10. The fear and ignorance which Lucretius mentions at 146 refer us back at least to 102ff., and thus to the "syllabus" for the whole poem.
11. The cause of so much historical criticism as has arisen on *De Rerum Natura* is perhaps more easy to postulate. The poet's biographical tradition and especially the suggestion of mental disorder must lie somewhere behind the persistent questioning of the text that has characterized modern scholarship in general.
12. This judgment must hold even in regard to Mewaldt's findings (see Chap. III, n. 15), since even these did not lead to anything like a relevant *Urplan.*
13. Alfredo Menzione, "Fisionomia del Poema Lucreziano," *Rivista di Studi Classici,* VI (1958), 253–286.

14. *Op. cit.,* 286.
15. *Op. cit.,* p. 80ff.
16. Similarly, the conviction of a disordered poetic imagination that studies like Regenbogen's have tended to instill has marred other provocative critiques of Lucretius. The very title of W. S. Anderson's "Discontinuity in Lucretius' Symbolism," *Transactions of the American Philological Association,* XCI (1960), 1–29, is symptomatic of the trend. Yet, given Anderson's evident sense and skill, a predisposition on his part to seek consistency rather than disarray in the very material which he handles would undoubtedly have yielded very profitable results. J. P. Elder in his "'Lucretius I, 1–49" *Ibid.,* LXXXV (1954), 88–120, provides, if anything, an even more definite case in point. Elder at once makes it known that he admires and is influenced by Regenbogen's notions and at the same time, without exploiting his discovery, discloses much of the essential substance of the creation theme in the work's proems. Again, then, it seems that a too trusting respect for the prevailing critical tradition has cut off valuable progress. Also, perhaps the fact that A. K. Michels in "Death and Two Poets," *Ibid.,* LXXXVI (1955), 160–79, can appreciate the cycle as the occasion of some of Lucretius' finest poetry and yet not pursue her insight is due to a mistrust of further pursuit, inspired by the critical tradition.

    In any case, all of these studies are immeasurably sounder than M. Rozelaar's, *Lukrez: Versuch einer Deutung* (Amsterdam, 1943), where, taking Lucretius' disorder to be self-evident, the author seeks to explain the person rather than the poem.
17. The "tensions" cited and the others mentioned by Regenbogen resolve themselves into a fundamental inner conflict of reason and emotion, and the true Epicurean, since reason is by definition ascendent in him, can know no such division.
18. Friedrich Klingner, *Romische Geisteswelt* (Munich, 1956), p. 173–99.
19. Henri Bergson, *The Philosophy of Poetry, The Genius of Lucretius,* trans., ed. and in part revised by Wade Baskin (New York, 1959). George Santayana, *Three Philosophical Poets* (Cambridge, 1910).
20. *Op. cit.,* p. 79.
21. *Op. cit.,* p. 23.
22. *Op. cit.,* p. 81.
23. *Op. cit.,* p. 42f.
24. *Ibid.*
25. Since full notice of universal destruction has already been given in the very argument (Book V) by the poem's end, the passage would look backward in substance as well as in form. Both *species* and *ratio,* therefore, would be made to consummate their lessons in the limp and the old.
26. See note 4.
27. McLeod, *op. cit.,* 150.
28. *Ibid.,* 152.
29. Taken together, fragments (Diels) 2, 6, 7, 8, 9, 10, 11, 12, 14, 15, 17, 21, 22, 23, 26, 29, 35, 36, 38, 57, 58, 59, 61, 62, 63, 66, 67, 68, 71, 77, 78, 79, 80,

81, 82, 86, 87, 89, 95, 98, 107, 109, 111, 112, 113, 115, 121, 124, 125, 128, 136, 137, 138, 139, 148 give strong indication of a thematic cyclical movement similar to that of *De Rerum Natura* in both Empedocles' *Poem on Nature* and *Purifications*. The evidence, however, is more definite for the former.

30. Steele Commager, *The Odes of Horace* (New Haven, 1962), p. 267f.

31. As we shall later see, Vergil's use of the word *primus* (10, 12) to claim originality is a direct piece of thematic borrowing from Lucretius.

32. Cf. Brooks Otis, *Virgil, A Study in Civilized Poetry* (Oxford, 1963), p. 213.

33. I owe these observations on the cycle in the *Georgics* to the suggestion of Prof. Paul L. MacKendrick of the University of Wisconsin.

CHAPTER II

1. The four-line coda (1114–17), while it obviates a strict close on the theme of destruction, produces actually more formal benefit than harm. First, we may *a priori* agree that such a protreptic is in place at the close of the first "lesson" in so rigorous and demanding a work. Second, as will presently become clear, the four verses, in their light-darkness imagery, themselves contain cyclical material and therefore do not depart from the general formal contours of the poem. Third, and this was probably the fundamental reason for their inclusion, they foreshadow the final four verses of Book V, which, as we shall see, are the most important formal hinge of the entire poem and are therefore in need of all the advertisement they can get.

2. In this passage, *grandis, cecidisse, vetulae, vietae, saeclum, antiquum, finibus* and *modus* are all to be regarded as thematic words; but this we shall better see when we have worked deeper into Lucretius' methods.

3. I use the word in its root sense to connote a falling, concluding movement in the theme.

4. The climatic movement is developed also by a progressive increase in the lengths of the terminal thematic passages. At the close of I, as we have seen, the theme is indicated by a relatively few verses; the *grandis arator* passage which I have quoted for III constitutes actually only the finale of a deep cyclical movement that begins with line 1105 and turns emphatically to the theme of destruction as early as line 1131; III's thematic close occupies the whole final segment of the book.

5. The couplet's function cannot be understood without awareness that the *guttae* here are a conscious formal reprise of the *dulcedinis gutta* with which the book's closing section began. On the matter of the verb's erotic suggestion cf. Catullus' far more blunt usage in 32.11.

6. A further, equally strong evidence of such accommodation lies in *morbo* (I, 133), which prefigures the plague itself, just as *sepultis* prefigures the results of the plague and VI's final lines. The accommodation, of course, would have been neater had Lucretius ended the first proem precisely with these lines, and it will perhaps be instructive to speculate on the

formal possibilities of his having done so. There would seem to be within the proem two possible alternative locations for the passage 136–45. The one is *post* line 49, the other *post* line 61. Might Lucretius have been tempted to transpose them to either place? We can make no worthwhile speculation on their movement to a position after 49, for, even as the text stands, there is the problem of a proper transition from an address to Venus to an address to Memmius—a problem, moreover, which this transition would hardly appear to alleviate. Meanwhile, there are strong formal grounds for not transferring them to a position after 61. As we shall presently observe, the words *primum* and *primusque* (ll. 66, 67) are extremely crucial to the creation theme. They are, however, not obviously so, and one means by which Lucretius tries to point their relevance is to juxtapose them to the same words employed in description of the atoms as creative bodies (ll. 58–61: *genitalia, semina, prima, primis*). To separate these clue words by the interpolation of several lines from the words they are meant to illuminate would clearly be poor formal practice—poor enough to Lucretius' mind, we may suppose, to outweigh the formal advantage of removing 136–45 from their present, obstructive position.

In sum, then, the structure of the proem would appear to have left no likelier place for the lines than the one in which they stand.

But rather than allow these inquiries to come to an indecisive close, we may cite yet more evidence of the accommodation of the proem's ending to that of the poem. The close of Book III shows that the correspondences we have seen in *morbus* and in notions of death and burial are not fortuitous. Here we meet many of the elements that were implanted in the close of proem I, and all that are to reemerge in Book VI's close. The *Acherusia templa* (I, 120) reappear (III, 978ff.); Homer (I, 124) reappears (III, 1037); burial (III, 1035, with *ossa* echoing I, 135) reappears and cremation (III, 906) appears, itself to reemerge at the poem's very end; *morbus* gets passing notice; and, finally, III, 1046ff. very evidently echo (with *mali* taking the place of *morbo* in the earlier lines) the crucial I, 132–33. The coincidences are too many to be fortuitous. Rather, surely, they are strands of the subtle web that binds the poem together into a meaningful unity.

7. Though it is true that Lucretius was at complete liberty to end, but not to begin, his books as he wished, this difference does not in itself explain the relative obscurity of the creation theme in the proems. As we shall see, his method was to blend the theme with the extraneous matter of the proems, mainly with the eulogy of Epicurus. When we observe its effects, we will agree that this blend was the poet's most urgent formal goal in the proems and that it was in order to achieve it that he risked veiling the theme.

8. It is to be noticed that this *primus* motif gets its start at line 12 in connection with Venus. Looking ahead, moreover, we may see a small but significant sign of its conscious development in the correspondence between *tam clarum extollere lumen/ qui primus . . .* (III, 1f.) and the *primum . . . tollere* here.

9. Included, of course, would be the "godhood" of the *Venus destructrix* of Book IV's close.
10. The identical passage occurs in the proem of I (44–49), but on this see the following note.
11. The reader may object that if I, 44–49 are to be accepted as genuine the rejection of Venus' deity becomes so blunt as to preclude entirely to gradualness of which I have spoken. This is true only if the lines are interpreted—as they must be at II, 646ff.—as an outright statement of Epicurean theology. They were not meant to be so taken, however.

The passage is this:

> omnis enim per se divum natura necessest
> immortali aevo summa cum pace fruatur
> semota ab nostris rebus seiunctaque longe.
> nam privata dolore omni, privata periclis
> ipsa sua pollens opibus, nil indiga nostri
> nec bene promeritis capitur, neque tangitur ira.

Certainly, no other verses in the poem have been regarded with as much suspicion. The history of their treatment can be fairly summed up by noting that Marullus was the first to suppress them and that they have recently been deleted without vestige in a *translation* of the poem.

The main inconsistency to be seen if they are a direct statement of Epicurean theology is that, by introducing such notions so abruptly after his appeal to Venus, Lucretius makes a mockery of the appeal itself, thereby stultifying everything he has attempted to accomplish so far. It does not beg the question, I think, to stress that nothing up to line 44 leads the reader to expect a declaration of Epicurean theology at this point. It follows that, if he appears to find one, his first response should be to try the snytax a second time. Herein lies the solution. The key to the lines lies in allowing *semota* and *seiuncta* a perfectly legitimate temporal force. The passage thus translates: "For it must necessarily be that the whole nature of the gods enjoys its everlasting life in fullest peace when removed and far disjoined from our affairs. For being (in that case) relieved of all pain and relieved of hazards, mighty in its own resources, lacking nothing of us, it is neither beguiled by virtuous service nor touched by wrath."

Taken thus, the passage follows naturally on the preceding appeal to Venus to intercede with Mars in the name of peace, which appeal amounts, after all, to a petition to remove him from mortal affairs. So taken, also, Mars is subjected to a piece of irony that would not be half so exquisite did it not come from the mouth of an Epicurean. He is represented as, by nature, best suited to live *summa cum pace*. So far, however, Venus is not at all impugned as goddess. But there remains an obvious second edge of the argument which introduces just the proper degree of doubt. It is evident that, if Venus is persuaded by the poet's fictive appeal to reason, she can comply with its requirements only by violating them. That is, she can remove Mars from mortal affairs only by surrendering herself to them. She is therefore left quite suspended in dilemma—and how better could the poet have left her? The all important fiction of her deity remains intact, and so surely does the poet's Epicureanism. It is precisely with this passage, then, that Lucretius commences to work the goddess gently out of the poem—all but her fiction. The technique of the whole is the more effective in that the same lines *become* the poet's absolute statement of Epicurean theology in Book II.

The problem of a probable lacuna after 49, it is true, remains. But, plainly, that difficulty is made no less vexing by the deletion of 44–49.

12. The symbolism is beautifully established by the association of light with *Venus genetrix* in the first proem and is clinched by the phrase *in luminis oras*. At times, Lucretius uses the image of light metaphorically to symbolize life. In other connections, also, it will take on other metaphorical significances. No serious confusion results, however, since the image will almost always be used in conjunction with images of darkness, the symbol of death, where it is intended to symbolize creation.

13. Bailey, *op. cit.,* I, 31. Bailey's groupings are I and II, III and IV, V and VI. G. Barra in his *Struttura e Composizione del De Rerum Natura di Lucrezio* (Naples, 1952), argues for a principal structural division into two parts, I–III and IV–VI. His grounds are that Lucretius mainfestly undertakes to set out the positive scientific essentials of Epicurean doctrine in the first three books, while reserving the final three for those phenomena the misunderstanding of which leads to injurious belief in the divine. The argument is not without merit. Even if accepted whole, however, it does not suggest the need of a different sort of proem for III. Indeed, given this division, the celebratory air that the proem possesses appears quite fitting as the poet looks ahead to the conquests of reason that follow.

There is, by the way, no reason why we cannot accept both Bailey's and Barra's observations side by side—a structural break both into threes and twos, but on different principles.

14. The proem is a nearly *verbatim* repetition of I, 926–50, but the lines cannot be said to establish as much there on the theme, because they occur before the pattern of thematic motifs has solidified. Also, the discrepancy in the final line detracts from the thematic force of the earlier passage.

15. That is, both are *primi* and, hereby, creators, and both range far (cf. *peragro* here and *peragravit* I, 75) into exclusive domains for the substance of their creation. The parallel is explicit. It is to be noted also that the *primus* motif as it relates to Epicurus first arose in connection with this passage in Book I. The parallel is important.

16. The oft-occurring phrase *nigror mortis* establishes it as such.

17. The marvel of it is that these difficulties appear not to have disturbed our poet in the least. Yet, not only does the same image arise perforce in I, 926–50, but twice also in the closing verses of proem I (136ff.). Their occurrence in the first proem, of course, is meant to give the first clue to an eventual tie between Epicurus and Lucretius in the creation theme

but the same criticism that applies to the symbolism in the latter passages applies here also and, meanwhile, the images here do not have the support of the thematic material that occurs in the later passages. It is especially striking that, though in all passages it is the word *obscura* that causes the difficulty (it does not matter that it *means* little more than "abstruse"), Lucretius seems to have had no temptation to change it. True, such a change would have destroyed the nice equipoise of the images, but this perhaps would not have been too great a cost for the resultant relief to the symbolism. The poet, however, appears not to have thought in terms of relief. As it would seem, he at the least felt that some formal symbolism yet clings to the images of light in all passages despite the difficulty of *obscura*. But even here, seeing that the very philosophy which, as he implies, his poetry causes to be life-giving is in the next breath linked with destruction, such symbolism as remains is not only purely formal but forced and arbitrary. There is no sign that the poet could have cared less.

A similarly cool aloofness to the resistance of detail is practiced in the proem of III, where, following Homer, the poet describes the abodes of the gods. There the words *semper ⟨que⟩ innubilis aether/integit et largo diffuso lumine ridet* magnificently capture the Homeric description; but, as V, 1188–93, when logically conjoined with the description in V, 1205, will clearly show, this *aether* cannot possibly be part of the actual Epicurean *intermundia.*

It seems, in sum, that this master of formal construction could wink at form where it stood in his way. But this is perhaps one of the secrets of his mastery.

18. That is to say, the turn on the "sweet honey of the muse" merely afforded Lucretius an attractive entry into the metaphor. Its importance is functional, not substantial.

19. It ought perhaps to be made explicit that, given the metaphor's structure, the *utilitatem* which the reader experiences corresponds directly to *recreata valescat.*

20. We must notice the thematic arrangement of the mythological allusions: first come Ceres and Liber (l. 14), signifying creation, and then, with Hercules as a bridge, the cluster of monsters (ll. 24ff.), emblematic of destruction.

21. I am proposing that to Lucretius, as to us, and in accordance with Epicurean tenets, Epicurus-as-god was a rational absurdity. That Epicurus (*qui princeps vitae rationem invenit*) had just claim to the title of creator, however, he believed implicitly. It is the two ideas working together that effects the mockery of religious persuasions. The hidden argument is: if one who genuinely creates is not a god, so much the less are they who do not create at all.

This is not to ignore Cicero's testimony (*Tusc.* I, 21, 48; *De Nat. Deor.* I, 16, 43) on the Epicurean tendency—Lucretius no doubt included in his charge—to revere the master as a god. (Bailey's suggestion —*op. cit.,* 1322—that they *worshiped* him as such is certainly based on an overinterpretation of the passages.) The only real question for us is whether or not Lucretius meant to represent Epicurus as one of the *true* gods, who can only be the inhabitants of the intermundia. Unless he was indulging himself in a mad illogicality, he obviously did not intend anything of the sort. Epicurus-the-god, then, is purely a figurative representation, a *persona* of the poem.

22. The fact that Lucretius later mentions attendance at the shrines of the gods (VI, 75) does not modify this assertion. The gods whose contemplation is involved are clearly not the Olympians of ancient belief.

23. Lucretius, of course, does not represent the plague as the cause of Athen's decline, but merely as its symbol.

24. The fact that the plague is a naturally, materially caused catastrophe renders it even more firmly an expression of the poem's own essence. How much more effective such an ending is than Santayana's suggested portrait of Mars sallying out in blind fury etc. (see Chapter I), the poem itself tells us in its every line. As for Bignone's suggested ending (see note 27), this would have been artistically far worse than Santayana's even though on the surface it might appear academically sounder.

25. The suggestion that Lucretius should have posed a cultural cycle and an atom-grounded natural cycle as participants in the very same process may at first seem startling or even absurd. To us, to be sure, they are quite separate logical propositions; but, just as surely, when dealing with Lucretian propositions, we must refer them to the Lucretian, not our own, view of things. Culture, whatever it is, must be the product of the application of mind to matter. In the Epicurean philosophy, the mind is explicitly held to be itself material. Hence, culture—an abstraction, by the way, to which the poet never specifically refers—is the issue of an interworking of matter and matter; manifestly, this interworking cannot but be subject to the laws that govern generally in matter. These, collectively, are the *ratio naturae*. Likewise, they cannot but show that outer configuration which the *ratio* always produces, the *species naturae*. We are thus on completely safe grounds when we infer that the cultural ebb and flow is just another *species* of the *ratio naturae* and that the *ratio,* the same that works within the movements of the atoms, works within the ebb and flow itself.

We therefore see that, in the Lucretian scheme of things, a cycle in culture, since it derives from the laws that govern in matter, is as fundamental a truth as a cycle of creation and destruction in nature, that, in fact, the two are the same cycle and the same truth.

As the final chapter will disclose, these conclusions, which are easily enough derived once the reader grasps the poem's formal principles, have a momentous influence on the work's final meaning.

26. The bodies of the various books are here left out of consideration, as they have been throughout this chapter, since they do not figure in the core of the poem's design.

27. See note 13.

28. What, then, of Lucretius' unfulfilled promise to "tell more about the gods?" Our main concern is to understand that, even if he in fact ever did contemplate such a description, he could not have meant to append

it, as most critics suppose he did, to the present close of the poem. This, as we may now see, would have entailed the deliberate ruination of the work's design. Next, it will be worth our while to inquire whether he ever proposed such a description at all, whether, in fine, the poem makes any promises that it does not quite fulfill. The answer, I think, is that it does not.

The passage in which the promise occurs (V 146–55) is this:

Illud item non est ut possis credere, sedis
esse deum sanctas in mundi partibus ullis.
tenuis enim natura deum longeque remota
sensibus ab nostris animi vix mente videtur;
quae quoniam manuum tactum suffugit et ictum,
tactile nil nobis quod sit contingere debet.
tangere enim non quit quod tangi non licet ipsum.
quare etiam sedes quoque nostris sedibus esse
dissimiles debent, tenues de corpore eorum;
quae tibi posterius largo sermone probabo.

Bailey translates the final line, ". . . all of which I will hereafter prove to you with plenteous discourse." That "prove" is the right word is well attested by the seven other uses of *probari* in the poem (I, 513, 858; II, 94, 499, 528, 934; IV, 477). It is a logical demonstration then, that we are to expect.

This understood, three preliminary facts concerning the passage and its implications must command our attention. First, if Lucretius is at all contemplating a treatment of things divine, the stress is decidedly on the godly abodes, not on the gods themselves. Second, as U. Pizzani perceptively points out—*Il problema del testo e della composizione del De rerum natura di Lucrezio* (Rome, 1959), p. 177—the passage is keyed to *negative* assertions concerning the divine abodes, the first and principal statement being that they *cannot* be located in any part of our world. Third (and it is stunning that this point should have been universally ignored before), it is quite evident that an outright description, however long, of the divine abodes would not fulfill the promise in the least, since merely to be told once more that these environs are different from ours because of their tenuity (which itself cannot be directly proven) would neither prove anything in itself nor add anything substantial to the proofs already given.

A fresh approach to the passage is therefore required. Clearly, the promised logical demonstration, the proof, must involve the following train of argument, which lies behind the *"quae"* of the final verse: 1. The nature of the gods is so fine as to be scarcely seen by the understanding of the mind; 2. Since this nature cannot be touched by the hand, it cannot touch anything which can be touched by us, since nothing can touch which cannot itself be touched; 3. Accordingly, the abodes of the gods must be different from our own (since there must be sensible contact between the gods and their abodes); 4. They must therefore be as delicately constituted as their bodies.

"*Quae probabo . . . ,*" says Lucretius. The words can only disclose that he does not feel the proof just given for the difference-because-of-tenuity of the divine abodes to be sufficient. Yet, it is not at all likely that he promises to strengthen it by bringing to bear other arguments of a similar kind. If this were so, we must first of all suppose that he had at his disposal an abundance (*largo sermone*) of material both similar and somewhat superior to that of proof already given. Beyond this we must assume that, having chosen to postpone his better arguments, he either forgot or abandoned them, or, perhaps, could find no place for their inclusion, or, last and most dismal, intended to subjoin them to the description of the plague as a kind of poetic postscript. More arguments like that of 146–54, then, are all but out of the question. Yet, again, unless *probabo* does not imply argumentation at all, which is impossible, neither does it predict a mere description of the divine abodes. This leaves but one possibility that will fulfill the implications of the word: a treatment *largo sermone* of the abodes of man. That is to say, if, following the reasoning (and the hither-worldly grounding) of the argument as already set down, Lucretius proceeds to demonstrate that our abodes are perfectly sensible to us, he will all the more convincingly demonstrate that they are unsuited to the gods, that they are therefore different from those of the gods, and that, by a condition already attached to the dissimilitude, the divine environment is fine according to the fineness of the divine nature.

The question naturally arises whether this will be a meaningful demonstration. For all the answer that is required, we need merely refer to the Epicurean imperative of argument according to directly sensible phenomena (*Ep. ad Hdt.,* 38). It is clear that the reasoning as so far proffered hardly fulfills Epicurus' requirement to the letter. It is founded wholly in appeals to the fact that we *do not* sense the nature of the gods. Accordingly, an implementation of the argument by way of immediately perceptible phenomena will constitute the methodological core of his proof. Hence the word *probabo*.

Now, such a continuation of the argument certainly exists. It may be said, in fact, that almost the whole remainder of the poem deals in some way or other with the abodes of man—that is, with the things (entities, phenomena, forces) with which he has sensible contact. If we want a list of those that are discussed explicitly (some of them occurring even before the point of the promise) we need merely refer to the very next place where Lucretius takes up the question of abodes (V, 1188ff.) to find a nearly complete one:

in caeloque deum sedis et templa locarunt,
per caelum volvi quia nox et luna videtur,
luna dies et nox et noctis signa severa
noctivagaeque faces caeli flammaeque volantes,
nubila sol imbres nix venti fulmina grando
et rapidi fremitus et murmura magna minarum.

The passage, however, represents immensely more than a simple list. To begin with, it is not fortuitous that here, as earlier, the context is negative. We are reminded of where the godly abodes are *not*, not told where they are or what they are. So much secures a tidy formal continuity of argument. Next, being so cast and representing the first reversion to the question of abodes, the passage naturally puts us on the alert for the promised proof. Nor is our attention unsolicited poetically. For, finally, the queer repetitiousness of the passage (in this quality there is none like it in *De Rerum Natura*) is anything but accidental. In their overlapping succession, the images contained become, as it were, an ever stronger radiance cleaving the darkness, then gradual day, then the weather of day in its full range, the whole passing from strictly visual images to strictly aural, from serenity to violence, the whole strikingly vivid. The verses are a deliberate assault on the senses. Can we doubt the reason, seeing that the whole argument hitherto has been rooted exclusively in the senses? These are our abodes. We are driven to sense them. Sensing them, by merely becoming conscious of their sensible existence, we *know* through our recollection of the former argument that they cannot be the abodes of the gods, that their abodes, being by nature insensible to us, are necessarily different, necessarily more delicate. Just so, when we become aware of the same and still other sensible phenomena of our environment in other contexts, as we do almost everywhere in the latter part of the poem, we deepen and expand that identical piece of knowledge.

Hence, through a brilliant piece of dialectical insinuation keyed to this passage, yet with complete canonical soundness, the promised plenteous logical demonstration is delivered. Seeing that it appears—and, indeed, can scarcely appear—in any other form, we may cease to look for it in any other form.

In view of these findings, Bignone's attempt to outline the sequel of Book VI in *Storia della Letteratura Latina* (1945), II, 318ff. is, of course, entirely out of place.

29. The chief studies of the meter have been those of Bailey (*op. cit.*, 109–123) and of W. A. Merrill: *The Lucretian Hexameter* (Berkeley, 1922–23); *The Metrical Technique of Lucretius and Cicero* (Berkeley, 1924); *The Characteristics of Lucretius' Verse* (Berkeley, 1924); *Lucretian and Virgilian Rhythm* (Berkeley, 1929). On the sound-pattern, Rosamund Deutsch's *The Pattern of Sound in Lucretius* (Bryn Mawr, 1939) is the main study. All are useful and unimaginative, leaving a great deal to be done in these areas.

30. E.g., warmth and cold, VI, 840–87; starting and stopping, II, 251–93; awakening and sleeping, the images of waking at IV, 927 and 995ff. amid Lucretius' discourse on sleep and dreams; blackness and whiteness, II, 757–94, 810–25; as for stillness, the master image and symbol would lie in III, 910.

31. The case for prolonged repetition is, I think, self-evident. Widespread repetition, meanwhile, would impart a sense of cyclical movement, if by

no other means, through the continual recurrence of the motif of repetition itself. Where it is used in conjunction with prolonged repetition, of course, it will derive cyclical force also from the latter.

A fair representation of the two types used in conjunction lies in Homer's *Iliad,* where, as I feel it, the repetition (in itself not appreciably longer in either quality, though it is of a different sort, than that of *De Rerum Natura*) gives rise to a very definite sense of cyclical movement.

32. The motive becomes quite explicit in the close of III (see especially 1024–52), where the poet takes his readers, all "defendants," to task for dreaming of that immunity to death that is given to no one, not even the most magnificent.

CHAPTER III

1. The question of Mars' precise intended symbolic value in the poem seems incapable of a sure answer. To take him as, *on a par with Venus and creation,* symbolizing the destructive principle in nature would be rash. Since he never reappears except, occasionally, to give his name to the phenomenon of war, he is, first of all, simply not the *persona* of the poem that Venus nor even that Epicurus is. Further, as Anderson well reveals (*op. cit.,* 11ff.) there are certain ambivalences in his (i.e., war's) symbolic value, stretching at times even to a tenuous association with creation. (Indeed, even in his appearance in the first proem, the god, since he is the father of Rome, takes some part in the creation theme.) Still, he is never posed as a creator outright in the manner that Venus represents destruction in IV, and, therefore, we cannot speak of an intended Mars creator-destructor to match the poem's Venus. It would therefore appears safe to say only that, regardless of its other associations, inasmuch as war represents a very frequent means and context of destruction in *De Rerum Natura,* Mars becomes an eminent if not quite an organic symbol of nature's destructive force.

2. Italics mine.

3. We should note that this summary recapitulates the final argument of this section as well, thus presenting a nice piece of formal economy on Lucretius' part.

4. Especially in lines 170 (*oras in luminis*), 179 (*in luminis oras*), 227–8, where Venus and the phrase *daedala tellus* reappear and in 250–61: *frondiferasque . . . silvas; pabula laeta; percussa*—but deep reminiscences of the proem are diffused generally throughout this last passage.

5. Among them, the images of 313f. prefigure the closes of Books II and IV.

6. *Natura* gives the creation motif by force of its etymology. The incidence of the word being legion in *De Rerum Natura,* I shall attempt to avoid superfluity by citing it principally where it does particular service in the movement.

7. Since mind, being itself of atomic composition, and its works are part of

nature, and since only mind in the nature of things can propose and effect design.

8. In its relation to the preceding *genitis,* the word affords a superb, if minor, specimen of the poem's intrinsic interdependence of form and meaning. The editors doubt the logic of the passage, Giussani rejecting 518–19 on the ground that they do not properly represent a conclusion to the present argument, which, he feels, should prove *soliditas.* Bailey, ever the poet's apologist in such matters, counters by observing that *soliditas* is covered in the relative clause, while 519 stands as an anticipation to the proof of *aeternitas* (528–39). Bailey's impressions are better, but close attention will show that Lucretius is in need of no apology whatever. At the beginning of the paragraph he stipulates that matter and, specifically, atoms can hold no admixture of void within. Next, he states that in *created* things, which can only be *concilia materiai,* void is inmixed. So far, we may logically infer that atoms are uncreated, and it is certainly a short and safe step from this point to assert that atoms can therefore be eternal. In brief, the editors have overlooked the importance to the argument of *creatis*—which the poem's *form,* however, does not permit. Hence, the form here helps clarify the argument and, conversely, the argument the form.

9. It is to be noted, however, that the *deus* motif is strictly withheld in regard to Heraclitus, whereas the divine ascription is abundantly lavished on Empedocles (I, 730ff.), Lucretius' poetic inspiritor.

10. Not all of these images denote atomic dissolution, it is true, but their thematic impress is made inescapable by the descriptive vividness of the verbs.

11. The ironic play on creation and destruction in regard to fire evident here in *creant incendia* is widespread in *De Rerum Natura.*

12. Bailey translates "created" in both places. The idea of a *finis,* however, has dubious thematic value at best in a passage where it is being refuted.

    It is perhaps worthy of note that the thematic *natura* occurs twice (ll. 962, 1002) to lend whatever force it can to the side of creation.

13. The thematic value of *suborire* is clarified in 1035–6.

14. A further objection to Santayana's suggested ending for the work (see Chapter I) is that Lucretius effects as much as it offered by the close of Book I.

15. J. Mewaldt in "Eine Dublette im Buch IV des Lukrez," *Hermes,* XLII (1908), 286–95, first brought the evidence to light.

    The main argument runs as follows: the awkward repetition of IV, 48–9 from IV, 29–30, and the fact that the second passage adds nothing substantial to the first reveal that lines 45–53 constitute a doublet of 26–44; since it is not reasonable that Lucretius would have omitted reference here to Book III if that book had been written and were intended to follow II at the time of IV's composition, and since 45–53 distinctly summarize the content of I and II, it is clear that 45–53 is the earlier version and represents the syllabus to IV at a time when IV was intended to follow II.

There are several important corroborating considerations. Since it clearly refers to the analogies commencing at line 54 and will not bear the interruption of 45–53, *hinc* in line 44 shows beyond doubt that a doublet exists. Seeing that 26–44 alone carries a reference to III, the word also strongly suggests that this passage is the finally intended version. Also, lines 44–48 occur almost *verbatim* in the syllabus to III (l. 31–4), and, since it is quite unlikely that the poet would have used the same verses to announce both III and IV, it follows that these lines could hardly have been intended as part either of an original or final version of the syllabus to IV in the present order of books. (The far greater probability is that, having been rejected here after their composition as a sequel to II, they were utilized as part of III's syllabus.) More, no syllabus to any book fails to make some reference at least to the book preceding (Book II, the only place where the recollection is not explicit, still manages a reference in the mention of the atoms and the void (ll. 62–65), the proof of whose existence constituted the main doctrinal matter of I). More indication, then, that 45–53 could scarcely have been either an original or final version in the present order. Further diminishing the likelihood of a final or even later but rejected version in these lines is the consideration that, as such, they would have represented a recasting of 26–44; it is inconceivable that Lucretius would have essayed a change that did not retain a reference to III.

It will seem that the only chance of resisting Mewald's conclusions is to insist on 45–53 as an original version of the syllabus in the present sequence. Lucretius in that case would be pictured as having made his first try at the passage without thought for III, but with the same introduction as employed in the announcement of III. True, this would have constituted an approach worthy of abandonment; but it is also unworthy of the poet himself.

Finally fortifying these thoughts is the fact that, however greatly the science of IV is clarified by a prior perusal of III, there are no references to *animus* or *anima* in IV (very frequent after line 720) which absolutely require the doctrinal stuff of III for their comprehension. A first-thought IV-III sequence is therefore not made impossible by reason of illogical exposition—much as the understanding of I is not impaired by the withholding of numerous details of Epicurean atomic doctrine till Book II.

A doublet exists, then, 45–53 is the earlier, rejected passage and, since the lines can show no reasonable relationship to the present order of books, they must be taken as having once announced IV as the sequel of II.

J. Schmid in "Altes und Neues zu einer Lukrezfrage," *Philologus*, XCII–XCIII (1937–39), 338–51, argues unconvincingly that 45–53 is a later interpolation. He envisions an *interpolator philosophus*, disturbed by the fact that 26–44 introduces only a small aspect of IV, borrowing the first four lines from III, reusing IV, 29–30 and adding 51–3 to form a new syllabus. Lines 51–3 are un-Lucretian, Schmid contends, and the *vehementer attinet* of line 49 does not follow logically on 45–8. Lines

51-3 are admittedly not up to Lucretius' best, but one cannot rest a case for interpolation on their awkwardness alone. And there is no other foundation. The phrase *vehementer attinet* follows convincingly enough on 45-8 in that the existence of images allows sensation of the created universe. As for the interpolator's motive, how could he have been inspired to his work by the lack of reference to IV and then have been satisfied with even less in his own version? Schmid's general appeal to the obtuseness of Lucretius interpolators (he sees perhaps half a dozen in the work) is not an adequate answer.

It will be noted that Mewaldt's conclusions are based on solid textual considerations, not, like those of so many others who have sought the *quondam* Lucretius, on incidental scraps of internal evidence. Yet, Mewaldt's very accomplishment points the folly of the quest. Even he did not nearly approach Lucretius' earlier plan, which will not be understood until a full evaluation of the *cyclical* movement in the order I, II, IV, III, V, VI is made.

16. Not only would this line of cyclical force have been lost in the earlier order but also the tendency of the books' terminal passages, culminating in III's finale, to close directly in on the reader toward the specific end of teaching him his mortality. It is true that even despite these sacrifices of power, III's close in the earlier sequence would yet have possessed impressive cyclical-didactic weight. The present order's *concentration* of cyclical energies, however, make it clearly the more forceful arrangement.

Other considerations also favor the transposition. The only loss entailed is the earlier suggestion of a general cyclical movement throughout the poem. No penalty is incurred by the retardation of the *Venus destructrix* close, since it cuts no different antithesis with proem I in its present place than in the earlier sequence. Meanwhile, like the closes, the proems gain by the turnabout. The earlier order would have allowed the poem's two thematically weakest proems to fall in succession. The present arrangement not only avoids this, but takes perfect advantage of poem IV's delicate mood of celebration (see Chapter II). Moreover, even the sequence of subjects is plainly improved. We are better taught the processes of sensation after exposure to soul and mind than before.

17. The creation of things, ll. 98–108; velocity of atoms, ll. 142–63; causes of motion, ll. 216–93.

18. *Op. cit.,* II, 898.

19. Such rhythm is already at least barely present in the recession and return itself of the sun images.

20. One advantageous effect of such a resolution would have been the corroboration of the darkness imagery, express and implied, in lines 115–36: *opaca* (115) *clandestinos caecosque* (128), *caecis* (129), *caecis* (136). It will be noted that, even as they stand, these images alternate either with the sun imagery or else with other thematic suggestions of creation, and so effect a minor movement of their own. The movement, of course, would have been greatly enhanced by a literal resolution in night.

21. The passage from 206 to 212 may well represent the inverse complement of the entry into the lacuna after 164. Note that *ardorem* and *ardor* (ll. 211f.) nicely reflect the suggestion of *fulgura* in 163.

22. The thematic intent is clinched by the use of *creari* in the same connection in line 269.

23. Since the word carries us subtly back to the earlier image of the stallion, we may be sure that we are dealing with a single conscious poetic construct.

24. There is considerable play on this motif up to line 260: *fatis* (l. 257); *tempore certo, regione loci certa* (ll. 259f.). Combined with the intervening impulses of creation, it adds to the paragraph's cyclical movement. Also, the motif returns by implication at the paragraph's close (l. 291), where, related to *innata* (l. 286), it gives yet another important dimension to the movement.

25. A particularly deft touch is the termination of the blackness-whiteness imagery (ll. 822f.) and our release into the destruction motif with allusions to ravens and swans, both of which bear suggestions of death.

26. The poet looks even further ahead in the book's great closing section. Lines 1115, 1123, 1129, resembling in language the final verses of V, key a cyclical movement that is scarcely different in kind than that which provides the poem's *denouement*.

27. E. K. Rand in "La Composition Rhetorique du troisième Livre de Lucrèce," *Revue de Philologie* (1934), 243–66, convincingly demonstrates a rhetorical structure for Book III. His divisions are: *Exordium,* 1–140; *Narratio,* (a.) 41–93, (b.) 94–416; *Argumentatio,* 425–633; *Refutatio,* 634–829; *Peroratio,* 830–1094. The device, which, given the substance and purpose of III, is perfectly appropriate in itself, becomes doubly effective in that the peroration, the rhetorical climax, is also the climactic movement of the cycle in the poem's first half. So studiously did Lucretius assemble every pressure possible to drive home the awesome message of III's cadenza.

It would be mistaken, however, to suppose that the rhetorical aspects of *De Rerum Natura* are concentrated entirely in III. The whole poem is designed toward an ultimate persuasion to the Epicurean life, which, as we shall see, is represented as precisely a persuasion to justice. III's rhetorical structure, then, is but an eminent fragment of a greater design.

28. The reader may easily test a more than etymological tie with the creation theme by noticing how often the word, so frequent in Book III, may not be nicely translated as "atomic texture" or just "texture"— and how rarely "nature" yields any definite or significant sense.

29. Bailey, *op. cit.,* II, 1047. Bailey misses even Lucretius' literal intention in this paragraph. For some reason, the editor supposes that the first two lines promise a discourse on the soul's communication of sensation to the body, along with a further development of the first line's hint that the body is the soul's shell. Lucretius' only purpose, however, is to show that body and soul have interdependent life. Everything in the paragraph contributes to the idea, and the idea itself is appropriate at this

point, first in that the passage heads a new section (ll. 323–416) on the relation of soul to body, and also as a prelude to the book's central argument on the mortality of the soul, where the idea is crucial.

30. Only *semina* (l. 496), *natura* (l. 561) and *primordia* (l. 568) give distinct signs of creation in lines 454–614. None are strong enough to constitute of themselves a movement of the creation theme.

31. See Chapter I.

32. Bailey (*op. cit.,* II, 1096) also criticizes paragraph 624–33 as interrupting the sequence of thought. As we have observed, however (see Chapter I), the sequence is kept well enough in that the passage concerns the vital structural unity of body and soul. His more specific criticism, that the argument would not be acceptable to anyone who held a non-material view of the soul, is surely applicable to any argument in this section of III. The argument, true, is not weighty, but neither is it despicable. Meanwhile, it has a worthy artistic function in that its reference to Acheron affords a return to the destruction theme on a solemn formal motif.

33. It will be noticed that lines 459–614 fall almost at the geometric center of Book III. Were it not for the signs of distress evident in 615–23, we might suspect an attempt to instill axial-symmetrical design in III—that is, a regular movement followed by a slow movement followed by a regular movement, all in linear proportion. The evidence of desperation in 615–23, however, suggests strongly that Lucretius did not originally intend the movement of 459–614 to be as slow as it turned out to be.

34. Here, as Bailey's notes help reveal (*op. cit.,* II, 1108), Lucretius was either napping in his science, or else allowed the theme to intrude on the science. As Bailey, through Giussani, shows, it is quite possible for one atomic compound to permeate another without loss of identity. Did Lucretius lose sight of this fact out of negligence or purposely to accommodate a distinctive movement of the theme?

35. Lines 819–23 make obvious reference to the conditions that hold in the *intermundia,* the abodes of the gods. So also do lines 811–13, even though the express reference there is to the void. This masked introduction of things divine and immortal in the midst of an argument against human immortality has great ironic point, which is all the greater because of the surface dissemblence. The editorial speculation, therefore, that 806–18, which reoccur in V, 351–63, were either never intended for III or else written first for V and then transferred here (a maneuver which Bailey—*op. cit.,* II, 1125—accepts as self-evident, chiefly because the argument is "much more appropriate" there) ought to be entirely eschewed.

36. The dominant cyclical motif in the close is constructed on references to past and future time, or to conditions that prevailed and will prevail before we were born and after we perish. The motif occurs first in lines 832–69, again at 972ff. in conjunction with the explicit statement of the cycle and once more, though this time less concisely, with lines 1024–44, which linger in the past, and 1071–75 together with 1085–94, which settle the state of the soul for all time that remains after its dissolution.

The motif emanates directly from the earlier arguments for the soul's mortality, which concerned the soul's state both before its birth (670–783 argue specifically against the pre-existence of the soul) and after its death. The passage of cyclical force from 964–77 to the final lines, therefore, begins to gather along this direct line of movement as early as verse 417, where Lucretius announces that he will undertake to prove the soul both *nativus* and *mortalis*.

37. This, to be sure, is not to say that *species* is not a reasonable consequence of *ratio* in nature or that it is not in itself a rationally apprehensible process. Lines 964–77 expressly recommend it as both. I imply only that its full impress, while comprising reason as far as reason can take us, lies beyond the scope of our rational faculties alone and that, as is only natural, Lucretius took full advantage of this further value in establishing the reader's final relationship to death.

38. The cycle, of course, helps implant the conviction in that it helps deliver the understanding that death is both inevitable and everlasting.

39. It is worthy of note that a peroration (see note 27) is distinctly the place where one is apt and even expected to stretch his evidence as far as ever his confidence will allow.

40. The traces of the leitmotif are *fit* (1. 274), *eliditur* (1. 296), *adlidat* (1. 297), *elisam* (1. 299), *exprimat* (1. 299), *elisa* (1. 315). There are indications, however, both that Lucretius provided and would have desired more. I suggest on the authority of identical emendations at IV, 143 and 159 that *geruntur* at 254 might reasonably be changed to read *genuntur*. The context is not the same as earlier, true, but it is notable that the idea of supreme speed is stressed in all three cases and that, meanwhile, the idea of true creation applies in all literalness to none. The emendation would allow one more thematic word. More significant are *eliditur* and *elisa*. In themselves they are strong thematic words. Very surprising, however, is the meaning, "reflected," which they are forced to carry in context. Nor do the intervening *adlidat* and *elisam* help very much to explain their extraordinary burden. Surely there is no better explanation for this diction than that, being conscious of the passage's formal weakness, Lucretius attempted with rather poor success to press these thematic words into good service. The result, though one of the most questionable pieces of craftsmanship in the entire poem, at least furnishes another proof of the cycle's intended presence.

41. The theme derives doubly from the suggested "creation" (*fingunt*) of the deities and the fictive rebirth of sound within the prevailing silence.

42. Nor, I think, would we ascribe anything unintended if we felt the whole movement from *primum* (1. 881) to the profound rest succeeding in lines 956ff. and even the ensuing dreams (ll. 962–1036) as one long implied cycle.

43. The image, however, artfully echoes the first image (ll. 1059f.) of the close (see Ch. II, n.5), and, recalling thence *frigida cura*, leaves no doubt as to the thematic intention.

44. Any implication of destruction in the word as used here, however, would admittedly be arbitrary.

45. It is evident that Lucretius placed the section on the world's mortality before that on its creation (we should *a priori* expect the opposite sequence) to accommodate a long movement from the beginnings of the universe through the development of human culture to its pinnacle (Athens), and thence to the final episode of the plague.
46. V, 1205 tells us so.
47. The same sort of evocation is seen at 509ff., where mention of stars brings on visions of night after the images of light (amounting to *flammantia moenia mundi*) in the description of the ether (495–508).
48. Save, of course, the indifferent gods.
49. It at first appears paradoxical that natural destruction should be at once represented as part of nature's outwardly visible aspect (*species*) and characterized as *abdita*. The difficulty dissolves, however, when we reflect that all yet unaccomplished destruction, being neither *yet* visible nor predictable as to its actual details, may legitimately be termed *abdita* and that nothing in this conflicts with the principle of *species,* which concerns in itself only destruction accomplished or in the process of accomplishment before our eyes.

    The ominous flavor of *abdita,* while it is perfectly functional in this particular context, where Lucretius is bringing the universe's own warning against ambition (the commander has *hybris*), and though it serves skillfully to anticipate the hidden force of the ruinous contagion to come, is quite neutralized in the earlier definition of piety (l. 1204): *pacata posse omnia mente tueri.* To attempt to settle the exact relation between the notions would require too much anticipation at this point. I will suggest, however, that in *vis abdita* and *pacata* we find exemplified the cycle's blended powers of compulsion and reconciliation.
50. The passage has not been well understood by the editors. In particular, Bailey's suggestion, however reluctant, that it may well betray symptoms of derangement must be resisted. Clearly, if on no other grounds, the lines would justify themselves as a vivid movement of destruction. But there is more to recommend them. Ever since line 1266, where the invention of weapons came into notice, Lucretius has been tacitly mulling over the ambivalent ends of human invention and discovery. In paragraph 1281–96, the antithesis of plough and sword express the ambivalence. In the ensuing paragraph it is the irony of a deliberate exercise of the creative instincts toward destructive ends. In short, the poet sees an absurdity at the heart of the cultural process and disapproves. The present passage, coolly posing as an actual historical description, deliberately allows the absurdity to evolve to its weirdest possible dimensions, and the reader's shock is not only intended but functional. He is being taught a moral lesson. For, even where the poet apologizes for the improbable historicity of his account (ll. 1341–49), he is merely saying that, if such things have not happened here, or if they have perhaps happened only in some other world, this is not to be explained by any convincing limit in the absurdity itself. The fact that the tactic depicted is futile and self-defeating is, of course, the passage's whole inner point.

In "Lucretius and Progress," *The Classical Journal,* LVIII (1962–63), 58, C. R. Beye appears to suggest somewhat the same idea, but the language is ambivalent.

51. Bailey's (following Giussani's) assertion that line 1434's intended meaning is, "and this, little by little, has advanced life to its highest plane . . ." is plainly incorrect and Munro's rendition (followed by Merrill and Leonard and Smith), "And this, little by little, has carried life into the deep sea . . ." is assuredly correct. Lucretius is merely asserting that the acquisitive instinct has imperiled life by generating fruitless toil and idle cares (ll. 1423f.) and by inducing war. According to Bailey's translation, the same instinct would be represented as the cause of cultural evolution. Seeing that Lucretius would have eradicated the instinct, however, unless we can accept with scant comfort from any other source that he here implies a willingness to forego the instinct's stated consequence as well, the evolution itself and its highest achievements, we must reject the translation.

52. Here more sensibly than in the section on earthquakes, since volcanic eruptions, unlike earthquakes, entail (in fire) the creation of a definite atomic entity.

53. As does the irony in the particular reference as well: the epithet associated with a place of destruction. Indeed, it was probably by the irony of this reference that Lucretius hoped to excite our recognition of the epithet's relevance to the poem's *exordium* and close.

54. Very definite indication that this is Lucretius' purpose comes with the notice that the image in 1256–58 is part of an intrinsic motif of the passage—ll. 1215f.; 1238; apparently 1247; 1263; and, by implication, 1272ff.—which culminates in the final piling of corpses upon the funeral pyres of others (1283ff.).

    The motif occurs in Thucydides as well, but is there confined entirely to II, 52. Lucretius obviously increased its incidence in order to deepen the impact of the parting scene, although, curiously, he there falls short of Thucydides' explicitness concerning the piling up itself of bodies upon the pyre.

    In his "Lucretius' Interpretation of the Plague," *Harvard Studies in Classical Philology,* XLVII (1957), 105–118, H. S. Commager Jr. nicely discloses the moral implications in Lucretius' description of the plague. In a word, Commager shows that the Athenian physical suffering is emblematic of a moral distress as well and that its lack of a *vera ratio* of cure represents its moral need of Epicurus' healing doctrines. To say as Commager does, however, that these implications comprise the poem's moral climax is excessive. As I trust the following chapter will indicate, the true climax can only reside in the moral transfiguration that Lucretius means to instill by the teachings principally, of nature's "outer form and inner law."

55. For a fuller citation of thematic evidence, see Appendices.

CHAPTER IV

1. Lest there be any mistake, I shall repeat that *species* nowhere works alone toward the final goal of moral salvation. *Ratio,* by giving the continued assurance of an orderly, atom-founded universe, by removing all agency and interest of the gods in the fact of death and its aftermath, as in all else that is human, and by establishing the complete dissolution of the soul after death, contributes its enormous part. But all of this, just as it is fundamental to the final goal, is also preliminary, leaving *species* to effect the finishing work.

2. This is not to say that the emotions clinging to birth and death have no part—or even no didactic part—to play in the poem. Clearly, they enlarge and deepen the movement of the cycle, which cannot but deepen its impact and meaning. But, though they may thus be seen as one of Lucretius' means to his didactic end, they constitute anything but the end itself.

3. There is no contradiction between the statement here that the rhythm works toward the end of instilling reason and the earlier statement that it offers a more than rational apprehension of death's place in the nature of things. The latter notion simply postulates that one's apprehension of the rhythm involves more than the merely rational faculties. Certainly, nothing deters such an apprehension from leading to reason. At the same time, as we shall see, nothing deters it from leading considerably beyond to a feeling of spiritual harmony with universal powers.

4. The essence, then, of Lucretius' improvement on the philosophy—always with the stipulation that the sources perhaps do not allow a fair estimate of the master's thought—lies in his introduction of a cleaner fusion between physics and ethics and a fuller line of development of the one from the other.

   It is clear, by the way, that Lucretius' explicit treatment of the ethics, spotty though it is, was sufficient for his purpose, which was to bring the reader psychologically and intellectually to a *position* where he was ready to accept the Epicurean moral life. As for the details of the ethics, the poet obviously assumed that, if the reader did not know them already, he would be inspired to the effort of seeking them out.

5. We might perhaps better ask what was *hybris* and *ate* other than a supernaturalized explanation of an observed reflex in the nature of things.

Appendix I

THE FULLER CYCLE

Offered herein is a fuller citation of thematic words, or of words that mark the incidence of the cycle in *De Rerum Natura*. No attempt has been made to furnish an absolutely definitive list—that is, one which would represent all the thematic clues intended by the poet and none else—, though all cited are taken to be definitely intended by the poet. In particular, no attempt has been made to cite all of the imagistic evidence for the cycle. Rather, in accordance with principles laid down in the second chapter, citation in this regard is limited to the occurrence of antithetical pairs of images that carry ready symbolic suggestions of birth and death. As the reader will discern, some previously uncited thematic words have been included (e. g., *genus* and its cognates). For the sake of simplicity, indications of increase have been grouped with the creation theme, indications of decline with the destruction theme. The abbreviation "C." indicates creation, "D." destruction, "C. and D." a word or phrase that captures both simultaneously and "Cy." a word or phrase that implies a cycle in itself.

This catalogue may appear to delineate a different face for the poem than that described in Chapter III. *It must be understood,* however, that the aim there was to mark the cycle's larger movement, not, as here, its mere incidence. Chapter III, then, remains the essential guide to the movement, while this list, where it expands upon earlier citations, will be useful as a guide to the incidence of the cycle within the main thematic movements.

References are to the 1947 edition of Cyril Bailey's text.

BOOK I

C. genetrix, 1; alma, 2; frugiferentis, 3; concelebras, genus, 4; concipitur, exortum, lumina, 5; adventum, daedala, 7; summittit, 8; verna, 10; genitabilis, 11; primum, 12; initum, 13; frondiferasque, virentis, 18.
Cy. saecla, 20.
C. propagent, 20; naturam, 21; luminis oras, 22; exoritur, 23; natura, 25.
D. mortalis, Mavors, 32; devictus, vulnere, 34.
C. patriai, 41; propago, 42; natura, 44; primordia, 55; natura, 56; natura, 57.
D. perempta, resolvat, 57.
C. genitalia, 58; semina, 59; prima, primis, 61.
D. mortalibus, 65.
C. primum, 66.
D. mortalis, 66.
C. primusque, 67; naturae, primus, 71; oriri, 75.
D. finita, 76; terminus, 77.

134

C. peperit, 83.
D. sanguine, 85.
C. prima, 86; patrio, princeps, 94.
D. concideret, mactatu, 99; finem, 107; morte, 111.
C. natura, 112; nata, nascentibus, insinuetur, 113.
D. intereat, morte, dirempta, 114; tenebras, Orci, 115.
C. insinuet, 116; primus, 117; gentis, 119.
D. Acherusia, 120.
C. naturam, 126; primis, 130; natura, 131.
D. sepultis, 133; morte, 135; obscura, 136.
C. inlustrare, 137.
D. noctes, 142.
C. lumina, 144.
D. occultas, 145.
C. solis, radii, lucida, diei, 147; gigni, 150.
D. mortalis, 151.
C. fieri, 152, 154; creari, 155, 157; fiant, 158; fierent, 159; genus, nasci, semine, 160; primum, oriri, 161; genus, 162, 163; partu, 164; ferre, 166; genitalia, 167; mater, 168; seminibus, creantur, 169; enascitur, oras in luminis, 170; prima, 171; gigni, 172; fundi, 175; semina, 176; creatur, 177; effert, in luminis oras, 179; fierent, exorerentur, 180; primordia, genitali, 182; augendis, 184; seminis, crescere, 185; fierent, infantibu', 186; exorta, salirent, 187; crescunt, semine, 189; crescentesque, genus, 190; grandescere, 191; laetificos, fetus, 193; natura, 194; propagere, genus, 195; principiis, exsistere, 198; natura, parare, 199.
D. divellere, 201.
C. gignundis, oriri, 204; fieri, 205; semine, creatae, 206; fetus, 209; primordia, 210; fecundas, 211; ortus, 212; fieri, 214.
D. dissoluat, interemat, 216; mortale, 217; periret, 218; discidium, exsolvere, 220.
C. semine, 221.
D. dissoluatque, 223; exitium, 224.
C. natura, 224.
D. amovet, 225; peremit, consumens, 226.
C. genus, generatim, lumina, 227; Venus, redducit, Venus, redductum, daedala, 228; auget, generatim, 229; ingenui, 230.
D. mortali, 232; consumpse, 233.
C. refecta, 235; natura, 236.
D. reverti, 237; conficeret, 239; leti, 241; dissolvere, 243.
C. principiorum, 244.
D. redit, 248; discidio, redeunt, 249; pereunt, 250.
C. pater, 250; matris, 251; surgunt, virescunt, 252; crescunt, fetuque, 253; genus, 254; florere, 255; frondiferasque, novis, 256; nova, proles, 259.
D. pereunt, 262.
C. natura, 263; gigni, 264.
D. morte, 264.
C. creari, 265; genitas, 266; primordia, 268.

D. ruit, 272; sternit, 274; silvifragis, 275; verrunt, raptant, 279; stragemque, 280.

C. propagant, 280; natura, 281.

D. fragmina, coniciens, 284; vim, 286; stragem, volvitque, 288; ruitque, 289; corripiunt, portant, 294.

C. calidos, 300.

D. frigora, 300.

C. natura, 303.

Cy. redeuntibus annis, 311.

D. tenuatur, 312; cavat, 313; decrescit, 314; detrita, 315; minui, detrita, 319; decedant, 320.

C. natura, 321; naturaque, 322; crescere, 323.

D. macieque, senescunt, 325; peresa, 326; amittant, 327.

C. natura, 328; natura, 330; genita, 344.

D. quiesset, 345.

C. crescunt, fetus, fundunt, 351.

D. rigidum . . . frigus, 355.

C. natura, 363; primum, 383; fiat, 386; primum, 389; fundet, 413.

D. resolvat, 415.

C. pertexere, 418; natura, 419; prima, 423; natura, 432, 446; cluent, 449.

D. permitiali, 451; discidio, 452.

C. adventu, 457

D. abituque, 457; quiete, 463.

C. Tyndaridem, 464; Troiugenas, gentis, 465.

Cy. saecla, 467.

D. abstulerit, 468.

C. Tyndaridis, conflatus, 473.

D. accendisset, 474.

C. partu, 476.

D. inflammesset, 477.

C. Graiugenarum, 477; primordia, 483; principiorum, 484; primordia, 485.

D. stinguere, 486; transit, 489; dissiliuntque, 491; solvitur, 492; liquescit, 493.

C. calor, 494.

D. frigus, 494.

C. naturaque, 498; semina, primordiaque, 501; creata, 502; natura, 503; prima, 510; genitis, 511.

D. dissoluantur, 519; dissolui, 528; retexi, 529; labare, 530; collidi, 532; frangi, findi, 533; conficiuntur, 535; temptata, labascit, 537.

C. prima, 538.

D. redissent, 541.

C. renata, 542; creari, 543; genitum, 544.

D. revocari, 544.

C. primordia, 545.

D. dissolui, 546.

C. reparandis, 547; reparare, 550; natura, 551.

D. frangendis, 552; frangente, 553.

Appendix I

C. conceptum, 555.
D. finem, 555; dissolvi, 556.
C. refici, 557.
D. fregisset, disturbans, dissoluensque, 559.
C. reparari, 560.
D. frangendi, 561.
C. refici, 562; generatim, 563; fiunt, 567; fiant, 568; primordia, 570; creari, 571; natura, 573.
D. frangendis, 577.
C. natura, 581; generatim, 584; crescendi, 585.
D. tenendi, 585.
C. naturai, 586; generalis, 590; primordia, 592.
D. commutari, revicta, 593.
C. oriri, 594.
D. finita, 595; terminus, 596.
C. generatim, 597.
Cy. saecla, referre, 597.
C. naturam, parentum, 598; natura, 602.
D. revelli, 608.
C. primordia, 609; conciliata, 611.
D. avelli, deminui, 613.
C. natura, semina, 614; natura, 626.
D. resolvi, 628.
C. natura, creatrix, 629; reparare, 630; genitalis, 632; consistere, 636; primus, 638; clarus, 639.
D. obscuram, 639.
C. creatae, 646; naturam, 649; fieri, 652; fierique, 661.
D. stingui, mutareque, 666; occidet, 668.
C. fient, creantur, 669.
D. exit, 670; mors, 671; redeant, 673.
C. renata, 674; naturam, 676.
D. abitu, 677.
Cy. mutant, 677.
C. aditu, 677; naturam, 678.
D. discedere, abire, 680.
C. attribui, 681; naturam, 682; crearent, 683; efficiunt, 686.
Cy. mutant, 686.
C. naturam, 687.
D. labefactat, 694.
C. naturam, 702; gignundis, 707; fingere, creare, 709; naturas, 710; primordia, 712; procrescere, 715; primis, 716; gessit, 717.
D. Charybdis, 722; murmura, 723; vomat, 724.
C. gentibus, 727; sanctum, 730; divini, 731; praeclara, 732; stirpe creatus, 733; divinitus, 736.
D. ruinas, 740; casu, 741.
C. primum, 742.
D. secandis, 746; fragori, 747.
C. primordia, 753; nativa, 754.

137

D. mortali, 755; reverti, 756.
C. renata, 757.
D. veneno, 759; peribunt, 760.
C. creantur, 763.
D. dissoluuntur, 764
C. primordia, 765; gignuntur, 767; naturam, 768; naturam, 772; creata, 773; naturam, 776; primordia, gignundis, 778; creatur, 781; primum, 783; gigni, creari, 784.
Cy. retroque . . . reverti, 785.
C. primum, 786.
Cy. mutare, meare, 787.
C. primordia, 789.
D. redigantur, 791; exit, 792; mors, 793.
Cy. commutatum, 795.
D. redeant, 797.
C. natura, 798; crearint, 799.
D. demptis, 800.
C. tributis, 800; facere, 801.
Cy. mutarier, 802.
C. crescere, 804, 808.
D. amisso, 810; exsoluatur, 811.
C. primordia, 815, 817; constituunt, 821; primordia, 828; creari, 829; patrii, 832; gigni, creari, 837; consistere, 839; concrescere, 840.
D. secandis, 844.
C. primordia, 847, 848; natura, 849.
D. pereunt, exitio, 850; mortem, leti, 852; mortalis, 855; victa, perire, 856; reccidere, 857.
C. crescere, 858; auget, 859; alienigenis, 865; crescunt, 867; alienigenis, exoriuntur, 869; alienigenis, 872, 873; exoriuntur, 873; auget, 874; primaque, 879.
D. franguntur, 882; terimus, 884; friatis, 888.
C. genera, 889.
D. praefracta, 892.
C. semina, 895; coorto, 900; semina, 902; creant, 903; facta, 904.
D. conficerent, cremarent, 906.
C. primordia, 908; creare, 911; fieri, 916; natura, 917.
D. pereunt, 918.
C. primordia, 918; avia, nullius, 926; integros, 927; novos, 928; nulli, 930; primum, 931.
D. obscura, 933.
C. lucida, pango, 933; recreata, 942; naturam, 950; natura, 962.
D. finitum, 968.
C. constituatur, 968; consisteret, 985.
D. finitumque, 986; requies, 992.
C. principiorum, 992.
D. finire, 998.
C. natura, 1002.
Cy. cursu, 1004. (The paucity of the theme between 951 and 1002 is to be

explained by the poet's focusing of his attention herein on another formal matter of cardinal importance, the cycle's setting, the infinite universe.)

C. natura, 1009.
D. mortale, 1015.
C. genus, 1015.
D. dispulsa, 1017; ferretur, soluta, 1018.
C. creasset, 1019.
D. disiecta, 1020.
C. primordia, 1021; genus, 1026; creata, 1028; integrent, 1032; fota, novet, fetus, gens, 1033.
D. amissa, 1037.
C. reparare, 1037; natura, 1038.
D. diffluit, amittens, 1039; dissolui, 1040.
C. suppeditare, 1040; conciliata, 1043; suppleri, 1045; principiis, 1047.
D. fugai, 1047; ferri, 1048.
C. naturam, 1054.
D. resolvi, 1055; reccidere, 1063.
C. solem, 1065.
D. noctis, 1065; noctes, 1067.
C. diebus, 1067; natura, 1080.
D. signis, 1089.
C. solis, 1090; frondescere, 1092.
D. diffugiant, soluta, 1103; ruant, 1105; subducat, 1106; ruinas, 1107; solventis, abeat, 1108; nil exstet, 1109.
C. primordia, 1110.
D. leti, 1112; se . . . foras dabit, 1113.
C. clarescet, 1115.
D. nox, 1116.
C. lumina, 1117.

BOOK II

D. noctes, 12.
C. dies, 12.
D. tenebris, 15.
C. naturam, 17, 20; natura, 23; igniferas, 25; lumina, 26.
D. nocturnis, 26.
C. conspergunt, 33.
D. febres, 34; mortisque, 45; tenebris, 54, 56.
C. luce, 56.
D. tenebris, 58; tenebrasque, 59.
C. radii, solis, lucida, diei, 60; genitalia, 62; gignant, genitasque, 63.
D. resolvant, 63; minui, 68; fluere, 69; subducere, 70; decedunt, 72; abeunt, minuunt, 73.
C. augmine, 73.
D. senescere, 74.

C. florescere, 74; novatur, 75.
Cy. mutua vivunt, 76.
C. augescunt, 77.
D. minuuntur, 77.
Cy. mutantur saecla *etc.,* 78f.
C. primordia, 80; progignere, 81; primordia, 84; prima, 91.
D. quies, 95.
C. semina, 678; primis, 681; 685; semine, 687; primordia, 696; con-108; conciliis, 110; lumina, 114; radii, 115.
D. opaca, 115.
C. radiorum, lumine, 117; conciliis, 120.
D. discidiis, 120.
C. primordia, 121; solis radiis, 126.
D. clandestinos, caecosque, 128; caecis, 129.
C. principiis, 132; primordia, 133; conciliatu, 134; principiorum, 135.
D. caecis, 136.
C. principiis, 138; lumine, 140; primum, novo, spargit, lumine, 144; luce, 148; lumenque, 150; primordia, 157; lumina, 162; fulgura, 164; primordia, 165.
Cy. tempora mutare, 170.
C. creare, 170.
D. mortalis, 171.
C. Veneris, 173.
Cy. saecla, 173.
C. propagent, 173; genus, 174.
D. occidat, 174.
C. primordia, 177; creatam, 180; naturam, 181; gignuntur, augmina, 188; crescunt, 189.
D. degustant, 192.
C. genus, 194.
D. sanguis, 194; cruorem, 195; nocturnasque, 206.
C. flammarum, 207; natura, 208.
D. cadere, 209.
C. sol, 210; conserit, 211.
D. vis flammea, 215.
C. natus, creata, 223; principiis, creasset, 224; gignere, genitalis, 228; natura, 237.
D. quietum, 238.
C. gignere, 241; natura, 242; exoritur, novus, 252; primordia, 253; principium, 254.
D. fati foedera, 254
C. progredimur, 258; principium, 262; patefactis, 263.
D. carceribus, 264.
C. prorumpere, 264; initum, creare, 269; primum, 270; procedimus, 272.
D. refrenavit, 276.
C. procedere, 278.
D. pugnare, obstareque, 280.
C. flecti, 282.

D. refrenatur, residit, 283.
C. seminibus, 284; innata, 286; fieri, 287.
D. prohibet, 288.
C. fiant, 288; principiorum 292; adaugescit, 296.
D. deperit, 296.
C. principiorum, 297; gigni, gignentur, 300.
D. commutare, 303.
C. genus, 304; naturam, 307.
D. mutare, vertere, 307.
C. primordia, 309.
D. summa . . . quiete, 310.
C. primorum, natura, 313; multigenis, 335; genus, 342; generatim, 347; matrem, 349; mater, prolem, 350.
D. mactatus, concidit, 353; exspirans, 354.
C. mater, 355; fetum, 358; genere, 372; genus, 374; natura, facta, 378; primordia, 379.
D. penetralior ignis, 382.
C. ortus, 383, 387; creatus, 387; almus, 390; primordia, 396; natura, 400.
D. rescindere, 406; perrumpere, 407.
C. perfecta, 409; figurant, 413; primordia, 414.
D. cadavera, 415.
C. semine, 419; principiali, creatast, 423; genere, 430; calidos, 431.
D. gelidamque, 431.
C. natast, 436; genitalis, Veneris, 437; semina, 439; principiis, 443; genere, primis, 447; prima, 448.
D. diffugere, 457.
C. principiis, 472; primordia, 476, 479; semina, 481; prima, 486; semina, 497.
Cy. saecla, 503.
D. superata, iacerent, 503.
C. novo . . . colore, 503.
D. oppressa silerent, 506.
C. exoreretur, 507.
Cy. cedere *etc.,* 508–511.
C. ignibus, 515.
D. pruinas, 515.
C. calor, 517.
D. frigus, 517.
C. creata, 519.
D. flammis, infesta, pruinis, 521.
C. primordia 523; naturam, 533; genere, 535; primis, 536; genere, 537; nativo, 542; progigni, concepta, creari, 545; procrescere, 546; genitalia, 548; conciliandi, 551.
D. naufragiis, 552; disiectare, 553; mortalibus, 556.
C. primordia, 560; concilium, 563; concilio, crescere, adaucta, 564; progigni, genitas, procrescere, 566; genere, primordia, 567; suppeditantur, 568.
D. exitiales, 569; sepelire, 570.

C. genitales, auctificique, 571; creata, 572; principiorum, 573; vitalia, 575.
D. superantur, funere, 576.
C. visentes, luminis oras, 577.
D. nox, noctem, 578.
C. diem, aurora, 578; vagitibus, 579.
D. mortis, funeris, atri, 580.
C. natura, 583; principiorum, 584; semine, 585; principiorum, 587; genera, 588; prima, 589; renovent, oriantur, 591.
D. succensa, ardent, 592; furit, 593.
C. gentibus, extollere, 595; generi, 597; mater, materque, 598; genetrix, 599; proles, 604; parentum, 605; matris, 609; gentes, 610; matrem, 611; primum, 612; creari, 613; matris, genitoribus, 615; progeniem, oras luminis, edant, 617; primum, 624.
D. mortalis, 625.
C. Matrem, 628.
D. sanguine, 631; mandaret, 638.
C. Matri, 639; Matrem, 640; patriam, 642; parentibus, 643; natura, 646; primordia, 653; matrem, 659; proles, 662; parentum, 665; generatim, 666; genere, 667; perfecta, principiorum, 672.
D. cremantur, 673.
C. semina, 678; primis, 681; 685; semine, 687; primordia, 696; constare, 698; genus, 699; egigni, 703.
D. flammam, spirantis, 705.
C. naturam, omniparentis, 706; genetrice, creata, 708; genus, 709; naturam, 714; natura, 720; genitae, 721; principiorum, 722; alba, albis, 731; principiis, candida, 732.
D. nigrant, nigro, 733
C. nata, 733.
C. & D. caecigeni, 741.
C. lumina, 741; ex ineunte aevo, 743.
D. caecis . . . tenebris, 746.
C. primordia, 750.
D. ad nilum redigantur, 752; exit, 753; mors, 754.
C. semina, 755.
D. redeant ad nilum, 756.
C. principiis, 757; natura, 758; genus, gignunt, 759; semina, 760.
D. nigro, 764.
C. candore, 765; canos, candenti, 767.
D. nigrum, 768.
C. principiis, 770; addita, 770.
D. demptaque, 770.
C. candens, album, 771; seminibus, albescere, 773; semina, 776; efficiunt, 777; efficitur, 779; principiis, 789.
D. occidit, 790.
C. albis, creantur, alba, 790.
D. nigra, nigris, 791.
C. exorientur, 792; candida, 793.

D. nigro, 793.
C. nata, 793; luce, 795; lucem, primordia, 796.
D. tenebris, 798.
C. lumine, 799; luce, refulget, 800; sole, 801; luce, 806; gignuntur, luminis, 808; genus, 810; album, 811.
D. nigrum, 812.
C. principiis, 815; natura, principiorum, 818; genus, genere, 821.
D. corvos, 822.
C. albis, album, 823.
D. nigros, nigro, 824.
C. fieri, semine, 824.
D. distrahitur, 827; evanescere, stinguique, 828; discerpitur, 829; disperditur, 831; efflare, 832.
C. semina, 833; constare, 838; prima, 843; teporis, 843.
D. frigoris, 844.
C. facere, 849; naturam, 851.
D. perdere, 853.
C. primordia, 854; gignundis, 855.
D. frigus, 858.
C. calidum, tepidumque, 858.
D. mortalia, 859.
C. principiis, 861.
D. redeant, 864.
C. principiis, constare, 867; gigni, 870; exsistere, 871.
D. putorem, 872.
C. & D. vertere, 874; vertunt, 875, 876.
C. naturam, 877.
C. & D. augescunt, 878.
C. natura, 879.
C. & D. vertit, 880.
C. procreat, 880.
C. & D. explicat, versat, 882.
C. primordia, 883; expromere, 887; gigni, 888; creant, 892; gigni, 893; primum, 894.
D. putrefacta, 898.
C. pariunt, 899.
D. permota, 900.
C. nova re, 900; conciliantur, gigni, 901; creari, 902.
D. mortali, 906.
C. creta, 906.
D. secreta, 912.
C. primordia, 917.
D. leti, 918; mortalibus, 919.
C. coetu, concilioque, 920; facient, 921; gignere, 923.
D. dimittunt, 924.
C. capiunt, attribui, 925.
D. detrahitur, 926.
C. vertier, ova, 927; effervere, 928.

D.   putor, 929.

C.   gigni, 930; oriri, 931; partu, 933; partum, concilio, 935; conciliatu, 936; genitam, naturam, 938; creatis, 940; congressa, 941; natura, 945.

D.   dissoluuntur, 947; solvit, 950; eiecit, 951; discutere, dissolvere, 953; leti, 958.

C.   accendere, 959.

D.   leti, 960.

C.   reverti, 961.

D.   decursum, ire, abire, 962.

C.   primordia, 967; principiorum, 969; almae, 971; principiis, 974; genus, auctumst, 975; primordia, 979.

D.   mortalibus, 980.

C.   seminibus, 988, 990; semine, oriundi, 991; pater, alma, 992; mater, 993; feta, parit, 994; genus, parit, 995.

Cy. saecla, 995.

C.   prolemque, propagent, 997; maternum, 998.

D.   cedit, 999.

C.   fuit, 999; missumst, 1000.

D.   receptant, 1001; interemit, mors, 1002; conficiat, dissipat, 1003.

C.   coniungit, 1004.

C. & D. convertant, mutentque, 1005.

C.   capiant, 1006.

D.   reddant, 1006.

C.   primordia, 1007; prima, 1011.

Cy. fluitare, 1011.

C.   nasci, 1012.

D.   perire, 1012.

C. & D. mutari, 1022.

C.   primum, 1026; primum, 1033.

D.   mortalibus, 1033.

C.   gentes, 1036; natura, 1051; seminaque, 1054; creatum, 1056; natura, 1058; semina, 1059; exordia, 1062; generisque, 1063; confieri, 1069; seminibus, 1070; natura, semina, 1072; conicere, 1073; coniecta, 1074; gentis, 1076.

Cy. saecla, 1076.

C.   gignatur, 1078.

Cy. saecli, 1079.

C.   genere, primis, 1080; genus, 1081; genitam, prolem, 1082.

D.   terminus, 1087.

C.   nativo, 1088; genus, generatimst, 1089; natura, 1090.

Cy. convertere, 1097.

D.   disturbet, 1102; exanimatque, 1104.

C.   genitale, 1105; primigenum, 1106; addita, 1107; semina, 1108; augescere, 1109; appareret, 1110; crescit, procudunt, 1115; crescendi, perfica, 1116; natura, creatrix, 1117; datur, 1118.

D.   fluit, recedit, 1119.

C.   natura, auctum, 1121; grandescere, adauctu, 1122; scandere, 1123; assumunt, 1124.

D. mittunt, 1124; remittant, 1126; dispendi, 1127.
C. vescitur, 1127.
D. fluere, recedere, 1128.
C. accedere, 1129; alescendi, 1130.
D. frangit, liquitur, 1132; adempto, 1133; dispargit, mittit, 1135; exaestuat, 1137.
C. suboriri, suppeditare, 1138.
D. pereunt, rarefacta, fluendo, 1139; succumbunt, 1140; grandi, defit, 1141; conficere, infesta, domare, 1143; expugnata, labem, putrisque, ruinas, 1145.
C. novando, 1146; sustentare, 1147.
D. nec . . . perpetiuntur, 1148.
C. natura, 1149.
D. fracta, effetaque, 1150.
C. creat, creavit, 1151.
Cy. saecla, 1152.
C. partu, 1152.
D. mortalia, 1153.
Cy. saecla, 1153.
C. crearunt, 1155; genuit, 1156; primum, creavit, 1158.
D. mortalibus, 1158.
C. fetus, 1159; grandescunt, aucta, 1160.
D. conterimusque, 1161; conficimus, 1162.
C. fetus, 1163; parentis, 1167; sator, 1168; genus, 1170.
D. tabescere, ire, 1173; capulum, defessa, vetusto, 1174.

BOOK III

D. tenebris, 1.
C. lumen, 1; primus, inlustrans, 2; gentis, 3; pater, patria, 9; floriferis, 11; naturam, divina, 15; lumine, 22.
D. Acherusia, 25.
C. natura, 29; exordia, 31; creari, 34; natura, 35; claranda, 36.
D. Acheruntis, 37; mortis, nigrore 39; tartara, leti, 42.
C. naturam, 43; patria, 48.
C. & D. parentant, 51.
D. nigras, mactant, manibu', 52; caeca, 59; noctes, 62.
C. dies, 62.
D. mortis, 64; leti, 67; caedem, caede, 71; funere, 72; tenebris, 77; intereunt, 78; mortis, 79; lucisque, 80; letum, 81.
C. patriam, parentis, 85.
D. Acherusia, 86; tenebris, 88.
C. luce, 88.
D. tenebris, 90; tenebrasque, 91.
C. solis, lucida, diei, 92; naturae, 93; primum, 94; exstant, 97; faciat, 100.
D. detracto, 119; relinquit, 123.
C. semina, 127.

D. moribundos, 129.
C. natura, 130; naturam, conficere, 137; exsistere, 154.
D. infringi, aboriri, 155; caligare, succidere, 156; concidere, 157.
C. naturam, 161; natura, 167.
D. disclusis, 171.
C. gignitur, 173; exsurgendi, 174; naturam, 175; unde constiterit, 177–8; factum, 180; natura, 185; constare, 186; seminibus, 187; creata, 190; natura, 191; exstat, 194; natura, 203; constare, 204; naturam, 208.
D. leti, quies, 211.
C. natura, 212.
D. recessit, 212; mors, 214.
C. seminibus, 217.
D. evanuit, 221; diffugit, 222.
C. semina, 226; creatam, 229.
D. fugiens, 230.
C. natura, 231.
D. moribundos, deserit, 232.
C. natura, 235; primordia, 236; natura, 237; creandum, 238; creare, 239; sensiferos, 240; natura, 241; sensiferos, prima, 245; prima, perfecta, 246.
D. perturbentur, 253; desit, 254; diffugiant, 255.
C. patrii, 260; primordia, 262; genus, 266; perfectum, augmen, 268; creant, naturam, 270; sensifer, oritur, primum 272; natura, 273; genus, 276; creatast, 278; facta, 279; fieri, 285.
D. interemant, diductaque, solvant, 287.
C. calor, 288; fervescit, ardor, 289.
D. frigida, 290.
C. effervescit, 295; genere, primis, 296.
D. frigida, 299; gelidas, 300.
C. natura, 302.
D. gelidis, 305.
C. genus, 307; naturae, prima, 309.
D. evelli, 310.
C. naturas, 315; principiis, oritur, 318; naturarum, 320; natura, 323.
D. pernicie, divelli, 326.
C. genus, 327.
D. evellere, 327; intereat, 328.
C. natura, 328; naturam, 329.
D. extrahere, dissoluantur, 330.
C. principiis, prima, 331; fiunt, 332; conflatur, 335; accensus, 336; gignitur, 337.
D. mortem, 338; convellitur, 340; discidium, relicti, 342; pereunt, putrescunt, 343.
C. ineunte, 344; maternis, alvoque, 346.
D. discidium, peste, 347.
C. naturam, 349.
D. dimissa, 356; expellitur, 358; sublatis, 369.
C. primordia, 372; nectere, 373; prima, 378; sensiferos, 379; exordia prima, 380; primordia, 392; semina, 393.

D. insequitur, discedit, 400; gelidos, leti, frigore, linquit, 401; caesis, lacer, 403; adempta, remota, 404; lacerato, 408; corrompas, 410; caedas, 411; pernicie, 412; peresa, 413; occidit, 414.

C. lumen, 414.

D. tenebraeque, 414.

C. splendidus, 415; nativos, 417.

D. mortalis, 417; mortalem, 423.

C. constare, 425; principiis, factam, 427; genus, 431.

D. quassatis, 434; discedit, 436; diffundi, perire, 437; dissolvi; 438.

C. prima, 438.

D. recessit, 439; conquassatum, 441.

C. gigni, 445; crescere, 446.

D. senescere, 446.

C. adolevit, 449.

D. ceciderunt, 452; deficiunt, desunt, 454; dissolui, 455.

C. naturam, 456; gigni, 457; crescere, 458.

D. fessa, fatisci, 458; leti, 462; dissolui, 470; leti, 472; exitio, 473.

C. genere, 481.

D. pereant, privata, 486.

C. semina, 496.

D. disiectatur, distracta, veneno, 501.

C. primum, 504.

D. distracta, 507; mortalem, 512.

C. naturam, 516.

D. exit, 519; mors, 520; mortalia, 521; ire, 526; deperdere, 527.

C. primum, 528.

D. leti, 530; scinditur, 531.

C. natura, 531.

D. mortalis, 532; dilaniata, dispargitur, interit, 539; moribundi, 542; mortalem, 543; pereat, dispersa, 544; deficit, 547; secreta, 552; liquuntur, tabe, 553.

C. natura, 561.

D. avulsus, 563.

D. primordia, 568; sensiferos, 570.

D. mortem, 571; resoluto, 576; eiectis, 577; dissolui, 578; discidium, tabescat, 581; emanarit, diffusa, 583; mutatum, putre, ruina, 584; mota, 585; emanante, 586; dispertitam, 589.

C. naturam, 589.

D. distractam, 590; prolapsa, enaret, 591; labefacta, 593; solui, 594; supremo . . . tempore, languescere, 595; exsangui, cadere, 596.

C. genus, 597.

D. liquisse, 598; conquassatur, 600; collabefiunt, 601; dissolvere, 602; prodita, 603; dempto, 604; moriens, 607; ire, 608; deficere, 610; dissolui, 612; moriens, dissolui, 613; relinquere, 614.

C. gignitur, 616; nascendum, 618; creatum, 619; creari, 622; gignier, 623; natura, 624.

D. infernas, Acherunte, 628; praecideret, 636; secernat, 637; dispertita, 638; discissa, dissicietur, 639; scinditur, discedit, 640.

C. naturam, 641.

D. abscidere, 642; tremere, 644; decidit, abscisum, 645; caedesque, 648; amissam, 649; abstraxe, 650; cecidisse, 651; adempto, 652; moribundus, 653; reddidet, 656; discidere, 659; tabo, 661; divisast, 667; mortale, 668; disciditur, 669.

C. nascentibus, insinuatur, 671.

D. leto, 676; interiisse, 678.

C. creatam, 678; gignimur, limen, inimus, 681; cresse, 683; originis, 686.

D. leti, 687.

C. insinuatas, 689.

D. exsolvere, 696.

C. insinuatam, 698.

D. peribit, 700; dissolvitur, interit, 701; dispertitur, 702; disperit, 704.

C. naturam, sufficit, 704; eunt, 706.

D. dissoluuntur, 706.

C. natura, creatur, 708; nata, 709.

D. periit, 710.

C. natali, 711; natura, 712.

D. funeris, 712.

C. semina, 713.

D. exanimo, 714; amissis, libata, 716; profugit, 717; cadavera, 719.

C. exspirant, 720; perfluctuat, 721; insinuari, 722; conveniant, 725.

D. recesserit, 725.

C. semina, 727; fabricentur, 728; perfectis, insinuentur, 729; faciant, 730; facere, 735; faciunt, 737; perfectis, insinuentur, 738; seminium, 742; patribus, 743; genere, 744; ineunte, generascunt, ingenioque, 745; semine, seminioque, 746; crescit, 747; semine, 750.

D. dissolvitur, interit, 756; dissolui, 758; intereant, 759.

C. ire, 761.

D. mortalem, 767; amittit, 768.

C. origine, 771.

D. exire, 772; putri, 773; obruat, 775.

C. Veneris, partusque, 776.

D. mortalia, 778.

C. prima, insinuetur, 780; prima, insinuetur, 782; prima, 783; crescat, 787; natura, oriri, 788; innasci, 792; crescere, 795; genique, 797.

D. interiit, periisse, 798; distractam, 799; mortale, 800; mortale, 804; dissociare, 809; discedere, dissoluique, 815; diffugiant, 817; dissolvere, 817; nigras, 829; mors, 830.

C. natura, 831.

D. ubi non erimus, 838; discidium, 839.

C. apti, 839.

D. erimus, 840; distractast, 844.

C. natura, 844; comptu, coniugioque, 845; apti, 846; collegerit, 847.

D. obitum, 848.

C. redegerit, 848; data, lumina, 849.

D. interrupta, 851.

C. semina, 857.

D. pausa, 860; deerrarunt, 861; mors, 864; morte, 866.

C. natus, 868.

D. mortalem, mors, 869; mortem, 871; interfiat, 872; morte, 875; tollit, eicit, 877; morte, 880; proiecto, 882; mortalem, 884.

C. creatum, 884.

D. morte, 885; peremptum, 886; morte, 888; non . . . accipiet, 894.

C. nati, 895.

D. non poteris, 897; ademit, 898; leto sopitus, 904; cine factum, 906; somnum, redit, quietam, 910; tabescere, 911; fuerit, 915; morte, 916.

C. primis, 916.

D. sopita, quiescunt, 920; soporem, 921.

C. sensiferis, primordia, 924; correptus, colligit, 925.

D. mortem, 926; nil, 927; disiectus, 928; leto, 929.

C. expergitus, exstat, 929.

D. frigida, pausa, 930.

C. natura, 931.

D. mortalis, 933; mortem, 934; interiere, 937; quietem, 939; periere, 940; pereat, occidat, 942; finem, 943; marcet, 946; confecti, lanquent, 947; moriturus, 949.

C. naturam, 951.

D. obitum, 953; marces, 956; elapsast, 958; mors, 959; mitte, 961; concede, 962; cedit, 964.

C. novitate, 964.

D. extrusa, vetustas, 964; ex aliis, 965.

C. aliud reparare, 965.

D. barathrum, Tartara, atra, 966.

C. crescant, 967.

Cy. saecla, 967.

D. perfuncta, sequentur, 968; cecidere, cadentque, 969.

C. alid . . . oriri, 970.

D. ex alio, 970.

C. nascimur, 973; natura, 974.

D. mortem, 975; Acherunte, 978; mortalis, 983; Acherunte, 984; lacerant, exest, 993; scindunt, 994.

C. naturam, 1003.

Cy. redeunt, 1006.

C. fetusque, 1006.

D. Cerberus, Furiae, lucis egestas, 1011; Tartarus, 1012; iactu', 1016; carnifices, 1017; terminus, 1020; finis, 1021; morte, 1022; Acherusia, 1023; reliquit, 1025; occiderunt, 1028.

C. gentibus, 1028.

D. adempto, moribundo, fudit, 1033; dedit, 1035.

C. repertores, 1036.

D. sopitu' quietest, 1038; vetustas, 1039; languescere, 1040; leto, 1041; obit, decurso, 1042.

C. genus, ingenio, 1043.

D. restinxit, 1044.

C. exortus, 1044.

D. obire, 1045; mortua, 1046.

C. naturam, primum, 1072.
D. mortalibis, 1074; mortem, 1075; finis, mortalibus, 1078; letum, obeamus, 1079.
C. nova, procuditur, 1081.
D. exitus, 1086; mortis, 1088; perempti, 1089; condere, 1090; mors, 1091; non erit, 1092; finem, 1093; occidit, 1094.

BOOK IV

C. nullius, 1; integros, 2; novos, 3; nulli, 5; primum, 6.
D. obscura, 8.
C. lucida, pango, 8; recreata, 17; naturam, 25; natura, 26; compta, 27.
D. distracta, rediret, 28.
C. prima, 28.
D. carentum, 35; Acherunte, 37; umbras, 38; mortem, 39.
C. natura, 40.
D. perempta, 40; discessum, 41.
C. primordia, 41.
D. diffusa, solute, 55.
C. nascentes, 60.
D. exuit, 61; spoliis, 62; cadant, recedant, 65.
C. prima, 71; corrident, 83.
D. correpta, 83; diffusae, abundant, 91.
C. ortae, 92.
D. scinduntur, 93; exire, 94.
C. coortae, 94.
D. discerpere, 96.
C. prima, 97; natura, 110; primis, primordia, 111; primum, 113; exordia, 114; primum, 116; primordia, 120; constet, natura, 121; gignuntur, 131; constituuntur, 132; formata, 133; concrescere, 134.
D. avulsaque, 138.
Cy. speciem mutare, 141.
C. genantur, 143; primis, 147.
D. scinditur, 149.
C. constant, 150.
D. scindi, 153.
C. genuntur, 159; origo, 160; lumina, 162; liquidissima, 168.
D. tenebras, Acherunta, 170.
C. coorta, 172.
D. nocte, 172; cycni, 181.
C. factas, 184; genere, lux, 185; primis, facta, 186; lumine, lumen, 189; fulgere, fulgur, 190; primum, 193; textura, 196; lux, 200; prima, 204; lumina, 208; primis, 209; primum, 211.
D. caelo stellante, 212.
C. radiantia, 213; sole, 219.
D. exesor, 220; requies, 227; tenebris, 231.
C. luce, claro, candore, 232.

150

D. tenebris, 235.
C. luci, 235; genuntur (?) 254; fierique, 262; genus, 271; fit, 274; primus, 275; primum, 279; confit, 291.
D. eliditur, 296; adlidat, 297; elisam, 299.
C. exprimat, 299; fieri, 303.
D. elisa, 315. (On the sparseness of the theme between 239 and 322, see Chapter III, note 40.)
C. natura, 322; splendida, 324.
D. turbantia, 328; adurit, 329.
C. semina, 330; gignunt, 331; semina, 334.
D. tenebris, 337.
C. luce, 337.
D. caliginis, 338.
C. candens, lucidus, 340.
D. nigras, 341.
C. luce, 344, 347.
D. tenebris, 348.
C. luce, 348.
D. calignis, 349; perit, 356; Umbra, 364.
C. lumine, 366, 368, 371; nova, lumina, 375; primaque, 376.
D. dispereunt, 376; spoliatur, 377.
C. lumine, 377; repletur, 378.
D. nigrasque, umbras, 378.
C. lux, 380.
D. umbra, 380.
C. lumina, 381.
D. umbraque, 382.
C. naturam, 385.
D. sidera, 391; obitus, 393.
C. exorta, 393.
Cy. revisunt, 393.
C. solque, 395.
D. luna, 395; ruere, 403.
C. iubar, erigere, 404; natura, 405; gentes, 413.
Cy. saecla, 413.
C. ortus, 432.
D. obire, condere, 433.
C. lumen, 433.
D. fractis, 437; refracta, 440; nocturno, 444.
C. splendida, 444; florentia, lumina, 450.
D. quiete, 454; noctis, caligine, 456.
C. solem, lumenque, 457.
D. noctis, 460.
C. genere, 462; crearit, 476; primis, creatam, 478; orta, 483, 484.
D. gelidum, 491.
C. fervensve, 491; primam, 505.
D. convellere, 505; ruat, 507; concidat, 508.
C. genere, 510; prima, 513.

D. ruere, ruantque, 518.
C. primis, 519; ortast, 521; constare, 526.
D. radit, 528.
C. coorta, 530; primordia, 531.
D. raditur, 532.
C. constent, 533; principiis, 534.
D. laedere, 534; auferat, 535; detrahat, 536; nigrai, noctis, umbram, 537; aurorae, exoriente, nitore, 538.
C. constare, 540.
D. amittit, 541.
C. fit, 542; creatur, 543; primordia, 544.
D. querellam, 548.
C. exprimimus, 550; daedala, 551; figurat, 552.
D. diffugit, 566; perit, diffusa, 569; adlisa, 570.
C. fingunt, 581.
D. silentia, 583.
C. rumpi, 583; fieri, 584; genus, 586; genere, 590; genus, 594.
D. perscinduntur, 601.
C. gignuntur, 604, exorta, 605.
D. obtunditur, 613.
C. exprimimus, 618, 620.
D. lacerantque, 625.
C. coorta, 625; cibus, 637.
D. venenum, 637; disperit, 639; venenum, 640.
C. auget, 641; semina, 644; generatim, 646; seminibus, constant, 648; semina, 649; textura, 657.
D. perturbatur, 666; commutantur, 667.
C. principiorum, 667; progignere, 670; apes, 679.
D. vulturiique, cadaveribus, 680.
C. pabula, 685.
D. veneno, 685.
Cy. saecla, 686.
D. perit, 692.
C. primum, 694.
D. fracta, 696; contrita, collabefacta, 697.
C. creatum, 698; principiis, 699.
D. refrigescit, 703.
C. calida, 704; generest, 707.
D. noctem, 710.
C. auroram, 711; semina, 715.
D. interfodiunt, 716; laedere, 718, 721.
C. veniunt, veniant, 723; iunguntur, 726; textu, 728; naturam, 731.
D. Cerbereasque, 733; morte, obita, 734.
C. genus, 735; fiunt, 736; confiunt, facta, 738; fit, 739; natura, 740; haerescit, 742; naturam, texta, 743; genere, creantur, 744; fieri, 751.
D. relicta, mors, 761.
C. natura, 762.
D. quiescunt, 763; mortis, letique, 766.

C. prima, 771.
D. perit, 771.
C. nata, 771; creat, natura, 785; prima, 800.
D. perit, 800.
C. nata, 800.
D. pereunt, 804.
C. fit, 806; generis, 819; factus, 820; creata, 825; genere, 832; natumst, procreat, 835; nata, 836; creatast, 837; origio, 838; creatae, 839; crescere, 842.
D. lacerare, cruore, 844; vulnus, 846.
C. natura, 846.
D. quieti, 848.
C. natum, 850; nata, 854; creari, 857; natura, 859.
D. fluere, recedere, 860; feruntur, 863; exhalantur, 864; rarescit, 865; subruitur, 866.
C. natura, 866; suffulciat, 867; recreet, 868.
D. restinguit, 873; abluitur, 876.
C. expletur, 876; primum, 881; fit, 883; movetur, 891; fit, 896.
D. quietem, 907; cycni, 910.
C. fit, 916.
D. distracta, 916; eiecta, 917; dissoluuntur, fluuntque, 919; perturbatam, 922; eiectamque, 923; frigore, leti, 924; cinere, 926.
C. reconflari, 927; consurgere, 928; novitas, confiat, 929.
D. perturbari, languescere, 930.
Cy. ducitur atque reflatur, 938.
C. primas, prima, 941; fit, 942.
D. ruina, 942; conturbantur, 943.
C. principiorum, 943.
D. eiciatur, 945; distracta, 946.
C. natura, 948.
D. abit, 949.
C. suffulciat, 950.
D. languescuntque, 951; cadunt, 952; resolvunt, 953.
C. efficit, 956.
D. conturbant, contusa, 958; eiectus, 960; divisior, distractior, 961.
C. naturam, 969; patriis, 970.
D. quiete, 991.
C. expergifactique, 995; propago, 998; seminiorum, 1005.
D. iugulentur, 1014; morsu . . . mandantur, 1016–1017; mortem, obeunt, 1020.
C. redeunt, 1023; semen, creavit, 1031; semine, 1034; semen, primum, 1038; semen, 1040; genitalis, 1044.
D. dira, 1046; saucia, 1048; cadunt, vulnus, 1049; sanguis, icimur, ictu, 1050.
C. Veneris, 1052.
D. ictus, 1052; feritur, 1055.
C. Venus, 1058; primum, 1059.
D. frigida, 1060; ulcus, 1068; furor, aerumna, 1069.

C. prima, 1070.
D. vulnera, 1070; Venere, 1071. (Since the close of IV is devoted essentially to *"Venus destructrix"* I list all citations of her name under the motif of destruction, with the exception of those appearances (1210ff.) where she explicitly resumes her earlier creative role. Also, words or images which imply the destructive power of love are included under the destruction motif.)
C. cures, 1071.
D. Veneris, 1073; poena, 1074.
C. primum, 1078; germina, 1083.
D. Venus, 1084; poenas, 1084.
C. origo, 1086.
D. restingui, 1087.
C. natura, 1088.
D. ardescit, dira, 1090; raptat, 1096; laborat, 1099; Venus, 1101; abradere, 1103; Venus, 1107.
C. conserat, 1107.
D. abradere, 1110; abire, 1111; Veneris, compagibus, 1113; labefacta, liquescunt, 1114.
Cy. redit, 1117.
D. rabies, furor, 1117; malum, 1119; Tabescunt, vulnere, 1120. absumunt, pereuntque, 1121; labitur, 1123; languent, aegrotat, 1124; teriturque, 1127; exercita, 1128.
C. parta, patrum, 1129; fonte 1133.
D. angat, 1134; remorder, 1135; perire, 1136.
C. vivescit, 1138.
D. ignis, 1138; plagas, 1146; retibus, 1147; nodos, 1148; implicitus, inque peditus, 1149; infestum, 1150.
C. primum, 1151.
D. Veneremque, 1157; adflictentur, 1158; mala, 1159; mortua, 1167.
C. genere, 1170.
D. Veneris, 1172; lacrimans, 1177; mortali, 1184; Veneres, 1185.
C. lucem, 1189.
D. Venerem, 1200; vinctis, excrucientur, 1202; compagibus, 1205; fraudem, vinctosque, 1207.
C. semine, 1209; matrum, materno, semine, fiunt, 1211; patribus, patrio, 1212; parentum, 1213; patrio, materno, crescunt, 1214; semina, Veneris, 1215; exsistere, avorum, 1218; proavorum, 1219; primordia, 1220; parentes, 1221; patribus, patres, stirpe, 1222; Venus, producit, 1223; maiorumque, 1224; semine, 1225; fiunt, 1226; oritur, patrio, semine, 1227; maternoque, exsistunt, creti, 1228; partus, semine, constat, 1229; creatur, 1230; suboles, origo, 1232; satum, genitalem, 1233; pater, gnatis, 1234; Venere, 1235.
D. sanguine, 1236; adolentque, 1237.
C. gravidas, semine, 1238; semine, 1240; semine, semen, 1247; Veneris, 1248; gravescunt, 1250; puellos, 1252; partu, 1253; fecundae, 1254; parere, 1255; natura, gnatis, 1256; semina, 1257; seminibus, genitaliter, 1258; concrescunt, semina, 1261.

D. extenuantur, tabentque, 1262.
C. concipere, 1266; semina, 1267; concipere, 1269.
D. Venerem, 1270.
C. seminis, 1273; gravidaeque, 1275.
D. Venus, 1276; Venerisque, 1278; labascit, 1285; pertundere, 1287.

BOOK V

C. repertis, 2; parta, 5.
D. mortali, 6.
C. cretus, 6; deus, deus, 8; princeps, invenit, 9.
D. tenebris, 11.
C. clara, luce, 12; divina, 13; Ceres, Liberque, 14; vitigeni, 15.
D. mortalibus, 15.
C. instituisse, 15; gentis, 17; deus, 19; gentis, 20.
D. leonis, sus, 25; taurus, pestis, 26; hydra, venenatis, colubris, 27; Geryonai, 28; Stymphala, 29; Diomedis equi, 30; serpens, 33.
C. genere, 37.
D. perempta, 37; victa, nocerent, 38; scindunt, 45; clades, 48.
C. divum, 51; divinitus, 52; naturam, 54; creata, 56; genere, primis, Natura, 59; nativo, primum, consistere, creta, 60.
D. reliquit, 62; mortali, 65.
C. nativumque, 66; fundarit, 68; exstiterint, natae, 70; genus, 71; coeperit, 72; insinuarit, 73; nativa, 77.
Cy. cursus lustrare perennis, 79.
C. augendas, 80.
Cy. volvi, 81.
D. finita, 89; terminus, 90.
C. naturam, 93; texta, 94.
D. exitio, 95; ruet, 96; exitium, 98; motibus, 105.
C. ortis, 105.
D. conquassari, 106; victa, fragore, 109; disturbent, 119; restinguere, 120; mortali, 121.
C. natura, 127; crescat, 131; natura, oriri, 132; innasci, 136.
D. putribus, 142.
C. natura, 148; parare, 156; naturam, 157; gentibus, 161.
D. evertere, 163.
C. genere, 164; novi, 168.
D. quietos, 168.
C. novis, 170; veteres, 171.
D. novitatis, 173.
C. creatis, 174.
C. diluxit, genitalis, origo, 176; natus, 177; creatum, 180; gignundis, 181; primum, 182; principiorum, 184; creandi, 186; primordia, 187; creare, 191; congressa, novando, 194; primordia, 195; paratam, 198; naturam, 199.
D. fervidus ardor, 204; assiduus geli casus, mortalibus, 205.

C. natura, 206; fecundas, 210; ortus, 211; exsistere, 212; frondent, florent, 214.
D. torret, 215; peremunt, 216.
C. genus, natura, 218; genti, 219.
D. infestum, 219.
C. alit, auget, 220.
D. morbos, 220; mors, 221.
C. & D. proiectus, 222.
C. infans, 223; primum, luminis oras, 224; alvo, matris, natura, profudit, 225; vagituque, 226; crescunt, 228; almae, nutricis, 230; parit, naturaque, daedala, 234; nativo, 238.
D. mortali, 238.
C. natura, 239; nativo, 241.
D. mortalibus, 241; mortalia, 242.
C. nativa, 243.
D. consumpta, 244.
C. regigni, 244; principiale, 246.
D. clademque, 246; mortalia, 248; perire, 249.
C. gigni, augescere, 250.
D. perusta, 251; dispergunt, 254; diluviem, 255; rodunt, 256.
C. alit, auget, 257; redditur, 258; omniparens, 259.
D. sepulcrum, 259; libatur, 260.
C. aucta, recrescit, 260; novo, 261; primum, 264.
D. tollitur, 265; diminuunt, retexens, 267; diditur, 268.
C. remanat, 269; caput, 270; detulit, 272.
D. fluit, 275.
C. retribuat, recreetque, 277.
D. resoluta, 278.
C. gigni, 279; reccidere, fluere, 280; fons, luminis, sol, 281; candore, recenti, 282; suppeditatque, novo, lumine, lumen, 283; primum, fulgoris, 284.
D. disperit, 284.
C. primum, soli, 286; radios, lucis, 287.
D. rumpere, 287; disperit, 288; inumbratur, 289.
C. splendore, novo, 290; primum, fulgoris, 291.
D. perire, 291.
C. sole, 292; suppeditet, lucis, caput, 293.
D. nocturna, 294.
C. lumina, claraeque, coruscis, 295; fulguribus, 296.
D. caligine, 296.
C. novum, lumen, 298; lux, 299.
D. rupta, relinquit, 299; exitium, 301.
C. origine, 301; lucem, iactare, subortu, 303; primum, 304.
D. perdere, 304; vinci, 306; ruere, putrescere, 307; fessa, fatisci, 308; finis, 309.
C. naturae, 310; dilapsa, 311; senescere, 312; ruere, avulsos, 313; caderent, avulsa, 315; fragore, 317.
C. procreat, 319.

D. perempta, 320.
C. nativo, 321.
D. mortali, 321.
C. auget, alitque, 322.
D. deminui, 323.
C. recreari, 323; genitalis, origo, 324.
D. funera, 326; cecidere, 328.
C. insita, florent, 329; novitatem, recensque, 330; naturast, exordia, 331; augescunt, addita, 333; peperere, 334; natura, 335; primus, primis, 336; patrias, 337.
D. periisse, torrenti, 339.
Cy. saecla, 339.
D. cecidisse, vexamine, 340; rapaces, 341; coperuisse, 342; exitium, 344; morbis, periclis, 345; cladem, ruinas, 347; mortales, 348; morbis, aegrescimus, 349.
C. natura, 350.
D. removit, 350; penetrare, 353; dissociare, 354.
C. naturam, 355.
D. discedere, dissoluique, 360; dissiliant, 362; dissolvere, 363.
C. naturast, 365.
D. corruere, turbine, 368; cladem, 369.
C. natura, 370.
D. exspargi, 371; pulsa, perire, 372; leti, 373.
C. nativa, 376.
D. mortali, 377; finem, 383; exsuperarint, 384; diluviare, 387; deminuunt, retexens, 389; siccare, 390; finem, 391; superantior, 394; regnarit, 395; superat, perussit, 396.
C. pater, 399.
D. deturbavit, 401.
C. recreavit, 404.
D. superare, 407; cadunt, revictae, 409; pereunt, exustae, torrentibus, 410; superare, 411; obruit, 412.
C. fundarit, 417; primordia, 419, 422; congressa, creare, 426; genus, 428; convecta, 429; fiunt, exordia, 430; generisque, 431; solis, lumine, 432.
D. sidera, 433.
C. nova, coorta, 436; omnigenis, principiis, 437; coniuncta, 441; discludere, 444; dividere, disponere, 445; secernere, 446; primum, 449; coibant, 450; perplexa, coibant, 452; expressere, 453; efficerent, 454; seminibus, 456; primus, sustulit, 458; primum, matutina, 461; rubent, lumina, solis, 462; conciliantur, 465; concreto, subtexunt, 466; exordia, 471; genus, 478; suffudit, 482; condensa, coiret; 486; expressus, 487; augebat, 488; densabant, 491; sidebant, crescebant, 492; succumbere, 494; concreto, 495; constitit, 496.
Cy. vertitur, 510; volvenda, 514; versantur, 520; volvunt, 521.
D. summania, 521.
C. creatis, 528.
D. evanescere, decrescere, 535.
C. naturam, 536; ex ineuente aevo, 537; prima, concepta, origine, 548.

D. concussa, 550; concutit, 551.
C. ex ineunte aevo, 555; natura, 561; solis, 564; lumina, 566.
D. libant, 568; contractior, 569.
C. solis, lumenque, 570; fulgent, 571.
D. lunaque, 575.
C. lumine, lustrans, 575; lucem, 576.
D. luna, 581.
C. claram, 582; clarus, 587; lumen, 593; patefactum, 597; fontem, scatere, erumpere, lumen, 598; capite, 601; fons, 603; genus, 608.
D. accidere, 609.
C. lucens, 610; fulgore, 612; solis, 614; aestivis, 615.
D. brumalis, 616.
Cy. vertat, 617.
D. lunaque, 618.
Cy. obire, 618.
C. sol, 619.
Cy. cursu, 619.
C. primis, 621; sancta, 622.
D. sidera, 623.
Cy. turbine, 624.
D. evanescere, 625; imminui, 626.
C. solem, 627.
D. signis, 627; signa, 628; lunam, 629; signis, 631.
Cy. reverti, 635.
D. signa, 636.
Cy. revisunt, 636.
C. aestivis, solem, 639.
D. signis, 639; brumalis, gelidumque, rigorem, 640.
Cy. reiciat, 641.
D. gelidis, frigoris, umbris, 641.
C. aestiferas, fervida, 642.
D. signa, 642; lunam, stellasque, 643.
Cy. volvunt, orbibus, magnos . . . annos, 644; magnos . . . orbis, 648.
D. sidera, 649; nox, obruit, caligine, 650.
Cy. cursu, 651.
C. sol, 651.
D. languidus, 652; concussos, labefactos, 653.
Cy. convertere, 654.
C. roseam, Matuta, 656; auroram, lumina, 657; sol, 658.
Cy. revertens, 658.
C. radiis, 659; semina, 660; nova, lumina, gigni, 662; genus, 663; orienti, lumine, 664; conficere, 665; semina, reparare, nitorem, 668; fiunt, 669; florescunt, 670.
D. dimittunt, 671; cadere, 672.
C. pubescere, 673; demittere, 674; fiunt, 676; exordia, prima, 677; origine, prima, 678.
Cy. redeunt, 679.
C. crescere, dies, 680.

D. tabescere, noctes, 680; minui, 681.
C. luces, augmina, 681.
D. noctes, 681.
C. sol, 682.
D. detraxit, 685.
C. reponit, 685.
Cy. relatus, 686; pervenit, 687.
D. signum, 687; nocturnas, 688.
C. lucibus, 688.
D. umbras, 688; aquilonis, 689.
C. austri, 689.
D. signiferi, 691.
C. sol, 692.
Cy. concludit, 692.
C. lustrans, 693.
D. signis, 695.
C. iubar, 697; ortus, 698.
D. noctes, hiberno, 699.
C. radiatum, insigne, diei, 700; faciunt, solem, surgere, 703.
D. luna, 705.
C. solis, 705; nitere, 705; lumen, 706; solis, 707; oriens, 709.
D. obitus, 709; condere lumen, 710.
C. solis, 711.
D. signorum, 712.
Cy. orbem, 712.
D. lunam, 713.
C. lumine, 715.
Cy. volvier, 716.
C. splendoris, 716.
D. cassum, 719.
C. lumine, 719.
Cy. versarique, 720.
C. candenti, lumine, 721.
Cy. versandoque, 722; vertit, 724; retro contorquet, 725.
C. luciferam, 726; nova, 731.
D. luna, 731.
C. creari, 731.
D. aborisci, 733.
C. creata, 733; reparari, 734; creari, 736; ver, Venus, Veneris, 737; Flora, mater, 739; calor, 741; Ceres, 742.
D. fulmine, 745; bruma, nives, rigorem, 746; hiemps, algu, 747.
C. gignitur, 749.
D. deletur, 749.
D. defectus, lunaeque, latebras, 751; luna, secludere, 753.
C. solis, 753; lumine, 754.
D. obstruere, 754; obiciens, caecum, 755.
C. radiis, 755.
D. cassum, 757.

C. lumine, 757; solque, 758.
D. dimittere, languidus, 758.
C. recreareque, lumen, 759.
D. infesta, 760; interstingui, perire, 761; lunam, spoliare, 762.
C. lumine, 763.
D. oppressum, 763.
C. solem, 763.
Cy. perlabitur, 764.
D. umbras, 764.
C. radios, 767.
D. interrumpat, 767.
C. lumenque, 767; fulget, 768.
D. luna, 768.
C. nitore, 768.
D. languescere, 769.
C. luminibus, 770.
D. inimica, 770.
C. fieri, 773; solis, 774.
D. lunaque, 774.
C. cieret, 775.
D. offecto, 776.
C. lumine, 776.
D. obire, 776; tenebris, 777.
C. lumine, 778; clara, candida, luce, 779; novitatem, 780; novo, fetu, primum, luminis oras, 781; tollere, 782; genus, 783; dedit, 784; crescendi, 787; primum, creantur, 788; nova, primum, 790; sustulit, 791.
D. mortalia, 791.
Cy. saecla, 791.
C. creavit, 791; coorta, 792; exisse, 794; maternum, 795, creata, 796; exsistunt, 797; concreta, 798; coorta, 799; nova, adulta, 800; genus, 801; ova, exclusae, 802; petentes, 804; primum, 805.
D. mortalia, 805.
C. crescebant, uteri, 808; infantum, petessens, 810; natura, 811; peperit, 814; novitas, 818.
D. frigora, 818.
C. ciebat, 818; aestus, 819; crescunt, 820; maternum, 821; genus, creavit, 822; fudit, 823; pariendi, 826.
Cy. mutat, 828.
C. naturam, 828.
Cy. excipere, 829; migrant, 830; commutat, 831.
C. natura, 831.
Cy. vertere, 831.
D. putrescit, languet, 832.
C. succrescit, exit, 833; naturam, 834.
Cy. mutat, excipit, 835.
C. tulit, tulit, 836; creare, 837; coorta, 838; genere, creabat, 845; natura, 846.

D. absterruit, 846.
C. auctum, 846.
D. nec potuere, 847; nec reperire, 848.
C. Veneris, 848; propagando, procudere, 850.
Cy. saecla, 850.
C. primum, genitalia, 851; semina, 852.
D. interiisse, 855.
C. propagando, procudere, prolem, 856; ex ineunte aevo, genus, 859; genus, 862.
Cy. saecla, 862.
C. genus, semine, partum, 865.
Cy. saecla, 866.
C. parta, 869; natura, 871; genus, 874.
D. praedae, lucroque, 875; fatalibus, 876; interitum, 877.
C. genus, 877; natura, 877, 879; alienigenis, compacta, 880; floret, 884.
D. senecta, 886; deficiunt, languida, 887.
C. florente, 888; vestit, 889; semine, 890; confieri, 891; genere, 893; florescunt, 895.
D. proiciunt, senecta, 896.
C. Venere, 897; pinguescere, 899.
D. venenum, 900; torrere, urere, 902.
C. genus, 902; nova, recenti, 907; gigni, 908; novitatis, 909; florere, 912; natum, 913; semina, 916; primum, fudit, 917; creari, 918; abundant, 920; genera, 921; creari, 922; procedit, 923; naturae, 924; genus, 925; creasset, 926; aestu, 929.
D. frigore, 929.
Cy. lustra, 931.
C. nova, defodere, 935.
D. veteres, decidere, 936.
C. dederant, crearat, 937; matura, 941; ferebat, 942; novitas, florida, 943; tulit, 944.
D. mortalibus, 944.
Cy. saecla, 947.
D. spoliis, 954.
C. Venus, 962.
Cy. saecla, 967.
D. nocturno, 971.
C. diem, solemque, 973.
D. noctis, umbris, 974; sepulti, 975.
C. rosea, sol, lumina, 976.
D. tenebras, 978.
C. lucem, gigni, 978.
D. nox, detracto, 981.
C. lumine, solis, 981.
Cy. saecla, 988.
D. linquebant, 989; pabula . . . praebebat, haustus, 991; sepeliri, busto, 993; adeso, 994; ulcera, 995; Orcum, 996; privarant, 997; vulnera, 998;

161

exitio, 1000; lidebant, 1001; fraudem, 1005; leto, 1007; mersat, 1008; venenum, 1009; dant, 1010.

C. pararunt, 1011; prolemque, creatam, 1013; genus, primum, 1014; Venus, 1017.

D. imminuit, 1018.

C. parentum, 1018; gigni, 1024; genus, 1026.

D. peremptum, 1026.

Cy. saecla, 1027.

C. propago, 1027; natura, 1028; expressit, 1029; infantia, 1031; nata, vitulo, 1034; catuli, scymnique, 1036; creati, 1038; genus, 1039; prima, 1042; insita, 1047; prima, 1048; genus, 1057.

Cy. saecla, 1059.

C. primum, 1063; catulos, 1067; florenti, 1074; genus, 1078.

D. cornicum, 1084.

Cy. saecla, 1084.

D. vetusta, 1084; corvorumque, 1085; mortalis, 1089.

C. detulit, 1092.

D. mortalibus, 1092.

C. primitus, diditur, 1093; incita, 1094.

D. fulgere, 1095.

C. exprimitur, 1098; emicat, 1099.

D. mortalibus, 1101; victa, 1104.

C. novis, 1106; condere, locare, 1108; inventast, repertum, 1113; creti, 1116.

D. deicit, 1125; Tartara, 1126; vaporant, 1127; sanguine, 1131; occisis, subversa, iacebat, 1136; cruentum, 1138; conculcatur, 1140.

Cy. redibat, 1141.

C. creare, 1143; genus, 1145.

D. defessum, 1145; languebat, 1146; pertaesum, 1150.

C. exortast, 1153.

D. revertit, 1153.

C. genus, 1156.

D. morbo, 1159.

C. gentis, 1161; compleverit, 1162.

D. mortalibus, 1165.

C. nova, suscitat, 1166.

D. mortalia, 1169.

Cy. saecla, 1169.

D. convinci, 1178; mortis, 1180.

Cy. verti, 1184; volvi, 1189.

D. nox, luna, 1189; luna, 1190.

C. dies, 1190.

D. nox, noctis signa, 1190; noctivagaeque, 1191.

C. sol, 1192.

D. fremitus, murmura, minarum, 1193.

C. peperere, 1197.

D. sanguine, 1201.

C. expergefactum, 1208; genitalis, origo, 1212.

D. finis, 1213; plaga, 1220; murmura, 1221.
C. gentesque, 1222.
D. poenarum, 1225; correptus, leti, 1232; vis abdita, 1233; proculcare, 1235; vacillat, 1236; concussaeque, cadunt, 1237; mortalia, 1238.
Cy. saecla, 1238.
C. repertumst, 1241.
D. cremarat, 1243.
C. & D. pandere, reddere, 1248.
D. interficere, 1249.
C. ortum, 1250.
D. exederat, 1253; percoxerat, 1254.
C. manabat, 1255.
D. liquefacta, 1262.
C. duci, 1265; parent, 1266.
D. caedere, 1266.
C. primum, 1270.
D. victa, 1271; retusum, 1274.
Cy. iacet, successit, 1275; volvenda, commutat, 1276; succedit, exit, 1278.
C. repertum, 1279.
D. mortalis, 1280.
C. natura, reperta, 1281
D. fragmina, 1284.
C. primum, 1285; reperta, 1286; natura, 1288; solum . . . tractabant, 1289.
D. belli, 1289; vulnera, 1290.
C. serebant, 1290; solum proscindere, 1295.
D. belli, 1296; 1299; vulnera, 1303; Martis, turbare, 1304.
C. peperit, 1305; gentibus, 1306.
D. belli, 1308; caede, 1313; turbabant, 1314; ora petebant, 1319; deripiebant, 1320; vulnere, victos, 1321; adfixae, 1322; terebant, 1323; hauribant, 1324; caedebant, 1326; infracta, sanguine, 1327; ruinas, 1329; succisa, 1332; concidere, casu, 1333; vulneribus, 1336.
C. genus, 1338.
D. mactae, 1339; malum, 1342.
C. creatis, 1345.
D. perire, 1348.
C. paratur, 1351; gigni, 1352; natura, 1354; genus, 1355; sationis, insitionis, origo, 1361; primum, natura, creatrix, 1362; pullorum, 1364; stirpis, 1365; defodere . . . virgulta, 1366.
D. succedere, 1370.
C. concedere, 1371; intersita, 1377; obsita, 1378; primum, 1382; pingebant, 1396; matrem, 1402; genus, 1409, 1411; terrigenarum, 1411; primis, 1413.
D. perdit, 1415; cecidit, 1418.
C. repertam, 1419.
D. letum, 1420.
C. primus, 1420.
D. obiret, 1420; distractam, sanguine, 1421; disperiisse, 1422; curis exercent, 1423f., belloque fatigant, 1424.

C. terrigenas, 1427; genus, 1430.
D. frustraque laborat, 1430; consumit, 1431; altum, 1434; belli, 1435.
Cy. versatile, 1436.
C. sol, 1437.
D. luna, 1437.
C. lustrantes, lumine, 1437
Cy. verti, 1438.
C. reperta, 1445; genere, 1449; protrahit, 1454; luminis oras, 1455; clarescere, 1456.

BOOK VI

C. Primae, frugiparos, fetus, 1.
D. mortalibus, 1.
C. praeclaro, 2; recreaverunt, 3; primae, 4; genuere, 5.
D. extincti, 7.
C. divina, 7.
D. mortalibus, 10.
C. gnatorum, 13.
D. corrumpier, 18; mortalibu', 29.
C. naturali, 30; natura, 31; genus, 33.
D. tenebris, 36.
C. luce, 36.
D. tenebris, 38; tenebrasque, 39.
C. solis, lucida, diei, 40; naturae, 41.
D. mortalia, 43.
C. nativo, 44; fiunt, fierique, 45; exsistant, 48.
D. placentur, 48; placato, 49; mortales, 51; finita, 65; terminus, 66.
C. unde volans, 87.
D. insinuarit, dominatus, 89; requies, 94.
C. fit, 99, 101; dant, 108.
D. perscissa, 111.
C. genus, 113; exierunt, 120.
D. concussa, 121; divulsa, 122; dissiluisse, 123.
C. dat, 129.
D. scissa, 129; fragorem, 129.
C. dat, 131.
D. displosa, 131.
C. faciant, 133.
D. fragorem, 136; perscindat, perfringens, 138; evolvens, haurit, 141.
C. dant, 143.
D. frangendo, 143; trucidat, 147.
C. calidis, 148.
D. gelidum, 149; comburens, 153; crematur, 155.
C. dat, 157; confercit, 158.
D. franguntur, 158.
C. concreti, 159; semina, 160; exsilit, 163.

D. caedere, 167.
C. natus, 172; spissescere, 176.
D. liquescit, 179; perscidit, atram, 180.
C. semina, faciunt, fulgura, 182; exstructa, 188.
D. sepultis, 193.
C. structas, 195; semina, 201.
D. divulsa, 203.
C. semina, 206; semina, faciunt, 213.
D. dissoluitque, 216.
C. semina, faciunt, 217; natura, 219.
D. accendunt, 223.
C. primis, 225; natura, 226.
D. transit, 228, 229; liquidum, 230; diffugiant, 232; collaxat, 233; soluens, differt, 235.
C. primordia, 235.
D. dominantior, 238.
C. gignantur, 239.
D. discludere, 240; disturbare, avellere, 241; commoliri, ciere, 242; exanimare, prosternere, 243.
C. genere, 244; gignier, 246; exstructis, 247; concrescunt, 250.
D. tenebras, Acherunta, 251.
C. coorta, 253.
D. atrae, 254; fulmina, 255; niger, 256; picis, 257; tenebris, 258.
C. trahit, 258; primis, 260.
D. caligine, 263.
C. inaedificata, 264; sole, 265.
D. abundare, natare, 267.
C. exstructis, 268; fiunt, 270; semina, 272; solis, radiis, 273; semina, 276; acuit, 278; accenditur, 279; maturum, 282.
D. perscindit, 283.
C. luminibus, lustrans, 284.
D. displosa, 285; opprimere, 286; diluviem, 292.
C. maturo, 296.
D. perscidit, 297.
C. igniscat, 301.
D. amittens, 302.
C. corradens, 304; faciunt, 305; fervida, 307.
D. rigoris, 307.
C. ignem, 308, 309; excitet, 309.
D. frigida, 310.
C. igni, 310; vaporis, 312; evolat, ignis, 314.
D. frigida, 315.
C. & D. accendi, 317.
D. frigida, 319.
C. igni, 321; tepefacta, calore, 322; colligit, eundi, 326; auctum, 327; exprimitur, 328; naturae, 331; natura, 335.
D. discutiat, 339.
C. semina, 343.

D. dissoluit, 352; confervefacit, 353.
C. facta, 353.
D. insinuantur, insinuata, 355; dissoluunt, relaxant, 356.
C. florentia, pandunt, 359.
D. frigore, 360.
C. ignes, calore, 360.
D. frigus, 364.
C. aestum, 364; fabricanda, 365; caloris, 368.
D. rigoris, 368.
C. vernum, 369; calor, primo, 371.
D. frigore, 371; hiemes, 373.
C. aestatibus, 373; fiunt, 375; naturam, 379; unde volans, 383.
D. insinuarit, dominatus, 385; quatiunt, 388; iaciunt, 389; perfixo, mortalibus, 392; inque peditur, 394; correptus, 395; opprimere, 408; discutit, 418; frangit, 419; demit, 420.
C. missi, 425.
C. veniant, 425.
D. periclum, 430; rumpere, 432; discidit, 436.
C. concinnat, 437; semina, 444.
D. dissoluitque, 446.
C. concrescunt, 451; faciunt, primum, consistere, 455; crescunt, 457; coortast, 458.
D. caligine, 461.
C. sufficiunt, conveniundo, 480; densendo, subtexit, 482; faciunt, 484; concrescat, 495; primum, semina, 497; crescere, 499; crescit, 501; semina, 507; convenere, adaucta, 508; facit, 512.
D. rarescunt, 513; dissolvuntur, 514; tabescens, liquescat, 516.
C. fit, 517; cumulata, 518.
D. retinere, longumque morari, 519.
C. semina, 520; sol, radiis, 524.
D. opacam, 524.
C. fulsit, 525.
D. nigris, 526.
C. arqui, 526; crescunt, creantur, 527; concrescunt, 528.
D. nix, gelidaeque, pruinae, 529; geli, 530.
C. fiant, creentur, 533; primis, 536.
D. tremit, concussa, ruinis, 544; subruit, 545; cadunt, 546; concussu, 547.
C. fit, 552.
D. provolvitur, 553.
C. exstructa, 561; naturam, 565.
D. exitiale, clademque, 566; exitio, euntis, 569; ruinas, 572.
C. causa, 577; coorta, 579.
D. diffindens, 584.
C. concinnat, 584.
D. disturbat, 587.
C. obortus, 587.
D. ceciderunt, 588; subsedere, 590; dissoluat, 598.

C. natura, 598.
D. distracta, dispandat hiatum, 599; confusa, ruinis, 600; pericli, 603; subtracta, feratur, 605; confusa, ruina, 607.
C. naturam, 609; veniant, 610; rigantque, 612; fontis, 613; adaugmen, 614; augescere, 615; sol, 616.
D. detrahit, 616.
C. radiis, solem, 618.
D. delibet, 621; tollere, 623; nocte, 625; tollere, 627.
C. venit, 633.
D. manare, 634.
C. caput, 636; redit, 637; detulit, 638.
D. clade, 641.
C. coorta, 641.
D. dominata, 642.
C. gentibus, 643.
D. scintillare, 644.
C. natura, 646.
D. febrim, 656.
C. coortam, 656.
D. morbi, 657.
C. semina, 662.
D. morbi, 663, 664; concussa, moveri, 667; abundare, flammescere, 669; ardescunt, 670.
C. coortu, 671; semina, 672; irritata, 680; primum, 682; natura, 683; fit, 685.
D. caligine, 691; extruditque, 692; subiectare, 700; exanimum, 705; leti, 707; interiisse, morbo, veneno, 709.
C. genere, 710; aestatem, 712.
D. aquilones, 715; gelidis, 720.
C. aestifera, 721.
D. aquilonum, 730.
C. mediam regionem, 732.
D. ningues, 736; tabificis, 737.
C. sol, 737; natura, 739.
D. contraria, 741; remittunt, 743; cadunt, 744.
C. natura, 745; almae, 750; natura, 755; primum, 757.
D. concidere, 758; mactata, 759.
C. naturali, 760; fiant, origo, 761.
D. Orci, 762; Acheruntis, 763; manis, 764.
Cy. saecla, 766.
D. morbos, 771; mortem, 772.
C. naturam, 775; primasque, 776.
D. inimica, 777; infesta, 778; gravesque, 782.
C. primum, 783.
D. gravis, 783; necare, 787.
C. surgunt, 788; semina, 789; gerit, tradit, 790.
D. nocturnumque, extinctum, 791.

C. lumen, 791.
D. morbo, 793; languentia, 797; solvunt, labefactant, 798; ruinas, 801; febris, 804; mactabilis, 805.
C. gignier, 807.
D. mali, 811; perire, 813; mortiferam, 819; venenet, 820.
C. primum, 821.
D. correpta, veneno, 822; cadat, 823; corruit, 824; aufert, 825.
C. primo, 826.
D. cecidere, veneni, 827.
C. fontis, 828.
D. vomenda, 828; mali, 829; claudicat, 834; proditur, 835; delabi, 837.
C. natura, 838.
D. dispergunt, 839; frigidior, 840.
C. aestate, 840.
D. rarescit, 841.
C. calore, semina, 841; vaporis, 842.
D. effeta, 843.
C. calore, 843.
D. frigidior, 844; frigore, 845.
C. calorem, 847; luce, 848.
D. frigidus, 849.
C. calidus, 849.
D. nocturno, 849.
C. sole, fervescere, 851.
D. nox, caligine, 852.
C. sol, calidum, 855; lumen, fervore, 856; percoquere, calido, 858; radiis, ardentibus, 860; semina, 863; roriferis, 864.
D. nox, 864; frigescit, 865.
C. semina, ignis, 867; calidum, 868; sol, radiis, 869.
D. dimovit, 869.
C. obortus, 869.
D. rarefecit, 870.
C. calido, 870.
Cy. redeunt, 871.
C. primordia, 871; ignis, calor, 872.
D. frigidus, luce, 873.
C. solis, radiis, 874; lucem, 875.
D. rarescit, 875.
C. aestu, 875; semina, ignis, 876.
D. gelum, 877; exsolvit, glaciem, relaxat, 878; frigidus, 879.
C. flammam, igni, 880; collucet, 882; vaporis, 883; semina, 884; calidus, 887; genus, 890; semina, 896, 899.
D. nocturna, 900.
C. lumina, 900.
D. extinctum, 901.
C. accendier, 901; vapore, 903; ardescunt, ignis, 904; naturae, 907; patrio, 908; patriis, ortus, 909; genus, 917.

D. frigus, 925.
C. calor, sole, 925.
D. exesor, 926; requies, 933.
C. claret, 937; primis, 939; crescit, 945; auget, 946.
D. frigus, 948.
C. calidumque, 948.
D. frigusque, 952.
C. vaposque, 952; ignis, 953.
D. morbida, 955.
C. insinuatur, 955; coortae, 956; sol, 962.
D. facessunt, 957; excoquit, are, 962.
D. glaciem, dissolvit, 963.
C. exstructas, 964.
D. nives, 964.
C. radiis, 964.
D. tabescere, 964; liquefit, 965.
C. vapore, 965; ignis, 966.
D. liquidum facit, resolvit, 966; trahit, conducit, 967.
C. iuvat, 970.
D. venenumst, 974.
C. recreare, 975; natura, 982; naturam, 983; natura, 995; naturam, 997; semina, 1003; primordia, 1006; primoribus, 1009; natura, 1011.
D. frigidus horror, 1011.
C. natura, 1042; creatur, 1048; genus, 1058; genere, 1066; primum, 1068; vitigeni, 1072; renovare, 1076.
D. morbis, 1090; mortiferam, cladem, 1091.
C. conflare, coorta, 1091.
D. morbida, 1092.
C. generi, 1092; primum, semina, 1093; vitalia, 1094.
D. morbo, mortique, 1095.
C. coorta, 1096.
D. morbidus, 1097; morborum, pestilitasque, 1098.
C. coorta, 1100; surgunt, 1101.
D. putorem, 1101.
C. patria, 1104.
Cy. saecla, 1109.
D. morbi, 1113.
C. generatim, 1113.
Cy. saecla, 1113.
D. morbus, 1114.
C. gignitur, 1115.
D. temptantur, 1116; inimicus, 1117.
C. concinnat, 1118.
D. inimicus, 1120; conturbat, 1122; corrumpat, alienum, 1124; clades, pestilitasque, 1125; pestilitas, aegror, 1132; adversa, 1134.
C. natura, 1135.
D. coruptum, 1135.

C. adventu, 1137. (To avoid an obviously needless catalogue of words *suggesting* destruction in the following lines, I shall hold the citations on this theme as far as possible to words of direct import.)
D. mortifer, 1138; funestos, 1139; vastavitque, exhausit, 1140.
C. veniens, ortus, 1141.
D. mortique, 1144; lababant, 1153; cadavera, 1155; languebat, leti, 1157; dissoluebat, defessos, fatigans, 1162; defessa, 1178; mortis, 1182.
C. primoris, 1193.
D. morte, 1196; reddebant, 1198; funera leti, 1199.
C. genitalis, 1207.
D. privat, 1209; mortis, 1212; inhumata, 1215.
C. genus, 1216.
D. languebat, morte, 1218.
Cy. saecla, 1220.
D. languebant, 1221; moriebantur, 1222.
C. primis, 1222.
D. extorquebat, 1224; funera, 1225; exitio, letumque, 1229; morti, 1232; funera, amittebat, 1234; apisci, 1235.
Cy. saecla, 1237.
C. primis, 1238.
D. funere, funus, 1238; mortisque, 1240; morte, 1241; mactans, 1242; ibant, 1243; leti, 1246.
C. genus, 1246.
D. sepelire, 1247; mors, 1251; languebat, 1254; morti, 1255; exanimis, exanimata, 1256.
C. parentum, 1256; matribus, patribus, natos, 1258.
D. edere, 1258; languens, 1260; mors, 1263; languida, 1268; perire, 1269; sepulta, 1271; mors, 1273; cadaveribus, 1274; sepulturae, 1278; humari, 1279; humabat, 1281.
C. exstructa, 1284.
D. subdebantque faces, 1285.

Appendix II

I offer below strands of a further proof for the cycle. The entries consist of thematic words already cited which cannot reasonably be taken as unconscious or inevitable in the composition of the poem. The implication, of course, is that they are deliberately intended—only more tellingly so than all other thematic words—to give the theme.

I do not cite every possible incidence of such words. The fact that the number cited or citable is small in relation to the total number of thematic words merely testifies to the deep harmony of form and substance in the poem and must therefore redound to the poet's great credit.

For the most part, the citations fall into distinct classes. Figurative usages represent the largest class. Others consist of coined words (e. g., *egigni*, II, 703), hyperbole (e. g., *conficiuntur*, I, 535; *occisis*, V, 1136), form impinging on science (e. g., *procreat*, II, 880; see Bailey, *op. cit.*, II, 939), words of strained meaning (e. g., *nativo*, II, 542; see Bailey, II, 867), thematic words not found in Lucretius' models (e. g., *requies*, VI, 94).

Individual citations include cases of strained compression (*recreavit*, V, 404), unparalleled syntax (*cladem . . . pericli*, V, 369; see Bailey, III, 1374), a rare verb form (*disperditur*, II, 831; see Bailey, II, 933), thematic words in lines not essential to the central thought (*propagent, occidat*, II, 173f.), a stronger word than the context requires, (*disperiisse*, V, 1422).

Three examples are given of poetic tactics of which many instances may be found in the poem: thematic words placed in emphatic positions (*Splendida*, IV, 324 together with *E tenebris*, IV, 337); a thematic image chosen out of numerous others possible (*exesor*, IV, 220); a thematic illustration chosen out of numerous others possible (*corpus . . . exanimum*, VI, 705).

BOOK I

peperit, 83.
silvifragris, 275.
propagant, 280.
conficiuntur, 535.

BOOK II

progignere, 81.
propagent, occidat, 173f.
conserit, 211.
natus, creata, 223.

caecigeni, 741.
gignere, 228, 241.
nativo, 542.
egigni, 703.
nata, 793.

gignuntur, 808.
disperditur, 831.
procreat, 880.
oriundi, 991.
primigenum, 1106.

BOOK III

gignitur, 173.
creatast, 278.
gigni, 457.
gignitur, 616.
nascendum, 618.

creatum, 619.
creari, 622.
gignier, 623.
natali . . . die, 711f.
funeris, 712.

BOOK IV

gignuntur, 131.
exesor, 220.
Splendida, 324.
E tenebris, 337.
perit, 356.
crearit, 476.

creatam, 478.
nascuntur, 495.
gignuntur, 604.
nata, 771.
procreat, 835.
natum, 850.

BOOK V

insita, 329.
peperere, 334.
cladem . . . pericli, 369.
diluviare, 387.
recreavit, 404.
gigni, 1024.
occisis, 1136.

creare, 1143.
peperere, 1197.
peperit, 1305.
gigni, 1352.
terrigenarum, 1411.
perdit, 1415.
disperiisse, 1422.

BOOK VI

requies, 94.
trucidat, 147.
sepultis, 193.

corpus . . . exanimum, 705.
almae, 750.
exanimis *etc.,* 1256–58.

Index

Index

Richard Minadeo took his Ph.D. at the University of Wisconsin. He has published articles in the classical journals and is Assistant Professor of Greek and Latin at Wayne State University.

The manuscript was edited by Louise Hemsing. The book was designed by S. R. Tenenbaum. The type face for the text is Mergenthaler Linotype Granjon redesigned by George W. Jones from a face cut by Claude Garamond; and the display face is Deepdene Italic designed by W. A. Dwiggins.

The book is printed on S. D. Warren's Olde Style Antique paper and bound in Columbia Mills' Bayside Vellum over binders board. Manufactured in the United States of America.